Jewish Law and Italian Local Laws

Studies in Jewish History and Culture

Edited by

Giuseppe Veltri

VOLUME 78

The titles published in this series are listed at *brill.com/sjhc*

Jewish Law and Italian Local Laws

From the Roman Age to the 19th Century

By

Vittore Colorni

BRILL

LEIDEN | BOSTON

The original *Legge ebraica e leggi locali* was published (in Italian) by Giuffrè Editore, Milan, 1945, which owns the copyright. Permission to re-publish the volume in English was given to the translator, Dr. Angelo Colorni.

Library of Congress Cataloging-in-Publication Data

Names: Colorni, Vittore, author. | Colorni, Angelo, translator.
Title: Jewish law and Italian local laws : from the Roman age to the 19th century / Vittore Colorni ; Angelo Colorni.
Other titles: Legge ebraica e leggi locali English.
Description: Leiden ; Boston : Brill, 2025. | Series: Studies in Jewish history and culture, 1568-5004 ; volume 78 | Includes index. | Summary: "From Roman times (when Jews first formed communities in Italy) throughout the 19th century (when Jews became emancipated individually but were deprived – as a group – of all their ancient autonomies), Jews remained tied to their separate judicial institutions. Administratively, Jewish communities sought control over their internal affairs (worship, charity, social welfare, schools, education, and their own communal rules) (administrative autonomy). Judicially, they sought recognition of their internal laws as applicable to their civic relations (regulatory autonomy), constantly striving to obtain from the State the authority to bring their community members to trial in their courts of law (judiciary autonomy)"– Provided by publisher.
Identifiers: LCCN 2024036401 (print) | LCCN 2024036402 (ebook) | ISBN 9789004677616 (hardback) | ISBN 9789004627154 (ebook)
Subjects: LCSH: Jews–Legal status, laws, etc.–Italy. | Jewish law–History.
Classification: LCC KKH2467.M56 C65613 2024 (print) | LCC KKH2467.M56 (ebook) | DDC 342.4508/5296—dc23/eng/20240821
LC record available at https://lccn.loc.gov/2024036401
LC ebook record available at https://lccn.loc.gov/2024036402

Typeface for the Latin, Greek, and Cyrillic scripts: "Brill". See and download: brill.com/brill-typeface.

ISSN 1568-5004
ISBN 978-90-04-67761-6 (hardback)
ISBN 978-90-04-62715-4 (e-book)
DOI 10.1163/9789004627154

This book is printed on acid-free paper and produced in a sustainable manner.

To the blessed memory of my father, Dr. Emanuele Colorni

Contents

Translator's Note

A significant part of this book was written by my late father ז"ל, Prof. Vittore Colorni, in occupied Rome while hiding from the Nazis with my mother and grandmother. He worked at the Biblioteca Alessandrina under a false name, at considerable risk to his life. Walking the streets of Rome in relative safety during 1943–44 required a residence permit, obtainable only if one could prove he was holding a job. My father presented the problem to Dr. Maria Ortiz, the Library Director, who bravely hired him as a "group A employee," providing him with the alleged status of a displaced civilian.

After the war, my father taught Ecclesiastical Law (1946–1956) and History of Italian Law (1956–1987) at Ferrara University. Between 1969 and 1971 he chaired as Faculty Dean. His favorite field of research was always the history of Italian Jewry. In this book, he investigated the Jews' special status and how Jewish law was recognized in Italy, tracing the history of rabbinical courts in medieval Italian states. He also wrote many articles on Mantuan Jewish history, the names and history of ancient Jewish families, and other general interest topics. His entire scope of studies remains unmatched due to his thorough research in countless libraries and state archives in Italy and abroad and his extensive analysis of every uncovered document.

My father was fluent in French and German and had a profound knowledge of several additional languages, especially Latin and ancient Greek. His effortless understanding of these languages, meant that in his writings he often switched from one language to another in the most natural and nonchalant way. Here, I occasionally ventured into the translation of a few quotes but, lacking my father's multilingual knowledge, the task of dealing with languages other than Italian, including archaic Italian, was far beyond my modest possibilities. For the vast majority, the quotes were therefore left in their original language. The AI-based translation applications available today can be used to make at least a rough and general sense out of those citations.

My father was both an eminent historian and a distinguished scholar, whereas I am a retired marine microbiologist more familiar with molecular methods for diagnosing aquatic organisms' diseases than with terminology of legal theory. "*Jewish Law and Italian Local Laws*" was written in the early 1940s, in Italian, for an Italian audience. Languages are evolving creatures with a life of their own. Writing styles have since changed in both Italian and English. Furthermore, mine is a translation, i.e., a rendition in readable English without losing sight of my father's interpretation of antique texts in Latin, ancient

Greek, archaic German, Italian and French. Therefore, while asking for your leniency for some word choices and sentence structures that may sound slightly odd today, for any doubts you may have about how I translated certain legal terms, I strongly urge you to check my father's original Legge Ebraica e Leggi Locali (Giuffrè ed., Milan, 1945).

Angelo Colorni, PhD

Vittore Colorni (1912–2005): a Historian of Law and (Jewish) Minority

Giuseppe Veltri

It was during the Enlightenment that the concepts of first the protection and then the full freedom of minorities came to the attention of our Western society as a matter requiring consideration, especially when investigating and observing societies of absolutist rule. Even today, a minority is often seen as a sign of instability and discord in a "nation," "culture," or society. The constitutions of contemporary democracies primarily contain stable principles that theoretically act as a brake on absolutist desires to assimilate or even eliminate minorities. Yet although it is repeatedly enshrined in UNO declarations, the principle of minority liberty often does not become a stable political force; rather, at best, minorities are simply tolerated.

In world history and in the perception and recognition of minority policy, Jewish history plays a significant role. Until the establishment of the State of Israel after the Shoah, Jews did not have their own state and government and lived as a mostly tolerated, though not entirely forcedly isolated minority, present in many states and regions. Living as a minority produced not only a strong sense of social identity but also a consequent legal, philosophical, and cultural reflection on the rights and duties of the individual when living in a state whose religion, culture, and way of life often differ from one's own. The dialectical contrast between the individual and the collective, identity and participation, own and common, is ever-present in its history and forms a pivotal element of the Jewish community.

Having lived first during the fascist regime, then in the Italian post-war period full of ideals and hopes, and finally in the turbulent democracy of the end of the second millennium, the historian of law and Judaism Vittore Colorni (1912–2005) was well acquainted with both the principles and the dangers listed above, having made them the main theme of his studies. There are few legal historians who have mastered more than one legal code. The difficulty lies less in the fundamental structures of legal language, which has many common connections, institutions, and logic, but rather primarily in the fact that scholars of bi-national legal systems have to be well acquainted with the historical events that led to certain legal decisions, with the internal and external discussions that took place in order to reach a consensus, with the institutions involved in them, and with the courses and recourses of the history of every law.

Colorni was well acquainted with the Greek, Latin, and Italian sources of the legal tradition of the Peninsula and with general and local Jewish laws. Born to an Ashkenazi family in Mantua on July 19, 1912, he studied jurisprudence at the University of Bologna from 1930 to 1934. During the Nazi/fascist years, 1943–1945, he and his family relied on the protection of Maria Ortiz, the director of the *Biblioteca Alessandrina*, which was also a haven for anti-fascist intellectuals (such as Gabriele Pepe, Franco Lombardi, and Vincenzo Ussani).[1] There, he was able to continue his studies. After 1945, he went back to Mantua, and in 1946, he received a university post in the faculty of law at the University of Ferrara. In 1956, he became ordinarius of the history of Italian law. He died on March 11, 2005.[2]

Vittore Colorni was a "jurist by profession and historian by passion," as Shlomo Simonsohn defined him.[3] Before the war, he published research on the Jewish community of Mantua. In 1945, he printed his groundbreaking work *Legge ebraica e leggi locali*, which has now been translated into English for the first time in this volume by his son, Angelo Colorni. As Simonson stated, Colorni's book is "the groundbreaking, still-definitive study of the application of Jewish law in Italy during almost two millennia. The author gives a detailed examination, with a careful and meticulous analysis of the sources, of the *status civitatis* of the Jews, the relationship between Jewish law and that of the state, and the judicial autonomy of the Jews."[4] Of relevance here is not only the state of the Jews (*status civitatis*), but also the sources of and the relationship with civil law. In 1956, Colorni published his complementary book on *Gli Ebrei nel sistema del diritto comune fino alla prima emancipazione*. During the very fertile period of the following years, he published many contributions, which were later republished in two volumes: *Judaica minora. Saggi sulla storia dell'ebraismo Italiano dall'antichità all'età moderna* (1983) and *Judaica minora. Saggi sulla storia dell'ebraismo italiano dall'antichità all'età moderna. Nuove ricerche* (1991).

---

1 Simonetta Buttò, "Ortiz, Maria," *Dizionario Biografico degli Italiani* 79 (2013), https://www.treccani.it/enciclopedia/maria-ortiz_(Dizionario-Biografico).

2 For bio-biographical notes, see Alberto Castaldini, "Cenni biografici," *Materia Giudaica* 1 (2005): 5–7 and idem, "Bibliografia degli scritti di Vittore Colorni," in *Una manna buona per Mantova. Man Tov Le-Man Tovah. Studi in onore di Vittore Colorni*, ed. Mauro Perani (Florence: Olschki, 2004), xvii–xxv. See also Guido Lopez, "Vittore Colorni: L'uomo che cerca le radici," *La Rassegna Mensile di Israel* 50 (1984): 53–57.

3 Shlomo Simonsohn, "Lo studioso e i suoi scritti," in Mauro Perani, "In Memoriam Vittore Colorni 19 Luglio 1912 – Mantova – 11 Marzo 2005," *Materia Giudaica* 10 (2005): 7.

4 In Italian in Simonsohn, "Lo studioso," 7.

Colorni's ability lay not only in his immense knowledge of both law and history but also in his weaving of both topics into particular studies and more general history. Although he dealt with local topics, he knew how best to place them into a more general framework of legal and general history. As David Bidussa put it years ago, Colorni prospected the binary backbones that formed the historical identity of the Jewish community, namely, self-government and written production. Hence, the local community's history is not only made up of the analysis of events but also of the "system of relationships that are maintained over time and that indicate the Jewish groups' involvement and belonging with the rest of society."[5]

Colorni's expertise in conjugating particular events with general history and local developments with the legal tradition over the millennia can be observed in two articles I would like to discuss here. The first is his interpretation of Justinian's *novella* 146, while the second is his almost unknown article on the first draft of a constitution of the Land of Israel and his caveats, a relevant topic today. Both articles have one point in common, namely, how to interpret the freedom or freedoms of a minority in the constitutions – and, hence, the decisions – of a government.

1 The Greek Version of the Torah and Roman Law

I first encountered Colorni's research during my studies of the Greek translation of the Torah, known as the Septuagint, during the 1980s, and it contributed to my understanding of the impact of this Greek Alexandrian translation on Rabbinic and medieval Judaism.[6] His work gave me useful details for a theory that I was developing, which states that Greek culture, language, and education (*paideia*) were widely accepted and disseminated in Rabbinic Judaism, in contrast to the ancient and modern Christian claims of their rejection. The Patristic thesis, which is still supported by scholars – namely, that Judaism before Constantine's seizure of power refused to use the Greek Torah because it was used by the Christians – was pure Christian propaganda. There is no

5 See David Bidussa, "Storia degli ebrei, identità di comunità e storiografia. A proposito di Vittore Colorni," *La Rassegna Mensile di Israel* 75 (2009): 143–57. This is my rendition of Bidussa's Italian text; see *ibidem*, 45.

6 See Giuseppe Veltri, *Eine Tora für den König Talmai. Untersuchungen zum Übersetzungsverständnis in der jüdisch-hellenistischen und rabbinischen Literatur* (Tübingen: Mohr, 1994); the main thesis of my dissertation is also present in idem, *Libraries, Translations, and "Canonic" Texts: The Septuagint, Aquila, and Ben Sira in Jewish and Christian Tradition* (Leiden and Boston: Brill, 2006).

Rabbinic source that can be incontestably dated to this period that expressly attacks the Septuagint for being – so to speak – "infected by Christianity," as the Patristic authorities would have it. On the contrary: the Greek language and the Greek text of the Torah were highly honoured in Palestinian and Babylonian academies insofar as they transmitted traditions about a version of the Torah that had been written for King Ptolemy, with no trace of blame or critical distance from it.[7]

Colorni's starting point, Justinian's *novella* 146, which restricts the liturgical activity of Jews, is obviously of a legal nature. On the ides of February 553, Emperor Justinian enacted *novella* 146 (known as *Peri Hebraiōn*), which was allegedly preceded by a Jewish controversy over the usage of Hebrew and Greek in the liturgy due to a difference of opinion. He permitted only the Greek language in both the Septuagint and Aquila versions, although the latter is of foreign origin and often deviates from the Septuagint.

Colorni's argument when unraveling the novella is historical, literary, and epigraphical. As already mentioned, the thesis to be proved is that Hellenistic and Rabbinic Judaism did not abandon the Greek language, but even used it in the liturgy. The evidence for this comes from the literature of the Hellenistic Diaspora, epigraphy, passages from Greek and Latin authors, and texts from the Rabbinic Jewish tradition. Colorni's conclusion is clear: Greek was used from the third century BCE to the eighth century CE. He was the first to debunk the thesis of the alleged abandonment or rejection of Greek (Hellenistic) life and culture in Rabbinic Judaism. According to him, a turning point in the evaluation of Greek in Judaism is found in the Venosa inscriptions from the sixth to seventh century, which display a revival of Hebrew rather than Greek.[8]

For Colorni, the dispute that Justinian raised was clearly between those who wanted to read the Torah in Greek and others who wanted to read it only in Hebrew. He concluded: "This was an attack launched by Hebraist Judaism against Hellenistic Judaism, not vice versa. It was not the Hellenists who wanted to innovate by introducing the official reading in Greek, ..., but the Judaizers who launched the anathema against the reading itself, which had been practised for centuries, with the intention of suppressing it."[9]

This is not the place to disentangle this difficult legal text which has challenged scholars as regards its historical value and its importance for the history

7 I am here summarizing the conclusion of the above-mentioned books (footnote 7). See the bibliography in my *Library* 104–5 and *passim* (quoted also above footnote 7).

8 Vittore Colorni, "L'uso del greco nella liturgia del giudaismo ellenistico e la novella 146 di Giustiniano," *Annali di Storia del Diritto* 8 (1964): 33–42.

9 In Italian in Colorni, "La novella," 70.

of Hebrew and Greek in Jewish communities in the East. However, there is one element that may be recorded as a turning point in the Christian evaluation of Aquila's translation of the Bible. The regular usage of Aquila in Christian texts made him an acceptable alternative to the Septuagint. Only Rabbinic teaching, meaning, undoubtedly, the oral Torah, is forbidden. The aim of the *novella* is precise: to bring about the conversion of the Jews, as the *deuterōsis* is the decisive point in distinguishing the non-Jewish world from Judaism.[10]

It is to Colorni's credit that he emphasized the importance of this Justinian novella and placed it in the historical arc in which the Greeks were an alive and flourishing presence among the Jewish community. He is also to be commended for his legal examination of it. What I find less convincing is his failure to consider Justinian's polemical intent. In my opinion, Justinian was not interested in settling the question of the use of Greek and Hebrew, whether historically or not, but rather – perfectly understandably, from his Christian point of view – in attempting to abolish the Jewish interpretation of the Bible expressed in the Hebrew tradition and emphasizing the Septuagint as the prophetic forerunner of the Christian message.

Their use of a language such as Hebrew, which was frowned upon by the majority, meant that the Jewish minority could not be controlled, something that Justinian and his theologians certainly must not have liked. There was great wariness regarding the possibility of insulting the Christian religion and especially Christian doctrine. Linguistic assimilation could have a more cogent effect than allowing a freedom that could not be controlled. Allowing Aquila as an alternative to the Septuagint was certainly a sign of compromise, because everyone knew that Aquila's translation was conducted by the school of the rabbis, like the Targum, and that it was definitely not the Christians' preferred choice.[11]

Justinian did not want to offer any protection to the minority Jewish community, because this went against his policy of controlling anything that challenged Christianity and ultimately his own rule. Rather, the intention of *novella* 146 was plausibly to restrain Judaism by setting language as the discriminating factor.

10 For details of my interpretation, see "Die Novelle 146 *Perì Hebraiōn*: Das Verbot des Targumvortrags in Justinians Politik," in *Die Septuaginta zwischen Judentum und Christentum*, ed. Martin Hengel and Anna M. Schwemer (Tübingen: Mohr, 1994), 116–30.

11 See my "Aquila" (with Alison G. Salvesen), in *The Oxford Handbook of the Septuagint*, ed. Alison G. Salvesen and T. M. Law (Oxford: Oxford University Press, 2021), 459–68.

2 The (Missing) Constitution of the State of Israel

Colorni also focused on the subject of the minority, especially when seen from the perspective of historical and intellectual Judaism in the logic of the history of law and its application, in his discussion of the new State of Israel, whose proclamation of independence had triggered enthusiasm not only among Diaspora Jews but also among Italian Catholics.[12] This matter is hugely topical for the conception and implementation of minority legislation and especially for the real armed conflicts that continue to rage to this day.

An early article by Colorni gives us the dimension of his conception of a free state, which includes minorities and not only protects them but also grants them all rights in the freedom of speech, thought, and action. This article is little known in the academic community not only because it was written in Italian but probably also because its subject matter, the attempts to draft a constitution for the newly created State of Israel, is no longer on Israel's agenda.

The Declaration of Independence was published by the Provisional Government of Israel in the first issue of the *Official Gazette* (5 Iyar 5708; i.e., May 14, 1948).[13] In it is written:

> WE DECLARE that, with effect from the moment of the termination of the Mandate being tonight, the eve of Sabbath, the 6th Iyar, 5708 (15th May, 1948), until the establishment of the elected, regular authorities of the State in accordance with the Constitution which shall be adopted by the Elected Constituent Assembly not later than the 1st October 1948, the People's Council shall act as a Provisional Council of State, and its executive organ, the People's Administration, shall be the Provisional Government of the Jewish State, to be called "Israel."[14]

Accordingly, the first constituent assembly, elected on January 25, 1949 (which became the Knesset on February 14, 1949), was intended to create a constitution by October 15, 1948, as required by the UN General Assembly Resolution 181 adopted on 29 November 29, 1947.[15] At the request of the leaders of the Jewish Agency, Leo (Yehudah Pinchas) Kohn (1894–1961), who served as the secretary

12 Mario Toscano, "'Un avvenimento grandioso e stupefacente,'" *La Rassegna Mensile di Israel* 85 (2019), 79–118, especially p. 105.

13 *Official Gazette* 1, Tel Aviv, 5 Iyar 5708 [5.14.1948]: 1.

14 I follow here the English translation published in: https://ecf.org.il/media_items/848.

15 Here, I am mainly following the detailed historical and legal analysis of Amihai Radzyner, "A Constitution for Israel: The Design of the Leo Kohn Proposal, 1948," *Israel Studies* 15 (2010): 1–24.

of the political department, was commissioned to draft the first text of the proposed constitution. This choice was not casual. In 1927, the Frankfurt-born Kohn had completed his dissertation in law at the University of Heidelberg dealing with the constitution of Free Ireland, the expanded version of which was published in 1932.[16]

The developments in the newly established State of Israel were communicated very quickly and effectively to the Jews who remained in the Diaspora, opening the horizon to new considerations and arousing excitement and even perplexities. Colorni was firmly convinced of the European nature of Judaism. Nevertheless, he paid particular attention to the birth of Zionism and the State of Israel.[17] Like many Jews after the Shoah, he was attracted by the new political format that existed first culturally in the British Mandate and then politically in the new State of Israel. However, his interest lay in the legal forms that were gradually being developed to support the state. He seized the opportunity to examine an account of the proposal for the constitution of the State of Israel published by Carlo Alberto Viterbo in the weekly *Israel* in 1948.[18] Given the importance of his paper,[19] which I feel has not received its due attention, I will summarize it in order to highlight the legal forms that Colorni believed should form the basis of a modern state.

Reading Leo Kohn's early draft of a constitution as summarized by Viterbo, Colorni praised Kohn's essential avoidance of a "purely emphatic enunciation of abstract and merely theoretical programs."[20] On the contrary, Kohn presented the draft as 'the effective basis of the political association, as the living source of all public powers and private rights,"[21] meaning the legislative, executive, and judiciary powers and the fundamental rights of individuals. However, his attention was concentrated on individual rights, which were to

16 Leo Kohn, *The Constitution Of The Irish Free State* (London: George Allen & Unwin Ltd., 1932): see Thomas Mohr, "Leo Kohn and the Law of the British Empire (March 13, 2019)," *UCD Working Papers in Law, Criminology & Socio-Legal Studies Research Paper* 12 (2019), https://ssrn.com/abstract=3352030 or http://dx.doi.org/10.2139/ssrn.3352030.

17 A very detailed article of the history of Zionism among Christian theologians is his "Teologi cristiani dell'ottocento precursori del sionismo," *La Rassegna Mensile d'Israel* 21 (1955): 170–85.

18 See Mario Toscano, "'Un avvenimento grandioso e stupefacente,'" *La Rassegna Mensile di Israel* 85 (2019): 79–118, passim.

19 Vittore Colorni, "Gli antichi principî giuspubblicistici ebraici e la nuova costituzione dello Stato d'Israele," *La Rassegna Mensile di Israel* 14 (1948), 379–386.

20 Colorni, "Gli antichi principî," 379: "pura enunciazione enfatica di programmi astratti e meramente teorici."

21 Colorni, "Gli antichi principî," *ibidem*: "la base effettiva della consociazione politica, come fonte viva di tutti i poteri pubblici e di tutti i diritti privati."

be considered a "legal limit on the legislative power, which in turn binds the executive and judiciary bodies."[22]

Adopting one of the cornerstones of Jewish claims from the eighteen century, according to which "it is high time that European Jews, and those in Germany especially, finally receive rights; namely, justice, and liberty, rather than rights and exemptions" (in the wording of the "father" of the *Wissenschaft des Judentums*, Leopold Zunz),[23] Colorni pointed out that the rights of individuals and minorities must be anchored in written laws and not in moral directives ("Freiheiten"; "rights" according to Zunz). This purely moral commitment would have the consequence that any legislative power could change any moral directive by replacing it with legally binding legislation.

That was the case for articles 24 to 32 of the Italian *Statuto Albertino* (Albertine Statute) on individual rights, which, Colorni added, had been considered in doctrine and jurisprudence alike as nothing more than a set of ethical brakes without legal compulsion. The reason for this relied on the fact that the Statuto was considered an ordinary law, subject to changes. In the Italian constitution of 1948 and in Kohn's draft, the constitution was considered to be a "rigid constitution," which could not be changed like an ordinary law and was "protected against any possible infringement by the legislative power by means of the attribution to the judicial power of the review of the extrinsic and intrinsic constitutionality of every act of the legislative power."[24]

The purpose of this power limitation was the defence of the individual; that is, ultimately, the defence of minorities "in the face of the possibility of an unjust action to their detriment by the law, which expresses, in its content, the not always impartial will of the majority."[25] Unlike the ancient concept of government, where the sovereign had total power, it would be via the

22 Colorni, "Gli antichi principî," *ibidem*; "un limite giuridico per il potere legislativo, vincolante a sua volta gli organi esecutivo e giudiziario."

23 "Es ist endlich Zeit, dass den Juden in Europa, insbesondere in Deutschland, Recht und Freiheit statt der Rechte und der Freiheiten gewährt werde: kein kümmerliches erniedrigendes Vorrecht, aber ein vollständiges, erhebendes Bürgerthum": Leopold Zunz, *Die gottesdienstlichen Vorträge der Juden, historisch entwickelt: Ein Beitrag zur Alterthumskunde und biblischen Kritik, zur Literatur- und Religionsgeschichte* (Berlin: Asher, 1832; repr. Hildesheim: Olms, 1966), 7; see Giuseppe Veltri, *Language of Conformity and Dissent: On the Imaginative Grammar of Jewish Intellectuals in the Nineteenth and Twentieth Centuries* (Boston, MA: Academic Studies Press, 2013); 143.

24 Colorni, "Gli antichi principî," 380: "tutelata contro ogni eventuale violazione da parte del potere legislativo a mezzo dell'attribuzione al potere giudiziario del sindacato sulla costituzionalità estrinseca ed intrinseca di ogni atto del potere legislativo."

25 Colorni, "Gli antichi principî," 380: "L'attribuzione di limiti all'azione di questo potere ha come finalità la difesa dell'individuo ossia, in ultima analisi, delle minoranze, di fronte

constitutions of the Americans and the French respectively, the 1776 Declaration of Independence and the 1789 Declaration of the Rights of Man and of the Citizen, that the defence of minorities would be achieved through a series of fundamental rights such as that of "freedom of conscience, of worship, of the press, of political opinion, of domicile, the inviolability of private property, of correspondence, etc., and by attributing to these rights the status of limits of the law."[26]

But even this was not new, Colorni continued. It could already be found in legal discourse between the Middle Ages and the modern era in the limitation of sovereign power in the figure of a monarch, oligarch, or democratic assembly. Colorni's argumentation is very stimulating because it aptly attributes to the schools of law a linear path from the Middle Ages to the nineteenth century, a process that begins with the "School of Bologna" in the twelfth century and ends with the Enlightenment. The argumentation is based on criteria that are formally different from but intrinsically identical to those devised since the nineteenth century.

Rather than arguing from rights by enumerating them and thus creating a limit to the law, requirements were placed on the legislative act, and the status of law was denied to all acts that were general in nature. At the end of the day, it was a matter of "indirectly proclaiming the principle of equality, which was equivalent to that protection of minorities against all arbitrariness of sovereignty that was later provided for with the system of declarations of rights."[27] Generality as an element of the law was affirmed by numerous Christian public lawyers of the so-called intermediate period.[28] Colorni argued that this new vision of jurisprudence with reference to public power was not only Christian, but was amply present in the world of the Halakhah.

This was a very important, albeit unknown element that could help the Israeli constituent assembly to regulate the law regarding minorities: the same perspective could also be found in the Jewish legal world, applied to the census. The famous principle *dina de malkhuta dina* ("the law of the state/kingdom is

---

alla eventualità di una ingiusta azione a loro danno da parte della legge, esprimente, nel suo contenuto, la volontà non sempre imparziale della maggioranza."

26 Colorni, "Gli antichi principî," 380: "con l'elencare una serie di diritti fondamentali, quali ad esempio la libertà di coscienza, di culto, di stampa, di opinione politica, di domicilio, l'inviolabilità della proprietà privata, della corrispondenza ecc.; e con l'attribuire a tali diritti la qualità di limiti della legge."

27 Colorni, "Gli antichi principî," 381.

28 See Vittore Colorni, *L'eguaglianza come limite della legge nel diritto intermedio moderno* (Milan: A. Giuffrè, 1946), 161. The principle of the generality of law is one of the important elements dealt with by Colorni in the book translated here. See pp. 43–45, 200–203.

(valid) law") enunciated in the Babylonian Talmud, *Baba Qamma* 113a,[29] was to be understood, according to Colorni, "not as being limited to the case in which the official acts not of his own free will, but on the basis of a general provision stipulating precisely the measure of the tribute."[30] In short, the law must be valid in a general way and not only applied to a group. He went further, quoting the French Tosaphists, who confirmed that if a tax collector is not fixed in advance, "there is no law of the state but violence of the state. Violence, even of the king, does not constitute law" (*ibidem*).

The same interpretative tendency was put forward by Maimonides: "Every law made by the king for all and not for a single individual separately is not robbery: on the other hand, he who takes from this single individual without relying on a law known to all, using violence, commits robbery."[31] Any general and preventive rule of taxation must be a valid law, otherwise the state command will be illegitimate. According to some jurists, the principle of generality could be interpreted in a local sense. R. Ya'acob ben Meir (Rabbenu Tam in 1100–1171) stated that "when the king makes equal decrees for all but makes different decrees for one province, he does not say: the law of the state is law," while R. Moshe ben Nachman (1194–ca. 1270) considered any law of a monarchic nation to be illegitimate and recognized only the ancient laws "that the antecedent kings applied and that are written in the annals of the kingdom."[32]

It was apparent, Colorni continued, that the new State of Israel constituted something new, suited to the circumstances and needs of everyday life. However, it had to take care to offer continuity with the tradition that founded the consciousness that has lasted eighteen centuries. Interestingly, Colorni, who was not an orthodox Jew, was at pains to point out that what was expected from the new State of Israel (at least by Jewish intellectuals) was consonance with tradition, a special tradition whose essence and existence are based its precisely in and on the Diaspora (as the Venetian rabbi Simone Simhah Luzzatto would say).[33] The following text is exemplary and paradigmatic in this sense:

29 See Babylonian Talmud, *Nedarim* 28a; Tosefta, *Nedarim* 3:4.

30 Colorni, "Gli antichi principî," 381–82: "si deve intendere limitato al caso che il funzionario agisca non di suo arbitrio, ma in base ad una disposizione generale statuente in modo preciso la misura del tributo."

31 Quotation from *Mishneh Torah, Seferv Nezikim, Gezelah we-Avidah* 5, according to Colorni, "Gli antichi principî," 381–82 and footnote 6 and 7, there.

32 Quotation from Colorni, "Gli antichi principî," 383.

33 Giuseppe Veltri, "'Identity of Essentiality of the Jewish People': The Diaspora and the Political Theories of Simone Luzzatto in the Jewish Thought of the 20th Century," *Civiltà del Mediterraneo*, n.s. 12/23–24 (2013): 249–69.

> It will be opportune to study carefully, to choose, to sift, to set aside what will prove to be irretrievably dead, while preserving what will still appear to be alive and capable of being maintained and adapted to the needs of modern life. In the pages of the Talmud, the *Mishneh Torah*, the *Turim*, the *Shulchan 'Aruch*, and all the countless other collections of casuistry and jurisprudence, the soul of our fathers is reflected, who dreamt every day, every moment of their lives of the great moment of the rebuilding of the State of Israel. The darkness of death descended upon their eyes without them being able to see their daily invocation fulfilled: "Vetechezena 'enenu be-shuvecha le-Zion vel Jrushalaim irecha":[34] while we have seen, we see the miracle hour by hour.[35]

Colorni saw a peculiarity of the law of the new state precisely in the continuity between old and new:

> Not an impossible intact revival, but not an indiscriminate repudiation for the sake of the new. A vast field of investigation is now open to Jewish legal scholars: from such research, a wonderful synthesis of the ancient and the modern can be created. The law of the Jewish state can be distinguished by its balance among the laws of all the states of the world. It is to be hoped that on this path, too, the reconstruction will proceed as happily as in all other fields of renewed Jewish life.[36]

As is well known, the constituent assembly did not reach an agreement on the constitution, a fact that Colorni discussed in this article. The reasons for this are well known and there is no need to repeat them here. The current Basic Law (in the version of March 17, 1992, amended March 9, 1994) based on the Declaration of Independence, which still has quasi-constitutional value today, precisely expresses Colorni's repeated desire to base laws on dignity and liberty: "The purpose of this Basic Law is to protect human dignity and liberty, in order to establish in a Basic Law tile values of the State of Israel as a Jewish and democratic state."[37] The Declaration of Independence states that the state must "ensure complete equality of social and political rights to all its inhabitants irrespective of religion, race or sex." Whether the Arab minority has to

34 Colorni's transcription of the Hebrew text.

35 Colorni, "Gli antichi principî," 386.

36 Colorni, "Gli antichi principî," 386.

37 Available at https://www.jewishvirtuallibrary.org/basic-law-human-dignity-and-liberty.

be considered as such is a *vexata quaestio* that goes beyond the purpose of an introduction to Colorni's masterwork.[38]

3 A Final Word

I would just like to end this brief look at the world of Vittore Colorni by emphasizing that his experience in fascist Italy had made him very aware of the Enlightenment and the liberal aspect of the freedom of minorities, which originated in Judaism in a paradigmatic way. The Jewish historical experience shows that minority freedom is an important pillar of modern state jurisdiction, which can only publish just and egalitarian laws if it respects the general nature of law.

Simonsohn concludes his eulogium with the following words: "Vittore Colorni's studies are distinguished by the methodology adopted, by the severe examination of texts and their scrupulous analysis, and by their lucid presentation of research results. His contribution to the historiography of Italian Judaism is profound and lasting as well as pioneering."[39] I have nothing further to add.

38 On this aspect, there is a great deal of literature. My suggestions are only intended to back the aspect of a *vexata quaestio*: see, for example, Amal Jamal, "The Contradictions of State-Minority Relations in Israel: The Search for Clarifications," *Constellations* 16 (2009): 493–507; Zeev Segal, "Israel Point of View Regarding Minorities – A Constitutional Perspective," *Israeli European Policy Network* (March 2010), http://www.macro.org.il/images/upload/items/86606597104836.pdf.

39 In Italian in Simonsohn, "Lo studioso," 8.

Jews, "Economy," and the Law in the Works of Vittore Colorni

Germano Maifreda

Vittore Colorni was undoubtedly a forerunner of the changes that Italian Jewish history saw beginning in the 1970s. In fact, all the salient features of that renewal – the identification of new, especially serial sources (notarial deeds, *estimi* books, other land registers), the emphasis on the relations between Jews and non-Jews, the in-depth study of Jewish communal life and its internal conflicts, the analysis of the relationship between Italian nation building and the histories of the minority groups present on the peninsular territory – are already discernible in the work of the distinguished scholar.[40]

In these pages, I would like to focus on the characters that Colorni's profound historiographical innovativeness takes on from the point of view of economic history: an operation that may seem paradoxical since in the text this volume presents Colorni never uses the category of "economy." Moreover, he employs the adjective "economic" only once, concerning an epoch that is very late in relation to the book's long chronological trajectory. Colorni speaks in fact of "the economic benefits that the existence of the national judiciary always brought to the Jews"[41] – where the "economic" is in a significant intertwining with the legal dimension – concerning a late eighteenth-century memorandum submitted by the Jewish Community of Mantua as a response to an attack brought by the Austrian emperor Joseph II on their jurisdictional autonomy. The same happens in Colorni's other post-war important monography on Jewish history, *Gli ebrei nel sistema del diritto comune fino alla prima emancipazione* (1956), where concerning the late eighteenth century the author evokes the "economic" sphere by recalling Giovan Battista Gherardo d'Arco's dissertation *Dell'influenza del Ghetto sullo Stato*, which insisted precisely (in

40 As David Bidussa has pointed out in "Storia degli ebrei, identità di comunità e storiografia. A proposito di Vittore Colorni," *La Rassegna Mensile di Israel*, vol. 75, 1/2 (2009): 143–157. Colorni welcomed the new historiographical season that resulted, among other things, in the 1979 founding of the Associazione italiana per lo studio del Giudaismo [Italian Association for the Study of Judaism], as attested by his correspondence quoted in Mauro Perani's "Cesare Colafemmina e Vittore Colorni," in M. Mascolo (ed.), *Ketav, Sefer Miktav. La cultura ebraica scritta tra Basilicata e Puglia. Mostra dedicata a Cesare Colafemmina* (Bari: Edizioni Di Pagina, 2014), pp. 20–22.

41 See below, p. 298.

Colorni's words) "rather on the defects of the Jews and the anomalies of their economic-social structure than on their right to freedom and equality."[42]

His acute historical sensitivity, therefore, enabled the famed Mantuan scholar to avoid, in *Jewish Law and Italian Local Laws, From the Roman Age to the 19th Century* and elsewhere, the anachronistic use of modern "economic" categories when speaking of eras that never knew them. In his oeuvre, he always considered the sphere we now define "economic" as inextricably intertwined, amongst Jews, with the legal and religious dimension, as well as embedded in the social texture. In the following pages, I will thus first attempt to illustrate how Colorni integrated the economic sphere into the legal-religious, moral, and social ones. I will then go on to briefly examine how the elements we now consider "economic" entered the framework sketched by this volume, finally succinctly relating them to today's knowledge and interpretations.

As early as 1938[43] Colorni proposed to reconstruct the history of the early modern Jewish Community of Mantua in its relations with the local majority reality, focusing also on the economic and social activities of Jews that he read in the framework of inner Jewish relational networks and forms of communal self-government. Establishing a significant renewal from the earlier scholarly tradition – one that had focused on the history of Jewish customs and traditions through an evenemential approach –, and by applying a long-term observation, Colorni posed here innovative questions: what had enabled Jews to maintain their settlement and internal and external relations over time? What does a Jewish group's belonging to a concrete geographical and civic space exactly imply?

Alongside the many historiographical paths opened by Colorni's work, the one concerning the economic behavior of European Jews was the one to which the scholar devoted some of his most innovative pages. The central economic theme he raised was that of usury and the transformation of credit practices, analyzed about the transformation of Jewish and non-Jewish community realities and local settlements. Colorni takes up at several points in his work the theories proposed in the second half of the 19th century by one of the founders

42 Vittore Colorni, *Gli ebrei nel sistema del diritto comune fino alla prima emancipazione* (Milan: Giuffrè, 1956), p. 70.

43 Id., "Le magistrature maggiori della Comunità ebraica di Mantova (Sec. XV–XIX)," 1938, now in Id., *Judaica minora: Saggi sulla storia dell'ebraismo italiano dall'antichità all'età moderna* (Milan: Giuffrè, 1983), pp. 257–327. To highlight, where I consider it appropriate, the year and original place of publication, in this chapter I will sometimes expressly quote Colorni's essays which later merged into this and the second volume *Judaica minora: Saggi sulla storia dell'ebraismo italiano dall'antichità all'età moderna. Nuove ricerche* (Milan: Giuffrè, 1991).

of the German Historical School, Wilhelm Georg Friedrich Roscher. According to Roscher, the economic role of Jews as money lenders must be read as an outcome of the conflict between medieval local economic actors. He presented an interpretation of the willingness of Italian Catholic rulers to historically tolerate Jews, arguing that the former protected the latter from popular violence not to enrich themselves, but to resolve a sort of imbalance between "advanced" medieval political institutions and "backward" commercial and financial markets.[44]

This reading of medieval political economy as a form of state intervention aimed at promoting commercial development against popular resistance reassessed the economic role of medieval Jewry as historically necessary and developmentally productive. This could be read in 1875 by Germans – more so than *Risorgimento* Italians – as an allegory of the so-called *Gründerkrach*: the 1873 stock exchange panic and subsequent financial crisis that triggered an economic depression in Europe and North America and lasted from 1873 to 1877 or 1879 in France and Britain. Roscher's presentation of Jewish creditors as performing a positive, nation-building function for past Europe sought to preempt the ransacking of European economic history for anti-Semitic ends. It was positively welcomed by – amongst the others – the economist and future Italian prime minister Luigi Luzzatti, the commercial law professor in Padua Adolfo Sacerdoti, and the director of the *Giornale degli economisti* Eugenio Forti. In his first monograph, focused on the activities of the Medieval Jewish bankers in Urbino, Gino Luzzatto – the founder of economic history in Italian academia – drew in 1902 an analogy between Jews in Italy, Huguenots in France, and Quakers in England citing from Roescher, which in turn was mentioned by Colorni in his 1935 essay published in the *Rivista di storia del diritto italiano*.[45]

44 Bidussa, "Storia degli ebrei, identità di comunità e storiografia"; G. Todeschini, "Teorie economiche degli ebrei alla fine del Medioevo," *Quaderni storici*, vol. 18, 52 (1983): 182–225. Particularly influential in Italy was the publication of G. Roscher, "La situazione degli ebrei nel Medio Evo considerata dal punto di vista della generale politica commerciale," *Giornale degli Economisti*, vol. 1, 2 (1875): 87–109. The article appeared first in Italy and shortly thereafter in Germany. See also Jonathan Zatlin, "The Usurious Jew. Wilhelm Roscher and the Historical Mission of Homo Economicus Judaicus," in Michael Wildt, Moshe Zimmerman, and Christoph Kreutzmüller (eds.), *National Economies: Volks-Wirtschaft, Racism and Economy in Europe between the Wars (1918–1939/45)* (Newcastle: Cambridge Scholars, 2015), pp. 18–32.

45 Tommaso Munari and Francesca Trivellato, "Gino Luzzatto and the Contested Place of Jews in the Economic History of Mediterranean Europe," *Mediterranean Historical Review*, vol. 37, 2 (2022): 203–228, 212; V. Colorni, "Prestito ebraico e comunità ebraiche nell'Italia

We are here at the heart of the coeval debate on the relations between religion and the rise of capitalism that would later be developed by figures such as Werner Sombart and Max Weber. Not coincidentally, the latter criticized Roescher for treating the *Volk* as "a homogenous and real entity of metaphysical character."[46] Roscher's treatment of "the Jews" as a unitary subject, as well as his portrayal of Jews as monopolists over capital markets, evoked the lasting specter of Jewish financial hegemony and connected anti-Semitic stereotypes. Colorni's early works are in continuity with Roscher's ideas, especially when they postulate that the outcome of medieval local economic actors' conflicts forced Jews to focus on lending activities, which had developed more slowly and residually than the trade in goods. The fact that an efficient money market implied the existence of extensive international relational networks would, in this paradigm, have been an essential prerequisite that made Jews competitively advantaged over their Christian lending counterparts. All this was seen by Colorni as a consequence of the diaspora – which in 1955 he defined as "the part of the Jewish people that lived for long centuries (and in some countries for millennia) dispersed among European peoples"[47] –, and of the forced demographic redeployment of the Jews that took place in the first centuries of the second millennium, and caused their displacement from the West to the Center of the continent. This entailed the consequent transformation of Jewish-Christian relations in new sociopolitical, institutional, and administrative contexts, and redefined the economic functions of the Jews in their 12th, 13th, and 14th centuries' landfalls.

It would, of course, be ungenerous to charge a young man in his early twenties, who was taking his first steps in historical research in the mid-1930s, with the responsibility for orienting the national historiographical debate on the role played by Jews in the development of the medieval and early modern economy. A debate that – Giacomo Todeschini recently noted – has "improperly"

centrale e settentrionale con particolare riguardo alla Comunità di Mantova," now in Id., *Judaica minora*, pp. 205–55, 209.

46 Zatlin, ibid., p. 21 and note 6; Nicolas Vallois "Jewish Social Science and the Analysis of Jewish Statistics in the Early Twentieth Century," *Journal of the History of Economic Thought*, vol. 43, 1 (2021): 1–26.

47 Vittore Colorni, "Il popolo ebraico è europeo," *La Rassegna Mensile di Israel*, vol. 21, 10 (1955): 403–09, 403. The article is in controversy with Guido Tedeschi's writing entitled "Siamo noi europei?," [Are we Europeans?] that appeared that same year in n. 5 of the same journal, to which Colorni resolutely objected: "The Jewish people is therefore not 'the closest to European civilization among all non-European peoples,' as Tedeschi asserts, but on the contrary, in my opinion, a distinctly European people, at least as far as its majority of them is concerned; made up of groups of Ashkenazi, Sephardic and, to a small extent, Italian descent" (408–09).

hinged on the assumption that medieval Jewish society was entirely conditioned by the decisions and idiosyncrasies of the Christian majority. Rather, it is worth noting that the early studies on the economic behavior of medieval Jews of Italy published by Colorni were elaborated in a very specific context. One later evoked in these words by the journalist Guido Lopez, brother of the United States-naturalized medievalist Roberto:[48]

> Published in 1935 and '38, [these studies] were reworkings of the two-subject thesis with which Colorni graduated in 1933. In the 1930s, the case of a Jew presenting himself to the graduate committee with a thesis concerning Jews or Jewish subjects was very rare: there was a kind of restraint in mixing one's private Jewishness with public studies. The topic of Jewish moneylending could appear even more embarrassing. The young Colorni approached it with great acumen, objectivity, and (we think it is fair to add) courage. His deductions were, moreover, against the grain of every previous coverage on the subject.

Moreover, the methodological framework presented in Colorni's 1935 study on moneylending is nuanced. Addressed here are the themes to which the Mantuan scholar will return several times in his later production, with an approach so much aimed at investigating the "origins" of Jewish economic behavior as its transformations over the long term, and in the different territorial contexts to which specific Jewish groups belonged. Particular attention is paid to migrations and resettlements of individuals, families, and networks of families. The "spread [*diffusione*] of the Jews" that induced them to reach northern Italy from Rome and Germany in the second half of the fourteenth century is still explained by him in a 1988 study as "[made] necessary in that they [the Jews] exercised a function, the lending of money on pledge, which Christians are forbidden to do by laws of the Church transposed everywhere,

48 Guido Lopez, "Vittore Colorni: L'uomo che cerca le radici," *La Rassegna Mensile di Israel*, vol. 50, 1/4 (1984): 53–57, 56. To be recalled in this regard are Colorni's own reconstructions "Sull'ammissibilità degli ebrei alla laurea anteriormente al secolo XIX," *La Rassegna Mensile di Israel*, vol. 16, 6/8 (1950), *Scritti in onore di Riccardo Bachi*: 202–16, and "Spigolature su Obadià Sforno: La sua laurea a Ferrara e la quasi ignota edizione della sua opera OR 'AMIM nella versione latina," *La Rassegna Mensile di Israel*, vol. 28, 3/4 (1962), *Volume speciale in memoria di Federico Luzzatto*: 78–88. Here the degrees awarded to Jews by Italian universities in the early modern era are described as "an ever-attractive theme because of its suitability for highlighting on the one hand the tenacious attachment of Jews to science [...]; on the other, the liberality shown by the organs of high Italian culture toward the members of a small minority everywhere continually persecuted" (78).

even in the civil sphere."[49] As much as this approach is challenged by more recent research, what should be noted is how local and continental scales are placed by Colorni in constant relation. When avoiding the shoals of an erudite, merely localist approach, he reveals the formative intellectual substratum that ideally connects him to the demological, anthropological, and statistical research carried on since the late nineteenth century by Italian scholars such as Giuseppe Pitré, Aldobrandino Mochi, and Riccardo Bachi.[50] "Such are the results of my research on Jewish moneylending and the spread of Jewish lenders in the quarters of Italy," Colorni could thus write as early as the conclusion of his '35 study. "I hope that this general picture [...] may serve as a starting point for further and broader studies of legal history, and history of Italian Jewry."[51]

It is undeniable that in Colorni's economic works moneylending takes on the character of the prime mover of Jewish dislocation between the late Middle Ages and early modern Italy. "Once it is understood that, from the fourteenth to the sixteenth century, the de facto monopoly of the moneylending activity drives Jews to all the major towns of the center and north of the peninsula," Colorni wrote in 1980 reviewing a study devoted to the Jews of Bagnoreggio, "the usefulness of research aimed at reconstructing the lines of such capillary diffusion appears clear. Thus, communities reappear in unsuspected localities."[52] But it is equally true that Colorni's study of Jewish lending activities, however epistemologically central, is never exhausted in a schematically functionalist form. Commenting in 1975 on Ariel Toaff's volume on Perugia, the historian made it explicit, for example, that he found it appreciable that the research was inspired by the "methodology followed by Cassuto in the exemplary and justly famous monograph around the Jews of Florence in the Age of the Renaissance, [since] the author [Toaff] follows the chronological line but also articulates the theme in a range of well-defined areas: the Jews in their relations with the civic authorities and with the state, economic life, the internal organization of the community, the cultural and scientific life of the individual members, and their professional and literary activity." However, the economic side assumes interpretive prominence here as well: in fact, Colorni went on to add that the

49 "Appunti sugli ebrei di Bozzolo," now in *Judaica minora. Nuove ricerche*, pp. 17–52, p. 17.

50 Bidussa, "Storia degli ebrei, identità di comunità e storiografia"; Fabio Dei, "Dal popolare al populismo: Ascesa e declino degli studi demologici in Italia," in *Meridiana*, vol. 77, 2 (2013): 83–100.

51 "Prestito ebraico e comunità ebraiche," 255.

52 Aldo Luzzato, Amedeo Tagliacozzo, "Gli ebrei in Bagnoreggio. Documenti di una comunità sconosciuta nel territorio dello Stato Pontificio," published in *Archivio della Società romana di storia patria* in 1978 and reviewed by Colorni in *La Rassegna Mensile di Israel*, vol. 46, 11/12 (1980): 365–66, 366.

"economic life of the Jews of Perugia" saw them "devoted above all to lending and, more generally, to banking. It is a general phenomenon that begins precisely in the 13th century, in connection with the canonical prohibitions of interest-bearing loans coupled with the Jewish abandonment of the trade and small industry previously exercised. Bankers are the pivot around which the whole life of the community revolves."[53]

However, the generalizations Colorni practices with reference to medieval periods saw many points where economic and political dimensions are paralleled. After depicting an extensive map of Italian Jewish settlements in the early Middle Ages in a paper published in 1980 among the proceedings of the *Settimane di studio del Centro italiano di studi sull'alto Medioevo*, he, for example, comments: "it is evident that these settlements, in their respective epochs, correspond to localities of a certain political and economic weight. [...] Jews drew their means of livelihood mainly from trade and cultivation, entrusted to settlers, of land they owned [...] or concessionaires *libellario* or *emphitheuticario nomine* of property owned by ecclesiastical bodies."[54] To the buying and selling of real estate by Jews "without any restriction whatsoever" is devoted, moreover, a good part of Coloni's study on Jews in Ferrara in the 13th and 14th centuries,[55] as well as his essay on the 1430 purchase of lands to be destined for cemetery use in Mantua.[56]

After pointing out that it would be a mistake to identify Jewish *libellario* or *emphitheuticario nomine* real estate ownership as "a lesser real right [... or] to the legal inability of Jews to be owners" (the same situation being peculiar to so many Christian possessors), Colorni identifies in the early thirteenth century

53 Vittore Colorni, "Gli ebrei a Perugia," *La Rassegna Mensile di Israel*, vol. 41, 11/12 (1975): 557–59, 558. The reference is to Umberto Cassuto's *Gli ebrei a Firenze nell'età del Rinascimento* (Florence: Galletti e Cocci, 1918). In *Gli ebrei nel sistema del diritto comune*, p. 9, Colorni wrote that Cassuto's monograph was "perfect and exemplary in every other respect," but had one flaw: a "defect of approach that leads the author to discern [...] an equality of rights between Jews and Christians which in reality is entirely nonexistent under the ius *commune*."

54 Id., "Gli ebrei nei territori italiani a nord di Roma dal 568 agli inizi del secolo XIII," now in *Judaica minora*, pp. 67–128: 100–01.

55 Id., "Nuovi dati sugli ebrei a Ferrara nei secoli XIII e XIV," *La Rassegna Mensile di Israel*, vol. 39, 7/8 (1973): 403–17, 413.

56 Id., "Una insospettata presenza ebraica nella campagna mantovana in età altomedievale," in *Judaica minora*, 129–46: 134–145, Colorni's sympathy for figures of farmers and farmhands derived perhaps from the positive relationship his bourgeois family had with those "trustworthy peasants" to whom the Colornis had left their Mantuan property in safekeeping – and who returned it to them safe – during their forced displacements in the years of World War II. I here quote from Mauro Perani's "In memoriam. Vittore Colorni 19 luglio 1912 – Mantova – 11 marzo 2005," *Materia Giudaica*, vol. X, 1 (2005): 5–8, 6.

the change in the socioeconomic basis on which the material existence of the Italian Jewish groups rested.[57]

> The emergence and intense expansion of a new local Christian trading class – he continues –, in fact, defeats, in that field, from the 13th century onward, the Jewish initiative that for many centuries dominated throughout the West. The Jews, obeying the general economic law enunciated by Roscher: according to which "highly civilized commercial peoples, when in the exchange of commodities they are overtaken by younger rivals, usually withdraw themselves with their capital into the money trade," and are induced, or rather forced, to seek in such trade their new basis of subsistence. From the 13th century onward, favored also by the hostility of the Church to any kind of interest-bearing employment of money [...] they become the principal and almost sole holders of the money-lending business.

The subject of moneylending, and the stereotypes built around it by the Christians in the long run, could elsewhere allow Colorni to dig into veins of irony. Reviewing an essay by Giuseppe Laras he observed:[58]

> This is a paper read at the Fourth Congress of Franciscan Studies, held in Loreto on April 25, 1972, and dedicated to the theme *The Montes of Piety and the Social Activities of the Franciscans in the 1400s*. On this occasion it was, with courtesy and breadth of vision, also requested that a suitable scholar be present at the Congress to represent the Jewish point of view, to guarantee as much as possible a sort of impartiality which was rather difficult, to tell the truth, if one considers that the Franciscans of the 15th century – from St. Giacomo della Marca to St. Giovanni da Capestrano, from Friar Michele da Milano to Friar Bernardino da Feltre – did not limit themselves, with regard to the Jews, to theoretical polemics, but constantly transcended to invective and plebs' incitement to fanaticism.

Having noted "the extreme poverty of episodes of warlike character that characterizes Jewish history in the Diaspora from the 3rd century of the Vulgar Era

---

57 "Gli ebrei nei territori italiani a nord di Roma," 101–02.

58 The reference is to G. Laras, "Evoluzione del concetto di usura nel giudaismo e riflessioni sui moventi della critica minoritica nei confronti del prestito ebraico" published in the journal *Picenum Seraphicum* in 1972: *La Rassegna Mensile di Israel*, vol. 39, 7/8 (1973): 475–76, 475.

onward,"[59] Colorni was a careful researcher of episodes of majority-minority conflicts. He employed them as probes into the historical declinations of both "the constant aspiration of the Jews of the Diaspora for autonomy," and the "fundamental characteristic of the Jewish tradition:" namely "the union of the religious element with the juridical element [...] perpetuating itself indefinitely, about changing times and situations."[60] Among the Jewish-Christian (but also Intra-Jewish) disagreements that proved in Colorni's view most fertile with economic consequences were disputes about the limits of the application of what he calls "Jewish law," especially in inheritance matters,[61] regarding both *ab intestato* and testamentary succession, Jewish law and what Colorni calls "local law" usually differed radically: hence continual conflicts especially around the richest inheritances. But Colorni's research also surfaces a number of medieval and early modern intra-Jewish conflicts related to mutual obligations. Significant is the emphasis he put on a case discussed in 16th-century Bologna about property leases. A Jewish landlord, having leased property to another Jew, had subsequently sold it. The buyer, a Jew himself, demanded that the tenant leave, based on the Roman law principle that the nature of the landlord's right was not real. But the tenant resisted based on Jewish law, according to which a lease is a *pro tempore* sale: that is, the landlord's right is real in nature and, for as long as the contract stipulates, prevails over that of the purchaser.

As has been authoritatively pointed out, an "unsurpassed," extremely innovative pinnacle of Colorni's work consisted of the research around the jurisdictional autonomy of Jews, within the framework of the "unstable balance of norms of permissibility and norms of restriction" established in Christian-European contexts.[62] This is a fundamental issue, which naturally has several repercussions in the field of economic history as well. "In deciding a dispute of a personal or patrimonial nature, the [Jewish] courts were constantly faced with the necessity of having to consider, along with Jewish laws of private law, also public law and administrative acts of the state about the private relations that had come into dispute," Colorni recalled in a poignant article published in December 1948, entitled *Gli antichi principi*

59 Vittore Colorni, "Shemuel (Simone) da Spira contro fra Giovanni da Capestrano," *La Rassegna Mensile di Israel*, vol. 38, 7/8 (1972), *Scritti In memoria di Paolo Nissim*: 69–86, 69–70.

60 Vittore Colorni, "Autonomie ebraiche in Italia nel Medioevo e nel Rinascimento," La Rassegna Mensile di Israel, vol. 32, 7 (1966): 306–17, 306.

61 See ibid., to which the following example also refers.

62 Diego Quaglioni, "Gli ebrei e la giustizia nell'età del diritto comune," in Mauro Perani (ed.), *Una manna buona per Mantova: Man tov le-Man Tovah. Studi in onore di Vittore Colorni per il suo 92 ° compleanno* (Florence: Olschki, 2004), pp. 21–40, 22.

giuspubblicistici ebraici e la nuova costituzione dello Stato d'Israele [The Ancient Jewish Jurispublicistic Principles and the New Constitution of the State of Israel].[63] This, he continued, "led Jewish doctrine to formulate those same constitutional theories which, for the same practical needs, were largely elaborated by coeval Christian publicists."

In the studies of Vittore Colorni the rewriting of general legal history to include the history of Jewish communities corrects the overemphasis on the economic dimension of community life itself, which is induced by distortions inherent in public sources. At several points in his scholarly career, he repeated what he wrote in no uncertain terms in his 1938 study of the Jewish magistracies of Mantua: that is, that European legal historians who primarily employ sources produced by the Christian majority – concessions, privileges, decrees, official correspondences, etc. – inevitably focus on the legal position of Jews as individuals. This "at best gives an idea of the relations of an economic nature between the community and the state, but does not at all consider the legal position of the community as such."[64]

In the case of Mantua, only one Hebrew writing thus attests that as early as the 15th century the local Jews – although recognized by the local government only and exclusively as individuals – had constituted a Community with their own leaders, and internal organization overseeing the economy both within and outside the community sphere. Colorni shows that the activity of the leaders of the Mantua Jewish Community was aimed overwhelmingly at protecting common economic interests within the community, also through a tax system that burdened single individuals. The opposite is, of course, also true: namely, that in 1466 - Colorni illustrates – the interests of the community were identified with those of the bankers. Among the community leaders themselves were established dynamics of competition and internal strife pertinent to the economic sphere and subsequently transposed, by spillover, into the community sphere.[65]

The theme of moneylending is also central to Colorni's research presented in this book. This is because a central point in Colorni's work, taken up by him in several publications, is that of the fullness of the right of citizenship enjoyed by medieval Jews in Italy. "Their citizenship was authentic," he argues, for example, further here, on p. 69. "Citizenship emptied, perhaps, of a good deal of its content by restrictive rules but one which always existed in all those elements that had not been expressly repealed." He continues:

63 *La Rassegna mensile di Israel*, vol. 14, 9 (1948): 379–86, 385.

64 "Le magistrature maggiori," 259–60.

65 Ibid., 264–65.

> By the end of the 13th century in central and northern Italy, a large number of Jews are engaged in money-lending. [...] The authorities conclude pacts (chapters) with them, regulating the duration of the concession – in most cases decennial – the modalities of the activity of money-lending at interest, and the rights that the holders of the concession and their families will enjoy for the period of their stay. Almost always explicitly listed is the right to be considered *tamquam cives* and to enjoy the benefits conferred in general upon citizens.

A reformulation of Colorni's theses in this regard, which are unanimously recognized as seminal, is offered by the contribution of Osvaldo Cavallar e Julius Kirshner.[66] The scholars here maintain that not all Medieval and early modern Jews became citizens of the localities in which they resided; and that we should rather speak of Jewish "inhabitants" (*habitatores*) who enjoyed a robust bundle of rights, privileges, and protections under the *ius commune*, local statutes, and Capitoli, whether or not they acquired citizenship. According to this view, the status of *cives* and that of long-term noncitizen *habitatores* were treated as virtually identical. Nevertheless, citizenship was only one of the potential sources of the legal rights and obligations of Jews in late medieval and Renaissance Italy.

From an economic point of view, this perspective leads us to highlight that focusing on the fullness of the right of citizenship tends to distort – based on a kind of modern "liberal" bias – a rather articulate framework of prerogatives and guarantees that were at the origin of a broad body of rights to own, transfer property, enter into contracts, test, inherit, confer and receive dowries. These prerogatives all belonged to the *ius commune* and were not necessarily transfused into the status of citizenship. As it is especially evident in the case of bankers operating at a supra-local level, Jews, in reality, enjoyed – as it has been observed – a sort of "plural membership." They in fact had the right to reside in several towns at once, as is shown by the toponymic indications typical of Jewish surnames referring to distinct places, even though economic actors were exponents of the same parental nuclei.[67]

After discussing it the first part the question of citizenship, *Jewish Law and Italian Local Laws* in its second part examines Jewish legislative autonomy,

66 O. Cavallar, J. Kirshner, "Jews as citizens in late medieval and Renaissance Italy: The case of Isacco da Pisa," *Jewish History*, 25 (2011): 269–318.

67 Ezio Claudio Pia, "Ai limiti della cittadinanza: Credito e appartenenza per Ebrei e Lombardi," *Mélanges de l'École française de Rome-Moyen Âge*, vol. 125, 2 (2013), https://doi.org/10.4000/mefrm.1305.

"namely – as the author wrote in the Introduction – the conflict between Jewish laws and local judicial norms."[68] In its third part this book evaluates examples of Jewish Mediterranean and continental-European normative or judicial autonomy collected from the antiquity to the late modern period, with emphasis on Italy.

In more than one passage, this book examines rulings concerning the conflict brought about by the local legislation, doctrine, and case law, also in economic matters. After surveying early (from the Babilonian diaspora) to medieval (including Maimonides') Jewish doctrine pronunciations on non-Jewish sovereignty and the validity of non-Jewish states tax laws, Colorni in the second part of the volume concludes that "the sages of Talmud outline the arbitrariness of government actions about taxes as emanating from incompetence and law violation,"[69] while considering legitimate all taxes imposed by the state within the limits of the law and collected by duly authorized (Jewish) officials. Medieval texts considered here seem to be in agreement that the coeval Jews were fully aware of their right to compliance with the judicial norms in force, as long as they depended on law and did not overstep its boundaries. In the framework of the constant aspiration by contemporary Jewish scholars to see the Jewish judicial and normative autonomy recognized by the state, Colorni highlights here that both Maimonides and Josef Caro – while reaffirming the generic Jewish prohibition against turning to state courts, even by mutual agreement – consider it legitimate to turn to them with the permission of the rabbinical court. We are here at the root of the well-known – even to scholars of pre-modern Jewish economic life – pluralism of Jewish recourse to Jewish and/or Christian (even Inquisition's) justice, which often depended on specific needs or momentarily convenience and was rooted in the (sometimes amazing) legal skills held by early modern Jewish people even of humble origins.[70]

Of course, since these pages have been first published in 1945 much new research has been conducted on these issues, some of which has surpassed the conclusions of this prominent scholar. Often, however, the reasons for apparent disagreement with Colorni's hypotheses are more due to questions of terminology or theoretical framing than to new empirical elements that have in the meanwhile emerged, or to radical differences in interpretation of those same facts. This is well highlighted by Bernard D. Cooperman with reference to the example of the Jewish judicial independence in late medieval Rome. Colorni was certain "that Jews never had the right to maintain rabbinic tribunals" in

68 See below, p. 2.

69 See p. 206.

70 G. Maifreda, *Italya: Storie di ebrei, storia italiana*, Rome-Bari, Laterza, 2021, esp. at pp. 126 ff.

Rome and refused to believe that Jewish rabbinic courts had existed since classical times, as some historians had suggested, without leaving any trace. Robert Bonfil similarly stressed that the church consistently refused to recognize any jurisdiction for a Jewish court, noting the institutional weakness of the communal rabbinate there. Though she acknowledges the limitations of Jewish courts in civil and certainly criminal matters, Anna Esposito, instead, declares that the Roman 15th century Jewish community possessed juridical autonomy that was recognized by the papal and municipal authorities, and that there was a "rabbinic court" for resolving internal disputes, especially in matters of matrimony and inheritance. "The disagreement among these historians is, on a certain level, a technical and terminological one," Cooperman concludes; "because each deal with the question of jurisdiction from a different perspective." They, in fact, all agree that Jews in Rome regularly made use of rabbinical authorities and halakhically defined procedures to resolve internal disputes, at least in the form of binding arbitration, even if they then relied on Christian notaries to document the results. "What we should like to know is whether Jewish courts had jurisdiction over recognized spheres, whether they had subpoena and enforcement powers, and whether they were linked to specific Jewish ethnic groups or to the entire community."[71]

The milestones set by this book constitute valuable references in today's historiographical debate, within which they continue to inspire new analyses and interpretations. To be hailed as welcomed is therefore the decision of the publisher and editor of the volume to make them finally available to an international audience, now almost eight decades after their Italian publication in that fateful year of 1945.

---

71 Bernard D. Cooperman, "Ethnicity and Institution Building among Jews in Early Modern Rome," *Association for Jewish Studies Review*, vol. 30, 1 (2006): 119–45, 134. Reference is to Roberto Bonfil, *Rabbis and Jewish Communities in Renaissance Italy* (Oxford: Oxford University Press, 1990); Anna Esposito, *Un'altra Roma: Minoranze nazionali e comunità ebraiche tra Medioevo e Rinascimento* (Rome: Il Calamo, 1995), quote from p. 244.

History of Italian Jews and History of Italian Law Revisited

Serena Di Nepi

In 1945, Vittore Colorni, an Italian Jewish historian from Mantua, published the volume *Legge Ebraica e Leggi Locali* [*Jewish Law and Italian Local Laws*] (Milan: Giuffrè). The aim of the work was to systematically record for the first time the relationship between Jewish law, which regulated the public and private life of Italian Jews, and the general law of the "Ancien Régime." The term Ancien Régime refers to the European society of the late 17th century and distinguishes it from the new social structures that emerged during the French Revolution and paved the way for today's society. Colorni's work, which represents the culmination of extensive research that was also carried out during the difficult years of 1938–1945, was published immediately after the Second World War. It was included in the series of the Institute of Roman Law of the "Reale Università degli Studi di Roma" [Royal University of Rome, now Sapienza University of Rome]. The decision to publish this text in such a prestigious place came at a time of complex transition from Fascist Italy to a new, still undefined Italy.[72] During this period, the question of the legal status and self-regulatory systems of Jews in the past went beyond academic interest and acquired great importance both for the author, who had devoted himself to this topic since his formative years in Bologna, and for the publisher, who had taken up and supported this innovative proposal.

A few years later, Colorni took up the subject again with a second volume entitled "Gli Ebrei nel sistema del diritto comune fino alla prima emancipazione" [The Jews in the system of common law up to the first emancipation], which was again published by Giuffrè (1956). This work aimed to provide a systematic synthesis of a complex subject. Building on his earlier research, this follow-up volume offered a comprehensive reflection and presented a plausible and convincing interpretation based on recent research on the history of the Jews in Italy. The centrality of the relationship with the Catholic Church, an enduring experience unbroken by expulsions, and the myth of the Italian Renaissance as a time of coexistence and friendship – celebrated by Cecil Roth in his "The History of the Jews of Italy" (Philadelphia, 1946) – made Colorni's analysis particularly timely. Criticism of this idealized view was soon voiced,

72 Umberto Gentiloni Silveri. *The History of Contemporary Italy (1943–2019)* (New York and London: Palgrave, 2019): pp. 5–53.

notably by Isaiah Sonne, an exceptional scholar and pioneer in the study of Jewish books and contemporary critical philology.[73] In the meantime, Attilio Milano had begun his research into Italian Jewish history with a series of articles on the ghetto in Rome, which he had published in *La Rassegna Mensile d'Israel* before the Second World War and which he later extended on.[74]

Compared to these main lines of research, Colorni took a unique path that was of great interest, although he remained somewhat isolated. After the Second World War, studies on the history of the Jews in Italy were influenced by the fundamental work of Salo W. Baron. As a result, historians focused mainly on the group's relations with the surrounding society, with particular attention to the economic and social perspectives rather than the history of institutions.[75] The researchers shed light on the widespread presence of Jewish communities throughout the Italian peninsula until 1492 and the subsequent expulsions from the south and the islands by examining local and central documents. This mapping of the Jewish presence was accompanied by studies of moneylending, material life and everyday Jewish existence, focusing on the networks and on the ability of individual Jews to establish and maintain relationships with local authorities.

The evolution of Catholic thought, theology, and legislation regarding the Jews has been a fundamental theme in reconstructing the history of Italy. The Papal State, one of the ancient Italian states, played an essential political and diplomatic role until the Unification in 1861. Since the annexation of Rome to the Kingdom of Italy in 1870, it has remained a significant, albeit hostile, interlocutor for both the monarchy and, after 1948, the republican governments. Over the centuries, Jews were permitted to reside within the Papal State under varying rules and discriminations, but there was never a general expulsion order. This range of restrictions and humiliations was underpinned by an extensive theological framework, which has been the subject of in-depth studies. The insoluble contradiction between the Christian-origin anti-Judaism – with its long history of persecution, censorship, ghettos, inquisition, forced baptisms, and more – and a practice of uncertain, fluctuating, and involuntary tolerance has intrigued scholars. Attention to the history of Jewish communities in the Papal State, particularly in Rome, has driven a long and still vibrant period of research. Overall, this rich historiographical field has explored the

73 Serena Di Nepi. "Jews, Italy, Renaissance. Parole antiche e nuovi paradigmi per una storiografia internazionale in movimento." *Studi e materiali di storia delle religioni*, 2021: pp. 737–745.

74 Attilio Milano. *Il ghetto di Roma. Illustrazioni storiche* (Roma: Staderini, 1964).

75 Salo W. Baron. *A Social and Religious History of the Jews* (New York: Columbia University Press, 1965, 2nd edition).

history of Jews in Italy through the lens of relationships: the dynamic between the oppressed minority group and the Christian world, as well as the internal dialectics within the Jewish community, marked by continuous tensions and social and cultural hierarchies.[76]

As we have seen, Vittore Colorni was concerned with an even broader topic. He sought a systemic reading of Jewish history through a legal-historical analysis of Jewish law within the framework of the *ius comune*. Methodologically, this approach required an examination of the history of Italy as a whole, thus calling into question the legitimacy of a unified Italian history for centuries in which the country as such did not exist. The analysis of customary law, particularly in the formulations of the Bolognese jurists, partially solved this problem by incorporating Justinian and canon law into its classical definition while taking local customs into account. However, this interpretative choice tended to downplay certain aspects related to the marginalization of Jews and Jewish-Christian relations in unfavorable circumstances – issues on that historian of Jewish societies and specialists in the history of anti-Semitism focused. By questioning the nature of customary law, its hierarchical, exclusionary and class-based structure became the necessary and obvious starting point for any further consideration. Since both of Colorni's works limited their temporal scope to the pre-emancipation period, they did not have to deal with the inequalities and privileges that formed the backbone of this legal system.

The boundaries of *civitas* in the ancien régime are the basic theme of Colorni's reflections, which center on the idea that the Jews possessed a weak *civitas*, but were not completely excluded from it. On the basis of the principles formulated in the Edict of Milan, the *iudaei* continued to be part of the *civitas*, albeit with certain restrictions, as they had chosen to remain outside the Christian community. This borderline status was ascribed to the Jews and repeatedly confirmed in the legal glosses of medieval jurists and treatise writers up to Giovanni Battista de Luca.

The recognition of this negatively conditioned difference corresponded to the logic of *ius comune*, which did not aim for anachronistic ideals of equality. This system recognized different *iura gentium* (specific law for specific people) and local customs, which paradoxically ensured the preservation of essential

76 See the classical work: K. R. Stow. *Catholic Thought and Papal Jewry policy, 1555–1593* (New York: The Jewish Theological Seminar of America, 1977); S. Simonsohn, *The Apostolic See and the Jews* (Toronto, Pontifical Institute of Mediaeval Studies: 1988–1990). And more recently: Germano Maifreda. *Italya. Storie di ebrei, storia italiana* (Roma-Bari: Laterza, 2022) and Marina Caffiero. *The History of the Jews in Early Modern Italy – From the Renaissance to the Restoration* (London and New York: Routledge, 2022).

features for Jewish survival. These included family law and the always recognized possibility of resolving disputes through internal arbitration, at least in the first instance. In addition, the basic Jewish principle of *dinà demalkutà dinà* (the law of the king is the law) facilitated the adaptation and continuation of their minority status and reduced tensions between one law and the other.[77]

In a society characterized by inequality, this was simply in the nature of things. As Tamar Herzog has recently shown, belonging to Christianity was a prerequisite for full inclusion in the *civitas*.[78] The political sphere was reserved for true faithful, and those who did not wish to belong deliberately chose to forego it. The Enlightenment called into question the appropriateness of this concept of society. The religious wars that had ravaged Europe for a century and a half made it clear that there was an urgent need to conceive and regulate a heterodox society. The debate about tolerance took place primarily within the Christian world and for a long time did not extend to the question of the place of non-Christians. Revolutions, Jacobin republics, Napoleonic codes and emancipation were necessary to bring about change. The equality guaranteed by these new rights brought unprecedented awareness and the challenge of maintaining religious differences in private life while respecting the rules of the new states, which nevertheless retained their Christian character in their legal systems.

In Italy, the profound contradictions of the time, the emergence of a new form of anti-Semitism and the seizure of power by the fascist regime culminated in the racial laws and the modern system of exclusion and persecution of the Jews. Colorni experienced this first-hand. As a college graduate, he was expelled and spent the months of the Nazi occupation in hiding in Rome, where he continued to develop his research. His work, which is undoubtedly imbued with personal nuances, reflects a civic consciousness that deserves reflection.

"The first volume, entitled *Legge Ebraica e Leggi Locali* [Jewish Law and Italian Local Laws], was already completed in 1942 – "hard times for everyone and impractical for the Jews," Guido Lopez recalled in 1984 in a concise but thorough review of the Mantuan author's works on Jewish studies.[79]

77 See also the "Introduction" by Ariel Toaff to the thematic dossier "Tra legge ebraica e leggi locali." Zakhor 11 (1998): pp. 5–8.

78 Tamar Herzog. *Defining Nations. Immigrants and Citizens in Early Modern Spain and Spanish America* (New Haven: Yale University Press, 2003) and more recently *A short history of European Law. The last two and a half millenia* (Cambridge, MA: Harvard University Press, 2018).

79 Guido Lopez. "Vittore Colorni: L'uomo che cerca le radici." *La Rassegna Mensile d'Israel* 50 (1/4, 1984): pp. 53–57.

Colorni's history of Jewish law had the merit of combining questions about the internal legal system with its interactions with the outside world, offering a perspective that simultaneously addressed elements of cultural, social and political history. The Jews in Colorni's work, despite their discrimination, were portrayed as active agents capable of negotiating with the surrounding society. They asserted their otherness while finding autonomous and negotiated ways to deal with their situation. This comprehensive and nuanced analysis moves skillfully between religious history and broader political and institutional history – an approach often lacking in Jewish historical scholarship in recent decades. Colorni's work reminds us how important it is to regain this integrative perspective.

Introduction

In Jewish tradition, the religious and political-judicial are typically blended.

By never turning secular, the legal system retained binding authority for Jews even outside their territorial State and even after the destruction of the second Temple in 70 CE.

Down to the 19th century, Jews everywhere in the diaspora remained tied to their separate judicial institutions out of combined religious and political motives. They sought everywhere a type of autonomy – administrative, legislative, and judicial – that would let them reproduce their ancient Jewish State in miniature. Administratively, Jewish communities sought control over their internal affairs such as worship, charity, social welfare, schools and education, and their own communal rules. They asked for a State's stamp of approval for these joint resolutions towards community members, including an authority to impose levies on them (*administrative autonomy*).

Judicially, the Jews sought recognition of their internal laws – constantly evolving under rabbinical elaboration – as applicable to their civic relations (*regulatory autonomy*).

Per that right, the Jews constantly strived to obtain from the State the authority to bring their community members to trial in their courts of law (*judiciary autonomy*).

As for time and location, legislators' attitude toward Jewish aspiration for autonomy has not always been consistent. Whereas in some places and periods, greater independence was granted in these three fields, other locations and eras were characterized by individualistic political conceptions or were contrary to the State surrendering even the slightest sovereign authority. In the latter case, scaled down to the character of mere consensual arbitrations, Jewish civil law and judicial rulings received no recognition, weight, or coercive power.

Leaving aside the study of administrative autonomy, in this work, I focused on investigating the limits where Italian Jews in various eras were allowed to live according to their own laws, applying them to internal private affairs within their courts.

Before discussing this topic, I deemed it appropriate to provide a foreword on Jews' *status civitatis* within the same geographic and chronological boundaries. This introduction was necessary to establish the meaning of recognizing Jewish personal law, as such recognition differed between Jews' status as foreigners and that of citizens.

This work, therefore, consists of three parts. First, geographically, it refers to Italy (and the ancient and medieval Roman Empire when – politically – Italy

 | DOI:10.1163/9789004627154_002

was merely one of its provinces). Second, chronologically, it focuses on the period from Roman times (when Jews first formed communities in Italy) throughout the 19th century (when, following the application of the democratic individualism principles, Jews became emancipated individually but were deprived – as a group – of all their ancient autonomies).

The first part discusses the question of citizenship.

The second part examines legislative autonomy, namely the conflict between Jewish laws and local judicial norms. In its first section, the rulings concerning the conflict brought about by the local legislation, doctrine and case law are generally described and whenever the multitude of sources allows, distinctively for each private law institution.

However, this issue has not been sufficiently explored since whenever local law stipulates that a given relation should be governed by Jewish law, the question arises, whether in concrete terms, the expression "Jewish law" should be understood only as of the substantive rules of private law or includes constitutional and conflict rules. Two new conflicts essentially emerge, one between local and Jewish constitutional rules and another between local and Jewish conflict rules (question of referral). The second section of the book second part deals precisely with these two further conflicts.

The third part refers to judicial autonomy; i.e., it includes the history of rabbinical courts in all ancient Italian states.

This study had been a strenuous undertaking for both data processing and the nature of research. Many publications – especially the 17th and 18th centuries' short German monographs and studies of Jewish law – were unavailable in Italy, so I could only find them in the libraries of Vienna and London. Others remained absolutely out of my reach despite my thorough research and extensive time devoted to them. All in all, I believe sufficient bibliographic material has been provided for authentication and further research.

As you can see, I provided complete document information in the footnotes to enable an immediate checkup of the statements made in the text. I know, from experience, how often references are approximate and incorrect.

In submitting these pages for publication, I would like to warmly thank the distinguished Prof. Gustavo Calò, rabbi of Mantua, who generously placed the treasure of his vast culture at my disposal and offered me valid and intelligent assistance in the search and interpretation of Hebrew texts. I would also like to thank the distinguished Prof. Emilio Albertario, director of the Institute for Roman law, East Mediterranean laws and history of law at the Royal University of Rome,* who most kindly agreed to include my work in the institute's publications.

* Today, Università degli Studi di Roma "La Sapienza."

PART 1

The Status Civitatis

CHAPTER 1

The Roman Empire and Italy in Particular

1 The Pagan Age

In the era before the victory of Christianity, Jews in the diaspora were usually not subject to special rules either concerning the *status civitatis*[1] or about exercising their political and civil rights.[2]

Based on Juster's fundamental study and general clarifications contained in other recent works, the principles concerning Jews' citizenship in the Roman pagan age can be summarized as follows:

1.1 *Until the Year 70*

1) Palestinian Jews have a right to their State citizenship and are included among the subjects (*peregrini*) with all other peoples who have entered the orbit of Roman sovereignty.[3]
2) In whatever state they settle in, Diaspora Jews can become citizens, which generally happens.[4]

   However, privileges of citizenship rights are sometimes challenged as, from a nationalistic and religious point of view, they are a separate community organized under their leaders and enjoying broad autonomy.[5]

---

1 Juster, *Les Juifs dans l'empire romain: leur condition juridique, économique et sociale*, Paris, 1914, vol. II, pp. 1–27.

2 Roman Jewish citizens – namely all Jews of the Empire after 212 – have access to all offices of the State (Juster, vol. II, pp. 243–290). The obligation of the pagan oath for the officials and any other possible acts in contrast with their faith are removed by Septimius Severus and Caracalla. D. 50, 2, 3, 3, *de decurionibus* (Ulpianus, *libro tertio de officio proconsulis*): "Eis qui Judaicam superstitionem sequuntur, divi Severus et Antoninus honores adipisci permiserunt, sed et necessitates eis imposuerunt, quae superstitionem corum non laederent." (Juster, II, p. 243, n. 4).

3 Juster, *Les Juifs dans l'empire romain: leur condition juridique, économique et sociale*, Paris, 1914, vol. II, pp. 1–2.

4 Juster, *Les Juifs dans l'empire romain:* vol. II, pp. 2–14.

5 For examples of disputes, see Juster, therein. The question of the *status civitatis* of the Alexandria Jews in Egypt has been widely discussed. Juster examines it in a lengthy note (ibid., pp. 7–11) and concludes that these Jews were not only citizens but belonged to the class enjoying the broadest political rights. On the subject, see also: B. Motzo, *La condizione giuridica dei Giudei di Alessandria sotto i Lagidi e i Romani*, in *Atti dell'Accademia delle Scienze di Torino*, 1912–1913, pp. 577–598; Engers, *Die staatsrechtliche Stellung der Alexandrinischen Juden*, in *Klio*, XVIII, 1923, pp. 79–90 (in the negative sense); G. De Sanctis, *Claudio e i Giudei*

 | DOI:10.1163/9789004627154_003

However, the contrasts are never lasting since, in antiquity, the pluralism of the state in nationalities and religious creeds is a normal situation. Before Roman law, these Jews, citizens of states controlled mainly by Rome, were likewise *peregrini*.

3) Similarly, Jews living in the metropolitan Roman State can become *cives romani*, whether by governmental concession or, in the case of slaves, by an act of liberation granted by their citizen masters.[6] Typically, the Jews of the Empire either retained the citizenship of the Jewish State, were citizens of the vassal states of Rome, or were Roman citizens.

There are, however, examples of Jews who enjoy both local and Roman citizenships.[7] The best known is that of the apostle Paul of Tarsus, who declares himself a Jewish national (Epistle to the Philippians, 3, 5; 2nd Corinthians, 11, 22), a citizen of Tarsus (Acts 21, 39) and a Roman citizen (Acts 22, 28).

In and of itself, there is nothing exceptional about it: as recently demonstrated in scores of documents by Schönbauer, since imperial times, granting Roman citizenship to *peregrini* does not cancel the original citizenship but overlaps it: as the Roman Empire is not unitary, but a complex state comprising a constellation of political entities joined under the sovereignty of Rome, the nationality of each of these political entities is not incompatible with Roman citizenship, and can quite easily coexist with it. Thus, when a subject is elevated to the rank of *civis romanus*, he does not cease to be a part of his original *civitas* or becomes alien to it. Instead, he remains in his previous judicial and political position, improved and enhanced, for himself and his heirs, in all political rights and privileges related to the quality of *civis romanus*.[8]

---

di Alessandria, in *Rivista di Filologia e Istruzione classica*, N. S., II, 1924, pp. 473–513 (in the positive sense); Neppi-Modona, *La vita pubblica e privata degli ebrei in Egitto nell'età ellenistica e romana*, in *Aegyptus*, II, pp. 253–75 and III, pp. 19–43, p. 265 et seqq. in particular. H. J. Bell, *Jews and Christians in Egypt*, London, 1924, pp. 10–16, with an extensive bibliography (intermediate solution: the Jews would be citizens as individual citizens, but foreigners as an entity); Goodenough, *The jurisprudence of the Jewish court in Egypt: legal administration by the Jews under the early Roman Empire as described by Philo Judaeus*, New Haven, 1926, pp. 15–16; and finally Segrè, *Note sullo status civitatis degli ebrei nell'Egitto Tolemaico e Imperiale*, in *Bulletin de la Société archéologique d'Alexandrie*, no. 28, Alexandria, 1933. Cf. Lucia Levi, *La lettera di Claudio e gli Ebrei di Alessandria*, in *Rassegna mensile di Israel*, vol. V, no. 7–8, 1930, pp. 382–391.

6 Juster, *Les Juifs dans l'empire romain*: vol. II, pp. 15–17.

7 Juster, *Les Juifs dans l'empire romain*: vol. II, p. 16.

8 Schönbauer, *Reichsrecht gegen Volksrecht? – Studien über die Bedeutung der Constitutio Antoniniana für die römische Rechtsentwicklung*, in *Zeitschrift der Savigny Stiftung*, 1931, pp. 330–333; same author, *Reichsrecht Volksrecht und Provinzialrecht*, in *Zeitschrift der Savigny Stiftung*, 1937, p. 309 et seqq. Even before Schönbauer, in the same sense, see Stroux and

Such a general state of affairs reflects the political dependency of several minor states on a larger and stronger one, a dependency, however, that has not progressed to the complete absorption of the states themselves and the destruction of their autonomy. Understanding this situation is sufficient to justify the dual nationality of some Jewish individuals or some Jewish communities in Palestine and the diaspora.[9]

1.2 *After the Year 70*

Mommsen's theory, by which all Jews of the Roman Empire after the 70 CE. war and the consequent destruction of the Jewish State became *dediticii*,[10] was quickly demolished by Juster, who showed undoubtedly that at least concerning the diaspora Jews' *status civitatis*, the disaster of 70 CE did not have the slightest effect.

As for Palestine, he notes that, perhaps, the most radical insurgents were reduced to the quality of *dediticii*, but even for them, this does not seem to have been a long-lasting measure. In fact, from Jewish and non-Jewish sources, the government does not appear to have enforced any of those restrictions on contracting marriages, wills, liberating slaves, etc. on any group of Palestinian Jews, whether according to Roman or local law, which defines the position of *dediticius*.[11]

Returning later to this question, A. Momigliano[12] fully confirms Juster's thesis regarding the diaspora but does not find the argument just mentioned very conclusive regarding Palestine since, in practice, the *dediticii* too, could marry, bequeath, etc. He tends to believe that the Romans have taken a different course towards the Jews, depending on the attitude taken during the war: only the rebels who surrendered early enough, the *security*, perhaps, were reduced to the permanent condition of *dediticii*. The others, those loyal to Rome, would not have changed their position. In an extensive review of Momigliano's

Wenger, *Die Augustus Inschrift auf den Markplatz von Kyrene*, in *Abhandlungen der Bayerischen Akademie der Wissenschaften*, XXXIV, 2, 1928, p. 44 et seqq. Also, cf. Wenger, *Nationales, griechisches und römisches Recht in Aegypten*, in *Atti del IV Congresso Internazionale di papirologia*, Milan, 1936, pp. 176–179. Wenger follows the integration of the Giessen 40, 1 papyrus as proposed by Wilhelm, in *American Journal of Archeology*, 38, 1934, pp. 178–180.

9 Schönbauer, *Rechrshecht Volksrecht und Provinzialrecht*, op. cit., 1937, p. 342.

10 Mommsen, *Gesammelte Schriften*, Berlin, 1905–13, vol. III, pp. 418–19; vol. VI, p. 168.

11 Juster, op. cit., II, pp. 19–23.

12 A. Momigliano, *Ricerche sull'organizzazione della Giudea sotto il dominio romano*, in *Annali della R. Scuola Normale Superiore di Pisa*, Series II, vol. III, 1934, p. 394.

work,[13] G. I. Luzzatto is even more specific in believing that it would not be possible "given the so different attitudes taken by individual communities towards Rome, to speak of the Jews as *dediticii* or not, but only of individual *dediticiae* communities."

In conclusion, no matter how the Palestine issue is resolved, scholars agree with Juster that diaspora Jews did not suffer any backlash from the events of 70 CE. Schönbauer's statement reiterating that after 70 CE, all Jews were *dediticii*, should be disregarded, as it ignores Juster and refers again to Mommsen,[14] even contradicting himself shortly afterward – again without mentioning Juster – restricting this quality only to Palestinians.[15]

1.3 *After the Year 212*

Any possible establishment and perpetuation of the quality of *dediticii* by some Palestinian Jews starting from 70 CE is relevant concerning the 212 CE. Constitution of Caracalla – granting Roman citizenship. In fact, while several judicial sources and literary notes state since ancient times that this emperor granted citizenship to all subjects of the Roman world without mentioning exclusions of any kind, from the text of the edict, found years ago in a Greek papyrus,[16] most scholars chose to deduce that the *dediticii* were excluded from the concession.

The central papyrus sentence, incomplete, was rebuilt in the following terms: δίδωμι τοῖ[ς συνάπα[σιν ξένοις τοῖς κατὰ τ]ὴν οικουμένην π[ολιτ]είαν Ῥομαίων, [μ]ένοντος [παντὸς γένους πολιτευμ]άτων, χωρ[ὶς] τῶν [δεδ]ειτικίων. Moreover, that exclusion was established by connecting the words χωρὶς τῶν δεδειτικίων to the main proposition δίδωμι etc., rather than to the secondary one μένοντος etc. However, this interpretation has been vehemently opposed by Segrè,[17] followed by Capocci,[18] who has shown in two excellent and argumentative studies that the fragment χωρὶς τῶν δεδειτικίων must be coupled with μένοντος etc., not with δίδωμι etc.

Therefore, they interpret this fragment as a provision relating the πολιτεύματα δεδειτικίων with which it is established that, unlike the constitution of

---

13 G. I. Luzzatto, in *Studia et documenta historiae et juris*, II, 1936, pp. 218–219.

14 *Reichsrecht gegen Volksrecht?*, op. cit., 1931, p. 335.

15 *Reichsrecht, Volksrecht, und Provinzialrecht*, op. cit., 1937, p. 342.

16 Pap. Giessen, no. 40, 1. Mitteis and Wilcken, *Grundzüge und Chrestomathie der Papyruskunde*, vol. II, Leipzig 1912, no. 377.

17 Segrè, in *Bollettino dell'Istituto di Diritto Romano*, 32, p. 210 et seqq., and by the same author, *L'Editto di Caracalla sulla concessione della cittadinanza romana ed il papiro Giessen* 40, 1, in *Studi Perozzi*, Palermo 1925, p. 159 et seqq.

18 Capocci, *La Constitutio Antoniniana*, in *Atti dell'Accademia dei Lincei*, series VI, vol. I, 1925, p. 104 et seqq.

other πολιτεύματα, their constitution should not remain unchanged, and they thus reject the thesis that this fragment implies the principle of excluding the *dediticii* from the benefit of citizenship.

Schönbauer also reaches similar conclusions through different paths.[19] In agreement with Mayer,[20] and contradicting Segrè and Capocci, he observes that Roman law knows no *civitates dediticiae* but only single *dediticiae* persons. Through a different reading and integration of the text of the papyrus,[21] he states that with his edict, Caracalla intended to grant the *civitas romana* to all members of the *orbis romanus*, simultaneously establishing the unaltered permanence of their citizenship and local autonomy. As a logical consequence, the *dediticii* are excluded from the provision. Since previously they had not belonged to any *certa civitas* (Ulpianus, Regulae, 20, 14), they will only enjoy the general citizenry.

According to Schönbauer, the edict generalizes the Roman and local dual citizenship system, enjoyed since the beginning of the imperial era by large numbers of members of the autonomous *civitates* subjected to Rome. However, it does not change the constitution of the state that even now does not become unitarian: the autonomous political communities (πόλεις) that existed within the various provinces before 212 CE continue to subsist with all their previous rights. Every citizen of these communities combines now the "Bundes- oder Reichsbürgerschaft" to his particular citizenship: only the *dediticius*, not having been a member of any previous πόλις "war künftigin nur ein 'Ρομαῖος, der einen Abstammungsort oder einen Heimatsort (ἰδία) hatte, aber keinen Heimatsstaat (πόλις)."[22]

Given these preliminary general remarks and starting from Mommsen's misconception that from 70 CE onwards, the Jews were *dediticii*, Schönbauer states that as a consequence of the Constitutio Antoniniana, they all became citizens of the Roman state. However, like other *dediticii*, they did not associate this "Bundesbürgerschaft" with the citizenship of a particular state.[23]

Although based on a different interpretation of the papyrus, both agree not to recognize the exclusion of the *dediticii* from the Antoniniana provision. Essentially and despite some differences in the construction details, they also agree upon affirming the immutability of the state's constitution, the persistence of the pre-existing autonomies and pre-existing citizenships and

19 Op. cit., 1931, pp. 310–11.

20 Paul M. Mayer, in *Zeitschrift der Savigny Stiftung*, vol. 46, p. 25.

21 μένοντος [πολιτκοῦ σφισι ἀπαραβ]άτως χωρὶς etc.

22 Op. cit., 1931, pp. 314 and 333–34.

23 Op. cit., 1931, p. 335; 1937, p. 343.

the subsequent coupling of these pre-existing citizenships with the general citizenship.[24]

We are only interested in clarifying that by accepting either point of view, we recognize that in 212 CE, all Jews of the Roman Empire became *cives romani* while remaining citizens of the political entities to which they previously belonged. When appropriate, we shall examine the consequences of this concerning the use of their law.

2 The Christian Age

While harassing the Jews, for following a different religion than the one declared official state religion, with complex political and civil prohibitions,[25] Christian emperors do not take away the quality of their *cives romani*.[26] This quality is actually explicitly recognized by *a*) imposing upon them rules applicable only to *cives romani*,[27] and *b*) overtly insisting, in the two laws of 393[28] and 398,[29] that they abandon their national law also in private relations and replace it with Roman law.

---

24 On this subject, see also Roberto Bozzoni, *La Constitutio Antoniniana e i dediticii*, Naples, 1933, p. 48; and more recently G. I. Luzzatto, *Epigrafia giuridica greca e romana*, Milan, 1942, pp. 30–44 and 301–321.

25 Juster's excellent work is devoted to studying these restrictions. The first (lost) law limiting the civil rights of Jews is that of Constantine (prohibition of owning Christian slaves: Eusebius, *Vita Constantini*, 4, 27, cf. C. Th. 16, 8, 22; Juster, op. cit. II, p. 72). The pagan rules that aim to curb proselytism (Juster, I, p. 254 et seqq.) cannot be considered detrimental to civil and political equality of the Jews.

26 Juster, *Les Juifs dans l'empire romain*: vol. II, p. 25, no. 1 and p. 246.

27 E.g., in succession issues, the laws *Furia testamentaria, Falcidia*, etc. L. 28 C. Th. 16, 8. Juster, II, p. 24, 83–84, 88–92.

28 L. 7 C. J. 1, 9: *Imppp. Valentinianus Teodosius et Arcadius. Intentio comiti Orientis.* Nemo Judaeorum morem suum in coniunctionibus retinebit nec juxta legem suam nuptias sortiatur nec in diversa sub uno tempore coniugia conveniat. *D. II. K. Ian. Constantinopoli Theodosio A. III et Abundantio conss.* [y. 393].

29 L. 10 C. Th. 2, 1: *Imppp. Gratianus Valentinianus et Theodosius AAA. Ad Eutychianum praef. praetorio.* Judaei romano et communi jure viventes, in his causis quae non tam ad superstitionem eorum quam ad forum et leges ac jura pertinent, adeant sollemni more judicia omnesque romanis legibus inferant et excipiant actiones: postremo sub legibus nostris sint. Sane si qui per compromissum ad similitudinem arbitrorum apud judaeos vel patriarchas ex consensu partium in civili dumtaxat negotio putaverint litigandum, sortiri eorum judicium jure publico non vetentur: eorum etiam sententias provinciarum judices exequantur, tamquam ex sententia cognitoris arbitri fuerint adtributi. *Dat. III Non. Feb. Constantinopoli Honorio A. IIII et Eutychiano V., C. Conss.*

The two laws reported by Justinian[30] show the constant will of the Christian emperors not to revive the category of *peregrini* by then already disappeared so as to apply it to the infidels, but rather to preserve for them their fundamental quality of citizens of the Empire. Except for matters where Jews are affected by a specific ban, in the times of Justinian, as in the past, they undoubtedly enjoy the benefits granted to *cives* and are subject to all obligations imposed upon them. Therefore, their citizenship is constricted only by special rules, but is always there and *ipso jure* resumes power only when a particular rule fails. Total judicial capacity remains the rule for Jews, whereas judicial incapacity remains the exception. The fact that the number of these legal 'disqualifications' keeps growing is irrelevant, because if they must be established one by one, this means the basic legal terms of qualification have not failed.

As for Byzantine Italy, fortunately, we have an extensive collection of documents between the end of the sixth and the beginning of the seventh century – the letters of Gregory the Great – attesting to the continuous application of the rules of the *Corpus Juris* to Jews.[31] One of these letters explicitly declares that they are living under Roman law,[32] which demonstrates their persistent quality of *cives*, beyond any possible uncertainty. This position appears to remain unchanged in later Byzantine legislation. In fact, the two cited laws

30 The first one, as we have seen, is only found in Justinian's Code. The second one is reported there (l. 8, C. J. 1, 9) with some variations, the principal of which is in the dropping of *non* before "tam ad superstitionem eorum." Accordingly, jurisdiction in purely religious matters is also taken away from the Jews. However, as Juster (II, pp. 152–153) rightly observed, such a restriction is completely illogical and must derive from an ancient error of copyists rather than from the will of the legislator. It nevertheless remained, as we shall see, in all subsequent compilations. The Greek version of the two constitutions, by the jurist Teleleo, a Justinian contemporary (about him, see Heimbach, *Prolegomena Basilicorum*, Heimbach, in volume VI of *Basilicorum libri*, pp. 13, 72–78) is published in the notes to Σίνοψις τῶν Βασιλικῶν in Zachariä von Lingenthal, *Jus graecoromanum*, re-ed. Athens, 1931, vol. V, p. 318 and it reads as follows:

l. 7, C. I. 1, 9. Μηδεὶς τῶν ἰουδαίων κατὰ τὸν ἴδιον θεσμὸν συζευγνύσθω, μήτε κατὰ τὸν ἴδιον νόμον γαμείτω, μήτε εἰς διαφόρους ἐν ἑνὶ καιρῷ γαμοὺς συνερχέσθω.

l. 8: Οἱ ἰουδαῖοι τῷ ρωμαικῷ καὶ κοινῷ νόμῳ βιοῦντες ἐν τούτοις τοῖς πράγμασι, ἁτινα πρὸς τὴν θρησκέιαν αυτῶν, καὶ τὴν αγορὰν καὶ τοῦς νόμους καὶ τὸ δὶκαιον ανήκουσιν, προσερχέσθωσαν τῷ εθίμῷ τρώπῳ τοῖς δικαστερίος καὶ πᾶσι τοῖς ρωμαικοῖς νόμοις ὑποπιπτέτωσαν καὶ λαμβανέτωσαν ἀγογάς· εἴ τινες δὲ τούτων κοινῇ συμφονία καθ' ὁμοιότητα τοῦ δικαστοῦ παρᾶ τοῖς ἰουδαίοις ἐν χρηματικῇ μόνον ὑποθέσει βουληθῶσι δικάσασθαι, καταλεγῆναι τοῖς αὐτοῖς κριτηρίοις δημοσίῳ νόμῳ μη κωλυέσθωσαν, καὶ ταῖς αυτῶν ψῆφοις οἱ ἀρχόντες ἐξακολουθείτωσαν, ὡσανεὶ ἐξ αποφάσεως ἄρχοντος αἱ ψῆφοι προενέχθησαν.

31 *Gregorii I Papae registrum epistolarum*, Ewald & Hartmann ed., two volumes, 1887–1889, in *Monumenta Germaniae Historica, Epistolae*, vol. I, II. See the list of the 24 letters concerning the Jews, in Juster, p. 81, no. 5.

32 Ep. II, 6 (Sept.–Oct. 591): Sicut romanis legibus vivere permittuntur.

prohibiting Jews from using Roman law in private relations appear in later Byzantine epitomes and elaborations with non-substantial variations.

Likewise, a *summa* of the l. 8 C. J., 1, 9 found in the fragments of the lost Breviary of Theodore Ermopolitan,[33] a sixth-century jurist,[34] and both constitutions are summarized in the *Collectio constitutionum ecclesiasticarum tripartita*,[35] composed between 578 and 610[36] and fully reported by the Basilici.[37]

All this demonstrates that the Jews in the Byzantine Empire never lost their *cives romani* status: here too, as already in the Western Empire, the various restrictive regulations imposed on them strongly affected this status, emptied its contents, but never reached the point of making it fail from its bases.

33 *Jus graecoromanum*, op. cit., ibid.:
Πᾶς ἑβραῖος κατὰ τοὺς ῥωμαίων νόμους πολιτεύσθω καὶ μὴ κατὰ μωσαικοὺς. Καλῶς ἐνάγουσι καὶ ενάγονται οἱ ἰουδαῖοι παρὰ τοῖς ἁρμοδίοις δικασταῖς, καὶ εἀν συναινέσωσιν ἀμφότερα τὰ μέρη δύνανται δικάζεσθαι παρὰ τοῖς πρεσβυτέροις αὐτῶν, ἂν δηλονότι αλλήλοις δικάζωνται· εἰ γὰρ χριστιανῷ δικάζεται ἰουδαῖος, οὐ κρίνεται παρὰ ἐβραίῳ ἀλλὰ χριστιανῷ.

34 Heimbach, Op. cit., ibid., pp. 17–18.

35 Voelli and Justelli, *Bibliotheca juris canonici veteris*, T. II, Paris, 1661, p. 1294.

36 Krüger, *Histoire des sources du droit romain*, Fr. transl., Paris, 1894, p. 492.

37 Basilici I, 1, 39 and 40.

CHAPTER 2

Italy – the Ostrogoth Age

As a natural consequence, the fall of the Roman Empire brings with it the collapse of the general concept of Roman citizenship. The Germanic monarchies that take shape on the ruins of the wrecked organism set themselves up as distinct autonomous states. In addition to members of the conquering people, every inhabitant already holding Roman citizenship is considered a citizen without distinction of nationality. Like there were Roman citizens of various nationalities in the Empire before, there are now citizens of different national groups in the individual Germanic kingdoms.

In other words, each ethnic group, each nation or fraction of nation residing within the borders of the new political entities acquires its respective citizenship, while the members of the same nation who have not become subjects of the same new sovereign become alien to each other.[38]

In this regard, the fate of the Jewish people spread in more or less extensive communities in every country of the Mediterranean basin does not seem to differ from that of other peoples of the former Empire. By 476, the shared Roman citizenship is gone and the Jews are incorporated into each of the new monarchies and considered citizens of each of them.

In Italy, the Jews are the only group that resides permanently in the peninsula alongside the Romans and enjoys Roman citizenship.[39] Alien as they are,

38 Cf. Tamassia, *Stranieri ed Ebrei nell'Italia meridionale dall'età romana alla sveva*, in *Atti del Reale Istituto Veneto di scienze lettere ed arti*, 1903–04, t. LXIII, part II, pp. 758–59 and 776–77, who rightly insists on the need to always keep the concepts of citizenship or subjection on the one hand and of nationality on the other hand well distinct. Besta, in *Le persone nella storia del diritto* italiano, Padua, 1931, p. 35: "Già sotto gli Ostrogoti … tutti quelli che, pure essendo di nazionalità romana, non erano insieme sudditi del re goto vennero reputati come *peregrini*." In *Storia e sistema delle fonti del diritto comune*, vol. I, *Le origini*, Milan, 1938, pp. 126–128, concerning Italy, Calasso correctly points out that in theory, from the Romans' viewpoint, Theodoric remains a simple *magistratus* of the Emperor in the East, whereas only for the Ostrogoths he is an autonomous *rex*. In reality, however, the Ostrogoth state is entirely independent of the Byzantine Empire and, therefore, regarding the Romans, we can speak of new citizenship.

39 On the indefinite continuation of Jewish individuality even after 212, e.g., the following texts of St. Augustine should be considered: *Enarratio in Psalmum*, on Psalm 58, sermon 1 (Migne, *Patrologia latina*, 36–37, col. 705): "Maneat gens Judaeorum; certe vincta est a romanis, certe deleta civitas earum; non admittuntur ad civitatem suam Judaei [on this ban see Juster, II, pp. 171–175] et tamen Judaei sunt. Nam omnes istae provinciae a Romanis subjugatae sunt. Quis jam cognovit gentes in imperio romano quae quid erant,

 | DOI:10.1163/9789004627154_004

in principle, to any unnecessary innovation, the Ostrogoths apply the norms of the Theodosian Code upon them, introducing a single, albeit very important, change which constitutes a partial implementation of the personality criterion of the law. This is contrary to the state's total judicial unity principle, which had eventually prevailed in the Roman Empire. They consider it thus normal that Jews live according to their national law in private internal relations and stipulate that their disputes be decided by experts in their law.[40]

Thus, by recognizing the validity of the law, the Jewish national individuality resurfaces *de jure* in Ostrogoth Italy, but without any change to their *status civitatis*. Romans, Goths, and Jews live together in Theodoric Italy, as citizens of the new monarchy, each group retaining the most typical expression of its ethnic personality with its private law.[41]

---

quando omnes Romani facti sunt et omnes Romani dicuntur? Judaei tamen manent cum signo; nec sic victi sunt, ut a victoribus absorberentur." And further on, sermon 2 (col. 706–707): "Per omnes gentes manent certe, et Judaei sunt nec destiterunt esse quod erant: id est gens ista non ita cessit in jura Romanorum ut amiserit formam Judaeorum; sed sic subdita Romanis est, ut etiam leges suas teneat, quae leges sunt Dei." The same author, *Contra Faustum Manichaeum*, book 12, ch. 13, Venice edition, 1730, vol. VIII, p. 233: "Multum mirabile est, quemadmodum omnes gentes quae a Romanis subiugatae sunt in ritum romanorum sacrorum transierint, eaque sacrilegia observanda et celebranda susceperint; gens autem Judaea, sive sub paganis regibus sive sub christianis, non amiserit signum legis suae, quo a ceteris gentibus populisque distinguitur; et omnis imperator vel rex qui eos in regno suo invenit, cum ipso signo eos invenit, nec occidit, id est non efficit ut non sint Judaei certo quodam et proprio suae observationis signo a ceterarum gentium communione discreti." In *Il Sacro Romano Impero*, It. transl., Naples 1886, p. 5, Bryce notes that after 212, following civil and political equalization, the peoples brought together in the Roman Empire gradually merge and lose their original ethnic individuality. The only exception is the Jews, "the only nation yet yearning for a national sentiment." Thus, failing the premise, Mommsen's thesis that after 70 C.E., all Jews of the Empire are reduced to the state of *dediticii*, that the Jewish nation is not longer recognized by the emperors, and that only the Jewish religion is, falls apart. Cf. Juster, op. cit., I, pp. 418–24 and II, pp. 19–23, and A. Momigliano, *Ricerche*, cit. pp. 394–396.

40 Edict of Theodosius (year 512), ch. 143: "Circa Judaeos privilegia legibus delata serventur: quos inter se jurgantes et suis viventes legibus, eos judices habere necesse est quos habent observantiae praeceptores." See further on pp. 108–110.

41 Juster's assertion, vol. II, p. 25, that the Ostrogoths "sous Théodoric en continuant à appliquer aux Juifs les dispositions du droit romain leur reconnaissaient, implicitement, la qualité de Romains" is therefore incorrect. By accepting in the edict and applying the rules of public law decreed by the Roman emperors to the Jews, the Ostrogoths only demonstrate their desire not to bring innovations into the political position of the Jews. However, with the granted faculty to live *suis legibus*, established by the edict in opposition to l. 10 C. Th. 2, 1 that decrees precisely the opposite, there is a clear desire to consider Jews as a distinct ethnic individuality. Conversely, only in the Visigothic Kingdom, this acknowledgment does not occur. There, the Alarician Breviary of 506 reports the mentioned l. 10 C. Th. 2, 1, together with the following *interpretatio*: "Judaei omnes qui romani esse noscuntur apud religionis suae maiores agant quod ad religionis pertinet

The Jews were indeed citizens, but as in the Roman Empire, i.e., without political rights and struck by a series of civil exclusions. Although of Arian faith, Theodoric does not feel like modifying the restrictive rules decreed for the Jews by Catholic emperors, in obedience to the dictates of the Church of Rome, and merely practices a broad tolerance.

A tombstone text from the Jewish catacombs in Venosa, published and expertly illustrated by Ascoli,[42] and subsequently taken into consideration also by Tamassia,[43] would have been an excellent proof of this, if it could be dated with certainty to the Ostrogoth Age.[44]

The headstone marks the grave of a 14-year-old girl, Faustina "que fuet pronepus [= neptis] Faustini patris, nepus [neptis] Biti et Acelli qui fuerunt majures cibitatis." It should be read as "heads of cities" rather than "heads of the Jewish communities of the city," which would make sense also to Tamassia,

disciplinam, ita ut inter se quae sunt hebreis legibus statuta custodiant: alia vero negotia, quae nostrae legibus continentur et ad forum respiciunt, apud judicem Provinciae, eo quo omnes jure confligant. Sane si apud maiores legis suae, consentientes ambae partes de solo tamen civili negotio audiri voluerint, quod, interveniente compromisso, arbitrali judicio terminatur, tale sit quasi ex precepto judicis sit definitum." The principle that Jews of the Kingdom who were *cives romani* before the conquest and lived under Roman law ("qui romani esse noscuntur," equivalent to "romano communi jure viventes" of l. 10 C. Th. 2, 1) is therefore reaffirmed, and by this law, they continued regulating their relationships. As in the past, the validity of Jewish law was not recognized except in religious matters. In civil matters, the exception to the rule was in explicit resorting to Jewish arbitration, subject to both parties' agreement and respective compromise. But this full confirmation of l. 10 C. Th. 2, 1 *in toto* assimilating the Jews to the Romans is a unique case apt only to the Visigothic *interpretatio*: as we shall see, all other epitomes of the Theodosian Code decidedly amend that constitution, introducing the Jewish-Roman antithesis, and recognizing the validity of Jewish law not only in the religious sphere but in the civil one as well.

42 G. I. Ascoli, *Iscrizioni inedite o mal note greche, latine, ebraiche di antichi sepolcri giudaici del napoletano*, Turin-Rome, 1880, no. 19, pp. 61–62.

43 Tamassia, op. cit., pp. 809–816.

44 The *ad quem* dating limit of the entire series of 21 hypogean graves can be put at 550 (Ascoli, op. cit., p. 46; cf., however, on p. 118: "Le catacombe di Venosa conducendoci in effetto, per le epigrafi sotterranee, in sino al VI secolo e probabilmente anche più in giù. …" That the one considered here is among the most recent ones, is demonstrated by the Hebrew phrase included in it. In fact, the Hebrew language, completely abandoned for centuries by the Jewish Hellenistic-Roman diaspora, following Palestinians' influxes, re-emerges for the first time in the West in these Venosa gravestones. And as time goes by, it asserts itself more and more at the expense of Greek and Latin, eventually becoming, once again, the only literary language, and thus also epigraphic, of the Jewish communities in Europe. On the abandonment of Hebrew and in general on the language spoken by the Jews of the Roman Empire, see Juster, op. cit., I, pp. 365–368. On the revival of Hebrew, see Ascoli, op. cit., pp. 11, 44–45, 91 and passim; cf. Tamassia, op. cit., p. 805; Ferorelli, *Gli ebrei nell'Italia meridionale dall'Età Romana al secolo XVIII*, Turin 1915, p. 29.

who mulls a great deal over that question. It would, in fact, be evidence of the disregard by the Ostrogothic government of the constitution of January 31, 438,[45] banning the Jews from holding any public office.[46]

The Jews' participation in the Byzantine-Gothic war and their strenuous, though unsuccessful, attempt to defend the city of Naples are certain, well-documented facts[47] and occurred in stark contrast to the Roman-Christian laws repeatedly excluding Jews from military service.[48]

Still, it is worth noting Theodoric's letter to the Jews of Milan (y. 523–26) regarding citizenship during the Ostrogoth Age. In this letter, upon request by the Jews, who complain about repeated illegal ecclesiastical interferences in their community's internal affairs, the king grants them his *tuitio*, aimed at safeguarding them from any undue harassment of that kind.[49]

45 Nov. Theod. II, 3, § 2 = C. J. 1, 9, 18, cf. Juster, II, p. 245.

46 Tamassia's conclusions are accepted by Roberti, *Svolgimento storico del diritto privato in Italia*, vol. I, *Le persone*, Padua 1935, p. 188. However, the expression "majures"could also be understood in its social significance, as "city elders."

47 Procopio, *De bello gothico*, 1, 10, Comparetti ed., (*Fonti per la Storia d'Italia*, no. 23), Rome, 1895.

48 C. Th. 16, 8, 16 (y. 404); C. Th. 16, 8, 24 (y. 418); Cost. Sirm. 6 at the end (y. 425). And later C. J. 1, 5, 12. The exclusion of all non-Christians and heretics has exclusively religious grounds, affecting the Jews not as a people but as a non-Catholic community. See Jo. Daniel Gruber (*praeses*) and Rodulphus Culemann (*submittens*), *Dissertatio juris publici de judeo milite*, Halae Magdeburgicae, 1723, pp. 37–44 and Juster, II, pp. 277–78. Culemann rightly observes (pp. 31–34) that, having become all Roman citizens under the Constitutio Antoniniana, from 212 until the cited Christian laws, the Jews of the Empire had enjoyed without exception the entire sum of political and civil rights, and therefore had also been admitted to the armed militia (p. 33: "Ex quibus omnibus apparet judeos a romanorum castris neque ob ignaviam aut imbelles mores, neque ob vitium quodpiam naturae, neque ob servilem conditionem, neque ob diversitatem sacrorum fuisse reiectos, quoad Roma idolorum cultui fuit dedita. Et licet olim peregrini jure civitatis destituerentur, quippe pro peregrinis reputati, ut adeo vel ex hac caussa arceri deberent a militia, ad quam neque servis, neque peregrinis aspirari licuit, tamquam munus et necessitatem civium ordinariam propriamque, remotum tamen hoc est obstaculum postquam primi Antonini beneficio non judei solum, sed etiam omnes peregrini civium juribus censeri coeperunt"). Culemann's brochure, very rare, is available at the Vienna University Library.

49 Cassiodoro, *Variae*, V, 37 in *Monumenta Germaniae Historica, Auctores antiquissimi*, XII, p. 163: "Judaeis mediolanensibus Theodoricus rex ...; Quoniam nonnullorum vos frequenter causamini praesumptione laceratos et quae ad synagogam vestram pertinent perhibetis jura rescindi, *opitulabitur vobis mansuetudinis nostrae postulata tuitio*, quatenus nullus ecclesiasticus, quae synagogae vestrae jura competunt, violentia intercedente pervadat nec vestris se causis importuna acerbitate permisceat, sed ut religionis cultu ita et actuum sint conversatione discreti: hac tamen moderatione principalis auxilii beneficium concedentes, ut nec vos quod ad praefatae ecclesiae jus vel religiosas certe personas legibus pertinere constiterit, inciviliter attrectare temptetis." *Synagoga* here is not meant as a place of worship but refers to the Jewish community. The word's dual meaning is

The Jews' situation is not unique: similar complaints are presented during the same years by the Jews of Rome[50] and the Jews of Ravenna[51] following the destruction of their synagogues, with similar attitudes adopted in both cases by the king. However, the formal indication of the *tuitio* granted to the community is the real innovation here. What is the meaning of this *tuitio*? What are its effects on the recipients? These are appropriate questions because, in later times, the royal protection of the Jews becomes increasingly frequent, forming the basis of their legal position. It will have significant repercussions on the social aspect, and there will be those who want to see in it a consequence of the reduction of all Jews to the status of foreigners.

Can this theory apply to our case that it is the first of its kind? Certainly not. Firstly, as apparent from Cassiodorus' formula,[52] the royal Ostrogoth *tuitio* is generally given exclusively for the protection of the weak and persecuted, not foreigners. Secondly, in this case, there is no need to insist on the indisputable fact that Milanese Jews request Theodoric's *tuitio* as means to be freed from any possible harassment, unrelated to their downgrading to the status of foreigners.

That is to say, in this request for *tuitio*, there is nothing even slightly resembling the act of the wargangus who, as we shall see, places himself *sub scuto potestatis* of the king to improve his judicial position, according to Longobard law (edict of Rothari, ch. 367).[53] Furthermore, under Theodoric, the Jews were

customary in the Roman Age (Juster, I, p. 414, no. 8) and corresponds to *ecclesia* = church and local Christian community.

50 Cassiodoro, *Variae*, IV, 43 (y. 509–511).

51 Anonimo Valesiano, c. 81–82, Mommsen ed., *M. G. H., Auctores Antiquissimi*, IX, p. 326. On these two episodes, see Juster's excellent observations, op. cit., I, p. 466, no. 3. Cf. as well Tamassia, op. cit., pp. 802–03. The citation of the *Variae* here is partially (p. 801, no. 1 and 2) incorrect.

52 Cassiodoro, *Variae*, VII, 39: "Superfluum quidem videtur tuitionem specialem a principe petere, cuius est propositi universos communiter vindicare. Sed quia securitatem tuam quorundam violentorum exsecranda temeritas inquietat, non piget dolentium querelis ad hanc partem pietatis adduci, ut quod omnibus praestare cupimus, supplicanti potissimum conferamus. Quapropter tuitionem tibi nostri nominis quasi validissimam turrem contra inciviles impetus et conventionalia detrimenta nostra concedit auctoritas. …" The hypothesis that this Ostrogothic *tuitio* sinks its roots in late Roman law is supported by Mommser, *Ostgotische Studien*, in *Neues Archiv der Gesellschaft für ältere deutsche Geschichtskunde*, 14, 1889, pp. 531–32, on the basis of C. Th. 1, 21, 1; 4, 15, 1; 13, 6, 36. Tamassia, *L'alta tutela del Re germanico*, in *Archivio Giuridico*, 1925, further tries to configure the institute to reflect Judeo-Christian principles that reached the Germans directly through the Church and indirectly through the Roman law they influenced.

53 Lastly, see on this point Giardina's two articles, *Il capitolo 367 dell'Editto di Rotari*, in *Rivista di Storia del Diritto italiano*, vol. VII, 1934, file 2; and *Osservazioni sull'expositio al c. 367 di Rotari e al c. 27 di Pipino*, in *Annali dell'Istituto di scienze giuridiche economiche, politiche e sociali della R. Università di Messina*, vol. IX, y. 1934–35.

not aliens, but citizens, which is unequivocally proven by the right they enjoyed to live *suis legibus*, whereas as a rule, it will be constant practice throughout the Middle Ages that foreigners live according to the law of the host State and not according to their own, even after they come under the King's shielded protection.[54]

It is therefore impossible to establish, for the Ostrogoth Age, any rapprochement between the legal position of Jews and that of the aliens; nor, is it legitimate to assume that granting the *tuitio* to a Jewish community reflects even a minimal reduction of freedom for its members.

Instead, it can be argued (and it could have actually been argued about the Roman Age) that the complex political and civil prohibitions imposed on them under the principle of state religion affected their legal position so heavily as to render the broader status of subjects, i.e., simple members of the state, more appropriate, as opposed to the status of *cives*, real citizens, which seems to imply full civil rights. However, there is uncertainty regarding the meaning of the words *civis* and *subditus*, and the relationship between them, to the point where every scholar interprets them differently. Thus, the terminological distinction does not deserve any additional importance. It is enough to understand that Jews constitute a national group, clearly distinct from foreigners, and even though it is considered legally inferior for religious reasons, it does *ipso jure* belong to the State, to which foreigners *ipso jure* do not.[55]

---

54 Cit. ch. 367 of Rothari: "Omnes waregang qui de exteras fines in regni nostri finibus advenerint seque sub scuto potestatis nostrae subdederint, legibus nostris langobardorum vivere debeant, nisi aliam legem ad pietatem nostram meruerint." Cf. Tamassia, Op. cit., p. 776 and Brunner, *Deutsche Rechtsgeschichte*, vol. I, II ed., Leipzig, 1906, p. 401.

55 *Ipso jure*, because Rothari hypothesizes in chapter 367 of the above the case of foreigners who came to live in the Longobard Kingdom and placed themselves under the subjection of the king to improve their legal status, thus becoming part of the State. This chapter has been interpreted in various ways, apart from the differences in viewpoints, also because of the swapping of terms *subditus* and *civis*. Agreeing with Giardina's thesis (*Il capitolo* cit., pp. 26–30), I also believe that we cannot speak of naturalization as, e.g., here want Besta, *Nuove vedute sul diritto pubblico italiano nel Medio Evo*, in *Riv. It. Sc. Giur.*, vol. 51, p. 56, and Finocchiaro-Sartorio, *Il diritto ereditario della Corte Regia nel periodo longobardo*, in *Circolo giuridico*, vol. 43, 1912, pp. 169, 171 no. 2, 189–90, who adhere to the interpretation of the *expositio*; and I think that the act of *subditio* is not sufficient to remove from these wargangi the quality of foreigners. Instead of giving them the status of *cives*, I prefer the status of *subditi*, since to support their *cives* status, a series of distinctions and boundaries of the *civis* concept need to be established, which can be avoided by merely separating genuine *cives* from simple subjects. The *wargangi sub scuto* actually belong to the latter category. In fact, with regard to these wargangi, Schupfer himself, *Guargangi e cives*, in *Riv. It. Sc. Giur.*, vol. 35, 1903, pp. 14, 15, 16, and idem, *Il diritto privato dei popoli germanici*, IV, p. 12, (passages cited by Giardina, p. 27, no. 60), talked about subjection and participation to political communion, but not about citizenship. Here, too, it is only a matter of agreeing on the content and value of the two terms.

CHAPTER 3

Italy – the Longobard Age

The Longobard Age is characterized by an almost absolute lack of news relating to the Jews.

They were not mentioned in the laws, and documentary materials add very little information. One literary source is notable, though, where King Bertarido's persecutory attitude towards them is reported,[56] an extraneous attitude to the judicial territory that renders the question of citizenship pointless for the time.

As for the later period, the doctrine[57] agrees in viewing the Jews as excluded from the category of wargangi mentioned in Rothari's ch. 367. In reality, this opinion is correct: apart from exceptional cases, had they been included in the wargangi category, they would have had to live according to the Longobard law. However, as we shall see, the question can be raised of whether they lived according to Roman law or Jewish law. Despite the absence of definite elements, it seems quite likely that they never lived according to the Longobard law. Even if we accept the latter hypothesis as accurate, it bears no proof of their reduction to the wargangi state, since it seems conceivable that just as the Visigoths did, the Longobards may have granted their Roman subjects – but not the Jewish ones – the right to live according to their law. In any case, one cannot deduce that they have lost the quality of citizens altogether.

56 *Carmen de Synodo ticinensi* in *M. G. H., Scriptores rerum longobardicarum et italicarum saec. VI–IX*, p. 190:
Subolis item Bertari in solium
Regni suffectus, imitatus protinus
Exempla patris ad fidem convertere
Judeos fecit baptizandos, credere
Qui renuerit, gladio peremere.

57 Ernst Mayer, *Italiänische Verfassungsgeschichte von der Gotenzeit bis zur Zunftherrschaft*, Leipzig, 1909, vol. 1, p. 147; Dahn, *Die Könige der Germanen*, vol. 12, *Die Longobarden*, Leipzig, 1909, p. 72.

 | DOI:10.1163/9789004627154_005

CHAPTER 4

The Holy Roman Empire and Italy in Particular

Let us now examine the question of the Jews' *status civitatis* in the Holy Roman Empire.

We must do this given that, *de jure*, the whole of Italy was always part of this entity, and many regions of the peninsula remained under imperial sovereignty for several centuries.

With the creation of the Holy Roman Empire, the ancient concept of a multinational political body tending to universality and governed by one supreme leader is reinstituted. In addition, the qualification of 'Holy' meant to emphasize that a new, Christian empire of Theodosius and Justinian is born, rather than the rebirth of the old empire of pagan Rome.

What then was the position of the Jewish nation amidst the nations of the Empire? Are Jews considered foreigners or citizens?

The union of Church and State already shaped the politics of the ancient Roman Empire (from 380 onward) and the barbarian monarchies afterward. Adopted again in the Carolingian Empire, indeed more rigorously and bluntly but not created *ex novo*, we would be sensible in considering the Jews as *cives* – second class perhaps, but still *cives*.

Instead, upon examining both the documentary material that has reached us and the doctrine that has elaborated it, we would face many questions to discourage us from making such a strong statement. Based on these documents, it seems especially necessary to consider the different periods separately and draw distinct conclusions for each one.

1 The Carolingian and Pre-feudal Age

Scholars dealing with the issue in this period rely on four letters of protection issued by Louis the Pious to individual Jews who had made specific requests.[58]

58 The first three are included in the collection of imperial formulas of Louis the Pious, (nos. 30, 31, 52; *M. G. H., Leges*, sect. V, *Formulae*, part I, Zeumer ed.). The fourth one is edited by Bouquet, *Recueil des historiens des Gaules et de France*, IV, 624, no. 252. All are reprinted by Aronius, *Regesten zur Geschichte der Juden im Fränkischen und deutschen Reiche bis zum Jahre 1273*, Berlin 1887, no. 81 (pp. 30–31), 82 (pp. 31–32), 83 (pp. 32–33), 102 (pp. 42–43). The three *formulae* are dated somewhat before 825. The fourth letter dates February 22, 839.

 DOI:10.1163/9789004627154_006

Interestingly, and so far unnoticed, these letters closely resemble the *tuitio* mentioned above, granted to the Milanese Jews by Theodoric three centuries earlier.

In these documents, the king takes those Jews under his protection,[59] forbids harassment, prohibits the seizing of legitimately owned property, and charges customs fees or other royal burdens upon them. He also lays down specific fundamental rules of civil and criminal law procedure which they must follow and guarantees them defense against the repetition of some serious abuses mentioned in their grievances.

In return for this safeguard, the protected join the service of *curtis regia*:[60] the primary consequence being that for the entire duration of the established relationship if one of them is killed, the wergild shall be paid not to the family of the dead but *ad partem palatii* of the king.[61]

Therefore, these documents prove the establishment of a protective relationship and correlative reliance between individual Jews and the king, constituting the prominent character of the Middle Ages in numerous different subspecies. The era is characterized by the rise and assertion of the patrimonial state as the sovereign's property. During this time, all individuals

59 "Omnibus notum sit quia istos Hebreos ... sub nostra defensione suscepimus et retinemus": formulas 30 and 31; "... quia suprascriptos hebreos sub mundeburdo et defensione nostra suscepimus ...": formulas 30 and 31;"... notum sit quia iste hebreus ... ad nostram veniens presentiam in manibus nostris se commendavit, ut eum sub sermone tuitionis nostrae recepimus et retinemus": formula 52. In the document of 839, the formal expressions are missing, but here too is a case of *tuitio* on the basis of *commendatio*. See text further on, footnote no. 78.

60 "Liceat eis sub mundeburdo et defensione nostra quiete vivere et partibus palatii nostri fideliter deservire": formulas 31 and 32. These Jews who joined the service of *curtis regia* and became thus *fideles* of the King are mentioned also in two other formulas of protection of Louis the Pious: formula 32 (Zeumer ed., cit., *M. G. H., Leges*, v, p. 311): "Sed liceat illi (the grantee of the letter of mundeburdio), sicut ceteris fidelibus nostris et his, qui sub nostra defensione recepti sunt, absque cuiuslibet impedimento, una cum rebus et hominibus suis cum honore residere et quieto ordine vivere absque cuiuslibet, sicut ipsi Judei, iniusta contrarietate"; formula 37 (ibid., p. 315): "Liceat eis, sicut judeis, partibus palatii nostri fideliter deservire." Tangl, however, in *Neues Archiv der Gesellschaft für ältere deutschen Geschichtskunde*, 33, 1908, pp. 197–205 claims, I do not know whether rightly so or wrongly, that the readings "sicut ipsi Judei" and "sicut Judeis" are erroneous and should be interpreted, respectively, as "sicut jam diximus" and "sicut diximus." Compare previous footnote of Sickel, *Beiträge zur Diplomatik*, III, in *Sitzungsberichte der Wiener Akademie*, 47, p. 254 et seqq.

61 "Ut jam quia suprascriptos hebreos sub mundeburdio et defensione nostra suscepimus, quicumque in morte eorum, quandiu nobis fideles extiterint, consiliaverit aut aliquem interfecerit, sciat se ad partem palatii nostri decem libras auri persolvere": formulas 30 and 31. Nothing of this appears in the other documents.

or categories of individuals who, for whatever reason, feel the need for particular legal protection turn to the king rather than the state organs, which were reduced in practice to powerless larvae. As the only owner of the territory, the king became the sole holder of State authority. That estate would later be transferred to the feudal lords or usurped by them, together with sovereign powers. However, the king is the only entity to whom one may turn in the hope for the actual protection.

The royal *mundeburdio* is therefore granted to clerics, churches, businessmen, women, orphans, pilgrims, strangers, and as Waitz[62] points out "überhaupt wohljedem der es wünsche, und der König es gewährte" (in general to anyone who wishes it, and the king granted it).

He continues saying that "Die Juden treten in den Schutz des Königs, ohne dass es deutlich wäre, ob das allgemein als nöthig angesehen ist" (The Jews enter the king's protection without it being clear whether this is generally considered necessary).[63]

Conversely, it seems that granting *tuitio* to certain individual Jews leaves no doubt and rather indicates the exceptionality of this relationship and lack of its normalcy.

Of all the writers who studied the letters of protection mentioned earlier, Scherer draws from them the neatest, most definite deductions in his comprehensive study on the legal position of Jews in Europe and in particular in the Austro-German lands during the Middle Ages.[64]

The work is deeply rooted in the partition of all Jews-related legislation into two distinct categories: *a*) laws considering Jews as belonging to a different religion; *b*) laws that start "von der Anschauung dass die Juden Angehörige einer fremdem Nation, Ausländer, und daher nach dem Fremdenrechte zu behandeln sind" ("from the view that the Jews are members of a foreign nation, foreigners, and therefore are to be treated according to the alien law").[65]

At the intersection of these two trends lies the complex of rules delineating Jews' legal status throughout medieval times. According to Scherer, all provisions relating to foreigners and laws that specifically refer to them as members

62 Georg Waitz, *Deutsche Verfassungsgeschichte*, vol. IV, *Die Verfassung des Fränkischen Reichs*, sect. I, Berlin, 1884, p. 237. On the various forms of royal protection, ibid., p. 234 et seqq.; on p. 238 the imperial formula 52 of request and granting of mundeburdio to a Jew is placed by Waitz alongside many other ones related to clerics and substantially equal to it.

63 Waitz, op. cit., IV, p. 343.

64 Scherer, *Die Rechtsverhältnisse der Juden in deutsch-österreichischen Ländern. Mit einer Einleitung über die Prinzipien der Judengesetzgebung in Europa während des Mittelalters*, Leipzig, 1901.

65 Scherer, op. cit., pp. 3–4.

of a religion different from the state's, apply. As for the origin of the general reduction of Jews to the status of foreigners, Scherer explains it as follows: "with the occupation of the Roman territories – he writes – the Germanic peoples encounter mainly those belonging to two foreign nations: the Romans and the Jews. In the new German States, Romans are recognized and officially legally matched with the *Volksgenossen*. In some states, such as in the Visigothic (*L. Romana Visigotorum*) and Burgundian (*L. Romana Burgundionum*) Kingdoms and in the Raetia Coirese (*Capitula Remedii*), special laws (*leges Romanae*) are issued for the Roman subjects. In the Ostrogoth, Visigoth, Burgundian kingdoms and most likely in the Longobard kingdom too, the Roman-Christian laws concerning the Jews remain in force. These judicial relations will change when the Germanic peoples, who have remained faithful to Arianism, convert to Catholicism. From that time on, Romans and Germans no longer divided by the difference of religion progressively and increasingly merge, so that Roman law slowly loses its meaning and validity.

Following this assimilation of Romans and Germans, Jews in the Germanic States established on Roman territory remain the only foreign people. Even though members of other foreign nations, especially traders, live in these states, Jews are considered individuals rather than people. Furthermore, Scherer concludes "Da die Volks- oder Stammesrechte – für sie nicht galten, die römische Judengesetzgebung aber mit dem römischen Rechte überhaupt ausser Kraft gesetzt worden war, so wurden die Juden nicht bloss als Fremde an sich, sondern auch, weil ihnen jeder Rechtsboden für den Verkehr mit der herrschenden Nation entzogen worden war, vollkommen rechtlos" (Since the people's or tribal rights did not apply to them, but the Roman Jewish legislation had been annulled along with the Roman law in general, the Jews became completely without rights, not only as strangers per se but also because they had been deprived of any legal ground for intercourse with the ruling nation).[66] Consequent to their sinking into the condition of foreignness since the Carolingian era, the Jews felt the need to put themselves under the *mundio regio*. The letters of protection cited above bear indeed the clear demonstration "dass die Juden *in allgemeinen* in der karolingischen Zeit als Unfreie, als Eigenleute in Gegensatze zu den Volksgenossen, daher nach den Fremdenrechte behandelt wurden" (that in general, during the Carolingian period the Jews were treated as unfree, as own people in contrast to the people's comrades, therefore according to the alien laws).[67] Scherer's conclusions

66 Scherer, op. cit., pp. 6–7. Cf. p. 62.

67 Scherer, op. cit., p. 63. Cf. pp. 64 and 67: "Die Juden *in allgemeinen* auch im fränkischen Reiche ohne specielle königliche Mund schutz- und rechtlos waren und dem Könige das freie Dispositionrecht über sie und ihr Eigentum zustand."

have been previously expressed by Klimrath[68] and Brunner.[69] Juster also agrees with the idea of complete identification of the two categories – Jews and foreigners – relying mainly on *Lex Romana Utinensis*.

In this law – he observes with von Salis[70] – "le Judaeus et sa lex est opposé au Romain et à sa lex" (the law of the Jews is contrary to the law of the Romans). Moreover, since, on the other hand, Jews previously had always been considered Romans, this means they now became foreigners.[71]

Furthermore, to the distinguished jurist – whose opinion comes close to Scherer's ideas – this change in the legal position of the Jews appears to be a historical necessity. If in fact non-assimilable Jews had continued to be legally Roman, this would have meant the indefinite persistence of Roman islets in a sea of Roman-Germanic assimilation. It would have entailed a false claim of the incompleteness of the whole merger process between the two nations, although it had already occurred in reality. For Juster, the configuration of the Jews as a nationally distinguished group, carved for the first time in the Middle Ages by the Roman-Udinese law, simultaneously means their reduction to the state of foreigners. The above naturally reflects on the merger between the Romans and Germanic nations, from which the Jews were excluded entirely.[72]

Still, to complete the picture of the best doctrine concerning our issue, it is worth mentioning some other opinions, utterly contrary to those previously cited.

---

68 Klimrath, *Travaux sur l'histoire du droit français*, Paris, 1843, vol. I, p. 405.

69 Brunner, *Deutsche Rechtsgeschichte*, cit., vol. I, 2nd ed., Leipzig, 1906, p. 402 and especially 403, no. 22. Cf. also what Schupfer writes about these formulas, *Il diritto privato dei popoli germanici con speciale riguardo all'Italia*, 1907, I, pp. 83–85. It seems to me that Schupfer does not insist sufficiently on the distinction to be made between those documents regarding individuals and other sources of general character and scope.

70 *Lex romana curiensis*, in *Zeits. der Sav. Stift., Germ. Abth.*, vol. VI, p. 143, no. 1.

71 Juster, *Le Juifs* cit., II, p. 26, no. 5. The same argument was used by Brunner, op. cit., p. 403, no. 22 cit.

72 Juster, op. cit., II, p. 27. "Si l'on avait maintenu aux Juifs leur qualité de Romains on aurait empêché de disparaître la notion de Romain dans son opposition à celle de Barbare et on aurait mis obstacle à la fusion complète entre Barbares et Romains; et si l'on avait continué à considérer les Juifs comme citoyens romains on aurait risqué de conserver à perpétuité des ilots de l'Empire romain dans les nouveaux Etats. Et c'est ce qui ne faillait pas. Aussi déclara-t-on les Juifs étrangers, serfs, etc. De sorte que la condition d'étrangers imposée aux Juifs est – sans paradoxe – un résultat de la lutte qui a abouti à la destruction de l'empire Romain: c'est pour avoir été les survivants de cet Empire que les Juifs furent littéralement "depaysés" dans les royaumes qui se les partagèrent." For Stobbe too, *Handbuch des deutschen Privatrechts*, vol. I, 3rd ed., Berlin 1893, p. 386, the Jews in the medieval German States are considered foreigners.

Thus Loening,[73] with the backing of the Alariciano Breviary text mentioned above, does not think of associating Jews with foreigners throughout the barbarian era. Instead, he considers them as Romans. Following Leoning, Zeumer deems it possible that the "lex corum," whereby the protégés of the imperial formula 31 must accordingly be considered of proven culpability,[74] refers to Roman law rather than Jewish law. Waitz, for whom the Jews in the Frankish Kingdom and the Visigothic Kingdom are "wahrscheinlich zu den Römern gerechnet werden" (probably counted among the Romans),[75] also embraces Loening's idea, with prudence.

Conversely, Mayer,[76] who relies on the cited lex Romana Utinensis, states that in the 9th century, Italian Jews no longer appear to be Romans. However, he adds: "ebensowenig sind sie *wargangi* in Sinne des langobardischen Ediktes" (nor are they wargangi in the sense of the Longobardian edict), so that it is incorrect to group them together, as Brunner does, with the protected foreigners.[77]

After uncovering the various theories expressed concerning the point in question, let us now take a brief critical examination of them, always bearing our sources in mind. The first point to consider is the idea, expressed by these last-mentioned writers, that Jews (up to the time of the *Lex Romana Utinensis* according to Mayer and Juster – throughout the entire Carolingian Age according to Loening and Waitz, who do not utilize that text) are considered Romans or at least equal to Romans.

Reviewing the arguments already discussed for the periods before the 9th century, I think I can positively discard this erroneous point of view. The Jews cease to be *cives romani* in the year 476, i.e., with the disappearance of the general *civitas romana* following the empire's collapse. Just like the Romans (now intended as nationals), they become Ostrogoth citizens (or – if you

73 Loening, *Geschichte des deutschen Kirchenrechts*, vol. II, *Das Kirchenrecht im Reiche der Merowinger*, Strasbourg, 1878, p. 51.

74 "Et nemo saepe dictis Hebreis flagellis cedere presumat, nisi probati fuerint secundum legem eorum, eos capitula, quae a nobis observanda promulgata sunt, violasse atque irrita facisse. …" Zeumer, l. cit. Note that this general legislation of Louis the Pious on the Jews is lost (Aronius, *Regesten zur Geschichte der Juden in fränkischen und deutschen Reiche bis zum Jahre 1273*, Berlin, 1887, no. 82, p. 32; Scherer, op. cit., p. 63 and 64). Archbishop Agobard of Lyon also refers to this legislation in a paragraph of his anti-Jewish article *De insolentia Judeorum* (y. 826–827, Migne, *Patrologia latina*, 104, ch. 2, pp. 70 et seqq.; Aronius, op. cit., no. 88, p. 36).

75 Waitz, *Deutsche Verfassungsgeschichte* cit., 3rd ed., vol. II, part 1, Kiel, 1882, p. 271.

76 Ernst Mayer, *Italiänische Verfassungsgeschichte von der Gothenzeit bis zur Zunftherrschaft*, Leipzig, 1909, I, p. 147.

77 Mayer, op. cit., ibid., no. 28.

like – subjects) in the Ostrogothic Kingdom, Longobard citizens in the Longobard Kingdom, Frankish citizens in the Frankish Kingdom, and so on. Their appearance as a *de jure* distinct nation is proven during the Ostrogoth Age when King Theodoric recognizes their national law. It is therefore incorrect to think, as does Juster, that only with the *Lex Romana Utinensis* the contraposition between *judaeus* and his *lex* on the one hand and the *romanus* and his *lex* on the other hand arises again, as it is already implicitly contained in § 143 of Theodoric's edict.

What could be argued is that with the founding of the Holy Roman Empire, the ancient generic concept of *civitas romana* reappears, again linking all nations included within the borders of the State of Charlemagne into a common bond. Furthermore, in this sense, the Jews become Roman again, just as Roman become Franks, Longobards, and all other nations of the Empire. Nevertheless, since every nation maintains its own law, and with it, clearly, its national individuality, it is safe to say that the renewal of the *civitas romana* has an unconvincing content. Of course, things will be very different after the 11th century when, in Italy and elsewhere, following the merger between the Roman and Germanic elements, Roman law resumes its ancient territorial value: but for now, to avoid confusion, those who, although belonging to the Holy Roman Empire, are not Roman by nationality can never qualify as Roman. The Jews, too, are never called Romans.

Let us now move forward to the second point. The Jews, re-emerging as a national individuality separate from the Roman-Germanic assimilation – as Scherer, Brunner and Juster maintain – sink from the position of Romans to that of foreigners. This is also untrue.

Just as it is impossible to argue that the Jews appear to the Germanic peoples at first as Romans of the Jewish religion. Hence, the idea that they become foreigners at some indeterminable moment is also unfounded. Juster's reasoning is well-designed and imprinted by the intuition and fineness of this writer. However, since it is based on an erroneous interpretation of the *Lex Romana Utinensis'* mentioned passage – with no other document being cited – it collapses promptly with the failure of the basis itself.

On the other hand, Scherer wants to find a brilliant confirmation to his thesis in the letters of Louis the Pious. But how can one deduce from the *tuitio* granted to four Jews and their families that all Jews of the Empire became foreigners and therefore in the position of placing themselves under the wings of the king's protection? As Waitz and any other good lawyer can teach us, do not clergy, merchants, widows, or anyone who needed protection, similarly enter the *mundio regio*? So, why should those Jews enter it as wargangi and not simply as harassed individuals and therefore need special defense? It would be enough to examine the contents of the four imperial formulas to become convinced that this is indeed the correct interpretation.[78]

In this context, the comparison with the *tuitio* granted by Theodoric to the Jews of Milan is beneficial. As already noted, no one would ever see in it a reflection of the Jews' reduction to the state of foreigners.

The whole argument on which Scherer has built his work does not hold up because the legislation division concerning the Jews into rules deriving from their religious denomination and rules deriving from their foreignness is arbitrary and artificial. In fact, the legislation on Jews stems solely from the difference in religion. It is only because of this difference in religion that in the Carolingian Empire, as elsewhere, among the other nations that make up the State, a notably inferior position is configured to the Jewish nation. Perceiving Jews as foreigners, as "Nichtvolksgenossen" (Non-Citizens), and *in addition* separately as members of a religion different from the State's,[79] means

78 Imperial formulas 30, 31 and 32: "ut neque vos neque iuniores seu successores vestri memoratos hebreos de nullis quibuslibet illicitis occasionibus inquietare aut calumniam generare praesumat." Letter of February 22, 839: "Proinde comperiat etc. quia dilectus frater noster Hugo venerabilis abbas et sacri palatii nostri summus notarius quosdam hebreos, Gaudiocum videlicet et Jacobum atque Vivacium filios suos, in nostram introduxit praesentiam, eorumque querimonias tam sua quam illorum relatione didicimus. Suggesserunt itaque culminis nostri clementiae, qualiter quibusdam adversitatibus, imo depraedationibus quorundam malivolorum praeceptum auctoritatis nostrae, quod eis olim super rebus quibusdam, quae dicuntur Valerianis sive Bagnilis, ex progenitorum suorum successione sibi jure competentibus feceramus, per quam eas quiete possidere valuissent, amiserint; suppliciter nostram expetentes mansuetudinem, ut eis memoratam auctoritatis nostrae praeceptionem denuo rescribi sibique tribui iuberemus, per quam memoratas res quieto ordine absque cuiuspiam contradictione aut inquietudine imposterum observare valerent. Quorum petitionibus ob divinum amorem libenter aurem accomodantes hos nostros imperiales apices eis fieri ac dari decrevimus, per quos praecipimus atque iubemus ut memorati hebraei eorumque posteritas memoratas res cum omnibus ad se pertinentibus vel aspicientibus ... absque cuiuslibet contrarietate aut detentione per hanc nostram auctoritatem teneant et possideant, et quidquid de iis jure proprietario ordinare, disponere aut facere vendendo donando vel commutando voluerint, liberam in omnibus habeant potestatem; neque quispiam eis de saepedictis rebus ullam calumniam aut inquietudinem generare audeat, sed liceat secure atque quiete (possidere)." Aronius, op. cit., no. 102, p. 43.

79 About the special modalities established for Jews in matters of judicial proofs, Scherer writes for example (p. 64): "Diese Vorschrift über die Beweisführung seitens des klagenden Juden hat wohl ihren Grund hauptsächlich in dem Misstrauen, dem die Aussagen eines Fremden, eines Nichtvolksgenossen gegen einen Volksgenossen begegneten, umsomehr, wenn dieser Fremde zugleich Angehöriger einer fremden Religion ist." Similarly, Juster, op. cit., II, pp. 26–27: "Toutes ces legislations (barbarian) finirent d'ailleurs, sous l'influence de l'Eglise, par considérer les juifs *ethniquement comme étrangers et réligieusement comme infidèles*, et, en ces qualités, privés de droits civiques et sujets à des déchéances speciales."

seeing things in a completely false light, quite obviously created by the erroneous retrospective projection of modern conceptions.[80]

All in all, we can conclude that even in the period and territories in question, Jews' status was of a national group whose members – if they resided for some time within a state's borders – were considered its subjects. This belonging to the state was not impaired by the fact that a whole series of special restrictions were imposed on these subjects due to their practicing a different religion.

Although the restrictions imposed on Jews had several points of contact with those imposed on foreigners, rendering the legal situation of both categories quite similar, they were hardly identical. While foreigners were still strangers to the state and – like today – they only became subjects for the duration of their residency, the Jews constituted a category of permanent subjects, distinct from *cives optimo jure*, but comparable to them with regard to citizenship.[81]

2 The Feudal Age

In our ongoing investigation, we must now focus our attention on the feudal age to determine whether we can retain the conclusions we have reached for previous periods.

During this epoch, Jews' status is one of unique dependency, which is why, since the 13th century, Jews have been called "servants of the Royal Chamber" or "of the Imperial Chamber."

We should dwell longer upon this relationship, trying to shed light on its precedents, genesis and nature, to detect any relationship with the subjects' *status civitatis*.

The term "servi camerae" appears for the first time in a privilege (protection) given by Frederick II to two Jews on the grounds, in 1234: "quod nos

80 Precisely to warn against false ideas of this kind, Juster, op. cit., II, p. 246, had written with regard to the Roman Age subsequent the victory of Christianity: "L'exclusion des fonctions a un motif réligieux et non national. Les Juifs sont Romains et continuent a l'être – le Juif désireux d'occuper une fonction publique qui lui est inaccessible, n'a qu'à se faire baptiser." Things don't change in the Middle Ages; at this time too the reason for the prohibitions established for the Jews is purely religious, and their constituting a nation apart is not at all relevant, being the barbarian monarchies – and even more so the Holy Roman Empire – pluri-national states in which all Christian nations enjoy the same rights.

81 This idea of permanent subjection, subspecies of the *civitas* and distinguished from the position of foreigners, must have intuitively crossed Tamassia's mind, as he fleetingly mentions it in the cited work *L'alta tutela del re germanico*, in *Archivio Giuridico*, 1925: "They (the Jews) might be considered as special subjects since they are permanent residents" (p. 20 of the abstract).

attendentes (sic) imbecillitatem gentis judaismi et quod omnes et singuli judaei degentes ubique per terras nostrae jurisdictioni subiectas christianae legis et imperii praerogativa, qua dominamur et vivimus, servi sunt nostrae camerae speciales."[82]

It is clear, however, that in a diploma dated September 1182 to the Jews of Regensburg, Frederick Barbarossa wanted to express the same concept by declaring his concession as a reflection of the Emperor's obligation to take care "omnium judeorum in imperio nostro degentium, qui spetiali prerogativa dignitatis nostre ad imperialem cameram dinoscuntur pertinere."[83]

From this moment on – as Scherer observes[84] – the expression "servi camerae" in Germany becomes the technical name by which the Jews are referred to in documents relating to them: it appears in the diplomas of Frederick II and Konrad IV,[85] William,[86] Richard,[87] and Konradin,[88] and constantly remains so until the fall of the Holy Roman Empire.

The obligations relating to this state of *servitus* mutate over times and places: however, their principal and invariable element consist in the full rights by the sovereign, not only on property matters, but also on the persons of the Jews; rights that are expressed with incessant spoils and continuous taxes, in exchange for a mere semblance of protection, almost always granted with an expiry date, and upon payment of large sums.

Since the end of the 13th century, this unrestricted right on property and lives of the Jews has been asserted in increasingly decisive terms by German emperors and kings, with all possible consequences. Thus, on December 6, 1268 Rudolph of Habsburg proclaimed that "cum universi et singuli Judei utpote camere nostre servi cum personis et rebus suis omnibus specialiter nobis attineant, ut illis principibus, quibus iidem Judaei a nobis et imperio in feodum sunt concessi, condignum et justum est utique consonum racioni, ut si aliqui judei huiusmodi facti profugi sine nostra sive domini sui speciali licencia et consensu se ultra mare transtulerint, ut se a vero dominio alienent, de illorum

82 Aronius, op. cit., no. 468, pp. 205–206.

83 Scheffer-Boichorst, in *Mittheilungen des Instituts für österreichischen Geschichtsforschungen*, x, pp. 459 et seqq. Aronius, no. 314 a., p. 139.

84 Scherer, op. cit., p. 77.

85 Document of May 1246 concerning the Jews of Frankfurt, Huillard-Bréholles, *Historia diplomatica Friderici Secundi*, vol. 6, part 2, Paris, 1861, p. 870; Aronius, no. 554, pp. 238–39; and another of January 20, 1251, concerning the Jews of Regensburg, Aronius, no. 582, p. 249.

86 March 15, 1255, Jews of Speyer, Aronius, no. 616, p. 260.

87 October 16, 1262, Jews of Haguenau, Aronius, no. 682, p. 284.

88 November 30, 1266, Jews of Augsburg, Aronius, no. 716, p. 297.

possessionibus, rebus et bonis omnibus, tam mobilibus quam immobilibus, ubicumque ea reperiri contingit, nos vel domini, quibus attinet, licite intromittere debeamus, ac ea non immerito nostre attrahere potestati."[89]

Similarly, Charles IV declares: "Und auch all Juden mit leib und mit güt in unser kameren gehören und in unserem gewalt und henden sein, daz wir von unser mechtichait damit tun und lazzen mügen was wir wellen."[90]

Based on this law, which generally stipulated that the Jews, in body and wealth, were considered the king's property, two hefty taxes known as "Goldene Opferpfennig" and "Kaiserehrung" were introduced in 1342 and 1434, respectively, by the German kings.[91]

Around the same time, the Jews' situation in other countries of Europe is no different. For example, in England, King John declares in a privilege of April 10, 1200, article 12: "et ubicumque Judaei fuerint liceat eis ire quocumque voluerint cum omnibus catallis (chattels) eorum sicut nostre res proprie et nulli liceat eos retinere neque has eis proibere."[92] On January 31, 1253, King Henry III likewise decrees, "quod nullus Judaeus maneat in Anglia nisi servitium regis faciat et quam cito aliquis Judaeus natus fuerit, sive sit masculus sive femina, serviat nobis in aliquo."[93]

Similarly, in France, starting from the 13th century, kings oppress the Jews in any way, imposing various taxes at whim, confiscating their properties and credits, and treating them as if they were slaves.[94]

---

89 Schunck, *Codex diplomaticus Moguntinus*, 1797, p. 122; *M. G. H., Leges*, sect. IV, T. III, no. 388, p. 368.

90 Scherer, op. cit., p. 80. J. J. Beck, *Tractatus de Juribus Judeorum*, Nuremberg, 1731, p. 41. A copy of this very rare work is preserved in Mantua Municipal Library.

91 Besides Scherer, op. cit., pp. 81–82 and 536, on these taxes, see in particular Isert Rösel, *Die Reichssteuern der deutschen Judengemeinden von ihren Anfängen bis zur Mitte des 14 Jahrhunderts*, in *Monatsschrift für Geschichte und Wissenschaft des Judentums*, 53 (1909), pp. 679–708; 54 (1910), pp. 55–81, 206–223, 333–347, 462–473. About the "Kaiserehrung," a declaration of 1463 by Achilles of Brandeburg proclaims: "Es sey kundig im Reich, so ein Romischer konig wirdt erkoren oder so er zu kejserlich wirde kompt und gekront wird, dass er die Juden alle mag brennen nach altem Herkomen oder Gnad beweisen den dritten Pfennig Irs gut zu nehmen, damit sie Ir Leben retten," Scherer, op. cit., p. 82; cf. Pertile, *Storia del Diritto Italiano*, Ist ed., vol. III, p. 180, note 16.

92 Scherer, op. cit., p. 88.

93 Tovey, *Anglia Judaica or the History and Antiquities of the Jews in England*, Oxford, 1738, p. 148.

94 For details and bibliography, see Scherer, op. cit., pp. 93–100. Also, in Grayzel, *The Church and the Jews in the XIII century*, Philadelphia, 1933, pp. 51–55 and 348–356.

The same occurs in the Iberian Peninsula, where any abuse of power is justified by claiming that Jews are a personal possession of the king.[95]

But then again, the continuous development of the feudal system and the subsequent natural absorption of sovereign functions from the secular and ecclesiastical lords bring about the passage of the *jus regale* on the Jews to these landlords – which in essence means: the right to squeeze as much money as possible out of them, poorly compensated by the correlative obligation (rarely practiced) to defend individuals and their assets.

As with all other royalties, this step is usually handled peacefully, and it is the king himself who gives or sells his rights or confirms *de jure* the transfer that had effectively already taken place.[96] However, it is frequently possible to capture in the documents an echo of a fierce fight for the possession of that royalty, which the king strives to preserve at all costs, as a source of a handsomely lucrative income.

From a passage of the *Annales Colmarienses* we learn that in the year 1292 the king "exactionem in Judaeos tentavit, sed non potuit resistente sculcteto francfordiano."[97] Article 25 of the English collection, known as *leges Eduardi Confessoris* (1042–1066), but more likely to be attributed to King Henry II (1154–1189), paints a clear picture of the rivalry between kings and landlords for the possession of the right of sovereignty-property over the Jews. "Sciendum est – this article proclaims – quod omnes Judaei, ubicumque in regno sunt, sub tutela et defensione regis ligie debent esse. Neque aliquis eorum potest subdere se alicui diviti sine licentia regis, quia ipsi Judaei et omnia sua regis sunt. Quodsi aliquis detinuerit eos vel pecuniam eorum, rex requirat tamquam suum proprium, si vult et potest."[98]

The struggle is sometimes resolved by agreements between the king and the feudal lords – or between the feudal lords themselves – where each party accepts not to keep the other party's Jews in its domains. This occurs especially in France, where feudalism has strengthened since the beginning of the

95 "Eorum persone domini regis sunt": *Fueros y observancias de las costumbres escriptas del Reyno de Aragon*, Zaragoza, 1576, f. 28 and 29 (of the time of King James I, 1213–1278). See Cassel, in *Allgemeine Encyklopädie der Wissenschaften und Künste*, sect. II, tome 27, Leipzig, 1850, sub voce *Juden-Geschichte*, p. 211 et seqq. In 1380, King John I of Castile (1379–1390) at the Cortes de Soria states "Los judios son nuestros, son cosa nuestra." *Cortes de los antiguos reynos de Leon y de Castilla*, 1863, II, p. 312. Scherer, op. cit., p. 102.

96 See the chart of 1286 just mentioned above.

97 Cassel, op. cit., p. 87, note 94. This treatise of Cassel is very valuable and, albeit aged, deserves particular consideration.

98 Reinhold Schmid, *Gesetze der Angelsachsen*, 2nd ed., Leipzig, 1858, pp. 505–06.

13th century to the point where feudal lords' power is at least equivalent to that of the sovereign, and acts of authority by him are no longer possible.[99]

Quite jarring in those agreements is the commitment that is expected from the Jews not to leave their sovereign's territory.[100]

The Jews' passage under the sovereignty of the feudal lords represents a new worsening of their conditions: unable to leave the territory of their master and lord without his license and forced to do so against their will whenever he cedes or donates them to some other feudal lord, they sink into a judicial status comparable to that of *adscripticii*, of serfs: and the less extended is the fief they inhabit, the more the public character of their serfdom fades to become confounded, at least in fact, with actual slavery of private nature. The sales of individual Jews[101] suggest precisely this, as does the claimed pertinence to the lord of the proceeds of their taxes, their property and even their lives.[102]

In this case, too, as in every aspect of life in the feudal period, this mutual penetration of the public and private law elements is typical of any pre-state political grouping and reappears when the state falls apart, making it difficult to determine the clear and precise nature of the institution.

Despite the profound investigations conducted by clever scholars,[103] we cannot say that everything is clear about its origins.

An attempt to explain the *servitus camerae* has been made during the Middle Ages, connecting it, no less, to Vespasian and Titus.

---

99 Scherer, op. cit., pp. 94–95; a collection of similar pacts is published by Grayzel, op. cit., pp. 351–356.

100 Grayzel, op. cit., p. 350. Year 1204, under Philip Augustus: "Apud Meduntam Jacob de Molinz tradidit in plegium residentie cartas de VIII libris et juravit super rotulum (the Bible) quod non recederet a terra domini regis." (Delisle, *Catalogue des actes de Philippe-Auguste*, Paris, 1856, nos. 890, 890 A).

101 In 1296, King Philip IV of France donates a Jew to his brother, count Charles of Valois, who then buys another one for 300 Liras from Peter from Chambly. Scherer, op. cit., p. 99. The number of examples could grow.

102 Princes speak of their Jews in the same sense they are used to speak of their lands, and the ways of disposal are the same: e.g., in 1247, Frederick II sells the Jews of the city "qui hactenus ad imperium spectare noscebantur" to the Bishop of Würzburg for 2300 marks, with a redeem agreement. Aronius, op. cit., no. 563, pp. 240–241. Nevertheles, we should not jump to conclusions.

103 Cassel, op. cit., l. cit.; Stobbe, *Die Juden in Deutschland während des Mittelalters*, 2nd ed., Leipzig 1902, pp. 8–10; Aronius, op. cit., pp. 139–142; Georg Caro, *Sozial- und Wirtschaftsgeschichte der Juden in Mittelalter und Neuzeit*, vol. I, Leipzig 1908, pp. 396–404; Grayzel, op. cit., pp. 51–55 and 348–351; and others who will be cited further on.

The Saxon Mirror (*Landrecht*, III, 7, § 3) states that Vespasian took the Jews under his protection to reward Flavius Josephus, who had managed to free his son Titus from gout![104]

Conversely, for the Swabian Mirror (*Landrecht*, ch. 260 and 261), it was Titus who, after the destruction of Jerusalem, declares the Jews to be servants of the Treasury and therefore takes them under his protection, granting them, again through the intercession of Josephus, various kinds of privileges.[105]

The idea that, in consequence of deicide and misbelief, the Jews have to be the slaves of the Christians soon appears in ecclesiastical writings: it is already found in the *Altercatio Ecclesiae et Synagogae*, a text of the fifth century.[106] It is, however, a purely theological opinion that finds no correspondence in the actual judicial field. Moreover, when we find it again with well-defined outlines in documents of the 13th century[107] and especially in St. Thomas,[108] it appears

104 *M. G. H. Fontes juris germanici antiqui*, Nova Series, T. I, file I, Hannover, 1933, p. 112.

105 von Lassberg Ed., Tübingen, 1840, pp. 116–118. Cf. *Specchio Tedesco, Landrechtstheil*, § 207, in *M. G. H., Fontes juris germanici antiqui*, Nova Series, T. III, p. 219.

106 The synagogue queries: "Sed dicito mihi, quomodo tibi servio, quae adhuc filios meos liberos esse recognosco. Vacant negotiis, navigandi potestas est libera, compedes nesciunt, nullus vineam laboriosae necessitatis fossuram discerpit, nescio an tibi sim servitute subiecta." The Church replies: "Alioquin si recte populo Israel Christianus populus regnat, constat te ancillam esse, non liberam, quam video servituti subiectam. Respice in legionibus signa, nomen Salvatoris intende, christicolas imperatores adverte et considera te de regno esse discussam: et nobis juxta Testamenti fidem quod servas, confitere: tributum mihi solvis, ad imperium non accedis, habere non potes praefecturam. Judaeum esse comitem non licet; senatum tibi introire prohibetur; ad militiam non admitteris; mensas divitum non attingis; clarissimatus ordinem perdidisti: totum non licet; cui etiam ad manducandum ut vel male viveres, paucula condonamus." Migne, *Patrologia Latina*, 42, 1133; on the *Altercatio*, see Juster, op. cit., I, pp. 73–74.

107 July 15, 1205, Innocent's III letter to the archbishops of Sens and Paris: "Etsi Judeos, quos propria culpa submisit perpetue servituti, cum Dominum crucifixerint, quem sui prophetae predixerant ad redemptionem Israel in carne venturum pietas cristiana receptet ..." (Grayzel, doc. no. 18, pp. 114–115); January 17, 1208, Innocent's III letter to the count of Nevers: "Blasphematores nominis christiani non debent a christianis principibus in oppressionem servorum Domini confoveri, sed potius comprimi servitute." (Grayzel, doc. no. 24, pp. 126–127); May 18, 1233, Gregory's IX letter to the archbishop of Compostela and his suffragans: "Judaei, quos propria culpa submisit perpetue servituti ..." (Grayzel, doc. no. 71, pp. 204–205). The section quoted from the letter of Innocent of 1205 is passed into the Decretals, ch. 13 X *de Judeis* 5, 6, influencing, with St. Thomas, the entire later doctrine.

108 St. Thomas, *Summa Theologica*, (*Opera omnia* ed., Rome, 1570, T. X) secunda secundae, quaestio X, art. X: The forced liberation of slaves who had been owned by Jews does not violate the natural law "quia, cum ipsi Judaei, sint servi Ecclesiae, (Ecclesia) potest disponere de rebus eorum"; ibid. art. XII: "Judei sunt servi principum servitute civili." The extreme consequences of the principle, such as the forced baptism of children *ante usum rationis*, however, are rejected.

as the reflection of change that has already occurred in practice, rather than the genetic factor of the change itself.[109]

In some authors' oversimplified view, the *servitus camerae* is considered a consequence of the Jews' reduction to the state of foreigners, as do Maurer[110] and later, in keeping with his conclusions relating to the previous period, Scherer.[111] Nevertheless, against Maurer's view, Aronius[112] rightly points out that Jews reside in the territory *ab immemorabili* and stably, and not as subjects to foreign state power: therefore, they cannot be considered as aliens. Grayzel, too, embraces this viewpoint.[113]

Deducing the quality of foreigners for the Jews from their submission to the *tuitio regia*, while on the other hand linking their state of servitude (i.e., of dependency on the monarch or princes) with the condition of foreigners – means arguing in a non-very clever vicious cycle, a fact that Scherer and his predecessors did not realize.

Far from such ideas, in the state of public servitude in which the Jews have fallen, the great historian Graetz sees the result of their spontaneous submission to the kings and feudal lords: in order to obtain protection against the pressure of persecutions caused by the Crusaders' fanaticism, and driven mainly by the massacres that in 1096 decimate their communities in Germany, Graetz writes,[114] the Jews, free until the 12th century, at this point trade their freedom for security.

---

109 St. Thomas, *De Regimine Judaeorum, Ad ducissam Brabantiae, Opera Omnia* ed., Rome 1570, vol. XVII, p. 192: "Primo ergo vestra requirebat excellentia, si liceat vobis aliquo tempore et quo exactionem facere in Judaeos; ad quam quaestionem sic absolute propositam responderi potest quia licet, *ut jura dicunt*, Judaei merito culpae suae sint vel essent perpetuae servituti addicti, et sic eorum res terrarum domini possent accipere tamquam suas: hoc tamen servato moderamine, ut necessaria vitae subsidia eis nullatenus subtrahantur … hoc servandum videtur ut, *sicut jura determinant*, ab eis coacta servitia non exigantur, quae ipsi praeterito tempore facere non consueverunt: quia ea quae sunt insolita magis solent animo perturbare. Secundum igitur huius moderationis sententiam potestis secundum consuetudinem praedecessorum vestrorum exactionem in Judaeos facere, si tamen aliud non obsistat." See further on, footnote no. 128.

110 In *Kritische Vierteljahrschrift für Rechtswissenschaft*, 9, pp. 565 et seqq.

111 Scherer, op. cit., pp. 70, 71. 84, 85. "Der einzige Erklärungsgrund für dieses Abhängigkeitsverhältnis der Juden, demzufolge nicht nur in Deutschland, sonder auch in den meisten übrigen Staaten des Mittelalters die Könige und andere Machthaber über ihre Personen und ihr Engentum nach freier Willkür disponierten und sie und ihr Eigentum wie eine ihnen gehörende Sache behandelten, kann nur in ihrer ursprünglichen Recht- und Schutzlosigkeit *als Fremde* liegen." (p. 85).

112 Aronius, op. cit., no. 314 a, p. 141.

113 Grayzel, op. cit., p. 348: "… the fact remains that the Jews were not foreigners. …"

114 Graetz, *Geschichte der Juden*, vol. VI, p. 183.

On the same line of thoughts are Stobbe[115] and Aronius,[116] who base themselves primarily on the new inclusion of the Jews since 1103 in the "peaces," i.e., the promises of sworn protection by the king to all categories of subjects in need of special protection.[117] Somewhat differently, however, Waitz,[118] Brunner,[119] Dahn[120] and Heusler[121] tend to relate the first traces of *servitus camerae* to the Carolingian period, connecting them with those requests previously discussed of *mundio* in Louis the Pious' times. In this, they dissent from an earlier opinion expressed by Cassel,[122] who vehemently denied any similarities between *deservire partibus palatii*, duty to be performed by the protected ludovicians, and the servitude later on. However, the relation would remain identical for these authors, and the difference would lie only in its generalization.

Apart from this chronological divergence, however, Graetz and Aronius, as well as other writers, share the idea that *servitus camerae* is a position the Jews enter at their own will. They do so through a spontaneous act of submission, which, performed at first only by a few individuals, under the impetus of the persecutions, is later practiced by the masses, to ultimately produce its consequences on the entirety of the Jews living in the Christian states.

In reality, plenty of good arguments support this thesis: against Cassel's idea, the substantial identity between the old ludovician *tuitiones* and the later *servitus camerae* seems to be confirmed by the fact that in a 1090 privilege to some Jews of Worms, drafted along the lines of those *tuitiones*, the protégés are declared as "related to the Imperial Chamber,"[123] as actually are all the Jews

115 Stobbe, *Geschichte der Juden in Deutschland*, 1st ed., Braunschweig, 1866, pp. 8 et seqq.

116 Aronius, op. cit., p. 141.

117 The peace of 1103 recites: "Juraverunt (Emperor Henry, his son and the great feudatories) pacem ecclesiis, clericis, monachis, laicis, mercatoribus, mulieribus ne vi rapiantur, Judeis." (*Mon. Germ. Hist., Leges*, II, p. 66; Aronius, no. 210, p. 97). Since this is the confirmation of a similar declaration where Jews are not mentioned, the novelty can be explained with the events of 1096 (Aronius, p. 141). Other general or provincial peaces that include the Jews are found in 1223 (Aronius, no. 422), 1224 (no. 428), 1224–32 (no. 458), 1254 (nos. 598, 599, 601, 602), around 1260 (no. 667), 1265 (no. 706), 1270–72 (no. 757), around 1275 (no. 771), 1251–78 (no. 772).

118 *Deutsche Verfassungsgeschichte*, vol. V, 2nd ed., p. 422, no. 1.

119 *Deutsche Rechtsgeschichte*, vol. I, 1st ed., Leipzig, 1887, pp. 275 et seqq.

120 *Deutsche Geschichte*, Gotha, 1883–1888, vol. I, part II, pp. 558 et seqq.

121 *Institutionen des deutschen Privatrechts*, Leipzig, 1885, vol. I, p. 149.

122 Cassel, op. cit., p. 84: "Es kann also kein zweifel obwalten dass hier *deservire* nicht mit *servi camerae* in Zusammenhange stehe, sonder von der besonderen Verpflichtung der Kaufleute an die Pfalz gegen kaiserlichen Schutz und kaiserliche Freiheit die Rede ist."

123 Hoeniger, *Zur Geschichte der Juden in früheren Mittelalter*, in *Zeitschrift für Geschichte der Juden in Deutschland*, I 1886, pp. 138 et seqq.; Aronius, cited work, no. 171, pages 74–77. The privilege has been lost and we have evidence of it from the confirmation of Frederick I on

of the Empire in a later privilege by Frederick I, for the Jews of Regensburg (1182).[124] On the other hand, the theory of voluntary extension of the relationship would find valid support in a passage of the *Deeds of Frederick I*, by Otto of Freising, stating that, in the year 1146, as a result of new massacres caused by the propaganda of a fanatical friar instigating the crowds to massacre the Jews, many of them resorted to the Emperor's *tuition*.[125] Even those *subditiones* to the feudal landlords prohibited by the king, mentioned in the above chapter of the so-called laws of Edward the Confessor, support the theory in question.

Nevertheless, I do not feel like adhering to this theory since I believe that a legal position, common to the Jews of all Europe since the 13th century, cannot derive from single contractual acts. In other words, I reject the correlation and substantial similarity between Louis the Pious' *tuitiones* and the *servitus camerae*, and seek elsewhere the foundation and prime source of this institution. To understand what that is, in my opinion, it would be worthwhile considering two things: first of all, the fact that in Carolingian times, as already in the Roman Empire, the Jews were required to pay a special annual tax,[126] and then also the trends that took place in the judicial life in general following

6 April 1157, Hoeniger, 1, c.; Aronius, no. 280, p. 123; *M. G. H., Legum sectio IV*, t. I, Hannover, 1893, no. 163, p. 226. The date cannot be determined with absolute precision. Aronius rightly observes that it is not a question of general privilege, since the *tuitio* is granted "Judeis de Wormacia et ceteris solidalibus suis," that is, to single individuals. The privilege is extended to all Jews of Germany by Frederick II in July 1236, *M. G. H., Legum sectio IV*, t. II, no. 204, p. 274. But there is no reason to see in this document, as Schupper does (*Manuale di Storia del Diritto Italiano, Le Fonti*, Città di Castello, 1908, page 334), as well as Bizzarri (*Il diritto privato nelle fonti senesi nel secolo XIII*, in *Bollettino senese di Storia patria*, year 33–34, 1926–27, file III, p. 280 = *Studi di storia del diritto italiano editi dalla famiglia*, Turin, 1937, p. 399), an imperial ordinance valid throughout the empire, to be considered perhaps also applicable to Siena in 1200.

124 Quoted above, p. 29.

125 "Radolfus monachus, vir quidem religionis habitum habens religionisque severitatem solerter imitans, sed litterarum notitia sobrie imbutus doctrinae suae non vigilanter interserens, quod Judaei in civitatibus oppidisque passim manentes tamquam christianae religionis hostes trucidarentur. Quod doctrinae semen in multis Galliae Germaniaeque civitatibus vel oppidis tam firmiter radices figens germinavit, ut plurimis ex Judaeis hac tumultuosa seditione necatis, *multi sub principis romanorum alas tuitionis causa confugerunt*." *Mon. Ger. Mist., Scriptores*, XX, p. 372. Aronius, no. 233, p. 109. On the persecution, sources and bibliography ibidem, no. 232, pp. 107–108.

126 Amulo da Lione, *Contra Judaeos* (around the year 846), c. 44 (Migne, *Patrologia Latina*, 116, 172): "propter annua tributa et exenia sua quae ab illis (the Jews) persolvuntur." The question of whether this tax can be considered a continuation of the *fiscus Judaicus* seems to me unsolvable and actually it is not very important. Even in the Visigothic kingdom, the existence of a special tax on Jews is certain, *Leges Visigothorum*, XII, 2, 18 (*Mon. Ger. Hist.* Zeumer ed.). Cf. Tamassia, cited work, p. 818. For the Byzantine Empire, see the writing

the progressive emergence of the ideas of patrimonial state and feudalism. The amalgamation of the idea of sovereignty with that of property, characteristic of the barbarian era and even more so of the feudal era, causes the relationship between all state members to the head of state to fall somewhat from the public into the private law domain. Thus, what in normal times is a relationship of subjection, becomes now a personal dependency, a servitude, in a sense. Consequently, an equalization of free and servile classes is established "in a relationship of dependency based on the common principle of subjection to the public authority of the lord"; such relationship "stands on a concept of sovereignty and dominance that depends on the confusion occurring in fiefdom between the public authority and the private authority."[127]

If this transformation affects the entire population, leading to a type of hierarchically ordered society and characterized by an intricate system of relationships of subjection, all the more it acts towards the categories on which a special tax is imposed: the mandatory payment by the Jews of this tax to the state turns into a particular dependency relationship upon the person of the sovereign-owner. Its proceeds, now regarded as the king's revenue – royalties – are ceded or sold by him to the feudal lords. As we have seen, this augments, even more, the private law aspect of the relationship. And when, for reasons whose genesis is hard to trace but that may be associated to the lack of any control in the exercise of powers, other taxes of personal character are associated with the taxation of patrimonial nature, the term *servitus* flows naturally from the Imperial Chancellors' pens. Nevertheless, it persists for centuries, surviving the system that generated it until the fall of the Holy Roman Empire.[128]

---

of Andréadès, *Les Juifs et le fisc dans l'empire byzantin*, in *Mélanges Charles Dhiel*, 1930, pp. 7–29.

127 Solmi, *Storia del Diritto Italiano*, 1930, pp. 238–39. Cf. pp. 115–116. Similarly, D'Amia, *Schiavitù romana e servitù medioevale*, Milan 1931, pp. 88–89: "We must not forget that if the distinction between sovereignty of public order and the rule of private character can conceptually be conceived, in reality the leveling work of the feud had merged them, so that if the classes are in fact become levelled, this happens in general in a way which is not different from a relationship of dependency. The actual fact of the proceeds that the feudal lord was receiving – despite his political supremacy – not exclusively under the sovereign power that he exercised, but also for the particular condition of *judicial* inferiority of those who had to pay them, confirms the contemporary and practical coexistence of the two motives of subjection. Hence, the two correlative categories of levies; and in the latter, the providing of certain services, as well as the performing of manual works, which are redeemable, that is reducible in the common financial expression of the levy."

128 The term *servitus* is probably drawn from ecclesiastical phraseology, whereas the substance of the relationship is of feudal origin. In the privilege for Vienna of April 1237,

Servitus is thus the new name by which a relationship is called at a certain point in its evolution and following some worsening of its content. It is rooted in ancient times and matures automatically in perfect correlation with the general development of feudal institutions. The subsequent stages of this evolution can be recognized through some documents. So, as we have seen, in the 9th century, the relationship between Jews and rulers still appears exclusively leaning on criteria of public law order, expressing itself in the sole mandatory requirement of a special tax. However, in the 10th century, the acquisition in the relationship of private law elements attesting the transfer to the king of the weregild of all Jews, or at least the tendency of a certain doctrine in favor of such cession, seems to be proved by a passage of Raterio, Bishop of Verona.[129] In the same century, the private law – or at least semi-private law – coloring of the king's lordship on the Jews, becomes clearer through their enfeoffments to the Church or the secular rulers: as such appear the donations of the Jews of Magdeburg and Merseburg made in 973 and 979 by Otto II to the respective bishops,[130] and the matching donation of the Jews of Merseburg made in 1004 by Henry II to the Bishop Wigbert.[131]

This process appears to advance around the end of the 11th century, after the massacres of 1096, when the Emperor ordered an investigation into the extent of the murdered Jews' looted goods, obviously emanating from the principle of his private right to such goods.[132]

Frederick II explicitly uses the language of the Church, stating that the imperial authority "a priscis temporibus ad perpetrati Judaici sceleris ultionem eisdem Judeis indixerit perpetuam servitutem," Aronius, op. cit., no. 509, p. 220. He too had previously used the expression "camerae nostrae pertinentes" (privilege of 1225 for the Archbishop of Arles, Huillard-Bréholles, *Historia Diplomatica Friderici secundi*, 1854, II, part 1, pp. 473–4). The ancient idea of the Church is thus realized in some way through the feudal relationship, which in turn borrows from the Church its specific name.

129 Raterio, *Qualitatis Coniectura* (Migne, *Patrologia Latina*, 136, 536), ch. 11: "Quale est autem quod clerico contendere pro Christo, Judaeo blasphamante Christum, pugnam consertam clericus Judaeum, Judaeus si percutit clericum, imo in coelo Christum (sic enim Saulo est dictum) Erimbertus noster verborum contortor, legum dicit distortor, triplam compositionem de Judaei percussione regi cedere, de clerici nullam alicui?"

130 Aronius, op. cit., nos. 132, 133 and 134, pp. 56–57. They are the most ancient *acta* of this kind that have reached us.

131 Aronius, no. 140, p. 139. The clarification contained in the following passage of a local chronicle is important, since it aptly confirms the particular character of these donations (Brotuff, *Chronica und antiquitates des alten keiserlichen Stiffts etc. Marsburg*, Augsburg, von 1557, f. 64, see Aronius, ibid.): "Auch gab Keiser Heinrich dem Bischoffe Wigberto die Juden zu Marsburg, das ist der Jüden jerlichen tribut."

132 May 1098: "Inquisitione facta Moguntiae ab imperatore de facultatibus Judeorum interfectorum, inter ceteros qui eas rapuerunt quidam ex consanguineis archipresulis incusati

We, therefore, get the notion that Jews are a pertinence of the Imperial Chamber (document quoted in 1182); from this, it is a short step to the term *servitus camerae*, which starts to enter the language in the 13th century.

In summary, the idea of *servitus* arises from the penetration, spontaneously occurring as it was linked to the complex medieval judicial dynamics, of private law elements into a specific obligation. An obligation whose origin was purely of public law: from a particular burden inherent to the subjection, we arrive to an exceptional servitude.[133]

The theory mentioned above that finds substantial identity between the relationship arising from voluntary *subditiones* of individuals to the royal *mundio* and the *servitus camerae* characteristic of all Jews, therefore fails to hold up. Hence the need to consider this particular relationship as superimposed on the pre-existing general one: which is evident from the fact that the individual *subditiones* continue uninterrupted for the entire period in which the *servitus camerae* lasts; and until the emancipation, in Germany, in the midst of the mass of *servi camerae* Jews, the so-called "Schutzjuden" continue to constitute a particular category of individuals possessing special protection papers, obtained at a very pricey cost from kings or princes.[134]

If at times the king opposes the *subditio* of Jews to lesser potentates, such as it appears from the aforementioned chapter of the "Leges Eduardi Confessoris," this does not happen because of the idea that this *subditio* is to replace that to the king and may therefore prevent the establishing of the *servitus camerae*

sunt ... Extiterunt autem qui dicerent etiam ipsum pontificem multam partem de pecuniis invasis accepisse et idcirco defensioni ceterorum tanto studio cor apposuisse." *Mon. Ger. Hist., Scriptores*, VI, p. 209. Aronius, no. 205, p. 95. We are not very distant from the right of escheat, but it is not legitimate nevertheless to infer that the Jews are in everything assimilated to the foreigners.

133 The expression "*special* servitude," i.e., characterized by special obligations, is used most often in the sources. In addition to the already mentioned Federician document of 1234, I shall quote, for example, the privilege of King Conrad of January 20, 1251 for Regensburg (... Judei, servi camere nostre specialiter ...; Aronius , no. 582, p. 249); and that of King William of April 3, 1251, for Goslar (... ad hec nullam indebitam molestiam sive captivitatem Judei civitatis sustinebunt a nobis, et defendemus ipsos amicabiliter et benigne tamquam speciales camere servos: sed sicut debitum est serviant nobis tamquam domino suo et romanorum regi ...," Aronius, no. 585, p. 249).sustinebunt a nobis, et defendemus ipsos amicabiliter et benigne tamquam speciales camere servos: sed sicut debitum est serviant nobis tamquam domino suo et romanorum regi ...," Aronius, no. 585, p. 249).

134 Beck, *Tractatus de Juribus Judeorum* cit., 1731, p. 29: "... und solche Juden werden Schutz-Juden, vergleitete Juden genennet, und bekommen den Schutz-Brief, und bezahlen dieserhalben jährlich gewiese Schutz-Gelder." For its persistence until the emancipation, cf. S. Dubnow, *Weltgeschichte des Jüdischen Volkes*, vol. VIII, § 1 = French transl., *Histoire Moderne du Peuple juif*, vol. I, Paris, 1933, § 1, p. 14.

relationship. Rather, it happens simply because the king fears that the spoils committed by the lords against the Jews who submitted to their "protection" are such as to put the Jews in the material impossibility to fulfill the obligations levied on them in favor of the Royal Chamber. Levied on them in virtue of that belonging to the Chamber asserted as existing *ipso jure* and thus foregoing such *subditio*.

If, as we have seen, the enfeoffments of Jews to the temporal lords and churches is to be regarded as a reflection of a special relationship of dependence – essentially identical to what will later in time be classified as "pertinence to the Imperial or Royal Chamber" and finally "servitude" – we can remark that in southern Italy the establishment of such a relationship in that – let's say – still anonymous form, dates back to the first decades of the Norman conquest.[135]

Donations are made mainly by the kings to churches and monasteries: in 1086, the Jews who were given by Robert Guiscard to his wife Sichelgaita as a dowry were ceded by her to the archbishop of Bari:[136] the concession is

135 This system of transfer of fiscal rights and jurisdiction on the Jews, however, is not unknown even in the Byzantine Empire, although no documents exist certifying its putting into practice in the Italian territories subject to the Empire. A precise news is provided by a chart of 1049, the Golden Bull of Monomakhos, published by Canellakis Χιαχὰ Ανάλεκτα, Athens 1890, pp. 350–51, and then by George Zolotas, Ιστορία τῆς Χίου, vol. II, Athens 1924, pp. 282–83 and taken into account by Andréadès, op. cit. (above, pp. 36–37, footnote no. 126), p. 22. "The Imperial Act – he writes – starts with explaining how the Jewish people forfeited God who to punish them surrendered them to the more faithful Christian people. Also the Emperor, having learned that the Jews of the island of Chios are παντάπασι ἐλεύθεροι καὶ μηδαμοῦ ὑποκείμενοι submits the fifteen Jewish families living on the island to the convent (of Néa Monè), and orders that in a sign of its sovereignty (ἵνα δὲ καὶ δεσπότης τῶν φαμιλιῶν δήλη ᾖ) the Néa Monè receives annually from them a κεφαλητιών; in addition, these families are exempted from any ἐπηρεσία (services in nature) or ἀγγαρεία (true corvée). The Act is confirmed in 1062, Zolotas, op. cit., pp. 297–98. Here too we are on the ground of feudal relations, to which, in retrospect, some kind of theological coloring is given; the annual tribute was probably there even before, although this is not evident with absolute certainty. (About the possible existence of the tax, Andréadès so concludes his research: "On peut invoquer, tant en faveur que contre l'éxistence d'un inpôt judaïque [in the Byzantine Empire] un certain nombre d'arguments serieux," op. cit., p. 20). For the Byzantine Italy, Tamassia, op. cit., pp. 818–820, considers the persistence *ab antiquo* of the fee likely, without, however, being able to bring documentary evidence.

136 *Codice Diplomatico Barese*, vol. I, Bari, 1897, no. 30; Tamassia, op. cit., p. 820; R. Strauss, *Die Juden in Königreich Sizilien unter Normannen und Staufern*, Heidelberg, 1910, p. 95.

confirmed in 1087 and in 1093.[137] Similarly, in the year 1090 Roger I donates the city's Jewish quarter with all its present and future Jewish inhabitants, apart from few exceptions, to the episcopal church of Salerno.[138] In Rossano, the passage of the Jews to the dependency of the episcopacy takes place around 1093, when Duchess Adelaide donates the Jewish tithes and, in addition, three Jews to the archbishop, and a Jew with his children, employees and all his belongings to the chaplain.[139] In 1093, Duke Roger also hands over the local Jews to the church of Melfi.[140] Similar donations of Jews to local churches were recorded in 1107 in Termini,[141] in 1113 in Cosenza,[142] in 1121 in Salerno,[143] and in 1127 in Reggio.[144]

The Swabians, who succeed to the Normans in the dominion of southern Italy, follow the same system. So does Henry VI, who in 1195 transferred to the S. Mary convent a fief "totam judaeam civitatis Neritoni (Nardò) cum omnibus et singuli Judeis, etc.,"[145] and in the same year, confirms to the Archbishop of Trani the right he holds on the Jewish quarter for the privilege of King William.[146] In 1198, Constance grants "in perpetuum judaicam civitatis" to

137 *Codice Diplomatico Barese*, I, nos. 32 and 35. The Jews are ceded to the bishop together with the entrustees "undecumque advenientes et quantoscumque habere potueritis" and the city's harlots. In relation to what I said above, this is one more reason to believe that Jews (and thus the harlots too) are *ipso jure* in that position of dependence, that has the payment of a tribute as end result, which for the entrustees is instead the result of the entrusting, of voluntary *subditio*. On these papers, see Besta, *Il Diritto consuetudinario di Bari e la sua genesi*, in *Rivista It. per le Scienze Giur.*, vol. 36, 1903, p. 63 and Tamassia, op. cit., pp. 819–20. On the protection and royalties of the entrustees, see Besta, ibid., p. 42 and Tamassia, *Jus affidandi*, negli *Atti dell'Istituto Veneto di Scienze, Lettere e Arti*, vol. 72, 1913, pp. 343–90.

138 Muratori, *Antiquitates Italicae Medii Aevi*, I, p. 899. The donation is confirmed in 1123 by Prince William and in 1221 by Emperor Frederick II. Muratori, op. cit., VII, p. 184. Ughelli, *Italia Sacra*, Venice, 1717–1722, vol. IX, p. 57; Huillard-Bréholles, *Historia dipl.* cit., II, part I, p. 112. Cf. Scherer, op. cit., pp. 103–104, and Pertile, *Storia del Diritto Italiano*, II ed., vol. III, p. 207, no. 14.

139 Ferorelli, *Gli ebrei nell'Italia Meridionale dall'età Romana al secolo XVIII*, Turin 1915, p. 44. Confirmation by Frederick II in 1223, Huillard-Bréholles, op. cit., II, p. 364.

140 Ughelli, *Italia Sacra*, vol. I, p. 923. Strauss, op. cit., p. 96.

141 Chalandon, *Histoire de la domination normande, en Italie et en Sicile*, Paris, 1907, vol. II, p. 563. Strauss, op. cit., ibid.

142 Ughelli, op. cit., vol. IX, p. 192. Strauss, op. cit., p. 97.

143 Paesano, *Memorie della Chiesa Salernitana*, II, p. 72, see Strauss, op. cit., ibid.

144 Cotroneo, *Gli Ebrei della Giudeca di Reggio*, in *Rivista Storica Calabrese*, 1903, November–December, pp. 391, 392 and 412. Ferorelli, op. cit., p. 44.

145 Ughelli, op. cit., vol. X, p. 298. Scherer, op. cit., p. 104; Strauss, op. cit., p. 100.

146 Strauss, op. cit., ibid.

the Archbishop of Capua, and in 1210, Frederick II donates the Jews with their dyeing industry to the Church of Palermo "ut de cetero homines vestri sint."[147] However, with this last monarch and from the time of his actual ruling (1215), a vigorous movement takes place tending to bring the Jews back under the Empire lordship,[148] a movement that provokes the papal wrath.[149] While remaining suspended in the period following the death of Frederick II, until the end of the Angevin domination characterized by a strong influence of the Church, the movement is then resumed by the Aragonese monarchs.[150]

Also, during the time of Frederick II, the Holy Roman Empire in general, thus, in Italy, the relationship between the Jews and the sovereignty began being qualified by the expression "servi camerae."[151] We find this term constantly used later in Aragonese documents of Sicily,[152] Sardinia,[153] and the Angevin documents of Naples.[154] Thus, we see that in those periods when, for one reason or another, the judicial pressure on the Jews becomes more robust, the consequences of the principle of *servitus* are drawn with greater vigor, developing into severe limitations of personal freedom.[155] In contrast,

147 Huillard-Bréholles, op. cit., I, p. 182. Confirmation in 1211 (p. 191, ibid.) and, for six years, in 1215 (p. 372, ibid.).

148 Tamassia, op. cit., pp. 838–839, who tries to explain the reasons for the transfer first to the Church and return to the Empire later.

149 August 17, 1236. "Series gravaminum Ecclesie contra Imperatorem, quam Papa (Gregory IX) episcopo Prenestino trasmisit." It includes the indictment: "de Judaeis ablatis quibusdam ecclesiis." Grayzel, op. cit., p. 224. On September 20, the Emperor replies: "Judaeos autem etsi tam in imperio quam in regno nobis communi jure immediate subiaceant, a nulla tamen ecclesia illos abstulimus que super eis jus speciale pretenderet, quod communi juri nostro merito preferretur." Huillard-Bréholles, op. cit., IV, p. 912. Aronius, no. 498.

150 Q. Sinigaglia, *La condizione giuridica degli ebrei in Sicilia*, in *Rivista It. per le Scienze Giur.*, vol. XLI, 1906, p. 81.

151 Huillard-Bréholles, op. cit., II, part 1, p. 473, Fontana, *Gli Ebrei in Catania nel secolo XV*, Catania 1901, p. 8. Scaduto, *Stato e Chiesa nelle due Sicilie*, Palermo 1887, § 39, p. 503. Sinigaglia, op. cit., p. 81.

152 For examples of the times of Frederick III (1355–1377) and Martin I (1392–1409), see Gregorio, *Considerazioni sopra la storia di Sicilia dai tempi normanni fino ai presenti*, 1805, p. 66 and passim. Cf. Roberti, *Diritto di naufragio*, in *Studi della R. Università di Cagliari*, 1912, p. 171.

153 See, e.g., the document mentioned further below, footnote no. 155.

154 Charles I of Anjou grants "Universitati Hebreorum Neapolis provisio quod non cogantur communicare cum aliis hominibus Neapoli, quia ipsi Hebrei cum immediate ad nostram Cameram pertineant, semotim nostre Camere solvant omnes impositiones." Strauss, op. cit., p. 114.

155 So, on January 3, 1485, while that storm that will lead to the expulsion of the Jews from the Spanish territories and therefore also from insular Italy is already about to be unleashed,

typically, the inherent obligations, with the hefty taxes, are practiced in some *servitia*, such as supplying banners to the galleys and royal castles and cleaning these buildings.[156]

The expression is common even in Northern Italy,[157] where during the 11th[158] and 12th[159] centuries, the Jews appear to be subjected to special tributes that Mayer[160] considers related to the ancient *fiscus judaicus*.[161] However, it would be more prudent to identify them with that tax which, as already shown, has been incumbent on the Jews of the entire Holy Roman Empire since the 9th century. The diplomas of the Imperial Vicariate from the 15th century mention the Jews as *servi camerae*, among the royalties and the possessions enfeoffed by the emperor to the lords.[162]

The generality of this Jewish *servitus* phenomenon, whether or not called by that specific name, and the consequent need to find an explanation of general character, undoubtedly rule out an opinion on its origin that, since it was formulated for Italy, is worth mentioning. It is put forth, with cautious reserves by Mayer,[163] who observes that in the Norman territories the Jews engage mainly

---

Ferdinand of Aragon declares that all the Jews dwelling in Sardinia are his servants and property of the Royal Chamber: in civil cases, therefore, they must be subject to the Attorney General and no longer to the Royal Vicar, under penalty of a heavy fine. Also, no Jew will be able to move to the continent without permission of the Royal Prosecutor, and once in possession of the permit, he must provide a suitable guarantor who guarantees his return within the period prescribed: nor can he take away from the island goods or assets. Spano, *Gli Ebrei in Sardegna*, in *Vessillo Israelitico*, 27, 1879, p. 231.

156 Zunz, *Geschichte der Juden in Sicilien* (in Volume *Zur Geschichte und Literatur der Juden*, 1845), It. transl. by Perreau in *Arch. Stor. Siciliano*, new series, IV, 1879, pp. 19 et seqq. Sinigaglia, op. cit., p. 80. Scherer, op. cit., p. 105. Lagumina, *Codice diplomatico dei Giudici di Sicilia*, Palermo, 1885–1909, doc. 144, August 19, 1398.

157 One should consider that until the 14th century, the number of Jews here was meager.

158 1015, Rimini, "Teloneum Judaeorum." Tonini, *Della Storia civile e Sacra riminese*, vol. II, Rimini, 1856, p. 48.

159 1134, Genoa, Tributo alla Cattedrale. *Liber Jurium reipublicae Genuensis*, Tome I, doc. 36, p. 47, in *Historiae Patriae Monumenta*, Turin, 1854, vol. VII. This too may be a case of transferring a tax already due to the imperial treasury – to the Church.

160 Mayer, *Italiänische Verfassungsgeschichte*, Leipzig, 1909, vol. I, p. 147.

161 On this issue, see the excellent treatise of Juster, op. cit., vol. II, pp. 282 et seqq.

162 1412, Vicariate of Louis Duke of Savoy (Lünig, *Codex Diplomaticus Italiae*, Frankfurt-Leipzig, 1725, vol. I, p. 643): "Auctoritatem Judeos servos camerae nostrae acceptandi, defendendi et tenendi ..."; 1495, Diploma of enfeoffment of the Duchy of Milan granted by the Emperor Maximillian to Ludovico Maria Sforza (Lünig, III, p. 815). Similarly, in the diplomas of Sigismund to Brunoro della Scala and the Venetians (Pertile, *Storia* cit., III, II ed., p. 207).

163 Mayer, op. cit., I, pp. 147–148.

in the craft of dyeing:[164] "now, because the dyeing workshop is a royalty of the lord of the territory, the possibility of disposing of the Jews could very easily be explained with the hypothesis that they are hereditarily linked to the State dyeing workshops: in fact, Jews and dyeing workshops are (sometimes) ceded together." Their treatment as *abhängige Leute* would derive from the incidental connection with that profession subject to royalties."

After what has been said above, it is unnecessary to insist on demonstrating the inadequacy of this hypothesis, linking a phenomenon of European nature to factors seen only in southern Italy. It is likewise to be discarded, as it has been,[165] any hypothesis that links the *servitus* of the Jews to the coinciding of their predominant commercial activity with the existence of special taxes levied on the merchants and with the fact that the Jews and the merchants are sometimes ceded together:[166] here too the sporadicity of the cases removes any possibility for the circumstance to be counted among the generators of the *servitus*.

It is now time to wrap things up.

What I have so far described seems sufficient to establish that even though, in some territories and times, this *servitus* of the Jews so intensely imbues itself with private law elements, generating a terminology that seems to outline the institution of true servitude, in its fundamental lines it nevertheless remains within the boundaries of public law. It maintains that character of political dependency relation, of subjection, which is unique because marked by special obligations. Such character will later manifest itself most clearly when private and public law separates again in a definite and precise way with the Middle Ages coming to an end. Nevertheless, even in feudal times, the fact

164 On the relations between the Jews and the dyeing workshops in Sicily, see Strauss, op. cit., pp. 66–74; and for southern Italy, see Tamassia, op. cit., p. 825 and Ferorelli, op. cit., p. 39.

165 Grayzel, op. cit., p. 348.

166 So in the mentioned sales of Otto II to the Merseburg bishops (973; the emperor cedes "quicquid merseburgensis murus continet cum Judeis et mercatoribus," Aronius, no. 132, p. 56) and Magdeburg bishops (973, June 4: "negotiatores vel Judei ibi habitantes"; 979, August, "negotiatoribus sive Judeis," Aronius, nos. 133–134, pp. 56–57) and of Henry II to the Merseburg bishop (1004: "insuper Wigberto antistiti mercatores et Judeos ... ab Gisilero primitus acquisitos ac diu commutatos reddidit," Aronius, no. 140, p. 59). A case occurs in Italy too: on January 9, 905, for the intercession of Queen Bertilla, King Berengar, inter alia, grants to the church of Treviso the teloneo due to the royal treasury "tam de Christinias quamque et de Judeis qui ibidem negotia exercere studuerint." (Schiaparelli, *I Diplomi di Berengario*, in *Fonti per la Storia d'Italia*, no. 35, Rome 1903, no. 52, p. 149). The donation is renewed by these exact words by Otto III, on April 18, 991 (*Mon. Ger. Hist., Diplomi*, T. II, part II, no. 69, p. 476) and confirmed on August 5, 996 (ibid., no. 225, p. 639).

that an almost complete judicial capacity of private law is acknowledged to the Jews is a fundamental event. They can sell, buy or otherwise dispose of movable or immovable property, draw wills or be their beneficiaries, stand trial, etc., without their sales or purchases being intended for the king or their personality being judicially integrated by the king. Despite some appearance to the contrary as a result – I repeat – of the confusion between public law and private law typical of the Middle Ages, we can thus safely state that the Jews can be categorized as freemen. The lords' power over them must be regarded as a demonstration, albeit taken to extremes, of the sovereign right.[167] Furthermore, this is the conclusion to which Stobbe[168] comes for Germany, followed by Aronius,[169] and to which Picciotto[170] comes for England, followed by Grayzel.[171]

Also, concerning Italy, where the *servitus* is never characterized by great harshness, its purely publicistic nature is established, by timely intuition, by Tamassia.[172] Sinigaglia,[173] too, hits the mark when he states that "the name (servants) should not presume a different legal status, lesser than the real one, a real servitude: the Jews were not slaves, but in an intermediate state somewhat reminiscent of the Germanic bondsmen *liti* or *aldi*, with the difference, however, that the *dominus* of the latter was domestic authority while in our case the king represented and impersonated the State. Whereas the relationships between master and *aldo* were personal and under private law, those between the sovereign and the Jews were collective and under public law."

Suppose it is true that even in feudal times, Jews did not sink to the status of serfs but essentially remained in the ancient position of freedom. In that

167 I shall note here that the thesis I refused, that the *servitus* derives from a general spontaneous *subditio*, would hardly be in agreement with the fact of this complete *jure civili* freedom. On the other hand, however, indeed, the Jews *sub mundeburdo* like the *Schutzjuden* of the following centuries are not in an actual state of servitude.

168 Stobbe, *Die Juden in Deutschland*, 1866, p. 8 (II ed., 1902, p. 13).

169 Aronius, op. cit., pp. 139–140.

170 Cyril M. Picciotto, in *Transactions of Jewish Historical Society of England*, 9, 1918–20, pp. 67 et seqq. (unreachable; quoted from Grayzel, op. cit., p. 351).

171 Grayzel, op. cit., p. 351. Scherer, op. cit., naturally holds an opposite opinion (see e.g., p. 70), but we know by now that his entire construction is based on a misunderstanding.

172 Tamassia, *Stranieri ed Ebrei* cit., p. 820: "Neither in Italy nor in France those subjected to taxes are to be considered as slaves, although due to their specific tribute, the Jews are often called servants of the Royal Chamber." Their position depends "on that curious fiscal concept that the Middle Ages had of incomes, according to which there was no other way to grant such incomes than to give the people from whom these incomes were coming."

173 Sinigaglia, op. cit., p. 81.

case, it is impossible to support the argument that they were no longer *cives* of either the Holy Roman Empire or of smaller political entities that formed within its boundaries. Now, more than ever, their *civitas* should be intended in a sense already outlined in the preceding paragraphs, i.e., as perpetual subjection having effects also outside the state territory, unlike that of foreigners, which was temporary and limited to that territory. And yet, it is far from being an *optimo jure* citizenship.

Furthermore, in the documents, Jews are often clearly defined as *cives*,[174] and as such, they are included, with all other categories of citizens, in the peace treaties between German cities,[175] sometimes taking part in the armed defense of the city in which they reside,[176] holding some municipal offices[177] and appearing as witnesses in notarial deeds.[178]

This situation, characteristic of the Holy Roman Empire and therefore also of northern and central Italy, which are not only *de jure* but quite significantly also *de facto* parts of it, applies as well to southern Italy. There, the *servitus* always remains within strictly public limits and relations between Jews and neighbors of another nation and religion were almost always excellent.[179]

In Sicily, the political situation of the Jews was exceptionally fortunate.

There, as Strauss notes, the existence of several groups different by nationality and religion made a high degree of mutual tolerance necessary, avoiding the usual rise of religious-political intransigence. So, during the Norman period, the island Jews appear "as free members of one of the nations that make up the State" rather than as a greatly inferior minority. This latter position is

174 On July 25, 1259, King Richard confirms the ancient privileges "civibus christianis et judeis" of Worms (Aronius, no. 637, p. 268).

175 April 1254; an alliance between Mainz, Worms, and Oppenheim (Aronius, no. 598, p. 256); July 13, 1254: an alliance between Mainz, Cologne, Worms, Speyer, Strasburg, Basle and other cities (ibid., no. 601, pp. 256–257); October 6, 1254, Rhenish Pact (ibid., no. 602, p. 257).

176 The same during the siege of Worms (1201), with permission of the rabbi, Jews carry weapons on Saturday (Aronius, no. 358 a, p. 159); and in 1252 in Cologne (ibid., no. 586, p. 249).

177 The same in the cities of Silesia (Grayzel, op. cit., p. 55, no. 71, who quotes Grünhagen, *Regesten zur schlesischen Geschichte*, II, p. 254, no. 1630).

178 Aronius, no. 341, p. 154.

179 For the qualification of citizen, see, e.g., a chart from 1183 (*Codice diplomatico barese*, vol. VIII, Bari, 1914, doc. 141, p. 185, lines 7–8): "adversus Samuelem ebreum f. Samuelis ebrei tranensem civem." One Adam bonus judeus is in the list of Bari dwellers to whom the Venetian doge, Domenico Michiel, vows protection in 1122 (*Codice* cit., vol. V, Bari, 1902, doc. 68, p. 118, line 58).

characteristic of the mainland.[180] The judicial equalizing of national and religious groups, deriving necessarily from their multiplicity, brings with it the "equality of all individuals before the state, whatever nation they belong to."[181] Consequently, the Jews of Sicily enjoy full recognition of their laws, like all other nations on the island.[182] In city legislations, they appear with a distinct *cives* status.[183]

In this favorable situation the Jews remained until the Swabians succeeded the Normans; then Sicily, too, gradually lost its "Nationalitätenstaat" character to achieve national and religious unity. Once the free Saracens had gone from the island in 1246[184] and the gradual merger between Greeks and Latins was completed, that "Vereinheitlichung der Bevölkerung ..., die Juden mehr als eine differente Minderheit denn als eine von vielen nationalen und religiösen Sonderngruppen erscheinen lies" became established.[185]

Later on, although similar to continental Jews, the legal position of Sicilian Jews remains good, and Scherer's thesis according to which in the 13th, 14th and 15th centuries, Jews in southern Italy, as in the other European States, were considered foreigners,[186] meets with a manifest refutation in the quality of citizens explicitly attributed to them by the sources[187] and consequently in the legal protection granted to them beyond the borders of the state territory.[188]

---

180 Strauss, op. cit., p. 18.

181 Strauss, ibid.

182 See further on, pp. 124–126.

183 *Consuetudini di Palermo*, La Mantia ed., Palermo, 1862, Tit. 77: "Judei, sive cives sint, sive exteri ..."; Tit. 15: "... si aliqua inter Christianos cives Panhormi et Judeos sive exteros sive cives, lis vel contencio in judiciis vel extra judicium oriatur. ..."

184 Amari, *Storia dei Musulmani di Sicilia*, vol. III, p. 620.

185 Strauss, op. cit., pp. 14–15; Neumayer, op. cit., p. 267.

186 Scherer, op. cit., p. 6.

187 G. and B. Lagumina, *Codice diplomatico dei Giudei di Sicilia*, Palermo, 1885, doc. 385, May 14, 1451: "Imperochè li Judechi [the Jewish communities] di lu dictu regnu su membru et chitatini in li chitati et terri di lu dictu regnu. Et li Judei concurrinu insemblamenti in tucti gravicii, carichi et pagamenti per loru prorata li quali scadinu in li dicti chitati et terri." Cf. ibid., doc. 85, June 28, 1392: "quia dicti Judei asserunt ab *aliis* dictae urbis civibus multis offensis laniari, etc."

188 In 1308, after a Syracusan Jew was killed in Zara, his relatives turned to Frederick III of Aragon, King of Sicily, to obtain through him, from the government of the Venetian Republic, the return of certain goods of the deceased that remained in the hands of the Count of Zara. Frederick took care of the matter and his request was satisfied. (From two letters of the Venetian Chancellory dated December 13, 1308, and March 17, 1309, and published by M. Lattes, *Di un mercante ebreo siracusano*, in *Archivio Veneto*, t. VI, 1873, pp. 322–23.)

3 The Intermediate Period (from the Glossators to the Emancipation)

Until now, in the study of our subject, we could only use data provided by laws and documentary sources, and based on those we tried to recognize the general principles governing the *status civitatis* of the Jews.

For the period that makes the subject of our examination in the present paragraph, however, it will also be possible to consider a broad range of doctrinal, civil law and canonic law sources, as several writers precisely examined the issue we are dealing with.

It is a known fact that all the legal system of common law writers gravitates around the basic idea of the Empire. With the resurgence of the old imperial law overlapping the last remnants of the dying barbarian rights, the ancient empire also reappears, giving relevance to Charlemagne's and Otto's *renovatio*: it is the ancient majestic body that, *de jure*, recommences to live in its unitary appearance, despite the minute compartmentalization that characterizes the reality of the political terrain in increasingly marked forms.[189]

It is precisely in the initial period when the old feudal autonomies are at the height of decadence, and the new autonomy of the *civitates* and the *regna* are still in their initial phase of development, that the idea of the Roman Empire's revival can assert itself in a more clear-cut manner: the gloss is, therefore, the text that allows us to grasp this important phenomenon in all its meaning.

As we can see from the glossators' commentaries, that dual concept of the empire was then to remain intertwined for centuries in writings relating to public laws. First, there is the idea of the empire's absolute universality as a presupposition of its theoretical sovereignty over all the states of the Earth.[190] "But alongside it – as Cavalieri cleverly writes[191] – in the gloss is a more concrete and more immediate idea: that of the relative universality, historically implemented by the Romans and with which the efficiency of imperial law has to confront. The dominion of Justinian represents the boundaries of its

189 Schupfer, *Manuale di Storia del Diritto Italiano. Le fonti*. Città di Castello, 1908, pp. 298 et seqq.; Solmi, *Stato e Chiesa negli scritti politici da Carlo Magno al concordato di Worms*, Modena, 1901, pp. 86 et seqq.; Ercole, *Impero e papato nel diritto pubblico italiano del Rinascimento*, 2nd ed., in the volume *Dal Comune al Principato*, Florence, 1929, pp. 139–149, with extensive literature.

190 M. Cavalieri, *Di alcuni fondamentali concetti politici contenuti nella glossa d'Accursio*, in *Archivio Giuridico*, 3rd Series, vol. XIII, 1910, pp. 152–153: Gloss to Rubr. D. 1: The imperial dominion is "perpetuus et generalis," Gloss to l. 9 D. 14, 2: The emperor is "caput mundi," etc., Ercole, op. cit., p. 141 and ibid no. 1, p. 145, no. 1.

191 Op. cit., p. 153.

sovereignty, and the *ratio imperii romani* constitutes the judicial title of subjection." Naturally, among the subjects of the Roman Empire, the members of those peoples who are now organized in completely autonomous political entities should also be counted.[192]

This full revival of Justinian's imperial idea, a reflection of the tangible accomplishment of the old judicial system, naturally also determines the actual reappearance of the ancient concept of Roman citizenship: this above and regardless of the citizenships of the individual political nuclei included within the borders of the great organism.

As per the glossators, Rome ideally reverts to identify with the Empire[193] and becomes the new "*communis patria*" according to fr. 33 D. 50, 1.[194]

As in the past, the *populus romanus* appears to be formed by the subjects of the Empire all together;[195] as already in Justinian's times, given the persistent effect of the Constitution of Caracalla, there is no gradation among them in their *status civitatis*: they are repeatedly proclaimed *cives romani*.[196]

As to the relationship with the Church, we are, of course, on the ground of unity and close coordination: the two powers, priesthood and Empire, collaborate intimately in the performance of their respective functions, which implies taking care of spiritual interests for the former and of material interests for the latter;[197] but union and coordination do not mean total and absolute identification of two societies. As it moves away from the curialistic theoretics of the previous centuries, the gloss rejects the idea of integral theocracy, does not confuse the *Ecclesia* and the *Imperium*, nor does it set the limits of the former,

192 Gloss to *Libr. feud., De pace tenenda*, (2, 53) see Imperio: "et ita videtur quod lex ista non habet locum nisi inter illos, qui subditi sunt. Sed numquid tenet Francigenas et alios ultramontanos? Videtur quod non, ex eo quod dicit: nostro subiecti imperio. Sed dicas quod eos similiter tenet: quoniam licet ei non sunt sacramento subditi, sunt tamen ratione imperii romani, cum ipsi fuerint de Imperio Justiniani."

193 Gloss to l. 3 D. 1, 7; cf. the gloss to l. 26 D 4, 6 according to which the empire is the only true organization of public law; the *civitates*, except Rome "loco privatorum sunt." The phenomenon of autonomy is not yet very much felt.

194 Gl. ibid. On this idea, see Trifone's note, *Roma communis patria nel pensiero dei giuristi dell'età intermedia*, in *Rivista di Storia del Diritto Italiano*, Yr. IX, 1936, vol. IX, dossier 3, pp. 357–364.

195 Gloss ad v. vel predones, 24 D. 49, 15: "Populus romanus: quod accipe pro toto romano imperio."

196 Gloss ad v. civium romanorum, 4 D. 1, 6: "Cives romanos dicas omnes subiecto imperio." Also in the comment to fr. 17 D. 1, 5 – Ulpian text of the Antonine Constitution reported with the erroneous reading "In urbe Roma" (instead of "in orbe romano") qui sunt cives romani effecti sunt" – the gloss notes: "sed hodie sunt omnes cives romani."

197 See texts in Cavalieri, op. cit., pp. 160 et seqq. and Ercole, op. cit., p. 148, no. 2.

to the latter, unifying the qualifications of *romanus* and *christianus* on the one hand, and of *extraneus* and *infidelis* on the other.

As we have seen, as in antiquity, the element that confers the quality of *civis romanus* is the objective fact of subjection, and not religion;[198] therefore, and although an explicit statement to that effect is not found in the gloss, we can logically consider *cives* also the infidel subjects of the Empire, and first among these the Jews, who already appeared as *cives* in Justinian's legislation.[199]

This relationship between subjection to the Empire and the quality of being Roman, typical of the risen-again judicial system, is highlighted for the first time concerning the Jews, where one might find very different principles, namely in the gloss to the *Corpus Juris Canonici*. Thus, while commenting on a definition of Isidore of Seville, included in *Decretum* (c. 12, Decr. Part 1, dist. 2), according to which "Jus quiritum est proprie romanorum, quod nulli tenent nisi quirites idest romani," the canonist notes that from l. 8 C. J. 1, 9 *de Judaeis*[200] it can be deduced that not only the Romans but also the Jews live in Roman law. He manages to harmonize the two texts basing the qualification as Roman not on the element of nationality but on that of subjection.[201]

Notoriously, in Bartolo we can generally see a regression towards the curial doctrines due to an accentuated systematic adhesion, possibly more opportunistic than intimately felt, to the political doctrines of the Church.[202]

198 I cannot, therefore, agree with Ercole, for whom the Justinian inspiration of the glossators is not substantial enough to break the now traditionally unitary conception of *populus romanus* and *christianus* at the same time. Ercole, *Studi sulla dottrina e sul diritto pubblico di Bartolo*, in vol. *Da Bartolo all'Althusio*, Florence 1932, pp. 68–69; and I accept instead the counter-argument of Woolf, *Bartolus of Sassoferrato, His position in the history of medieval political thought*, Cambridge, 1913, pp. 15 et seqq.

199 What is said about the glossators can be repeated for the post-glossators, including, first among them, Cino da Pistoia. As Chiappelli notes, *Vita e opere giuridiche di Cino da Pistoia*, Pistoia 1881, p. 149, these writers "sought to elevate the universal empire and the public law of the Romans against the universal denomination of theocracy and the ecclesiastical public law." Thus, an unthinkable trend at that time – if not toward separation, at least toward the distancing from the theocratic idea. Cf. Ercole, *Impero*, cit., pp. 148–149.

200 It is the well-known law: "Judei romano communi jure viventes, etc."

201 Gloss ad v. quod nulli: Contra *C. de Judeis, l. Judei*, ubi dicitur quod Judei utuntur romano jure. *Sed ibi omnes vocantur Romani, subiecti romano imperio*: prout dicitur proprium Romanorum est habere filios in potestate: prout etiam gentiles sunt sub romano imperio. Nam imperator est princeps totius mundi ... sed in diversis provinciis diversi reges sub eo constituti sunt." The dependence of the Jews on the Emperor is affirmed also by the gloss ad v. in Germanos in ch. 34 x, 1, 6: "Ipse (the Emperor) enim est princeps mundi et dominus ... et etiam Judei sub eo sunt. *C. de Judeis, l. Judei.*"

202 Ercole, *Studi sulla dottrina politica e sul diritto pubblico di Bartolo*, cit., p. 62 and texts cited in the notes from pp. 40–44.

Are the clear and absolute identification of Christianity and Romanness and the assimilation of the *infideles* to the *extranei* therefore present in his thinking? For Ercole, the answer to this question is affirmative. "In Bartolo's thinking – he writes[203] – the whole of Christianity, i.e., the consortium of all men who profess the Christian religion, forms the *populus christianus* or *romanus*. *Christianity* and *Romanness* are equivalent concepts: one ends where the other ends. *Romanus* is the *Christianus* people, because for a divine destination, Rome is the center of Christianity, and Romanity ceases where Christianity ceases: by Christianity, it should substantially be intended *Catholicity*: that is, recognition of the religious sovereignty of the Pope, or Bishop of Rome, as the immediate representative or Vicar of Christ on Earth. He who does not recognize this sovereignty, is outside Christianity (outside the *populus christianus*) and outside Romanity (outside the *populus romanus*). Hence the straight demarcation line marked by Bartolo between *Populus Romanus* and *Populi extranei*: *extranei* are those peoples who not only do not recognize the sovereignty of the Emperor but also, and especially, do not recognize the sovereignty of the Bishop of Rome: indeed, those do not recognize the former because they do not recognize the latter: *extraneus* people and infidel or *non-Catholic* people are once again equivalent terms.

The *populus romanus* is therefore not *universal*, that is to say, it is not encompassing the entire humankind, if not in the sense in which the Church of Rome is Catholic: as it has in itself the power to extend to all humankind, which has the religion of Christ led by his Vicar on Earth as divine destination: it is as Catholic as the Church is. However, being in fact infidel people, they are also *extranei* to the *populus romanus*."[204]

I deemed it appropriate to report here Ercole's entire passage because frankly, it does not seem to be in line with Bartolo's thought, as it appears to us from that fundamental passage of the commentary on fr. 24 D. 49 15, on which Ercole mainly bases his reconstruction.

I carefully reread this text.[205] Bartolo places the dichotomy *populus romanus* – *populi extranei* and identifies in the gloss (cf. above no. 13) the

203 Op. cit. pp. 50–51.

204 Cf. also Ercole, *Impero*, cit., p. 190 and here, footnote no. 189.

205 Bartolo, *Commentaria in secundam Digesti novi partem*, Lyon, 1552, in *l. Hostes. ff. De captivis et postlimio, et redemptis ab hostibus* (D. 49, 15, 24): "Vos debetis scire quod duo sunt genera gentium principaliter: primo populus Romanus; secundo populi extranei ... Circa primum quaero quis dicatur populus Romanus. Glossa dicit: hic accipitur pro toto Imperio Romano ... Sed diceres tu: cum modicae gentes sint, quae Romano Imperio obediant: ergo videtur quod sit parvus populus Romanus. Respondeo: quaedam sunt gentes, quae Imperio Romano obediunt: et iste sine dubio sunt de populo Romano. Quedam

populus romanus with all subjects of the *imperium*. Clearly, Bartolo is subsequently led to reflect on the natural objection of the small number of people actually submitted to the imperial authority. Such paucity is in too stark a contrast with the majestic vastness of the idea of the Empire and with the wide spreading of Roman law. Faced with the same consideration, as we have seen, the gloss[206] had concluded by positively awarding the old borders of Justinian to the Empire, proclaiming *cives romani* the subjects of the states included within those borders. Faced with an entirely new category of autonomous political entities, Bartolo must instead adopt a different criterion. He, therefore, declares "*de populo romano*" those peoples who recognize in any way the imperial authority. In addition to those who obey *in totum*, "de populo romano"

---

sunt, quae non obediunt Romano Imperio in totum, sed in aliquibus obediunt: ut quia vivunt secundum legem populi Romani, et Imperatorem Romanorum esse dominum omnium fatentur, ut sunt civitates Tusciae, Lombardiae, et similes: et istae etiam sunt de populo Romano. Nam cum populus Romanus in eis exerceat iurisdictionem in aliquo articulo, totam iurisdictionem retinet … Quidam sunt populi, qui nullo modo obediunt Principi, nec istis legibus vivunt, et hoc dicunt se facere ex privilegio Imperatoris: et isti similiter sunt de populo Romano: ut faciunt Veneti. Nam cum illam libertatem ipsi habere se dicant ab imperio Romano, et privilegio quodammodo precario tenent ab eo, et posset privilegium illud revocare quando vellet, cum liceat ei mutare voluntatem suam … Praeterea illud privilegium eis concessum, debet eis esse ad commodum, ut non priventur civitate Romana … Quidam sunt populi, qui non obediunt principi, tamen asserunt se habere libertatem ab ipso ex contractu aliquo, ut provinciae, quae tenentur ab ecclesia Romana, quae fuerunt donatae ab Imperatore Constantino ecclesiae Romanae: posito pro constanti quod donatio tenuerit, quodque revocari non possit: adhuc dico istos de populo Romano esse. Nam ecclesia Romana exercet in illas terras iurisdictionem, quae erat Imperii Romani, et istud fatentur: non ergo desinunt esse de populo Romano: sed administratio istarum provinciarum est alteri concessa. Videtur in simili: iurisdictio in clericos est concessa totaliter Papae: desinunt ne propter hoc clerici esse cives Romani? Certe non, quod apparet, quia retinent ius succedendi … Et idem dico de istis aliis Regibus et principibus, qui negant se esse subditos Regi Romanorum: ut Rex Franciae, Angliae, et similes. Si enim fatentur ipsum esse dominum universalem, licet ab illo universali dominio se subtrahant ex privilegio vel ex prescriptione, vel consimili, non desinunt esse cives Romani, per ea quae dicta sunt: et secundum hoc quasi omnes gentes quae obediunt sanctae matri ecclesiae, sunt de populo Romano. Et forte si quis diceret dominum Imperatorem non esse dominum et monarcham totius orbis esset haereticus: quia diceret contra determinationem ecclesiae, contra textum sancti Evangelii, dum dicit: "Exivit edictum a Caesare Augusto, ut describeretur universus orbis," ut habes *Luca*, II et III c. Ita etiam recognovit Christus Imperatorem ut dominum … Secundo dixi quod alii populi sunt extranei. Sunt et populi extranei proprie, qui non fatentur Imperatorem Romanum esse dominum universalem: ut Graeci, qui non credunt Imperatorem Romanum esse dominum universalem, sed dicunt Imperatorem Constantinopolitanum esse dominum totius mundi. Item Tartari, qui dicunt Grant Chan esse dominum universalem. Et Sarraceni, qui dicunt dominum eorum esse dominum totius mundi. Et idem in Iudaeis."

206 See above, p. 69, no. 13.

are also those living under Roman law and "imperatorem Romanorum esse dominum omnium fatentur," those who – despite being completely independent, and while not living in Roman law – are aware of the fact that they do so because of imperial privilege (Venice) or contract (provinces of the Church), and finally those who, while proclaiming their full and complete autonomy from the Empire, agree to place a slight theoretical limit to this autonomy by recognizing the universal nature of the imperial authorities (like: France or England). In light of this policy, "de populo romano" are *almost* all faithful to the Church. Nevertheless, this is an a posteriori observation: they are – and, noteworthy, not all of them – not for the mere fact of belonging to the Church, but precisely because they are members of states whose rulers have somehow recognized the Empire's high authority. Which ones are, in fact, the "populi extranei"? They are those who are unbending before an even theoretical recognition of the Emperor's universal sovereignty, attributing the quality of *dominus mundi* to their leader: namely, the Greeks, who confer such quality to the Emperor of Byzantium, the Tatars, who empower with it the Gran Khan, the Saracens, who do the same with their sovereign, and finally – the Jews.

In parallel to the almost complete overlapping of Romans and *fideles Ecclesiae* just noted, here there is a sense of identification between the *extranei* and *infideles*. However, in this case it should be noted that the identification is not intentional and that these *infideles* are *extranei* not because of *infideles*, but because they do not recognize the supreme authority of the Roman emperor. External to the Church and not recognizing the authority of the Pope, they are not, as Ercole claims, the reason for their estrangement. Nor is there a link between the disavowal of the emperor and that of the pope. Furthermore, the proof is that on the one hand, Bartolo denies the quality of Romans to the peoples mentioned above, taken as a whole, as political collectivities, based on their not-even-theoretical obedience to the emperor. But, on the other hand, he accepts the quality of *cives romani* to those members of the same infidel peoples who, residing within the boundaries of States *de jure* or *de facto* subject to the emperor, objectively find themselves under his authority. Thus, this happens to be the situation of the Jews: excluded from the *civitas romana* as an oriental and distant people,[207] they are made equal to *cives romani* when they find themselves to be permanent subjects of the empire.[208]

207 It is likely that after his attention was drawn to the Tatars and the Saracens, Bartolo meant the bulk of the Jewish people living in the Persian Empire.

208 In fact, only in this way one can reconcile the inclusion of the Jews – found in the passage cited – among the *populi extranei* with the statement: "Judei habent ea quae sunt civium romanorum" which is the summary of Bartolo's l. 8 C. J. 1, 9. It is evident that in this

This explicit declaration by Bartolo about the *status civitatis* of the Jews of the Empire aims to remove any doubt about the possibility of extending them to the entire Roman legal system. However, such declaration is not among those promptly accepted later on by the doctrine. Many of the later writers abstain from offering their opinion on the general question of whether the Jews are or not *cives romani*: this, therefore, generates many discussions in their treatises, about the opportunity to recognize to the Jews those faculties and those rights that the ancient sources allegedly confer only to Roman citizens.

For example, this is what happens with respect to the patria potestas: can this institution, jurists wonder, repeatedly proclaimed in the *Corpus Juris* as "proprium civium romanorum,"[209] be also recognized with the Jews? Addressing the problem in his commentary on the Digest, Baldo favors an affirmative answer. Nevertheless, his opinion is not based on the generic presumption of the inclusion of Jews among the *cives*, but on the consideration that since a marriage is an institution of natural law, all those born in a marriage are subject to patria potestas.[210]

law, the Jews are mentioned as subjects and *cives* of the Empire; Bartolo sticks to it and recognizes them as *cives*, while keeping for the Jewish people the quality of *populus extraneus*. Bartolo's argument is followed almost word by word by Uberto da Lampugnano (… 1375–1385 …, Besta, *Fonti*, I, p. 859) in his *quaestio "Utrum omnes principes reges et populi quicumque Christum colentes sunt* (sic) *de imperio Romano, an vero dicamus quod aliqui sunt exempti ab Imperio Romano privilegio prescriptione vel quocumque modo alio,"* published by Dolliner, *Einige Nachrichten über den Rechtsgelehrier Ubertus v. Lampugnano*, in *Zeitschrift für geschichtliche Rechtswissenschaft*, tome II, 1816, pp. 246–256. However, as he wanted to demonstrate that all peoples, or more precisely the Christian states, depend on the Empire (the position of Christians *ut singuli* is not taken into account), da Lampugnano definitely suppresses Bartolo's *quasi* (p. 255: Et secundum hoc *omnes gentes* Christum colentes sunt de Imperio Romano et subditi Romano Imperio), denying in an absolute way the possibility of a Christian political association that is not subject to the Emperor and therefore is not *de populo romano*. However, if in so doing he affirms that all Christians are Roman, even he does not claim the reciprocality, i.e., that all Romans are to be Christians. In fact, the dependence on the Emperor of non-Christians, namely the Jews, serves him as an *a fortiori* argument to assert the Romanity of all Christian peoples (p. 249: Praeterea hoc – that is "Quod omnes principes et populi quicumque Christum colentes sint de Imperio Romano" – I advocate for l. 8 C. *de Judeis* ubi quod nedum omnes naciones christianorum sunt sub imperatore, sed eciam omnes naciones Judeorum).

209 Ist. 1, 9, 2: Jus autem potestatis, quod in liberos habemus proprium est civium romanorum: nulli enim alii sunt homines, qui talem in liberos habeant potestatem quam nos habemus. – D. 1, 6, 3: Item in potestate nostra sunt liberi nostri, quos ex justis nuptiis procreavimus: quod jus proprium civium romanorum est (Gaius, *Institutiones*, 1, 55).

210 Baldo degli Ubaldi, *Lectura super primam partem digesti veteris*, Venice 1493, p. 32 v.; commentary to fr. D. 1, 6, 4: "Omnis qui ex matrimonio nascitur est in patria potestate, sive sit fidelis, sive infidelis; unde judei sunt in potestate parentum. Idem in paganis qui sunt sub

The canonist Giovanni d'Anagni comes to the same affirmative conclusion by examining two requirements covered by the passage mentioned above D. 1, 6, 3 as essential for the institution of the patria potestas: the *justae nuptiae* and the quality of *cives romani*. Regarding the first requirement, it can be concluded that it also exists with the Jews. Although in conflict with the canonical norms, the dissolubility of their marriage is not contrary to the civil law, which is always valid despite the factual prevalence of Church law in the regulation of marriage.[211] Moreover, the same can be said of the second requirement, based on the gloss that makes the quality of *civis romanus* dependent on the objective fact of subjection.[212]

---

imperio romano; cum enim matrimonium sit de jure naturali non distinguitur an sit natus ex judeo vel ex christiano; ... ergo filiisfamilias judeorum non possunt testari impediente patria potestate; sunt enim judei sub jure communi." In the commentary to the previous fr. D. 1, 6, 3, Baldo states, however, that the patria potestas is established only if the Jewish marriage is performed according to Roman law: "Quaerunt doctores utrum judei habeant filios ex suis uxoribus in potestate; et videtur quod non quia non contrahunt matrimonium. Contrarium est verum dummodo contrahant secundum judeorum ritum et secundum legem romanam et ideo filii eorum sunt successibiles secundum Jacobum de Rave. [Revigny] et alios." (More briefly in another commentary to the same text "An Judei habeant filios in potestate dic quod sic, si contrahunt matrimonium secundum ritum romanorum, secundum Jaco. de Rave. et Cyn.") In another place, Baldo proclaims if not the quality of *cives* for the Jews, something essentially not much different from it: see commentary to the l. *spadonem D. de excusatione tutorum*, § *jam autem* (D. 27, 1, 17): "In humanis actibus judei nobiscum participant, non in divinis, neque in aliquo actu superioritatis. In hoc apparet quod judeus potest esse procurator christiani, et intervenire in judicio pro eo et contra." (However, regarding this matter, the state law orders exactly the opposite. See my work in *Rivista di Storia del Diritto Italiano*, VIII, 1935, vol. VIII, file 3, pp. 417–418. The prohibition to fulfill the position of attorney strikes the Jews not as such but because they are money-lenders at interest.)

211 Giovanni da Anagni, *Lectura super quinto Decretalium*, Milan, 1492, f. 69, Commentary to *c. etsi judeos x de judeis* (c. 13 × 5, 6): "Circa primum de justis nuptiis communiter dicitur quod sacramentum coniugii apud fideles et infideles existit, *ad Corinth, c. VI*, ... tamen non est omnino matrimonium perfectum quia in illis non verificatur illud dictum: quod Deus coniunxit homo non separet ... Possunt ergo judei dato libello repudii uxorem dimittere ... Considera tamen quod licet quo ad hoc non conformet cum jure canonico tamen consonat cum jure civili in *l. consensum C. de repudiis* (C. J. 5, 16, 8) et patria potestas videtur regulari potius secundum jus civile quam secundum jus canonicum. Et sic videtur posse dici quod matrimonium sit justum sive legitimum secundum jus civile, secundum quod permittitur quod filii duorum fratrum coniunguntur, quod licet etiam Judeis. *Insti. de nuptiis*, § *duorum*; secus de jure canonico. Et isto respectu videtur satisfactum textui qui loquitur de justis nuptiis; hodie vero in christianis matrimonium regulatur jure poli, non jure fori."

212 Idem, ibidem: "Circa secundum, quia textus dicit quod est proprium civibus romanis, dic quod glossa in *dist. jus quesitum* (sic per *jus quiritum*, c. 12 Decretum 1, 2, see above p. 69

Contrary to this quality of *cives*, alleged to sustain that Jews were entitled to the patria potestas, d'Anagni remains strangely silent concerning the text of the Decretals in which the Jews are defined as servants. This text that we already know to be the only reflection of that unique state of dependence – the *servitus camerae imperialis* we studied in the previous paragraph – that entered the *Corpus Juris Canonici* and that characterizes the legal position of Jews in the late Middle Ages.[213]

Without contesting that the quality of *cives* decidedly excludes servitude and therefore, if the Jews are *cives*, they cannot be servants, d'Anagni still realizes that the text cannot speak of an absolute servitude of private law.[214] He then rejects the likelihood that it may produce those significant consequences that would otherwise be authorized by a literal interpretation of the text: namely the legitimacy of the forced baptism of Jewish children[215] and the right of the Prince to drive the Jews out of his territory without plausible reasons.[216]

Concerning the latter point, Oldrado Da Ponte had previously reached similar conclusions as he had well figured out the peculiar character of Jewish servitude, seeing in it only the expression of the particular requirement of a tribute to the Prince.[217]

About the issue of recognizing the right of patria potestas to Jews, on the same line of thought, one would note Alessandro Tartagni, who, after referring to the arguments of Baldo and Giovanni d'Anagni,[218] also denies any actual

---

and note 13 therein) tenet quod judei orientales (?) habent filios in potestate et debet exponi: civium romanorum, idest omnium qui subiecti sunt romano imperio."

213 It is the ch. 13 × 5, 6. See above, p. 49, no. 26.

214 Idem. Commentary to the *c. sicut judei x de judeis* (c. 9 × 5, 6), p. 65, t.; "Non est verum quod judei sunt taliter servi, quod possent vendi, sed, quicquid sit de jure, de consuetudine non servatur quod habeantur pro servis. Dominus Abbas (Nicolò de' Tedeschi) hic dicit se de hoc multum dubitare quod non sunt proprie servi; ymo ab eis coacta servitia exigi non possunt." Cf. the above mentioned passage by St. Thomas, footnote no. 109.

215 Idem. Ibidem. Conversely, Udalrico Zasio, *Singularia responsa*, Basel 1541, is in favor of the thesis of the complete servitude, and consequently of the legitimacy of the forced baptism. Quaestio I: an judei etc., pp. 396–97. He bases himself in particular on the mentioned ch. 13 × 5, 6 (*Etsi judeos*) and on ch. 11, Decretum, Part II, cause 23, quest. 8: "Hi [the Jews] vero ubique servire parati sunt."

216 Idem, commentary to ch. 13 × 5, 6.

217 He calls the Jews "servi aut tributari" of the Emperor. *Consilia*, s. l., 1543, no. 264, f. 84.

218 Alessandro Tartagni, *Consilia*, Book II, Venice, 1580, cons. 213, col. I, § iam autem: "Judei dicuntur esse in patria potestate parentum cum vivant jure romano, *l. judei C. de judeis* (l. 8 C. J. 1, 9) iuncta *l. item in potestate* cum. *l. sequenti ff. de his qui sunt sui vel alieni juris*. (D. l, 6, 3 and 4, see above, footnotes nos. 209–210) et ibi in ispecie firmat Baldus et in *l. nam et civium* (D. 1, 6, 4, see above footnote no. 209), hoc etiam vult glossa *c. jus Quiritium* (see above). Nam omnes qui nati sunt ex i(u)stis nuptiis sunt in patria potestate; quod jus paternae potestatis est proprie civium romanorum, ita habent Institutiones, *de patria potestate*, in principio; ... et sacramentum coniugii est apud fideles et infideles ... licet possent hebrei dato libello repudii uxorem dimittere ... et hoc fieri poterat ex dispositione

value to the servitude in question,[219] and Felino Sandeo, who finds support on the same texts and the conclusions of Baldo and Pietro d'Ankarano.[220]

By contrast, the later civilist Lancellotto Gallia adopts Bartolo's affirmation mentioned above, and, based on the complete assimilation of the Jews to the *cives*, declares that both the right of patria potestas and the set of rules governing donations between spouses[221] are extensible to them.

With time going by, the theory of the *status civitatis* of the Jews, slightly nebulous up to this point, becomes clear and explicit.

---

juris civilis iuxta *l. consensu C. de repudiis* (C. J. 5, 16, 8) et *ff. de divortiis* per totum; et tamen nati ex illo matrimonio erant in patria potestate." Equal principles in cons. 72 of book V.

219 Tartagni, ibid.: "Non obstat quod interdum jura dicunt judeos esse servos *c. etsi judeos, x, de judeis*; 14, *q.* 3, § *sed qui*; 28, *q.* 8, § *dispecte*; ergo si sunt servi non possum habere alios in potestate 32 *q.* 3 *et ibi nota et l. sic evenient ff. de adulteriis*; quia potest responderi quod jura non loquuntur de illa servitute propter quam quis amittat penitus libertatem. Nam et uxoratus in servitute esse dicitur *l.* 11 *de lib. bo. exhib.* et tamen non est dubium quod retinet filios in potestate. Unde videmus quod judei non retinentur in servitute nec venduntur ut reliqui servi."

220 Felino Sandeo, *Tertia in quinque libros Decretalium*, in *cap. Judei* (*the second*), *de Judeis* (c. 5 × 5, 6), p. 235: "Utrum Judei habeant filios in potestate … Baldus et Petrus de Ancharano in dicta *l. qui in potestate* (D. 1, 6, 3) (dicunt) quod tale jus patriae potestatis est penes omnes romano imperio subiectos. Item et tales sunt Judei, *l. Judei C. de Judeis*." Similarly, referring to the Jews, Nicolò de' Tedeschi, *Super tertio libro Decretalium*, Venice 1477, comm. in c. 2 × 3, 3: "In ea glossa ibi *de jure quiritium* (c. 12 × 1, 2) dic: quiritum idest romanorum … et dicuntur quo ad istud effectum romani omnes qui sunt sub romano imperio: alii vero non recognoscentes romanum imperium non habent filios in potestate: unde dubitatur de venetis et quibusdam aliis de quibus vide per glossam *Insti. de pa. po.* (Ist 1, 9, 2)." On the issue of the servitude and patria potestas, see also Marquardus de Susanis, *Tractatus de Judeis*, in *Tractatus universi juris*, Venice 1584, t. XIV, part III, ch. IV, nos 9–11, p. 65; and Caspar Ziegler (praes.) – Christian Caspar Mascovius (resp.), *De juribus Judeorum*, dissert. Leipzig 1721, ch. II, § 13: "Quod patria potestas in liberos aeque Judaeis ac Christianis competat, propterea non dubito quod illa ex jure naturae originem suam trahat, et apud omnes gentes introducta, et demum a jure civili adaucta sit, ut propria romanorum civium sit facta, l. 3 D. 1, 6. Cum Judei itaque non tantum jure naturae et gentium, sed etiam civili utantur, et romanorum jure vivant, *l.* 8 *C. de Judeis*, utique patria potestas illis denegari non debet, sed is, qui ex Judeo et eius uxore nascitur in eius potestate est per *l. 4 ff. de his, qui sui vel alieni juris*, ut in specie de Judeis concludit Abbas (Nicolò de' Tedeschi) in *c. 2 x de conversione infidelium* (c. 2 × 3, 3). Only for contingent purposes related to the legal practice, Andrea Barbazza denies the patria potestas to the Jews, on the basis of the previously mentioned text that declares them "servi principis" (c. *etsi judeos, de judeis* [c. 13 ×. 5, 6]), *Consilia*, Venice, 1581, vol. IV cons. 68.

221 Lancellotto Gallia, *Praefationes in consuetudinem Alexandrinam prohibentem maritum ultra certum modum uxori relinquere, T. U. J.* cit., Venice 1584, vol. II, p. 300, quaestio VII, nos. 4–8: "Redeundo tamen ad institutum, dubio procul hebreos hic comorantes hac nostra prohibitione (prohibition of donations between spouses) fore comprehensos dicendum est, propterea quod ipsi communi jure romano vivunt, ac habent ea quae sunt civium romanorum, *l. Judei C. de Judeis* et ibi, nota Bartoli … unde fit quod patriae potestati subsunt … et rei propius accedendo, videmus quod donatio inter coniuges judeos non secus ac inter Christianos prohibita habetur."

While remaining sound, the principle already enunciated by the gloss that, due to the persistent effect of the Constitution of Caracalla, *civis romanus* shall be understood to mean anyone who is a citizen of the Empire, that is, who belongs in the *orbis romanus*,[222] the Jews are openly declared "*de populo romano*."[223] The immediate result removes any doubt about recognizing all rights of the *cives romani*, with the sole exception of those rights of which they were stripped with specific provisions for the usual religious reasons.

This recognition is complete: so much in fact, that concerning the faculty of *condere jus*, derogating from the common Roman law and from living according to this special *jus*, not just a few single writers but the near totality of them arrives at the most important admission of the equality of the Jewish people with the other peoples enjoying the *civitas romana*. Common law is recognized as valid only in a subsidiary way, that is to say, in those fields where the rules themselves do not predispose. Just like all the peoples or rather, all political associations included within the *orbis romanus* can establish legal standards of derogatory and innovative nature, so can the Jewish people. While not constituting a political association or a state, the Jewish people have, nevertheless, a legal system of their own; as members of the *orbis* and *populus romanus*, the right in civil matters to live according to their own law is recognized as valid. As in royal or state law, this conferred the power to prevail over Roman law with regard to all institutions where the Roman law has not taken upon itself the regulation with a special provision, specifically canceling Jewish norms.[224]

---

222 Cf. for example Francesco Zoanetti, *De Romano Imperio, T. U. J.* vol. XVI, pp. 21–24, 25: no. 105 "Cives romanos omnes illos censendos qui in orbe Romano sunt atque Caesari obediunt: immo etsi non obediant dummodo legibus romanis vivant"; "… quum hodie omnes qui in orbe romano homines sunt, intellige, et Caesari obediunt ex Antonini imperatoris constitutione cives romani sint, *l. in orbe romano ff. de statu hominum* …"; no. 118: "cives romani dubio procul illi sunt, quos romanae leges tenent."

223 Marquardo Susani, *Tractatus de Judeis* cit., part I, ch. VII, no. 5, p. 35: "Domini terrarum non possunt expellere mercatores forenses sine causa …; ita dicendum est de ipsis judeis et aliis infidelibus post quam sunt in terris Christianorum recepti, ne sine causa expellantur; facti sunt enim de Populo Romano et de eodem corpore civitatis ut per glo. in *cap. jus Quiritum, I dist.* (note 201 above)"; ibid., part II, ch. I, no. 3, p. 41: "Dicuntur enim judei etiam ipsi de populo Romano, et subiecti imperatori et aliis principibus ut per glo. in *cap. Jus Quiritum, I dist.*; et notatur per glo. in *cap. venerabilem* in verso "transtulit in Romanos" (sic, instead of : Germanos), *de electione*." (See footnote no. 201 above.)

224 The subject will be dealt with in the second part. Here I will only mention the interesting passage by Lauro Palazzi, *Tractatus de Statuto communiter per Italiam vigentem, quod extantibus masculis foeminae non succedant*, in *T.U.I.*, Tome II, Venice 1584, nos. 262–263, p. 283: "Quod (Judei) possint statuere contra jus commune, ubi non sint superstitiones, est textus hic. Solum enim reprobantur jure civili eorum leges circa matrimonia, ut non contrahant secundum leges eorum, sed secundum legem communem, *l. nemo, la prima, C. de Judeis* (l. 7 C. J. 1, 9). Ergo in aliis remanet quod possint statuere, quia exceptio firmat regulam in non exceptuatis, ut in *c. in nostra, de sepul.* (c. 10 × 3, 28); quodque possint, ut alii populi, etiam contra jus commune legem condere, istud est secundum dispositionem

Founding the quality of *civis romanus* on the element of subjection and not on that of faith allows non-Catholics to be counted among the citizens, too, and this theory is so widespread and reiterated by common law scholars that we are taken aback in our encountering a discordant voice out of the large and homogeneous choir.

This is the voice of Andrea Alciato, certainly a voice of undisputed authority, but doomed to find a small and narrow echo indeed.

Alciato exposes his theory on the *populus romanus* and, after mentioning the organization of the Empire, until 212 divided into nations connected to Rome by subjection bonds of diverse types and intensities, he notes that the Constitutio Antoniniana removed every internal distinction, granting citizenship to all those who were included in the Roman world.[225] Since these are facts and not ideas, most writers obviously agree. This divergence, however, becomes apparent in the consequence drawn by Alciato from his premises: in principle, following the granting of the *jus civitatis*, the *populus romanus* is actually made up of all the Christians. As the primary outcome, this implies that only the wars between Christians and infidels must be genuinely considered as such. Those fought by Christians among themselves, being civil fights between members of the same people, are not considered real wars, nor will they find a place in the postliminium.[226]

---

juris communis, *l. omnes, de justitia et jure* (D. 1, 1, 9) unde si est facta exceptio in matrimoniis, quod non possint statuere contra, in aliis remanet jus commune, ut possint et maxime quando consuetudo hebreorum longissimo tempore sic fuit; *habent enim judei omnia quae sunt civium romanorum, l. Judei C. de Judeis, et quod populi subditi romano imperio possunt condere leges, et introducere consuetudines, de hoc videtur textus in c. sicut judei, eodem titulo, ibi* (c. 9 × 5, 6); *aut eorum bonas consuetudines immutare, etiam contra dispositionem communem juris civilis, est textus in l. omnes populi, de justitia et jure*, et ideo statutum vel consuetudo judeorum potest excludere dispositionem juris communis, quod filia non habeat bona materna, sed potius pertineant ad eorum parentes contra dispositionem *l. 1 C. de bonis maternis*, etc."

225 Andrea Alciato, *De verborum significatione* [D. 50, 16] *libri quatuor et commentaria*, Lyon, 1535. Commentary to *l.* 118, *hostes* (D. 50, 16, 118), p. 180.

226 Idem, ibid.: "At cum Antonini constitutione omnes qui in orbe Romano erant cives Romani effecti sunt, sequitur *omnes Christianos hodie populum Romanum esse*: quo jure exciderunt qui in Asia, Africave, caeterisque provinciis fidem Christi non agnoscunt: hi enim hostes Populi Romani sunt et civitatis Romanae jus amiserunt. Hincque est quod cum Turcis et Sarracenis indictum nobis est bellum; suntque vicissim jura postliminii, et capti in bello efficiuntur capientium. At inter Christianos aliud est: cum enim ex lege Christi omnes sint fratres, quae inter eos moventur arma, plusquam civilia (non) sunt, unde jus postliminii in his non est. Hincque videmus antiquissima consuetudine introductum, ut capti libertatem non amittant, sed prestita victori pecunia (λύτρον Graeci vocant) veniam recedendi impetrent." The same concept is expressed in the commentary to *l.* 215, *Potestatis*, p. 244: "Hoc jus (parental authority) proprium civium romanorum est, quoniam a lege XII tabularum introductum; sed cum constitutione Antonini, qui in orbe romano sunt cives romani effecti sunt, sequitur ad omnes Christianos hodie illud

We are therefore in full theocratic idea, which Ercole thought he had noticed, in our view, incorrectly, in Bartolo's thought and that is expressed here in a clear and precise form: identification of *fidelis* with *civis* and *infidelis* with *barbarus* and *hostis*: an absolute identity of *romanus* and *christianus*.

To the best of my knowledge, this theory, the developments of which would have been quite interesting, especially in respect to the legal position of the infidels living in the Christian states, is not followed but by a historian from Vicenza, Sebastiano Monticuli, and two others he mentions, Giorgio Vivienne from Antwerp and Lancellotto Corrado from Lodi,[227] whose writings have remained inaccessible to me.

As for the Jews, however, the only one who draws the logical and necessary consequences of the principles raised by Alciato is Monticuli, who not only denies the actual quality of *cives* to the Jews but through reasoning denoting a specific historical sense, also maintains that they never had it, even in ancient times. This writer continues to argue that polygamy has never been a typical institution of the Romans: but if in 393 with the l. 7 C. J. 1, 9 Theodosius forbids it to the Jews, this means that before it was lawful; and if it was legitimate, it means they were not *cives romani*; only some of them may have sometimes been able to obtain citizenship, individually, by special granting of the Prince.[228]

The reasoning is acute, and if we did not know – for sure – on the one hand, that the Constitution of Caracalla gave the Jews citizenship[229] and on the

pertinere. Quapropter et Francis communicatum est, qui licet regibus Germanorum, quos Imperatoris titulo Romani pontifices insigniverunt, non subsint, Romani tamen imperii et ipsi pars sunt, eoque jure vivunt."

227 Sebastian Monticuli, *De patria potestate*, in *T.U.J.*, Tome VIII, part II, p. 136, no. 67: "Quod facit ut vocemus hodie cives romanos illos qui vere sunt Christiani: non scismatici, non haeretici, neque Christi fidem aut dogmata ullo pacto abnegantes. Ita Alciatus in *l. potestatis et l. hostes, de verborum significatione*, cuius expositioni assentitur nuperrime Georgius Viviennus, antverpianus, hic (i.e., probably, in the commentary to the same laws included in the work *Enchiridion de verborum ac rerum significatione*, Cologne, 1570, listed by Fontana, *Amphiteatrum legale*, part II, p. 419), et Lancillottus Conradus laudensis in suo opere inscripto *Templum omnium judicum*, lib. I, cap. I, de Imperatore, § 1 et libr. I, cap. 2 de rege, ubi tractat an reges Galliae et Hispaniae subditi sint imperatori." (Venice 1575 and Frankfurt 1600, according to Fontana, ibid., p. 546).

228 Sebastiano Monticuli, op. cit., p. 138, no. 133: "atque errant maximopere qui contendunt unquam Judaeos fuisse cives Romanos per textum in *l. judei C. de Judeis*. Immo non sunt per alium textum eiusdem tituli *C. de Judeis, l. nemo Judeorum*, ubi Theodosius imperator vetat Judaeis rito suo veteri plures ducere uxores. Si id vetat Theodosius ergo ante Theodosium licebat judaeis, quod certe nullo unquam jure civili licuit civibus Romanis plures ducere uxores ... Ex Judeis nemo unquam civis Romanus fuit nisi princeps jure singulari adlegisset."

229 Juster, *Les Juifs dans l'Empire Romain*, cit., II, pp. 23–25; cf. pp. 8–10 above.

other hand, that the use of their legal institutions – including polygamy – was allowed, at least in the East, for quite some time even after 212,[230] there would be good reason for perplexion. But, since the modern doctrine has certainly clarified these issues, we can disregard Monticuli's reasoning, as a brilliant attempt to find historical support to Alciato's thesis.

A thesis which, I repeat, remains entirely isolated. Writers in the following centuries do not refer to it nor refute it.

In Italy, the assertion that Jews are "*de populo romano*" is widespread among 17th and 18th-century publicists;[231] and is found at greater frequency among German authors, for whom the Empire and thus the concept of *populus romanus* always remain live and effectively operating realities, much more in fact than what happens outside Germany.

Moreover, in Germany, having the Jews remained under the emperor's authority, the theory of *servitus camerae* is kept alive, whereas in Italy, it soon wears off. This occurs following the different configuration of their dependency relationships, publicly conceived on a basis free from those medieval influences that, as we have seen, lead to the interweaving of the idea of servitude with that of subjection.

The German jurists must thus clear the field first by insisting on the *sui generis* character of the *status servitutis* of the Jews, and only after this necessary premise can they assert the Jews' quality of *cives romani*.

So do Mynsinger,[232] Wehner,[233] Brunnemann,[234] and Reinkingk,[235] a famous public law historian. Apart from some uncertainty[236] and some isolated

230 As it will be demonstrated further on, pp. 91–96.

231 Jemolo, *Stato e Chiesa negli scrittori italiani del seicento e del settecento*, Turin-Milan, 1914, p. 284.

232 Joachim Mynsinger, *Observationum singularium centuriae sex*, Helmannstadt, 1599, Centuria 5th, observ. 6.

233 Paulus Matthias Wehner, *Practicarum observationum liber singularis*, Frankfurt, 1624, entry: Juden.

234 Johannes Brunnemann, *Commentaria in Codicem*, Leipzig, 1663, ad l. 7 C. 1, 9. He follows Ippolito Riminaldi.

235 Teodoro Reinkingk, *Tractatus de Regimine seculari et ecclesiastico ... circa hodiernum S. Imperii Romani statum ac gubernationem*, Giessae Hessorum, 1619, Book II, class I, ch. II, p. 240, nos. 23–27: "Denique ita tractandi Judei ut Christianis subiiciantur et ab iis pro sola humanitate foveantur *c. Judei x. de testibus* ... utpote quos perpetuae servituti propria submisit culpa, *c. etsi x de Judeis*. Quod tamen non de servitute illa civili, sed subiectione quadam suppressionis intelligendum venit, ut interpretatur ... Nam quod dominia, possessiones, commercia, matrimonia, et potestatem patriam, liberorum non servorum jure censentur ... Et in Germania sunt cives romani ex stylo et consuetudine ... ac juris communis fere sunt participes, tamquam cives romani."

236 Georg Theodor Dietrich, adviser of Hesse, *De jure et statu judeorum in republica christianorum discursus*, Marburg, 1648, ch. IV, *De statu Judeorum in republica christianorum, an*

opposing opinions,[237] the authors dealing *ex professo* with the legal position of the Jews of the Empire in special monographs, such as Kitzel,[238] Gercken,[239]

sint cives et fruantur privilegiis civitatis, denies (p. 66) that the Jews are servants in the proper sense, declaring them (p. 75) "de populo romano" but then (p. 80) does not recognize their quality of citizens, observing that a statute "de civibus loquens, de veris civibus accipi debere, non de his qui in oppido tantum commorantur, quales sunt die Pfalbürger et Judei." Similar is Lochner's uncertainty, *Dodecas legalis de judeorum receptione ac tolerantia, von Judenschutz, quam ... in alma Jenensium universitate sub presidio ... domini* Christiani Wildvogelii, *die 26 octobris 1700 examini sistit* Johannes Carolus Lochner, Jena, s. a., p. 17: "At respondeat adversarius: Judeos ex consuetudine et stylo Camerae pro civibus romanis habere, verum sine acribia."

237 The quality of Roman-Germanic citizens is explicitly denied to the Jews only by Jung, *Tractatio juridica de jure recipiendi judeos, quam in Academia Georgia Augusta ... sub presidio* Georgii Henrici Ayrer *publico examini subiicit* Johannes Henricus Jung, *ad diem x Febr. 1741*, Göttingen, s. a. p. 68: "Non desunt doctores qui corrasis undique testimoniis ... demonstrare conantur Judeos in numero civium romano-germanicorum ponendos esse. Sed non est ... Excipe tamen Judeos qui per specialia privilegia jus civitatis impetrarunt, quales sunt qui Wormatiae, Spirae, Francofurti et alibi habitant ..."; p. 70; "Non ausim tamen affirmare ut nonnulli sibi persuadent Judeos apud Germanos cum servis romanorum plane ac omnino comparandos ... Non obstat denominatio servi Camerae, ex qua quidem et aliis cognominibus summa imperatorum in Judeos potestas, qualis ea prisco aevo fuit, haud obscure colligi potest" and probably originates from the special tribute from the Frankish and Saxon era [as I demonstrated, see above pp. 36–39]..."; p. 73: "Quid sunt vero Judei? Peregrini, et, si recipiantur, Schutzverwandte, Schutzgenossen. ..." Similarly on page 10. The discussion on the *status civitatis* presupposes the other one, on the opportunity or not to admit the Jews in the State, as already resolved in the affirmative. In addition to the authors of general monographs, the following authors deal *ex professo* in various ways on this question: Johann Kitzel, *Oratio panegirica de regali habendorum Judeorum, quatenus inter Christianos sustineri possint, habita a J. K., juris utr. doct. et professore in Academia Giessena 2 dicembris* 1616, printed following Dietrich's work (cit. in the previous note), pp. 150–200. Other Giessen edition 1617; Kornmann, *Ueber die frage: Ob und wie die Iuden unter christilichen Obrigkeit zu dulden*, Marpurg, 1622; Paolo Crusius, *Discursus politicus Judaeos in republica non esse tolerandos, dissertaz., preside* M. Martinus Siebenhaar, October 3, 1657, Leipzig s. a.; Conrad Friedrich Kollmann, *Judeus in Christiana republica tolerandus, dissertaz. preside* M. Johann Dünnehaupts, May 5, 1688, Wittenberg, s. a.; Rüdolf Friedrich Ziegler, *De judeorum in rebus christianorum publicis tolerantia, dissertaz., preside* Johann Heinrich Tiemeroth, Sept. 22, 1703, Erfurt s.a.; Johann Andreas Bastineller, *Dissertatio juridica de cauta judeorum tolerantia, dissertaz., preside* Justus Henning Böhmer, March 1708, Halae Magdeburgicae, 1717.

238 Kitzel, op. cit. p. 175.

239 *Dissertatio juridica de Judeis quam ... preside ...* Bernhardo Schultzen, *consil. Hassiae, eruditorum examini subiiciet* Philippus Otto Gercken, s. l. 1677, p. 57: "Habentur enim pro civibus romanis ... etiam habent jus patriae potestatis."

Weber,[240] Beck,[241] Klipstein,[242] and Mascovius,[243] all express a similar viewpoint. Nor can a different orientation be found among the most famous writers

---

240 *De Judeis, circularis disputatio quam discutiendam proponunt a. d.* 16 *septembris* 1705 *praeses* Jo. Christ. Wagenzelius ... *in altdorfina Academia ... ac respondens* M. Andreas Weberus, *heldburgo-francus*, s. l. et a., thesis VII , p. 4: "Falluntur vero qui Judeos veros servos Christianorum esse statuunt. Quippe satis constat ipsos jure communi civili et jure statutario illius loci ubi degunt uti, bona propria possidere, liberos habere in potestate, commercia exercere, inter se et cum aliis contractus inire, ac omnia propemodum facere posse quae cives romanae reipublicae peragunt: haec autem universa a servis aliena sunt."

241 Iodoch Beck, *Tractatus de juribus Judeorum*, Nurimberg, 1731, ch. V, pp. 40–41: "In denen alten Teutschen- Rechten werden sie (the Jews) genennt des Reichs-Knechte, dess Römischen Königs Cammer zu eigen gegeben ... Allein, dass die Juden keine leibeigene Knechte, sondern freye Leute seyen, ist daraus abzunehmen, dass die alten Jura servitutis sich auf selbige nicht appliciren lassen. Dann sie haben ihre eigene Güter, acquiriren sich selbst, nicht aber denen Christen, können Contracte schliessen, und freye Commercia treiben, Testamenta und andere letzte Willens-Verordnungen aufrichten, Recht-und Gesetzmässige Ehen contrahiren, mit denen Christen solemni more active und passive vor Gericht stehen, seynd dess Römischen Rechts und anderer Reichs-üblichen Gesetzen, Statuten und Gevohnheiten theilhafftig, und, wo sie in einer Republique oder Land einmahl aufgenommen, daselbst als Schutz-und Schirms-Verwandte unter dem Nahmen der Unterthanen mitbegriffen: gleichwie sie auch, nach der Gewohnheit im Teutschen Reich, und dem Stylo dess Kayserlichen Cammer-Gerichts, pro Civibus Romanis geachtet werden ... Dass sie aber Kayserliche Cammer-Knechte genennet worden, das kommt daher, weilen sie damahln niemanden als dem Kayser unterworffen, und in dessen, als ihres allgemein Ober- und Schutz-Herrns, Königliche-Cammer, die Cronen-Steur und järliche Opfer-Pfennige zu geben pflichtig und Schuldig gewesen." Similarly on p. 181.

242 *De autonomia Judeorum, commentatio Academica quam praeside doct.* Jo. Fried. Kayser, ... *ad diem* 17 *dec.* 1739 *publice ventilabit* Jacob Christian Klipstein, Giessae, s. a., p. 90, who, granting to the Jews – with a bizarre construction – only the *jus civitatis* of the Empire, not the local one, distinguishes: "Cives enim in imperio nostro sunt in triplici differentia: alii sunt cives imperii, alii provinciales, alii municipii, vici aut communitatis ... Judei autem per suam receptionem nacti sunt jus civitatis generale non speciale. Deinde judei quoque procul dubio in Christianis rebuspublicis non habent jus in fundationes in gratiam pauperum, orphanorum factas et huius generis alias: quia haec sunt beneficia ex intentione fundatorum tantum singulari favore erga Christianos introducta, non sub consideratione indigentiae generalis." Similarly, Johann Sigismund Thiel, *Principia jurisprudentiae judaicae per Germaniam communis, sive conspectus jurium et obligationum in Germania singularis*, Halae Saxonum, 1790, § 42, p. 70, observes that Jews "ex stylo Camerae imperialis pro civibus romanis existimantur" and that "servi Camerae dicti sunt, quia nemini subiecti erant olim nisi imperatori, et Camerae illius tributa dederunt, tamquam census supremo gentis judaicae protectori et unico judici debitos." But, in relation to the citizenship of the particular States, he had earlier stated (§ 9, p. 14): "Pro civibus autem in sensu stricto Judei in Germania neutiquam habentur, quia in regula ad juramentum civicum non adstringuntur, sed solummodo ad homagium; ubi enim homagium facit subditum ita quoque juramentum facit civem. Sunt itaque Judei (ut cum perillustri Cramero loquar) quidem *in civitate* non vero *de civitate*."

243 Mascovius, *De juribus Judeorum*, Leipzig, 1721 cit., ch. II, § 1. The following monographs have remained inaccessible to me: Heinrich Hahn, *Diatagmata Judeorum sive de rebus*

of the time, whether canonists like Reiffensthuel[244] or civil law jurists like Samuel Stryk[245] who maintain in a clear-cut way that the Jews are Roman citizens and therefore enjoy the whole complex of rights that the law recognizes to the citizens with the exception, of course, of those expressly taken away from them by special provisions.

•••

So far, we have examined the question of the Jews' *status civitatis* concerning the Empire, but we know that this empire is neither an actual state nor a super-state exerting a practical authority over its member states. More than anything else, it is an idea kept alive by the rebirth of Roman law, which must find in it the rationale of its persistent vitality. Within the considerable ideal body, the political reality is represented by a myriad of independent state entities, connected to the empire only by the theory of public law with clever dialectical tricks proper to that need for a *reductio ad unum* arising from everyday use of Roman law.

---

judaicis ex jure etc., Halmstadt, 1661; Miri, *An christianus magistratus in republica tolerare aut in eam recipere debeat judeos*, Wittemberg, 1682; E. Otto, *Dissertatio prima et secunda de statu Judeorum publico ad l. 3 fin. D. de decurionibus*, Traject. ad Rhenum, 1721; Jacob August Franckenstein, *De juribus singularibus circa judeos maxime in Germania*, dissertation, Leipzig, 1772; Heusch, *De publico Judeorum statu ab eo tempore quo primum gens romana victa est*, Argentorati, 1745; Behlen, *De statu odierno Judeorum in Germania*, Moguntiae, 1764; W. Burchard, *De regali judeis incolatum largiendi jure*, Herbornae, 1766; Löwenstein, *Observationes quaedam de Judeis eorumque diversa conditione secundum jus romanum et germanicum*, Bützow, 1768; Gatzert, *De juribus judeorum*, Gissae, 1771; Schneidt, *De juribus judeorum ex legibus in primis Franconicis*, Würzburg, 1776; Starck, *De judeorum tolerantia legum series temporum ordine digesta*, Tubingae, 1782; Biener, *De jure regio recipiendi Judeos*, Leipzig 1790.

244 Anacleto Reiffenstuel, *Jus canonicum universum*, Venice, 1717, t. V; in X. 5, 6, *de Judeis et Saracenis et eorum servis*; p. 129, no. 21: "Judaei semel recepti frui valent jure civium aliorum, ita ut rerum dominia non tantum habere sed de iisdem tam inter vivos, quam mortis causa libere disponere, et quosvis contractus tam inter se, quam cum Christianis inire, matrimonia inter se rito suo contrahere, actiones instruere et excipere etc. ... *l. Judei Romano jure*; desumitur id ipsum etiam ex *c. de terris* 16, *de decimis* et *c. quanto, in fine, de Usuris* et confirmatur universali consuetudine quae est optima legum interpres."

245 Samuel Stryk, *Dissertationum Juridicarum*, vol. IX, *Opera Omnia* ed., Frankfurt 1746, disputatio IX, part II, Ch. I § 9, p. 124: " Deinde Antoninus dedit civitatem omnibus in orbe romano viventibus ... Hinc et Judaei habentur pro civibus romanis ...; idem vol. X, Disp. XIV, ch. II, § 3, p. 189: Judaei ... jure civili romano utuntur, juxtaque illud judicantur *l. 8 C. de Judeis*; sunt enim in Germania cives romani. Quaecumque igitur beneficia civibus imperii ut civibus concessa sunt, ea quoque judaeis indulta censentur."

Consequently, determining who is a citizen of the Empire essentially means determining who has the potential to become a citizen of one of the various states composing the Empire itself: being declared "de populo romano," *civis romanus*, constitutes the necessary prerequisite for being also recognized as "de corpore civitatis," that is – a citizen of one of the states of the Empire.

Therefore, if all those who belong to the *populus romanus* can, under the conditions laid down which vary from place to place, become citizens of the lesser political entities, by the concordant opinion of the Romanistic and canonistic doctrine examined above, this is also possible for the Jews who are part of the *populus romanus*.

This local citizenship (distinguishing it from that of the Empire, discussed until now) has also been considered by many writers and mentioned in legislative texts.

Let us start with the doctrine.

After Baldo, who, without theorizing, states "quod immunitas concessa incolis certi loci extenditur ad judeos, quemadmodum gravamen,"[246] we find the explicit declaration of Giovanni d'Anagni that the Jews are part of the *corpus* and *populus* of the state, that is, they are citizens of it.[247]

Repeated by Andrea Barbazza[248] and by Mariano and Bartolomeo Socini,[249] the theory becomes habitual in the late doctrine[250] and finds its most authoritative and clear exponent in Cardinal De Luca.

246 Baldo, *Commentaria*, on fr. 17 D. 27, 1 (*l. spadonem, ff. de excusatione tutorum, § jam autem*).

247 John of Anagni, *In librum Quintum decretalium*, Milan 1492, p. 63 v.: Judei dicuntur esse de eodem populo et corpore ipsius civitatis quamvis non dicantur esse de corpore spirituali in *l. Christianis C. de paganis* < *ri. tollen.* > (C. 1, 11, 6); sunt ergo de massa et civitatem faciunt magis populosam ut probat textus in *auth. De questore*, post princ. ibi civitas nostra populosa est turbis diversorum hominum, *collatio VI* (novel 80).

248 Andrea Barbazza, *Consiliorum volumina quatuor*, Venice, 1581, vol. I, cons. 15, and vol. IV, cons. 63.

249 M. and B. Socini, *Consiliorum volumina quatuor*, Lyon, 1551, vol. I, cons. 63, nos. 12–13; cons. 71, nos. 3–4.

250 See e.g., Bermondo Choveronio, *De publicis concubinariis*, in *T.U.J.*, tome XI, part I, p. 149: "Judei dicuntur esse de eodem Populo et corpore civitatis, quamvis non sint de corpore spirituali"; Alderamo Mascardi, *Communes conclusiones ad generalem quorumcumque statutorum interpretationem accomodatae*, Ferrara 1608, conclusion VI, no. 210, p. 279: "Limita conclusionem (regarding the rules on foreigners), ut non procedat quoad judaeos, nam licet respectu divinarum rerum sint quoad nos Christianos, nedum forenses, sed omnino extranei, cum nobiscum in illis minime participent, tamen in actibus humanis secus, et habitantes in aliquo loco non dicuntur, quoad statuta et forum illius loci forenses, sed potius uti incolae et cives quoad ea reputantur, ideo statuta illos ligabunt"; Cf. Giulio Ferretti, *De Gabellis*, in *T.U.J.*, tome XII, p. 86 v,, no. 271; Francesco Bursati, *Consiliorum volumina quatuor*, Venice 1586, cons. 452, no. 58 and the authors cited by

With the insight that distinguishes him, De Luca asks himself the precise question: "An hebrei in aliqua civitate fixum habentes domicilium dicantur cives, utrumque usum activum et passivum seu onerosum et favorabilem habentes, ad instar aliorum civium Christianorum, legum statutorum et consuetudinum civitatis"; and against the doubts of some, he clearly resolves it in the affirmative by stating: "*quod hebrei originarii seu veri domiciliarii civitatis dicuntur veri cives in omnibus, exceptis illis juribus honorificis et praeminentialibus a quibus tantum per viam limitationis regulae exclusi sunt*, praesertim vero circa usum activum et passivum legum sive communium sive municipalium et consuetudinum in prophanis et mere temporalibus."[251] Elsewhere, referring specifically to the Jews of Rome, relying Pius IV's provision (Constitution 48, § 5) which states "Judeos comprehendi sub statutis et decretis generalibus Urbis," De Luca repeats that "de jure, quicquid plures dixerint distinguendo inter leges et statuta continentia rigorem vel equitatem, verius est, exceptis iis, quae concernunt forum spiritualem seu internum, hebreos dici in omnibus cives, tam in odiosis et onerosis quam etiam in favorabilibus et privilegiativis, ideoque sub legibus, statutis et consuetudinibus aut indultis comprehendi."[252] He is true to form in his conclusions whenever he deals with the subject again.[253]

Andrea Tiraqueau, *De jure primigeniorum*, quest. 66, no. 4, *Opera omnia* ed., Frankfurt am Main, 1597, p. 545.

251 De Luca, *Theatrum veritatis et justitiae*, Venice, 1726, book IV, part I, *De servitutibus praedialibus*, Disc. 70, nos. 2 and 3, p. 89 with the list of the most ancient literature.

252 Idem, op. cit., Book II, *De regalibus*, disc. 160, nos 30 and 32, p. 264.

253 Idem, op. cit., Book II, *De regalibus*, disc. 182, nos 9 and 10, p. 320: "Quamvis apud Deum judei criminosi et delinquentes censendi sint, utpote in eorum perfidia perseverantes, atque veritatem redemptionis agnoscere nolentes, ac propterea servi reputentur: attamen id improprie procedit ad predictum, scilicet effectum fori interni apud Deum et Ecclesiam, sed in foro externo habentur tamquam liberi et cives eodem modo quo Christiani, adeout gaudeant omnibus favoribus et privilegiis, ac statutis et legibus, quibus alii etiam in iis quae fundata sunt in aequitate ... Atque discurrendo etiam per rationes, dicebam quod quamvis Judaei sint infideles, non tamen sunt publici hostes generaliter, et in generica prohibitione commercii, ut Turcae, dum Ecclesia in ipsamet Urbe eius Metropoli et in multis locis permittit eorum commercium adeout habeantur, potius tamquam cives et pacifici amici." Idem, book VI, *De dote*, disc. 132, no. 9, p. 202: "Judei dicuntur cives atque in eis servanda est dispositio juris communis, vel statutarii eodem modo quo in reliquis civibus, quoniam exceptis spiritualibus, quoad temporalia dicuntur de populo ac de corpore civitatis." Idem, book IX, part III, *De legitima, trebellianica, et aliis detractionibus*, disc. 15, no. 6, p. 240: "favore Populi Romani, et civium romanorum, sub quorum nomine veniunt Judei, qui generaliter comprehenduntur sub omnibus legibus, statutis et consuetudinibus, praeter quam in respicientibus forum animae." Similarly, book VII, part III, *De alienationibus*, disc. 60, nos. 3–4, p. 321 and book VIII, *De credito et debito*, disc. 102, no. 3, p. 161.

References to the local legislation in these dissertations of the doctrine are very scarce: the reasoning is almost always abstract, and the conclusion that the Jews are citizens is self-evident and rests on more or less anguished Roman texts. However, if we carefully examine that legislation, we can see that it agrees in the most precise and clear-cut way with the doctrine we have just outlined.

Thus, it is in Pisa, where three documents of 1317 speak of "Judei olim facti cives" and of one Angelo and one Musetto Jews "cives pisani de Urbe."[254] Even more explicit is the statement contained in a decree of Boniface IX for the Jews of Rome (April 15, 1402) under which "omnes et singuli Judei et Judeæ in Urbe habitantes et moram trahentes cum eorum familia in Urbe, tractentur et tractari debeant et sint et esse intelligantur cives Romani, in omnibus et per omnia habeantur et reputentur et gaudeant et gaudere possint privilegio civium Romanorum, non obstantibus quibuscumque statutis et juribus in contrarium loquentibus."[255] Similarly, in a provision between the residents of Anagni and Pope Boniface IX on May 4, 1399, Jews are entitled to all privileges and dignities enjoyed by the other citizens.[256] This rule is later reported in even more precise terms in the Anagni statute of 1517.[257] Also, in the Kingdom of Naples, Jews are considered citizens and often appeal to the rights inherent in their quality.[258]

254 P. M. Lonardo, *Gli ebrei a Pisa sino alla fine del secolo XV*, in *Studi storici* (by Crivellucci), VII, 1898, p. 179.

255 H. Vogelstein and P. Rieger, *Geschichte der Juden in Rom*: 139 *v. Chr. bis* 1870 *nach Chr.*, Berlin 1896, vol. I, p. 493. The decree was confirmed by Martin V (ibid.). Cf. also the provision decided in Cividale on August 3, 1321 and inserted in the municipal statute under the heading "De non faciendis iniuriis Judeis": "Die tertio intrante Augusto. In civitate Austria, in domo communis. Ordinatum fuit per Gastaldionem, et consilium et firmatum quod judaei qui morantur in Civitate cum loco et foco, tractentur et sint in protectione Communis, et de eis fiat justitia tamquam debet fieri vicinis, si eis in personis, vel in rebus iniuria, vel violentia fieret aut gravamen in Civitate vel districtu. Si vero extra terram gravarentur, communis eos adiuvet bona fide. Et hoc pro eo quod annuatim circa Festum S. Georgii dare debent camerae Communis quinque vel tres marchas denariorum aquilegensis monetae." Giuseppe Bianchi, *Documenti per la storia del Friuli dal* 1317 *al* 1325, Udine, 1844, p. 483, no. 277.

256 Theiner, *Codex diplomaticus dominii temporalis S. Sedis*, vol. III, p. 981: "Judaei civitatis Anagninae gaudeant privilegis et dignitatibus dictae civitatis sicut et alii cives dicti loci pociuntur et gaudent." Cf. Rezasco, *Del segno degli Ebrei*, reprint from *Giornale ligustico di Archeologia, Storia e Belle Arti*, XV (1888), p. 27.

257 *Statuto di Anagni*, De Magistris ed., Rome, 1880: "Et ipsi Judei in civitate nostra habitantes vel morantes cum familiis suis pro nostris civibus penitus habeantur et civium immunitatibus statutis et beneficiis singulis decernimus eos gaudere." In accordance to an unclear odd reasoning, Rezasco, op. cit., p. 28, gives the term "penitus" a negative connotation and infers a radical change in the position of the Jews, whereas it is not but a confirmation.

258 Ferorelli, *Gli ebrei nell'Italia meridionale*, Turin, 1915, p. 98.

Mantuan legislation also offers interesting testimonies, where the "jus civilitatis" is frequently granted to stranger Jews in absolute equal terms to those used for the naturalization of Christian foreigners,[259] with the consequences of such award consisting mainly in the obligation to pay taxes and in the right, denied however to foreigners,[260] to purchase real estate in the Mantuan territory.[261]

Before this perfect concordance of legislation and doctrine awarding Jews the quality of citizens, deprived only of those rights that have been taken away from them, as De Luca states, "per viam limitationis regulae," stands the observation made by the late Bizzarri. In her study on citizenship, which to this day is the only comprehensive historical treatise on this matter, she states that the citizenship concessions granted by some towns to Jews brought about "a remarkable deviation from the principle of law by which the Jews were considered foreigners, the religious confession having an impact on the granting of citizenship." Such observation seems incorrect.[262] Nevertheless, after what has been described so far, there is no need to insist on the fundamental point that the theocratic doctrine identifying the *civis* with *fidelis* never took roots either in the doctrine or the legislation of the period which we are dealing with and that consequently a perpetual exclusion from citizenship for religious reasons never took place. It is actually in agreement with what Bizzarri maintains in another chapter about the contractual character of the citizenship, whose

259 See the documents published in the Appendix. The first Jew who settled in Mantua, Abraham of Bonaventura from Forlì, in the documents of 10 years from his settlement (on this issue see my work cit. p. 449) is also said "civis et habitator Mantuae" (Notarial Archive of Mantua, vol. of 1399, May 30, dossier 27, f. 18 v.; vol. of 1405, II semester, October 20, dossier 20, f. 4 v.).

260 *Statuti Gonzagheschi di Mantova*, (1393–1404, Torelli, *L'Archivio Gonzaga di Mantova*, p. 72; kept in several manuscripts in the Gonzaga Archive and in Mantua municipal library) rubric *De alienationibus prohibitis in personis non subditis jurisdictioni communis Mantue* (copy of 1643 kept in the Gonzaga Arch., p. 82), modified with a decree of Ferdinando Carlo Gonzaga on June 3, 1684 (ibid., pp. 112–113).

261 Sometimes permission to buy real estate in the territory is granted exceptionally to foreign Jews, without resorting to the naturalization. See for example the Decree of Gianfrancesco Gonzaga of the year 1428, for Angelo di Dattolino, a Jew from Serrmide (Gonzaga Archive of Mantua, *Books of the Decrees*, III, p. 254) and the other similar one of August 12, 1433, for Moisè son of the late Benjamin, Jews from Revere (ibid., Book VI, p. 19 v.). But since these are measures which are taken countless times also for Christians, the possibility that they might still be considered a reflection of a peculiarity in the legal *status* of the Jews must be ruled out.

262 Dina Bizzarri, *Ricerche sul diritto di cittadinanza nella costituzione comunale*, in *Studi senesi*, vol. XXXII, 1916, p. 64. = *Studi di storia del diritto italiano editi dalla famiglia*, Turin 1937, p. 101.

benefits, conceived as the correlative payment of taxes and the fulfillment of other civic duties,[263] extend to all those – Christians or Jews – who voluntarily subjected themselves to these burdens.

Bizzarri is not the only one claiming the Jews were not citizens: the majority of the writers cannot easily solve this problem. Faced with the complexities of political and civilian prohibitions imposed on the Jews, most of the authors are reluctant to admit they could have been granted actual citizenship.[264]

We know, however, that their citizenship was authentic. Citizenship emptied, perhaps, of a good deal of its content by restrictive rules but one which always existed in all those elements that had not been expressly repealed.

Instead, another circumstance should be taken into account, contributing to tangle the web further – at first glance: by the end of the 13th century in central and northern Italy, a large number of Jews are engaged in money-lending. United in societies supplied with large capitals, they spread from Rome towards the North, making their way into every important town and village and, with the permission of the governments, founding local banks that offer money loans at interest. The authorities conclude pacts (chapters) with them, regulating the duration of the concession – in most cases decennial – the modalities of the activity of money-lending at interest, and the rights that the holders of the concession and their families will enjoy for the period of their stay.[265] Almost always explicitly listed is the right to be considered *tamquam cives* and to enjoy the benefits conferred in general upon citizens.[266]

---

263 Bizzarri, op. cit., p. 33 (ed. 1916).

264 See e.g., Lonardo, op. cit., p. 179: "It seems that by special privilege some Jewish residents in Pisa were granted citizenship, a very singular fortune since in other cities they were always considered strangers"; Pertile, *Storia del diritto italiano*, vol. III, ed. I, p. 182; Bar, *Teoria e pratica del diritto internazionale privato*, Buzzati transl., in *Biblioteca di scienze politiche e amministrative*, vol. XI, I, p. 41, no. 4.

265 My study *Prestito ebraico e comunità ebraiche nell'Italia centrale e settentrionale*, in *Rivista di Storia del Diritto Italiano*, yr. VIII (1935), vol. VIII, dossier III, is devoted to this subject.

266 Urbino, March 28, 1433, request by two Jews to the count of Montefeltro for the opening of a money-lender bank: "Magnificentia vestra sibi concedat quod ipse vel frater ... qui contingent residere in dicta civitate et ut supra mutuare habeantur tractentur et reputentur ut cives et pro civibus dicte vestrae civitatis Urbini. ..." In the reply it is said: "Quod dictus supplicans et frater habeantur et tractentur ut cives Urbini," G. Luzzatto, *I banchieri ebrei in Urbino nell'età ducale*, Padua, 1902, doc. I, pp. 51–52; Reggio Emilia, July 30, 1413, pacts stipulated by the Municipality with Muso (Moisè) from Leuccio and associates: "Item che li dicti possano gaudere tutti li statuti e ordene del Comune de Rezzo e benefieri de quelli, como fa li altri citadini e de questo no possano sere privati," A. Balletti, *Gli Ebrei e gli Estensi*, II ed., Reggio E., 1930, p. 22; Piove di Sacco, ca. 1373, decennial pacts stipulated by Francesco da Carrara, Lord of Padua, with the Jew Abraham: "Item quod antedicti mutuator, factor, socii, familli et famillia dicti banchi habeantur et reputentur

As the doctrine of the time already realized,[267] it can be noted that in this way, these Jews have not been declared citizens but only made equal to native citizens for the duration of their precarious residence, which is quite different. However, in this temporary character of assimilation to the *cives*, applying a principle excluding the Jews as such from real citizenship cannot be viewed as Luzzatto[268] and Bizzarri seem to be viewing.[269] The reason is simply that if granting a permit for the money-lending activity was restricted to a given term, accordingly, equating them to citizens should have also been temporary: once

---

in omnibus velut alii cives Padue et Plebis Sachi"; and can buy real estate like other tax-paying citizens. A. Ciscato, *Gli ebrei a Padova*, Padua 1901, p. 24 and Doc. I, pp. 229–230; Udine, July 6, 1387, pacts stipulated by the Municipality with the Jew Moisè: "ceterum promiserunt prefati domini nomine dicti Comunis ipsi Moissi ipsum Moissem mantenere et deffendere et tractare in jure contra quoscumque tamquam vicinum terrae, et quod prefatus Moisses possit emere et vendere in terra tamquam vicinus, et aliis conditionibus gaudere possit quibus gaudent alii cives terre." *Statuti e ordinamenti del Comune di Udine*, yr. 1425, Udine, 1898. Appendix VII, *De judeis*, p. 125; Pisa 1400, decennial pacts for two Jewish money-lenders: "Item quod ipsi Judey habitantes in civitate pisana ad prestandum et fenerandum, ut dictum est supra, fiant et fieri possint et debeant pisani cives et in dicta civitate pisana tractentur et tractari debeant in omnibus et per omnia prout et sicut alii facti cives pisani feneratores," Lonardo, op. cit., p. 171; Perugia, 1381: "quod dicti infrascripti Judei et eorum descendentes et familie ipsorum et cuiuslibet eorum in omnibus et per omnia gaudeant omnibus et singulis beneficiis, immunitatibus et exemptionibus in civilibus prout quemadmodum veri et originarii cives dicte civitatis Perusii, et pro veris civibus nec aliter quomodolibet possint aggravari." A. Fabretti, *Sulla condizione degli ebrei in Perugia dal XIII al XVII secolo*, Turin 1891, p. 100; Siena, pacts of 1457: "Et cosi s'intendessero esser veri et originarii cittadini di Siena, durante el tempo dei predetti capitoli," Mengozzi, *Il monte dei Paschi in Siena*, 1906, I, p. 148. These statements of temporary recognition as citizens are constantly accompanied by the exemption from all sorts of taxes, according to the custom in force with regard to the strangers whose immigration is encouraged. See for example the cited Pisa pacts of 1400: during the concession, the holders will enjoy royal and personal immunity "eo modo et sicut sunt immunes ibi forenses, qui de novo venerint ad habitandum." Provisions similar to those mentioned are found in all the Jewish money-lending pacts all over Italy, a large number of which has already been published and studied. A list of these chapters is given by Cassuto, *Gli Ebrei a Firenze*, Florence 1918, pp. 120–121; cf. Gabrieli's bibliography, *Italia judaica*, Rome, 1924, and my above-mentioned work.

267 Felino Sandeo, *Tertia in quinque libros decretalium*, in *cap. Quoniam, de ufficio judicis ordinarii*, (X 1, 31, 14), nos. 3–4: "An quilibet in dubio presumatur civis ... et ratio scribendi ibi ponit quod incola dicitur qui non subiit munera: et non est civis; unde Judeus stans in loco et dans ad usuram non dicitur civis sed incola." Alessandro Tartagni, *Consilia*. Book V, cons. 75, Venice ed. 1580, p. 81 pleads the cause of a Jew from Massa, maintaining that albeit "advena," having this person a domicile, he must enjoy the rights of citizens.

268 Luzzatto, op. cit., p. 30. Cassuto, op. cit., p. 122, no. 2, merely points out that this is not real citizenship, without, however, investigating the reasons determining the special *status*.

269 Bizzarri, op. cit., pp. 64–66.

the term had expired without any renewal, the money-lenders had to leave the country, it was, therefore, logical that all the facilities established for the period of their stay would also be gone: in short, something akin to what was happening for students or traders, considered *cives* in several cities, limitedly to the time of their residence.[270]

All this does not affect the principle that, as De Luca says, all non-money-lender Jews born in a given place or residents in it *ab immemorabili* – "fixum domicilium habentes" are included in the ranks of *cives* and enjoy all the rights due to the citizens, with the only exception of those specifically taken away from them because of the difference in religion: this, as we have seen, can safely be stated based on a concomitant testimony of legislation and doctrine, both ancient and recent.[271]

Therefore, all those who argued that revolutionary emancipation turned the Jews from foreigners into citizens[272] were wrong. In reality, it did nothing but repeal the oppressive restrictions on the already existing right of citizenship, giving it, after fifteen centuries, the possibility of expanding again in all its fullness.

•••

As a rule, citizenship is granted to the Jews, as to anyone else, by competent state bodies: because of its purely political nature, the autonomy accorded to

270 Pertile, op. cit., 1st ed., vol. III, p. 117.

271 Among the later writers, the following ones should be mentioned: Sessa, *Tractatus de Judeis*, Turin 1717, ch. 2, no. 7, p. 4; Reinkingk, *Tractatus de regimine seculari et ecclesiastico*, cit., class II, ch. III, no. 26, p. 240; and Stryk, *Dissertationum* etc., cit., vol. VII, p. 559, disput. 24, ch. V, § 8. I shall recall here also another question that the doctrine presents and that has some correlation with our subject: the question, that is, of whether an infidel foreigner, having gotten baptized in a city, becomes *ipso jure* citizen of it. In *l. municipem D. ad municipalem et de incolis* (D. 50, 1, 1) Bartolo resolves it in a dubitatively negative sense, whereas Marquardo Susani (*Tractatus de Judeis* cit. part III, ch. II, § 13, p. 64) together with Luca da Penne favors an affirmative interpretation. A precise provision in the latter sense, of Paul III (1542), is reported by Pertile, op. cit., vol. III, p. 116, note 84.

272 And so, looking to France, state Brun, *La condition des Juifs en France*, Paris, s. d. and Maignial, *La loi de 1791 et la condition des Juifs en France*, Paris, 1903. The thesis of the latter was victoriously refuted by M. Liber, who in a large study (published in *Révue des Etudes juives*, t. 63, pp. 185–210; t. 64, pp. 89–108 and 244–277; t. 65, pp. 89–133 and t. 67, pp. 161–212) demonstrated that in France the Jews were considered subjects of the Kingdom even before the revolution, which had only to repeal the restrictive laws affecting them. See, in the same sense, the interesting pages of Baruch Hagani, *L'émancipation des Juifs*, Paris 1929, pp. 187 et seqq.

the Jewish communities, even where very broad, does not generally include the right to confer naturalization to foreign members of the communities.

As already done by others,[273] it is fascinating to observe the major communities of Tuscany, i.e. Pisa and Leghorn, obtained such an exorbitant privilege by the Grand Dukes. Under it, compared to the higher federal political authority, their autonomy succeeded in establishing an even broader basis than that which a member state would usually have enjoyed in a confederation.

Ever since the gates of Leghorn and Pisa were opened to merchants of every nation and religion with the licenses of February 12, 1591, and June 10, 1593, it was determined the enlisting in Jewish communities by vote decided on by the respective assemblies through a ballot (ballotage) would have conferred to the individuals for whom the vote has cast the use of the rights listed in the same license.[274] The individual rights then progressed towards the configuration of unique, comprehensive citizenship rights and joining the community was considered apt to confer the quality of Leghorn or Pisa citizens to these people *ipso jure*, without even the need for a decision taken by the state authorities.

This privilege was confirmed in 1614,[275] 1715,[276] and 1761.[277] However, it was repealed by the French in 1808 by a general provision revoking all privileges.[278]

Specifically, a decree of February 9, 1811, laid the principle "that all foreigners without any distinction of a cult, who took residence in those [Tuscan] provinces, could not acquire the French quality if not according to the rules laid down by the general laws of the empire"; while recognizing the validity of the acquired citizenships in the past through ballotage.[279] Even odder is that while the ancient Jewish autonomies suppressed by the French along with the *privilegia odiosa* were not revived by the governments of the Restoration,

---

273 Isacco Rignano, *Della naturalizzazione acquistata in Toscana col mezzo della ballottazione e dei suoi effetti sotto la legislazione italiana*, in *Archivio Giuridico*, vol. 44, 1890, pp. 394–409.

274 Art. 31 of the first license and 35 of the second one, Rignano, p. 394. The second license can be found published in *Collezione degli ordini municipali di Livorno corredata dagli statuti della Sicurtà* etc., Leghorn, Carlo Giorgi ed., 1798, pp. 237–255.

275 Royal rescript May 12, 1614. Rignano, ibid. no. 2.

276 Art. 15 of the December 20, 1715 motuproprio on the "Riforma del Governo della Nazione ebrea di Livorno," Rignano, ibid. no. 2. For the entire text of the motuproprio, see *Collezione degli ordini* etc., cit.

277 Royal rescript of November 1761 in Affare Corcos, Archives of the Jewish University of Leghorn, dossier 4 of the rescripts, no. 104, Rignano, ibid., note 2.

278 Rignano, p. 395.

279 Rignano, p. 401.

in Tuscany, except for the jurisdiction whose repeal was retained, from 1814 onwards the old way returned in every respect.[280]

Therefore, the privilege of the community to confer Tuscan citizenship by ballotage was also revived. That privilege was upheld in 1836[281] and 1846, when this concession by ballot was subject to the condition that those individuals for whom the ballot was cast settled in the Grand Duchy as permanent residents.[282]

As late as the 19th century, the actual application of that privilege is attested by numerous examples. Thus – Rignano writes[283] – with a note by the Secretariat of State dated April 28, 1837, addressed to the Governor of Leghorn, to a certain Isach Raffael Zabban from Ancona settled in Pisa, who had requested that the government grant him the naturalization, it was replied: "that for the resolution requested, he would have to submit the application to the representatives of the city's Jewish University because the ballotage produced the effect of conferring the quality of Tuscan subjection on the individual Jews."[284] And with a resolution of the Ministry of Justice dated January 12 of that year, to Emanuele Modigliani, a native of Rome, for several years domiciled in Leghorn, who in 1853 had pleaded with the Grand Duke for being granted Tuscan naturalization, it was replied: "that since he was a Jew, he accordingly had to go through the formalities of ballotage by the Governing Council of the Jewish University of Leghorn"; and while informing him of that resolution, the royal advocacy let him know that once he had obtained the ballotage, he would have been declared a Tuscan citizen without the need for

280 Decree of December 17, 1814, reported by Rignano on p. 395.

281 Royal motuproprio August 10, 1836, reported by Rignano, p. 396.

282 Royal resolution of January 16, 1846: "S. A. I e R. il Gran Duca occasionalmente all'esame di un affare relativo ad alcuni israeliti sudditi naturali del Vice Re d'Egitto, i quali ballottati in Livorno con animo di acquistare la sudditanza toscana a forma dei privilegi del Gran Duca Ferdinando I, non fissarono il domicilio nel Granducato, ma tornarono in Egitto, con veneratissima Risoluzione del 16 gennaio corrente, si è degnata dichiarare che il privilegio nascente dal bando del 10 gennaio 1593, per cui gli ebrei esteri, ottenuta la ballottazione dall'Università Israelitica di Livorno, vengono aggregati all'Università medesima ed acquistano per ciò la sudditanza toscana, deve intendersi subordinato alla condizione che gli israeliti forestieri ballottati stabiliscano la loro permanente dimora nel granducato, questa essendo la causa finale del privilegio medesimo. Ha inoltre la prelodata A. S. I. e R. dichiarato che una tale intelligenza del bando su riferito, la quale dovrà servire di regola nei casi futuri, deve ritenersi ancora come operativa all'effetto di togliere alle ballottazioni già eseguite l'efficacia di rivestire della nazionalità toscana tutti quelli ebrei, che dopo averla ottenuta non soddisfecero alla rammentata condizione di stabilirsi nel Granducato." Rignano, p. 398.

283 Op. cit., pp. 398–399.

284 The related documents are in the archive of the Jewish University of Leghorn, year 1853, lot 11, no. 82.

a royal rescript. He, therefore, turned to the Jewish University of Leghorn and asked for the ballotage, which was granted to him by decision of October 9, 1853, no. 132; and with the local Government's letter dated November 23, he was awarded the appropriate diploma.[285]

Eight more naturalizations were subsequently granted by the Jewish Community of Leghorn, until in 1859, with the annexation to the Kingdom of Italy, according to the equality to all citizens principle, the privilege came to an end definitively.[286]

The Italian government, like its Napoleonic counterpart, nevertheless, recognized the full validity of naturalizations obtained by ballotage, and in two responses to questions of Jewish applicants requesting the naturalization after they already had been balloted by the Community of Leghorn, declared that they did not need naturalization since they already were citizens following the deliberation of the community.[287]

285 The documents concerning this question are in the same Archive, file Rescripts, no. 28, doc. no. 82.

286 Rignano, p. 399.

287 Ibid., p. 402. First case: application by the brothers Raphael and Abraham Scialom, of Tunisian origin, domiciled in Leghorn and balloted by the community with January 1, 1857, no. 138 and May 2, 1858, no. 140 deliberations respectively, to obtain Italian citizenship. The Minister of Justice with dispatch of February 2, 1861, with copy to the applicants from the Government Office of Leghorn on the 5th of the same month, states "che i prenominati Scialom non avevano bisogno della naturalizzazione e che si valessero dei diritti a loro derivanti dalla ballottazione cui erano stati sottoposti negli anni 1857 e 1858 per conseguire, conforme conseguirono per questo mezzo, la naturalizzazione in ordine alle leggi già esistenti in Toscana" ["that the above mentioned Scialom brothers did not need naturalization and could make use of the rights derived to them from ballotage which they had undergone in 1857 and 1858 to achieve, and in this way subsequently obtained, naturalization according to the laws already existing in Tuscany"]. Second case: similar application of the German Ludovico Bernheimer already balloted in Leghorn with deliberation of April 4, 1836, no. 123. The Ministry of the Interior, with a dispatch of November 26, 1868 (Div. 3. Section. 1, n. 28572) declares: "di riconoscere in lui la qualità di suddito italiano, per la circostanza che il medesimo, fin dal 4 aprile 1836 era stato sottoposto alla formalità della ballottazione per parte dei rappresentanti la Università Israelitica di Livorno: atto che per antiche leggi e consuetudini vigenti in alcuni paesi della Toscana dava agli israeliti certi privilegi in forza dei quali erano equiparati ai cittadini del Granducato, e perciò in seguito all'annessione devono essere considerati come cittadini italiani" ["to recognize in him the quality of an Italian subject, by virtue of the fact that, since April 4, 1836, he underwent the formalities of ballotage by the representatives of the Jewish University of Leghorn: an act that for the ancient laws and customs applicable in some towns of Tuscany gave the Jews certain privileges by virtue of which they were treated as citizens of the Grand Duchy, and therefore following the annexation they must be considered as Italian citizens"].

In other Italian states, too, the Jewish communities were empowered with specific authority for strangers and received from the state the faculty to make the settlement of strangers subject to their consent, establish the modalities of aggregation to the community, revoke the aggregation granted to undeserving members and, in general, to punish members of their communities charged with misconduct, with the severe penalty of exile. For example, that was the situation in Mantua from 1560 onwards[288] and in Piedmont from 1564.[289] In Mantua, the autonomy of the Jewish group was the broadest and so were the faculties concerning strangers. However, not even in Mantua was the faculty of conferring state citizenship *ipso jure* through aggregation to the group seems to be included. With the ballotage by one of the town districts, the community first granted permission to "settle down,"[290] or be domiciled;[291] it then decrees

288 July 28, 1560. Ducal decree stating that no stranger Jew can settle down in the city without prior informing the Judge of the Jews as for the probity, costumes, etc., which will be based on the opinion of the Jewish massari and bankers (Jewish Archive of Mantua, *Libro E*, sheet 6, ch. 1). Confirmation April 26, 1566; July 22, 1579 (ibid. sheet 7); April 4. 1587 (*Libro M*, sheet 1); Sept. 1, 1580 (ibid. sheet 3). Commissions of August 3, 1615 and December 3, 1618, confirmed with decree February 16, 1689: "Che in avvenire non possa nè debba esser accettato in questa città nè in questo Ghetto alcuno forestiere hebreo, sia di che conditione esser si voglia, con famiglia o senza, ancorchè per qualche tempo havesse tenuto casa et habitatione in qual si sia città o luogo dello stato di S.A.S., quale non sarà conceduta se prima non vi saranno precedute le esate informationi della qualità trafico et costumi dello stesso hebreo forestiere o di sua famiglia da prendersi secretamente dai massari, o deputati dalla Convocazione più ristretta degli ebrei, e queste ad effetto che detta Università possa mantenersi coi suoi trafici e che il numero di essa non si accresca in pregiuditio di quelli che già vi sono e che si possano mantenere con decenti regole e governo, ecc." (*File* 149, no. 3). Government rules of the Community 1758–1761: "Desiderando alcun forestiere di venire a domiciliarsi in questo Ghetto et aggregarsi all'Università eziandio per il solo corso delle regole triennali, dovrà esser balotato nella Vicinia Generale della medesima, nè si intenderà ammesso se non riporterà quattro quinti dei voti della medesima" (ibid.).

289 Duboin, *Raccolta per ordine di materie delle leggi, provvidenze, editti, ecc. ... della R. Casa Savoia*, t. 2, Turin, 1825, p. 289, privilege May 19, 1564: "Primo che resti servita V. A. dichiarar e confermar che non sia permesso a nessun altro ebreo forestiere di qualsivoglia stato e condizione di venir ad abitar nei stati di quella, senza il consentimento e volontà d'essi Ebrei, quali al presente fanno residenza in detti suoi stati, atteso che vi potria venir ad abitar alcuno di mala condizione e la sua mala vita potrebbe causar e portar danno agli abitanti, ecc." Numerous later confirmations (ibid. pp. 295, 356, 364, 376, 541, 546, 559, 592).

290 So for example October 29, 1634 (Mantua Jewish Archive, *libro Am.*, sheet 7 v., ch. 6), Dic. 15, 1637 (ibid., sheet 15 v., § 6); Oct. 1 and November 6, 1639 (ibid. sheet 19, §§ 5 and 7), etc.

291 For example, 1702, 1st Sivan (*Libro Am.*, sheet 179, § 4), August 25, 1753 (*libro Ap.*, sheet 143 v., § 22), etc.

aggregation, also known as "citizenship,"[292] transforming the foreigner into a member of the community with all the related rights and burdens – fiscal ones in particular. However, although permanently aggregated to the community, the person balloted remains a foreigner to the state and must apply to state bodies to obtain naturalization.[293]

According to a Ferrara document from 1741, settling in the ghetto without the permission of the Jewish University's general congregation is forbidden to Jews even if they had already become citizens of the state by royal concession.[294] This document shows that in Ferrara, too, unlike in Tuscany, aggregation to the community and acquisition of citizenship are two distinct acts that must be requested separately from two different authorities.

---

292 For example 1746, 28 nov. (*libro Ap.*, sheet 123, § 4); June 5, 1759 (*libro Cd.*, sheet 5).

293 So, on January 5, 1652, the ducal magistrate, "in causa civilitate petite per Angelum Laudadeum Vivantem hebreum ferrariensem," established by means of witnesses that the mentioned "per decennium et ultra in hac Mantue civitate habitasse ... censuit describendum esse et pro descripto habere in numero civium civitatis predictae, ita quod potiatur omnibus privilegiis et prerogativis quibus ceteri hebrei cives originarii gaudent et in futurum gaudebunt" (Jewish Archive, *File* 30, no. 37).

294 Edict of Cardinal D'Elci, Apostolic legate in Ferrara, March 24, 1741, in print, § 5: "E finalmente ordiniamo e comandiamo che nessun Ebreo forestiero di qualunque condizione possa in avvenire accasarsi e venire ad abitare nel Ghetto di questa città, se prima non sarà passato per partito dalla Congregazione Generale della suddetta Università, intendendosi anche di quelli che fossero cittadini *ex privilegio*."

PART 2

Jewish Law and State Law

SECTION 1

The Conflict between Jewish Law and Local Laws in General and with Regard to the Norms of Private Law

CHAPTER 5

The Roman Empire and Italy in Particular

In several chapters of his excellent work, Juster dealt with the application of Jewish law in Roman times.[295] Here are the conclusions of his research:

According to general principles, Jewish law is applied throughout the Empire to the Jews who remained Palestinian citizens, as *peregrini*,[296] and also, to a small extent not precisely determinable, to Greek Jewish citizens who acquired the citizenship as a group.[297] In contrast, it is not applied to Roman Jewish citizens, on whom the Roman civil law is imposed without exception.[298]

From passages where the faculty granted to the Jews by emperors to live according to their own laws is discussed, in particular by Josephus[299] and the Fathers of the Church,[300] it is clear these "laws" should be understood as religious rules and nothing more. It is, in fact, only a ceremonial and cultural freedom, and not the autonomy law, that the State is ready to guarantee to Jews.[301]

Only after the year 212, with the edict of Caracalla, will the Jewish peregrini obtain citizenship en bloc, that the use of some Jewish legal institutes will be tolerated, albeit not recognized *de jure*[302] not only to these *former peregrini*, but also – in the impossibility of making distinctions – to all other Jews who were previously citizens of the Empire.

In matrimonial matters, the marriage between uncle and niece, levirate and polygamy (banned in Roman law) will therefore be tolerated throughout the diaspora,[303] and possibly even the divorce according to Jewish norms.[304] As for all other private legal institutions (personal rights, inheritance, the enfranchisement of slaves, guardianship, bonds, etc.), the Jews, as Roman citizens, must follow Roman law.[305]

295 Juster, *Les juifs dans l'empire romain*, cit., vol. II, ch. VI–XIII, pp. 29–92.
296 Juster, II, p. 30.
297 Id., p. 31.
298 Id., p. 32.
299 Collected ibid., vol. I, p. 252, no. 1, 2 and 7 and vol. II, p. 28, no. 1.
300 Collected ibid., vol. II, p. 36, no. 1 and 2.
301 Id., II, pp. 28–29 and 36.
302 Id., II, pp. 33–34.
303 Id., II, pp. 49–50, 51.
304 Id., II, p. 59.
305 For the respective institutions, see ibid., vol. II, p. 62, 65–67, 83–84, 87–92.

 | DOI:10.1163/9789004627154_007

Even the tolerance for Jewish matrimonial institutes will soon come to an end under a specific law,[306] so by the end of the 4th century, all Jews of the empire, indiscriminately, appear as living in Roman law.

On the other hand, Juster argues, based on some non-legal texts,[307] some Talmudic sources,[308] and in particular, the law 10 C. Th. 2, 1,[309] that until the year 398, both in Palestine and in all the locations of the diaspora subject to Rome, the Jews enjoyed the privilege of their own jurisdiction for internal civil disputes. He claims that jurisdiction was omnipresent in conjunction with the civil courts and the submission of a lawsuit to one or the other judicature was biased.[310] And so "tout en y étant soumis en droit ou en fait, les Juifs se soustrayaient, dans beaucoup de matières, aux règles du jus civile romain, en portant leur affaires devant les tribunaux juifs,"[311] that ruled according to the Jewish law.

It is precisely to avoid such inconvenience that in 398, the emperors abolished such Jewish jurisdiction, prescribing from then onward the need for prior parties' agreement to deem a ruling valid.[312]

It seems to me that Juster's construction, aside from any remark on the sources, fails to stand up to simple logical analysis. On the one hand, Juster claims that Roman Jewish citizens lived in Roman law and were judged accordingly in state courts. However, on the other hand, he claims they also had the faculty of bringing their internal disputes before Jewish courts that ruled according to Jewish law. This means one must assume that the same disputes were resolved according to either Roman or Jewish law, depending on the court to which the lawsuit was filed (and since the two were concurrent jurisdictions, the choice was free). Quite clearly, this is an absurdity.

If Jewish judges had passed sentences exclusively as arbitrators, that is to say, if a preliminary agreement between the parties was required, then it could be said the State disregarded Jewish law. It could be said that while applying the Roman law in its courts also to the Jews, it then allowed the application of

306 The l. 7 C. J. 1, 9 of 393. See text above, footnote no. 28.

307 Strabone in Giuseppe, *Antichità giudaiche*, 14, 7, 2 (court of the ethnarch of Alexandria); Id., *Ant.* 14, 10 (year 49 – court of Sardi); Bardesane, *Liber legum regionum*, § 44, transl. from Syriac by F. Nau, *Patrologia syriaca*, vol. III, 1897, pp. 605–606 (jurisdiction in general); S. Giovanni Grisostomo, *Adversus judaeos*, 1, 3, Migne, *Patrologia greca*, 48, p. 848 (court of Antioch of the time). Juster, II, pp. 111, 112 no. 4, 114 no. 1.

308 Jerusalem Talmud, Sanhedrin, 3, 2 (court of Antioch); Babylonian Talmud, sanhedrin (court of Rome). Juster, II, p. 113, no. 1. Cited are also Toseftà Ghittin 1, 4 = Babylonian Talmud, Ghittin 11a, and Jer. Talmud, Ghittin 1, 3; I do not see, however, how anything can be deduced about the jurisdiction from these passages.

309 See text above, footnote no. 29.

310 Juster, II, pp. 110–114 and 119 no. 1.

311 Id., II, pp. 37–38.

312 Id., II, pp. 38, 101–102, 104–105.

Jewish law by the Jewish arbitrators only upon consent of the parties, and to the same extent to which, in the arbitration, it generally admitted the derogation of the will of private individuals to state law. In this case, we could speak of a voluntary evasion of Roman law and submitting to Jewish law brought back to life in the aforementioned precise limits.

Actually, the Jews exercised a real jurisdiction recognized by the State, which was imposed on a party even against the other party's will. Therefore, the application of Jewish law took place not only with the parties' prior consent and within certain boundaries but was rather imposed on the contenders even against their will. Moreover, that application was not subject to any restrictions since it dealt with their personal statute that the State seemed to recognize by recognizing their particular jurisdiction. Well then, if this personal statute was imposed upon the contenders before the Jewish court, is it conceivable that a different personal statute was imposed to the same parties before the concurrent Roman court? This would have entailed the unjust faculty for the plaintiff to choose and force one of two applicable jurisdictions most favorable to him on the opponent: and the same lawsuit would have been resolved to the detriment or benefit of one side, depending on the court to which the lawsuit had been presented, and the law consequently applied.

Since this is logically impossible, it must be concluded that in the topographic limits within which, until 398, the Romans recognized the Jewish jurisdiction in concurrence with the State jurisdiction, they also recognized Jewish law as the sole law governing internal private relations between the Jews. And such a law they did apply also in their courts, whenever the controversy between Jews was brought before them rather than before the Jewish court.[313]

---

313 This is undoubtedly evident from some Jewish texts (for which see also H. Strack und P. Billerbeck, *Kommentar zum Neuen Testament aus Talmud und Midrash*, vol. III, 1926, p. 362, commentary to I Corinthians, 6, 1) reproducing all, attributing it to different sages, the same rule based on same homiletic exegesis of a biblical passage:

a) Babylonian Talmud, Ghittin, f. 88b: "R. Tarfon [y. 70–130, Bacher, *Die Agadá der Tannaiten*, vol. I, 2nd ed., Strasbourg, 1890, pp. 342–352] said: "Wherever you find non-Jewish courts, *even if their rulings are equal to those of the Jews* [i.e., pronounced according to Jewish law], you must not turn to them, as it is written, "These are the laws that you shall put before them" [Exodus, 21, 1], them [the Jews] and not unto the Gentiles [non-Jews]."

b) Midrash Tanhumà [9th century rabbinical commentary on the Pentateuch], S. Buber ed., Wilna, 1885, vol. II, p. 81, mishpatim, f. 93 a: the same text attributed to R. Shim'on [bar Jochai, y. 130–160, Strack, *Einleitung in das Talmud*, p. 93].

c) Idem, Mishpatim f. 91a: "On what basis it is forbidden to the Jews who have a dispute between them, to call upon non-Jews, to be judged, *even if they know that they will judge the dispute according to Jewish law*? The scriptures [Ex. 21, 1] teach: "These are the laws that you shall put before them"; "them," the Jews, but not unto the Gentiles; because the person who leaves the judges of Israel and runs to the Gentiles denies God and denies the Torah. ... God spoke to the Jews: If you have a court case and don't go before the courts of

If they had not adhered to this principle and had judged according to Roman laws, they would have committed – and may have done so[314] – a grave error in terms of legal logic.[315]

---

the Gentiles, then I will [re]build the Sanctuary and with it the Sanhedrin will start working again, as it is written [Isaiah, 1, 26]: "I will reinstate your judges as in the past."

d) Mechiltà [rabbinical commentary to Exodus; for editions and translations, see Juster, I, p. 21] f. 81b, treatise of Nezikin, section. 1 (available as a trans. into Latin, in part erroneous, in Ugolini's *Thesaurus Antiquitatum Sacrarum*, Venice, 1744–69, t. 14, p. 432): "Rabbi Eliezer ben 'Azariah [Palestinian scholar who teaches between 90 and 100, Bacher, op. cit., I, 219–240] says: Behold, *when the Gentiles judge according to the Jewish laws*, are their rulings to be considered valid? The text [Exodus, 21, 1] refers to this: "These are the laws that you shall put before them" [which is to be understood]: You will judge their disputes, but they shall not judge yours. [Therefore, these sentences are invalid]. Hence, they said [Mishnah, Ghittin, 9, 8]: A cause of divorce from husband to wife according to a sentence by a Jewish court is valid, whereas by a pagan court is invalid; but if the Gentiles beat him [the husband] and say: do what the Jews [i.e., the Jewish court ruling] tell you to do, then the ruling is valid.

Utilizing the first part of this text of the Mechiltà, Juster, II, p. 95, no. 3, rightly draws the confirmation that the Jewish law in Palestine continued after 70 CE, the attestation that this jurisdiction was exercised concurrently with the Roman one, and the proof that in their rulings the Romans applied the Jewish laws. However, in the eyes of the Jews, the exercise of their jurisdiction was not seen as legitimate. But the second part of the text should also be considered, which quotes a passage of the Mishnah, reported with minor and non-substantial variations, confirming in a particular case the rule enunciated before in general. Since according to Jewish law, a divorce could not be pronounced by a sentence of a court of law, but only by virtue of a release given by the husband to the wife (Deut. 22, 1–4 and, accordingly, Bab. Talmud, Eruvin, f-15b), the wife could go to court, which after examining the cause, ruled, if necessary, to force the husband to give the said release. Once the executive power moved into the hands of the Roman rulers, they were the ones who, with the use of force, were imposing on the husband to execute the ruling of the Jewish court: and the Mishnah finds this legitimate. But having the jurisdictional duality established itself in Palestine after 70 CE, and judging the Jewish civil courts and the Roman ones concurrently, it could happen that in order to get the sentence against her husband the wife would prefer to go to Roman courts, which judged according to Jewish law and possibly condemned the husband to give the release, coercing him, if he would not obey, by means of force. The cited text shows that in the eyes of Jews, while the activity of the Roman executive power, that became the instrument of the will expressed by the rabbinical jurisdiction, appeared legitimate, the judicial activity of the Roman court was conversely regarded as illegitimate, even though the decision was rendered in accordance with Jewish civil law. Since the texts recalled here belong to a time prior to 212, it appears natural that as *peregrini* the Jews live according to their own law, and according to it they are judged both in their own courts and in the Roman ones; but as we will see immediately, things do not change even after 212, i.e., even after the general attainment of Roman citizenship. See further on, footnote no. 324.

314 Indeed, from the guidelines mentioned in the previous note, it seems that the criterion followed by the Roman courts was not constant and that they sometimes applied the Jewish law, and other times – the Roman law.

315 On the same question, which came up in practice throughout the Middle Ages and the modern age until 1800, compare the extremely precise observations of an 18th century

These considerations now enable seeing the meaning and scope of the law of February 3, 398 (l. 10 C. Th. 2.1) more clearly. It states that for legal disputes the Jews, "romano communi jure viventes" must go to court only according to the Roman jurisdiction: except for religious matters, the special Jewish jurisdiction is canceled and turned into a simple arbitration, for the formation of which the consent of the parties is required. Clearly, the special jurisdiction is suppressed here to get rid of the special personal statute. From now on, this is the sense of the law; the Jews shall live in Roman law and bring their disputes

---

Alsatian jurist: J. F. Fischer, *Commentatio de statu et jurisdictione Judeorum secundum leges romanas, germanicas, alsaticas*, Argentorati, 1763, p. 109: "Accidit saepe ut Judaeus adversarium suum coram judice christiano persequi malit, in causis praecipue ubi leges nostrae a moribus judaicis longissime abeuntes magis ipsi favere videntur. Ast recte agunt illi judices, qui causas tales, non secus ac rabbinus fecisset, ad normam consuetudinum judaicarum decidunt. Harum enim usum genti repetitis vicibus confirmaverunt Reges nostri: summa autem iniquitas esset, Judaeum eundem mox christiana lege, mox iterum judaica vivere, prout vel illam vel hanc suis commodis aptiorem animadvertit; neque quicquam amplius inter Judaeos certum foret ac stabile, si in causis cotidie obvenientibus aliud in foro rabbini, aliud in foro christiani judicis justum haberetur. Atque in hanc sententiam Curiam Supremam, quae Metis est, et plura tribunalia primae instantiae in Alsatia nostra decidisse novimus." Similarly, J. Chr. Dohm, *Ueber die bürgerliche Verbesserung der Juden*, 1783 (work of political nature, which calls for the complete emancipation of the Jews) so expresses himself (Italian translation titled *Riforma politica degli ebrei*, Mantua, 1807, pp. 116–118): Jews regard as constantly indisputable divine precepts not only the laws written by Moses, which concern not only Palestine and the religious and civil constitution of early times, but also the laws that have been preserved by oral tradition. In addition, this nation has attached a legal authority to many explanations and comments to these laws, made by renowned Jewish scholars. If we want to grant this nation the full enjoyment of human rights, it will be necessary to let it live and be judged according to its own laws. Then the Jews will not be more separated from the other citizens of the state than what a town or a community may be, that has the privilege to govern itself according to its own statutes. Moreover, experience in the early days of the Roman Empire as well as in certain modern states, has revealed that the *Autonomy* granted to the Jews does not cause any disgusting or uncomfortable consequence. And although, according to these laws, it is not necessary that the distribution of justice be placed in the hands of the judges of this Nation, there is nevertheless no doubt that they would handle it more willingly. It would help avoid the serious drawbacks that would turn up, should Christians judges exercise the Jewish legislation with which they are unfamiliar, which is very complicated and requires a deep knowledge of the Hebrew language and rabbinical matters. In the particular disputes of the Jews, it therefore seems more appropriate to let their own judges examine them, and let them rule in the court of first instance with the faculty, if they want, to bring their grievances before ordinary Christian judges. *But it is natural that these judges, as well as those of the Supreme courts to whom they could appeal the decision of the Jewish judge, would pass their sentences according to no other law than that of the Jews, since if they would rule in conformity with the ordinary jurisprudence, a huge mess would infallibly follow and the plaintiff would always have the unfair advantage of being able to bring his grievances before that court from which he would hope for the most favorable ruling*. Cf. further on all what is explained concerning the intermediate period.

before the Roman court that shall judge according to this law; by mutual agreement, they may, however, choose the patriarchs[316] or any other Jew as arbitrators and request from them to resolve a possible dispute according to Jewish norms: however, the State will ignore this law and will acknowledge its application by the arbitrators only within the limits allowed in general for the derogation from Roman norms, following the will of private individuals.

Therefore, it is for the will to completely suppress the Jewish civil law that the Roman emperors took away from the Jews the special jurisdiction they had always enjoyed up to 398. Unsurprisingly, it corresponds with the trend toward a judicial unification of the empire, based on Christian principles to which the emperors growingly aimed after the victory of the Catholic Church.

A proof of this tendency was already demonstrated with the suppression of the rules of Jewish marriage, especially polygamy, in 393.[317]

Therefore, it is inevitable that the Jews enjoyed judicial autonomy until a specific time: and if this is so, they must have also enjoyed their particular personal statute.

But how could this be harmonized with the sources, researched by Juster, demonstrating the *in toto* submission of the Jews to Roman law?

In my opinion, the enigma can be resolved if we make an appropriate topographical distinction between East and West instead of considering laws and testimonies from the sources as applying to the whole empire.

316 Given that the law speaks of "patriarchas" in plural, it evidently does not refer to the supreme patriarch, who is one and resides in Palestine, but to the lesser patriarchs, Jewish leaders in each province. This quality of lesser Patriarchs is clarified by Juster I, pp. 402–405 who identifies them with the "primates." Already before, Gotofredo, *Commentaria in C. Theod.*, ad 1. 2 C. Th. 16, 8, vol. VI, p. 220 had called them "regionarios, qui scilicet uni alicui regioni seu Provinciae parti praeerant," but identified them as the *patres synagogae*. In the text of Justinian law, these patriarchs are no longer mentioned, which suggests that none exists akin to the supreme patriarch.

317 According to a hypothesis – probably destined to remain as such – by Israel Oestersetzer, *La Collatio legum mosaicarum et romanarum*, in *Révue des Etudes Juives*, 1934, pp. 93–96, the compilation of the Collatio would have to be linked to the provision of 398 and would represent an attempt by the Jewish side to demonstrate the perfect conformity between Jewish norms and Roman norms in order to avoid the suppression of the Jewish law by the government. The Jewishness of the author of the Collatio was supported with many arguments by Volterra, *Collatio*, etc. in *Memorie della R. Accademia dei Lincei*, Class of Moral Sciences, Rome, 1930.

First of all, it should be noted that since the law of 398 suppressing Jewish jurisdiction is addressed to a praetorian prefect of the East,[318] it must be considered as enacted only for the eastern regions of the Empire.[319]

Upon careful examination, we see that the other sources attesting to the existence of the Jewish civil jurisdiction refer solely to Eastern countries.

As for Palestine, the testimonies from which evidence can be drawn of the uninterrupted persistence of that jurisdiction until the repealing law of 398 are plentiful and reliable.[320] As for the diaspora, in the pre-70 era, the Jewish court was only mentioned in Alexandria and Sardis and in the 4th century in Antioch.[321] Therefore, I would not feel confident to generalize, as Juster does,

---

318 Eutichiano. On him, see Bartolomeo Borghesi, *Oeuvres*, t. 10, *Les préfets du prétoire*, Paris, 1897, pp. 279–297.

319 The thesis that, save expressed declaration, the imperial constitutions have no general strength but were rather limited to the province or provinces for which they have been issued, was advanced by Cuq. He also theorized that in the absence of any declared specification, such a limit is determined by the recipients of these constitutions, *Les préfets du prétoire régionaux*, in *Mélanges Boissier*, 1893, pp. 147 et seqq., and *De l'utilité des schede de Borghesi sur les préfets du prétoire pour l'histoire de la législation du Bas Empire* in *Atti del congresso internazionale di scienze storiche*, Rome, 1904, vol. IX, pp. 339–346, and by Gilson, *L'étude du droit romain comparé aux autres droits de l'antiquité*, Paris, 1899, pp. 120 et seqq., cf. pp. 257–296. Rejected without precise arguments by Juster, I, p. 236 no. 1, the thesis has now been forcefully resumed byVolterra in his volume *Diritto romano e diritti orientali*, Bologna 1937, pp. 275–296, and more recently – despite the opposing views of Orestano, *Il potere normativo degli imperatori e le costituzioni imperiali*, Rome, 1937 and Idem, *Gli editti imperiali. Contributo alla teoria della loro validità ed efficacia nel diritto romano classico*, in *Bull. Ist. di Dir. Romano*, N. S. III, 1937, pp. 219 et seqq. – in another work specifically devoted to the topic: Volterra, *L'efficacia delle costituzioni imperiali emanate per le provincie e l'istituto dell'expositio*, in *Studi in onore di E. Besta*, vol. I, Milan s. a. [1939], pp. 449–477.

320 On them, see Juster, II, pp. 95–106, who on firm documentary foundations refutes the opposite thesis by Chajes, *Les juges juifs en Palestine de l'an 70 à l'an 500*, in *Révue des Etudes juives*, 39, 1899, pp. 39–52 and by Graetz, *Geschichte der Juden*, vol. IV, 2nd ed., footnote 20 of page 471. The fact that third century scholars repeat the teaching of the Mishnah about the case (cited above, footnote no. 313) of concurrence of Jewish and Roman jurisdiction in cases of divorce (see further on, footnote no. 324) would be enough on its own to attest to the unchanged persisting of the Jewish jurisdiction.

321 See the above-cited texts in footnotes no. 307–308. The sense of Bardesane passage, *Liber legum regionum*, § 44, varies depending on the translators and it is not well understood whether it alludes to the fact that on Saturday Jews do not judge or to the privilege obtained not to appear in court that day. See the discussion on the various versions in Juster, II, p. 112, no. 4. As for the text that mentions the Court of Rome (Babylonian Talmud, Sanhedrin, f.. 32 b) it is as follows: "Insegnano i nostri Maestri: dicendo la Torà [Deut. 16, 21]: Giustizia, giustizia persegui, vuol dire: Va presso un buon tribunale, dietro R. Eliezer a Lidda, Jochanan ben Zaccai a Berur Hail, R. Jehoshua' a Peki'in, Gamliel a Javnè, 'Akivà a Benè Berak, R. Mattia [ben Heresh] a Roma, Haninà a Sicnin, Josè a Zeffori,

chronologically and topographically, stating that Jews throughout the diaspora enjoyed the jurisdictional privilege up to 398. Because, as I said before, where a special jurisdiction exists, the special personal statute also had to be there. Such a statute had to be drawn up by some academy, reported in some text, and applied by Jewish and Roman courts.

As for Palestine, we particularly know the activity of the Jewish legal academies that set the law giving rise to the Mishnah and then, in the subsequent development, to the Gemara of Jerusalem. We can also note – something of importance and gone hitherto undetected – that these academies' coming to an end and the closure of the Palestinian Talmudic canon takes place just at the end of the IV century,[322] coinciding with the enactment of the law of 398, which repealed Jewish jurisdiction and its related personal statute.[323]

Jehudà ben Betera a Nisibi, Josua a Pumbedita, Rabbenu Hakkadosh a Beth Shearim, il Gran Sinedrio nella sala delle pietre tagliate." From the text it is not possible to determine whether each of these authorities exercised a real jurisdiction recognized by the State in civil matters or had, instead, the right to judge only as an arbitrator or limitedly to ritual matters: the fact that the Grand Sanhedrin undoubtedly had jurisdictional competence does not allow to draw inferences about the above-listed scholars who belong to different eras and to different places. Mattia ben Heresh is a scholar native of Judea who settled in Rome at the beginning of the 2nd century CE, teaching the traditional Jewish disciplines and acquiring wide fame for himself. He may also have quite certainly arbitrated civil cases among Roman Jews: but proclaiming him, on the basis of the aforementioned passage, the founder of a civil court, as the two historians of the Jewish community of Rome (Berliner, *Geschichte der Juden in Rom*, 1893, vol. I, p. 96 and Vogelstein and Rieger, *Geschichte der Juden in Rom*, 1896, vol. I, p. 111) and Juster, II, p. 113, no. 1, do is a haphazard and arbitrary statement.

322 For the date, see Strack, *Einleitung in das Talmud*, IV ed., Leipzig 1908, p. 63.

323 The closure of Palestinian Talmudic canon reflects the end of the elaboration activities of the Jewish law by the sages of the Academies of that country. It is evident that such an elaboration is a practical necessity that lasts as long as the same law is applied in the Rabbinic and State courts; as soon as the State abolishes that law (and therefore also the special jurisdiction) to replace it with the Roman law, the necessity ceases for its elaboration by the rabbinical Academies: which brings about the closure of the canon. The closure of the Babylonian Talmudic canon followed as well a provision, entirely analogous to the Roman one, by which in Persia the Jewish personal statute and the rabbinical jurisdiction were abolished. This was pointed out already by Shemuel David Luzzatto, in the first part of his Hebrew introduction to the *Formulario di orazioni di rito italiano*, Leghorn, Belforte, 1856: "The text of the prayers and blessings – he writes – remained oral until after the closure of the Talmud, i.e., until a king of the Persians came about who shut down the academies and removed from Israel the power of legislature and decreed that the Jews submit to the Persian courts. Then the sages [no longer creators of judicial tradition nor judges] became disciples [of the more ancient sages]; and even though Jewish scholars secretly judged Jewish causes, they had to be called "disciples of the sages" [talmudè hahamim instead of hahamim]. Then the Talmud was closed and the

Furthermore, with regard to Palestine, we do have clear evidence of the application to the Jews of their national personal statute by both Jewish and Roman courts after 212.[324]

But what evidence do we have for the diaspora?

As for Alexandria, there were some who wanted to see in the treatises of Philo, in particular in *De specialibus legibus*, nothing more than a collection of the legal practice of the Jewish court in that city:[325] which appears very

---

legal ruling ended: namely, the Jews had no longer authority to judge and decide. These scholars [without jurisdictional power] were called Saborei, i.e., students. They closed the Talmud, which occurred in the year 500 CE." This refers to the persecution that started at the time of King Peroz, who in the year 474 closed the academies and took vexatious measures against the Jews in order to force them to convert to Parseeism. This brought about the end of the Jewish doctrinal activity and induced the surviving Jewish sages to draft the Talmudic canon in writing. See S. Funk, *Die Juden in Babylonien*, vol. II, Berlin, 1908, p. 118; S. Ochser, in *Jüdisches Lexikon*, entry Babylonien and S. Assaf, ibidem, entry Gelehrtschulen in Babylonien.

324 The Ghittin 9, 9 Palestinian Gemara in fact reproduces the already (above, footnote no. 313) examined Mishnah rules on divorce, enunciated by sages of the late third century: "R. Jirmija [a Babylonian sage of the late third century, who also lived in Palestine, Bacher, *Die Agadà der Palestinensischen Amoräer*, vol. III, pp. 582 et seqq.] says on behalf of Rav [Babylonian sage]: the divorce given by a Jew upon compulsion by the Gentiles [i.e., according to the ruling of a court of Gentiles] is nil. This [i.e., the imposition] happens following the wife's appeal in the case that [the husband] says: I will not give alimony. R. Hijà [a Palestinian sage of the late third century, Bacher, op. cit., vol. III, pp. 174–201]: But if the Gentiles have imposed according to the Jewish imposition [i.e., they just enforced the ruling issued by the Jewish court] the sentence is valid even (?) if the husband says: I will not give alimony. Says R. Josè [a Palestinian sage who teaches between 130 and 160, Bacher, *Die Agadà der Tannaiten*, vol. II, pp. 150–190]: It is the Mishnah that says that expressly: the Gentiles beat him and say to him: do what Israel tells you to do. R. Hijà says: he who refuses to give alimony is forced to give divorce." Thus also at the end of the third century the two jurisdictions were concurrent, the Roman court examined the cause according to the Jewish law, and the Jews continued to consider unlawful the ruling of that court whereas considered legitimate the coercive action of the government enforcing a sentence issued by the Jewish court. The translation and interpretation that Juster (II, p. 57, no. 5) gives of these texts do not seem to me entirely accurate.

325 According to Ritter, *Philo und die Halachà*, Leipzig, 1879, p. VIII and p. 92, the Philonian interpretations of the Jewish law would reflect the practice of the Jewish court of Alexandria. Although rejected by Juster, I, p.5, this argument is largely taken up and developed by Goodenough, *The jurisprudence of the Jewish Court in Egypt: legal administration by the Jews under the early Roman Empire as described by Philo Judaeus*, New Haven, 1929, p. 26: "I disagree with Juster altogether and think that in the *De specialibus legibus* Philo is thinking throughout of the law used in the Jewish courts in Alexandria." Cf., however, the broad review by Heinemann, *Jüdisch-hellenistische Gerichtshöfe in Alexandrien*, in *Monatsschrift für Geschichte und Wissenschaft des Judentums*, vol. 74, 1930, pp. 363–369.

likely but does not offer the certainty that that law and that court have continued to exist until the end of the 4th century.[326]

Of a Jewish personal statute in Asia Minor, to which the above-mentioned Sardi court would seem to have referred, we have no trace: it must therefore have been an exceptional privilege of short duration; or, perhaps, a concession made to Jews who remained Palestinian citizens.

Some more certain data, on the other hand, are offered by the sources with regard to Syria: The Jewish court of Antioch is named both in the Talmud and in a Christian text;[327] and if there is a court, there must also be the recognition of the Jewish civil law. In addition, apparently, the Talmud mentions as well the state courts of Syria, noting their lack of familiarity with Jewish law: that would seem to confirm the use by such courts of Jewish law for the resolution of disputes between Jews; a far from perfect use since they had to deal with rules different from the usual standards.[328]

---

326 Also, the Talmudic sources, however, provide us with details regarding the judicial rules in use in Alexandria: So, in Babylonian Talmud, Bavà Mezi'à, f. 104a, it is said that in Alexandria marriage contracts were drafted at the time of the engagement, which agrees with what Philo says, *De specialibus legibus*, 3, 12, Juster, II, p. 42, no. 4. The Jerusalem Talmud, jebamot, 15, 3, reports that such contracts in Alexandria were drafted in Greek (Juster, II, p. 43, no. 2). These are undoubted proofs of the recognition of Jewish personal statute in Egypt too.

327 Jerusalem Talmud, Sanhedrin, 3, 2: Saint John Chrysostom, *Adversus Judaeos*, 1, 3 (*Patrologia Graeca*, 48, 848), above cited texts nos. 307–308.

328 In Babylonian Talmud Sanhedrin, 23a, it is said that the right to refuse to be judged by the court of his own city, choosing another court, only exists for the creditors, not the debtors. The latter have that right too, however, "when it comes to 'Arkaot she be-Suria (courts of Syria) but not when it comes to courts practical [of Jewish law]." Jerusalem Talmud, Sanhedrin, 3, 2 is similarly in agreement. In rabbinical sources, the word 'Arkaot, plural of 'Arkàa (= ἀρχή) always designates the non-Jewish courts: these are thus the ones that apply, albeit in a way that is not satisfactory, the Jewish law. This actually makes sense, since if there were in Syria real rabbinical courts judging according to Jewish law, the same law had to be enforced by the state courts, where a lawsuit between Jews was brought to their knowledge. I do not understand then why Schwab in his French translation of the Jerusalem Talmud, t. 10th, p. 254 renders the expression "'arkaot shebe-Suria" with "vulgaire, ἀρχεῖον, de Syrie." From this text, in *Jesodè ha-mishpat ha-ivri*, [The foundations of Jewish law], Berlin, 1923 et seqq., vol. IV, p. 27, Gulak deduces the following points: 1) In Palestine, in Talmudic times, in addition to Jewish courts, there are Roman courts called "'arkaot shebe-Suria" because operating under the jurisdiction of the Roman Governor residing in Syria; 2) These courts judge Jews according to Roman law; 3) In such courts Jewish judges are present who are called laymen because they are not experts in Torah law; 4) Although the expression "'arkaot" usually indicates real courts, it might also signify "courts of arbitrations established under the laws of Syria and Rome." I really do not understand the meaning of these deductions, and I observe: 1) "'arkaot shebe-Suria" can only mean: [State] courts located in Syria. Nothing to do thus with the Palestinian

Based on these observations, we can conclude: that in the West, Jews throughout the Roman period had neither a particular personal statute, nor jurisdictional autonomy, and as citizens, they were subjected to the provisions of the local law. We can also conclude that in some eastern regions of the empire, for sure in Palestine and probably in the neighboring provinces of Syria and Egypt,[329] even though enjoying the right to local and Roman citizenship, up to 398 the Jews, maintained their personal ethnic-religious statute and had their own courts that applied such statute concurrently with the State jurisdiction.

The existence of the Jewish jurisdiction until 398, that Juster sees extended to all the diaspora, needs to be somewhat restricted to the above-mentioned eastern provinces; whereas for those countries, the *de jure* recognition by the Roman government of the Jewish personal statute, necessarily connected to personal jurisdiction even after the year 212, should be acknowledged. According to the institutes, such recognition, that Juster erroneously does not admit, or admits partially or considers as resulting from an actual tolerance, concerning Palestine, also fits, in general, to the Roman system of preservation of local rights even after the granting citizenship to all *peregrini*.

As recently been made clear, granting Roman citizenship, both before and after Caracalla's constitution, did not include changes in the personal statute of individuals or groups who received it. This new citizenship was added to the original one without the latter being canceled, and therefore the personal statute continued to be governed by local rules and not by Roman rules. By extending Roman citizenship to all, the *Constitutio Antoniniana* simply generalized this situation: with the result that the provincials, although having become Roman citizens, continued to be at the same time citizens of their *civitates* and act in accordance with those laws.

---

courts. 2) As stated by the text and confirmed by logic, sentences are issued according to Jewish law, not to the Roman one, even though knowledge of Jewish law is not deep. 3) There is not the slightest element to affirm that the Roman court makes use of Jewish judges. Untenable is therefore also the affirmation by D. M. Shohet, *The Jewish court in the middle ages*, New York, 1931, p. 101; relying on Gulak's interpretation, he considers the text in question as a proof of the validity, in accordance with the Jewish doctrine, of the ruling pronounced by the mixed courts, of Jews and non-Jews. 4) "'arkaot" never designates Jewish courts, much less so then the simple arbitrations.

329 This situation of provinces bordering the Jewish State explains quite clearly the local Jews' stronger attachment to the Mosaic-rabbinic rules of law and the tendency – to which the authorities complied – to formal recognition of them, limitedly of course to the internal relations of civil character.

When unified citizenship had been established, Caracalla's provision did not intend to either abolish or diminish the autonomy of political groups brought together under the empire: their political structure remained unchanged, and so did their legislative autonomy.[330]

In light of this concept, the circumstance of the persistence of local rights in the various provinces after the edict of Caracalla, hitherto poorly explained, is thus clarified.

Starting from the idea of an absolute connection between the quality of Roman citizens and the subordination to Roman private law, from Voigt[331] to Mitteis[332] throughout Taubenschlag,[333] the scholars who noted the survival of provincial rights even after 212, and mainly based on papyrological sources sought to determine its borders, perceived this survival as the result of an ongoing struggle between the *Volksrechte* and the *Reichsrecht*, tending to impose itself everywhere.[334]

On the other hand, Schönbauer's considerations allow for an understanding that keeping the rules of the various subjected peoples, even after citizenship had been granted to all members of the Roman world, is part of the imperial political system and should not be perceived as something contrary to

330 Schönbauer, *Reichsrecht gegen Volksrecht ? Studien* cit., in *Zeitschrift der Savigny Stiftung*, 1931, pp. 314 et seqq., 330, 333–335; Schönbauer, *Reichsrecht, Volksrecht und Provincialrecht, Studien über die Bedeutung der Constitutio Antoniniana für die römische Rechtsgeschichte*, in *Zeitschrift*, cit., 1937, pp. 309 et seqq.

331 Moritz Voigt, *Das jus naturale aequum et bonum und das jus gentium der Römer*, vol. II, part II, 1856, pp. 786–827. The problem is already accurately tackled by Spanheim who discusses it largely in his *Orbis romanus, seu ad Constitutionem Antonini imperatoris, de qua Ulpianus leg. XVII Dig. de statu hominum, exercitationes duae*, in Johann Georg Graevius' *Thesaurus antiquitatum romanarum*, T. XI, Venice, 1735, 2nd exerc., ch. XI–XVIII, pp. 101–151. As for the persistence of national rights after 212, see pp. 131 et seqq. Voigt resumes the question, distinguishing (pp. 790–809) nine cases "in denen eine Rechtsverschiedenheit und beziehentlich ein Fortbestand des nationalen Rechtes auch nach der *lex antoniniana* in dem römischen Rechte fortfindet," and examining (pp. 816–827) their surviving in the various provinces of the empire. Priora's article *Dei rapporti fra cittadinanza e diritto privato secondo la legislazione romana*, Pisa, 1883 and Degenkolb's article *Rechtseinheit und Rechtsnationalität in altrömischen Reich*, Tubingen, 1884, are not important.

332 Lüdwig Mitteis, *Reichsrecht und Volksrecht in den östlichen Provinzen des römischen Kaiserreiches*, Leipzig, 1891.

333 Taubenschlag, *Le droit local dans les constitutions prediocletianiennes*, in *Mélanges Cornil*, II, pp. 499 et seqq. and many other important works by him that can be found listed in Volterra's *Diritto romano e diritti orientali* cit., p. 79, no. 1.

334 Voigt, op. cit., p. 809: after the *lex antoniniana* the *de jure* abolition of any national right is in no doubt: "das national-peregrine Recht der einzelnen Pertinenzen des Reiches seinem Untergang erfährt und höchstens noch als fremder Rechtsstoff in einem römischen *jus speciale* fortlebt." Similarly Mitteis, op. cit., p. 110 et seqq.; cf. Albertario, *Introduzione allo studio del diritto romano giustinianeo*, 1935, p. 96.

the will of the rulers:[335] Roman law continues to apply only for metropolitan citizens: for the provincial citizens, as before, the rights of their respective *civitates* apply instead.[336] Of course, Rome can impose all sorts of changes in these provincial rights with specific rules, with general provisions throughout the empire, or contingencies issued for all provinces, or a single province, by the central government or by the head of the province itself, it can limit their sphere of validity. However, within those limits imperatively established by Rome, the provincial rights *de jure* also exist after 212[337] and will not be

335 Schönbauer, op. cit., 1937, p. 345: "Die Sondernormen der πολιτεύματα hatten sich nicht gegen den Willen der römischen Kaiser und des römischen rechts durchgesetzt, sondern wurden in der Regel anerkannt oder wenigstens geduldet." The *de jure* prevalence of the provincial *civitates* law over Roman law is fully confirmed in two passages of the sources (D. 50, 1, 21, 7 and C. 11, 32, 1) where the general validity of the decreed rules is demanded only "si civitas nullam propriam legem habet" (ibid., p. 336). Schönbauer, op. cit. 1931, pp. 277–299, rightly observes that had Caracalla with his edict really meant to violently suppress all local rights, he would have operated a senseless and brutal reform which would have brought many hostilities upon himself: whereas all judicial and literary sources attest that the constitution on citizenship was appreciated as a great benefit by all the subjects and not suffered as an oppressive measure.

336 Schönbauer, op. cit. 1931, pp. 330 et seqq., and 1937, p. 336. Against this thesis, accepted by Wenger, *Nationales, griechisches, und römisches Recht in Aegypten*, in *Atti del IV Congresso Internazionale di Papirologia*, Florence, 1935, pp. 176–179 (cf. also *Archiv für Papirusforschung*, XII, 1936, p. 156) and by Wilhelm, in *American Journal of Archeology*, vol. 38, 1934, pp. 178 et seqq., stands Weiss, *Grundzügen des römischen Rechtsgeschichte*, Reichemberg, 1936, p. 105, who wrongly considers the condition of Roman citizens living under a private law, different from Roman law, unthinkable. Conversely, De Visscher, *La condition juridique des nouveaux citoyens d'Orient*, in *Comptes rendus de l'academie des inscriptions et belles lettres*, Paris, January–February 1938, pp. 24–29, notes how Schönbauer's thesis that the provincials-made-citizens have continued to live under their national laws, found a good confirmation in an edict of Octavian discovered in the necropolis of Rhosos. With this edict (published by Roussel, in *Syria*, 1934, pp. 38 et seqq. and re-published by De Visscher, ibid.), to reward a Syrian navarch, Seleucus of Rhosos, for services rendered, Octavian grants Roman citizenship to him, his family and his descendants, with the right to continue to live ἐν οἰκῶι τοῖς ἰδίοις νόμοις. In all likelihood there isn't here an exceptional case but the usual formula of granting citizenship, in which the right to continue to live as before according to his national law is expressly granted to the holder. *Addendum*: Only after the final drafting of this work of mine did I receive the book by G. I. Luzzatto, *Epigrafia giuridica greca e romana*, Milan, 1942, in which in the light of many epigraphic sources, (part I, chap. I, pp. 30–44 and part II, chap. III, pp. 301–321), the issues of dual citizenship and *de jure* persistence of the provincial rights after the year 212 are extensively reviewed. The author (p. 306) is inclined to credit to Schönbauer's thesis "much more than a simple basis of truth," but as far as the edict of Rhosos is concerned in particular, he does not believe that any support for the claim in question can be drawn from it, as the right to live according to their own laws seems to him quite an exceptional concession granted *ad personam* rather that an act of confirmation of the general rule.

337 Schönbauer, op. cit. 1937, pp. 349–353. The relationship between the different kinds of legal systems from which the provincials are governed can be settled as follows: 1) State norms explicitly declared valid throughout the empire (Reichsrecht): they prevail over

abolished until later, at different times, with different provisions from province to province.[338]

Now, suppose we keep in mind that Rome permitted the use of one's own law to autonomous *civitates* (*liberae* and *foederatae*), non-autonomous ones, and territories ruled by kings, princes and clerics,[339] we must infer that Palestine was not excluded from the general principle and that Jewish law must have been in force, *de jure*, as national law, both after 70 and, following the theory above, after 212.[340] The limits of its validity will sometimes be modified

---

any other norm; 2) State norms intended to have effect in all provinces (gemeines Provinzialrecht) or in one province (partikuläres Provinzialrecht, e.g., the Gnomon of the Idios Logos): they prevail over the rights of the political communities (πολιτεύματα and σῶματα); 3) Rights of the political communities (Volksrechte). "Die Gerichtsbarkeit des Statthalter [the head of the Province] und ihr Verfahren is es zusammen mit dem Amtsrecht, das weitens mehr als das Reichsrecht die Bedeutung des Volksrechtes immes stärker aushölt. Die Constitutio Antoniniana brachte mit dieser Entwicklung nicht zu brechen. Die volksrechtlichen Sondernormen blieben durch die Cost. Ant. unangestaltet, aber reichsreichtlichen Sätze und Sätze des Amtrechtes des Statthalter engen das Gebiet der Volksrechte so sehr ein, dass sie besonders nach der Neuordnung von Diokletian den Charakter von lokalen privilegien annahmen" (Schönbauer, op. cit. 1937, p. 353). Also, Volterra, *Diritto romano e diritti orientali*, cit., pp. 280 and 288 no. 2, notes that even after the year 212, the imperial constitutions were valid throughout the empire only when they contained a specific claim of generality; and sometimes they explicitly claimed to yield to the local norm. I would like to point out that this state of affairs is not much different from what shall occur in the late Middle Ages, with the rise anew of the Roman Empire and the Justinian legislation on the one hand, and the development on the other hand of genuine autonomy of the *civitates*, ideally reunited in the *orbis romanus*: even then all members of these *civitates* will be Roman citizens and at the same time citizens of the individual autonomous political entities and will live according to the law of the latter, before which the Roman-Canon Law will only have a subsidiary character. There will be, however, this difference: that while in the ancient Roman Empire, as the central power kept the real political control, the autonomy of the *civitates* could be restricted and modified at will by it, in the Middle Ages the *civitates* will end up becoming completely autonomous, therefore backing out of any imposition of the emperor's authority, reduced to a pale and impotent ideal simulacrum.

338 The ways and times of abolishing are not mentioned by Schönbauer. Volterra, *Diritto romano* cit., pp. 294, 303–305, states that only with Diocletian an attempt begins to unify the empire also in the field of private law. The work stops with the death of this emperor and is later resumed by Theodosius II. It is interesting to note for example that the Armenian inheritance law continues its existence until the time of Justinian who decreed its abolition with two constitutions (edict 3) of 535 and 536 (Nov. 21). V. Güterbock, *Römisch-Armenien und die römischen Satrapien in 4–6-en Jahrhundert. Eine rechtsgeschichtliche Studie*, in *Festgabe der juristischen Fakultät zu Königsberg für J. Th. Schirmer*, Königsberg, 1900; Karst, *Grundriss der Geschichte des armenischen Rechts*, in *Zeitschrift für vergleichende Rechtswissenschaft*, XX, pp. 47–48.

339 Mommsen, *Droit public romain*, vol. VI, part II, pp. 284, 323 and ibid. no. 1, 361, 383–384 and ibid., no. 2 and 4.

340 Of course, the scholars earlier than Schönbauer hold a contrary opinion. For Voigt, op. cit., pp. 794–795 and 823–828, Jews have no jurisdiction, their law persists against the will of

by general[341] and special[342] norms, but it will be rescinded entirely only in 398.[343]

---

the State and is recognized only as a norm applicable in Jewish arbitration judgments: the constitution of 398 abolishes it "selbst als Norm compromissorischer Entscheidung." Such claims are each more absurd than the other, since the use of a law limited to arbitrators is not an actual law in force and cannot possibly be either in collision with the State law or repealed by coercion. Juster also states that after 212, the Jewish law both in Palestine and the diaspora was only partially tolerated and gradually suppressed (op. cit., II, pp. 33–34, 53, 65, 83, 88 no. 3). But Schönbauer (op. cit., 1931, pp. 335 and 1937 pp. 342–343), ignoring Juster and following Mommsen, *Gesammelte Schriften*, III, pp. 418–419, believes that after 70 the Palestinian Jews had become *dediticii*; consequently, he states, they did not enjoy any specific citizenship and therefore could not live by a particular law. "Durch die Constitutio Antoniniana werden sie alle Reichsbürger, erhalten aber keine Heimatsstaat, so dass sie auch weiterhin in derselben öffentlichrechtlichen Stellung wie die andere Bewohner des Reiches ohne Heimatsstaat bleiben." Consequently, from 212 it is the Roman law that is imposed upon them entirely, as evidenced by the two laws of 393 (C. J. 1, 9, 7) and of 398 (C. J. 1, 9, 8). No need to dwell on the inadequacy of a similar construction based entirely on a claim proven incorrect by Juster. In addition, the laws of 393 and 398 abolishing the Jewish matrimonial law and jurisdiction demonstrate the opposite of what Schönbauer claims, giving proof that earlier that law and that jurisdiction – within topographic limits that were just clarified – were admitted and recognized.

341 That is to say by the provisions imperatively declared as addressed "*omnibus* (or *omnibus civitatibus*) *qui sub imperio populi romani sunt*": e.g., the l. 2, C. 5, 5 forbidding polygamy, which is from 285. Hans Zucker, *Untersuchungen zur Organization der Juden von Babylonischen Exil bis zum Ende des Patriarchats* (dissertation, Berlin), Leipzig, 1936, pp. 183–184 remarks a Talmudic passage that reflects an aspect of the relations between local Jewish law and Roman norms. The passage is the following (Babylonian Talmud, Bavà Batrà, f. 58a; year ca. 200: "On the city's gate was written: Every judge who is indicted may no longer be judge. To the objection of R. Banaa that one may be accused falsely, they added: the leaders of the Jews say: every judge who has been indicted and sentenced to pay a sum may not longer be judge." The rule, modified as a result of the objection of the Jewish sage, according to Zucker, would be part of the *Edictum provinciale*, that in the East used to be put, engraved on tablets, at the gate of the city; and it would correspond to the following passage of Salvio Giuliano (lib. 36th of the *Digesti*) found in D. 5, 1, 75: "Si praetor jusserit eum a quo debitum petebatur adesse et ordine edictorum peracto pronuntiaverit absentem debere, non utique judex, qui de judicato cognoscit, debet de praetoris sententia cognoscere: alioquin lusoria erunt huiusmodi edicta et decreta praetorum." Frankly it seems to me that this fragment has nothing to do with the Talmudic rule, which, nevertheless, does not detract from the likelihood of the hypothesis about the Roman origin of the rule itself.

342 For example, l. 1 C. J. 11, 51, (50) to be placed between 384 and 388 (Juster, II, p. 79). With this law, the *colonatus aeternitatis*, unknown to the Jewish legislation, is introduced in Palestine. The special kind of colonatus in Jewish law is studied by L. Löw in *Graphische Requisiten und Erzeugnisse bei den Juden*, Leipzig, 1870–71, vol. II, pp. 92–94 [inaccessible, cited by Juster, ibid.].

343 In support of his argument that also in Palestine Jews were generally subjected to Roman law, after 212, Juster observes how in the Talmud itself there are institutes taken straight from Roman law, that retain their Greek and Latin names: in fact, certain Roman rules regarding testament (דיאתיקי=διαθήκη) can be found (Juster II, p. 88 no. 3), and the

Concerning the diaspora regions mentioned above, such recognition of the Jewish personal statute and special jurisdiction for Jews who were Roman citizens has a peculiar character. It appears as an exception to the general principles of Roman public law, made as a result of the religious nature of the Jewish law. Conversely, far from being an unusual thing, Palestine is included in the set of common principles followed by Rome in recognition of provincial laws. The highlighted connection between recognizing special Jewish jurisdiction and that of the special law, and the issue of topographic limits assigned to such recognition, can receive further clarification by a brief reference to the imperial measures relating to the judicial activities of the Christian bishops.[344]

validity of manumission for בנטוקטא (*vindicta*) and for טבלא (*tabulae*, in the meaning of testament) (Juster, II, pp. 83–84) is recognized. But these highly learned and interesting observations do not serve the purpose to which Juster aims: they only demonstrate the reception in Jewish law of some Roman institutions that are adopted along the national ones but without replacing them at all. This is not the abolition of Jewish law by the Roman law carried out imperatively by the government, but the spontaneous incorporation of some Roman elements in the theory and practice of the judicial Palestinian Jewish life.

344 On the bishop's jurisdiction in civil cases in the Roman age, the literature is considerably abundant. The specific studies of major importance are, in chronological order, the following: Le Gendre, *Episcopale judicium adversus calumnias Jacobi Gothofredi acerrime defensum, nec non ab omni falsa suspicione plenissime vindicatum*, Paris 1690, re-printed in Meermann, *Thesaurus juris civilis et canonici*, t. 3rd, 1752, pp. 333–368; A. D. Alteserra, *Ecclesiasticae jurisdictionis vindiciae*, Paris 1703; Hebenstreit, *Historia jurisdictionis ecclesiasticae ex legibus utriusque codicis illustrata*, Leipzig 1773–78; B. Schilling, *De origine jurisdictionis ecclesiasticae in causis civilibus*, Leipzig 1825; Fr. Aug. Jungk, *De originibus et progressu episcoporum judicii in causis civilibus laicorum usque ad Justinianum*, Berlin 1832; Siciliano-Villanueva, *Studi sulle vicende del foro ecclesiastico nelle cause dei laici*, in *Antologia Giuridica*, Palermo, 1896; Same author, in *Studi giuridici dedicati a F. Schupfer*, vol. II, 1898; Martroye, *S. Augustin et la compétence de la jurisdiction ecclesiastique au V siècle*, in *Mémoires de la Société des Antiquaires de France*, t. 70, Paris 1911; De Francisci, *Per la storia dell'episcopalis audientia fino alla Novella* XXXV (XXXIV) *di Valentiniano*, in *Annali della Facoltà di Giurisprudenza dell'Univ. di Perugia*, XXX, 1915, series 3rd, vol. XIII; Bell, *The episcopalis audientia in Byzantine Egypt*, in *Byzantion*, I, 1924, pp. 139–144; Vratislav Busek, *Cirkevni soutnictvi ve vecech civilnich v risi rimske v I–V stoleti po Kr.*, Bratislava 1925, with summary in French, pp. 77–82; A. Steinwenter, *Zur Lehre von der episcopalis audientia*, in *Byzantinische Zeitschrift*, XXX, 1929–1930, *Festgabe Heisemberg*, pp. 660–668; F. Lammeyer, *Die audientia episcopalis in Zivilsachen der Laien in römischen Kaiserrecht und in den Papyri*, in *Aegyptus*, XIII, 1933, pp. 193–202; G. Vismara, *Episcopalis audientia*, Milan, 1937; G. Masi, *L'udienza vescovile nelle cause laiche da Costantino ai Franchi*, in *Arch. Giur.*, vol. CXXII (II series, vol. II), files 1–2.

It is common knowledge that the Catholic Church, considering itself heir to the Jewish theocracy,[345] the new Israel, grows as a social entity based mainly on the Jewish one. So, likewise, it is upon the Jewish type that at least in the early period, the Christian community structure is modeled,[346] and by following the example of the Jews, Christians of the first centuries aspire to an autonomous civil jurisdiction that may remove the disputes among the faithful from the ruling of the pagan courts, as well as from a criminal jurisdiction for certain offenses related to spiritual matters.

It is out of concern, similar in all respects to what led Jewish leaders to urge their followers to submit to Jewish courts rather than to Roman courts, that St. Paul exhorts the Christians to refer their civil disputes to the judgment of a member of the Church.[347]

The exhortation, repeated by innumerable canonical texts,[348] produces a practice in the desired direction, and bishops often become the judges of causes between Christians, just as the Synagogue elders were the judges of causes between Jews.[349] Furthermore, like the Jews apply the

---

345 "Die Kirche ... war die Fortsetzung der jüdischen Theocratie, von der sie den Namen entlehnte, und als deren Nachfolgerin sich betrachtete." Wellhausen, *Israelitische und jüdische Geschichte*, 8th ed., 1921, Berlin and Leipzig, p. 370.

346 In this sense, against the widespread theory of the derivation of the Greek and Roman associations, see Loening, *Die Gemeindeverfassung des Urchristentums*, Leipzig, 1888; Juster, I, p. 418, no. 2 and La Piana, *La successione episcopale in Roma e gli albori del primato*, Rome, 1922, p. 29 and *Foreign groups in Rome during the first centuries of the empire*, in *The Harward theological Review*, year XX, 1927, pp. 183 et seqq. = *Ricerche religiose*, a. 2, 1926, pp. 485 et seqq.; a 3, 1927, p. 36b et seqq.; a 4, 1928, p. 193 et seqq. The recent observations to the contrary moved by Frey, *Corpus inscriptionum judaicarum*, Rome 1936, pp. CII–CXI, to Juster and La Piana do not seem justified on the basis of the erroneous assumption of the solely politico-national character of Jewish communities and purely religious one of the Christian communities: conversely, the universalisation of Judaism on the one hand and a clear willingness by the Church to totally supplant the Synagogue place the two types of communities absolutely on the same level: for the similarities between the structure of the Jewish communities and that of the primitive Christian communities cf. the old but still useful work of Vitringa, *De Synagoga vetere libri tres*, Franqueferae, 1696 and Leucopetrae 1726.

347 First Epistle to the Corinthians, 1, 6 et seqq.; to be compared with the texts cited above, footnote no. 313.

348 For examining these, see Vismara op. cit., pp. 7–21; 59–63. For the patristic texts, ibid., pp. 63–82.

349 That the bishops' judicial activity grew on the model of the Jewish patriarchal jurisdiction is highlighted by several of the scholars dealing with either jurisdiction. Cf., e.g., Lammeyer, op. cit., pp. 194–195; Steinwenter, op. cit., p. 661; Vismara, op. cit., pp. 4–6. (However, Vismara's assertion, pp. 5 and 16 no. 2 in the end, that "the jurisdiction of the Jewish patriarch was opted for only with the consent of the parties" is incorrect, as up to

Jewish civil law in their rulings, so the bishops apply the *lex christiana*, that is, a special private law[350] that molds itself as a rule upon the Jewish

the law of 398, such consent was not requested by the Roman legislation). Also, the procedure of the courts of bishops, at least at the beginning, carries a strong Jewish imprint (in this regard see primarily B. Wilanowski, *Rozwoj Historyczny procesu kanoniczego*, 1: *Proces koscielnj w starozytnosci chrzescijanskiej*, in *Rozprawy wydzialn III Towarzystwa Przyjacol Nank w Wilnie*, III, Wilna, 1929, accessible through the review of H. F. Schmid in *Zeit. Sav. Stif.*, vol. 50, kan. Abt., vol. 19, 1930, pp. 834–841) and only later, especially since the 4th century it appears influenced by the Roman court system: Steinwenter, *Der Enfluss des römischen Rechtes auf den antiken Kanonischen Prozess*, in *Atti del Congresso internazionale di Diritto Romano*, 1934, vol. I: cf. Vismara, op. cit., pp. 97–121.

350 Mention of such private law of the Church can be found in quite a lot of patristic texts that under different qualifications (ἡμητέροι νόμοι, leges Christi, leges evangelii, lex divina) set it against the State private law (ρομαίων νόμοι, leges Caesarum, lex saeculi, lex humana, lex imperialis, οἱ τῶν ἔξωθεν νόμοι). Cf. the following texts collected by A. Tabera, *Professio monastica causa divortii in jure Justiniani*, in *Acta congressus juridici internationalis*, vol. I, Rome, 1935, p. 192, no. 4; St. Gregory Nazaianzus, *Epist.* 176, Migne, *Patr. Gr.*, 37, col. 290: "Τὸ ἀποστάσιον ὅ τοῖς ἡμετέροις ἀπαρέσκει πάντως νόμοις κἂν οἱ ρωμαίων ἑτέρως κρινῶσι" St. Justin, *Apologia I pro christianis*, Migne, *Patr. Gr.*, 6, col. 349: "Ὥσπερ καὶ νόμῳ ανθρωπίνω διγαμίας ποιούμενοι ἁμαρτολοὶ παρὰ τῷ ἡμετέρῳ Διδασκάλω εἰσί, καὶ οἱ προσβλέποντες γυναικὶ πρὸς τὸ επιθυμῆσαι αὐτῆς." Saint Jerome, *Epist. LXXVII ad Oceanum*, Migne, *Patrol. latina*, 22, 691: "Aliae sunt leges Caesarum, aliae Christi. Aliud Papinianus, aliud Paulus noster praecipit." St. Augustine, *De nupt. et concup.* I, c. x: "Quod si quisquam fecerit (divortium) non lege huius saeculi, ubi interveniente repudio sine crimine conceditur alia copulare connubia, sed lege evangelii reus est adulterii"; Id. *Expositio ad Lucam*, lib. VII, no. 5: Dimittis ergo uxorem quasi jure, sine crimine; et putas id tibi licere, quia lex humana non prohibet; sed divina prohibet." St. John Chrysostom, *De libello repudii*, III, 1 (Migne, *Patr. Gr.*, 51, col. 218, who gives only the Latin translation of the phrase): "Καὶ οἱ τῶν ἔξωθεν δὲ νόμοι etc." Idem, ibid., col. 219: "Μὴ γάρ μοι τοὺς παρὰ τοῖς ἔξωθεν κειμένους νόμους." Idem, *Laus Maximi*, (attributed to St. John Chrysostom by Migne), *Patr. Gr.*, 51, col. 226. Add to this the following provision of the Council of Carthage (year 406; Bruns, *Canones apostolici et concil.*, p. 186): "Placuit ut secundum evangelicam et apostolicam disciplinam neque dimissus ab uxore neque dimissa a marito alteri coniungantur, sed ita permaneant aut sibimet reconcilientur. Quod si contempserint ad poenitentiam redigantur; in qua causa legem imperialem petendum est promulgari." Very interesting is also the 1st similarity of the Shepherd of Hermas, effectively outlining the psychological extraneousness of Christians to the pagan State and the antagonism between their laws – religious and civil – and State laws: extraneousness and opposition born out in the Christians in imitation of analogue Jewish diaspora tendencies, and in every respect similar to these, although in the Christians the real exile from their terrestrial Palestinian homeland is replaced by the sense of symbolic exile from heavenly homeland. *Shepherd of Hermas*, French translation by A. Lelong, Paris 1912, pp. 139–141, Simil. I: "Vous savez, me dit le Pasteur, que vous, les serviteurs de Dieu, vous habitez sur une terre étrangère: vôtre patrie en effet, est loin d'ici. Si donc vous connaissez vôtre cité, cette cité que vous devez un jour habiter, pourquoi achetez vous ici des champs, des meubles somptueux, des palais, et des habitations superflues ? Qui fait ces acquisitions pour la cité d'ici, ne songe evidemment pas à retourner dans sa propre patrie. Insensé, indécis, infortuné ! Ne

law,[351] retouched by the Gospel precepts and later combined with rules drawn from various provincial laws and Roman law, modified by Christian *equitas*.[352]

It is understood that during the first three centuries, as the Roman Empire does not recognize the Church, so it also totally ignores its jurisdiction. The bishops may certainly judge Christians, but only if they agree, while the disengagement from the law by the parties is admitted in the ruling only with their prior consent and to the extent to which arbitrators are in general allowed to break away from the law naturally imposed on the contenders. If brought before state courts, in the resolution of the same lawsuit, the law corresponding to the parties' *status civitatis* is applied rather than the *lex christiana*, which is entirely unknown.

Nevertheless, at the beginning of the 4th century, after the recognition of the Church by the state, things change radically: in disputes between Christians, the bishop's ruling is recognized as a valid jurisdiction which is imposed upon the defendant even against his will, and concurrently with that of the

vois tu pas que tous ces biens te sont étrangers et au pouvoir d'un autre ? Le maître de cette cité te dirà en effet : Je ne veux pas que tu habites dans ma ville : sors d'ici, puisque tu ne reconnais pas mes lois. – Possesseurs de domaines, d'habitations et de beaucoup d'autres richesses, quand tu te verras ainsi banni que fera tu de ton champ de ta maison et de toutes les autres acquisitions ? Car il aura raison le maître de la cité de te dire: Observe mes lois, ou sors de mon pays ! – Que feras tu donc, toi qui as une autre loi, celle de ta propre cité ? A cause des tes domaines et des autres richesses, renonceras-tu absolument à ta loi pour suivre celle de la cité d'ici ? Prends garde que ce ne soit un malheur pour toi d'abandonner ta loi : car si tu veux un jour retourner dans ta patrie, tu n'y seras pas reçu, pour avoir repudié ta loi, et tu en seras exclus." An acute, fundamental study of this Christian civil law, its application in the courts of bishops, and its influence on Roman law and other secular rights is the one by F. Bossowski, *Quo modo usu forensi audientiae episcopalis suadente non nulla praecepta ad instar juris graeci aut hebraici etc., in jure romano recepta sint exponitur*, published in *Acta Congressus juridici internationalis*, vol. I, Rome, 1935, pp. 361–410.

351 Bossowski, op. cit., p. 364: "Attamen Christianorum communitates praeceptis juris privati ad commercium veluti ad contrahendam emptionem, venditionem etc., ad hereditatem defuncti etc., spectantibus carere non potuisse, palam est ideoque Christianorum antistites in litibus ex causa privata dirimendis consuetudine suadente praecepta juris mosaici porro observare soliti esse videntur." Cf. ibid., pp. 368–369, 377. Some talented scholars recently highlighted the Jewish origin of certain Christians judicial institutions. Particularly interesting are Volterra's work, *Studio sull'arrha sponsalicia*, part III, Rome 1930, pp. 28–91, that has shed light on the influence of the Jewish *mohar* on the Christian institution of the *arrhae sponsaliciae* and Vismara's work, *La donazione nuziale nel diritto ebraico e nelle fonti cristiane in relazione al diritto romano postclassico*, Milan, 1934, in which the relation between the Jewish *ketubà* and the Christian-Roman *donatio propter nuptias* were studied.

352 Bossowski, ibid., pp. 364–380.

state,[353] just like the ruling of the Jewish leaders for causes between Jews;[354] consequently, that *lex christiana* that had previously been applied only *inter consentientes* and within the limits listed above becomes the personal law of Christians that the bishops apply in internal civil relationships, regardless of the parties' agreement.[355]

---

353 L. 1 C. Th. 1, 27, of July 27, 318 (Sirmondina Constitution 17th) and Sirmondina Constitution 1st of 333. The authenticity of this 333 Constitution, that explicitly recognizes the episcopal jurisdiction *inter nolentes*, has been questioned and scholars have argued a lot about it. Bernhard Matthias, *Die Entwicklung des römischen Schiedsgerichts*, in *Festschrift ... Windscheid*, Rostock, 1888, part III: *Das bischöfliche Schiedsgericht*, p. 134, admitted it without difficulty stating consequently that "da die Competenz des Bischofs durch einen einseitigen Willensacht der Partei begründet ward, so kann von einem schiedsgerichtlichen Verfahren nicht die Rede sein. Es handelt sich vielmehr um eine wirkliche Gerichtsbarkeit der Bischöfe, die ihnen vom Kaiser übertragen ist in Concurrenz mit allen ordenlichen Gerichten. Die Competenz ist in allen civilen Rechtssachen begründet, sofern nur eine Prozesspartei den Anstoss gibt durch Provokation." Similarly, Martroye, op. cit., l. c. Against the latter, De Francisci, *Per la storia*, cit., pp. 11–18 (of the reprint) supported instead the apocryphal nature of this constitution, thus insisting on the character of pure arbitration of the bishops' rulings. But that thesis (which is still supported by Savagnone, *Studi sul diritto romano ecclesiastico*, in *Annali del seminario giuridico dell'Università di Palermo*, 14, 1930, p. 63, no. 1; Scialoja, *Procedura civile romana*, Rome, 1936, p. 313, and Salvioli, *Storia della procedura civile e criminale*, Milan, 1925, p. 28) is concordantly rejected by more recent writers, who recognize the constitution as authentic and thus see the bishops' rulings as a real jurisdiction, concurrent with that of the State": Chénon, *Histoire générale du droit français public et privé des origines jusqu'à 1815*, Paris 1926, I, p. 99; Busek, op. cit., pp. 4–31 and 77; Vismara, op. cit., pp. 32–30 [TN: sic] and Steinwenter, *Zur Lehre*, cit. p. 661, who points out how the bishops' jurisdiction even against the *pars refragans* is thinkable only by restricting the extent to cases between Christians (correct observation) and between diocesans (groundless observation). In my opinion, the authenticity of Sirmondina I is also logically evident from the fact that, once it recognized the Church, the Roman State could not treat the Christians with less deference than that used toward Jews. Once the Jewish jurisdiction was admitted, the Christian civil jurisdiction had obviously to be admitted too, at least within the same limits. The equalization occurred precisely with the law of 318, confirmed by the law of 333. Masi, op. cit., pp. 105–107 and passim, still insists on the character of pure arbitration of the bishops' sentences, but his argument does not stand on solid ground and is unacceptable. Similarly, G. Ferrari dalle Spade, *Immunità ecclesiastiche nel diritto romano imperiale*, in *Atti del Reale Istit. Veneto Scienze Lettere e Arti*, t. 99, 1939, pp. 224–232, refuses to recognize the judicial character of the bishops' sentences, noting that the l. 1 C. Th. 1, 27 of 318 does not admit the *provocatio inter nolentes*, while the authenticity of Sirmondina I, which, alone, admits it, has not been proven.

354 The Jewish law is also exercised *inter nolentes* until the law of 398, which by establishing the obligation of the consensus between the parties, suppresses it by transforming it into simple arbitration.

355 L. 1 C. Th. 1, 27: "Si quis ad legem Christianam negotium transferre voluerit, etc." The first text of legislation that makes mention of private Christian norms is Galerius' Edict of Toleration (year 311) in which it is noted that by rejecting their ancestral laws, Christians

Once the Christian law has become a personal law, with reasoning akin to that done above regarding Jewish law, it must necessarily be applied in disputes between Christians also by the civil court: that is to say that after the law of 318, the attitude of the State towards the two laws, the Christian and Jewish, turns to be thoroughly equal.

However, is this recognition of the bishops' judicial activities throughout the empire, or is it also circumscribed to certain site limits?

The issue has never been considered, and the authors who, recognizing the Sirmondina I as authentic, support the jurisdictional character of the bishops' rulings and do not think at all about making topographic distinctions.

In my opinion, however, a distinction between East and West is in order in this area, too.

It should also be noted that, firstly, the most important normative laws of the institute are directed to the eastern Praetorium prefects:[356] the Sirmondina I to Ablavio,[357] the suppressive constitution of 398 to Eutychianus,[358] like the analogous provision of the same year regarding the Jewish jurisdiction. Secondly, it is a fact that the rare papyrological testimonies of *episcopalis audientia* relate to eastern regions, in particular Egypt.[359]

Yet, there is still another subject, and in my opinion the most important one.

Throughout the Middle Ages, in the wholly Christianized West, the bishops do not exert but act purely as arbitrators, and no civil law of the Church exists,

"ἑαυτοῖς νόμους ποιῆσαι, καὶ τούτους προφυλάττειν" (see Eusebius, *Hist. Eccl.*, lib. VIII, ch. 17). A reference to the Christian civil law concerning inheritance is included in a canon of the Council of Nicaea (penalties and additional decrees, ch. 15, Mansi, *Conciliorum omnium amplissima collectio*, II, p. 1045): "Si autem pro indiviso instituti sunt haeredes, sive nullo facto testamento suo jure succedent defuncto, dividant haereditatem inter se secundum legis et aequitatis praecepta et morem. Porro si avaritia et aviditate distenti inter se non conveniant, adeant simul judices, qui in divinarum scripturarum et legum lectione studium et meditationem impendunt et Dei sunt vicarii, ut *dijudicent inter eos secundum leges veritatis*, et sciat unusquisque quod suum est, et acquiescant judicio et patienter ferant, etc." In criminal matters too, which are not of our concern here, the sources refer to a gap between ecclesiastical and State norms: see e.g., a letter from Constantine to Pope Athanasius about the misdeeds of a schismatic sect (St. Athanasius, *Apologia contra Arianos*, no. 68, *Patrologia graeca latine tantum edita*, t. 15, p. 1047: "Si quid ejusmodi ultra moverint, *non juxta ecclesiasticas, sed secundum publicas leges, meipsum meamet opera causam auditurum etc.*").

356 And thus, they must have been issued for Eastern regions. See footnote no. 319 above.

357 On him, see Bartolomeo Borghesi, *Oeuvres*, cit., t. X, Paris 1897, *Les préfets du prétoire*, pp. 199–203.

358 See footnote no. 318 above.

359 See Vismara, op. cit., pp. 90–96 and the bibliography cited therein. To be honest, from these documents no really clear news and irrefutable evidence about the judicial character of the *episcopalis audientia* transpire.

unlike the State's civil law. Contrariwise, in the East, where Christians live under pagan, Islamic or any multi-faith political entities, we can see the prevalence of personality law, according to confession, under which each religious or ethnic-religious community lives according to its own civil law, applied by the heads of the respective ecclesiastical hierarchies.[360]

The various Eastern Christian national churches have special collections of civil laws – the so-called nomocanons – drawn up in the various languages of the peoples belonging to the same churches (Syriac, Coptic, Arabic, Armenian, Georgian, to name a few). These laws represent the personal statutes of the Christians in civil matters and are enforced on them by courts of bishops.[361]

The oldest of these collections is the one called the Syro-Roman Law Book,[362] a nomocanon compiled originally in Greek, between 476 and 480,[363] most likely in the chancellery of the Patriarchate of Antioch,[364] in order to serve as a manual of civil law for the episcopal hearing of the Syriac Church.[365]

360 For the courts of the Syriac and Persian Churches, see Partsch, in *Zeits. Sav. Stif.*, 30, 1909, pp. 360 et seqq., and Taubenschlag, ibid., 1925, pp. 494 et seqq.; for those of the Coptic Church, see Riedel, *Die Kirchenrechtsquellen des Patriarchats Alexandrien*, Leipzig, 1900, pp. 48, 64, 86, 114 and passim. Cf. Steinwenter, *Zur Lehre* cit., p. 665.

361 The nomocanons of the Syriac Church are known especially from the edition and translation of Sachau, *Syrische Rechtsbücher*, vol. III, 1880 et seqq.; for the Armenian nomocanons, see Karst, *Grundriss der Geschichte des Armenischen Rechts*, in *Zeitschrift für vergleichende Rechtswissenschaft*, XIX, p. 313 et seqq. (bibliography on p. 313) and XX, p. 14 et seqq.; Idem, *Armenisches Rechtsbuch*, I and II, 1905 (on the Sempad Code); broader literature is available in Kohler and Wenger, *Allgemeine Rechtsgeschichte*, 1914, Berlin-Leipzig, p. 153.

362 E. Sachau, *Syrische Rechtsbücher*, cit., vol. I; the studies on that are listed by Bossowski, op. cit., p. 375, nos. 45 and 46. Latin translation by Ferrini, in *Bull. Ist. di Dir. Romano*, 1900, re-edition reviewed by Baviera, in *Fontes juris romani antejustinianei*, Florence, 1940, vol. II.

363 On the compilation of the Syro-Roman Law Book, see the authors cited by Bossowski, op. cit., p. 375, no. 45 and above all Nallino, *Sul Libro Siro-romano e sul presunto diritto siriaco*, in *Studi Bonfante*, vol. I, pp. 202 et seqq. On the date, the various authors are in agreement; only Bossowski considers the code "jam ante Constantini tempora conscriptum, postea vero IV et V saeculo p. Chr. multis novis praeceptis interpolationibusque auctum esse" (ibid., p. 375).

364 Kübler, *Geschichte des römischen Rechts*, 1925, pp. 398–399.

365 In this sense Bruns and Sachau, *Das Syrisch-römische Rechtsbuch*, vol. II, p. 330; Manigh, in *Zeits. Sav. Stift.*, 30, p. 357. Setting himself against them, Nallino, op. cit., l. cit., supports instead the purely theoretical character of the nomocanon, compiled, according to him, only for educational purposes, and having come into practical use only in the 8th century, when it was translated into Syriac. But this viewpoint it is rightfully rejected by Bossowski, op. cit., p. 375, no. 46.

Very ancient appear as well the law sources of the Coptic Patriarchate of Alexandria.[366]

This is a unique pertinence of the medieval Christian legal sources to the East that lays the foundation for the hypothesis of an analogous topographical limitation of ecclesiastical jurisdiction, even in Roman times.

Moreover, the fact that the earliest traces of Christian law and jurisdiction are found in those two provinces – Syria and Egypt – seemingly the only extra-Palestinian locations of Jewish special jurisdiction in the Roman Empire, is also significant.

It seems only natural that the recognition of the *episcopalis audientia* as an actual activity of real jurisdiction had started and maintained in Roman times only where the similar recognition of *audientia* of the Jewish leaders existed *ab antiquo*?[367]

---

366 About them, see Riedel, *Die Kirchenrechtsquellen des Patriarchats Alexandrien*, Leipzig, 1900.

367 In support of the hypothesis of the identity of topographic limits set to the recognition of the two jurisdictions – Jewish and Christian – is the fact that the law of eastern nomocanons appears predominantly interwoven with Jewish principles characteristic of the Mishnah and the two Gemarot, of Jerusalem and Babylonian. For the study of Jewish elements penetrated in the Syro-Roman book and then subsumed, through the practice of the ecclesiastical tribunals, in later Roman law, see Bossowski, op. cit., passim and in particular. pp. 366–369 and Idem, *Suntne in jure romano suadente usu forensi audientiae episcopalis quaedam praecepta ad instar juris privati hebraici introducta?* in *Odbitka z tomu x Rovznika Prawniczego Wilenskiego*, 1939, p. 2 et seqq. (accessible as an abstract in the library of Bologna Judicial Institute). Cf. the summary that the same author gives of these researches of his in the booklet: *Quomodo multa in jure romano postclassico ad instar praeceptorum ab episcopis ex compromisso lites dirimentibus observatorum, innovata sint auctoris opinio breviter exponitur*, s. l., s. d., pp. 7. In general, the reception of Mosaic-Talmudic law in the judicial sources of the eastern Churches has been extensively and minutely studied by Victor Aptowitzer in following works that Bossowski unfortunately overlooked: *Beiträge zur Mosaischen Rezeption in Armenischen Recht*, in *Sitzungsberichte der K. Akademie der Wissenschaften in Wien*, Band 157, Abhand. IV, 1907; *The influence of Jewish law on the development of jurisprudence in the Christian Orient*, in *Jewish Quarterly Review*, I, 1910, pp. 217–229; *Die Rechtsbücher der nestorianischen Patriarchen und ihre Quellen*, in the *Anzeiger der philosophisch-historischen Klasse der K. Akademie der Wissenschaften in Wien*, 1910, jahrg, VII; *Die Rechtsbücher der Syr. Patriarchen und ihre Quellen*, in *Wiener Zeitschrift für Kunde des Morgenlandes*, XXVI, 1910, pp. 181–224; *Die Syrischen Rechtsbücher und das mosaisch-talmudische Recht*, in the *Sitzungsberichte der K. Akademie der Wissenschaften in Wien, Philosophisch-historische Klasse*, Band 163, Wien, 1909, p. 108; *Jüdisches in Syrischen Rechtsbüchern*, in *Scripta universitatis atque bibliothecae hierosolimitanarum*, vol. I, Jerusalem, 1923 (in German, Hebrew translation by A. A. Kaplan); *The controversy of the Syro-Roman Code*, in *Jewish Quarterly Review*, N.S., II, 1911, pp. 53–73.

The thought that Rome may have allowed Christians governed by their provincial laws to follow the Christian personal statute instead of the personal ethnic statute does not appear illogical. It is ambitious to think Rome may have allowed such a thing to the Christians of the West, where Roman civil law was applied.

Recognizing the *episcopalis audientia* in the West, thus enforcing the Christian law as a personal statute governing the internal relations of civil nature between Christians, meant abolishing all Roman private norms regarding relations between the Christians themselves, at once. This was, too, revolutionary for the emperors, however Christians, to wish for.

After the edict of Milan, the emperors more wisely start a gradual transformation in the West of the entire Roman public and private legal system in the Christian sense, while striving to drive the ethical and judicial beliefs of the Catholic Church into all branches of the state organization.[368]

Such adaptation of the *leges saeculi* to the *canones* – which will appear in all its extent and evidence in Justinian's legislation[369] – is already quite advanced at the end of the 4th century. So advanced in fact that, in 398, eager to unify the empire judicially, based on the new Christian law, the emperors revoke the personal statute of Eastern Christians, considering it already transfused into the new state law, and therefore superfluous. To that purpose, they abolish the bishops' courts that had hitherto applied it concurrently with civilian courts.[370]

---

368 In the last few decades, the action of the Christians ethical and legal principles on Roman law starting from the 4th century has been the object of a large number of studies that would be too long to list here. See the most recent writings collected in the volume *Cristianesimo e diritto romano*, Milan, 1935, the memoirs collected in vol. II of *Atti del Congresso internazionale di diritto romano*, Rome, 1935 and in the first two volumes of *Acta Congressus juridici internationalis*, Rome, 1935, as well as the literature listed by Volterra, *Diritto romano e diritti orientali*, cit., p. 268. Also, to be considered Troplong's reservations, *De l'influence du christianisme sur le droit civil des Romains*, Paris, 1843, and Baviera's, *Concetto e limiti dell'influenza del cristianesimo sul diritto romano*, reprint from *F. P. Girard Mélanges*, Paris, 1912, in particular pp. 45, 50–51, 54.

369 See for all Alivisatos, *Les rapports de la législation ecclésiastique de Justinien avec les canons de l'eglise*, in the cited volume of *Atti Congr. Int. di dir. romano*, Rome 1935, and Biondi, *Giustiniano primo imperatore cattolico*, Milan, 1937.

370 C. J. 1, 4, 7 (year 398): "Imp. Arcadius et Honorius A. A. Eutychiano p. p. Si qui ex consensu apud sacrae legis antistitem litigare voluerint, non vetabuntur, sed experientur illius (in civili dumtaxat negotio) arbitri more residentis sponte judicium." As I have already pointed out and as Lammeyer, *Die Audientia* cit., pp. 194–195, believes too, the Constitution refers only to the East; it is confirmed by l. 1 C. Th., 16, 11 of 399, addressed to Apollodorus proconsul of Africa. The transformation of episcopal jurisdiction in simple arbitration appears incontrovertibly from the law 398, and arguments to the contrary of

Since all subjects, even if not Christians, must submit to the new Roman-Christian state law, the Jewish law (and jurisdiction of Jewish Patriarchs) are abolished in the same year 398 with the aforementioned law.[371]

It is therefore for the same reasons and at the same time that *jus christianum* and *jus judaicum* and their respective jurisdictions are repealed by the Roman emperors: the difference, however, is that while the former disappears as a particular law to reappear as transfused in the general law, the latter disappears totally and definitely from the practical use.[372]

Vismara, op. cit., pp. 31–39, whose work is all aimed at supporting the thesis of the persistent jurisdictional character of the *audientia episcopalis* from 318 to the Justinian era, are groundless. That since 398 in East and 408 in the West (to which l 8 C. J. 1, 4 of that year, addressed to Theodorus, praetorian prefect of Italy, relates, Lammeyer, l. cit.) the bishops' arbitration presents special characteristics is beyond doubt, but the various features are not such as to confer to it real jurisdictional nature, given the issue of the required agreement of the parties which is precisely the typical element of arbitration. And the reason for this reduction of *episcopalis audientia* within the limits of consensual arbitration is actually clear: to recognize the function of judge in the bishop meant also to recognize the existence of the special private law he applied in his rulings; in order to abolish this law and unify the empire judicially, it was therefore necessary to remove from those rulings the jurisdictional character that had previously been recognized.

371 As it was already noticed by several scholars and lately also by Busek, op. cit., p. 36, the expressions used in the two constitutions of 398 (C. Th. 2, 1, 10 [= C. J. 1, 9, 8] and C. J. 1, 4, 7) are absolutely equivalent, and indeed demonstrate the complete identity of the fate suffered by the Jewish and the Christian jurisdictions. From 398 onward, the Jewish jurisdiction too is transformed into consensual arbitration and this to the purpose, rightly noted by Juster, op. cit. II, p. 101, of suppressing the Jewish civil law. It is incomprehensible how, after that just observation, Juster will then argue, ibid., pp. 102–105, that the law of 398 only restricts without abolishing the Jewish law. It is a mistake very similar to that made by Vismara regarding the episcopal jurisdiction and based on the same matter of the peculiarity of Jewish rulings versus those of simple arbitration. It is enough here to observe that the request for the parties' prior consent unequivocally shapes the arbitral character of those rulings. Without standing on any solid ground, Vismara, op. cit. pp. 34–35, insists on the difference of position outlined by the Roman state for the Jewish and Christian jurisdictions, trying to find in the two cited constitutions of 398 substantial differences which in reality do not exist at all.

372 A law from 415 (C. Th. 16, 8, 22) stipulates that the Patriarch of the Jews "inter Christianos nullam habeat copiam judicandi et si qua inter eos ac Judaeos sit contentio, a rectoribus provinciae dirimatur." The norm is reproduced by Justinian that replaces the missing Patriarch with the *seniores* (C. J. 1, 9, 15): "Si qua inter Christianos et Judaeos sit contentio non a senioribus judaeorum sed ab ordinariis judicibus dirimatur." One could conversely infer the legality of the jurisdiction of the Patriarch and of the *seniores* for the internal disputes among Jews. But the law of 398, reproduced also by Justinian (C. J. 1, 9, 8) shows that this later prohibition refers to the simple arbitral activity that the Patriarch and the Jewish *seniores* may not exercise, in mixed lawsuits, even with the consent of the parties.

Based on what has been described so far, we can quite safely establish the following issues:

1) The existence of a real special jurisdiction, exercised upon the impulse of only one part "etiam si altera pars refragatur" is necessarily connected with the existence of a special personal statute. As a result, in the chronological and topographic limits within which the existence of Jewish and Christian jurisdictions are recognized, it should also be possible to see that Jews and Christians lived according to particularly personal statutes.
2) The limits and the vicissitudes of these two jurisdictions appear entirely similar.

The Roman state admitted Jewish jurisdiction and the associated personal statute, up to 398, both in Palestine and in some other Eastern provinces, most likely in Syria and Egypt.[373] Regarding Palestine, such recognition fits the general system followed by Rome on the preservation of local laws. The use of these laws was left to the provincial subjects, not only as long as they remained *peregrini*, but, according to a recent theory, also after they became citizens, individually or in groups, and finally in toto with the Constitution of Caracalla.

As for other regions, on the other hand, it represents a unique exception in the system of Roman law, which never granted separate personal statute and special jurisdiction to Roman citizens, nor their own jurisdiction to *peregrini* outside their province; an exception established as a sign of respect to religious freedom intended in the broadest sense, taking into account the confessional foundations of the Jewish personal statute.

Christian jurisdiction and the associated customary personal statute, ignored by the Roman state as long as it generally ignores the Catholic Church, are recognized a few years after the edict of Milan in imitation of the recognition of the Jewish jurisdiction, for the same confessional reasons, and, apparently, within the same topographic boundaries (East).

---

373 The only writer who, with respect to the recognition of the Jewish jurisdiction in the diaspora in the Greco-Roman era, sets topographical boundaries consistent with those that I established (Persia, Palestine, Egypt, Syria), is Leopold Löw, *Dinà demalchutà dinà*, in *Gesammelte Schriften*, vol. III Szegedin, 1893, p. 347. To come to that conclusion, he relies only on four texts of Flavius Josephus: a) *Ant.* 11, 8, 5 (Alexander the Great allows the Jews of Palestine, Babylon and Media to χρῆσθαι τοῖς πατρῴοις νόμοις); b) *Ant.* 14, 7, 2 (the passage of Strabo on the powers of the ethnarch of Alexandria cited above, no. 13); c) *Bell.* jud. 7, 3, 3; d) Id., 7, 5, 2 (cited off the point because in them, respectively, only the ἰσοπολιτεία is mentioned, granted by the successors of Antiochus Epiphanes to the Jews of Syria, and the attempt on their rights committed just after the war of 70, by the Greeks of Antioch and frustrated by Titus. The paucity and inadequacy of these textual supports explain the research that I made again on this issue.

With their respective statutes, both jurisdictions were abolished in the same year, 398.

•••

All this rather long dissertation was necessary to clarify that during the Roman period, the Jews of Italy did not live according to their ethnic-religious statute, but, as citizens, according to Roman law; nor, therefore, did they have a special jurisdiction. Claims to the contrary[374] are based on elements too tenuous to be acceptable[375] and must therefore be rejected based on the considerations set out above.[376]

374 In the magazine *Der Katholik*, 1903, I, 220 (cited by Juster, II, p. 86) Bludau argues that the Jews of Rome and their proselytes followed the Jewish law of succession based on Juvenal, *Satira* 14, verses 100–102 (year 128): "Romanas autem soliti contemnere leges, Judaicum ediscunt et servant ac metuunt jus, Tradidit arcano quodcumque volumine Moses." For Krüger, *Histoire des sources du droit romain*, p. 160, "la réforme [of Caracalla] n'eut que très peu d'effet par rapport aux juifs; St. Ambroise, Ep. 5, 29, nous rend compte de leur situation légale en ces mots: Ipsi romanis legibus teneri se negent ita ut crimina leges putent." In *Istituzioni di diritto romano*, vol. I, 2nd ed., 1928, p. 558, without documenting, Perozzi even claims, without providing evidence, that the Justinian law "compels (the Jews) to live not according to Roman law, but Mosaic law."

375 Precisely because it is built on too frail foundations, Juster, II, p. 86, rejects Bludau thesis, and notes (II, p. 36 and I, p. 462, no. 3) that from the context of which the phrase of St. Ambrose is part, the inference drawn by Krüger is not possible: in that passage, it is observed how unfair it is that the Jews, who customarily refuse to obey Rome's – public – laws, try then, when the right time comes, to use them against the Church. At issue is a criminal arson of a synagogue that St. Ambrose, with deplorable zeal, wants to remain unpunished, whereas the Jews insist on enforcing the laws that oversee such crime. As for Perozzi, he probably intends to refer to the law of 398, reported by Justinian (C. J. 1, 9, 8) and just an oversight makes him say the exact opposite of what the law itself expresses.

376 The only text that seems to really demonstrate the subordination of all Jews of the diaspora to the Jewish laws is that of Bardesane, *Dialogo delle leggi dei paesi*, Italian translation by G. Levi della Vida, Rome, 1921, pp. 48–49: "Disregarding the law of the country ... the Jews abide by the law that was given to their fathers." One should not forget, however, that Bardesane is a Persian, and before his eyes are the Jews in his country, who actually enjoy a wide regulatory and judicial autonomy, and at most the Jews of other eastern countries (Syria, Palestine, Egypt) whom we know they had such autonomies. An extension of his observations also to western Jews should be considered risky and unwise. The fact that an entirely analogous observation is made by Bardesane (ibidem) for the Christians ("in any country and place they are, the laws of the countries do not separate them from the laws of their Christ"), and this at a time (approximately the year 200) in which the latter have not yet developed a particular civil law, suggests that, as in the patristic texts collected by Juster (II, p. 36, no. 2), also for this writer the expression "laws" refers only to the religious and ceremonial norms and not to the judicial ones.

CHAPTER 6

The Ostrogothic Age

After decreeing the confirmation for the Jews of the privileges granted by the Roman emperors, chapter 143 of the Edict of Theodoric (y. 512) goes on setting the principle that they "inter se jurgantes et suis viventes legibus, eos jufices habere necesse est, quos habent observantiae praeceptore." Scholars are not unanimous as to the interpretation of this passage. Attributing to the word "legibus" the most apparent meaning of "judicial norms," some believe that Theodoric has repealed the l. 10 C. Th. 2, 1 and re-established things in the state (in the East, in our opinion) they were before 398, allowing Jews the use of their private law in internal relations and validating rabbinical arbitration in civil matters as proper jurisdiction.[377] Others argue that that word refers only to the "religious norms" and that the chapter does nothing but confirm the principle of the rabbinical jurisdiction restricted to ritual matter, as set by the aforementioned Roman law.[378] Proponents of this latter viewpoint argue that the purely religious meaning attributed to the *leges* mentioned by Theodoric comes from the subsequent expression "observantiae praeceptores," which must necessarily refer only to the ritual side.

377 Dahn, *Die Könige der Germanen*, vol. IV, *Die Edikte der Könige Theodorich und Athalarich und das gotische Recht in gotischen Reiche*, pp. 98–99 and 152. Bethmann-Hollweg, *Der germano-romanische Civilprocess*, vol. I, p. 275. Pertile, *Storia del diritto italiano*, vol. III, I ed., 1885, p. 186. Vogelstein and Rieger, *Geschichte der Juden in Rom*, vol. I, Berlin, 1896, pp. 129–130. Tamassia, *Stranieri ed ebrei*, cit., pp. 800–801, also shares the same opinion. He believes, however, that far from innovating, Theodoric only sanctioned a de facto already existing state of affairs. Meaning, he thinks that in Italy, the use of Jewish law in private relations between Jews continued even after 398. However, it should be observed to the contrary: 1) that, as we had seen, such use before 398 was admitted only in the East and not in Italy; 2) if, as deductible from the law of 398, for the arbitration the consent of the parties is necessary, we cannot speak of the validity of the Jewish law. This law will always be ignored by state courts and applied by Jewish arbitrators only with the explicit agreement of the parties. Therefore, it will be limited to the area where the will of those parties could derogate from the mandatory norms of the Roman law, according to standard rules of arbitration.

378 Cassel, in Ersch and Grüber, *Allgemeine Encyclopädie der Wissenschaften und Künste*, II Section, vol. 27, entry Juden-Geschichte, Leipzig, 1850, pp. 54–55. Glöden, *Das römische Recht im ostgotischen Reiche*, Jena, 1843, p. 36. Gaudenzi, *Gli editti di Teodorico e di Atalarico*, 1886, pp. 83–86.

 | DOI:10.1163/9789004627154_008

To begin with, it seems this correlation between the content of the *lex* and the word "observantia" is not as logical or necessary after all. Altogether, I consider the consequence sought to be drawn from it quite far-fetched.

We should not forget that the supporters of this view are the same ones who assert the territorial value of the edict and deny any application to the Goth law.[379] They seek to avoid the completely obvious objection that had Theodoric left the use of their civil rights to the Jews, the more so he should have made such a concession to his Goths, who ruled the country and by far outnumbered the Jews.[380]

Now, the conclusions by most recent scholars are contrary to the territoriality theory and unanimously admit that, at least in private relations between them, the Goths were able to maintain their own law and jurisdiction: the Roman norms would apply only to Roman relations among themselves and to those between Romans and Goths.[381]

Therefore, given this incomplete system of legal personality for the Goths, the possibility of a similar system for the Jews becomes conceivable: consequently, the strongest argument against the interpretation of the "lex judeorum" in purely religious terms fails. This interpretation is also contradicted by the fact that later elaborations of the Theodosian code unequivocally transform, as we shall see,[382] the l. 10 C. Th. 2, 1, re-establishing the validity of Jewish civil law and introducing rabbinical jurisdiction in internal relations of private character in place of purely consensual arbitration.

In conclusion, I think the following can be drawn from the aforementioned chapter 143 of the edict: 1) that the phrase "suis viventes legibus" refers to civil law and sets an opposite principle to that established with the Roman law of 398 ("romano et communi jure viventes"); 2) that the application of such right seems to be entrusted by Theodoric exclusively (necesse est) to the jurisdiction of the "observantiae praeceptores," that is, of the rabbis, while before 398 the

379 In this sense, Glöden and Gaudenzi in particular, ops. cit., II, cc.

380 The objection is raised, for example, by Dahn, op. cit., p. 99.

381 Del Giudice, *Sulla questione della unità o dualità del diritto in Italia sotto la dominazione ostrogota*, in *Mélanges Fitting*, Montpellier, 1907 = *Nuovi studi di storia e diritto*, Milan, 1913, pp. 326–340. Besta, *Storia del diritto italiano* (Del Giudice), vol. I, part I, Milan, 1923, pp. 91–92. And already before, Dahn, op. cit., in particular pp. 137–190, and Troya, *Storia d'Italia*, IV, part II, *Codice diplomatico longobardo*, Naples, 1853, p. 325. Calasso, *Storia e sistema delle fonti del diritto comune*, vol. I, *Le origini*, Milan, 1938, pp. 126–128 points out that, given the special position of Theodoric compared to the Romans (cf. above, footnote no. 38) under the Goths we cannot talk of personality of law in the true sense, but only of de facto co-existence of both legal systems.

382 See further on, footnote no. 412.

Jewish courts of the empire, wherever recognized, judged *in concurrence* with the state courts.

However, there is reason to believe that even under Theodoric, once invested with full knowledge of a civil case between Jews; state courts would unlikely refuse to rule; in which case they must have applied Jewish law. Once restored to life, Jewish law could not be considered by one court and ignored by another. It would have offered the plaintiff the unjust opportunity of presenting the contentious legal question before whichever of the two jurisdictions would apply the law in a way favorable to him in that particular case.

CHAPTER 7

The Longobard Age

As I have already noted, the Longobard laws maintain absolute silence on the Jews, and scarce are also documentary records relating to it under their rule. Learning then whether in the Longobard territories the Jews lived according to Roman, Longobard or Jewish law is a question that is extremely difficult – if not impossible to solve – in the current state of documentation.

Theoretically, it is not unthinkable that the Longobards recognized the use of Jewish private law to the Jews: if as most modern scholars have clarified[383] against Troya's old opinion,[384] they, too, applied the principle of the personality of the law; if they recognized the right to live *suis legibus* not only to their Roman subjects[385] but also to the Gothic ones,[386] at least for the part relating to family law, it is quite possible that the Jewish subjects too may have benefited from the general rule, of course to the same small extent and exclusively relating to internal relations.

Nevertheless, what confirmations, even indirect, can we bring forward to validate this hypothesis?

Tamassia's keen eye has focused on a short note by Erchempert, who says that after marrying the Greek Wantia Prince Grimoald, "more hebreico, dato ei libello repudii, ad proprios lares eam vi transvexit."[387] "Such a meaningful allusion to Jewish customs, writes Tamassia,[388] more than knowledge of the

383 Besta, *Storia del diritto italiano*, cit., I, pp. 144–148; Solmi, *Storia del diritto italiano*, III ed., 1930, p. 120; Leicht, *Storia del diritto pubblico italiano*, Milan, 1938, pp. 91–93.

384 Troya, *Storia d'Italia*, vol. IV, part II, *Codice diplomatico longobardo*, Naples, 1853. The territoriality of the Longobard law is affirmed countless times. Compare especially pp. 325–326.

385 Chapters 204 and 226 of Rhotari; Chapters 91 and 127 of Liutprand; Besta l. c.; Solmi l.c.

386 Compare the profession of Gothic law of 769, erroneously considered Visigoth by Schupfer, *Una professione di legge gota nell'anno 769*, in *Riv. it. per le scienze giur.*, II, 1886; and that even more significant of a document from Goito (Mantua) of 1045. Tamassia, *Una professione di legge gotica in un documento mantovano del 1045*, in *Atti dell'Istituto veneto*, t. 61, part II, pp. 131–155 = *Archivio Giuridico*, IX, 1902; Schupfer, *Ancora di una professione di legge gotica nell'Età longobarda*, in *Riv. it. per le scienze giur.*, 1902, vol. 34, pp. 162–182; Tamassia, *La professione di legge gotica in Italia*, in *Atti dell'Accademia di Padova*, vol. 19, 1902–1903, pp. 31 et seqq.

387 Year 793, *Historia langobarda Beneventanorum*, c. 5, in *Mon. Germ. Hist., Scriptores rerum langobardicarum et italicarum saec. VI–IX*, Hannover, 1878, p. 236.

388 *Stranieri ed ebrei*, cit., p. 834.

 DOI:10.1163/9789004627154_009

Mosaic law sources, highlights and demonstrates the daily life of the Jewish element in its historical background, which he had the opportunity to study *de visu* and without difficulty, given the not small number of Jews in the southern Longobard region." Tamassia is therefore convinced that in their internal relations, also in southern Italy, Jews were living according to Mosaic law.[389]

This opinion, however, is not shared by another scholar, Marongiu, who recently revisited the issue.[390] He remarks that being a monk, Erchempert knew for sure the Jewish biblical laws regarding divorce; thus, there is no need to think his expression necessarily reflects practice used in his country during his time.[391]

While rejecting Tamassia's argument, Marongiu did not deem it impossible that Jews lived according to Jewish law limitedly to "private law relations, having a direct or indirect link to religious elements: so did perhaps the marriage, despite the l. 7 C. J. 1, 9 and, almost certainly, the oath." Apart from these relations, Morangiu did not doubt that in Longobard territory, Jews lived according to the *lex et consuetudo romanorum*: he believed that the professing of Roman law stated respectively in 1193,[392] 1268,[393] and 1272[394] by two married Jewish women from Salerno testified to that. In fact, if these wives lived by Roman law, their husbands would most certainly align to the same law, owing to the communication to the wife of her husband's law, established by Rotari's chapter 27. Furthermore, suppose those three Jews lived by Roman law; In that case, there is no reason to believe this did not reflect a general state of affairs, which is also confirmed – according to Marangiu – by the important assertion of the contemporary jurist, Andrea da Isernia, that "Judei vivunt et vivere debent communi jure romano."[395]

389 And this, he added, although in the contracts with the Longobards, they give vadia [TN, or wadia or guadia] and guarantors. "It is enough to mention that also the Duke of Naples gives the launegild [TN, or launechild] to the Longobard donor."

390 A. Marongiu, *Gli ebrei di Salerno nei documenti dei secoli X–XIII*, reprint from the *Archivio Storico per le provincie napoletane*, year 62, 1937, pp. 8–13.

391 Ibid., p. 9, no. 21.

392 Cerone, *Sei documenti inediti sugli ebrei di Salerno dal 1125 al 1269*, in *Studi di Storia napoletana in onore di Michelangelo Schipa*, Naples, 1926, docum. III, pp. 62–63. Jewess Bonafata is obliged "secundum legem et romanorum consuetudine, qua vivit."

393 Carucci, *Codice diplomatico salernitano del secolo XIII*, vol. I (1201–1281), Subiaco, 1931, no. 185, p. 329 "Suprascripta fecit ipsa Gemma [hebrea, uxor Melis hebrei] secundum legem et romanorum consuetudinem qua vivit."

394 Carucci, op. cit., no. 265, p. 404 "Suprascripta fecit ipsa Gemma secundum legem et romanorum consuetudinem qua vivit."

395 *Constitutiones regni utriusque Siciliae glossis ordinariis commentariisque* Andreae de Isernia, Lyon, 1559, p. 32.

All these considerations by Marangiu are indeed very perceptive but, in my opinion, undecisive. Therefore, one may look at them contrariwise, even asunder from Erchempert's short note, which I also deem too vague to initiate any discussion: 1) There is no contrast between l. 10 C. Th. 2, 1 = l. 8. C. J. 1, 9 and l. 7 C. J. 1, 9 and the possibility of a different system in Longobard territory, given these laws belong in public legislation and are certainly not among the Roman norms left in force by the Longobards.

2) The relationships to which the three professions of law refer are mixed between Jewish women and Christian counterparts: it is logical, therefore, that in this case, the Jewish law does not apply, and Jewish parties must declare a different law by which the relationship is established. Nothing can be inferred about the private relations of the Jews *inter se*.

3) As for the phrase by Andrea da Isernia, it should be considered a quote of the principle "Judei Romano communi jure viventes" of law 8 C. J. 1, 9, which reappeared following the rebirth of the whole Roman law. Reality, however, could be very different: the analogous claim of the earlier scholars from Bologna, expressed in the theoretical illustrations of the Justinian Code, corresponded, as we shall see, to a totally opposite practice, destined to be recognized and assimilated into the doctrine only later.

We can then conclude by reaffirming the lack of any element apt to solve the problem: on which seemingly cardinal news contained in a local source from that era is not going to shed light.

Achimaaz Ben Paltiel provides the news from Oria, a Jew who lived in the 11th century in Puglia and author of a Chronicle,[396] completed in 1054, describing the events of his family over the past two centuries in the frame of Jewish community life in southern Italy. Among other things, Achimaaz talks about an influential Jew from Bagdad, Aron, son of the Nassi – that is of the supreme leader – of the Jews of Babylon, Shmuel, and "father of the mysteries," who arrived in the mid-9th century[397] in southern Italy and after staying in Gaeta and Benevento, settled in Oria. "There – Achimaaz verbatim says[398] – he took up his residence and his wisdom spread and his teaching was established and

396 Titled "*Sefer Juchasin*" (Book of generations). It was published by Neubauer, *Medieval Jewish Chronicles*, in the collection "*Anecdota Oxoniensia*," vol. II, Oxford, 1895, pp. 110–132; by Abraham Kahana in his miscellanea "*Sifrut ha-Historija ha-Israelit*," vol. I, Warsaw 1922, pp. 117–140, and – with English translation – by Salzmann, *The Chronicles of Achimaaz*, in *The Columbia University's Oriental Studies*, vol. XVIII, New York, 1924. On it, see David Kaufmann's study, *Die Chronik des Achimaaz von Oria. Ein Beitrag zur Geschichte der Juden in Süd-Italien* (850–1054), Frankfurt a. M., 1896.

397 From Kaufmann's reckoning, op. cit., p. 10.

398 Neubauer ed., p. 114.

there he displayed rigor and exceptional judgments [sic: afsakat dajanim], just like when the Urim were there [reference to Exodus 28, 30] and the assemblies of the Sanhedrin and the law of the Sotà [adulterous woman, referring to Deut. 22, 13–21]. And there he pitched his tent and instead of the soil dust of the tabernacle, he prepared the dust of the basis of the ark (of the synagogue); and once Theophilus committed an offense and had a relation with a married woman and Aron judged him in the assembly in the presence of the congregation, ordering that he be annihilated by means of strangulation. And a man leaped up against a woman and killed her, and he passed judgment for his ruin and ordered that he be killed by the sword. And another committed sodomy acting like the pagans do and his cause was discussed and examined and he was sentenced to death by stoning. Another man had a relation with his mother-in-law, thus transgressing the laws of God and his doctrine and the Master passed his judgment and they gathered around him and they burned him."

Clearly, by accepting this testimony as correct, we should necessarily acknowledge a Jewish judicial autonomy so extended as to assume even the existence of an independent Jewish State. But, in fact, only complete political independence allows a people to use the *jus gladii* for common offenses: and it is well known that such exorbitant privilege was never granted to any Jewish community in the diaspora.

True, there are some examples of enjoyment by the Jews of relatively broad criminal judicial autonomy;[399] but that occurs at different times and is restricted to questions of religious infractions.

Instead, it is noteworthy that the legendary character of Achimaaz's chronicle concerning events non-contemporary to his lifetime and the ample space he accorded to the fabulous factor are recognized unanimously by scholars who studied that document:[400] and finally, it is remarkable the fact that the four sentences attributed to Aron from Baghdad, each involving a different

---

399 See e.g., the information provided by Fritz Baer, in *Encyclopedia Judaica*, entry Gemeinde – Mittelalter, that attests to the use by the Jewish communities of Spain, in the 12th–15th centuries, of a vast criminal jurisdiction, that goes all the way to capital punishment: but this only for crimes of religious nature. Also, synchronously in Germany, some Jewish communities obtain the right to condemn "evil and pernicious" Jews to extremely severe corporal punishment (mutilations, blinding and the like). Wiener, *Regesten zur Geschichte der Juden in Deutschland während des Mittelalters*, Hannover, 1862, no. 86, p. 36; Scherer, op. cit., p. 255.

400 Kaufmann, op. cit. p. 3, notes Achimaaz's constant eagerness to shroud his family's origins with an aura of legend to boast its nobility and antiquity. In the same sense, Cassuto, in *Encyclopedia Judaica*, entry Achimaaz ben Paltiel.

death penalty and such as to show, when taken together, the practical application of all four death sentences considered under Talmudic law,[401] appears to be too rigid an oversimplification to be considered corresponding to the truth.

All in all, Achimaaz's news should be considered a fantasy: and yet, since all legends have a kernel of truth, I believe that some deductions may be drawn from it. Perhaps, the reality of a genuine autonomy enjoyed by the community of Oria or by all the communities of the territories placed under the Longobard influence, although nominally Byzantine, is reflected in Achimaaz's exaggerations: autonomy, however, that may have not necessarily crossed the limits of the purely civil field.[402]

The likelihood of such a hypothesis is supported by information about Jewish culture's revival, which, as a result of immigration from Babylon, occurs in Apulia starting from the 9th century, and spreads from there throughout southern Italy. For the first time in Europe, the Jews, who had hitherto only known Greek and Latin, resume to Hebrew as a literary language.[403] Moreover, the Jewish literary monuments, foremost among them the Talmud, begin to be actively studied and commented: judicial-ritual academies are founded,[404] and soon the fame of the Apulian Jewish scholars reaches such stature as to rival the unchallenged Babylonians sages.[405]

---

401 Mishnah, Sanhedrin, 7, 1: "Sentences to four kinds of death are handed down for different crimes by the courts: stoning, burning, decapitation, strangulation."

402 With the exception of possible arbitrary trespassing also into criminal matters: of which – if there weren't too many reasons to deem it a pure invention – the episode reported by Achimaaz could provide an example.

403 Ascoli, *Iscrizioni inedite* cit., pp. 11, 44–45, 91 and passim. Cf. Tamassia, *Stranieri* cit., p. 805; Ferorelli, *Gli ebrei nell'Italia meridionale dall'Età romana al secolo XVIII*, Turin 1915, p. 29; Cassuto, *Storia della letteratura ebraica postbiblica*, Florence, 1938, pp. 66–67.

404 In 846, Nathan ben Ephraim, head of a Talmudic Academy (yeshiva), dies in Venosa. For the tombstone, see Ascoli, op. cit., no. 26 pp. 71–72. Learned Talmudists are attested as early as 900 in Bari, Otranto and Oria. See Cassuto, op. cit., p. 67. Three Talmudists from Bari, Shemarià, Chushiel and Moshè, flourishing around 960, were mentioned by Landauer, in *Literaturblatt des Orients*, VII, p. 3.; S. D. Luzzatto, *Della letteratura ebraica in Italia*, reprint from the first booklet of "*Giudaismo illustrato*," II ed., Padua 1908, pp. 32–35, and Eppenstein, in *Monatsschrift für Gesch. und Wiss. des Jud.*, 1906–1907. From Bari, Chushiel migrated to Al-Qairawan, in present-day Tunisia, importing there the methods of judicial systematics already in use in Babylon and Italy. His teaching was developed by his son Chananel and by Nissim ben Jacob, his disciples. Some legal consultations of the latter two are found in *Responsi dei Gheonim*, edited by D. Cassel, Berlin, 1847, with an introduction by Rappaport. Cf. Steinschneider, in Ersch und Grüber, *Encyclopaedie* cit., II series, vol. 27, p. 387, entry Jüdische Literatur.

405 Proof of this is the saying, reported by Rabbenu Tam, famous among French Talmudists of the XII century, in his *Sefer ha-Jashar*, f. 74, col. 2: "from Bari, the law will come out, and from Otranto the word of the Lord" (paraphrase from Isaiah 2, 6 and Michea 4,2). Most of

Therefore, it is not inconceivable that all this fervor of theoretical studies of Jewish law may have to be juxtaposed with the existence of a specific sphere of the practical application of such law permitted by consuetude if not by special legal provisions.

We nevertheless remain in the field of pure hypotheses, that for the time being, were just worth mentioning while waiting for some fortunate discovery to provide a more intense textual enlightenment for the solution of this interesting problem.

---

the information related to Jewish culture in Italy in the early Middle Age can be found in the collection of Güdemann, *Geschichte der Erzihungswesens und der Cultur der Juden in Italien während des Mittelalters*, Vienna, 1884, ch. 1, pp. 9–55. For the Babylonian derivation of this culture, see pp. 15 et seqq.

CHAPTER 8

The Holy Roman Empire and Italy in Particular

1 Carolingian and Feudal Age

It is known that in the Carolingian Empire, the principle of legal personality according to the lineage is one of the cornerstones of public law. In the field of private relations, and for some parts also in the penal and procedural field, subjects of the state live according to the law of their people:[406] and according to certain principles, these laws – whose rules may be amended by state legislation through constitutions either general (*capitularia per se scribenda*) or aimed explicitly at altering a single law (*capitularia legibus addenda*) – also regulate the relations between members of different nations.[407] Conversely, to whatever nation they may belong (even to one of those represented in the Empire), foreigners did not have this faculty, and according to chapter 367 of the above-mentioned edict of Rotari, still in force, must be judged by the law of their protector, the head of State.[408]

---

406 Capitolare missorum (792 or 796) in *Mon. Germ. Hist., Capitularia regum francorum*, Boretius ed., vol. I, p. 67, ch. 5: "Ut unusquisque homo suam legem pleniter habeat conservatam"; Italic capitulary of Pepin (782–786), ibid., p. 92, etc.; compare the *index rerum et verborum*, entries lex nationis, lex personalis, at the end of volume II of the Capitularies. The criterion is always as mentioned above, which applies to the entire barbaric and feudal era until the resurgence of Roman law. On this issue, the works are notable of Brunner, *Deutsche Rechtsgeschichte*, I, 1st ed., pp. 261 et seqq.; Tamassia, *Stranieri ed Ebrei*, cit., p. 776 and *Una professione di legge gotica in un documento mantovano del 1045* in *Atti Ist. veneto*, vol. 61, 1901–1902, part II, p. 153; Besta, *Fonti del diritto italiano dalla caduta dell'impero romano ai tempi nostri*, Padua, 1938, pp. 64–70 (see literature on p. 64); and Calasso, *Storia e sistema*, cit., pp. 122–125. Less noteworthy is Calisse, who by stating that "as foreigners had to be intended all those whose nation was not annexed to the empire" (*Storia del diritto italiano*, vol. I, 2nd ed., p. 90), on one hand sets an inaccurate demarcation and, on the other hand, seems to believe by contrast that citizens were all the members of the nations aggregate to the empire itself even when they were not its subjects; that means precisely falling into that confusion between diversity of nation and diversity of subjection, which Tamassia warned about.

407 On this issue, see Karl Neumayer, *Die gemeinrechtliche Entwicklung des internationalen Privat- und Strafrechts bis Bartolus*, I, *Die Geltung der Stammerrechte in Italien*, München, 1901.

408 Tamassia, l. cit., On the persistence of Rhotari's chapter 367, see Giardina, *Osservazioni sull'expositio*, cit.

 | DOI:10.1163/9789004627154_010

Does this provision also apply to Jewish subjects? Again, why not consider the sources?

First, we should examine a provision of Charlemagne that sets the following principle: "Si judeus contra judeum aliquod negocium habuerit, per legem suam se defendat. Si vero contra christianum, christianus, si necesse fuerit, cum idoneis testibus super sanctorum pignora, per sacramentum aut cum ferro ignito se exoniet."[409]

According to this provision, we can deduce the following two principles: 1) In civil causes between Jews, the judges will apply the substantive Jewish law and comply with it even in the procedural part concerning the evidence; 2) In mixed relationships, the substantive non-Jewish law will be applied; as for the evidence, however, the Christian (that is, he alone) will resort to the means established by the Germanic tradition; whereas the Jew will conduct himself according to Jewish law.

It could be observed that the expression "per legem suam se defendat" has only a procedural content and that the second part of the rule concerning mixed relationships similarly refers only to the procedure.

However, apart from theoretical consideration, applying Jewish procedural rules in internal relationships would appear extremely illogical when not accompanied by a parallel application of the substantive ones, a provision (II, 1, 8) of the *Lex Romana Utinensis*[410] clarifies this matter. The provision corresponds to l. 10 C. Th. 2, 1, but radically transforms it by establishing, in opposition to the Roman law, the rule that in internal relationships the Jews

---

409 Capitulary of Charlemagne *de Judeis* (not datable precisely, but a little earlier than 814), § 6, in *Mon. Germ. Hist., Leges*, section II, *Capitularia Regum Francorum*, Boretius ed., t. I, p. 259. Reprinted in Aronius' *Regesten zur Geschichte der Juden im fränkischen und deutschen Reiche bis zum Jahre* 1273 Berlin, 1887, no. 78, p. 29. Boretius considers this provision spurious as it contrasts the Ludwigian formulas that we will soon cite and § 13 of the "Capitulare missorum acquisgranense alterum," of 809 (*Mon. Germ. Hist.*, ibid. p. 152) which disposes: "De judeis constitutum est ut si aliquis judeus super christiano propter suam querellam aliquid interpellaverit et cum testibus fuerit ei judicatum adprobare, III testes idonei christiani illi sufficiant et habeat judeus secundum aestimationem rei IIII aut VIIII aut VII. Si vero christianus judeum interpellare voluerit et de qualibet re, similiter cum tribus testibus idoneis christianis vel tribus judeis illi sufficiat." But there is no reason to doubt the authenticity since the two norms of capitularies, far from contradicting themselves, integrate, and provisions appear in each of the formulas (see below, footnote no. 416) which repeat, except for slight and insubstantial changes, the contents of both of them together.

410 *Mon. Germ. Hist., Leges*, Zeumer ed., t. V of the ancient collection. It is a text probably in Italian, in use in the Holy Roman Empire, to be placed between the 8th and 9th centuries. On the question of the date, see Besta's recent *Storia del diritto italiano, Le fonti*, vol. I, pp. 269–271; and Idem, *Fonti del diritto italiano*, Padua 1938, pp. 62–63.

live according to their law: "Judei qui apud romanos conversant inhabitandum, suam legem inter se ipsos custodiant: nam omnes alteras causas, quae apud christianos habuerint, judices christianorum inter eos judicent."

Therefore, in internal relationships, the Jews are obliged to live according to Jewish law and (it is argued *a contrario*) its application, as a rule, is handed down by Jewish judges.[411] In mixed relationships, the jurisdiction goes to Christian judges and – as clarified by the text of another epitome of the Theodosian, the *Epitome Monachi*[412] – State Civil Law is applied;[413] with the exception, it is fair to add based on Charlemagne's text, of the reference to Jewish procedure rules relating to evidence.

The picture drawn based on the conjunction of three cited texts is fully confirmed by the privileges granted to individual Jews or Jewish communities by German emperors and kings established in this instance. Privileges which, in this matter like many others, were granted in harmony with the general rule, to ensure better application, rather than, as some have thought,[414] to establish exceptions.

As in the aforementioned Ludovician formulas, the principle is established that the Jews benefiting from the privilege live according to their own law[415] and that, in case of controversy with Christians, are not forced to submit to

411 Which does not exclude concurrence with state courts, that will have also applied the Jewish law since, as I have already observed, it is not possible to devise a personal status ancipital and variable depending on the jurisdiction employed.

412 Epitome Monachi, *Mon. Germ. Hist.*, ibid.: "Judei omnes negotia quae inter se habent lege sua definiant. Quae vero cum christiano habent nostris legibus apud judicem provinciae confligant."

413 Which one? Probably one of the lineages to which the Christian counterpart belongs.

414 Scherer, op. cit., pp. 64–69 believes – erroneously as we have seen – that as foreigners the non-privileged Jews are deprived of all rights and that the privileged ones, by entering the royal *tuitio*, acquire the rights guaranteed by the king. However, the existence of general rules relating to the Jews, such as the capitulary of Charlemagne mentioned before and the lost legislation of Louis the Pious (on which, see above, footnote no. 74), belie this original "Rechtslosigkeit" claim for all the Jews. And also, by reasoning logically, if it looks natural that protection letters bring more security guarantees and greater privileges of public law to the beneficiaries, it does not seem possible that they decree a change of personal statute. It seems quite unthinkable that the unprotected Jews lived according to a law – let's say the state law, that is the lex franca – and those protected according to Jewish law. And besides the above-mentioned general texts disprove this shaky construction of Scherer.

415 *Mon. Germ. Hist.* Leges, section V, *Formulae imperiales e curia Ludovici Pii*, no. 30, p. 309, no. 31, p. 310: "... liceatque eis secundum legem eorum vivere"; no. 52, p. 325: "... liceat etiam ei secundum legem suam vivere." Cf. Waitz, *Deutsche Verfassungsgeschichte*, III, *Die Verfassung des fränkischen Reichs*, section II, 2nd ed., Kiel, 1883, p. 347 and ibid. no. 2 and Scherer, op. cit. pp. 66–67.

the trial by ordeal practice of evidence. They must instead adduce evidence according to Jewish law.[416]

Likewise, in Henry's IV, two privileges granted to the Jews of Speyer in 1090,[417] and of Worms probably on the same date,[418] the same rule is established, namely the prohibition in mixed relationships to submit the privileged to the trials by ordeal and their right to adduce the evidence according to their law, particularly about swearing under this same law; in internal disputes, the right to be judged by Jewish leaders, of course under Jewish law.[419]

---

416 Form. 30, pp. 309–310: "Quod si Christianus causam vel litem contra eos habuerit, tres idoneos testes christianos et tres ebreos similiter idoneos in testimonium suum adhibeat et cum eis causam suam vindicet. Et si illi causam vel litem contra christianum habuerint, christianos testes in testimonium sibi adsumant et cum eis eum convincant ... et nullatenus volumus ut predictos judeos ad nullum judicium examinandum [*sic*, per examinetis (Zeumer)], id est nec ad ignem nec ad aquam calidam seu etiam ad flagellum, nisi [sic, to be corrected with sed] liceat eis *secundum legem eorum vivere* <vel> [et probationem] ducere. Form. 31, p. 310 and 52, p. 321. The same passage "Quod si. ... convincant," to which it follows: "Nam si aliquis illorum, christianus aut judeus veritatem occultare voluerit, comes loci illius per verissimam inquisitionem faceat unumquemque illorum *secundum legem suam* veritatem dicere"; form. 31 finally adds: "... et nemo saepe dictis hebreis flagellis caedere praesumat, nisi probati fuerint *secundum legem eorum*, eos capitula, quae a nobis eis observanda promulgata sunt (see above, footnote no. 74) violasse atque irrita fecisse." There is not the slightest element to consider, as Löning does, *Geschichte des deutschen Kirchenrechts*, II, pp. 51 et seqq. and with him, though with some reservation, Zeumer, cit., p. 310, no. 2, that this *lex eorum* is in fact the Roman law. We saw that the idea that the Jews were considered as Romans in ethnic sense is absolutely false. They could be acknowledged as Romans only as subjects of the Holy Roman Empire, but this had no influence whatsoever on the personal law. Besides, all the scholars that we are going to mention here do not doubt that *lex judeorum* is in fact the Mosaic Rabbinic Law. See e.g., Waitz, 1, cit.

417 Hilgard, *Urkunden zur Geschichte der Stadt Speier*, I, no. 12; Stumpf, *Regesta*, no. 2902; Waitz, *Deutsche Verf.*, V, *Die deutsche Reichsverfassung*, I, p. 421 and II, p. 518, no. 4.

418 Lost; accessible in the act of confirmation of Frederick I, of April 6, 1157, *Mon. Germ. Hist., Constitutiones et acta publica imperatorum et regum*, I (911–1197), L. Weiland ed., Hannover, 1893, pp. 226–229. Cf. Waitz, op. cit., V, p. 421. On the two privileges, there are three articles by Hoeniger, Bresslau and Stobbe, respectively, in Geiger's *Zeitschrift für Geschichte der Juden in Deutschland*, I, 1886, inaccessible to me.

419 § 11. Quod si judeus contra christianum vel christianus contra judeum contenderit uterque prout res sua est, secundum legem suam justiciam faciat et rem suam probet. Et sicut licet unicuique christiano per suum et unius testis utriusque legis publicum juramentum probare fidejussores judeo per eum positos absolvisse, sic etiam judeo liceat per suum et unius judei et unius christiani publicum juramentum probare, fidejussores christiano per eum positos absolvisse, nec amplius ab actore vel judice sit cogendus. § 12. Et nemo judeum ad ignitum ferrum vel ad calidam aquam vel frigidam cogat nec flagellis caedat nec in carcerem mittat, sed juret secundum legem suam post quadraginta dies ... § 14. Quod si ipsi judei litem inter se vel causam aliquam habuerit determinandam, a suis

Even the privilege granted by Emperor Frederick II in August 1238 to the Jews of Vienna,[420] privilege mainly based on that of Worms just mentioned,[421] contains similar provisions;[422] while the later Germanic documents agree in showing the internal disputes of Jews decided under Jewish law, whether they are brought before rabbinical courts or instead judged by State tribunals.[423]

The private and procedural Jewish law in the Holy Roman Empire – and therefore in Italian territories of which they are part – is granted a rather broad sphere of validity[424] extending, as for the procedure, also to mixed relationships.

However, does this validity reflect an application to the Jews of the principle of the personality of the law in force, as we have said, for all citizens of

---

paribus et non ab aliis judicentur. Et si aliquando inter eos perfidus alicujus rei inter eos geste occultare voluerit veritatem, ab eo qui est episcopus eọrum veritatem fateri cogatur.

420 Printed in Hoeniger, op. cit., pp. 145 et seqq. and Scherer, op. cit., pp. 135–137 (who on p. 135, no. 1, points out the older editors).

421 Scherer, op. cit., pp. 137–143.

422 § 6. Si judeos in christianum vel christianus in judeum contenderit, uterque prout res est secundum legem suam justitiam faciat et rem suam probet. § 7. Et nemo judeum ad ignitum ferrum vel ad calidam acquam vel frigidam probet nec flagellis caedat vel in carcerem mittat, sed juret secundum legem suam post quadraginta dies. § 9 . Et si judei ipsi litem inter se aut causam aliquam habuerint determinandam coram eo qui praeest eis judicentur. On these paragraphs, see Scherer, op. cit., pp. 162–163 and 170–171.

423 Scherer, op. cit., p. 242, no. 2. So, in 1364 Rudolf IV takes in his hands "nach rat der jüdischen meister und der pesten juden, die wir zu den zeiten bei uns gehaben möchten" an inheritance civil lawsuit between two Jews and rules on it "nach jüdischen recht." Scherer, pp. 381–382. As a historical commentary to Frederick's II mentioned articles 11, 12 and 14 of the privilege dated 1238, the general rules in force in the various states of Europe about the jurisdiction on the Jews are reported in Scherer's work (pp. 249–312). Unfortunately, it is a chaotic presentation that cannot quite distinguish between administrative and judicial functions of the Jewish communities, offers a very confusing picture and is thus of very scarce usefulness.

424 Goldlast, *Imperatorum ... recessus, constitutiones etc.*, Frankfurt, 1673, t. III, p. 255 reports about a constitution *De nuptiis*, that he attributes to Ludwig II and dates 826, which enjoins the Jews to celebrate their weddings according to Christian ritual and canon law requirements, baptize their children and the like. The editor claims this bill to be "ex sacrarum institutione legum," book 12, tit. 3, chapt. 15. However, Ludwig has nothing to do with this constitution that is part of the terrible and oppressive legislation on the Jews of the Visigothic king Erwig (Lex visigothorum, XII, 3, 8, *Mon. Ger. Hist.* Leges, section I, t. 1, pp. 435–436). It loses all meaning if taken out of the context of the accompanying regulations that prohibit Jewish worship, force the Jews to baptism and impose the observance of the Catholic religion upon them. The Carolingians never thought anything like that. An acceptance on their part of the mentioned law on matrimony is to be discarded categorically. Of this opinion were, obviously, all modern editors of Carolingian legislation, who never included that constitution in their compilations.

the Empire, or the result of gracious concession? In other words, do Jews live according to their own law by right or by tolerance?

In the two pages dedicated to this issue, Brunner[425] expresses himself somewhat confusedly. While on the one hand, he states that the Jews are not Romans as maintained by Loening, but foreigners as maintained by Klimrath, and the Roman law is not their personal law, on the other hand, he argues that "in those matters in which Roman law has retained its strength, it has remained valid for the Jews." In contrast, however, in the territories in which the judges followed German law, it was the latter, and not the Roman law, applied to the Jews. But then again, Brunner adds that in their internal legal relationships, the Jews put the Roman law aside and, wanting to be Jews and Romans, used the Jewish law. However, the latter's application did not occur *de jure* but for mere tolerance, and its position before German and Roman laws constituted a an exceptional stance. As everyone can see, the picture is quite unclear.

Conversely, Goldschmidt[426] believes that the use of Jewish law by Jews derives simply from the general principle of the personality of the law and does not reflect the exception, made in their favor, to a general rule that would have subjected them to German law. The same viewpoint is also expressed by Stobbe, who includes the Jews among the foreigners.[427]

Heusler[428] opposes Goldschmidt in noting that Jews were not, in fact, subject *de jure* to German law, not because they could use, *de jure*, another law, but because they did not have any right to which to appeal. Jews, Heusler maintains, were not treated like other German peoples, nor were they allowed to use their law like the Romans or the Saxons were permitted to do so. On the contrary, the recognition of their law occurred by privilege and tolerance and was always so limited as to exclude that it resulted in applying the general personality principle.

Heusler's and Brunner's views are shared by Gierke,[429] for whom "the Jewish national law was a merely tolerated law " that the ordinary judge was not at all applying like he was applying the German law. According to Schröder,[430] Jews

425 Heinrich Brunner, *Deutsche Rechtsgeschichte*, I, 2nd ed., Leipzig 1906, pp. 402–403 and ibid., no. 22.

426 Goldschmidt, *Der Erwerb dinglicher Rechte*, in his *Zeitschrift für das gesammte Handelsrecht*, VIII, pp. 266 et seqq.

427 Otto Stobbe, *Handbuch des deutschen Privatrechts*, vol. I, 3rd ed., Berlin, 1893, p. 386: "Da die Juden im deutschen Staat als Fremde galten, standen sie in alter Zeit, nach dem Princip des Persönlichkeit des Rechts, unter dem jüdischen Recht."

428 A. Heusler, *Institutionen des deutschen Privatrechts*, Leipzig 1885, pp. 151–152.

429 O. Gierke, *Deutsches Privatrecht*, vol. I, Leipzig 1895, p. 439.

430 Richard Schröder, *Lehrbuch des deutschen Rechtsgeschichte*, 7th ed., reviewed by von Küntsberg, Berlin – Leipzig 1932, pp. 245 and 709.

could not appeal *de jure* to either the Roman law or Jewish law as their national law but received a personal statute only by privilege.

This German doctrine is followed by the Italian scholars Calisse,[431] Besta,[432] Solmi,[433] and Giardina.[434]

In summary, on the point in question, we have three different opinions:

1) In the Carolingian Empire, the Jews are regarded and treated as foreigners, and, as a rule, they cannot refer to their national law: this may be permitted to them only for an exceptional arrangement. (Klimrath, Scherer, Brunner, Schröder, Heusler, Gierke and all the Italians; for Stobbe, on the contrary, they can refer to their own law precisely because they are foreigners.)
2) The Jews are recognized as Romans and live under Roman law (Löning).
3) The Jews are neither Romans nor foreigners but citizens, and in their internal relations they live according to their law (Mayer,[435] referring to Italy from the 9th century and basing himself on the Lex Romana Utinensis; Goldschmidt who is referring to Germany).

Therefore, the most significant number of scholars favor the first of these theories.

Can this prevailing point of view now be maintained, after examining the Jews' *status civitatis* and the texts relating to using their law in the Carolingian Empire?

It does not look like it. These scholars, who want to rule out the extension of the principle of legal personality to the Jews, whether explicitly or implicitly, all assume that the Jews were considered aliens or treated as foreigners. Yet, we have shown that this is untrue. Jews were subjects, suffering from particular incapabilities, but still subjects. In principle, they were entitled to refer to their national law in all areas where this was allowed to the Christian subjects. Since the rules of these laws were very different from the Roman and Germanic ones, written in a language unknown to non-Jews and therefore generally unknown to all Christians, it was seen as appropriate that in mixed relationships – about rights and obligations – this law should not be taken into consideration, but would give way to the law of the Christian counterpart. How could have a Christian in fact checked the regularity of an obligation assumed by the Jewish counterpart according to Talmudic law rules? How could he have known, for

---

431 Calisse, *Storia del diritto italiano, Le fonti*, p. 91.

432 Besta, *Storia del diritto italiano, Le fonti*, vol. I, 1925, p. 206.

433 Solmi, *Storia del diritto italiano*, 3rd ed., 1930, pp. 122 and 301.

434 Giardina, *Osservazioni sull'Epositio al c. 367 di Rotari e al c. 27 di Pipino*, in *Annali dell'Istituto di Scienze giuridiche, economiche e sociali dell'Università di Messina*, vol. IX, y. 1934–1935, p. 26 of the reprint.

435 Mayer, *Italiänische Verfassungsgeschichte*, cit., vol. I, p. 147.

example, the age set by the Talmud to the capacity to contract and the deeds deemed necessary by this code to pass property ownership?

This would be possible if the Talmud were translated into Latin and at least in the civil law section, abridged in such a way as to be made accessible to Christians, a challenging undertaking, which had never been attempted.

It was deemed preferable to exclude the use of the Jewish law from mixed relationships, restricting it to internal disputes and empowering, as a rule, Jewish judges with the right to settle such disputes, both to satisfy the wishes of the Jews themselves, and more than anything else to overcome the difficulty that would have derived for Christian judges to apply the unknown and inaccessible Jewish rules.

After all, it can be asserted that the situation of the Jews, as for the use of their national law, appears to be *sui generis*: but here too their equalization to foreigners is unsustainable, since – unlike the foreigners, forced to live under the law of the ruler – in internal relations, they could follow the rules of the Jewish law.

This limitation in the use of their own law to the internal relations is, in fact, the only difference between the position of the Jews and that of the other citizens: the only one, I say, because the allegation that the principle of the personality of the law applicable to the Christian nations was *ipso jure* valid, and that the faculty left to the Jews to use their law, with the above-mentioned limitations, was an exceptional privilege, does not look very sound to me. However, in reality, neither the rule: "unusquisque homo suam legem pleniter habeat conservatam" nor the arrangement established, as we said, for the Jews, appears as a norm issued by the Imperial Chancellery in the standard form of fundamental state laws: they have a similar nature, and it is, therefore, illogical that a particular character of precariousness is attributed to only one of them.

•••

The application of the personality principle of the law to the Jews is documented accurately in Sicily, where, as has already been observed, the population's multinational and multi-faith composition determines the equality of the various groups and the admission of their respective laws on shared bases. The Sicilian citizens are divided into the groups of Latins, Greeks, Saracens and Jews; designations that have been rightly pointed out, refer to the commonality of language and confession than to nationality.[436]

---

436 K. Neumayer, *Die gemeinrechtliche Entwicklung des internationalen Privat- und Strafrechts bis Bartolus*, vol. 1, München 1901, pp. 261–262.

The term Latinos refers to the Latin-speaking followers of the Church of Rome, that is, Romans, Longobards and Franks, each of whom lives according to his own law.[437] The Greeks are members of the Church of Constantinople, Greek-speaking and living under Byzantine law.[438] The Saracens are Muslim Arabs, who also speak their own language and live according to their religious law. Finally, there are the Jews, whose law is fully recognized, alongside others, in internal relations and relations with members of other nations.

A document of 1168 from Catania[439] and a chapter of the Palermo Consuetudes provides direct attestations to that state of affairs, as they attribute full validity to the deeds stipulated in Arabic, Greek, and Hebrew according to the modalities of the respective laws.[440] This plurality of laws confirmed by Norman Assizes[441] entails typically also the plurality of notaries. Therefore, there are notaries of the Greeks, Latins,[442] Saracens and Jews.[443]

Of course, using one's own laws also includes taking the oath according to specific formulas.[444]

---

437 Id., op. cit., pp. 262, no. 2 and 266.

438 Id., op. cit., p. 264.

439 Episcopal privilege: "Latini, Graeci, Judaei et Saraceni, unusquisque secundum legem suam judicetur." De Grossis, *Catana sacra*, p. 88; Lagumina, *Codice diplomatico dei Giudei di Sicilia*, Palermo, 1885, doc. 15; R. Strauss, *Die Juden in Königreich Sizilien*, cit. p. 15; Neumayer, op. cit., p. 267.

440 *Consuetudini delle città di Sicilia*, La Mantia ed., Palermo, 1862, p. 19, Consuetudini di Palermo, ch. 36: "Venditiones quae factae sunt vel fient in posterum per Saracenos, judaeos et Graecos Siciliam habitantes de rebus stabilibus et mobilibus ab eis possessis omnimodam obtineant firmitatem; et instrumenta confecta de venditionibus vel permutationibus eorum aut quibuscumque contractibus aliis in lingua arabica, graeca et hebraica per manus notarionum Saracenorum, Graecorum vel Hebreorum vel Arabicorum, etsi sollemnitatibus careant Christianorum, nec non et instrumenta quae in posterum fient modo prescripto, firma et stabilia perseverent." La Mantina himself reports the text, *Cenni storici su le fonti del diritto greco-romano e le Assiste e leggi dei re di Sicilia*, p. 108, no. 1, and it is used by many scholars (Strauss, op. cit., l. c., Scherer, op. cit., p. 283, and others). Although only differences of language and form are allegedly dealt with, the judicial content of the documents is undoubtedly dealth with as well.

441 Brandileone ed., 95: The new law has only value as a subsidiary of common law "moribus, consuetudinibus, legibus non cassatis pro varietate populorum nostro regno subiectorum, sicut usque nunc obtinuit." Neumayer, op. cit., p. 266.

442 Doc. of 1271, 1282 and 1290: Benedictus publicus tabellio civitatis Panormi tam ad graecos quam latinos civitatis predictae. La Mantia, *Consuetudini*, cit., p. 227; C. A. Garufi, *I documenti inediti dell'epoca normanna in Sicilia*, I, 27; Neumayer op. cit., p. 267.

443 Consuetudini di Palermo, ch. 36 cit. A "publicus urbis Panormi notarius judeorum" can be found in 1321, Neumayer, p. 267, in Siciliano, *Consuetudini di Sicilia*, I, p. 320a.

444 Palermo 1286 and 1296: Jewish citizens are sworn in as interpreters and experts in judicial matters for the translation of Arabic documents into Latin, Giuseppe Spata, *Le pergamene greche esistenti nel grande Archivio di Palermo tradotte e illustrate*, Palermo, 1862, p. 451 and Garufi, op. cit., l. c. Neumayer, op. cit., p. 271.

However, this state of affairs does not continue indefinitely: in the mid-13th century the Arabs disappear, and the Latins and Greeks merge gradually, with the consequent disappearance of their respective laws, with the exception of some no longer personal but locally surviving norms.

Only for the Jews, since no assimilation is there, the difference in legislation persists:[445] as we shall see, in the 15th century, its recognition will remain restricted to internal relations and probably limited to matrimonial matters.

•••

During this period, the validity of Jewish law in Italy is confirmed by the substantial development that the study of the Talmud receives there, a development undoubtedly associated with the practical application of the law itself.[446] Although the Italian-Jewish Talmudic doctrine of the 11th, 12th and 13th centuries flourishes, especially in southern Italy, it cannot compete with contemporary Spanish, French and German schools, it can nevertheless boast the names of famous commentators. Izhak Ben Malkizedek of Siponto[447] and of Jesajà senior from Trani (d. ca. 1272), one of the most fruitful Talmudists of the Middle Ages, author of glosses (Tossafot) as celebrated as the classic ones of the French school[448] are among the most distinguished names. Traces of the Talmudic culture can also be found in northern Italy: in the 13th century, El'azar Ben Shmuel da Verona, grandfather of the famous philosopher Hillel da Verona and the glossator Moshe Ben Meir da Ferrara are the most well-known representatives of this era.[449]

2 Intermediate Period

2.1 *Generalities*

The *in complexu* revival of the Roman legislation determines the reappearance of the laws 7 and 8 C. J. 1, 9 that require Jews to live according to the State's law and suppress their judicial autonomy.

---

445 Neumayer, op. cit., p. 267.

446 Just like the resumption of studies of Roman law, which takes place in Italy right at the same time is a reflection of the renewed practical vigor of such a law.

447 Güdemann, *Geschichte der Erzihungswesens und der Kultur der Juden in Italien während des Mittelalters*, Vienna, 1884, p. 65.

448 Id., op. cit., pp. 184–189 and 320–326.

449 Id., op. cit., p. 185.

Although in contrast, as we have seen, with a centuries-old practice, these laws are accepted by earlier commentators as in force and considered applicable, without any restriction.

So, commenting on law 7 concerning Jews' marriage, Azone states that this must be contracted according to common law and not according to Jewish law.[450] By the same point of view, Jacopo de Ravanis (Revigny) and Cino da Pistoia abide, adding that if the marriage has not been concluded according to state law, the offspring who may be born to such couple, as illegitimate children, would not have the right to succeed to their parents.[451] Concerning the degrees of kinship prohibited, Cino da Pistoia furthermore raises the question of whether in the marriage Jews should observe the provisions of Roman civil law that allow marriages between first cousins,[452] or those of canon law that have declared such marriage incestuous and therefore forbidden.[453] Finally, he concludes that since the canon law prevails on the civil law for the Christian,[454] the Jews too are required to comply with it.[455]

Bartolomeo da Saliceto from Bologna,[456] who wants Jews to be submitted to common law in general, holds the same opinion, noting, however, the opportunity to derogate from the rule concerning swearing, given the religious basis of the institute.[457]

---

450 Azone, *Summa*, Venice, 1566, in C. 1, 9, f. 21: "Item permittitur eis [to the Jews] contrahere matrimonium inter se secundum jura nostra communia, non secundum leges suas, sed non cum christianis, ut in *l. nemo, de judeis* (C. 1, 9, 7)."

451 Jacopo da Revigny, *Lectura super Codicem* (attributed to Pietro da Bellapertica), Paris, 1519, in *l. celebrandis C. de nuptiis* (C, 5, 4, 20): "nisi Judei contrahant matrimonium secundum ritum nostrum liberi eorum non eis succedunt." Cino da Pistoia, *Super aureo volumine Codicis*, Venice, 1493, in *l. nemo C. de judeis* (C. 1, 9, 7): "Judei debent contrahere matrimonium secundum jus nostrum, alias filii non succedent."

452 C. 5, 4, 20 (y. 405) of Constantine, Arcadius and Honorius who, by repealing previous laws, allow marriages between first cousins.

453 Decretum , causa 35 *cum igitur*, q. II and III, ch. 20 (Letter from Gregory the Great to Augustine, Bishop of the Anglos). The l. 20 C. 5, 4 is expressly repealed.

454 The gloss "celebrandis" of the l. 20 C. 5, 4 notes: "haec lex hodie non servatur iure canonico," and cites precisely the Decretum, causa 35, q. II and III, ch. 20.

455 Cino, in *l. celebrandis de nuptiis* (C. 5, 4, 20): "Lex ista obtinet jura nostra fori, sed non jure poli. Sed quid in judeis qui contrahunt secundum hanc legem? Nunquid filii nati ex tali matrimonio succedunt tamquam legitimi? Dicendum est quod non, quia judei debent contrahere secundum ritum nostrum, ut supra *de judeis, l. nemo judeorum* (C. 1, 9, 7)."

456 Bartolomeo da Saliceto, *In primum et secondum codicis libros*, Venice, 1574, in *l. nemo C. de judeis* (C. 1, 9, 7): "Nuptiae inter christianos prohibitae similiter inter judeos prohibentur sua lege cessante."

457 Idem, in *l. nemo C. de judeis* (C. 1, 9, 8): "Causa judeorum secundum jura nostra est agitanda ... sed per quem jurabunt in sacramento columnie? Dicit Bart. quod per Moysen vel Deum non per Evangelia que non colunt."

Evidently, these scholars are sticking to the text of the two laws considered in their abstract expression that never wondered whether the denied vitality of Jewish legislation was contrary to the practice in force throughout the Holy Roman Empire before the laws reappeared. Furthermore, I think I can explain the reason for this attitude. Except for the Frenchman da Revigny, the scholars mentioned belong to northern and central Italy, where with rare exceptions, the Jews do not begin to take stable residence before the 14th century and do not form numerically significant communities till much later.[458] Those jurists did not have the opportunity to practically deal with the conflict between Jewish law and local law and detect the contrast between Roman and medieval principles concerning the resolution of the conflict itself. Consequently, they do not see any reason to break away from the provisions of two Roman laws and fully abide by them.

As soon as Jewish communities settled in northern and central Italy and determined the rise in litigations among Jews before district courts, the aforementioned conflict between the two legislations was set there concretely by Romanist doctrine. Hence the need for a further examination of the matter, which generally determines abandoning of the negative solution, set by the two Roman laws and the affirmation of an opposite doctrine, in favor of recognizing the vitality of Jewish civil law.

In the intermediate period, the first jurist who hits the new road is the canonist Giovanni Calderini from Bologna (b. late c. XIII, d. 1365). He presents his conclusions concerning practical questions that probably arose in Bologna itself or some recently formed communities of Umbria, Tuscany and Marche. For Calderini, the Jewish law is a special law that, under Roman and canonical rules,[459] derogates from the general and common law like a species from its genus. He concludes that, just like in cases of controversy among Christians, where according to *l. omnes ff. de justitia et jure* (D. 1, 1.9) first the municipal

---

458 Toward the end of the 1200s, some Jewish families migrated from Rome and settled in various locations of Lazio and Umbria in order to engage in the money-lending business. Moving from Rome, the migratory current continues its spread in those regions in the following century, and then touches Marche and Romagna. Finally, in the second half of the 1300s, it reaches Emilia, Lombardy and Veneto, meeting another flow of migrants coming from Germany. It is precisely from the continuous flow of these two currents that the communities of northern and central Italy originate. See on this, my extensive work *Prestito ebraico e comunità ebraiche nell'Italia settentrionale e centrale* (Jewish money loaning and Jewish communities in Northern and Central Italy) in *Rivista di Storia del Diritto italiano*, y. VIII, 1935, pp. 431–444.

459 D. 50, 17, 80: "In toto jure generi per speciem derogatur." Decretales, VI, book 5, tit. 12, *de regulis juris*, reg. 34: "generi per speciem derogatur."

law applies as a special law, and then, subsidiarily, the common law,[460] so in cases of dispute between Jews, their law needs to be applied first and, in the absence of norms adequate to the case, the common law thereafter. The application of Jewish law should be precluded only in areas where it is expressly repealed by local law but not in the other areas.

This critical faculty of seeing one's own law applied by derogation from the common law in what is not *expresse reprobatum* is not recognized to the Jews *ex novo*: Calderini wants it based on Roman and canonical texts that are naturally interpreted in a forced manner.

So, the phrase of the *l. Judeos C. De Judeis* (C. 1, 9, 11) "ritos suos citra contemptum Christianae legis retineant amissuri sine dubio hactenus permissa, nisi ab illicitis retractaverint" referring generically to the privileges granted to the Jews is turned to mean "quod lex sua inter eos debet servari nisi in his quae non sunt eis permissa sed prohibita." To support it without many splitting hairs on the circumstances of time and place, Calderini quotes the Gospel (John 19, 7) about the request made by the Jews before Pilate to rule on Jesus according to their law "quasi dicatur lex nostra debet servari nobis." Nor do the laws 7 and 8 C. 1, 9 stand in the way. According to them, civil law enforcement is imposed since they must be understood as referring to mixed disputes between Christians and Jews or even in internal matters, to matters in which the civil law expressly derogates from the Jewish laws.[461]

---

460 This well-known passage taken from Gaius (*Ist.* 1, 1) was initially meant to highlight how in all nations' legal systems, a core of peculiar rules, and another core of common rules can be found. However, in the intermediate period, it was instead intended as proclaiming the priority of particular municipal laws over Roman common law, and it became the basis of the autonomy system.

461 Giovanni Calderini, *Consilia ... secundum decretalium rubricas digesta*, s. l., 1536, *De constitutionibus*, cons. 10, f. 3v.: "Lex mosaica est specialis judeorum; ergo inter eos derogat legi generali et communi sicut species generi; in *l. toto ff. de regulis juris* (D. 50, 17, 80) et eodem titulo generali Lib. VI (VI, 5, 12, reg. 34). Hinc est quod ut scribitur in Evangelio [John 19, 7] judei de diversis legibus loquentes dicebant Pilato: legem habemus et secundum legem debet mori, etc., quasi dicatur lex nostra debet servari nobis. Non obstant contraria: quod in his quod expressim contra legem eorum sunt eis per legem communem prohibita, lex communis debet servari. In his vero in quibus lex communis legi judaicae non derogat, tunc inter <christianos et> [oversight] judeos lex est communis: et sic a christianis servari debet lex judaica ut eorum specialis: sicut inter christianos servarentur primo eorum jura municipalia. Lege vero judaica deficiente recurrendum est ad jus commune: ita debet intelligi *l. judeos C. de judeis* (C. 1, 9, 11) in fine: "amissuri sine dubio permissa hactenus nisi ab illicitis retractaverint." Nam ex illa littera datur intelligi quod lex sua inter eos debet servari: nisi in his quae non sunt eis permissa sed prohibita: sic et inter christianos jure municipali deficiente recurrimus ad jus commune, *l. omnes ff. de justitia et jure* (D. 1, 1, 9)." Similarly, Id., *De testamentis*, cons. 30, f. 41 and *De consuetudine*, cons. 2, f. 6v.

Not long afterward, another renowned canonist, Giovanni d'Anagni, is drawn to deal with the problem. While advocating, with many reservations, the disregard of Jewish law alongside opposite arguments, he diligently lists those arguments, which in his opinion could support the thesis of the application of the law.[462]

It is worthwhile considering these texts individually since, along with those cited by Calderini, they will subsequently constitute with a few others the constant basis of the arguments in favor of the application of Jewish law; and we will find them again in many scripts of theoretical and practical nature.

1) A first argument is taken from the Decretum (45, *dist. qui sincera,* § *Judei* = Decr. 45, 3). It is a letter by Gregory the Great (book 11, Epist. 15) to Pascasio, bishop of Naples, with which the Pope recommends leaving the Jews the freedom to observe their festivals and ceremonies. The original meaning of lex is expanded from the religious and ritual norm to the judicial norm; thus, the ground is laid for Jews' right to live according to their civil law.

2) A second argument is that already used by Calderini, who rests on the passage by Gaio (Ist. 1.1) quoted in the Pandects (*l. omnes populi ff. de justitia et jure* = D. 1, 1, 9). According to the usual arbitrary[463] interpretation of the intermediate period, as I have said, this passage sets the principle of the prevalence of civil law distinctive to each people over the common Roman-Canon Law that would assume a simply subsidiary value. Such civil law, adds another canonical text (1, *dist. Jus civile* = Decr. 1, 8), may have a human as well as a divine origin,[464] and for the Jews, it is constituted by the laws of the Old Testament revealed by God to the people through Moses (7, *dist. Moyses* = Decr. 7, 1).[465] According to the general rule, these laws prevail over common law and only when they are lacking it is necessary to resort to common law.

The principle outlined here that concerning the Roman-Canon Law, Jewish civil laws are on the same level alongside the rules of the *civitates* included in the empire is of enormous importance. Through these laws, that very same legislative autonomy that the *civitates* had painfully been gaining with a bitter political struggle was attributed unchallenged to the Jewish communities, even though they did not constitute territorial entities.

---

462 Giovanni d'Anagni, *Lectura super quinto Decretalium*, Milan, 1492, f. 63–63-v, commentary to *c. Judei, il secondo, x de judeis* (c. 5 ×. 5, 6). D'Anagni also repeats verbatim all of Calderini's arguments.

463 See no. 460 above.

464 "Jus civile est quod quisque populus vel quaeque civitatis sibi proprium divina humanaque causa constituit."

465 "Moyses gentis hebreae primus omnium divinas leges sacris literis explicavit."

After Calderini and d'Anagni many others will repeat that,[466] and in fact, the Jews themselves will resort to it when, with the emancipation policy, their autonomy will be questioned.[467]

In further support of the thesis, Anagni also cites the *l. de quibus ff. de legibus* (D. 1, 3, 32) that in lawsuits where there is no written law, prescribes to use that common law first, then – if a particular rule is missing in it – the principles learned from it by analogy, and then the "jus quo urbs Roma utitur." Through an interpretation that has nothing to do with the original meaning of the passage, probably here, too, one wants to see in Jewish law a customary law that must prevail over Roman law.

3) Another support is drawn from the passage of 1, *dist. jus Quiritum* (Decr. 1, 2, 12) that reserves the use of quiritarian Roman law to the Romans only.[468] We understand the text initially intends to exclude non-citizens, i.e., the *peregrini*. But d'Anagni intends the qualification of Roman not in the political-state sense, but the national sense and he thus excludes the Jews from the use of Roman law since, although Roman citizens, as members of the Holy Roman Empire, they are not nationally Roman and therefore must adhere to their national law.[469]

4) Finally, to give a semblance of validity to the thesis of the prevalence of Jewish law over common law, one can base himself, says d'Anagni, on the statement that Jews "non humanis sed divinis constitutionibus subiciuntur" made

466 So does Lauro Palazzi, *Tractatus de statuto communiter per Italiam vigentem, quod extantibus masculis feminae non succedant*, in *T.U.J.*, tome II, Venice, 1584, nos. 262–263, p. 283 (passage reported above, footnote no. 224). Still at the end of the 18th century, in the passage already quoted (above, footnote no. 315) of his article *Riforma politica degli Ebrei*, Italian transl., Mantua, 1807, pp. 116–118, in addition to the right to equality, we see Dohm also supporting the right for the Jews to legislative and jurisdictional autonomy. He does not find anything illogical that, albeit in the complete equalization policy, they are granted the same faculty that various cities and communities usually enjoy.

467 And precisely to the argument of Dohm, the Jewish communities of Mantua will appeal in 1804, when the French Government, *in toto* equalizing the Jews to other citizens, seeks to suppress the legislative and judicial autonomy that the community had enjoyed for centuries. See further on, part 3, chap. 3, § 11, footnote no. 1082.

468 "Jus quiritum est proprie romanorum, quod nulli tenent nisi quirites idest romani."

469 Conversely, as we have seen (above, p. 50), noting that in the l. 8 C. 1,9 it is stated that the Jews too are "romano communi jure viventes," the gloss (in "quod nulli") concludes that the word "romani" in the text does not refer to nationality, but rather to subjection. In this sense, as subjects of the Roman Empire, the members of Jewish lineage can also be considered Roman.

in texts 12 *dist. omnia* (Decr. 12, 12),[470] and 7, *dist. si solus Christus* (Decr. 8, 9) with the gloss "hominum."[471]

5) Lastly, D'Anagni presents the contrary thesis "quod illa quae scripta sunt in veteri testamento non ligant in novo nec aliter sunt observanda nisi sint in novo repetita," but he notes that one may oppose to it considering "hoc verum inter christianos, vel judeum et christianum, secus inter judeos."

This important point is connected with a theological matter that deserves more careful consideration and clarification.

The Catholic Church's fundamental doctrine that the whole Mosaic Law was abolished "per adventum Christi."[472] Since Paul of Tarsus proclaims that the soteriological effectiveness of the Law has expired, replaced by that of faith in Christ,[473] the Christian community that had been hitherto entirely faithful

470 Epistle of St. Augustine to Januarius (Epist. 119, c. 19). When founded neither on the Scriptures, nor on Councils, nor on the general custom, but only on the particular *mos*, the practices established in the Church must be abolished in order not to become a burden to the faithful "ne tolerabilior sit conditio Judeorum, qui, etiam si tempus libertatis non agnoverint, legalibus tamen sacramentis non humanis praesuptionibus subiciuntur." Here it is simply pointed out that the Jews are more reluctant than the Christians to submit to burdensome and extensive human interpretations of the divine law; but, taken out of context, the sentence "legalibus tamen sacramentis non humanis praesumptionibus subiciuntur" serves quite well to support the thesis that the Jews should be governed by their divine laws rather than by the local human ones.

471 Not human tradition, but the word of Christ is to be followed, as Isaiah says: "sine causa colunt me mandata et doctrinas hominum docentes." Gloss to "hominum": "ergo Judei reguntur humanis constitutionibus et sic est contra infra-12, *dist. omnia* [Decr. 12, 12, see previous note] ubi dicitur quod Judei tantum divinis constitutionibus reguntur: sed verum est quod olim regebantur constitutionibus humanis, scilicet Scribarum et Phariseorum, ut hic dicit, sed hodie non, ut ibi." The effort to find common ground in such disparate texts, as we can see, leads to highly devious reasoning: but the conclusion is always the same.

472 On this point there are three old particular studies, Wilhelm Zepper, *Legum mosaicarum forensium explanatio; ubi quaestio an et quatenus abolitae illae sint ventilatur*, Herbornae, 1604, 2nd ed. 1617; Nitzsch, *Ueber die Ungültigkeit des mosaischen Gesetzes*, Wittemberg, 1800; Christian Hermann Friedrich Bialoblotzky, *De legis mosaicae abrogatione commentarius*, Göttingen, 1825 (quite unimportant for our point of view since it only deals with ceremonial rules and not legal ones).

473 As it is well known, that is the central point of Pauline theology. It is mainly developed in the Epistle to the Galatians (2, 15–16, 21; 3; 4; 5, 1–7) and *Acts* 13, 38–40; but it dominates in all apostles' writings. For Paul, no longer the precepts of the law but only the faith in Christ can bring salvation. The Ancien Covenant (Old Testament, as it will be termed later, interpreting in a different sense the Greek διαθήκη that translates the Hebrew *brith*) made by God with the Jews through the Law, is replaced now by the new Covenant – the New Testament – sealed by the martyrdom and the blood of Christ, son of God. Thus, the Jews are no longer the true people of God but all those who believe in Christ. Jews and

to Judaism[474] detaches itself from it as it began its autonomous journey.[475] Breaking free from the Judaizing tendencies continually springing up within it is indeed its constant concern during the first centuries.[476]

Of the Mosaic precepts, only those of moral character are considered valid (and this, furthermore, only by the later theological elaboration): the ceremonial and legal provisions are proclaimed null and devoid of binding

---

Gentiles alike will join this new people since with his sacrifice, "of the two peoples Christ made one (the Church) and with the abolition of ... the law he has knocked down the wall of separation (Ephesians, 2, 14–15). Therefore, it is impossible to go the two ways at the same time: either you believe in the salutary efficacy of the Torah, and then you stay – if you are Jewish – or walk with the ancient people of God – if you are a Gentile – in the synagogue; or you believe in that of Christ, and then, you join the new people, the Church. It is either one thing or the other.

474 The opposition of the Judaizers to Paul's radical thesis brings about the Conference of Jerusalem (*Acts*, 15, 1–36); on this and on early Jewish phase of Christianity in general, see Hoennicke, *Das Judenchristentum in ersten und zwetten Jahrhundert*, Berlin, 1908.

475 Breaking away from Judaism, the Church claims the quality of chosen people for itself. In its relationship with God, the Church has replaced Israel and has inherited the qualities of a "chosen generation, Kingdom of priests, consecrated lineage" (*I Petri*, 2, 9, cf. *Exodus* 19, 5–6); now, it carries on its history. No longer the Jews but the Christians are the true Israel; the Church, not the Synagogue owns the divine promises. This consciousness of the integral replacement of Christianity to Judaism is overly emphasized in the first centuries and gives rise to violent polemics with the Jews who are unwilling to admit their abandonment by God. On the Christians as a people, as the "true Israel," see the interesting chapter by Harnack, *Missione, e propagazione del cristianesimo nei primi tre secoli*, Milan 1906, pp. 183–211, with an extensive collection of texts that might still be greatly enriched (cf., for example, Justin, *Dialogo con Trifone*, ch. 11, 123, 135; Afraate, *Omelia* 16, § 6, etc.); N. Bonwetsch, *Der Schriftbeweis für die Kirche aus den Heiden als das wahre Israel bis auf Hippolitus*, in the *Theologische Studien Theodor Zahn dargebracht*, Leipzig, 1908, pp. 3–22 (which I haven't seen). On their claims to the succession and the subsequent controversies with the Jews, see Juster, I, p. 44, no. 2, 227 no. 6, 292 and 294 no. 1; Volterra, *Collatio Legum Mosaicarum et Romanarum*, in *Memorie dell'Accademia dei Lincei*, Cl. Scienze morali, 1930, pp. 91–95 and Idem, *Considerazioni teologico-giuridiche di Asterio di Amasea*, in *Riv. It. per le Scienze giuridiche*, N.S., year IV, 1929, dossier 1–2. Nevertheless, the idea remains one of the primary points of Catholic theology, and we can find it repeated by theologians and jurists in every century. Cf., e.g., Bartolo, *Prima super Codicem*, in l. 6 C. 1, 8 *de Paganis*: "Dices tu: qualiter Ecclesia inducit bellum contra Saracenos? Respondeo: Quia Saraceni tenent terram nostram. Nam terra Hierusalem est terra promissionis, quam promisit Deus Abrahae et semini eius: et debita nobis: quia sumus filii Abrahae secundum Apostulum."

476 On the various Christianizing Jewish sects (Nazarenes, Ebionites and others) and Judaizing Christian sects (Ipsistarians, Eufemites, etc.), see sources and bibliography in Juster I, p. 287, no. 1, and 288, no. 2. On the struggle by the Church against all Judaizing currents, see ibid., pp. 277 and seqq.

effectiveness:[477] they may be brought back to life sometimes and adopted by the Church but, in this case, they are not in force *ipso jure* but under this call back.[478]

---

477 The ecclesiastical theory on the value of the ancient law is extensively developed by St. Thomas, *Summa Theologica*, prima secundae, quest. 98–105 (Opera omnia, Rome, 1570, pp. 211–242). The abolition of the *praecepta ceremonialia* is examined particularly in question 103; that of the *praecepta judicialia* in question 104. After stating that they must be intended in a figurative sense (art. II: Judicialia illi populo tradita magis sunt figuralia quam judicia aliis populis tradita: sicut etiam bella et gesta illius populi exponuntur mistice, non autem bella, vel gesta Assyriorum vel Romanorum, quamvis longe clariora secundum homines fuerint), St. Thomas proclaims the complete repeal of the latter (Art. III: Dicendum quod judicialia praecepta non habuerunt perpetuam obligationem, sed sunt evacuata per adventum Christi, aliter tamen quam caeremonialia. Nam caeremonialia adeo sunt evacuata, ut non solum sint mortua, sed etiam mortifera observantibus post Christum, maxime post Evangelium divulgatum. Praecepta autem judicialia sunt quidem mortua, quia non habent vim obligandi, non tamen sunt mortifera: quia si quis princeps ordinaret in regno suo illa judicialia observari, non peccaret, nisi forte hoc modo observarentur, vel observari mandantur, tamquam habentia vim obligandi ex Veteris Legis institutione. Talis enim intentio observandi esset mortifera et huius defferentiae ratio potest accipi ex praemissis). For an even more complete treatise, see Francesco Suarez, *Tractatus de legibus ac de Deo legislatore*, book IX, *De Lege Divina positiva vetere*, Lyon 1619, pp. 634–715. On the abrogation of the law in general, see pp. 667 and seqq.; of the *praecepta judicialia*, p. 671 ("Circa praecepta judicialia potest esse nonnullum dubium an mortua sint ... Nihilominus certa conclusio est, legem veterem cessasse seu abrogatam esse quaod praecepta judicialia"). In a similar way Reiffenstuel expounds, *Jus canonicum universum*, Venice 1704, tome I, ad lib. I Decretalium, title II, § 3, nos. 47–48, p. 66; E. Pirhing, *Jus canonicum in quinque libros Decretalium distributum*, Dilingae, 1722, tome I, p. 4; Devoti, *Institutionum canonicarum*, 4 Books, 5th ed., Florence 1816, tome I, p. 25: "Judicialia ac ceremonialia praecepta adventu Christi sublata sunt; et si qua adhuc vigent, ea servantur quod ab ecclesia recepta sunt, non tamquam mosaicae legis reliquiae, sed tamquam apostolorum atque Ecclesiae mandata. Moralia tamen praecepta perpetuo manent; nam ea sunt mandata ipsa juris naturae." Note that in the preface of the Eastern nomocanon known under the name of *Leges Saeculares* or *Libro siro-romano di diritto* it is stated that "all laws [i.e., not only the Mosaic ones but also those of other peoples] have been abolished since the advent of our Lord, and one law has been given to all men, that of the Messiah, starting from the Blessed King Constantine." (German ed. and transl. in E. Sachau, *Syrische Rechtsbücher*, vol. I, pp. 47–49, Berlin, 1907; Latin transl. by Ferrini in *Bull. Ist. di Dir. Romano*, 1900, re-ed. in *Fontes juris romani antejustinianei*, Florence, 1940.)

478 See e.g., the text of St. Thomas mentioned in the previous note. In *Corpus Juris Canonici* numerous rules taken from the Mosaic code can be found (e.g., ch. 1–5 × 5, 36 *de iniuriis et damno dato*; ch. 1 × 5, 15 *de adulteriis*; ch. 1 × 5, 18 *de furtis*; ch. 1 × 5, 12 *de homicidiis*, etc.; from Exodus, ch. 21 and 22), whose the influence is often directly exerted on civil laws (for the Byzantine law, cf. the 36 chapters of Mosaic law included in the *Ecloga ad Procheiron mutata*, title 39, Zachariaä von Lingenthal, *Jus graeco-romanum*, vol. IV; for the Irish law, see Fournier, *Le Liber ex Lege Moysi et les tendences bibliques du droit irlandais*, in *Révue celtique*, XXI, 1900, pp. 728 et seqq.). Despite the dogma of abolition, the strength of the

To the dogmatic reasons mentioned for the abolition of Mosaic Law, Christian theologians consistently add the Law's national and local character, contrary to the Gospel's universality.

Centuries later, but in terms substantially identical, so do Eusebio,[479] St. Thomas,[480] Suarez,[481] and Zepper,[482] to name a few.

Mosaic norms was such as to render sometimes necessary a specific prohibition to eliminate them. See the curious provision of Frederick II King of Prussia dated August 20, 1751: "Thus it is my firm intention that in the future such cases be handled absolutely according to my orders and my prescriptions and no one should turn for advice to Moses and the prophets, such as those who have nothing to do in this country." Friedberg and Ruffini, *Trattato di diritto ecclesiastico*, Turin, 1893, p. 102, no. 10.

479 Eusebio, *De demonstratione evangelica*, ed. Paris, 1581, ch. III, p. 283: The Jewish Law has local character because it imposes obligations that can be implemented only by residents in the country. So e.g., the feast of Pentecost: "Quum igitur eum locum tam multis signis ostendat, totiesque illuq ire cum toto genere, totaque domo oportere praecipiat, qui fieri potest, ut ea quae dicit, vel iis conveniant qui brevi intervallo a Judea distant, nedum gentibus, quae in toto orbe terrarum, degere intelligantur? eo magis quod ne veniam ullam tribuit iis qui transiliant quaecumque praescripta sunt ... Quod quidem quum ab omnibus quicumque sunt in terra plane effici non posse, ipse auctor legis videret, tum perspicue significavit legem inducens, non infinite adversus omnes, sed adiiciens: "Si anima peccaverit nolens, *ex populo terrae* ...; p. 284: "... plane perspicis ut vel ipsis Hyerosolima incolentibus atque in una Judea versantibus et degentibus, mosaicum vivendi illud institutum servatu difficile esset, nedum tale ut posset a reliquis observari."; ch. V, p. 286: "Ita quidem ostensum iam est, quemadmodum Vetus illud Testamentum lexque mosaica uni iudaicae genti, et huic ipsi propriam terram incolenti accomodari posset, ac neque reliquis gentibus, quae toto terrarum orbe tenentur, neque alienas terras Judaeis incolentibus conveniret." The same concept is expounded in ch. VI and VII (pp. 293 and 294) where the contrast with the universality of the Gospel is emphasized, "ab initio propriam non solum Judaeis sed etiam Graecis et Barbaris et quaecumque sub sole sunt, gentibus inclamans legem, vide quid dicat: O homo, et universum mortalium genus!"

480 St. Thomas, *Summa Theologica*, prima secundae, quaest. 98, artic. 4: Utrum lex vetus dari debuerit soli populo Judeorum; artic. 5 "Utrum omnes homines obligabantur servare legem veterem": Dicendum quod lex vetus manifestabat precepta legis naturae et superaddebat quaedam propria praecepta. Quantum igitur ad illa, quae lex vetus continebat de lege naturae omnes tenebantur ad observantiam veteris legis, non quia erant de veteri lege, sed quia erant de lege naturae: sed quantum ad illa quae lex vetus superaddebat, non tenebantur aliqui ad observantim veteris legis, nisi solus populus Judeorum. cuius ratio est: quia lex vetus, sicut dictum est (art. 4) data est populo Judeorum, ut quandam praerogativam sanctitatis obtineret propter reverentiam Christi, qui ex illo populo erat nasciturus."

481 Suarez, *De legibus ac de Deo legislatore*, cit., p. 651: "Atque ex dicta legis promulgatione, et forma eius colligi potest primo legem illam non esse datam pro universo mundo, sed pro solo populo Israel, ut tradit divus Thomas quaest. 98, art. 4 et sumitur aperte ex forma ejusdem legis *Exodi*, 19, 20 et seqq. ubi ad illum populum solum sermo legis dirigitur, et *Deuteronomio*, 1: "Haec sunt verba quae loquutus est Moyses ad omnem Israel," et cap. 5: "Audi Israel. ..." Deinde lex illa soli illi populo promulgata est, tantumque praecipiebat eis,

Besides, this abolition of Mosaic Law is established by the Church as concerning only Christians. Therefore, although Jews are not banned from conforming to it in the legal field, since once the principle is accepted that their religion – based precisely on that law – is tolerated, it is irrelevant for the Church whether this tolerance is exerted only *quoad ceremonialia* and not *quoad judicialia*, too. Thus, we see that the Church lets the State free to determine as it pleases, with political criteria, if and to what extent the validity of the Jewish law can be accepted for the Jews, as it also recognizes that certain relations between Jews – marriage in particular – should more appropriately be regulated by their law.[483]

The arguments of Calderini and d'Anagni constitute excellent support to the thesis of the validity of the Jewish norms, as opposed to the provisions of the old Roman laws of 393 and 398; and we see the majority of scholars, both canonists and civilists, agreeing in this viewpoint proclaiming the viability of the whole Mosaic-rabbinical civil law.

Among the civilists, the first who accepts the thesis is Baldo degli Ubaldi, in a council we shall talk again later.[484] He will be followed by Floriano da S. Pietro, from Bologna, in his comments to the Digest and the Code,[485] and

quibus dabatur, ut eam docerent filios suos et nepotes, ut dicitur *Deut.* 4 ... Ratio autem ob quam lex illa data est particulari populo, et non omnibus hominibus reddi potest primo, quia illa non est data ut simpliciter necessaria ad salutem: nam sine illa potuerunt homines salvari ante illam, et gentiles illa durante ... Deinde data est illi populo potius quam aliis, non propter justitiam eius, sed ex divina electione ... Ratio enim inde sumi potest quia ex illo populo erat Christus nasciturus, in cuius honorem Deus voluit specialiter disponere illum populum, mediante lege ... Advertendum est autem, licet illa lex non fuerit gentibus imposita, nihilominus voluntarie potuisse illam amplecti, idque duobus modis. Primo per imitationem, acceptando v. g. in suis regnis, vel rebuspublicis, et in eis similiter leges statuendo, hoc enim nec per se malum erat, nec prohibitum. Tunc autem leges illae in talibus populis humanae essent non divinae quia ibi non obligarent ex vi divinae legislationis sed ex voluntate alicuius principis humani, sicut nunc lex solvendi decimas in Ecclesia quoad quotam humana est, licet in populo Israel fuerit divina. Secundo potuerant gentes legem illam voluntarie profiteri, assumpta prius circumcisione, ut constat *Exod.* 12, tum autem licet legis professio esset voluntaria, postea observatio esset necessaria, juxta illud *Pauli, ad Gal.* 5."

482 Zepper, op. cit., p. 24 et seqq.

483 See further on, footnotes nos. 547–554.

484 Baldo degli Ubaldi, *Consiliorum volumina*, vol. v, no. 428, Venice ed. 1575, p. 114. It should be noted that this consultation is also included in those by Floriano da S. Pietro, *Facumdissima ac eximia in tres secundae partis infortiati insigniores titulos ... commentaria, cum ... quibusdam aliis eiusdem in iure civili responsa sive mavis consilia*, Bologna, 1576, cons. 18, f. 278–279, so that its authorship is in question.

485 Floriano da S. Pietro, *Commentaria in primam et secundam partem Digesti veteris*, Bologna, 1576–1578, comm. in D. 1, 6, 3 and *Commentaria in primam et secundam Codicis partem*, in C. 6, 28, 4.

in a consultation relating to an important lawsuit of 30,000 ducats, also subscribed – besides by himself – by his colleagues Pietro d'Ancarano, Raffaele Fulgosio and Gaspare Calderini.[486]

The mentioned scholars' authority induces the contemporary canonist Felino Sandeo[487] to side with them, not adding any new argument but rather summarizing his predecessors. We learn from him that Paolo di Castro[488] had already previously agreed with the theory.

Also, based on the authority of Calderini, whose entire quoted cons. 30 *de testamentis* is reported, is the consistent conclusion by Alessandro Tartagni from Imola that "ubi habemus legem mosaycam non debemus ab ea discedere quoad actum celebratum per judeum sine christiano, et solum debet attendi ipsa lex mosayca, non autem lex humana, nisi quatenus expresse lex humana prohiberet judeis."[489]

Interestingly, this doctrinal current in favor of recognizing the Jewish law keeps gradually strengthening to the point of including even those who initially admitted to having an entirely contrary opinion. We see in fact the old adversary Bartolomeo of Saliceto[490] adhere to it in a council also undersigned by Francesco Ramponi, Giovanni Fantuzzi and Pietro d'Ancarano.

All these scholars repeat the arguments of Calderini and d'Anagni listed above, passing them with very few variations from predecessor to successor; argumentations on which subsequent lawyers, whom we shall meet in the following paragraphs, will also rely on. Only in the case of local privileges allowing the Jews to use their precepts and rites, the doctrine sometimes also relies on these concessions, maintaining that the Jewish legal rules are also recognized in them.[491] Still, others resort to *c. lex imperatorum, 10 dist.* (Decr., part

---

486 As he reports in the cited comm. to l. 4 C. 6, 28. The news can be found also in Felino Sandeo, *Tertia in quinque libros decretalium*, Lyon, 1547, in *c. Judei el secundo, de Judeis* (c. 5 × 5, 19), p. 234v. = id., in *c. canonum statuta, de constitutionibus* (c. 1 × 1, 2).

487 Locations cited in the previous note.

488 Cons. 103, incip. "Visa quadam scriptura." I was unable to track down this consultation.

489 Alessandro Tartagni, *Consiliorum seu responsorum libri*, Venice 1590, Book 6, cons. 6, nos. 2–5, p. 5.

490 This consultation, which begins with the words "Mathesias hebreus civis perusinus" is mentioned only by Andrea Tiraqueau, *De jure primigeniorum*, in *Opera omnia*, Frankfurt am Main, 1597, vol. 1, quest. 66, pp. 453–458, with a simple "dicitur consuluisse etc." He also adds: "Idem quoque ferunt consuluisse Petrum Ancharanum consilio incipiente: 'Decessit judea ab intestato,' et ei quoque subscripsisse Jacobum a Salyceto, quod tamen consilium non repperi inter consilia ipsius." In fact, the consultation is not included in those sent to the press.

491 Opinion shared by Ansaldo Ansaldi from Florence, *De commercio et mercatura*, Coloniae Allobrogorum, 1698, discursus 40, pp. 158–160, with reference to the use granted by the *princeps* to the Jewish nation of Leghorn "di tutte le cerimonie, precetti, riti, ordini e costumi di legge hebrea." (Ch. 20 of the privileges of 1593, *Collezione degli ordini municipali*

1, dist. 10, c. 1), in which it is stated that the law of the emperors "non est supra legem Dei," interpreting this "lex Dei" not in the most obvious sense, given the location of the text, of canon law, but in that of Mosaic law and referring the text, that had been reserved to something else entirely, to the Jews, and the *l. si qua C. de judaeis* (C. 1, 9, 15), in which, as Riminaldi puts it "casus est a contrario sensu, quod si inter ipsos judeos sit contentio, a senioribus judeorum debet judicari, merito jura et consuetudines eorunt debent attendi."[492]

However, the prevalence of the doctrine in favor of the recognition of the validity of Jewish law is not absolute. Further to the early jurists already mentioned, representatives of the opposite current want Jews subjected to Roman and local laws.

The argumentations and texts used by this side of the doctrine, whose names we shall also encounter in the following pages, are as follows:

1) First of all, the explicit provision of the two Roman laws of 393 and 398 (l. 7 and 8 and C. 1, 9) that these authors are unwilling to interpret in elaborately. On these laws rely among others Giovanni da Imola,[493] Alberto Bruni[494] and later Andrea Alciato, who, as a representative of the Scuola Culta, cannot remain silent in the face of the alterations, so frequent in practice, of the literal sense of the Roman norms. For Alciato, Calderini's opinion is unsustainable as blatantly inconsistent with the aforementioned law 8 "quam Calderinus non interpretatur sed pervertit, ut merito modernus apostillator ad Alexandrum [Tartagni], cons. 6 vol. 6 dixerit hanc opinionem non esse veram, nisi in his in

---

di Livorno, Leghorn, Carlo Giorgi, 1798, p. 247). He adds that it is not only a matter of the "facultas preservandi veteres leges mosaycas inter ipsos vigentes, sed etiam condendi fortasse nova statuta et consuetudines." Similarly, on the basis of the Mantuan concessions, Francesco Ciriaco Negri, *Controversiarum forensium liber II*, s. l., 1652, dispute 241, pp. 165–169.

492 Ippolito Riminaldi junior, *Consiliorum seu responsorum volumen secundum*, Venice 1576, cons. 119, pp. 47v.-54.

493 Giovanni da Imola, *Consilia*, Venice, 1581, cons. 1, p. 7v., nos. 12–14.

494 Alberto Bruni from Asti, *Commentarii super statutis excludentibus foeminas et cognatorum lineam a successionibus*, art. VI, no. 60, in *Tractatus utilissimi de statutis*, Lyon, 1554, f. 179 = *T.U.J.*, tome 2, f. 179: "Ad predicta facit *l. Judei*, secundum quod verba sonant, *C. de Judeis*: (C. 1, 9. 8) ubi dicit Judeos communi romano jure uti et tam de causis ad eorum fidem spectantibus, quam ad forum et leges et jura adire debere judices christianos; et sic tam ad ea quae sunt ordinis judiciarii, dum dicit forum, quam quo ad ea, quae concernunt decisionem, dum dicit leges et jura copula interposita; et sic eorum ritus et superstitiones ad eorum fides eis preservantur et juri communi in coeteris subiciuntur."

quibus inter eos [ebrei] a superiore loci toleratur dumtaxat."[495] The German Moscovius will also express himself the same way.[496]

2) The texts quoted by St. Thomas concerning the abolition of the Mosaic law "per adventum Christi," joined by Gratian's opinion expressed in the Decretum (Decr. 6, 3). The abolition is conceived in a general sense and thus extended also to the Jews,[497] without giving much thought to the fact that, as it refers not only to *precepta judicialia* but also to the *cerimonialia*, the logical result would be to declare expired, next to the Jewish law, the very same Jewish rite.

3) The gloss to *c. jus quiritum*, Dist. 1 (Decr., part 1, dist. 1, ch. 12) and the other texts we have already cited,[498] from which it follows that Jews are Roman citizens; hence it is deduced that they live according to Roman law.[499] The reasoning is more than questionable since all members of the Empire are Roman citizens, yet people live according to their own local law prevailing over common Roman law.

4) Finally, a consideration of somewhat historicist flavor, that the Jewish law cannot survive once the state that gave rise to it has fallen.[500]

495 Andrea Alciato, *Responsa*, Lyon, 1561, resp. 123, f. 105–106.

496 Caspar Ziegler (praes.) – Christian Caspar Mascovius (resp.), *De juribus Judaeorum*, Wittemberg, 1684 (other editions therein 1742 and Leipzig 1721), ch. I, § 7: "Judei communi romano jure vivere omnesque suas actiones romanis legibus conferre et excipere jubentur in l. 8 C. *de Judeis*, quae legis dispositio est generalis, neque ad solum judiciorum ordinem adstringi se patitur, sed omnino ad decisionem causarum etiam est extendenda cum "conferre actiones legibus romanis et excipere," sit ita aliquid proponere, prout vel legibus romanis prohibitum vel permissum est."

497 Like that e.g., the gloss and Guido da Bayso (Archdeacon) in the commentary to the text of Graziano (*dist. 6, c. finali, § his ita respondetur*): Giovanni da Imola, cons. 1 cit., and in his commentary to the *c. fin. de consuetudine* (ch. 11 × 1, 4) and to the *l. stipulatio hoc modo concepta ff. de verborum obligatione* (D. 45, 1, 61) dubitatively Giovanni d'Anagni, l. cit., Alberto Bruni, l. cit. and many others who follow these scholars. Practical application in decis. 414 of the Sacra Rota dated January 1, 1612 reported in full by Sessa, *Tractatus de Judeis*, Turin, 1717, p. 85.

498 See above, p. 69, no. 13 and p. 73, no. 20.

499 Giovanni d'Anagni and Alberto Bruni, ll. citt., followed word by word by many others. On the other hand, there is Natta (*Consilia*, t. 3, Venice 1583, no. 621, p. 155) who relies on the same texts to affirm that, precisely because they are citizens, the Jews may follow their own laws, whereas they would not be able to do so "si essent forenses quoad populum christianorum, quia ex quo nullum aliud jus haberent, tenerentur servare jus loci."

500 Bruni, l. cit.: "Ad illud autem quod dicitur in Evangelio passionis D. N. Jesu Christi, per quod apparet quod Judei habebant legem diversam a communi, potest responderi ... quod cum Judei haberent proprium territorium poterant particularem legem habere, etc." Similarly, the cited ruling 414 of the S. Rota and Ziegler, l. cit., "De lege forensi notandum quod ea, postquam Politia mosaica esse desiit, sit sublata; translato enim regno aliquo tollitur

In theory, and even more so in practice, the discussions between the followers of the two different currents expounded here are still widespread;[501] and it is often not the intimate persuasion as much as the client's interest that induces the lawyer to support one or the other of the conflicting theses in his legal advice.

The opposition between the two tendencies can also be followed in the late monographic literature of the seventeenth and eighteenth centuries.

Of the Italian authors of studies on the legal position of Jews, Susani[502] and Sessa[503] generally accept the thesis of the prevalence of Jewish law over common and statutory law, whereas Ricciulli[504] is inclined towards the opposite opinion.

Discordant opinions and conclusions are also noted in German doctrine, where such dissertations are plentiful. Relying on the arguments already known to us and on the conclusions of the Italian doctrine, some scholars deny the validity of the Jewish law entirely, like Dietrich,[505] Mascovius,[506] and Klipstein.[507] By contrast, the majority admit it entirely: among these, Kitzel,[508]

---

quoque lex regni, nisi novus rex legem antiquam confirmat. Quousque ergo imperatores everso Judeorum regno expresse aliud statuerunt, eousque lex mosaica abrogata est."

501 Cf. De Luca, *Theatrum veritatis et justitiae*, Venice, 1726, t. 15, *De judiciis*, disc. 35, no. 52, p. 114: "In istis itaque intrat quaestio an, cessante mixtura christianorum, adeout agatur de casibus, qui inter eos contingant, tam in ordinatoriis, quam in decisoriis in judicando procedi debeat cum lege mosaica eiusque interpretibus, vel potius cum eiusdem legibus cum quibus eiusdem loci populus christianus regitur; atque in hoc magna dignoscitur scribentium lucta; multis unam multisque alteram opinionem tenentibus; adeout eadem Rota Romana desuper variaverit, in secunda tamen opinionem maturius persistendo, ut dicto jure mosaico jam evacuato, in rebus presertim indifferentibus, eodem jure quo alii vivunt ipsi vivere debeant, juxta declarationes de quibus in respectivis sedibus." De Luca, on the other hand, favors the thesis of the applicability of the Jewish law in matrimonial matters (T. 14, *De matrimonio*, disc. 15, pp. 165–166) and inheritance matters (T. 6, *De dote*, disc. 132, nos. 6–9, p. 202) as long as there is for the case in question a precise norm of the Bible or a custom "probata cum suis requisitis."

502 Marquardo Susani, *Tractatus de Judeis* cit., Venice, 1584, ch. 4, nos. 1–4 and 11, pp. 43v.-44; ch. 5, no. 10, p. 45; ch. 6, nos. 21–25, pp. 47v–48; ch. 8, nos. 3–4, p. 49.

503 Sessa, *De Judeis*, cit., Turin, 1717, pp. 79, 81–83, 109–112, 139–141.

504 Ricciulli, *Tractatus de personis extra ecclesiae gremium*, Rome, 1622, book II, ch. 15, pp. 63–67.

505 Georg Theodor Dietrich, *De jure et statu judeorum* cit., 1648, ch. 5: Quatenus Judei lege mosaica forensi adhuc ligentur, ubi de eorum consuetudinario et municipali jure, pp. 83–97.

506 Mascovius, op. cit., ch. II, §§ 14, 15, 23; ch. III, §§ 11 and 20.

507 Jacob Christian Klipstein, *De autonomia judeorum*, cit., pp. 91–125.

508 Kitzel, *De regali habendorum Judeorum*, 1616, cit., pp. 174–175.

Weber,[509] Fuchs in a dissertation dedicated *ex professo* to our question,[510] Beck,[511] Fischer,[512] and Thiel.[513] Finally, the third category of authors strictly abides by the principle of the permissibility of the Jewish law in all matters in which it has not been repealed explicitly by Roman law. Thus, with a bizarre construction, it gets to the point of admitting the right of inheritance but not that of marriage, as *specialiter reprobatum* by law 7 C. 1, 9. In this group belong Gercken,[514] Nerlich,[515] and Lochner.[516]

Once the recognition of the Jewish law is admitted, recognition that is naturally done concerning biblical law as well as the later Talmudic-rabbinic entire evolution,[517] the problem arises by the Court called upon to decide the dispute between Jews of the knowledge of the judicial post-biblical norms, directly inaccessible as they are written in Hebrew, a language habitually unknown to civil courts.

509 Weber, *De Judeis*, cit., 1705, thesis 9, p. 5, and thesis 15, p. 6.

510 *De causis in quibus Judaei legibus mosaicis et institutis propriis adhuc relinquendi sunt*, dissert., Königsberg, September 1719, praeses Balth. Tilesius, respondens Daniel Fuchs, Königsberg, s. a., pp. 14–38.

511 Beck, *De juribus Judeorum* cit., Nuremberg 1731, ch. 4, p. 38: "Jedoch sind gewisse casus, in welchen die Juden einig und allein nach denen mosaischen Gesetzen zu richten [sind]: und zwar: 1) in Sachen die ihre Ceremonien und Kirchgebräuche betreffen, 2) in Ehesachen, Aussteuerungen, und Ehescheidungen, 3) in Erbschaftlichen-Successionsfallen; 4) in Testaments-Sachen und in Stritt und Irrungen, so die Juden unter sich selbst haben; es wäre dann in denen Reichs-Rechten und Landes-Constitutionen, der Juden halbers, ein anders verordnet zu finden."

512 Fischer, *Dissertatio inauguralis de statu et iurisdictione Judeorum secundum leges romanas, germanicas, alsaticas*, Argentorati, 1763, p. 109. (see footnote above no. 315).

513 *Principia jurisprudentiae judaicae per Germaniam communis seu conspectus jurium et obligationum Judeorum in Germania singularibus*, Halae Saxonorum, 1790, pp. 119–120, 203, 210. Thiel only rejects (§ 172, p. 111) the Jewish norms about coming of age.

514 Philippus Otto Gercken, *Dissertatio inauguralis juridica de Judeis*, 1677, cit., pp. 44–47; 53–56.

515 *Periculum legale de Judeis*, dissert. praeside Georg Adami Struven, resp. Johannes Henrich Nerlich, May 1680, Jena, s. a., § 23 (without page numbering). Drawing from Gercken.

516 Johannes Carolus Lochner, *Dodecas legalis de Judeorum receptione ac tolerantia*, 1700, cit., thesis 11, pp. 36–40. The same conclusion had previously been reached by Lauro Palazzi, *Tractatus de Statuto*, cit., l., cited above, p. 58.

517 Giovanni Calderini, *Consilia* cit., *De consuetudine*, cons. 2, is the first to acknowledge both the Jewish written law and consuetudinary norm. In the cited passages, Natta, Ansaldi, Negri, Riminaldi, De Luca talked about "lex vel consuetudo judeorum." Similarly, Ruini, *Responsorum sive Consiliorum*, T. II, Venice 1571, cons. 4, pp. 7–8 and Rocco Curzii (or de Curte) who precisely warns that "ubi esset consuetudo inter judeos illa attendenda esset, et sic tolleret nedum legem suam mosaicam, sed etiam tolleret jus commune." (Curtii Rochi, *De consuetudine ad materiam statuti faciente*, in *T.U.J.*, Venice, 1584, vol. II, sect. IX, nos. *36–37, p. 379 v.).

It is generally the rabbis of the local community, consulted by the Court on the point in question, who provide the translated Talmudic and post-Talmudic texts about the case, confirming under oath the faithfulness to the original text. Sometimes their opinion is supported by the confirmation of some non-local Jewish jurist of evident fame; while in some cases, for texts needed, the court turned to converted Jews is known for their expertise in Jewish law.

And so, in 1578 in Venice, the municipality's Avagador enjoins to the rabbis to communicate the provisions of the Jewish law concerning the husband's inheritance to his wife;[518] and the respondents reply with a brief statement, also signed by the famous doctor Abraham Ben David Provenzali of Mantua and by other rabbis of that city.[519] So also, in Venice, in 1697, three Mantuan friars, Jewish by birth, are consulted by the court to clarify the Jewish norms on the same issue,[520] while other translations of Maimonides' Mishneh Torah and

518 Venice State Archives – Search on the Jews. No. 38: Dossier titled: "Ritti e cassi a favor dei mariti per l'eredità della dote ad esclusion dei figli a norma dei ritti ebraici": Die 18 decembris 1578 Josephus Cattaneus famulus officii retulit de mandato Clar.mi domini Antonii Emiliani Honorandissimi Advocatoris Communis precepisse ut infra: Si fa comandamento a voi Dottori et Rabini de Ghetto novo et Levantini che dobbiate dare per scritto e far fede de quel che dispone la leze de Moisè in materia che li mariti heredita la sua moglie, et darla a Cervo Levi Ebreo banchier in Istria per poterla usare avanti li magistrati ove farà bisogno overo farla registrare a suoi spese nell'Officio dell'Avogaria. Leon da Padova – Vitale Cevidale – Jacob Abram – Gabriel Menachem – Josef Iferera (sic) – Josef Sameggia.

Marcus Bembo Officii advocatoris communis notarius."

519 Ibid.: "1578, 25 Dicembre – Facciamo fede noi Dottori Ebrei di Ghetto che per la legge nostra morendo la donna incinta il marito eredita la sua facoltà, ogni volta però che non vi fosse tra loro qualche espresso patto o conventione in contrario, e così sempre è stato osservato da noi universalmente, in fede di che havemo fatto fare la presente che sarà sottoscritta di nostra mano propria.

Io Samuel Giuda affermo ut supra
Io Jacob del qm. Abram " " "
Io Vidal de Cevidal " " "
Io Joseph de Pery (sic) " " "
Io Abram dell'Ecc.te Dr. Rabi David Provenzali Ebreo da Mantova
affermo ut supra
Io Gabriel de Menachem Levantin " " "
Io Josef Semegia " " "
omissis
altra fede dei Rabini di Mantova."

520 Ibid., Search on the Jews. No. 39, dossier titled: "Casi a favor dei figlioli eredi della dotte de loro madri, e non li maritti, e rispettivi padri." The text further on, section 2, ch. 2, § 2, footnote no. 900.

Caro's *Shulchan 'Aruch* bear the signature of the translator "elletto dagli Ill.mi et Ecc.mi Signori Presidenti sopra gli Offitii."[521]

Mantua, 1626: the rabbis were consulted on the issue of the final appeal, *jure hebraico*, of the arbitration rulings[522] and in 1692, in a case brought before the Commissioner for the Jews by a Jew, against the Jewish University, the Commissioner resorted to the rabbinate of Modena to obtain information on the Jewish laws regarding the case. Later on, when a new issue came into dispute, he contacted the rabbis of Mantua themselves.[523] In the same city, in 1783, the praetor consulted the Rabbinical Academy twice on the aforementioned issue of succession of husband to wife.[524] In Rome, no doubt on the occasion of an actual case that occurred before the state court, the well-known rabbi Tranquillo Corcos writes and prints a brief memorial in Italian on the Testament in Jewish law.[525] Again in 1850, a memorial of the rabbi of Rome I. M. Hazan is submitted to the court of Ancona, in a case of succession between

521 Ibid., no. 38, cited dossier.

522 A. Bertolotti, *Curiosità storiche mantovane*, no. CXCVI, *La Corte di cassazione ebraica*, in the little Mantuan magazine *Il Mendico*, December 1, 1890. Document drawn from the Gonzaga Archive of Mantua: "Ricercati per verità noi Rabini Hebrei infrascritti da Messer Jacob Cuzzar hebreo d'atestare se una sentenza arbitrale data fra un Hebreo all'altro riceve appelatione; Affermiamo che per legge et Rito Hebraico et conforme al solito stile di questa Città di Mantova tra Hebrei non patiscono nè ricevono le sentenze d'arbitri appelatione alcuna, bensì se alcuna delle parti si tiene gravata, può ricorrer in qualsivoglia tempo per la recessione dinanzi a Rabini, come anco per ciò avanti di noi è ricorso il suddetto Cuzzar, et havendo noi inteso, et ben considerato il fondamento d'una sentenza data tra il suddetto Cuzzar et gli fratelli Colorni sotto il dì 21 Gen. 386 al piciol numero [that is according to Hebrew dating] data dalli Magnifici Jacob Rabeno et Angel Jarè, affermiamo la detta lor sentenza dichiarandola per ben giudicata et che a Rito Hebraico non è più in potere di alcuno il prettender altra revisione, et per fede habbiam sottoscritto la presente. Adì 19 di Maggio 386 al piccol numero in Mantova.
Io Gratiadio Finci Hebreo dichiaro et affermo come di sopra.
Io Lazaro Provenzali Hebreo dichiaro et afffermo come sopra."

523 See further on, pp. 183–184.

524 Archive of the Jewish Community of Mantua, *Dossier* 193, f. 3, 1783, January 27. Lawsuit between Iseppe Levi and his aunt Brunetta Volta. The Academy is consulted by the Praetor on "whether, according to Jewish law, in case of the wife's pre-dying, the husband or the child is heir to the dowry." The Academy replies "by law to be the husband's heir to his wife's dowry, to the exclusion of their children, but subject to change in cases." July 1, 1783, similar question but with Christian participants in the lawsuit. The Academy replies that in this case the local law prevails.

525 *Informatione del Rabino* Tranquillo Corcos, *ebreo romano per provare che l'ebreo può far testamento e disporre delle sue facoltà*, Romae, Typis R. Camerae Apostolicae, 1699, p. 11. A copy is preserved in the Archive of the Jewish Community of Mantua, *Dossier* 57, no. 9.

Jews, containing a thorough account and discussion of Jewish judicial sources referring to the particular case in question.[526]

I cited these examples because they are those of which a more detailed memory remained. However, it is mathematically certain that in civil cases between Jews brought before state courts, once it was decided in a prejudicial way that the Jewish rules were to be applied, for the knowledge of the sources, the courts would always have resorted to rabbis and other experts in Talmudic and post-Talmudic law.[527]

Printed translations of these sources are not available in Italy. Even in Germany, where Jewish law was widely applied, it is necessary to reach the end of the 18th century to find a couple of them; more precisely, a Latin version of the succession rules of the *Shulchan 'Aruch*,[528] and a broader account on the whole Jewish civil law recognized as current by the state, which Rabbi Hirschel Lewin, in collaboration with the famous philosopher Moise Mendelsson,[529] was officially charged with working on.

After these general remarks, it is essential to note that the doctrine in favor of the recognition of the Jewish law entirely agrees in limiting such recognition to civil relations:[530] as a mere curiosity, Rocco Curzii's opinion should be thus

526 *Successione per Israele, Voto dell'eccellentissimo signore* I. M. Hazan, *membro del tribunale superiore di Gerusalemme, attuale rabbino maggiore dell'Università Israelitica di Roma*, Ancona, tip. Baluffi, 1851. Lawsuit between the heirs of the late Jacob Israel Gallico. The request that judgment takes place according to the Jewish law is made by one of the two parties, relying on the memorial of Hazan; yet it is unknown whether the Court has ruled in this sense.

527 Cf. Sordi, *Decisiones Sacri Mantuani Senatus*, Piacenza, 1598, decis. 133, p. 299: "At in facto presenti sex Rabbini de hoc a senatu interrogati, responderunt et suo juramento affermarunt etc."

528 Ch. Gottlob Mayer, *Sententiae rabbinorum de successione ab intestato et testamentaria, collatae a* R. Yoseph Caro *cum prefatione* Dan Nettelblatt, Halae Magdeburgicae, 1775. As Shemuel Eisenstadt, *En mishpat. Repertorium bibliographicum literaturae totius juris prudentiae hebraicae*, Jerusalem, 1931, no. 3994, p. 358, observes, Mayer was a Jew from Posen, later converted and turned pastor in Germany. I consulted this extremely rare work in the Library of the British Museum in London.

529 R. Hirschel Lewin and Moses Mendelssohn, *Ritualgesetze der Juden betreffend Erbschaften, Vormundschaften, Testamente und Ehesachen, insoweit sie das Mein und Dein angehen*, Berlin, 1778. Other editions 1792, 1799, 1819, 1820, cf. Marcus Cohn in *Jüdisches Lexikon*, entry Recht, jüdisches. Jacob Georg Christian Adler's translations, *Sammlung von gerichtlichen jüdischen contracten, rabbinisch und deutsch*, must also have had a practical scope. Mit einer Vorrede von Olaf Gerhard Tychsen. Hamburg, 1773, 2nd ed. Altona, 1792 (Eisenstadt, *Repertorium*, no. 244); and those of Lehmann-Glückstein, *Eduth Aschereth, oder Sammlung von ehecontractlichen Formulen, aus dem hebraïschen übersetzt*, Bremen, 1818.

530 Which does not mean, however, that the conflict between Jewish law and local laws is considered and settled only in relation to the substantive rules of private law: the conflict

mentioned, since he claims to be in favor of the application of the Jewish rules over the local ones in the criminal area as well, in case of offenses committed by Jews toward other Jews.[531] Those views, stemming from an excessively primitive and privatistic idea of penal relations, had no follow-up either in theory or in practice.

Obviously, the Jews were declared exempt from imputability only concerning offenses linked to prohibitions raised by local civil law, with which the application of personal norms allowed them to get away.[532]

In Italy, the viability of Jewish law declines in the early decades of the 19th century. In general, however, there is no explicit repeal. As already happened centuries before with the recognition, the rejection of the application of that law by civil courts is now accomplished not by law but by the doctrine and the jurisprudence. Only the rabbinical courts, where they exist, are suppressed: and this precisely to end the use on their part of the special law. At the same time, state judges and with them the doctrine ceases further to consider Jewish rules on reflection that for the Jews, the persistence of the autonomy legislation such as that of jurisdictional autonomy would conflict with the realized principle of civil and political equality of all citizens. As we shall see, the Jewish marriage law generally lasts the longest, at least for certain relations, due to its closer connection to the area of religion and the similarly ecclesiastic

also arises regarding constitutional principles and rules of conflict, as we shall have the opportunity to expose later on (see the second section of this second part).

531 Rocco Curzii (or De Curte) *Enarrationes in celeberrimum cap. cum tanto, Tit. de consuetudine*, Lyon, 1550, Sect. 9, § 44, f. 118, no. 36: "In quantum autem dixi quod consuetudo civitatis liget judeos, intellige verum: nisi lex mosaica repugnaret: quia respectu judeorum in primis lex mosaica servanda est inter ipsos judeos ... et credo premissam declarationem procedere etiam in criminalibus, scilicet ut si una poena imponatur judeo delinquenti contra alium judeum per legem mosaicam, illa preferri debeat poenae impositae per legem civilem vel canonicam et moveor quia rationes assignatae per Calderinum in dicto cons. 30 [see above footnote no. 461] militant etiam in criminalibus." Curzii adds that this is also the opinion of Felino Sandeo, in c. 1 × 1, 2. But this is a misunderstanding since in his commentary to that passage (*Commentarii in quinque libros decretalium*, vol. I, Venice, 1600, no. 38) Sandeo only affirms that the canon law punishes the Jews "quando delinquunt contra legem suam" that is to say in case of non-observance of the ritual precepts, and cites as an example of such punishments the burning of the Talmud decreed by the Pope "quia male interpretabatur legem mosaicam."

532 And so, once the divorce is admitted, the remarriage of divorcees went free from penalties established for bigamy. A controversial case about this is reported by Baldo degli Ubaldi, *Consiliorum volumina*, Venice, 1575, vol. V, cons. 428, p. 114 (see footnote no. 484 above and further on, pp. 154–156).

regulation that the marriage bond between Christians typically receives in Italy until 1865.[533]

2.2 *Marriage*

Let us now briefly analyze the conflict between Jewish marriage norms[534] and local norms regarding both form and substance of this institution.

2.2.1 The Form

The post-biblical Jewish marriage always maintains the ancient nature of a simple purchase contract of the woman from the person having authority upon her, and ends with the same forms of contracts of immovable property rights, i.e., with one to be chosen from the following means: either payment, or the deed in writing, or the appropriation, which, in this case, translates into the

533 The legal value of the husband's commitment in the *Ketubah*, guaranteeing the dowry brought by his wife by pledge and mortgages on all his properties, was recognized by the Court of Grosseto on May 8, 1828, in the lawsuit Nepi-Frascati against Sadun. Cantini, *Tesoro del foro toscano ossia Raccolta delle decisioni del Supremo Consiglio e delle R. Ruote civili delle prime appellazioni di Toscana*, T. XXII, Florence, 1830, decis. 63, pp. 364–370. Cf. the mentioned Hazan memorial of 1850. Some survival of practical effectiveness of Jewish law in dowry relations is still traceable in notarial deeds of the late last century. See Guido Tedeschi, *Il diritto ebraico nell'Italia contemporanea*, in *Rassegna mensile di Israel*, 1938, special volume of *Scritti in onore di Dante Lattes*, p. 148. Also, in many German states, Jewish law continues to be applied by the courts of the State for several decades since the 19th century. See in this respect the valuable historical and dogmatic note of Bessel, *Ueber das bürgerliche Recht der Juden in Deutschland nach gemeinem deutschem Rechte*, in *Rheinisches Museum für Jurisprudenz*, vol. III, 1829, pp. 443–457. See also Beseler, *System des gemeinen deutschen Privatrechts*, vol. I, 3rd ed., Berlin, 1873, p. 224; and Stobbe, *Handbuch des deutschen Privatrechts* vol. I, 3rd ed., Berlin, 1893, pp. 386–389. Cf. the authors cited by Windscheid, *Diritto delle Pandette*, vol. I, part I, Turin, 1902, § 55, no. 4-a, p. 222.

534 For a comprehensive literature on marriage in Jewish law, see Eisenstadt, *Repertorium* cit., pp. 321–360 (nos. 3535–4014). Among the foremost general works, the following ones are noteworthy: John Selden, *Uxor ebraica seu de nuptiis et divortiis ex jure civili idest divino et talmudico veterum ebreorum libri tres*, London, 1646, 2nd ed., Frankfurt an der Oder, 1673, 3rd ed., ibid., 1695; Ludwig Lichtschein, *Die Ehe nach mosaisch-talmudischer Auffassung und das mosaisch-talmudische Eherecht*, Leipzig, 1879; Leopold Löw, *Eherechtliche Studien*, in *Gesammelte Schriften*, vol. III, Szegedin, 1893, pp. 13–334; H. M. Luckock, *The history of marriage, Jewish and Christian, in relation to divorce and certain forbidden degrees*, London, 1894 and 2nd ed. 1895; Moses Mielziner, *The jewish law of marriage and divorce in ancient and modern times and its relation to the law of the state*, Cincinnati, 1884, and New York-Cincinnati, 1901; Jocob Neubauer, *Beiträge zur Geschichte des biblisch-talmudischen Eheschliessungsrechts. Eine rechtsvergleichend-historische Studie*. (Judicial dissertations, Leipzig, 1920–1921 = *Mittheilungen der vorderasiatischen Gesellschaft*, 24 und 25 Jahrg.), Leipzig, 1920.

carnal conjunction;[535] moreover, only the pronunciation of a given formula is required.[536] This in theory: in practical use, only the first of these three means of conclusion remains, namely the payment of the price, which has become symbolic in the form of a ring and which is now made directly to the woman.[537]

This (*kiddushin* or *erussin* = *sponsalia de praesenti*) is the actual act of marriage, not the subsequent *traditio sponsae* (*nessuin*) that can be performed even after quite a long time.

To celebrate a marriage, Jewish law does not require the intervention of any minister or other public official: religious blessing is customary, but *de jure* not required.[538]

---

535 Mishnah, Kiddushin, 1, 5: "Realty can be purchased either with money, or by a written deed, or by appropriation"; ibid. 1, 1: "Marriage is finalized either with money, or by a written deed, or by copulation." Cf. Josef Kohler, *Die Kaufehe nach dem Mishnatraktat Kiddushin*, in *Zeitschrift für Vergleichende Rechtswissenschaft*, 26, 1911, pp. 456–460. It should be noted that the written document (*shetar*) constitutive of the marriage should not be mistaken with the regulatory writing of the patrimonial relationships between spouses (*ketubah*). Into such a confusion, against which Juster, op. cit., vol. II, p. 43, no. 2, had already warned, Vismara, *La donazione nuziale nel diritto ebraico e nelle fonti cristiane in relazione al diritto romano postclassico*, Milan, Vita e pensiero ed., 1937, pp. 20–47, recently fell. According to this author, the *ketubah* would be comprehensive of the constitutive document of marriage (in case of a marriage contracted by written deed) (pp. 25–27), of the document (no more substantial but only of evidence) proving the finalizing of the marriage that occurred using "money," i.e., by paying the woman's purchase (the biblical *mohar*) (pp. 28–30), and the deed containing the obligations of the husband towards his wife (pp. 31 and seqq.). All this is erroneous. The *ketubah* has no relation with the finalization of the marriage act, nor does it have it with the *mohar*, but rather only contains a list of various obligations that the husband must assume as a result of the marriage, the principal of which are the payment of the "pretium pudicitiae" (the German *Morgengabe*), the guarantee for the dowry brought by his wife, her alimony, her clothing, etc. In any Rabbinic Law texts, the marriage *shetar* and *ketubah* are treated elsewhere. So, for example, in Caro's *Shulchan 'Aruch*, Eben haezer, mentions the marriage by *shetar* in ch. 32 and *ketubah* in ch. 66 and seqq. Inaccurate, since incomplete, is also the translation by Bloch, *Der Vertrag nach mosaisch-talmudischem Rechte*, in *Jahrebericht des Rabbiner-Seminars in Budapest für das Jahr* 1892–1893, pp. 104–105 of the abstract, which renders *ketubah* with *Morgengabe*.

536 The formula that the husband pronounces to the woman is the following: "Be my wife according to the law of Moses and Israel" or "Behold, be consecrated to me according to the law of Moses and Israel." On these formulas, see L. Löw, *Eherechtliche Studien*, in *Gesammelte Schriften*, vol. III, p. 24. Cf. Juster, op. cit., vol. II, p. 42, no. 6.

537 Cf. Marcus Cohn in *Jüdisches Lexikon*, vol. II, pp. 254–259, entry Eherecht, § 5, Eheschliessung.

538 Löw, op. cit., p. 281; Juster, op. cit., vol. II, p. 43, no. 4. It is interesting to recall what the 16th century Venetian Rabbi Leon da Modena writes around the celebration of marriage in his *Historia dei Riti hebraici*, part 4, ch. 3, re-ed. in *Rassegna mensile di Israel*, April 1933, p. 560: "Contratto che si ha il matrimonio [i.e., once the engagement is made], si fa scrittura tra

Notoriously, in Roman law, marriage is perfected by simple consensus, and no specific form of manifestation is required: a conflict, even theoretically, with Jewish law is thus not possible. Therefore, in the Italian territories where Roman tradition prevailed (with the decline of the personality of the law), Jewish marriage would be considered valid as a perfect marriage, according to Roman law. Where Longobard tradition prevailed, the validity of the marriage was subjected to its celebration by a public official,[539] and conflict was likely to emerge. As we shall soon see, since the validity of Jewish norms was also admitted with regard to the substance of the institution, indeed, these were even more so recognized in the form. Moreover, in the only known case of controversy between Jews, on marriage celebrations, the state courts do not discuss which law to apply but rather examine the rabbinical sources necessary to the case's solution.[540]

---

lo sposo e parenti della sposa, e poi va lo sposo a toccar la mano e riconoscer la sposa. In alcuni paesi usano all'hora ponergli l'anello in dito e sposarla [in this case engagement and actual wedding coincide], ma in Italia e Thedeschi per ordinario non lo fanno. Stanno poi così promessi chi un anno, chi due, chi sei mesi, più e meno secondo la volontà e comodo delle parti, che così pattuiscono; in questo tempo lo sposo visita e pratica la sposa e scherza con lei, ma non la conosce carnalmente. Giunto il tempo delle nozze, e deputato il giorno. … all'hora che si vuole, si riducono gli sposi in una sala o camera, sotto un baldacchino con suoni et alcuni usano con certi fanciulli appresso con torce accese in mano che cantano. Concorsa la gente d'intorno, si mette uno di quelli manti quadrati con pendacoli detto Taled che copre il capo dello sposo e sposa insieme. Li Rabini del loco, o il cantarino della Scuola, o 'l più stretto parente, preso una tazza o una caraffa di vino in mano, dice una benedittione a Dio, che ha creato l'uomo e la donna et ordinato il matrimonio, etc. e dà da bere di quel vino allo sposo et alla sposa. Poi lo sposo gli mette l'anello in dito alla presenza di due testimonij, che sogliono esser i Rabini, dicendole: Ecco tu sei sposata a me, come il Rito di Mosè e d'Israel. Leggono la carta di dote [*Ketubah*], nella quale si obbliga lo sposo per la dote ricevuta e di alimentarla, e star seco, etc. e ne ricevono obbligo da lui. E poi con altro vaso di vino cantano altre sei benedittioni, in tutto sette, e danno altra volta da bere ad ambi li sposi, et versano il vino per terra per bon segno d'allegrezza, e il vaso vuoto si dà in mano allo sposo, il quale lo getta forte in terra, per raccordarsi nell'allegrezza della morte che rompe e frange noi come vetro, per non insuperbire. Et all'hora tutto il popolo grida: Mazal tov, che vuol dire: sia con buona ventura, e se ne vanno."

539 Brandileone, *Saggi sulla storia della celebrazione del matrimonio in Italia*, Milan, 1906, pp. 41 et seqq.

540 De Luca, *Theatrum veritatis et justitiae*, Venice 1726, T. 14, *De matrimonio*, disc. 15, pp. 165–166: Lawsuit between two Jews on the validity of a marriage. The wife, abused by her husband, wants the separation, or even more, to have the marriage declared null and void. She claims that the acts of *aras* [*erussin*] and *chidussin* were not followed by the act of *nessuin*: and that therefore there is only the promise and obligation for the woman not to concede herself to another man under the death penalty, but not a real marriage, which stems only from *nessuin*. The husband counters that the first two acts are sufficient

2.2.2 The Substance of the Matrimonial Relationship

2.2.2.1 *Impediments Due to Family Ties*

According to Jewish laws, the following relative marriages were allowed:

a) Between the children of brothers: This marriage was initially forbidden; later allowed under Roman law;[541] and ultimately forbidden under canon law.[542]
b) Between uncle and niece: This marriage was banned in both Roman law[543] and canon law.[544]
c) Between a widower and his deceased wife's sister: This marriage was likewise forbidden in Roman law[545] and canon law.[546]

---

to constitute an actual marriage. The consulted rabbis (wrongly) side with the wife's opinion and consider them only as preparation acts. De Luca follows them, comparing *erussin* and *kiddushin* to the *sponsalia de futuro*, of which, however, he says, they are less mandatory, given that "sponsalia inducunt obligationem, etiam per censuras aliasque coactionis species, cessante justa causa, ad matrimonium"; and he too thinks that since the two were not followed by the other necessary acts, the marriage was not yet finalized. As to the objection of the prohibition of divorce, affirmed by Sanchez and other *morales* against Marquardo Susani, *De judeis* cit. part 2, 8, 4, based on Matthew, 19, he states that, in that case, the ban applies to full-fledged marriage, not just a promise. And to the objection that Deut., 22 establishes the death for the woman who after the *erussin and kiddushin* lies with another man, which seems to confirm that those acts constitute marriage and the penalty is imposed as punishment for adultery, he responds that it can be sustained "ut etiam sponsa de futuro dictae penae subiaceat, ob iniuriam, quae irrogari quoque dicitur sponso, qui in vim sponsalium, matrimonio deinde contraendo, ita deceptus inveniretur ducendo mulierem ab alio corruptam." The judge, however, "stante longaeva plurium annorum cohabitatione, cum verisimili subsecuta copula, (licet pro parte mulieris negata, utpote illicita, donec dictae aliae sollemnitates sequerentur). ... pro matrimonii validitate pronuntiavit. Neque causa ulteriorem habuit progressum." The parallelism stated by De Luca between *sponsalia de futuro* and *kiddushin* is inaccurate since the *kiddushin* correspond in reality to the *sponsalia de presenti* (= *desponsatio* = *subarratio cum anulo*). As for the *sponsalia de futuro* (in Hebrew: *shiddukin*), they are just an obligation to contract the marriage, but not the initial act of marriage itself. (Cf. the beginning of the passage by da Modena quoted above). Like any other contract, they are stipulated also by the Jews sometimes in front of the notary, as for example the script drafted in Recanati in 1473, and published by Brandileone, op. cit., p. 567, no. 1, demonstrates. In it, the Jew Servo promises "se facturum ita et taliter ... quod dicta Bellarosa, filia ipsius Servi, contrahet sponsalia de praesenti et matrimonium cum dicto Manuele, etc."

541 C. 5, 4, 19 (*l. celebrandis C. de nuptiis*) that allows such marriages "revocata prisci juris auctoritate." (y. 405).

542 Decretum, ca. 35, quest. 2–3, ch. 20; c. 8 × 4, 14.

543 C. Th. 3, 12, 1.

544 c.8 × 4, 14.

545 C. Th. 3, 12, 2 (y. 355); C. J. 5, 5, 5 (y. 393).

546 c. 1 × 4, 14 (Alexander III).

Unless a liberating ceremony (*halizah*) is performed, it furthermore imposes the marriage between a childless widow and the brother of the deceased husband (a levirate marriage), this type of marriage was also forbidden by both Roman law[547] and canonical norms.[548]

As we have seen, the Roman emperors had explicitly vetoed the application of Jewish matrimonial law with l. 7 C. 1, 9. Moreover, many of the earliest civilists of the intermediate era, such as Azone, Jacopo da Revigny, Cino da Pistoia and Bartolomeo da Saliceto accept the provisions of this law unobjectionably.

Yet, in the Middle Ages, as we know, the Roman Constitution provisions fall into total disuse and, under the new legislation, an opposite practice based on a broad acceptance of Jewish law takes hold for centuries. The Church does not sanction this new direction with explicit declarations of a general nature: but a great Pope, Innocent III, shows that he is not against it by issuing decisions that implicitly recognize the full force of Jewish matrimonial law in the area of the internal relations between Jews. On these rulings, which had later become part of the Decretals, that the canonists base themselves on declaring the Roman norm opposing them null and void.

The first ruling is driven by the question submitted to the Pope of whether converted Jews, who contracted the marriage before their conversion according to their law in the degrees allowed by this law but forbidden by canon law, "debeant separari post baptismum." On January 3, 1198, Pope Innocent responds

547 C. Th. 3, 12, 2 and C. J. 5, 5, 5, cit.

548 Decretum, ca. 35, quest. 2–3, ch. 10 (Gregory the Great). On the Jewish levirate marriage, see bibliography in Eisenstadt. *Repertorium* cit., pp. 340–343. Main studies: Benary, *De Hebreorum levirata*, Berlin, 1835; G. M. Redslob, *Die Leviratsche bei den Hebräern*, Leipzig, 1836; Cruveilhier, *Le lévirat chez les Hebreux et chez les Assyriens*, in *Révue Biblique*, 34, 1925, pp. 524–546. On the *halizà* in particular, see A. Geiger, *Dispensation von der Schwagerehe und Weigerung der Unmündigen*, in *Jüdische Zeitschrift*, I, 1862, pp. 88–112. On the practice in Italy, see Leon da Modena, op. cit., part IV, ch. 7, in *Rassegna* cit., ibid., pp. 564–565. On the levirate in general among the primitive peoples, see I. Flach, *Les institutions primitives. Les origines de la famille. Le lévirat*, in *Annales des sciences politiques*, 15, 1900, pp. 316–340. On the comparison between the kinship degrees forbidden in Roman, Canonical and Jewish laws, see Karl August Schlegel, *Critische und systematische Darstellung der verbotenen Graden der Verwandschaft und Schwägerschaft bei Heiraten nach dem mosaischen Gesetzen, dem römischen und dem canonischen Rechte und der protestantischen Kirchenordnung*, Hannover, 1802; Rosin, *Beiträge zur Lehre von der Parentelenordnung und Verwandschaftsberechnung nach deutschem und österreichischem, jüdischem und Canonischem Rechte*, in *Zeitschrift für das privat- und öffentliche Recht der Gegenwart*, vol. 28, Vienna, 1901; Ladislaus Szepansky, *Impedimenta matrimonii alia apud hebreos et in jure canonico*, in *Mélanges de l'Université de St. Joseph* [of Beirut], T. X, 1925, file 3, pp. 55–75.

that the marriage so contracted before baptism must not be dissolved to avoid disobeying the divine word that proclaims "Quod Deus coniunxit homo non separet."[549]

In the same year, the second ruling also concerns the validity of the marriage of Jewish converts who, before the christening, married the widows of their brothers, according to Jewish custom, which the Church forbids Christians to do. This time, again, Pope Innocent concedes these marriages must not be dissolved; provided, however, that they were celebrated in accordance to Mosaic law, i.e., only where there is no offspring "ut semen defuncti suscitarent," but also enjoining on the spouses to abstain, after the baptism, from sexual relations.[550]

Finally, with his third ruling, in 1201, *utilitate publica suadente*, Pope Innocent declares legitimate the offspring born to Jews converted who, before the baptism, married in degrees permitted by Jewish law and prohibited by the Church.[551]

From these texts, it can be deduced that the Church considers it normal for Jews to contract marriage according to the provisions of their law and not according to those established by canonical law concerning the prohibited degrees. It also recognizes the persistence of the validity of these marriages even after baptism.

549 *Registrum Innocentii III*, Baluze ed., Paris, 1863, vol. I, p. 514 = c. 4 × 14, 4 (*c. de infidelibus x de consanguineitate et affinitate*): "Innocentius III Archiepiscopo et Capitulo Tirensi. De infidelibus ad fidem conversis utrum, si ante conversionem suam secundum legis veteris instituta circa gradus consanguineitatis a canone renotatos coniuncti fuerint, separari debeant post baptismum: consultationi tuae duximus respondendum quod matrimonium sic contractum non est post baptismi lavacrum separandum. ..." The prohibited kinship degrees are dealt with in the Decretum, part 2, c. 35, q. 2 and 3, ch. 1–14. In chap. 2, it is stated that the Church considers prohibited unions those which are forbidden by the laws of God, Roman laws and Greek laws. Upon those guilty of such unions, the Church imposes excommunication and curse, the secular laws infamy and instability.

550 *Registrum*, cit., Baluze ed., I, p. 604 = c. 9 × 4, 19 (*c. finali x de divortiis*). Innocentius III Livoniensi episcopo et eis qui cum ipso sunt fratribus. Deus etc. ... "Quia dispar est ritus Livoniensium de novo ad fidem catholicam conversorum a nostro: propter infirmitatem gentis ejusdem concedimus ut matromoniis contractis cum relictis fratrum utantur; si tamen fratribus decedentibus sine prole, ut semen defuncti juxta legem mosaicam suscitarent, cum talibus contraxerint, ne tales sibi de cetero, postquam ad fidem venerint, copulent, prohibentes." (year 1201).

551 *Registrum*, cit., Baluze ed., I, p. 604 = c. 15 × 4, 17 (*c. gaudemus x qui filii sunt legitimi*) = c. 8 × 4, 19 (*c. gaudemus x de divortiis*). Innocentius Tiberiadensi episcopo. "Ceterum prolem de infidelium coniunctionibus natam, qui secundo, tertio vel ulteriore gradu secundum opinionem illorum matrimoniali contraxerunt affectu, post fidem receptam (utilitate publica suadente) legitimam volumus reputari."

The contrast between these practices, collected in the Decretals, and the law 7 C. 1, 9, and the resulting fall into disuse of the latter are immediately grasped by Enrico da Susa (from Ostia, d. 1271), who mentions the issue repeatedly in his *Summa*.[552] Somewhat later, basing himself on the same texts, Nicolò de' Tedeschi similarly states that before the christening, the Jews, "licite contrahunt matrimonia in gradibus prohibitis humana lege," nor does the baptism dissolve the marriage because a relationship contracted under the imperative of an old law cannot be dissolved by the onset of a new one.[553]

Floriano da S. Pietro, a civilist, also follows in the canonists' footsteps proclaiming the validity of Jewish marriage between uncle and niece, as the Mosaic law prohibits only those marriages between direct line ascendants and descendants, not those between collaterals.[554] Andrea Barbazza also reaches the same conclusion, in a consultation defending a Jew accused of having contracted marriage at a degree canonically forbidden and consequently threatened of *publicatio bonorum*. Relying on the conclusions of Giovanni D'Andrea and Nicolò de' Tedeschi, Barbazza declares l. 7 c. 1, 9 no longer in force. Against the interpretation of this law by Bartolomeo da Saliceto and Raffaele Fulgosio, maintains that in the area of marriage, Jews can follow their law in its entirety, regardless of contrary rules whether canonical or civilian. There is no doubt then, he argues, that despite the rules contained in the title *De incestis nuptiis* of the Justinian Code, Jewish marriages between uncle and niece, between the

552 Ostiense, *Summa*, ed. 1490, *De judeis*, § in quibus tolerentur, vers. sed addit lex: "Sed addit lex quod hoc matrimonium facere debent secundum legem romanam non juxta ritus suos ... ut in *C. l. nemo* ... (C. 1, 9, 7) sed decretalis permittit quod juxta ritum suum contrahant ut supra, *de consanguineitate, de infidelibus* (c. 4 × 4, 14)." Similar considerations in the same *Summa, de divortiis*, § quot modis, verbo non solum; and *de consanguineitate* § usque quartum gradum, versic. si verum infra hos gradus. In the same sense Innocent IV, comm. in ch. 8 × 3, 34 *de voto et voti redemptione*; Guido da Bayso (*Archidiaconus*) comm. in Decretum, part 2, ch. 30, q. 1; and Giovanni d'Andrea, comm. in ch. 13 × 2, 13 *de restitutione spoliatorum*.

553 Nicolò de' Tedeschi (Abbas Siculus, Panormitanus), *Lectura in quartum et quintum Decretalium*, Venice ed., N. Jenson, [1477] ad *l. de infidelibus, de consanguineitate et affinitate* (4 × 4, 14). "Nota primo judeos non astringi legibus canonicis circa sacramentalia et concernentia animam; unde licite contrahunt matrimonia in gradibus prohibitis humana lege; tamen ad hoc *c. gaudemus, de divortiis*, ubi bonus textus. Nota secundo quod per superinventionem nove legis non debet mutari quod gestum est secundum legem antiquam ex quo adhuc non emanaverat nova lex. Judeus enim non astringitur ad servandam legem canonicam nisi post baptismum; id ergo quod gessit antequam se subiiceret legi christianae debet tenere ex quo non est gestum contra legem divinam."

554 Floriano da S. Pietro, *Commentaria in primam et secundam digesti veteris*, Bologna, 1576–1578, in *l.* 3 *ff. de his qui sunt sui vel alieni juris* (D. 1, 6, 3). The Jewish sources are: Leviticus, 18, 12–14; 20, 19–20; Babylonian Talmud, jebamot, f. 62b.

children of brothers, and between a widower and his deceased wife's sister are to be held valid: and no charge can therefore be brought upon a Jew who has contracted a marriage of this kind.[555]

On a similar matter relating to a marriage between an uncle and *ex sorore* niece, Giovanni da Imola, on the other hand, declares himself in disagreement. His pettifogging argument, however, does not have any doctrinal value. He argues that such degree of relationship prevents marriage both in the Mosaic law – which, being untrue, he tries to prove through the contortion of various passages of the *Corpus Juris Canonici* – and in civil law, according to the *l. nemini C. de nuptiis* (C. 5, 4, 17) and the provision in *Ist. de nuptiis*, § *inter, eas, vers. fratris vel sororis* (1, 1, 10, § 3), as well as in canon law according to the *c. non debet* x *de consanguineitate et affin.* (c. 8 × 4, 14).[556] Now, he continues, according to the known c. 8 × 4, 19, *de divortiis*, it is certain that Jews need not heed the canonical prohibitions: only the divine (Mosaic) law and the civil law remain then to be considered, according to both of which the marriage in question is to be considered null and void. In this way, the particular question is resolved, but not the general conflict between matrimony in civil law and Jewish law.

Overall, however, despite the contrary opinion of some early jurists and a few uncertainties among the more recent ones, based on the passages mentioned, the intermediate doctrine concurs in the thesis that recognizes the in-full application, among Jews, of the Mosaic-rabbinical matrimonial law.

Generally speaking, the reasoning is as follows: the civil law indeed denies the referral to the Jewish marriage law, but canon law, on the other hand, does admit such passing on. Now, in matrimonial matters, the canonical norm must prevail; therefore, Jewish law should be applied since the canonical norm has recognized it.

Indeed that is the way Marquardo Susani, the earliest among the authors of comprehensive monographs on the legal position of the Jews, argues: he recalls and discusses the canonical texts and the opinions of the authors just mentioned and agrees with them "quicquid contra premissa videatur dixisse Petrus de Bellapertica in *l. celebrandis C. de nuptiis* (C. 5, 4, 20, see above, footnote no. 451) et Salycetus in *l. nemo, la prima, C. de Judeis* (C. 1, 9, 7; see above, footnote no. 456) circa judeorum matrimonia, ut ibi per eos, quorum dicta

555 Andrea Barbazza, *Consilia*, Venice, 1581, vol. IV, no. 13. Likewise, Felino Sandeo, *In quinque libros decretalium*, notation 2, comm. in c. 8 × 5, 6 *de judeis*.

556 Giovanni da Imola, *Consilia*, Venice, 1581, no. 3, p. 8.

sustineri possunt attento scilicet jure civili, secus attenta canonum dispositione, cui in hoc standum est, ut *c. de infidelibus* (c. 4 ×, 4, 14) *et c. gaudemus* (c. 8 × 4, 19."[557]

On top of the already cited authors, Alessandro Tartagni,[558] Mariano Socino,[559] Roberto Maranta,[560] and cardinal Domenico Toschi[561] repeated the arguments of their predecessors.

2.2.2.2 *Divorce*

The application of Jewish law implies the possibility of marriages in prohibited degrees and that of divorce,[562] an institution contemplated both in the Deuteronomy and the Gospel.[563] Jurists recognize this without hesitation, admitting even the possibility of a second marriage when the legitimately repudiated first wife is still living.[564]

---

557 Marquardo Susani, *De Judeis et aliis infidelibus*, in T. U. J., vol. XIV, Venice, 1584, part II, ch. 4, no. 1, p. 44.

558 Alessandro Tartagni from Imola, *Consiliorum seu responsorum libri*, lib. VI, Venice, 1590, cons. 6, no. 5, p. 5, on the basis of the canonical texts cited above nos. 16, 17, 18.

559 Mariano and Bartolomeo Socini from Siena, *Consiliorum volumina*, vol. I, Venice, 1571, cons. 72, nos. 6–7, p. 136 v.

560 Roberto Maranta, from Venosa, *Tractatus de ordine judiciorum, intitulatus Speculum aureum et lumen advocatorum*, Venice, 1540, tertia pars principalis, no. 58, p. 25.

561 Card. Domenico Toschi, *Practicarum conclusionum tomus IV*, Rome 1606, conclus. 369, pp. 702–703, nos. 3, 4, 5, 21. He relies in particular on the argumentation of Baldo which, as in ecclesiastical causes, shall be decided in accordance with the canons, whatever the judge may be. And so must the matrimonial causes among Jews be dealt with *juxta mores suos*, even if the judge is Christian.

562 On the Jewish divorce, see the complete literature in Eisenstadt, *Repertorium*, cit., pp. 351–354. Cf. Juster, op. cit., vol. II, p. 57, no. 2. Main works: Roberto Cenalis, *De divortio matrimonii mosaici per legem evangelicam reputato axioma*, Paris, 1549; Chr. Gottl. Wolfius, *Schediasma philologicum de divortio Judeorum*, Leipzig, 1739; P. L. B. Drach, *Du divorce dans la synagogue*, Rome, 1850; Mielziner, *The Jewish law of divorce in ancient and modern times, and its relation to the law of the state*, Cincinnati, 1884; Amram David Werner, *The Jewish law of divorce according to Bible and Talmud with some reference to its development in posttalmudic times*, Philadelphia, 1896; Leopoldo De Feis, *Del libello del ripudio nella legge mosaica*, Florence, 1906; Ludwig Blau, *Die jüdische Ehescheidung und der jüdische Scheidebrief. Eine historische Untersuchung*. 2 Theile. In: 34 *Jahresberichte der Landes- Rabbinerschule in Budapest für das Schuljahr* 1910–1912. For the Italian praxis of the XVI century, cf. Leon da Modena, *Historia dei riti hebraici*, cit., in *Rassegna mensile di Israel*, April 1933, pp. 563–564.

563 In general, the authors cite Deuter. 23 [*recte*: 22, 1–4], Matthew 18 (admission of the divorce *cum causa*), and the two canonical texts that report the evangelic precept, that is Decretum, part 2, ca. 32, q. 1, c. 2 and ibid., q. 7, ch. 7.

564 Nicolò de' Tedeschi, op. cit., l. cit.: In glossa finali in fine [gloss "esse matrimonium inter eos"] sentit haec glossa quod si judeus contraheret cum judea pacto expresso ut liceat

However, this matter must not have been seen natural to the people accustomed by the Christian principles to consider divorce a monstrosity and a tremendous sin, including the authorities in those locations where Jewish communities had settled not long before. As proof of that, there are numerous examples of Jews accused of bigamy and arrested for having contracted a second marriage after their divorce.

Precisely a case of this kind refers to a consultation by Baldo, which we have already mentioned.[565] In defense of Vitaluccio, the Jewish defendant, Baldo notes that bigamy is indeed prohibited by Roman laws[566] in general and to Jews in particular.[567] But the ban does not apply to the case, such as the current one, in which his wife "legitima causa subsistente repudiata fuit in forma solemni secundum ritus et consuetudines Judeorum." They may, in fact, do this according to their law, especially when the wife has not produced children; that said, it should be noted that for the divorce to be valid, the act of handing over the bill of divorcement following the biblical norm is insufficient, but the parties must consult the priest – meaning, of course, the Jewish minister, not the Christian bishop – "qui de hoc inter eos sententiam facere debebit": this was possible according to the *l. judei* 8 C. 1, 9 *de judeis*, that allows Jewish judges to rule in lawsuits between opposing parties of the same religion "quae respiciunt eorum ritus et consuetudines, scilicet circa matrimonia et similia." However, Baldo adds, the matrimonial lawsuit may be connected to other ones "quorum cognitio ad judices seculares pertineret." Well, in this case, these judges remain entrusted, incidentally, also with the cognizance of the matrimonial cause which "sive per iudices christianos, sive per alios cognoscatur, debet secundum eorum ritus et consuetudines decidi." Apart from being proven by the aforementioned canonical texts, it is also proven by the analogy of principle sanctioned by both civil and canonical laws.[568] Therefore, even if presented to a secular judge, the ecclesiastical or spiritual lawsuits must be defined not according to laws but according to canons.

Baldo concludes by proclaiming the complete innocence of the Jew who, having acted in obedience to his law, cannot be found guilty of any crime.

---

dare libellum repudii secundum ritum eorum, quod non teneat matrimonium quia apponitur pactum contra substantiam matrimonii. Doctrina tenet oppositum quia ex quo eorum lex hoc permittit licite deducitur in pactum: non nam consequitur effectum vi pacti sed vi legis.

565 See above, footnote no. 484.

566 C. 9, 9, 18; I. 1, 9, 10, 6; C. 5, 3, 5; C. 5, 5, 2.

567 C. 1, 9, 7 (*l. nemo C. de Judeis*).

568 C. 1, 2, 6; c. 8 × 2, 1; c. 11 × 3, 26. Cf. Ostiense, *Summa, de maledicis* (x 5, 26) at the end.

The later judicial literature just mentioned unanimously admitting Jewish divorce,[569] and in practice, the institution continues to be viable up to the 19th century, only yielding with the unification of legislation introduced by the new codes.

2.2.2.3 *Polygamy*

The Jewish law admitted polygamy until the early Middle Ages.[570] In 1040 the respected rabbi Ghereshon of Worms banned it with a decree that, with rare exceptions,[571] was accepted by all the European Jewry.[572] The case of those who sought to take a second wife because of the sterility of the first one, made evident by at least ten years of unfruitful marriage, remained nevertheless excluded from the ban.[573] Although without definitely acknowledging the institution, too stridently contrasting with Christian principles, the state occasionally granted permission for those special unions.[574]

Though not entirely unknown polygamy in Italy was rarely practiced.[575] The documents so far uncovered report altogether only two cases.

---

569 For all of them, see Sessa, *Tractatus de judeis*, Turin, 1717, pp. 109–112 and Beck, op. cit., pp. 136–140.

570 For the bibliography see Eisenstadt, *Repertorium*, cit. pp. 343–344. Main work: L. Löw, *Eherechtliche Studien: Die Einehe und die Vielweiberei in der biblischen Zeit*, and Id., *Die Einehe und die Vielweiberei in der talmudischen Zeit*, in the magazine *Ben Chananja*, vol. III, Szegedin, 1860 = *Gesammelte Schriften*, vol. III, 1893, Szegedin.

571 Zacharias Frankel, *Bigamie noch in 14-ten Jahrhundert, Notizien.*, in *Monatsschrift für Geschichte und Wissenschaft des Judentums*, vol. XIV, 1865, p. 390.

572 F. Rosenthal, *Einiges über die Tekanot des Rabbi Ghereshom ben Jehudà*, in *Jubelschrift zum 70 Geburtstag des Dr. I. Hildesheimer*, Berlin, 1890, pp. 37–53.

573 Rashì on Mishnà, jebamot, 6, 6 and Ghemarà ibid. (jebamot, f. 64a), on the basis of Genesis 16, 3. Similarly, Caro, *Shulchan 'Aruch*, Eben haezer, ch. 154, § 10: "If one married a woman who remained with him for 10 years and has no given birth he should give her a divorce paying her the *ketubah*, or marry another one likely to have offspring." It should be noted that, in theory, rather than a right, it is an actual obligation.

574 Wilhelm Pappenheim, *Staatliche Bigamiedispense für Juden in Europa*, in *Zentralblatt für die juristische Praxis*, in *Festschrift für den 35 deutschen Juristentag*. (Salzburg, September 12–15, 1928), pp. 177–183.

575 Cf. Leon da Modena, *Historia dei Riti Hebraici* cit., part IV, ch. 2, re-ed. in *Rassegna mensile di Israel*, April 1933, p. 559: "Gli è lecito pigliar più d'una e quante mogli vogliono, come da molti luoghi della Scrittura si vede la licenza, et i casi seguiti, e così fanno Levantini; ma tra Tedeschi non si permette nè si usa et in Italia rarissimi, e solamente in caso che sia molt'anni stato con la prima et non habbia potuto haver figlioli." However, art. 6 of the decisions taken at the Congress held in Ferrara on June 21, 1554 by the deputies (2 for every city) of the major Jewish communities of Italy (Rome, Venice, Bologna, Modena, Reggio Emilia, Mantua, Ferrara and Padua) is in contrast with this statement. With regard to the opinion of some ritual authors allowing a new union after 10 years of marriage

In 1416 the king of Sicily granted a Jew of Malta permission to take a second wife, being the first resident in another State.[576] Furthermore, in 1578, the bishop of Feltre granted the Jew Lazarus from Bologna similar permission, having the first wife, now old, remained infertile for ten years.[577]

---

even in case the first wife had given birth to children – and this against the censorship of Rabbenu Gereshon of Worms – the above-mentioned deputies decree that the new union cannot take place without the full consent of the wife and of one of her closest agnates, given in front of witnesses. The text of the resolutions was published by Izhak Baruch Levi, תקנות חכמים – תקנות וגזרות שגזרו רבני איטליה על היהודים שבארצם בפירארא בשנת שי״ד [*Norms of the Scholars, norms and rules established for the Jews in their countries by the rabbis of Italy in Ferrara in 1554*], Brody, 1879. The booklet is nowhere to be found in Italy, and I have drawn from a manuscript copy of the deliberations themselves, kept in the archives of the Jewish community of Mantua, File 1, no. 14. See the directory of this archive, vol. IV, pp. 271 and 284.

576 G. and B. Lagumina, *Codice diplomatico dei Giudei di Sicilia*, Palermo 1885, doc. 264, July 3, 1416: Infans Johannes serenissimi domini etc., capitaneo, judicibus et juratis aliisque officialibus civitatis et insulae Meliveti aliisque officialibus et personis quibuscumque dicti regni, etc. Comparendo noviter davanti la nostra excellencia Ruben da Marsala judeu havitaturi di quissa insula et chitati di Malta mi exposi essiri dispostu voliri stari et habitari in la dicta chitati et insula et illocu conduchiri et prindiri mugleri in la dicta chitati et insula di Malta. Nui veru havendu havutu informacioni da Judei prout in quista chitati esseri permisu per ligi musayca chasquidunu Judeu putiri prindiri plui di una mugliri et maxime in diversi chitati et regni pur ki li poza sustiniri et dari loru vita havimu ad tali supplicacioni graciose condixisu et per li presenti permictimu et damu licencia ki lu dictu Ruben judeu poza et vagla senza incurriri in pena alcuna prindiri et conduchiri mugleri et habitari et stari cum ipsa in la dicta chitati et insula di Malta quantunqui haia mugleri in Gerusalem; però ki comandamu ki alu prenominatu Ruben judeu servati et exequiti la presenti licentia et permissioni et non permictati esserli facta hac de causa novitati nè molestia alcuna per nixunu tractandulu como li altri Judei et habitaturi di la chitati et insula. Dat. Cathanie III Julii nonae indictionis."

577 *Archivio veneto*, vol. XXXIV, 1887, pp. 215–217: BC, *Aneddoti storici e letterari*. The Bishop of Feltre ... "visa instantia D. Benjamin qm. Lazari de Bononia, mariti dominae Annae qm. Jacobi Scaletta, hebrei degentis ad presens in burrallis Ausugii dioecesis feltrensis; visis dispositionibus testium super eo quod predicta Anna qm. Jacobi Scaletta eius uxor nunquam habuit filios, et quod nulla spes ob aetatem jam ingravescentem est relicta quod possit amplius concipere et partorire ... per has nostras literas patentes auctoritate nostra ordinaria declaramus licere dicto domino Beniamin juxta formam sacro sancti Veteris Testamenti aliam superinducere uxorem, priori retenta pro suscitanda et suscipienda prole, ipsique domino Beniamin eadem nostra auctoritate damus licentiam plenam et omnimodam aliam uxorem superinducendi, et cum ea legittime matrimonium contrahendi priori etiam retenta, secundum formam et ritum hebreorum ad supradictum effectum prolis iuxta formam et legem predictam sacrosancti Veteris Testamenti quo conceditur hebreis id posse tuto et impune fieri. Venezia, 4 marzo 1578." Sessa mentions another case, *Tractatus de Judeis*, cit., p. 110, as he reports having heard "a quamplurimis tam Hebreis quam Christianis jamdiu fuisse dispensatum quemdam Hebreum divitem de familia Murenorum, qui ex secunda uxore prolem inde suscepit, ac uxorem dimissam

The doctrine has rarely had to deal with this point.[578]

• • •

On the particular question of whether matrimonial law was admissible or not concerning the general theme of the conflict between Jewish and state laws, controversies abound in German doctrine of the 17th and 18th centuries. As already noted, this admissibility was rejected, not only by the opposers of Jewish law en bloc[579] but also by some who had recognized it in certain fields. They considered the l. 7 C. 1, 9 to always be in force and draw the consequence that, unlike the other norms, the matrimonial ones were "specialiter reprobatae."[580] The unique monograph, dedicated to Wagner's end of this issue,[581] is conducted precisely on this line of thought.

• • •

At least concerning form, the institution of marriage is the most resistant unifying legislative wave of the 19th century. In the Austrian civil code, which took effect in the Kingdom of Lombardy-Venetia on January 1, 1816, the Jewish marriage is governed by special rules that partly accept and elaborate the traditional Jewish law.[582]

---

nihilhominus, honorabat et victui necessaria providebat." But from these latest expressions, it seems that rather than bigamy, it was in fact a divorce followed by remarriage.

578 Cf. Beck, *Tractatus de juribus Judeorum*, cit. pp. 103–104, who observes that after the ordinance of R. Ghershon, polygamy is no longer practiced by the Jews of Europe; and Sessa, op. cit., l. cit.

579 Ibid., pp. 140–141.

580 Ibid., pp. 141–142. Beck, *Tractatus* cit. is not among these and admits (p. 63) the validity of the Jewish matrimonial law.

581 Johann Tobias Richter (praes.) and Johann Gottlieb Wagner (respondens), *Jus matrimoni Judeorum in Germania tum inter se tum si alter coniunx ad sacra christianorum transiit*, Leipzig, 1751, 32 pp. German translation by the title: *Abhandlung von dem Rechte der jüdischen Ehe in Teutschland so wohl unter sich als wenn ein jüdischer Ehegatte zur christlichen Religion getreten ist. Aus dem lateinischem übersetzt*, Leipzig 1779.

582 Art. 123–136. Upon previous licensing by the civil court, the divorce by bill of divorcement is also admitted. See J. Grassl, *Das besondere Eherecht der Juden in Oesterreich*, Vienna, 1835, 2nd ed. 1849. At the time of Joseph II, consistent with the policy of suppression of autonomies and of legislative unification, Jews are bound to abide by the general rules stipulated for the marriage and in particular, for each case of marriage between relatives in degrees prohibited by civil law, to ask for the permission of the provincial court. See the edict published in *Gazzetta di Mantova* of May 31, 1786 (a copy available in the archives of the Jewish community of Mantua, lot 209, no. 48). The provision is perfectly analogous, in the substance and in the reasons that determine it, to the Roman law of 393 (l. 7. C. 1, 9).

In Piedmont, the Albertine code of 1837 (art. 150) provides that the nuptials and marriages between individuals professing state-tolerated religions be ruled by the customs and regulations relating to them.[583]

In Parma, the civil code of July 1, 1820 (art. 31) establishes that the marriage of Jews is celebrated according to their rituals.[584]

In Modena, a decree by Francesco V of October 25, 1851 (art. 9) confirms to the Jews the use of their law on matters of marriage and divorce.[585]

Finally, in the Grand Duchy of Tuscany, an act of December 17, 1814 (art. 3), confirmed by a circular dated September 2, 1822, establishes "that in the causes of marriage and divorce between Jews, the Jewish rite should prevail for everything that relates to religious bonds."[586]

The last vestiges of Jewish matrimonial law disappear from the judicial field, returning to the purely religious one with the codification of 1865, which, by establishing the obligation of civil marriage, excludes the validity of any law for the marriage other than that of the state.

2.3 *Coming of Age*

The conflict we have discussed in relation to marriage sometimes also arises for the coming of age, fixed by Rabbinic Law at the time of alleged puberty, i.e., at thirteen years for men and twelve for women,[587] in accordance with the practice of the most ancient laws;[588] and at 25 by Roman law.[589]

---

583 See *Collezione completa dei moderni codici civili degli stati d'Italia*, Turin, 1845.

584 *Collezione*, cit.

585 *Codice civile per gli Stati estensi*, 2nd ed., Modena, 1852, p. 374.

586 I. E. Rignano, *Sulla attuale posizione giuridica degli israeliti in Toscana*, Florence, 1847, p. 18. According to this provision, in Rignano's interpretation, celebration of marriage, impediments and its dissolution were to be governed by Jewish law, whereas the judicial content of the bond, i.e., the mutual obligations of the spouses and their patrimonial relations, was to depend upon the civil law. It seems to me that the recognition of the legal status of the obligations assumed by the husband towards his wife with the ketubah, made still as late as 1828 by the Court of Grosseto, contrasts with this interpretation. See above, footnote no. 533.

587 Maimonides, *Mishneh Torah*, Ilchot ishut, ch. 2: "The female from birth to twelve years of age is called a minor or young girl; by twelve years and one day, if she displays signs of puberty, she is defined as girl up to the following six months. After the six months she is defined as *boghered* (mature). The male from birth up to age thirteen is defined as *katan* or *tinnoc* (a minor). From the age of thirteen and one day, he is called a man." Mendelssohn, *Ritualgesetze der Juden*, cit. part II, § 1, p. 36; S. Tibi, *Le statut personnel des israélites et spécialement des israélites tunisiens*, tome I, Tunis, 1923, p. 146.

588 Post, *Giurisprudenza etnologica*, Bonfante transl., Milan, 1906, vol. II, pp. 24–25.

589 The term was established by *lex Pletoria* issued around 200 BC. Previously, coming of age coincided with the age of puberty, calculated at 14 years for males, at 12 for females. Cf. the title "De minoribus vigintiquinque annis" of the Digest (D. 4, 4). Ferrero, *La lex Pletoria e la cura minorum*, in *Filangieri*, 1889, pp. 456 et seqq.

The debate primarily arises about the capacity to be bound in contracts concluded by Jews, minors under common law, whereas already of age in accordance with their law. If Jewish law is applied, the obligation must be binding; if common law is applied, the legal act is to be considered null and void and, where appropriate, the *restitutio in integrum* may be put into effect.

On this point, the authors were quite divided.

Ippolito Riminaldi *junior* of Ferrara ruled that a bond contracted by Jewish brothers under 25 years of age but over 14 (i.e., passed puberty) with a fellow Jew had to be considered fully binding as here, like in other institutions of private law, Jewish law should be applied.[590]

Ettore Felici concurred, as expressed not in a council but rather in a doctrinal treatise.[591]

The opposite principle was advocated with a great display of doctrine by Pietro Sordi from Mantua, who maintained the inapplicability of Jewish law both in general, with the usual arguments, and in particular with regard to the issue of coming of age. About the latter point, he claimed among other things that the conflict was all about non-substantial, procedural norms, so that the application of the local rules was obvious. He also pointed out that the Roman statute setting the minors' age limit to twenty-five years responded to rational criteria going beyond which was not appropriate. He concluded with the observation that, since a decree of the Duke of Mantua ruled that Jews were "jus reddi modis et formis quibus redditur christianis," a law other than the common law could not possibly be applied.[592] The Senate of Mantua, before which the case was discussed, decided in the sense advocated by Sordi, and, considering the Jews under 25 years as minors, according to Roman law, granted them their *restitutio in integrum* request.[593]

The same question came up again later, again in Mantua, again in a request for *restitutio in integrum propter minorem aetatem*. It was discussed by the jurist Francesco Negri, who adopted a strategy opposite to that of his predecessor Sordi and refuted his arguments point-by-point both in general and in particular.[594] With regard to the specific subject, it was easy for Negri to

590 Ippolito Riminaldi *junior*, *Consiliorum sive responsorum liber quartus*, Venice, 1581, cons. 399, nos. 11–12, p. 181. Lawsuit between the Jews Galli and Samuele da Siena.

591 Ettore Felici, *Tractatus de communione seu societate deque lucro et quaestu damno ibidem ac expensis*, Turin, 1610, ch. 5.

592 Pietro Sordi, *Decisiones sacri mantuani senatus*, Piacenza, 1598, decis. 133, pp. 296–300. Lawsuit between the Sacerdoti brothers and sisters.

593 Idem, ibidem.

594 Francesco Ciriaco Negri, *Controversiarum forensium liber secundus*, s. l., 1562, controv. 240, pp. 162–164 and controv. 241, pp. 165–169.

clarify that this was not a procedural but rather a substantial point "vel saltem quid emergens valde diversum ab ordinatoriis judicii, quod venit decidendum secundum leges ac mores hebreorum." As for the issue of the rationality of the limit placed by Roman law to the *aetas perfecta*, he replied that there was no lack of statutes in which the same limit was moved to a younger age.[595] If that was possible – and there was no shortage of lawyers[596] who recognized the full legality of the statutory modification – this meant that the Roman law was not absolutely intransgressible and for relations between Jews could therefore be replaced by Jewish law. Finally, as for the prescription to judge Jews in the same way and under the same forms as Christians, that had to be understood in the sense of treating equitably, without bias, applying to both not the same law but to each their own law.

The *restitutio in integrum* therefore was not to be granted to applicants who, *jure hebraico* were adult and therefore fully capable.

Such disparity of views between jurists on the question of which law to apply to Jews in the issue of coming-of-age was later reported by De Luca, who recalls the debate between Sordi and Negri and deems prevalent, in doctrine and jurisprudence, the opinion of the former, opposing the recognition of the Jewish law.[597]

This opinion is shared by later Italian and German authors of monographs on Jews, like Sessa,[598] Thiel,[599] and Mascovius.[600] The latter points out, as did Sordi before, that the age posed by Roman law perfectly responds to natural reason and social needs, confusing puberty with maturity a blatant mistake and considering thirteen or twelve-year-old boys capable "cum fragile et infirmum sit huiusmodi aetatis consilium et multis captionibus suppositum" (according to the expression contained in D. 4, 4, 1). The Jewish norm is not in the Bible but belongs in the traditional Rabbinic Law and is therefore observable with less rigor.[601]

595 These are the statutes reflecting the German norms.

596 See e.g. Sforza Oddi from Perugia, *De restitutione in integrum tractatus*, Venice, 1584, quest. 2, art. 6.

597 De Luca, *Theatrum veritatis et justitiae*, vol. VII, *De donationibus*, disc. 19, nos. 10–11, p. 41, and *De alienationibus*, disc. 60, no. 10, p. 320.

598 Sessa, *Tractatus de Judeis*, Turin, 1717, ch. 46, p. 149, who observes that such was the praxis in the State of Piedmont.

599 Thiel, *Principia jurisprudentiae judaicae per Germaniam communis*, cit., Halae Saxonum, 1790, § 172, p. 111.

600 Johann Caspar Mascovius, *De juribus Judeorum*, cit. Wittemberg, 1684, ch. 2, § 23.

601 Mascovius, ibidem.

In essence, therefore, the thesis prevails that the limit for being of age is a matter not of particular but of general public policy; that is to say, it is an imperative and mandatory standard not only for Christians living in Roman law but also for all other citizens of the State living in different laws. We are currently in the field of provisions that we nowadays call international public policy, from which even foreigners cannot derogate, unlike the rules of internal public policy, from which the permissibility of derogation is excluded only for citizens.

2.4 *Guardianship*

According to Jewish law, the guardianship terminates at the coming of age, that is, as we said, at the age of thirteen years for males and of twelve for females: from this moment on, the period of total capacity begins.[602]

In Roman law, the tutelage ends with puberty (fourteen and twelve years respectively), but up to twenty-five is followed by guardianship.

The German authors just cited above, who see the Jewish being of age conforming to Roman law, think that up to twenty-five years as required by Roman law, or up to an age possibly established by local regulations, the authority of the guardian should be applied upon them as well.[603] In Italian authors, the question is not examined.

On the other hand, in Andrea Barbazza, we find discussed the validity of the appointment of a woman as guardian. According to the general rule, observes Barbazza, Jewish law is applied to the Jews when their law explicitly settles a moot point; in the absence of a particular provision, one shall resort to the *jus commune*. In the case in question, therefore, either the Jewish law explicitly acknowledges women's capacity or incapacity regarding guardianship, and this Jewish norm will thus be observed, or such explicit provision is absent. In the latter case, it will be necessary to make use of l. 2 C. 5, 35 that allows women to be guardians of their children and their descendants. In any case, Barbazza points out that it is common among Jews to entrust guardianship to the mother, the fact that he observed, especially in Bologna, where "sunt

---

602 Mendelssohn, op. cit., ibid. On guardianship in Jewish law, see Keyzer, *Dissertatio de tutela secundum jus talmud*, Leyden, 1847; M. Bloch, *Die Vormundschaft nach mosaisch-talmudischem Recht*, Budapest, 1904 (*Beilage zum 27 Jahresberichte der Landesrabbinerschule*) (that I have not seen); see complete literature in Eisenstadt, *Repertorium* cit., pp. 361–362.

603 Thiel and Mascovius, op. and books of both cit.. Inaccessible to me, as it was to Juster, op. cit., vol. II, p. 63, no. 6, was Johann Friedrich Mayer's work *Gekrönte Preisschrift von den Unterschieden zwischen Tutel und Kuratel Unmündiger und Minderjärigen nach römischen und deutschen Recht für die Juden*, 1803, Frankfurt a. M.

multae hebreae habentes tutelas filiorum; et illud quod est consuetudinarium non est arbitrarium."[604]

2.5 *Successions*

2.5.1 Ab Intestato

Inheritance[605] is the one area where the question of which law should apply in relations between Jews arises most frequently, and there are as many authors discussing it in one sense or the other, but constantly rummaging in the same arguments, which are handed down for centuries, though unchanged in substance and form. Firstly, there is the question of female heirs to their fathers in concurrence with their male siblings: Jewish law (Numbers 27, 8–11) denies it, whereas Roman law (*l. maximum vitium C. de liberis praeteritis* = C. 6, 28, 4) accepts it, not recognizing gender differences in heritage issues. On the other hand, in a large number of Italian statutes, norms can be seen as diverse in their particular determinations but in agreement with the general principle, which delineates a disadvantageous position for females, competing with male siblings for an inheritance, pushing them back, not only behind their brothers, as required by biblical law, but sometimes behind the descendants, ascendants and even collaterals.[606]

---

604 Andrea Barbazza, *Consiliorum sive responsorum libri*, vol. I, Venice, 1581, cons. 15, nos. 1 and 2.

605 For the complete literature on successions in Jewish law, see Eisenstadt, *Repertorium*, cit., pp. 355–360. Main studies: John Selden, *De successionibus in bona defuncti seu jure hereditario ad leges hebreorum*, 2 volumes, London, 1631, 2nd ed., London 1636, 3rd ed. Leyden, 1638, 4th ed. Frankf. a. O., 1673, 5th ed. 1695; Hirschel Lewin and Moses Mendelssohn, *Ritualgesetze der Juden betreffend Erbschaften, Vormundschaften, Testamente und Ehesachen, insoweit sie das Mein und Dein angehen*, cit. above (footnote no. 529); Eduard Gans, *Die Grundzüge des mosaisch-talmudischen Erbrechts*, in *Zeitschrift für die Wissenschaft des Judentums* (by Zunz), vol. I, 1823, dossier 3, pp. 419–471; L. Bodenheimer, *Die Erbfolge bei den alten Hebräern*, in *Literaturblatt des Orients*, 1843, pp. 353–390; A. Wolff, *Das jüdische Erbrecht, zugleich ein Beitrag zur biblisch-talmudischen Exegese*, Berlin, 1888, 80 pp.; Moses Bloch, *Das mosaisch-talmudische Erbrecht*, in *Jahresberichte der Landesrabbinerschule in Budapest für das Jahr* 1889, Budapest 1890, 70 pp.; M. Mielziner, *The rabbinical law of hereditary succession*, Cincinnati, 1900; M. W. Rapaport, *Der Talmud und sein Recht*, part 2: *Grundsätze des Intestaterbrechts*, in *Zeitschrift für vergleichende Rechtswissenschaft*, vol. XIV, 1900, pp. 33–93. Not all of these works are available in Italy.

606 Pertile, *Storia del diritto italiano*, vol. IV, 2nd ed., pp. 93–95; Besta, *Le successioni nella storia del diritto italiano*, Padua, 1935, pp. 51–56; Leicht, *Il diritto privato preirneriano*, Bologna, 1933, pp. 278–280. For the old literature, see Alberto Bruni, from Asti, *Commentarii super statutis excludentibus feminas et cognatorum lineam a successionibus*, in *Tractatus illustrium ... jurisconsultorum* (*T.U.J.*), Venice, 1584, t. 2, f. 165–245; Lauro Palazzi, from Fano, *Commentarii super statuto communiter per Italiam vigentem quod extantibus masculis*

This provision is of the Longobard origin,[607] characteristic of all primitive laws,[608] on which Germanic and Hebrew laws partially agree, precisely because they both reflect the same archaic, patriarchal, degree of social evolution, in which the female inheritance is excluded or restricted in order to keep intact the tribal or gentile heritage (cfr. Numbers 36, 1–12).

Now, shall the provisions of the statutes, either Roman law or Jewish law, be applied to Jews?

Giovanni Calderini is the first to argue that, since Jewish law sustains all relations between Jews, it is the Biblical norm that should apply, not the Roman one, to the point in question.[609] Not long afterwards, Pietro d'Ancarano, Raffaele Fulgosio, Gaspare Calderini and Floriano da S. Pietro also reach the same conclusion, in a council concerning a matter of 30,000 ducats.[610] However, we know that in the same sense, a complicated dispute was judged in Mantua in 1461.[611]

By contrast, Giovanni d'Anagni, the canonist who adopted the "*evacuatio to adventum Christi*" thesis of Jewish law also among Jews (though with some reservations), in the case of a daughter in concurrence with her brothers for their father's inheritance, favored the application of the local statute. However, he noted that in this specific case, "talia statuta reponuntur in dispositione legis mosaycae et iste reditus est comendabilis" according to the rule laid down in the *l. lege C. de legi. here* (C. 6, 58, 14).[612] It should be noted that d'Anagni is wrong when considering the Jewish and statutory laws entirely equal: in fact, there are differences in detail that make that "reditus" only partial. Giovanni Campeggi from Mantua was also wrong with him. While supporting the

femine non succedant, ibid., f. 272–282; Giovanni Campeggi, *Commentarii super eadem materia de statutis excludentibus feminas a successionibus*, ibid., f. 273–271 [TN, sic].

607 Leicht, op. cit., l. c., and already, among the old ones, Bruni, op. cit., art. 2, nos. 1, 2, 3, f. 167v. Cf. F. Nicolai, *La formazione del diritto successorio negli Statuti comunali del territorio lombardo-tosco*, Milan, 1940.

608 Extensive documentation in Post, *Giurisprudenza etnologica*, vol. I, pp. 192–193.

609 Giovanni Calderini, *Consilia ... secundum decretalium rubricas digesta*, s. l., 1536, De testamentis, cons. 30, f. 41: "An si judeus reliquit filios et filias ab intestato filie pariter succedant cum masculis. Et videtur quod non quod ex lege mosaica habetur quod solus masculus succedat exclusis feminis et dixit Dominus quod hec lex sancta esset perpetua: hoc habetur Numeri, XXVII. Cum igitur hec lex fuerit data judeis et Ecclesia illos tolerat et papa et imperator ut inter se legem suam servent, ergo secundum illam succedant, etc."

610 This is reported by Floriano da S. Pietro, *Commentaria in primam et secundam Codicis partem*, in l. *maximum vitium C. de liberis praeteritis* (C. 6, 28, 4).

611 Campeggi, *De statutis* cit., quest. 60, no. 241, f. 271v. = *De dote*, part 5, quest. 114 and last, in *De dote tractatus ex variis juris civ. interpretibus*, Lyon, 1585, p. 474.

612 Giovanni d'Anagni, *Lectura super quinto Decretalium*, Milan, 1492, f. 63–63v., in *c. judei, il secondo, de judeis* (c.5 × 5, 6).

opposite of Calderini's thesis (i.e., the recognition of the Jewish law), Campeggi considers the provision of statutes applicable as being equal to that of the Bible.[613] Likewise wrong is Merlino Mercuriali from Forlì for whom, concerning the point in question, the Bible and statutes coincide perfectly, so much, in fact, as to render vain the question of conflict between the two provisions.[614]

Alberto Bruni accurately understood the distinction between the significance of the two exclusions, abiding, however, by neither and asserting that Jews must follow through with the Roman law that equalizes both genders. This does not seem too logical since, as a rule, in the occurrence of a statutory norm, it is this that must prevail over common law; therefore, once the application of Jewish law is excluded, one would think most appropriate to rely on the statute and not on the Roman norm.

Bruni argues that the exclusion of females would turn out in favor of Jewish males, and this cannot coincide with the principle established by the final gloss c. 2 × 5, 19, that prescribes, for Jews, the use of "rigor" and not of "equitas."

Furthermore, and this is what matters most, "etiam suadet ratio, propter quam factum censetur tale statutum, quae est ut dignitas familiarum conservetur, cum ipsi [Jews] non aspirent ad dignitates, ut dixi; nec publica utilitas versetur in conservatione suarum agnationum et familiarum." If the brothers had converted to Christianity, however, the statute should be applied differently "quia bene tunc militaret familialis intentio statuti."[615]

In a council on a court case regarding the succession of an aunt to a nephew as *adgnatus proximus* of the latter, Ansaldo Ansaldi moves along the same line of Bruni's thought.[616] The woman is entitled to the inheritance, both according to Jewish law which, in the known text (Numbers, 27), with regard to close agnate makes no gender distinction, and to Roman law, which in the whole area of inheritance is gender equal (*l. maximum vitium C. de lib. praeter.* = C. 6, 28, 4).

For local – Florentine – statute "precipiens quod agnati remotiores feminas excludant," the heir would rather be a more distant male relative of the *de cuius*.

On the one hand, Ansaldi supports the applicability of Jewish norm-based, besides on general arguments, also on the specific provision of the privilege

---

613 Campeggi, op. cit., l. c., and quest. 36, nos. 158–160, f. 269.

614 Merlino Mercuriali, *De legitima*, Venice, 1651, book 3, title 1, quest. 7.

615 Bruni, *Commentarii*, cit., art. 6, nos. 55–62, f. 179v.–180.

616 Ansaldo Ansaldi, *De commercio et mercatura*, Coloniae Allobrogorum, 1698, discourses 40 and 41, pp. 158 et seqq. Court case discussed in Loghorn, for the inheritance of Beniamino Barzillai, between Gabriele Arias (donee of a *de cuius*' aunt, Sara Barzillai) and Abramo Barzillai, a *de cujus*' more distant relative.

of the Grand Duke of Tuscany, who grants Jews of Leghorn permission to use "di tutte le cerimonie, precetti, riti, ordini e costumi di legge hebrea," where Jewish law is also included. But, on the other hand, he denies the applicability of the statute, since the exclusion of females established by it "ut dignitas familiarum conservetur," while "in conservatione agnationis et familiarum judeorum publica utilitas non servatur." Jews – he presses on – are subject only to those statutes concerning the matter "aeque proportionabili judeo ac christiano"; but since the statute in question has only the purpose of "conservatio agnationis et splendoris familiarum," it would be inappropriate to apply it to pass the inheritance on "ad masculos judeos remotiores, in quibus nulla dignitas reipublicae, nullus splendor familiarum concurrit." Nor should it be objected – Ansaldi concludes – that that statute refers to the Mosaic law, which too "favebat agnationi," since this favor had a meaning in an era when Jews had a state and a government of their own, and does no longer have it today.

Conversely, regarding the point in question, the application of Roman norm, except for the Jewish one, is supported in a decision of the Sacra Rota dated January 1, 1612, concerning a lawsuit brought before that court. The dispute was between a Jewess, and her brother-in-law, about the succession to the woman's son, predeceased to her.[617] The ruling favored the woman, based on the common law admitting the mother to the succession, in opposition to the contrary Jewish norm. Besides the general argumentation of the "evacuatio per adventum Christi" of the entire Mosaic law, also in relations between Jews, the specific argument was the consideration that the biblical inheritance law should not be applied anymore "quia hodie non est divisio tribuum, nec divisio illa bonorum, nec causa ex qua dicta lex promulgata est. Nam precepta judicialia ab hominibus instituta habent perpetuam obligationem durante illo statu regiminis, sed si civitas vel gens ad alium regimen deveniat oportet leges mutari." Indeed, an argument permeated by a historical sense rare for its time, slipping from its author's pen probably without him grasping its intimately revolutionary depth and significance.

On the issue of conflict between Jewish law, Roman law and local law in the succession area, the position of the firstborn is another point on which the discussion of authors focuses.

Here too, we have a similar situation of female succession: like almost all archaic statutes,[618] Jewish law favors the firstborn, who must receive

617 Reported by Sessa, *Tractatus de judeis*, Turin, 1717, p. 85.

618 Post, *Giurisprudenza etnologica*, vol. I, pp. 191 and 194–195 and M. W. Rapaport, *Der Talmud und sein Recht*, in *Zeitschrift für vergleichende Rechtswissenschaft*, vol. XIV, 1900, p. 53. For a helpful consultation, see the old work of Hermann Johann Friedrich Schulze, *Das Recht*

twice what it is due to other sieblings.[619] However, according to Roman law (Nov. 118), all children are equal; and the statutory law often contains rules of German origin – germinated from the same social situation of which the Jewish norm was a reflection – that place the firstborn in a favorable condition to his brothers.[620]

What, then, is the law that applies to the Jews?

This issue is considered for the first time, I believe, by the French Andrea Tiraqueau (Tiraquellus) in connection with the general issue of conflict between Jewish law, common law and statutory law, which he extensively discussed. In this case, he concludes that Jewish law should be applied like all other cases where there are no contrary provisions expressly relating to Jews. The rule is also valid if the children have converted to Christianity, and if the Christian is only the second-born, to avoid that, he converts to double his share.[621] Nor can it be objected that birthright does not compete with the Jews because it is a *dignitas*, and the *dignitates* are banned by the *l. ultima C. de Judeis* (C. 1, 9, 18), since the *dignitates publicae* but not the *privatae* ones are mentioned therein.[622]

The same opinion expressed by Tiraqueau is shared by Alberto Bruni. This appears somewhat strange, since, as we have seen, he refused to accept the Jewish norm regarding female succession.[623]

After discussing the conflict in general, Jean Le Cirier reached the same conclusion as Tiraqueau, that Jews should use "quocumque jure primogeniturae sive veteris sive novi vel legis communis aut particularis"; which does not

der Erstgeburt in den deutschen Fürstenhaüsern und Seine Bedeutung für die deutsche Staatsentwiklung, Leipzig, 1851.

619 Deuter. 21, 15–17. Maimonides, *Ilchot nechalot* (Inheritance norms), ch. 2 and 3; Caro, *Shulchan Aruch*, Hoshen Mishpat, ch. 277 and 278. V. J. H. H. Hottinger, *De primogenitis*, Marburg, 1711; D. Gerdes, *De variis S. Scripturae locis in quibus mentio primogenitorum occurrit*, Duisburg, 1730; J. J. Schröder, *De veterum hebreorum primogenitis*, Marburg, 1741; Kirsch, *Der Erstgeborene nach mosaisch-talmudischem Rechte* (dissertation, Bern), Frankfurt a. M., 1902; Rapaport, op. cit., pp. 53–57; and M. Cohn, in *Jüdisches Lexikon*, entry Erstgeburtrecht. For the complete literature, see Eisenstadt, *Repertorium*, cit., pag. 320.

620 Pertile, *Storia del diritto italiano*, vol. IV, 1st ed., Padua 1874, pp. 146 et seqq.

621 Andrea Tiraqueau, *De jure primigeniorum*, in *Opera omnia*, Frankfurt a. M., 1597, vol. 1, quest. 66, pp. 453–458, nos. 35–41. This argument is considered very convincing by Sessa, *Tractatus de judeis* cit., p. 141; from it he is drawn to follow Tiraqueau's view, rejecting Ricciulli's contrary opinion, *Tractatus de personis extra Ecclesiae araemium*, cit., book 2, ch. 15, no. 2, in which Ricciulli supported the appropriateness to apply the Roman law to the case in point.

622 Tiraqueau, op. cit., 1, cit.

623 Bruni's view on this issue is quoted by Jean Le Cirier, *De primogenitura*, in *Tractatus universi juris*, T. 10, part 1, Venice, 1584, book 1, quest. 16, pp. 31v.-32.

resolve the issue unambiguously. Le Cirier also understands that Jews cannot be excluded from the dignity of private character, such as birthright, and noted that "inter se possunt habere dignitates" as proved by the law *si qua C. de Judeis* attributing to Jewish *seniores* the decision power in internal court cases.[624]

A third point of dissent between Roman and Jewish inheritance laws is inheritance between spouses.

A. According to Jewish law, *if a wife predeceases her husband*, the latter is the heir *in toto* of both the dotal properties and the paraphernalia.

Neither the children nor – in their absence – ascendants or collaterals can claim any right over these possessions.[625]

In contrast, according to Roman law, the children are the heirs to their mother while the surviving husband receives nothing.[626] A decision by the Sacra Rota mentioned by Bruni[627] rules for applying Roman norms, whereas, per the Jewish norm, Antonio Roselli contends that the right of a surviving husband to the defunct mother's inheritance should prevail over that of his daughter.[628] From Jewish sources, we know that, when questioned concerning a practical case, on the conflict at issue, the rabbinic doctrine refused to apply the principle of reference to local law permitted in other areas and reaffirmed the thesis of the precedence of the husband rights, denying restitution of the dowry to his deceased wife's father.[629]

---

624 Le Cirier, op. cit., l. c.

625 See e.g., Bab. Talmud, ketubot, f. 50a; Maimonides, *Mishneh Torah*, Ilchot nechalot, ch. 1, § 8; Caro, *Shulchan Aruch*, Eben haezer, ch. 90, § 1: "The husband is his wife's heir, both of the dotal possessions and the paraphernalia." See Rapaport, *Der Talmud und sein Recht*, cit., part 2, *Grunsätze des Intestaterbrechts*, in *Zeitschrift für vergleichende Rechtswissenschaft*, vol. XIV, 1900, pp. 60–70; Tschernowitz, *Das Dotalsystem nach der mosaisch-talmudischen Gesetzgebung*, in *Zeitschrift für vergleichende Rechtswissenschaft*, vol. XXIV, 1912, pp. 470–472; M. Cohn, in *Jüdisches Lexikon*, entry Erbrecht, § III, Erbrecht des Ehemannes. Cf. Olaf Gerard Tychsen's dissertation, *Die Erbfolge eines Ehemannes in dem Nachlasse einer ohne Kinder und Testament verstorbenen Ehefrau, nach jüdischen Gesetzen beurtheilt*, Rostock, 1804.

626 Nov. 117, c. 5 repealing that of Nov. 53, c. 6, according to which also the needy husband was entitled to the *quarta uxoria*. Conversely, the German law provides in a sense more akin to the Jewish one; as a result, many Italian statutes of the intermediate period, that uphold the Germanic system, with regard to the succession to the wife, place the husband in a much more advantageous position than that established by Roman law. See for example Ciccaglione, in *Digesto italiano*, entry Successione, diritto intermedio, no. 133, pp. 345–346.

627 Bruni, *Commentarii super statutis* cit. art. 1, no. 14, f. 166.

628 Antonio Roselli, *Arbor consanguineitatis*, cited by Bruni, ibid. This *Arbor* will be included in the treatise *De Successionibus ab intestato* by Roselli, which remained unpublished. See Schulte, *Geschichte der Quellen und Literatur des canonischen Rechtes*, vol. II, p. 305.

629 See the sources cited further on, Second Section, ch. 2, § 2, footnote no. 889; and further back, footnote no. 519.

However, in litigation brought before the Tribunal of Venice in 1697, the court judges established the appropriateness of applying Jewish laws, and having some friars, formerly Jews, been consulted as experts, they claimed that while the Jewish law indeed established the principle of exclusion of the children from the maternal inheritance, it was then generally deferred to statutory norms. Once the deferment was accepted, these were the ones that were ultimately applied.[630] By giving the husband the right to become his wife's heir, the Jewish provision gives him the possibility, in the event of a new marriage, to pass the assets of the defunct wife, rather than on her children, on any possible offspring from his second marriage. To avoid this, a clause is often found in the dotal deed, whereby: in the event of the wife's predeceasing, while in homage to the law, her husband is declared her heir and upon the death of their father, the exclusive right of succession over their mother's inheritance is attributed to the children of first marriage.[631]

B. *If the husband predeceases his wife*, by Jewish law, she is entitled to the restitution of the dowry upon her swearing that nothing she has taken away from her husband's assets during the marriage period. Lacking such oath, an amount equivalent to the dowry is presumed to have been taken away by the wife, and the dowry remains in the bulk of the deceased's possessions.[632]

---

630 See the texts cited further on, Second Section, ch. 2, § 2, footnote no. 900.

631 Such clause is called *ketubà benin dichrin*. See M. Cohn, in *Jüdisches Lexikon*, entry Ketubbà and Vismara, *La donazione nuziale nel diritto ebraico e nelle fonti cristiane in relazione al diritto romano postclassico*, Milan, 1934, pp. 46–47. Cf. the dotal deed drafted in Recanati in 1475 before a notary and published by Brandileone, *Saggi sulla storia della celebrazione del matrimonio*, cit., p. 567, no. 1: "Moyses Aleutii [not Alcutii] judeus de Recanati ... confessus fuit recepisse ... a Servo Angelerii, judeo de Auximo, presente et interrogante, pro parte dotis d. Bellerose, filie dicti Servi, uxoris Manuelis, filii dicti Moysis, et pro matrimonio jam contracto et carnali coppula consumato inter eosdem Manuelem et Bellamrosam, ducatos ducentos monete ... quos ducatos ducentos ... prefatus Moyses ... restituire promisit dicte Bellerose ... si dictum matrimonium ... divideretur per mortem dicti Manuelis, extantibus vel non extantibus filiis ex dicto matrimonio ... sed si divideretur morte dicte Bellerose, supervenientibus filiis vel filiabus ex dicto matrimonio ... tunc dicta pars dotis tota sit, et esse voluerunt, et remaneat ipsi Moysi, pro filiis ipsius Manuelis et d. Bellerose. Et hoc secundum stilum, ritum et morem atque consuetudinem Ebreorum."

632 Mishnà. ketubot, ch. 13, § 1; Caro, *Shulchan Aruch*, Eben haezer, ch. 89 and 96. Cf. Josef Kohler, *Güterrecht und Ehescheidungsrecht der oesterreichischen Juden*, in *Zeitschrift für vergleichende Rechtswissenschaft*, vol. 33, 1915–1916, pp. 285–286. This, of course, unless otherwise expressed in an arrangement by which the restitution of the dowry is agreed upon even without the oath by the widow. See, e.g., the document cited in the previous note.

In a consultation, Paolo di Castro claimed precisely that, in the case in question, not having wanted the widow to take the oath required by Jewish law, her dowry was not to be subtracted from her husband's inheritance bulk.[633]

In the area of inheritance, the conflict we are discussing finally arises relative to the position of natural children that Jewish law equalizes to the legitimate ones,[634] whereas by contrast, Roman law deprives them of any rights, when in concourse with the legitimate ones, to their father's inheritance, except for alimony.[635]

Andrea Alciato reports such a practical case in one of his consultations.[636] After their father's death, a natural son is hushed up by the legitimate brothers with a sum, and by a deed drafted in Hebrew, he waives any further claim. He later changes his mind and takes his brothers to court to obtain the annulment of the waiver, as it was vitiated by a great prejudice, given his right to a succession equal to that of the legitimate brothers according to Jewish law. Hence, the disproportion between the hush-up amount already received and the portion of inheritance claimed.

Defending the brothers' interests, Alciato rejects the thesis of the applicability of Jewish norms based on the explicit provisions of l. 7. C. 1, 9 and of the "reprobatio" of the entire Talmud repeated several times by the Church. In any case, he adds, even if, per the provisions of Rabbinic Law, the right of the natural son to his father's inheritance were admitted, this could only be exercised in the absence of other legitimate children, but not in competition with them: and this is also by a provision of the same biblical law that does not admit the "filius ancillae" to the succession with the "filius liberae" (Genesis, 21, 10).

The authors cited thus far are the ones known to have most often carried out specific arguments in favor and against applying the Jewish inheritance rules. However, in many others, the usual arguments in favor or against the Jewish

633 Paolo di Castro, *Consiliorum volumen secundum*, Venice, 1570, cons. 378, f. 175v.: The restitution of the dowry occurs "quando mulier que remansit vidua juravit se nihil habere de bonis mariti ultra dotem, alias secundum eos et eorum ritum dos remanet in bonis mariti, quia presumitur tantundem subtraxisse; et sic erit judicandum hic, tamquam de bonis mariti, cum non juraverit ut mihi asseritur."

634 Babylonian Talmud, jebamot, f. 22 ° and b; Maimonides, *Ilchot nechalot*, ch. 1, § 7; Selden, *De successionibus*, cit., ed. 1673, ch. 3, pp. 9–11; Saalschütz, *Das mosaische Recht*, Berlin, 1853, vol. II, p. 825, no. 1058; S. Mayer, *Die Rechte der Israeliten, Athener und Römer*, Leipzig, 1866, vol. II, p. 463; Rapaport, *Der Talmud und sein Recht*, cit., in *Zeitschrift für vergleichende Rechtswissenschaft*, vol. XIV, 1900, pp. 46–47. The incestuous ones are also equalized to the legitimate ones.

635 Nov. 18, c. 5; Nov. 89, c. 12. S. Mayer, op. cit., vol. II, pp. 463–464. Perozzi, *Istituzioni di diritto romano*, Milan, 1928, vol. I, p. 378. A better position in the Longobard and statutory law, Pertile, *Storia del diritto italiano*, II ed., Turin, 1893, vol. IV, pp. 65–67.

636 Andrea Alciato, *Responsa*, Lyon, 1561, resp. 123, f. 105–106.

law in general are available, from which the inference on the particular point at issue is drawn.

Accordingly, Felino Sandeo,[637] Pietro Filippo Corneo,[638] Alessandro Tartagni,[639] Tommaso Diplovataccio[640] side with the proponents of the application of biblical norms, including Lauro Palazzi, who recapitulates on everything Anagni says on this issue, while then concluding in the opposite sense.[641]

Paolo di Castro[642] and Giovanni da Imola[643] contrarily declare themselves in favor of the application of common law.

No new argument on this issue can be found in the aforementioned Italian authors of monographs on Jews. They just report the earlier doctrine and statute extensively. After reporting the different viewpoints, Susani declares himself in favor of the observance of the Mosaic law.[644] Sessa discusses the subject extensively without showing a marked preference for one solution or another, merely noting that in practice it very rarely happens that Jews bring internal succession issues before courts: they will usually adjudicate them amicably or through rabbinical arbitration "et impensas quas litigando erogarent libentius in anserum comestione convertunt"![645]

German authors of monographs also deal with the conflict in the matter of succession. Moscovius,[646] contrary to admitting the validity of Jewish law also in the area of marriage, denies it, as Dietrich already did,[647] in a clear-cut way in *ab intestato* succession issues, noting that, with the merger of the tribes, the reasons of the biblical rules that excluded the daughters from paternal

637 Felino Sandeo, *Tertia in quinque libros decretalium*, Lyon, 1547, in *c. judei*, the second one, *de judeis* (c. 5 × 5, 6) = in *c. canonum statuta, de constitutionibus* (c. 1 × 1, 2), no. 37, p. 13.

638 Pietro Filippo Corneo, *Consiliorum sive responsorum volumen secundum*, Venice, 1572, cons. 180, nos. 12–13.

639 Alessandro Tartagni from Imola, *In digestum vetus lecturae*, Lyon, 1558, Lettura seconda, in *l 1 ff. si certum petatur* (D. 11, 1, 1), f. 120v.

640 Tommaso Diplovataccio, *Note alle "lecturae"* cit. by Tartagni, l. cit., note to the words "legi mosaicae": "illa lex hodie servatur inter judeos et ita practicavi, et obtinui bis, et ita consului et subscripsit meo consilio excellens dominus Petrus Philippus Corneus, incipit: ad decisionem presentis consultationis. Et vide etiam P. Corneus in cons. 180, in secundo vol."

641 Lauro Palazzi, *Commentarii super statuto* cit., pp. 285v.–286.

642 Paolo di Castro, *Consilia*, Venice, 1570, cons. 378, vol. II, f. 175v. However, regarding the issue of restitution of the dowry, di Castro thinks it is the Jewish norm that should be followed: see above footnote no. 633.

643 Giovanni da Imola, *Consilia*, Venice, 1581, no. 1, p. 7v., nos. 12–14.

644 Marquardo Susani, *De judeis* cit., part 2, ch. 4, no. 4, pp. 43v.–44.

645 Sessa, *Tractatus de judeis*, cit., cap. XXVI, pp. 81–83.

646 Mascovius, *De juribus judeorum*, cit., Wittemberg, 1684, ch. 3, § 20.

647 Dietrich, *De jure et statu judeorum* cit., 1648, ch. 5, no. 56.

inheritance and attributed double share to the firstborn have vanished. Therefore, such rules must be regarded as revoked "legis ratione cessante." Room should therefore be made to the application of the opposite Roman norms, i.e., respectively of the l. 4 C., 6, 28 and Nov. 118.

Conversely, Beck has no doubts about the appropriateness of recognizing the Mosaic-Talmudic succession norms.[648] Lastly, Thiel,[649] in the face of the disparity of opinions among both ancient and recent jurists and despite the contrary opinion of his authoritative teacher Hommel,[650] supports the thesis of the applicability of Jewish law, relying on argumentation that senses the fresh aura of the new times, the freedom of conscience. For Jews, he notes, heeding the biblical norms, both ritual and judicial, is a religious precept: declaring the abolition of Jewish law, therefore, means violating freedom of conscience, "quae ex ipsa natura est et illis abripi a nemine potest." Based on the evidence collected by Fischer,[651] he also notes that the right, indeed the obligation, for the Jews to follow their own law in internal legal matters is established by many provisions and particular statutes, among which Frederick the Great's privilege for Prussia dated April 17, 1750[652] deserves special mention.

2.5.2 Testamentary Dispositions

Like all primitive laws,[653] including the Germanic law,[654] known due to Tacitus' brief mention of it,[655] the Jewish biblical law does not know the testament.[656] In the Hellenistic period, the Jews borrowed from the Greeks the institution of the διαθήκη, bearing the same name (דיאתיקי) in Hebrew.[657] It is, in fact, an

648 Beck, *Tractatus de juribus judeorum* cit., pp. 206–207.

649 Thiel, *Principia jurisprudentiae judaicae per Germaniam communis*, cit., pp. 119–120, § 184.

650 Carlo Ferdinando Hommel, *Rapsodia Questionum*, vol. IV, note 556.

651 Fischer, *Dissertatio inauguralis de statu et jurisdictione judeorum* etc., cit. §§ 62, 64, 65, 85.

652 Available in *Corpus Constitutionum Borussico-Brandeburgicarum*, vol. III, pp. 118 et seqq.

653 On those, see Post, *Giurisprudenza etnologica*, vol. II, pp. 144–149.

654 See Post, op. cit., p. 145; Solmi, *Storia del diritto italiano*, Milan, 1930, pp. 337–344.

655 *Germania*, c. 20.

656 Leonard van Wolde (*auctor respondens*) and Ravius Sebald (*praes.*), *Dissertatio antiquaria de testamentifactione Hebreis veteribus ignota*, Trajecti ad Rhenum, 1760 (which I was unable to consult); and the works cited in the following note.

657 L. Bodenheimer, *Das Testament unter Benennung einer Erbschaft ... nach rabbinischen Quellen bearbeitet*, Crefeld, 1847–1849 (which I was unable to consult); David Castelli, *Il diritto di testare nella legislazione ebraica*, Florence, 1878, 60 pp.; Idem, *Nullità secondo il diritto ebraico del testamento del fu Conte Caid Nissim Samama*, Florence, 1882; Idem, *La legge del popolo ebreo nel suo svolgimento storico*, Florence, 1884, pp. 396–399; Elia Benamozegh, *Delle fonti del diritto ebraico e del testamento del fu Conte Caid Nissim Samama*, Leghorn, 1882; Idem, *Controreplica alla replica del prof. David Castelli sul testamento del fu Conte Caid Nissim Samama*, Leghorn, 1883; Israel Michel Rabbinowicz,

institution closer to the *donatio mortis causa* than the actual *testamentum*),[658] and Jews further restricted its weight concerning both the subject and the object. Indeed, by Talmudic-Rabbinic Law, only the ailing person can dispose of his assets after death unilaterally, without the need for symbolic compensation (*Kinyan Sudar* = launegild) for the deed to acquire validity like in the donation of the healthy person. Lacking the *Kinyan Sudar*, the act of marriage is not irrevocable, and in the case of recovering, it becomes invalid *ipso jure* and can thus be replaced by another without any further formalities.[659] Also, the testator cannot change the order of the individuals entitled to the succession, order established by the Bible and the later tradition, e.g., he cannot equalize the firstborn to the other children or designate his daughters as heirs versus male offspring. Instead, to the best of his abilities, he can only distribute the required inheritance's share among members of the same order of entitled individuals.[660] Any other non-public form of testament is also excluded.[661]

Le testament olographe selon le Talmud, Observations concernant le testament du Caid Nissim Samama, Paris, 1884; M. Cohn, in *Jüdisches Lexikon*, entry *Erbrecht*, § 6: Letzwillige Verfügungen. See also all the literature listed above footnote no. 605.

658 Bonfante, *La διαθήκη ellenica e la donatio mortis causa*, in *Scritti misti*, vol. I, pp. 422 et seqq. A comparative study on the Hellenic διαθήκη and the rabbinical *diatiki* would certainly generate fruitful results and valuable clarifications.

659 Castelli, *Il diritto* cit., pp. 35–36, 39; M. Cohn, op. cit., ibid. The universal donation of assets by the seriously ill is valid without *Kinyan*; for a partial donation one must specify that it is done *causa mortis*. See the text cited further on, Section Two, ch. 2, § 2, footnote no. 889.

660 Castelli, *Il diritto* cit., pp. 21 et seqq.; Idem, *La legge* cit., p. 397; M. W. Rapaport, *Der Talmud und sein Recht*, in *Zeitschrift für vergleichende Rechtswissenschaft*, vol. XIV, 1900, pp. 45–46; M. Cohn, op. cit., ibid. Conversely, no limit is put by the Jewish law for donations *inter vivos*. But these are done by means of *Kinyan Sudar* and the checklist is at that moment in time and irrevocable. See Castelli, *Il diritto* cit., pp. 37 et seqq. The same principles had clearly been affirmed in a *Informatione del Rabino* Tranquillo Corcos *ebreo romano per provare che l'ebreo può far testamento e disporre delle sue facoltà*, Romae, Typis R. Camerae apostolicae, 1699, 11 pp. (Archives of the Jewish Community of Mantua, Dossier 57, no. 9). Against the claim by an unknown plaintiff that a Jew cannot bequeath and that therefore at his death no lawful inheritance can take place, Corcos demonstrates the opposite, although with the due limitations, relying on Mishnah Bavà Batrà, ch. 8, no. 5; on Maimonides, *Mishneh Torah*, Ilchot nechalot, ch. 6, no. 1; and on Jacob ben Asher, *Arba' Turim*, Hoshen mishpat, ch. 281. "Da queste dottrine – he concludes (p. 8) – chiaramente si raccoglie la ferma conclusione che all'ebreo è permesso di disporre delle sue facoltà con titolo di donatione, a favore di chi che sia, benchè estraneo; e con titolo di successione hereditaria, puole escludere gli eredi legittimi e naturali quando però disponghi d'un erede consimile. La legittima poi da darseli agli esclusi è arbitraria del testatore, suffragando ogni minima cosa. Non so dunque come mai possa affermarsi che all'ebreo *de jure mosaico* è proibito fare testamento."

661 Castelli, *Il diritto* cit., pp. 34–36.

Within those limits, respected even while in constant search for artifices that made it possible to increase the freedom of disposition so mortified by the law, the Jews constantly used the testament. By being similar to the Hellenic διαθήκη, but well apart from the Roman-canonical *testamentum*, the testament rules lay the foundations for the usual conflict between the two legislations. This conflict is felt both with regard to the form and the substantial rules.

2.5.2.1 *The Configuration of the Will*

2.5.2.1.1 The Language

The Jews sometimes make their wills through deeds drawn up in Hebrew by Jewish scribes and certified by Jewish witnesses, according to the rules of Jewish law, other times, it is done through notarial deeds written in Latin. As long as the limits mentioned above on capacity are respected, Jewish law recognizes nuncupative wills as valid, even more so accepts notarial wills as such.[662] Also, for deeds drawn up by Jewish scribes, it matters not if drawn up in Hebrew or any other language since as a rule of thumb, the language of deeds is not a formal judicially relevant element.[663]

Intermediate law authors – deducting from l. 21 C. 6, 23 that recognizes wills in Greek as valid, the faculty to use any other language[664] – admitted for the Jews the faculty to make valid wills in Hebrew:[665] but generally, they did not make it a prerequisite, leaving the freedom to choose the language to those concerned.

Only one writer, Carlo Ruini, in a consultation claimed the invalidity of the will of a Jew, drawn up in Latin, stating that in the specific case, being the lawsuit between Jews, the Jewish law had to apply, which in fact made the use of the Hebrew language in testamentary matters absolutely compulsory.[666]

---

662 See Jacob ben Asher, *Tur*, Hoshen mishpat, ch. 253, § 50 and Caro, *Shulchan 'Aruch*, Hoshen mishpat, ch. 253, § 32, texts reproduced further on, Second Section, ch. 2, § 1, nos. 30 and 32.

663 Maimonides, *Mishneh Torah*, Ilchot malvè ve-lovè, ch. 27; the text is reported further on, Second Section, ch. 2, § 1, footnotes nos. 851 and 853.

664 The observation is due to Carlo Ruini, *Responsorum sive consiliorum tomus secundus*, Venice, 1571, cons. 4, pp. 7–8.

665 Calderini, *Consilia*, cit., De consuetudine, cons. 2, f. 6v. "Consuetudo que habet quod inter hebreos periti legis Abrahe vel alii habeant potestatem scribendi testamenta et taliter scriptis adhibeatur plena fides valet. Et tali consuetudini est standum ... Et maxime quod Ecclesia tolerat judeos et eorum cerimonias et observantias eis permittit."

666 Op. cit., l. c.: "Si ergo per legem Judeorum vel eorum consuetudinem testamentum inter eos non valet nisi scriptum sit lingua hebraica, et quod scriptum lingua latina sit nullum, debet inter illos dicta lex vel consuetudo conservari."

Furthermore, as we have said, this did not correspond to the actual provisions of the Jewish sources.

Against Ruini, Susani notes that although it is true that in matters of succession between Jews, whether legitimate or testamentary, Jewish law must be applied, in Numbers, passage 27, nothing is said about that. As for the Talmud, it is not to be considered, having this work been repeatedly repudiated by the Church. The language difference does not matter: it suffices that the Jew knows the language in which the will is drawn up. "Et ita – Susani adds – vidi servari in pratica circa testamenta judeorum, quae solent communiter scribi per notarios christianos et executioni mandari, prout de testamento illius Vitae hebrei Patavini opulentissimi, quod fuit scriptum per quendam presbiterum, sive plebanum, notarium in civitate Padue."[667]

In reality, as we still say, the issue of language does not engender a conflict since the will which was drawn up in Latin is also valid according to Jewish law.

2.5.2.1.2 The Number of Witnesses

On this point, the principles are as follows: for each deed, Jewish law requires the signature of only two witnesses[668] but stipulates signatories must be Jewish.[669] However, it also recognizes the validity of deeds endorsed by Gentiles, provided they are issued by a public authority (court or notary).[670] On the other hand, the common law requires seven witnesses in all cases.[671]

Consequently, while in the eyes of the Jews, a notarial testament is formally always valid, Christian jurists discuss and express opposite opinions on matters of Jewish wills made by two or three witnesses.

Noting the Jewish norm in the law of the Church – that the Church had made its own, by proclaiming valid the wills drawn up "coram presbytero" in the presence of two or three witnesses[672] – some consider it applicable to the Jews,

---

667 Marquardo Susani, *De judeis* cit., part 2, p. 4, pp. 43v.–44.

668 Deuter. 19, 15. See the passage of Leon da Modena, *Historia dei riti hebraici*, part 2, ch. 6, reported further on, Second Section, ch. 2, § 2, footnote no. 880. M. Cohn, in *Jüdisches Lexikon*, entry Schetar (document).

669 Maimonides, *Mishneh Torah*, Ilchot 'Edut (rules of testimony), ch. 11, excludes the non-Jews from testimony relying on the Talmud, abodà zarà, ch. 2.

670 See further on, Second Section, ch. 2, § 1, footnotes nos. 823 and 824.

671 C. 6, 23, 21 and 31. Five are required for the codicils, l. 8 C. 6, 36.

672 C. 10 and 11 × 3, 26, letters from Alexander III to the Bishops of Ostia and Velletri, in which it is imposed on the ecclesiastical judges to judge wills not according to the civil law that wants them endorsed by seven or five witnesses, but according to the divine, Mosaic, evangelical law (Matthew, 18, 16) and canonical (c. 1, Decretum, part 2, c. 2, q. 4) according to which: "in ore duorum vel trium testium stat omne verbum."

contrary to Roman laws. Thus, Marco Antonio Natta, a jurist from Padua,[673] decides to establish the prevalence of Jewish law over common law in lawsuits between Jews based on the usual argumentations. Alessandro Tartagni, relying on the authority of Calderini, had previously championed the validity of a will drawn up following the forms prescribed by Jewish law, endorsed by a smaller number of witnesses than required by Roman law.[674] Natta foresees the objection "quod in respicientibus ordinationem et solemnitatem actus servanda est lex loci, in quo actus fit – according to the provisions of fr. 6 D. 21, 2 and of l. 2 C. 6, 32, passed into the proverb: lex est ipsa regio – et per consequens Judaei existentes in terra Christianorum adhibere debent, in testando, numerum testium requisitum da jure communi, si jus commune servetur." However, he rejects it by noting that the rule would apply if the Jews were foreigners, which is not the case, as they are "de corpore christiani populi, licet non de corpore spirituali." Therefore, according to the law *omnes populi ff. de justitia et jure* (D. 1, 1, 9), "servandum est sibi jus corum speciale postposito communi." In his rebuttal, Natta is targeting Paolo di Castro in particular, who declared in a previous consultation that a testamentary provision drafted according to Jewish norms was valid, just because it had been authenticated in front of a notary, with the due solemnity; demonstrating that he would not have recognized it if no such a *confirmatio* had taken place.[675]

Agostino Berò relies on di Castro interpreting his thought precisely in this sense. For Berò, both the form and substance of testamentary dispositions must be governed by the local law: this is because, on the one hand, the provisions of the laws and imperial constitutions on testamentary matters are binding on all those who reside in the towns and castles of the Roman Empire, as it can be evinced by l. 31 C. 6, 23; and on the other hand the Jews themselves of the location where the cause is discussed (Bologna) are accustomed to drawing up their wills before Christian notaries who use form and common law. It is thus absurd for Berò to think that the Mosaic law was followed instead of the Roman law concerning the number of witnesses.[676]

Berò's numerous argumentations, however, are insufficient for leading the doctrine toward the disavowal of Jewish norms: they are invoked by Ippolito Riminaldi in a consultation related to a lawsuit between Jews of Ferrara, noting,

673 Marco Antonio Natta, *Consiliorum sive responsorum volumina*, Venice, 1583, vol. III, no. 621, p. 155.

674 Alessandro Tartagni from Imola, *Consiliorum seu responsorum libri*, Venice, 1590, lib. 6, cons. 6, nos. 2–5, p. 5.

675 Paolo di Castro, *Consiliorum seu responsorum volumina*, Venice, 1571 = Turin, 1580, cons. 377, f. 175–175v.; in other more recent editions the consultation carries the no. 395.

676 Agostino Berò [Berous or Berojus], *Consiliorum volumina*, Bologna, 1567, vol. III, cons. 28.

that about the point in question, the l. 31 C. 6, 23 concerns only the testament of rustics and cannot be interpreted in a broad sense; while on the other hand, the practice of Jews drawing up their wills before Christian notaries according to the Roman norms is not constant, since there are examples of wills by Jews "per suos scribas secundum ritus eorum facta."[677]

The same disparity of views can be found among later German authors: some of whom like Reinkingk, following Natta, admit the validity of the Jewish testament undersigned by only two witnesses,[678] whereas others, like Mascovius, claim compliance with local legislation on form and substance, therefore denying validity to a will which is not undersigned by seven witnesses, as required by Roman law.[679] Lastly, Sessa's opinion, too, settles in this sense.[680]

2.5.2.2 *The Substance of Testamentary Dispositions*

We have already mentioned the lack of freedom that Jewish law leaves the individual to modify the order established for the succession *ab intestato* by testament.

Sometimes the limits were surpassed, becoming prejudicial to the legitim to which heirs were entitled *jure hebraico*, so they filed a lawsuit. In the preliminary rulings, the defendants would, of course, claim, in the specific case, the thesis of the application of the Roman norms, much more favorable to them for the greater freedom allowed to the testator.

Alessandro Tartagni already had to deal with such a case: the case of a father who bequeathed the firstborn a portion of inheritance equal, rather than double, to that of the other siblings. Nevertheless, in the consultation, his ruling is missing.[681]

Gian Maria and Jacopo Riminaldi will later declare themselves in favor of the Jewish norms, examining the question that arose following the testamentary disposition of a father "qui substituerat filiis decedentibus sine liberis filios superviventes, vel illorum liberos." Against the claim of his daughters, the two jurists think that with those words, the deceased had not intended to include the females in the substitution "quia in sua dispositione videtur convenire voluisse cum lege mosaica, quae, stantibus masculis, feminas ab intestato

677 Ippolito Riminaldi *junior*, *Consiliorum sive responsorum* vol. II, Venice, 1576, cons. 119, pp. 47v.-54.

678 Theodor Reinkingk, *Tractatus de regimine seculari et ecclesiastico*, Gissae Hessorum, 1619, book 2, class 2, no. 9.

679 Mascovius, *De juribus judeorum*, cit. Wittemberg, 1684, ch. 3, § 11.

680 Sessa, *De judeis*, cit., ch. XXV, p. 79.

681 Op. cit., book 2, cons. 304.

excludit." As a supportive argumentation by analogy, they produce the following: just as if there are statutes contrary to common law, the testator's will is interpreted according to the statutes. Therefore, for Jews, their will should be interpreted according to Jewish norms, standing these – for them – vs. common law in the same place, where statutory law is in place for Christians.[682]

Already long before, Paolo from Monte Pico had expressed himself in the same way. Debating whether the so-called Bulgarian custom – stipulating that if a person appoints his children as heirs and his wife as usufructuary, the latter is entitled only to alimony – was to be also applied to the Jews, he had maintained that a possible interpretative criterion had first to be sought after in the Mosaic law, "atque ea deficiente" that rule had to be applied.[683]

Conversely, in the decision already mentioned, Berò reaches a distinctly opposite conclusion, invoking, among other things, an unpublished request for consultation (No. 11) of Calderini, who was said to have declared the nullity of the testament of a Jew "qui praeteriit filium," whom by common law he should have either expressly designated as heir or disinherited.[684] Berò also notes that a man "de jure naturali et gentium" is entitled to freedom to bequeath, and such freedom cannot, therefore, be suppressed; consequently, a Jew can also bequeath to his wife, against Jewish rules.

This last point was the subject of extensive consideration by Ippolito Riminaldi *junior*, particularly in a consultation request concerning a lawsuit for the hefty sum of 40,000 scudi, discussed in Ferrara; an interesting lawsuit also because of the notoriety of the disputing parties, don Isacco Abravanel *junior* and his stepmother, doña Benvenida.[685] Shortly before his death, Isacco's father, don Samuele, had designed his second wife, doña Benvenida, as his sole heir leaving only 500 scudi to his son from his first marriage. Hence a cause brought by the latter as the inheritance was deemed prejudicial to the legitim guaranteed to him by Jewish law.

Backing the son's reasons, Riminaldi takes care of patiently refuting, one by one, the general argumentations in favor of the application of Roman law by invoking all authors supporting the opposite thesis, from Calderini downwards; and on the particular issue, he relies on Ruini, on da Monte Pico

682 Giovan Maria and Jacopo Riminaldi, *Consiliorum seu responsorum juris volumen primum* (by Jacopo), cons. 186, pp. 250v.–251.

683 Paolo da Monte Pico, *Repetitio in l. Titia cum nuberet ff. de legatis et fideicommissis*, 11, (D. 31, 34, 7), in tome 4 of *Repetitionum in varias juris civilis leges a* Pompeo Limpio *compilatarum volumina* 8, Lyon 1553 and Venice 1603.

684 Berò, op. cit., cons. 28. It is unlikely that Calderini, who is the first to support the application of Jewish law and who repeatedly insists on such thesis of his, adhered to the opposite thesis on this particular issue.

685 Ippolito Riminaldi, op. cit., cons. 119, pp. 47v.–54.

and his namesakes, the Riminaldi *seniores*. He pins his critique especially on Berò, noting, among other things, that the *libertas testandi* is indeed *jus gentium*: but it has to be understood limitedly to the form, – according to the laws *nemo potest ff. de legatis etc.* (D 30, 1, 55 [57]) and *l.* 1 *C. de sacr. eccl.* (C. 1, 2, 1: in verbis liber est stilus) – and to the will, not as to the substance that must be expressed *secundum leges et bonos mores*, as Accursio intends; laws that, in this case, are the Jewish ones, that specifically prescribe the exclusion of the wife from an inheritance when in concurrence with the offspring. It is unknown which of the two conflicting theses were adopted by the court in the resolutive ruling of the dispute.

2.6 *Obligations*

The conflict appears to have been discussed less frequently in consultations and monographs in contractual matters. In fact, in this area, the same Jewish law, even without operating an en bloc referral for certain relations, recognizes the state norms' authority.[686]

However rare, disputes are nevertheless not lacking also in this field.

The most curious among them is a lawsuit between two Jews from Forlì for a gambling debt. After paying out, the loser claims the refund of the amount paid because the civil statute prohibits gambling and therefore invalidates the obligation. This is contrary to the common law, which admits this debt as natural while denying, in case of spontaneous payout, the right to recover what was disbursed. Andrea Barbazza, the winner's lawyer, argues that since the case is about relations between Jews, their law should also be applied in obligatory matters when it expressly provides for the case in question, in preference to local or common law. "Tunc concludo – he writes – quod si lex mosaica disponit specialiter super hoc, quod judeus vincens aliquid alteri judeo ludendo, si sine falsitate aut dolo aut fraude vincat, non teneatur ad restitutionem, tunc servabitur lex mosaica specialis et non lex civilis aut statutaria generaliter disponens, tamquam non liget ipsos hebreos; et ista videtur indubitata veritas. Et ita concludo in favorem ipsius judei vincentis."[687]

---

686 See further on, Section Two, ch. 2, § 2.

687 Andrea Barbazza, *Consiliorum sive responsorum volumen tertium*, Venice, 1581, cons. 66. In reality, the rabbinical sources disagree about the recognition of the validity of the obligation arising from gambling. As J. Jacobsohn reports, *Aleatorische, insbesondere Glücksverträge nach jüdischem Recht*, in *Zeitschrift für vergleichende Rechtswissenschaft*, vol. 40, 1923, pp. 331 and 336 the tossafot are for the validity (on sanhedrin, f. 25), R. Asher ben Jechiel (*Responsi*, no. 66, § 18), and Jacob ben Asher (*Tur*, Hoshen mishpat, ch. 207; cf. the glosses to Caro's *Shulchan Aruch*, ibid., by R. Moshè Isserles. Maimonides, *Mishneh Torah*, Ilchot ghezelà ve-avedà, ch. 6, § 10, declares himself against the validity. All the authors, however, unanimously agree in considering gambling – and bets – forbidden

Tiberio Deciani invokes applying common, i.e., post-biblical, Jewish law to support the validity of specific mortgage contracts at interest drawn up between Jews. He notes that, against the provisions of the Mosaic law, the later Jewish tradition does not consider these contracts illegal, and as such, they must be recognized "quia de his qui foris sunt nihil ad nos."[688]

The same thesis is supported by Berò and Gozzadini, both from Bologna, concerning real estate leasing with greater depth of doctrine. The question these two authors deal with concerns whether the Roman rule "emptio tollit locatum" is applicable or not to the relations between Jews. In the present case – the parties' identical names reveal that both consultations refer to this same specific case – first a lease, then during its course , the sale of the rented premises was made by an owner. Can the buyer evict the tenant? It would seem he could, according to common law, since, under it, the farmer or tenant has no right in rem over the immovable property such as to prevail over the buyer's right in rem. However, the law to be applied should instead be the Jewish one, according to which things are done differently. Having consulted experts of Talmudic law, both Berò and Gozzadini know this law considers the lease as a *pro tempore* sale and establishes a right on the item that had been leased equal to that which arises from the item purchased in a market sale. Consequently, in the absence of an express agreement to the contrary, the buyer is obliged to comply, for the whole time of the lease, with the right of the lessee, equal to his own and prevailing by chronological priority.[689] Therefore, coming to the point

---

as immoral. Cf. M. Cohn in *Jüdisches Lexikon* entry Spiel und Wette. It is interesting to note that precisely in Forlì a particular prohibition was issued by a rabbinical synod of 1418, see S. J. Halberstamm, *Antiche costituzioni emanate dai rappresentanti di tutta Italia in Bologna e Forlì negli anni* 1416 *e* 1418 (in Hebrew) in *Graetz-Jubelschrift*, Breslau, 1887, Hebrew part, pp. 53–61, quoted by Samuel Rapaport, in *Jüdisches Lexikon*, entry Spiele.

688 Tiberio Deciani, *Responsorum volumen quartum*, Venice, 1602, cons. 76, nos. 3–5. Having become the loan at interest one of the few activities permitted to the Jews, without being able to abolish the ban placed by the Bible and Talmud, the post-Talmudic Jewish law bows to the demands of time and recognizes the validity of fictitious contracts of association in participation, which palliate the loan. For the rabbinical sources, see Moses Hoffmann, *Der Geldhandel der deutschen Juden während des Mittelalters bis zum Jahre* 1350, Leipzig, 1910, pp. 64–236; J. Bernfeld, *Das Zinsverbot bei den Juden nach talmudisch-rabbinischem Recht*, Berlin, 1924; and cf. my work *Prestito ebraico e comunità ebraiche nell'Italia centrale e settentrionale*, in *Rivista di Storia del Diritto italiano*, dossier 3, note 3 on page 454, where some company contracts concluded between Jews are examined, which obviously conceal the loan at interest, and are drawn up in order to fall within the provisions of *Tur*, Jorè de'à, Ilchot ribbit, ch. 167, § 1, later transfused by Caro into the *Shulchan Aruch*, ibidem. For a more extensive literature, see Eisenstadt, *Repertorium*, cit., pp. 309–311, and *Jüdisches Lexikon*, entry Zins.

689 "A lease is a pro tempore sale": Babylonian Talmud, Bavà Mezià, f. 56b (not 56a, as cited by Rapaport); similarly Maimonides, *Mishneh Torah*, Ilchot sechirut (norms on renting),

more precisely in dispute, the two authors conclude that no action is possible by the purchaser against the seller for the resistance of the tenant since the purchaser himself was required to know what his law was commanding.[690]

---

ch. 7, § 1; and Caro, *Shulchan 'Aruch*, Hoshen mishpat ch. 227, § 35, ch. 315, § 2. See M. W. Rapaport, *Der talmud und sein Recht*, in *Zeitschrift für vergleichende Rechtswissenschaft*, vol. xv, 1901, p. 39a of the reprint (2nd ed., 1912), who notes that, as a consequence of the principle, the consent is not enough to perfect the lease and acquire the right on the item leased, but rather the same means as those required for the purchase of the right to property are necessary. He cites about it Babylonian Talmud, Bavà Kammà, f. 79a and idem, Bavà Mezià f. 99a. On this point, see also M. Bloch, *Der Vertrag nach mosaisch-talmudischem Rechte*, in *Iahresbericht des Rabbiner-Seminars in Budapest für das Jahr* 1892–1893, Budapest, 1893, pp. 50–51 of the reprint (available at the Brera Library in Milan).

690 Agostino Berò, *Consiliorum volumen primum*, Bologna, 1567, cons. 2, pp. 7–8: "Et ex predictis infertur quod cum lex mosaica hebreorum disponat, quod quandocumque locatio rei ad certum tempus facta fuit, durante locatione dominus et locator non possit ex aliqua causa etiam justa conductorem expellere, dummodo conductor servaverit locatori promissa, etiam si locator et dominus rem locatam pro usu et necessitate sua, vel illam reparare vellet juxta *l. eadem C. loc.* (C. 4, 65, 3) quae lex in hoc est contraria legi hebreorum, quae (ut ab eorum peritis habuit) disponit locationem, ea durante, judicari esse venditionem, ergo haec lex et consuetudo hebreorum erit inter ipsos servanda, et non lex civilis: infertur itaque, quod et si secundum legem civilem emptor rei locatae non teneatur stare locatori, quia potest illum expellere, ut in *l. emptorem* cum ibi not. *C. loca.* (C. 4, 65, 9) tamen secus erit inter ipsos judeos propter legem, et consuetudinem, quae vult conductorem ante finem locationis a nemine posse repelli, ergo in casu nostro Vitalis emptor domus, et cessionarius jurium, quae Davit habebat, non poterit excludere Simonem hebraeum conductorem domus et cessionarium jurium dicti Davit ad certum tempus, quia priora jura in domo et juribus predictis habuit. Preterea ex quo Vitalis emptor scivit legem suam, et consuetudinem hebreorum, vel scire debuit ... et consequenter quod emptores rerum alteri locatarum colono, seu inquilino stare tenebantur, censetur ipsum Vitalem emisse domum et acceptasse cum hac lege, si aliud expresse non fuerit conventum." Then "cum Vitalis hac lege emerit, nullo pacto poterit Simonem conductorem expellere, sed tenebitur illum usque ad finem locationis ei factae pati ... Accedit ad haec quod si verum est, prout mihi pro vero presupponitur, quod hebrei secundum eorum legem vel consuetudinem contractum locationis ad certum tempus pro illo tempore judicant esse contractum venditionis, seu naturam eius penitus habere, quia secundum eos nulla est differentia inter contractum locationis et venditionis, nam uterque dicitur venditionis contractus, et solum respectu temporis differunt, quia alia dicitur venditio rei perpetua, alia venditio rei ad tempus, quam nos locationem appellamus, sequitur quod inter ipsos hebreos locum non habebit regula illa, quod emptor non tenetur stare locationi juxta *l. emptorem C. locati.* (C. 4, 65, 9) et ea quae habentur in *lege si filio* § *si vir ff. solu. matrimo.* (D. 24, 3, 25 [26], 4). Sed habebit locum illa alia regula, quod secundus emptor stare tenetur primo emptori, quando res illi tradita fuit, ut in *l. quoties C. de rei vindica.* (C. 3, 32, 15) ubi si duobus res vendita fuit, ille est potior, cui res tradita fuit; sed in casu nostro res fuit prius Simoni tradita: ergo ipse respectu temporis, pro quo sibi fuit concessa, potior dici debet." – Ludovico Gozzadini, *Consilia seu responsa*, Venice 1598, cons. 24, pp. 59–60: "Quaeritur an Davit hebreus qui vendidit domum cum jurisdictione retinendi et exercendi bancum fenoris Vitali de Fano hebreo, si jam locaverit dictam domum per prius

Alongside these arguments favoring the application of Jewish law, there is, however, also an argument to the contrary, which Bursati, from Mantua vigorously supported, in a case between Jews about the execution mode of an instrument.[691]

2.7 *The Oath*

As evident, all tribunal matters are handled by local law. However, the oath makes an exception due to its connection with the faith.[692] How exactly did

cum jurisdictione exercendi foenus per novem annos Simoni hebreo, an teneatur d. Davit ad interesse vel ad penam ipsi Vitali; et videtur dicendum quod sic, primo ... etc., septimo. ... Quibus tamen non obstantibus que vere in casu nostro non obstant, contrarium puto de jure fore verius, videlicet quod iste Davit nullo modo inciderit in aliquam poenam conventionalem, nec posset agi per emptorem de evictione, vel ad aliquod interesse contra ipsum Davit venditorem." And this for the following reasons: "Quoad secundum, an iste Simon possit expelli ab emptore et emptor non teneatur stare colono, vel inquilino, et videtur quod sic quia colonus, seu inquilinus nullum jus habet in re, sed solum habet obligatam personam domini locantis, merito emptor non cogitur stare locationi, ita dixit Bertolus in *l. emptorem C. loca.* (C. 4, 65, 9) ... Contrarium puto fore verius, videlicet quod nullo modo possit expelli. Et primo. ... Secundo principaliter, quod in contractibus celebratis inter hebreos servari debetur lex mosaica, et consuetudo et usus eorum. ... Qui facit aliquem actum, videtur astringere se legi loquenti de illo actu, sed cum isti hebrei inter se contraxerint, certe videtur contrahere secundum eorum leges, et velle se astringere legi mosaicae, qua lege sunt astricti, ut supra late deductum est; si ergo ita est, sequitur quod cum lege mosaica venditio non rescindat locationem, etiam si [locatio] fuerit ad modicum tempus, et nullum jus in re habeat talis conductor, et sic emptor nullo modo potest eum expellere, sequitur ergo quod inter eos servari debet talis lex tamquam specialis inter eos, derogans juri civili et communi romanorum. ... Sed sic est, quod secundum leges hebreorum locatio facta de aliqua re dicitur venditio, sed ad tempus, et nullo alio differt a venditione, nisi quia alia est perpetua, alia temporalis, quae lex, ut dixi, inter hebreos indubitanter servanda est, si ergo fuit facta venditio Simoni, sequitur quod tradendo illam, prout fuit tradita, et reperitur fuisse in possessione per biennium, et ibi exercuit foenus publicum, et habitavit, ergo dominium est in eum translatum juxta no. in *l. 1 ff. de contrah. emp.* (D. 18, 1, 1) ex quo sequitur quod si postea res fuit vendita Vitali et perpetua sit venditio, quod prefertur primus, cui fuit per prius red tradita, et quia jus habet in re idest dominium, et non poterit molestari durante tempore dictae venditionis ut dixi. ... secundo respondeo, quod dicitur habere dominium nedum utile, sed directum rei locate ... cum secundum jura et consuetudines hebreorum talis locatio dicatur venditio, ergo non potest aliquo modo expelli. Preterea et tertio dico, quod et si nullum jus haberet in re Simon conductor, tamen quia jura hebreorum non sinunt ipsum posse expelli, quae inter eos observanda sunt, ideo non habet locum legem emptoris."

691 Francesco Bursati, *Consiliorum sive responsorum libri*, Frankfurt a. M., 1579, book 2, cons. 182, pp. 218–218v. Lawsuit between the Jews de Attis from S. Felice sul Panaro and the Jews Bordulani from Mantua. The application of the Jewish law in the inheritance area is admitted as expressly provided by the Mosaic law (Numbers, 27). "At secus in judicando super contractibus et executionibus instrumentorum hebreorum, cum in his jus civile et municipale terrae, quam inhabitant, omnino attendatur ad superius congesta, et quia id in patria mantuana semper servatum fuit."

692 For the literature on the oath in Jewish law, see Eisenstadt, *Repertorium*, cit., pp. 203–208.

the Jews take an oath in Roman times is unclear,[693] but already in the 9th century, the oath formula of *more judaico* is found in the capitularies,[694] which is the same one that, with some variations, the jurists of the intermediate period report many centuries later.[695] That the Jews must take an oath according to this formula is widely agreed by all these authors, who generally make no distinction between form and substance of the institution: the distinction is set only by Moscovius, who applies his principle of general invalidity of Talmudic law here too and notes that also the oath of the Jews, for all that is not the simple formula, that is to say as for capacity and effects, should be understood as governed by Roman law.[696]

In some places, the Jewish norms on oath are recognized until the mid-19th century.[697]

2.8 *The Community Tax Rules*

All disputes that may arise between Jews and their communities about the taxation or the internal rules of other kinds set by the communities themselves and provided with the executive support of the government are evidently resolved according to the rules themselves.

The lawsuit brought to court in Mantua in 1692[698] therefore seems curious.

A Jew and father of twelve children refused to pay taxes to the Jewish University. Sued by it before the Commissioner for the Jews,[699] he alleged that the Gonzaga government exempted the fathers of such numerous offspring

---

693 See Juster's scholarly research, op. cit., vol. II, pp. 124–126.

694 Capitulare de Judeis, *Mon. Germ. Hist., Leges*, sect. II, vol. I, pp. 258–259.

695 Marquardo Susani, *De Judeis* cit., part 2, ch. 5, no. 10, p. 45. The Jews take an oath "secundum suam legem, vel secundum legem Moysis, vel per Deum, vel per patrem omnipotentem Sabaoth, vel per Deum qui apparuit Moysi in rubo, vel verum Adonai patrem, vel per Deum Eloy; et respondeat: juro; vel sic: si tu periurus es, vel culpabilis, sis dispersus inter gentes, et moriaris in terra inimicorum tuorum, et sic terra te absorbeat sicut Dathan et Abyron, et ipse respondeat: Amen. ...: denique vel sic: lepra te apprehendat, sicut Naaman Syrum [2 Kings, 5, 1–27]. Likewise, with several others, Sessa, *Tractatus de judeis* cit., p. 60, who also reports the formula: and in the same way, Maranta, *Tractatus de ordine judiciorum, intitulatus speculum aureum et lumen advocatorum*, Venice, 1540, Tertia pars principalis, no. 50, p. 24; Tuschi, *Practicarum conclusionum tomus quartus*, Rome, 1606, conclus. 369, no. 16, pp. 702–703, and others cited by them. Cf. Joh. Henr. Wolfart's monography, *De juramentis Judeorum judictalibus cautionibusque iisdem adhibendis vel improbandis*, Frankfurt a. M.-Leipzig, 1743, mentioned by Eisenstadt, l. cit.

696 Mascovius, *De juribus judeorum* cit., ch. 1, § 7.

697 See for example the circular letters of Nov. 11, 1815 and April 18, 1842 of the Grand Duchy of Tuscany. I. E. Rignano, *Sulla attuale posizione giuridica degli israeliti in Toscana*, Florence, 1847, p. 18.

698 This is reported by A. Bertolotti, *Curiosità storiche mantovane*, no. CXCVI, *Il pagamento delle tasse presso gli ebrei*, in the Mantuan magazine *Il mendico*, December 1, 1890.

699 Kind of Minister for Jewish Affairs, who, as rightly notes Bertolotti, ibidem, "was always a Catholic, mostly a Senator, chosen not because he had special knowledge of Jewish

from taxes in his defense. The Commissioner deemed it correct to judge according to the Jewish law and, unable to ask for directions at the University that was a party in the suit, turned to the rabbis of Modena. These responded that Jewish law knew no such exemptions,[700] and, based on this declaration, the Commissioner condemned the defendant to pay the taxes, authorizing the impounding. However, the loser did not accept the ruling and appealed before the Commissioner himself, claiming the seizure had taken place during a holiday and was therefore illegal according to the local law. Placed before this new position of conflict between local norms and Jewish norms, the Commissioner relied on the latter and in order for the matter not to take too long by turning again outside the Gonzaga domains, he asked the rabbis of Mantua for information. Moreover, having attested that the Jewish law permitted the distraints for paying taxes even on holidays,[701] the Commissioner sentenced the unlucky defendant to pay the amount claimed by the University.

---

matters, but for a bureaucratic or other reason totally independent of the novel office granted to him."

700 The text of the reply, reported by Bertolotti, ibidem, is as follows and is certified by the municipal authority of Modena: "Noi sottoscritti Rabini dell'Università degli Hebrei di Modena facciamo ampla et indubitata fede a chi si spetta, così per uerità ricercati come secondo li riti de gl'hebrei tutti indifferentemente devono concorrere al pagamento di qualsivoglia tassa dell'Università loro etiandio quelli che avessero numero compito di dodici figliuoli, come pure attestiamo che secondo i medesimi riti non può qualunque hebreo procurar dal Principe gratia dell'essentione de gl'aggravii o impetrata valersene a pregiudizio e danno de gl'altri hebrei e così è etc.
Dato nell'Accademia nostra li 8 luglio 1692
Salomon Levi hebreo affermo
Leon Padoa hebreo affermo
Abram del quondam Raffael Rovigo affermo
Bonaventura Salitti affermo."

701 Bertolotti, ibidem: "È verità indubitata che il ritto e consuetto hebraico apporta indispensabile il sforzare quelli hebrei che fossero morosi e renitenti a voler concorrere al pagamento di quanto potesse occorrere per il sovvenimento de loro poveri et altresì per la direzione e conservatione della propria legge e ritti, essendo ciò di precetto; e però si puonno sforzare non solo realmente ma anco personalmente senza riguardo ad alcun tempo, etiandio nei giorni feriali; e come nel corpo della legge di R. Mosè di Egitto, [Maimonides, *Mishneh Torah*], Trattato d'elemosina, ch. 7; Tur e Bed Josef, Tomo 2 °, cap. 248. In Fede Mantua il 21 luglio 1692.
Leone Brielli affermo et attesto come sopra.
Raffael Fano affermo et attesto id.
Sanson Guastalla attesto quanto sopra
Efraim Levi-Ostiglia attesto q. s."

SECTION 2

The Conflict concerning Constitutional Principles: the Question of Referral

In the previous section, we examined the boundaries set by the local legislation, doctrine and jurisdiction to recognize Jewish law, underscoring how this recognition of civil nature is restricted to internal relations between Jews only.

Should this be understood that only private Jewish law is invoked and recognized? On this point, one should bear in mind that when regulating legal relations between two individuals, not only provisions of private law, but also norms of public law, administrative proceedings, judicial deeds may concur. A state's referral to the laws of a given group to set the judicial negotiation between individual members of such group can be understood in two ways:

1) referral restricted to the norms of private law only;
2) referral extended not only to these, but also to the principles – that we shall call constitutional – set by that legal system about the validity and acceptability of the legislative, administrative and judicial deeds of the state, and also to the principles – that we shall call of private International Law – by which the same legal system would, in turn, postulate the referral to given private state norms.

In the Jewish law of the diaspora, especially in medieval law, a whole theory is just going to take shape, parallel to what happens in the common law, about the deeds of the government, and precise limits are set, within which the state deed must be maintained to be deemed legitimate. Legislative, administrative and judicial deeds considered illegitimate according to given constitutional standards, it is stated, should not receive the application by the judges; claims, that are based on such deeds before the courts, must be rejected.

Moreover, on specific subjects, the Jewish law finds the deferment to the state's private law appropriate, especially if optional, thus recognizing the local judicial rule as valid (a possibility, in matters of form) alongside the Jewish one. We know for a fact that, in addition to the right to live according to their own law (*normative autonomy*), the right to apply this law in their courts was very often recognized to Jews, concurrently with the courts of the State (*judicial autonomy*).

In these courts of theirs, not only the private Jewish norms were undoubtedly applied, but also the constitutional principles and the norms on referrals to the local law mentioned before. But, whether the judges also applied those principles and those norms when ruling in lawsuits between Jews in state courts is not easy to establish. Once admitted the concurrence of the two jurisdictions and the faculty for the plaintiff to apply to one or the other, logic would have dictated that not only the same private law but also the same public law principles ruled the proceedings in both courts, to avoid that between the two jurisdictions the plaintiff could choose the one that applied the principles most favorable to him in the case in question.

 | DOI:10.1163/9789004627154_011

We have no evidence to draw safe conclusions from, although, as we shall see, concerning the norms on deferment to private law, one might be more inclined to believe that they were indeed taken into consideration.

Remaining in doubt, and given the particular application before rabbinical courts, it is appropriate to deal with the constitutional principles and those on referral, considering the Jewish law generally integrates the treatment of both into a single interpretation of the principle: דינא דמלכותא דינא (dinà demalchutà dinà = the state law is [the valid] law), set by a renowned jurist of the third century, Shemuel Jarchinai, from Babylon.

Here we will deal first with the constitutional principles, following the various changes in this regard of the judicial-political thought of medieval Judaism. We will also emphasize the consonance or the conflict between the principles themselves and the parallel conceptions of coeval Christian political doctrine.

Then, we shall review the deferral issue, with the appropriate distinctions, and endeavor to shed light on an area where, due to the generally non-judicial background of the many who delved into this subject, the greatest darkness still reigns.[702]

---

702 The theme of the relations between Jewish law and law of the State according to the rabbinical doctrine has been treated by different scholars but in an incomplete and unsystematic manner. In addition, each work totally ignores those written previously, so that a study in depth on the subject has never been reached. I have consulted the following works: I. M. Hazan, *Successione per Israele. Voto dell'ecc.mo signore I. M. Hazan membro del tribunale superiore di Gerusalemme, attuale rabbino maggiore dell'Università israelitica di Roma*, Ancona, 1851, sect. 3, pp. 65–74; Hirsch B. Fassel, *Das mosaisch-rabbinische Civilrecht*, 2 volumes, Vienna, 1852–1854, vol. I, pp. 9–10; Leopold Löw, *Dinà demalchutà dinà*, in *Gesammelte Schriften*, vol. III, Szegedin, 1893, pp. 347–358 (already printed in the Hebrew periodical *Ben Hananjà* of Szegedin, y. V, 1862, pp. 36–40); Elia Benamozegh, *Delle fonti del diritto ebraico e del testamento del fu Conte Caid Nissim Samama*, Leghorn, 1882, pp. 84–203; David Castelli, *Nullità secondo il diritto ebraico del testamento del fu conte Caid Nissim Samama*, Florence, 1882, pp. 65–84; Benamozegh, *Controreplica alla replica del prof. David Castelli sul testamento del fu Caid Nissim Samama*, Leghorn, 1883, pp. 138–183; Hamburger, *Realencyclopädie des Judentums*, Abt. 2, Neustrelitz, 1896, entry Obrigkeit, p. 867; J. H. Greenstone, in *Jewish Encyclopedia*, vol. IV, entry Conflict of Laws, London, 1903, pp. 224–225; Israel Abrahams, *Studies in Pharisaism and the Gospels*, Cambridge, 1917, vol. I, ch. VIII: "Give unto Cesar," pp. 62–63; D. M. Shohet, *The Jewish Court in the Middle Ages*, New York, Bloch Publ. Co., 1931, pp. 83, 96–117. Herbert Finkelscherer, *Zur Frage fremder Einflusse auf das rabbinische Recht. Samuel und das sassanidische Recht*, in *Monatsschrift für die Geschichte und Wissenschaft des Judentums*, 1935, pp. 381–383 and 441; Ismar Elbogen, entry Judaism, in *Encyclopedia of Social Sciences*, vol. VIII, New York, 1935, p. 436 (mention); Isaac Herzog, *The Main Institutions of Jewish Law*, vol. I, *The law of property*, London, 1936, pp. 24–32. Ph. Biberfeld's writings, *Dinà demalchutà dinà*, in *Schriftenreihe des Bundes jüdischer Akademiker*, II, Berlin, 1925, 42 pp., and those of Jacob Töplitzky, *Dinà demalchutà* (in Hebrew) in the magazine *Ha-shiloach* from Warsaw, 5673

(=1913), pp. 505–512 (listed by Eisenstadt, *Repertorium* cit., pp. 213 and 214) were inaccessible. A large collection of texts is provided by the entry "Dinà demalchutà dinà" of the excellent Talmudic encyclopedia *Pahad Izhak* by Izhak ben Shemuel Lampronti (a Jew from Ferrara, b. 1679, d. 1756) vol. II, Venice, Izhak Foà and Shelomò ben Moshè David Askenazì editors, Bragadina Printhouse, 1753. It is useful to note that, similarly to the Jewish law, Canon law faces the same problem of relations with the state law. For the question of referral to the norms of civil law, see in particular Jo. Bapt. Bartoli, *Institutiones juris canonici*, Ausugii, 1749, pp. 371–407, and concerning the current law of the Church, see M. Falco, *Introduzione allo studio del Codex Juris Canonici*, Turin, 1925, pp. 89–92 and V. Del Giudice, *Il diritto dello stato nell'ordinamento canonico*, in *Archivio giuridico*, 1924, dossier I.

CHAPTER 9

The Constitutional Principles

1 General Principles on the Legality of the State and Its Organs and the Constitutionality of the Laws

In the beginning, diaspora Jews assumed an attitude of total subservience towards the states to which they belong, believing that it was their duty to obey the authorities to an unlimited extent, without questioning the legitimacy of the power or the legality of its acts.[703]

Living under a non-Jewish government by free choice and not by force, they accepted its laws and decrees without arguing. Although certain opponents sometimes accuse them of disobedience to state rules,[704] only the accidental provisions violating their freedom of conscience they go up against, not the sovereignty in general, which they fully recognized.[705]

A well-known echo of these political principles of Judaism in the diaspora is the theory of St. Paul, who preaches total obedience to pagan authorities and

703 Jeremiah, 29.7: "Seek the good of the city where I have lead you in captivity and pray the Lord for it: for on the wellbeing of it your own wellbeing depends." As an execution of this command, in everyday Jewish liturgy a prayer is included for the prosperity of the state. The first text of this prayer is available in *Aboth derabbi Nathan*, II, p. 36, Schechter ed., p. 68. Abrahams, op. cit., p. 64.

704 Esther, 3, 8: "and Aman said to the King Ahasverosh: there is a people secluded and scattered among the peoples of all the provinces of your kingdom, whose laws are different from those of any other people, and that does not heed the laws of the king. …" The clear contrast between Jewish (private) national laws and (public) state laws is of interest. The composition of the book of Esther is to be set between 200 and 150 BC. Cf. S. Bernfeld, *Storia della Letteratura ebraica*, It. transl., Turin, 1926, pp. 82–87; Salvatorelli and Hühn, *La Bibbia*, Milan, s. a., p. 212.

705 It is constant, e.g., the refusal of the imperial cult; cf. Daniel, ch. 3 as a whole. On the text of Ecclesiastes 8, 2 ("Obey the laws of the king) the Midrash Tanhumà [see on that Strack, *Einleitung in Talmud und Midrash*, pp. 204 et seqq.] commentary on Genesis 8, 16, Noah § 10, Buber ed., p. 33, demands obedience to the government laws even if they are harsh, except in matters of religion: "If the government decides to abandon the commandments and deny God, then you will not obey, but you will say: I obey the laws of the king only for those things that are necessary to the government." Cf. Abrahams, op. cit., p. 63. On the special forms of imperial cult by Jewish subjects of Rome, see Juster, op. cit., vol. I, pp. 339–354.

 | DOI:10.1163/9789004627154_012

full recognition on the part of the Christian community of the legality of any form of government.[706]

It is precisely among diaspora Jews and, particularly, Babylonian diaspora, that (perhaps due to not readily verifiable influences of local Persian concepts) the theory of the divine origin of every government and political authority emerges for the first time.[707] Christian communities espouse and maintain this theory, just like Jewish communities, for as long as they remain small minorities distant from the idea of their possible successful expansion.

The principle will be abandoned by Christians as soon as their increased numerical strength and expansion begin to make them judge the pagan state as an enemy entity to conquer and then shape anew according to their principles: the Augustinian theories will then start to develop, representing the earthly city as an organism with no more divine imprint but devilish, against which, as an irreconcilable enemy, the heavenly city, the Church, God's only creation stands out. Furthermore, only later, after the definitive triumph of Christianity, the State, no longer pagan but Christian, reappears as a divine creation and the Augustinian principles will be overtaken by other ones more responsive to the changing circumstances.[708]

However, the Jews, despite some proselytizing success,[709] were promptly curbed by pagan emperors[710] and later stopped altogether by the Church

706 Epistle to the Romans, 13, 1–7; Ep. to Titus, 3, 1. Cf. 1 Petri, 2, 13. Carlyle's idea, *History of medieval political theory in the west*, Edinburgh and London, 1903 and seqq., vol. I, pp. 91–93 that the Christian principles are in contrast with the Jewish ones simply stems from inadequate knowledge of the rabbinical sources.

707 Babylonian Talmud, Bavà Batrà, f. 91b: "The water superintendent is also designated by the heavens"; cf. idem, berachot, f. 58a (text by Shemuel Jarchinai); idem, Sanhedrin, f. 20b (text by Josè ben Chalaftà the chronicler, 2nd century C.E.). These last two texts are quoted by Löw, *Dinà* etc., cit., pp. 353–354.

708 These variations of orientation in the political thought of early Christianity are not usually given the due eminence by scholars who address this issue. Cf. Carlyle, op. cit., vol. I, pp. 89–94 and 147–174. Wonderful, on the contrary, is Salvatorelli, *Lo stato e la vita sociale nella coscienza religiosa d'Israele e del cristianesimo antico*, Pavia, 1913 (from Crivellucci's journal *Studi storici*); Idem, *Il pensiero del cristianesimo antico intorno allo stato*, in *Bilychnis*, y. IX, 1920, dossiers 10 and 11.

709 Schürer, *Geschichte des jüdischen Volkes in Zeitalter Jesu*, vol. III, 1909, pp. 150–188 (bibliography on p. 167, no. 47); Juster, op. cit., vol. I, p. 253–290 (bibliography on p. 253, no. 10, complete up to 1914); G. Rosen, *Juden und Phönizer; Das antike Judentum als Missionreligion und die Entstehung der jüdischen Diaspora*, Tübingen, 1929, pp. 22–69 (bibliography in the notes, pp. 130–152, in particular p. 132, no. 12).

710 D. 48, 8, 11 pr. (Modestinus); Paulus, Sent. 5, 22, 4; cf. Spartianus, Vita Severi, 17, 1. Juster, op. cit., I, pp. 258–259 and 266–267.

and Christian emperors.[711] In fact, they never managed to emerge from their minority status and had no reason to change their original attitude. So they continued proclaiming total acceptance of the laws of the state[712] and considered any rebellion against the established authority a severe crime.[713]

This only occurred in the diaspora. In Palestine, things worked differently. During the Mishnah scohlars' era, the Jews were governed by conquerors who exercised their power with iron fists, imposing exorbitant tolls and taxes. In the face of such a fiscal over-exploitation, while reaffirming the general principle of recognizing the state's legitimacy,[714] practically the entire rabbinic doctrine considered all government-imposed taxes illegitimate. From a religious viewpoint, it would be legitimate – the doctrine proclaims – to avoid the tax collection through fraud,[715] and conversely, it would be religiously forbidden to trade money from the taxman's bank, for the same reason that prohibits trading in stolen money.[716] The contrary opinion of the Tanna, R. 'Akivà, is far from

711 C. Th. 16, 8, 1 (315); 16, 8, 7 (357); 16, 7, 3 (382); 16, 8, 19 (409); Nov. Th. 3, § 4 (438), Juster, op. cit., I, pp. 260 et seqq.

712 Babylonian Talmud, Bavà Kammà, f. 113a and b = idem, nedarim, f. 28a = id., Bavà Batrà, f. 54b = id., ghittin, f. 10b: "Says Shemuel [Jarchinai]: the State law is the law" (Dinà demalchutà dinà). On this famous scholar, b. ca. 165 CE in Nehardea (Babylon) where he was head teacher, d. ca. 257, physician, lawyer, astronomer, see D. Hoffmann, *Mar Samuel*, Leipzig, 1873; Sigmund Fessler, *Mar Samuel der bedeutendste Amora*, Halle, 1879; Felix Kauser, *Beiträge sur Kenntnis des Rechtssystem und der Etik Mar Samuels*, Bern, 1895; Bacher, *Die Agadà der Babylonischen Amoräer*, Strasbourg, 1878, pp. 37–45; I. Z. Lauterbach, in *Jewish Encyclopedia*, entry Samuel Jarchina'a, and the above mentioned article by Finkelscherer.

713 BabylonianTalmud, Sanhedrin, f. 49a: "He who rebels against the king's authority is guilty of a crime deserving the death penalty."

714 Mishnà, Pirkè Avot, 3, 2: "R. Haninà [d. in the year 68] president of the priests used to say: Pray for the well-being of the government, because if it were not for the fear of it, men would swallow one another alive." Without wishing to exaggerate the ideological weight of this phrase, I seem to see in it a conception of Hobbes' type in a nutshell, setting the *status naturae*, characterized by the *bellum omnium contra omnes* against the *status societatis*, achiever of peace and order by means of legislative compulsion.

715 In Mishnà, Nedarim, 3, 4, in princ. the permissibility is affirmed of fraudulent misappropriation of property from the tax collectors, who are compared to thieves and murderers. The fraud consists in swearing falsely that the goods are consecrated or belong to the king. In Mishnà, Chilaim, 9, 2, it is declared that not even for the purpose, considered generally permissible, of defrauding the tax collection, it is permitted to wear, even momentarily, a garment woven with a ritually forbidden mixture.

716 Mishnà, Bavà Kammà, 10, 1: "It is forbidden to trade your own money with the small change from the coffer of the tax collector or from the purse of the state treasurers: it is permissible, however, to exchange their private money with them. The reason for the ban and the distinction is to be found in the equalization of tax money to stolen money, from which it was considered sinful to draw, even though for a simple exchange."

certain.[717] As to Jesus' attitude, I believe his famous answer to the question about the legitimacy of tributes[718] cannot be understood either as an explicit proclamation of intrinsic tax equity.

This total disavowal of the validity of state tax laws by the Palestinian tannaites could not but impact the Babylonian sages who started out from principles very different from those of Palestinian doctrine with regards to the state.

Once their comments and debates on the Mishnah reached the principles enunciated above, finding themselves in need to consider those principles always in force[719] and therefore unable to use historical explanations, they must somehow bring them into conformity with the opposite principle of Shemuel Jarchinai, which states that the state law is valid without exceptions. To manage this reconciliation, projecting backward what their innovative distinction is, they assert that the Mishnah will not reject all taxes, but only those exacted unlawfully.[720]

With that, the Talmud scholars proclaim the sole invalidity of administrative deeds contrary to the law while at the same time reaffirming their full acceptance of the laws, that they do not submit to any question of constitutionality.

Medieval French Talmud commentators (the so-called Tossafists),[721] also embrace this view which rejects only the government's illegal executive

717 Babylonian Talmud, Bavà Kammà, f. 113a: "This opinion [i.e. the legality of tax fraud deductible from the passage of the Mishnah, Chilaim, 9, 2, cited above no. 14] is not conforming to what says R. Akivà that it is forbidden to evade taxes. On R. Akivà's name, however, R. Shim'on says: it is permitted to elude."

718 "Render unto Caesar what is Caesar's and to God what is God's" (concerning the question of taxes): Matthew, 22, 15–22 = Mark, 12, 13–17 = Luke, 20, 20–26. The comparison between Jesus' viewpoint and that of Judaism is accomplished by Abrahams, *Give unto Cesar*, cit.

719 According to the Jewish teaching, the Mishnah is in fact divine law, just like the Torah, and can be interpreted but not repealed.

720 Babylonian Talmud, Bavà Kammà, f. 113a (Gemara of the passage cited of Mishnah, Bavà Kammà, 10, 1) = Id. Nedarim, f. 28a (Gemara of the passage cited of Mishnah, Nedarim, 3, 4 in princ.): "And yet Shemuel says: The State law is the law. Responding on behalf of Shemuel, R. Haninà ben R. Kahanà: the Mishnah meant a tax collector who has no fixed fee. Conversely, the school of R. Jannai said that the Mishnah meant a tax collector who acts on his own behalf (unauthorized). R. Ashè said that it referred to a pagan tax collector (nochrì)." The same concepts are found in Toseftà Nedarim, 3, 4.

721 About the French school of the glossators of the talmud (Tossafists), which begins with R. Shelomò ben Izhak from Troyes, called Rashì (1040–1105) and reaches the late XIV century, see L. Ginzberg, in *Jewish Encyclopedia*, entry Law, codification by: P. Buchholz, *Historischer Ueberblick über die mannigfache Codificationen des Halachastoffes*, in *Monatsschrift für Geschichte und Wissenschaft des Judentums*, y. 13, pp. 202–217; U. Cassuto, *Storia della letteratura ebraica postbiblica*, Florence, 1938, pp. 100–102.

action,[722] while collectively accepting, without setting constitutional requirements, its legislative activity. They do, however, draw attention to the fact that this integral acceptance comes not so much from an inner persuasion of fairness of every tax law but rather from the need to avoid causing possible harm to any tax collection contractor, or to the tax collector who is accountable for the sum whose collection was entrusted to him.[723] Acceptance itself, they add, is agreed upon only concerning a non-Jewish state, where the principle is in force that, in addition to sovereignty, the king retains the private ownership of the lands and can therefore banish anyone who unconditionally refuses obedience to him. This would not be admissible in a Jewish State "because all Jews are collectively the owners of the land of Israel."[724]

In this interesting text, the right to unlimited taxation – provided it is legally exercised – is recognized based on the feudal principle of the eminent sovereign dominion over private lands. Another French Tossafist expresses the same concept, R. Eliezer Ben Shemuel from Metz (d. 1198),[725] who states that in his state, the king can impose any royal or personal tax, since, in his view, he is the owner of all the lands, of which private owners have nothing but the

722 Tossafot [glosses to Bab. Talmud, Nedarim f. 28a. cit., gloss to "amar Shemuel" [Shemuel said]: "Precisely because it does not have a fixed fee, it is not State law but State violence. And violence, even by the king, does not constitute law." Rashì's gloss to "dinà demalchutà dinà" of the same text: Therefore, a Jew who has received the king's tax contract with a certain amount a year as a fixed fee is not a robber." The tossafot and Rashì's commentary accompany as a rule the old editions of the Talmud, which are very numerous.

723 Tossafot, gloss to "mohes a'omed meelav" [tax collector acting on his own] of the same Talmudic text: "That is without royal permission … If they apply the principle: The State law is the law, it is only for this, that if a Jew bought the contract of this tax we are obliged to pay him the fee; and so even if he has not bought it but he is responsible for the collection of the taxes, the Jew [taxpayer] cannot swear [falsely, as on the contrary the Mishnah, Nedarim, 3, 4 admits in principle, cit. above no. 14] that the item object of the tax is consecrated [and cannot, therefore, be delivered], because there is no compulsion and in this case, we apply the principle: the State law is the law [unlike the Mishnah which allowed tax evasion]. But if this civil servant cannot let the Jew evade the tax to be paid to him, this is just because of the fear of the king [to whom he is responsible for the accuracy of the tax collections, and not because the tax is intrinsically fair]."

724 Tossafot, ibidem: "and the tossafot [meaning the oldest] write that the principle: The State law is the law, is valid only with reference to a gentile king, because the land is his, and he can tell them [the subjects]: if you do not carry out my order I throw you out of the land. But to the Kings of Israel, this does not apply, because all the Jews share ownership of the land of Israel."

725 On this author, who was a disciple of Rabbenu Tam, see A. Peiginsky in *Jewish Encyclopedia*, entry Eliezer from Metz.

mere use of them.[726] However, as we have seen, acceptance of the principle in practice does not undermine its rejection in theory. We see the same refusal implemented from the outset by the near totality of the Romance doctrine.[727] In the later rabbinical scripts, that principle is no longer mentioned.[728]

Rather than setting general principles on the state and the validity of the laws, the texts examined so far usually only consider the government's action in tax matters. Also, in judicial relations between private individuals, the texts do not appear to draw practical consequences from the attitude assumed regarding the constitutionality or unconstitutionality of the state norms.

---

726 R. Eliezer ben Shemuel from Metz, *Commento al Talmud*, Nedarim, ch. 4 [sic, but is likely ch. 3, being certainly the well-known passage of f. 28a], in Mordechai ben Illel, *Sefer Mordechai*, (ed. with the *Alachot* of R. Izhak Alfasì, Sabbioneta, Foà, 1554), commentary on Bavà Kammà f. 113b, §§ 190–194 (the passage, slightly abridged, is also reported by R. Asher ben Jechiel, § 11 of the commentary on ch. 3, f. 28a of the Talmudic treatise cited Nedarim; and by Josef Caro, *Bet Josef*, ch. 369): "We do not say that his law is valid unless it concerns the lands and is within the norms relating to them, such as the tax, or if it says: no one passes if he does not pay, or as it is said in hezcat ha-battim [Bab. Talmud, Bavà Batrà, f. 55a, see further on, footnote no. 873] that the statute of limitations is up to 40 years, or if it says: let whomever pays the fee enjoy the land; and also for private lands, if it says: it is forbidden to dwell there without paying so and so. And the reason is because the land is his and no one is allowed to pass through without his order. But if he rules about things that do not belong to him or imposes a levy on one who doesn't want to stay, this is robbery and he does not have the right [to act like that]. But the Kings of Israel cannot make laws for the lands because the land was not allocated to each one and does not belong to the king. Conversely, the Gentiles are owners of the land, and if the king imposes a tax we must pay it, and taxes can also be imposed on private owners. And so Shemuel [Jarchinai] interprets it this way, that the land belongs to the king; in fact in ch. Ha-Gozel Batrà [Babylonian Talmud, Bavà Kammà, f. 113b, see further on, footnote no. 767] it is said: they cut palms down and make bridges, because these palms belong to the king, just like the lands." Projecting the medieval concept backward, here too the recognition the Talmud of the legality of the acts of expropriation of trees, ordered by the king is based on the doctrine attributing the private ownership of all assets of the subjects to the king. On the similar principles of the Christian jurists from the same era concerning expropriation for public utility, see Nicolini, op. cited in the following note.

727 On the negative response to the question "An princeps sit dominus rerum particularium" in the intermediate doctrine and in the jusnaturalists who refer to it, see the comprehensive chapter 2 of part 2 of the recent work of Nicolini, *La proprietà, il principe e l'espropriazione per pubblica utilità*, Milan, 1940, pp. 107–134. Cf. Georg Mayer, *Das Recht der expropriation*, Leipzig, 1868, pp. 86 et seqq. and Gierke, *Das deutsche Genossenschaftrecht*, III, p. 616 = pp. 239–240 of the French transl., *Les théories politiques du moyen age*, Paris, 1914.

728 Only R. Nissim ben Reuben Gherondi of Barcelona (d. 1380), in his *Commento alle Alachot* (Talmudic compendium) *di R. Izhak Alfasì*, ed. with text commented, Sabbioneta, Foà, 1554, on Nedarim f. 28a, repeats verbatim the words of the tossafot on the same passage, reported above, footnote no. 723. On R. Nissim, see entry I. Z. Lauterbach in *Jewish Encyclopedia*.

Instead, they just consider the moral aspect of the matter, asserting the lack of any sinful element in the evasion of taxes arbitrarily imposed and conversely asserting the presence of such an element in the use of tax money regarded as stolen goods.

We must get to Maimonides' (1135–1204) coding, the Mishneh Torah,[729] to find political principles of general order and see a clear connection set between the issue of the legality of governmental acts and private relations.

It establishes that any expropriation based on an invalid law or an unlawful administrative act is considered theft, thus null and void Therefore, the person expropriated may recover his possessions, as he would from a recipient of stolen goods, from those the state had anyway handed over the goods: by contrast, the original owner of a lawfully taken asset will not be entitled to any right.[730]

But what is the criterion by which the validity of law should be judged?

According to Maimonides, to assume the quality of valid law, a state provision must:

a) Have a general character.[731]

b) Must be issued by a legitimate government, that is, from a government whose head has been recognized and freely accepted by the people.[732]

---

729 On Maimonides as a jurist and on Mishneh Torah, see: Adolf Schwarz, *Der Mishnè Torà, ein System der mosaisch-talmudischen Gesetzlehre. Zur Erinnerung an den 700 jährigen Todestag Maimonis*, in XII *Jahresberichte der israelitisch-theol. Lehranstalt in Wien*, Vienna, 1909. Also in a separate reprint, Vienna and Leipzig, 1909; the articles by Bernhard Ziemlich, Moritz Peritz, Ferdinand Rosenthal and Ludwig Blau in the collection *Moses ben Maimon, sein Leben, seine Werke, und sein Einfluss, Zur Erinnerung an den 700 Todestag des Maimonides*. Herausgeg. von der Gesellschaft zur Förderung des Judentums, vol. I, Leipzig, 1908, vol. II, 1914; M. W. Rapaport and J. Levin in *Jüdisches Lexikon*, entry Maimonides als Codificator. (Bibliography listed by Eisenstadt, *Repertorium* cit., pp. 85–90, that also adds the literature in Hebrew and Yiddish). The translations, all partial, in European languages of the juridical parts of the Mishneh Torah are listed by Eisenstadt, op. cit., pp. 27–29 and 395–396, but the passages used in this study of mine cannot be found in any of them. The work of J. R. Fürstenthal, *Das jüdische Traditionswesen*, Breslaw, 1892 that Eisenstadt defines (ibid. p. 28, no. 189): Targum Ha-Yad Ha-Chazakà (translation of Yad Ha-Chazakà or *Mishneh Torah*) is rather only the translation of Maimonides' introduction to the treatise Zera'im of the Mishnah, as I have checked myself on the copy of the work kept in the library of the British Museum in London.

730 *Mishnè Torà*, Venice ed., Marco Antonio Giustinian, 1551, Ilchot Ghezelà veavedà (Norms on robbery and lost items, ch. 5 cited further on, footnotes nos. 774 and 775).

731 Idem, ibid. "Any law made by the king for all and not for an individual separately is not robbery; conversely, he who takes from this individual only, not according to a law known to all, using violence, commits robbery." Cf. other parts of the text cited further on, pp. 207–209.

732 Idem, ibid., at the end: "All this [i.e. the rules on executive acts] was said for any case in which the State law is the law; which happens when his [the King's] currency is legal

By setting these requirements, Maimonides fits perfectly in the political doctrine of his time.

The first constitutes a defense against the omnipotence of state power, since denying validity to government provisions if issued only for individual citizens and not for the collectivity of citizens means disavowing the privileges on the one hand and, on the other hand, opposing the execution of arbitrary acts: in other words, it means setting the principle of equality. Some ten years later, Accursio (1185–1259), prompted by the same concern, facing the dangerous statements of the Digest "Princeps legibus solutus est" (D.2, 3, 31) and "Quod principi placuit legis habet vigorem" (D.1, 4, 1) clarifies in terms substantially similar to those of Maimonides, that to maintain the character of law, the prince's will must be expressed in general norms, not in special orders addressed to individuals.[733]

Bartolo later affirms that the *jura quesita* and, particularly, that of ownership, cannot be touched by a *civitas* unless "condendo jus commune,"[734] or "generaliter faciendo statuta" or "faciendo legem universalem" and not "faciendo legem privatam contra unum" or "specialiter contra aliquos" or "praecipiendo uni vel quibusdam hominibus."[735]

---

tender in those lands, i.e. when the citizens agreed that he be their Lord and they his subjects and gave him their vote. But if his currency is not recognized as having legal tender [lit.: doesn't come out], he is a robber and a performer of violence; and just like in companies of bandits their laws are not laws, so this king and all his servants are by any means thieves." The first part of the passage is explained by bearing in mind that coin mintage is one of sovereignty's essential attributes, and thus accepting the currency means for a population accepting sovereignty: which is even more explicitly clarified in the text that follows.

733 Accursio, gloss "Quod principi placuit," in D. 1, 4, 1: "Ut esset jus generale et commune; nam si placeret ei concedere non est lex." Cf. the gloss "Placuit" in Ist. 1, 2, *de jure naturali*: "causa faciendi communem legem et generalem; alias non esset lex communis. ... et sic non omnis vox principis est lex." M. Cavalieri, *Di alcuni fondamentali concetti politici contenuti nella glossa d'Accursio*, in *Archivio Giuridico*, series 3, vol. XIII, 1910, p. 156; and Nicolini, *La proprietà* cit., p. 141, no. 1, and p. 158.

734 Bartolo, *Commentaria*, Lyon, 1552, in C. 1, 22, 6: "Circa hoc an princeps possit mihi auferre dominium rej meae, dic: aut vult mihi auferre dominium jus commune condendo, et potest, ut in toto titulo *ff. de bonis damnatorum* (D. 48, 20), etc." Nicolini, op. cit., p. 222. Perfectly analogous is the construction of Maimonides who supports the lawfulness of retrieving, by general law on the norms regulating the confiscation of the assets of the sentenced. Cf. the text reported further on, footnote no. 778.

735 Bartolo, in D. 42, 5, 37: "Quaero utrum civitas posset facere statutum per quod auferatur jus privati ...; veritas est quod potest facere faciendo legem universalem, ut hic et *l. venditor ff. comm. predior.* (D. 8, 4, 13). Sed faciendo legem privatam contra unum non potest, *ff. de pollicit., toties* (D. 50, 12, 6), *ff. de quibus, si privatus* (D. 40, 9, 17)." Bartolo in D. 50, 12, 6: "civitas per suum statutum non potest auferre ius alterius. ... singulariter praecipiendo

Concerning the first requirement, there is a total agreement between Maimonides and the best representatives of the oldest intermediate Roman judicial doctrine. As to the second one, however, the thinking of the Jewish scholar finds no match in the political theories of the Christian civilists who now have relinquished the democratic views of the previous era and are not any longer making the legitimacy of the sovereign's power a condition to the election and the investiture of the people.

What Maimonides reflects is both the theory and practice of early medieval monarchies, among whose fundamental constitutional principles is that power comes from God, but by mediation, through the election or widespread recognition. Therefore, there can be no succession in the government without election or recognition by the people or by the elements that represent them.[736]

He very clearly expresses the medieval concept of *pactum subjectionis*, by which "any legal authority is based on submission of the community to its sovereign, a voluntary submission resulting from a contract stipulated between these two parties."[737]

Maimonides, therefore, requires that people recognize the sovereign. Once the recognition has been established, he is a legitimate sovereign and may decide whatever he likes, as long as his provisions have a general character. Meaning no limit is placed to the legislative omnipotence of a king duly invested with his authority.

Maimonides does not ask for more, but other scholars go farther and affirm the king's obligation to follow the ancient laws of the kingdom, deny the validity of any provision, even of general character, if issued *ex novo*.

---

uni homini vel quibusdam hominibus. ...; sed generaliter faciendo statuta bene posset." Idem, in D. 8, 4, 13, § 1: "Nota quod per consuetudinem vel per statutum potest quis cogi ad vendendum res suas. Quod est verum per statutum generale non autem si fieret specialiter contra aliquos, ut *l. fi. ff. Ad legem Juliam* (recte: *De lege Julia*) *de annona* (D. 48, 12, 3); *C. de Judeis l. nemo* (C. 1, 9.9); *ff. de rei vindic. l. item si verberatum*, § 1 (D. 6, 1, 15, § 1). Nicolini, op. cit., pp. 327–328.

736 Ercole, *Per la storia del pensiero politico medioevale*, in the volume *Da Bartolo all'Altusio*, Florence, 1932, pp. 29, 33–34, already published in *Politica*, y. 5th, 1923, nos. 50–51, Nov.-Dic. Carlyle, op. cit., vol. I, ch. XX, pp. 240–250; vol. II, ch. VII, pp. 56–74; vol. III, pp. 11 and 150–153; cf. then idem, vol. V, part I, ch. VII, pp. 86–106.

737 Gierke, *Les théories politiques du moyen âge*, cit., p. 169 and no. 138, p. 171 and no. 143, pp. 174–175 and nos. 151–153. Carlyle, op. cit., vol. III, pp. 12–13, 166–169, 185.

A proponent of this point of view is R. Moshè Ben Nachman (Nachmanides), from Gerona (b. 1194, m. in Palestine ca. 1270),[738] a scholar of great authority among his contemporaries and in posterity.[739]

Even though not expressed in an entirely precise manner, here is yet another fundamental principle emerging already since the 9th century, both among authors of public law and in the reality of the political life of western monarchies. The principle is that the law should emanate not from the king, but the will of the people expressed either tacitly in customs or expressly in parliamentary deliberations. That means the king should adhere, not only to the divine and natural laws, but also to the positive ones of his State.[740]

In the same order of Nachmanides' ideas, but only examining tax levying, R. Meir Ha-Levì (Ramà)[741] writes that "a new tax or an increase in the fee fixed and used to be paid every year, even if levied on everyone, is not considered as

738 R. Moshè Ben Nachman, in Josef Colòn, *Sheelot utshuvot* (questions and answers, namely legal consultations), cons. no. 66, Venice ed., 1519, p. 61: "But it seems to me that the principle: the State law is the law, only applies to rules laid down throughout the kingdom, which the preceding kings have applied and so are written on records. But what the king does at the moment or a new statute that he does at the moment for fining the people and that has not been done by his ancestors is violence by the kings and the principle: the State law is the law, does not apply." The passage abridged is quoted also by Vidal di Tolosa (Rav Hamagghid), in Josef Caro, *Bet Josef* (commentary to Jacob ben Asher's *Tur*), Hoshen Mishpat, ch. 369, no. 14. Neither Colòn nor Vidal mentions the precise site of the passage. It is worthwhile to compare the concept of Moshè ben Nachman – to which also R. Jacob Israel concurs in a consultation quoted by Caro, *Bet Josef* Hoshen Mishpat, ch. 369 cit. (the passage is reported further on, footnote no. 884) – to the principles repeatedly expounded by John Locke, in ch. XI of his *Saggio sul governo civile*: § 136: "The supreme authority ... must administer justice according to laws promulgated and fixed"; § 137: "The sovereign power must be exerted according to laws issued and of public reason rather than by means of decrees devised on the spot and by arbitrary resolutions"; § 142: "The sovereign must govern according to the laws enacted and stable not likely to vary capriciously in every single case."

739 On him, see entry Broydè in *Jewish Encyclopedia*.

740 Ercole, op. cit., pp. 28–32. Hence the obligation, for the king upon ascending the throne to take the oath of obeying the laws of the state. About this fundamental issue of the participation of the people to the legislative function and subsequent superiority of the law over the Prince, see in particular Carlyle, op. cit., vol. I, ch. 18 and 19, pp. 219–238; vol. III, introduction , pp. 10–12, ch. 3, pp. 41–48 and pp. 153–154; vol. V, part I, ch. IV–IX, passim. Cf. by the same author, *Some aspects of the relation of roman law to political law to political principles in the Middle Ages*, in *Studi per Besta*, vol. III, Milan, 1939, pp. 185 et seqq. For the opinions of the jurists of the intermediate period, see Nicolini, op. cit., pp. 135–177.

741 Di Fulda, 1320–1390. About him, see Jacob Freimann, in *Jüdisches Lexikon*, entry Meir ben Baruch ha-Levi.

state law [i.e., valid law]."[742] Another Spanish sage from Gerona-based family, R. Nissim Ben Reuben Gerondi (Ran), who flourished in Barcelona between 1340 and 1380,[743] distinguished between "state law" (*dinà de-malchutà*) and "king's law" (*dinà demalcà*), rejecting the latter and accepting as legitimate only the former, i.e., considering as valid only the rules emanating from the people by custom or the will of national parliaments, rather than those issued by the king. With the usual process of retrospective projection of his own ideas, he wants to find the distinction already in Samuele Jarchinai's principle, noting that he would have said appropriately: *dinà demalchutà dinà* (the law of the State is the law) and not: *dinà demalcà dinà* (the king's law is the law).[744] However, it is easy to realize this is a new principle and that Samuele and the other Talmud scholars had no idea such a distinction.

Nachmanides' opinion, perhaps because it was expressed in a too clear-cut way, as an absolute denial to the sovereign of any legislative power, had little consequence. Izhak Ben Baruch of Worms[745] had earlier pondered the viewpoint in question, concluding "that a king's decree, even if new, when it concerns the whole kingdom is a valid law."[746] Vidal of Toulouse (Rav Hamagghid; second half of the 13th century), commentator of Maimonides,[747]

742 Ramà, in Jacob ben Asher, *Tur*, Hoshen Mishpat, ch. 369, no. 14, Venezia ed., Gioan Grifio, s. a. (16th century). The passage is reported by Izhak Lampronti, op. cit., l. cit.

743 About him, see I. Z. Lauterbach in *Jewish Encyclopedia*, entry Nissim ben Reuben Gerondi. His fame is linked in particular to his *Commento alle Alachot di R. Izhak Alfasì* (that is Isacco di Fez, called Rif).

744 R. Nissim Gerondi, *Commento* cit. *a R. Izhak Alfasì*, (on ghittin ch. 1) f. 557a: "And if we say: the State law is the law, we mean what the king does in conformity to the laws of his kingdom, but not what he does not according to the law. This is exactly what the expression: *dinà demalchutà* [State's law] means, therefore they did not say: *dinà demalcà* [king's law], because if [the king] acts not according to the law, this is violence and not law." The passage is reported also by Josef Caro, *Bet Josef*, Hoshen Mishpat, ch. 369, no. 14, Sabbioneta ed., 1553, and by Izhak Lampronti, l. cit.; and, a little abridged, by R. Josef Colon, *Consulti* cit., cons. 66. The distinction between *lois du roi* and *lois du royaume* is customary in the French public law specialists starting from the 14th century. Duguit, *Traité de droit constitutionel*, Paris, 1923. vol. III, pp. 642–643.

745 German talmudist who flourished around 1200, from the glossators (tossafists) school, born in Worms but lived at Regensburg, a pupil of the French tossafist Izhak ben Shemuel of Dampierre. Author of glosses and of a celebrated *Sefer hatterumà* (Book of charity).

746 Baruch of Worms, *Sefer hatterumà*, cited – without a precise indication – by R. Josef Colon, *Consulti* cit., cons. 66.

747 Author of a classic commentary to Maimonides' Mishneh Torah, titled *Magghid Mishnè* (hence the name of Rav Hamagghid), always printed together with the Mishneh itself. *Editio princeps* Constantinoples, 1509. V. S. Ochser in *Jewish Encyclopedia*, entry Vidal of Tolosa.

after having interpreted the passage of Nachmanides, he adds: "This is not the opinion of our master [Maimonides] and the great sages. He [the king] can make a new law and say: those who do not follow it are liable to such punishment, and the penalty imposed is lawful.[748]

In principle, the Jewish sages require that the sovereign's measures do not affect any particular individual but all citizens in general.[749] Based on a rigorous application of this principle of generality, they sometimes even go as far as to deny the validity of laws emanated non-statewide, but for a particular province.[750] This is, for example, the opinion of R. Jacob Ben Meir, also called Rabbenu Tam [= man of integrity] (b. at Ramerupt, Seine, in 1100, d. in Troyes in 1171), head of the school of the French Glossarists.[751] While a later scholar, also of French origin, R. Josef Colòn, rabbi of Mantua,[752] in a consultation concerning a practical matter, seems to deny validity to a law that he considered as non-general, since it was not addressed to the totality of the citizens but only to a particular category, in that specific case to the shopkeepers.[753] Likewise, R. Jacob Israel denies the quality of valid law to a state measure relating to the money lenders at interest, on the reflection that this measure "is not general

748 Vidal di Tolosa, *Magghid Mishnè* on Maimonides, *Mishneh Torah*, Hilchot Ghezelà Veavedà, ch. 5 cit. The passage is available also in Josef Caro, *Bet Josef*, on *Tur*, Hoshen Mishpat, ch. 369, no. 14, cit.

749 Cf. the opinions of R. Asher Ben Jechiel and his son R. Jacob Ben Asher, author of the *Tur*, contained in the passages cited further on, pp. 210–211.

750 R. Tam, in Josef Caro, *Bet Josef* cit., in *Tur*, Hoshen Mishpat, ch. 369, no. 14: " R. Tam explains that it is said: the State law is the law, only when the king makes decrees equal for all, but if he makes them different for a province, it is not said: the State law is the law." The passage is also mentioned by Lampronti, op. cit., and by Löw, op. cit., without site indication.

751 About him, see entry Max Schlesinger in *Jewish Encyclopedia*.

752 Son of R. Shelomò Trabot (da Trevoux), was born in Chambéry ca. in 1420, died in Pavia [handwritten correction by V. Colorni] in 1480. Rabbi in Piove di Sacco, Mestre, Bologna, and for several years in Mantua. Author of celebrated legal consultations collected by his pupils and printed several times. *Editio princeps* Venice, 1519. See L. Ginzberg in *Jewish Encyclopedia*, entry Colon, Joseph ben Salomon and U. Cassuto in *Encyclopedia Judaica* at the same entry. For some biographic elements, see my work *Note per la biografia di alcuni dotti ebrei vissuti a Mantova nel sec. XV*, in *Rivista di studi ebraici*, vol. I, Rome, 1934, pp. 169–173.

753 R. Josef Colon, *Sheelot Utshuvot* cit., cons. no. 66, at the end: "... and the majority of opinions are in agreement that it is not said: *dinà demalchutà dinà*, unless it is a generality; so that this law, which is not general but a royal decree imposed on shopkeepers, remains excluded."

law throughout the kingdom, but aimed only at those who lend money at interest, not at other merchants."[754]

Alongside these variously restrictive opinions, but in agreement with objecting to the recognition of an unlimited and arbitrary expression of the state's legislative power, others interpret Shemuel's principle according to which "the

754 Consultation in Caro, *Bet Josef*, in *Tur*, hoshen mishpat, ch. 369. With respect to this criterion of generality, on which both the Jewish juridical doctrine and the Christian one base themselves to distinguish the law from administrative regulation, it is worth noting that, upon careful analysis, the identity of views between the two doctrines appears to be less complete than it might seem at first glance. For the Jewish authors as we have seen, only that provision which concerns all citizens is to be intended as general, i.e. legislative; and this in order to avoid unfairness by the state not only against individual persons but also against individual categories. Conversely, as it has been well observed, (opinion in rotal cause, see De Luca, *Tractatus de officiis venalibus vacabilibus romanae curiae*, Venice, 1735, p. 85, nos. 38–39) the Christian authors are indeed in agreement in considering "quod ad essentiam legis requiratur universalitas, ne in odium potius unius quam alterius suspicari possit promulgata, unde concludunt eam omnes comprehendere, ad differentiam praecepti, quod particularibus dirigitur …" but then, in conclusion, "non descendunt ad hoc, an requisita universalitas talis esse debeat ut omnes cuiusvis generis omnino comprehendat, vel potius sufficiat ut intra aliquod genus neminem excludat." Among those who ask themselves this question, few are those who resolve it in the first sense, claiming that, to assume validity of law, the rule should be directed to all the subjects without exception. The vast majority, on the other hand, follow the second interpretation and consider as law any provision that does not affect concretely and specifically an individual person but is directed to a group or a category mentioned abstractly, even when composed of very few individuals; which, as it can be easily understood, makes arbitrary acts legitimate, if not against individuals, at least against minorities. As conclusions in the first sense, I will mention those of Gaspare Turco (opinion in the mentioned rotal case, in De Luca, op. cit., p. 98, no. 26) who, starting from the opinion that the law "referri debet ad omnes subditos, alias, amissa propria natura, degeneraret in preceptum particulare," does not consider the suppression of a *collegium* of 24 people as having taken place by law, albeit operated mentioning abstractly the college itself and not concretely the individual members. Still concerning the same case in question, Ciriaco Lancetta (opinion ibid., p. 111, no. 28) and Domenico Taurusio (opinion ibid., p. 122, no. 17) express themselves in the same sense. It is interesting the viewpoint of Angelo da Perugia (that can be compared to that of the Jewish doctor R. Jacob ben Meir), *In Primam et secundam partem Digesti veteris commentaria*, Venice, 1580, in *l.* 1 *ff. de legibus* (D. 1, 3, 1) for whom "Civitas non potest facere statutum quod liget unum quarterium civitatis tantum." He is followed by Giasone del Maino, *In primam et secundam partem Digesti veteris commentaria*, Venice, 1580, in *l.* 1 *ff. de legibus* (D. 1, 3, 1) and, with others, by the Rota, *Decisionum novissimarum diversorum Sacri Palatii Apostolici auditorum volumina tria*, Venice, 1590, part II, vol. II, decis. 50, no. 19, p. 33v. In the opposite sense, in conformity with the majority of the views, De Luca (*Discorso avanti la Rota romana* in the above mentioned cause of abolition of the college, op. cit., p. 239, no. 23) expresses himself as follows: "Non niegano gli avvocati [avversari]… la verità di questa distinzione, come certa ed irrefragabile, ma ne niegano l'applicazione al caso, dicendo che la legge generale di sua natura deve abbracciare tutti i

law of the State is the law" as complete acceptance of any manifestation of the will of the State, as it may be expressed.

On this line of thought, which finds its parallel in the theories of the Christian absolutists,[755] moves R. Shemuel Ben Meir (Rashbam),[756] who interprets the *pactum subjectionis* as an ultimate alienation of all rights by the people and states that precisely as a result of such a pact, the people must accept all laws and royal statutes as valid.[757]

No new opinions were issued after those hitherto considered, and the later writers just quoted the opinion of one or the other of the sages we cited. Even

---

sudditi ed a tutti generalmente pregiudicare, non già nel caso presente che il pregiudizio è solamente di 24 persone particolari; però che si contiene un equivoco manifesto, posciachè la legge e la provisione generale si dice quando abbraccia tutto un genere, sicchè non vi sia parzialità od eccettuazione di persone comprese in quel genere, altrimenti una legge la qual si faccia per una religione, o per un monastero, o capitolo o altra simile università, non meritarebbe di dirsi legge e pur sarebbe una mera vanità il dirlo; nè perchè il Papa sopprima una religione si potrà dire che non sia legge e provisione generale perchè non si supprimono tutte le altre, e con simiglianti esempi." Similarly, Tommaso Maurizio Richeri, *Universa civilis et criminalis jurisprudentia*, Venice ed., 1841, p. 39, § 43: "[Lex] praeceptum commune est: lex enim pro omnibus ferri debet, nec principis singulare imperium legis nomine donatur. Non tamen necesse dixerim ad legis rationem ut omnes omnino subditos perstringat; cum sufficiat si eius vis pertrahatur ad quandam universitatem. Quare constituuntur leges pro solis magistratibus, judicibus, militibus, pro unius vel alterius generis opificibus." Conversely, Udalrico Zasio, *In aliquot Digesti veteris titulos lecturae*, Basel, 1537, in *l. jura ff. de legibus* (D, 1, 3, 1), relying on Angelo da Perugia's and Giason del Maino's viewpoint mentioned above, denies law validity to the decree issued "contra unum ex collegiis civitatis" while admitting nevertheless "certos casus in quibus statui potest certarum personarum ratione habita." The quality of law also for the norms concerning members of certain professions, social classes, or groups, on the other hand, is affirmed by Suarez, *De legibus et de Deo legislatore*, Lyon, 1613, book I, ch. VI, p. 23. About the substance of the law, it is therefore evident the contrast between most conclusions of the Christian jurists and those of the Jewish jurists just mentioned even under the apparent reigning accord concerning the prerequisite of generality.

755 Gierke, *Les théories politiques*, cit., pp. 176–178.

756 French exegete, brother of R. Jacob ben Meir (R. Tam), b. ca. in 1085, d. ca, in 1174, who lived in Ramerupt. Author of various commentaries to the Talmud (printed with the text), among which, one to the treatise Bavà Batrà (from folio 29a to the end). See S. Ochser in *Jewish Encyclopedia*, entry Samuel Ben Meir.

757 Shemuel Ben Meir, commentary to Bavà Batrà, f. 54b: "And yet Shemuel said: dinà demalchutà dinà, that is, all the levies and taxes and uses of the laws by the kings with which they usually govern in their kingdom are legal, because all the subjects of the kingdom accept the king's statutes of their will and his laws and therefore [the law in question] is a perfect law. Consequently, anyone who holds partner's assets under state law is not a robber."

the latest codifier, Josef Caro,[758] in the *Shulchan 'Aruch*,[759] follows Maimonides word for word[760] reproducing, perhaps without quite realizing it, remarkably democratic principles, in a time when throughout Europe, the democratic institutions and idealities had significantly been wanting. The same goes for

758 Top of the codifiers of the diaspora, whose *Shulchan 'Aruch* still represents the sum of the Jewish ritual and juridical laws. He was born in Spain in 1488 and died in Safed in 1575. Major works:

a) *Bet Josef*, commentary to the *Arba' Turim* (Four orders) or *Tur* (Order) by Jacob ben Asher (see further on, footnote no. 784), very broad since more widely based on the Talmud and on the subsequent jurisprudence, begun in 1522 in Adrianople, finished in 1542 in Safed. *Editio princeps* part 1 and 2, Venice 1550–1551; part 3 and 4, Sabbioneta 1553–1559. In *Bet Josef*, Caro followed *Tur* rather than Maimonides since the latter's authority was limited to the Spaniards, whereas *Tur*'s authority was recognized by Spaniards, Germans and Italians.

b) *Shulchan 'Aruch*, more concise codification than *Bet Josef*, written by the author in his old age and completed (Steinschneider, *Catalogus librorum hebraicorum … in Bibliotheca Bodleiana*, 1852, col. 1480) in Biri, Palestine, 1555. *Editio princeps*, Venice 1565. It follows the *Tur*'s framework, reproducing its subdivision into four parts, with corresponding chapters in each part, but it is more concise and dogmatic. For further information, see L. Ginzberg in *Jewish Encyclopedia*, entry Caro, Joseph Ben Ephraim.

759 About *Shulchan 'Aruch* in particular see Creizenach, *Shulchan 'Aruch oder encyclopädische Darstellung des mosaischen Gesetzes, wie es durch die rabbinischen Satzungen sich ausgebildet hat*, Frankfurt a. M., 1833–1840; M. Gaster, *The origines and sources of the Shulchan Aruch*, 1893; S. Back, *Die religionsgesetzliche Literatur der Juden in dem Zeitalter vom 15 bis 18 Jahrhundert mit besonderer Berücksichtigung des Shulchan 'Aruch*, Treviri, 1893; Ch. Tschernowitz, *Die Entstehung des Schulhan Aruch*, Bern, 1915. (Literature listed by Eisenstadt, *Repertorium* cit., pp. 85–90, where the bibliography in Hebrew, Yiddish and Russian can also be found, as well as other minor texts concerning the *Shulchan 'Aruch*).

760 *Shulchan 'Aruch*, Mantua ed. 1723, part IV: Hoshen mishpat, ch. 369, nos. 2 and 8. The translations into European languages of this 4th part of the *Shulchan 'Aruch*, regarding civil law are as follows: in German: Heinrich G. F. Löwe, *Schulhan Aruch* (all 4 sections), 1st ed. Hamburg 1838, 2nd ed. Vienna 1896; Johann Pawly, *Choshen Mishpat, oder Civil-Strafrecht* [of Judaism], *zum ersten Male aus dem Original frei ins deutsche übersetzt*, etc., St. Ludwig i. E., 1893 (who only gives the first numbers of each chapter). In English: Kadushin, *Hoshen Ha-Mishpat, Jewish Code of Jurisprudence*, New York, 1919 (unavailable in Europe). In Polish: Ignaz Debicki, *Hoszen Hamiszpat, czyli prawo zydowskie*, Krakow, 1900. The work of Johann Pawly, *Code civil et pénal du judaisme. Traduit pour la première fois sur l'original chaldéo-rabbinique avec notes et commentaires*, Paris, Leroux, 1896, is not, as it might be believed and how in fact Eisenstadt, *Repertorium* cit., p. 31, no. 214, thought it was, a translation of Caro's code, but rather a summary composed by Pawly with provisions of all the post-biblical Hebrew legislative collections and divided according to the Romanist and modern criteria in 729 articles. I examined this work of no value in the library of the British Museum in London.

Polish codifier Mordechai Jaffè[761] in his *Levush*,[762] representing contemporary views among Ashkenazi Jews in Eastern Europe before the *Shulchan' Aruch* took over everywhere.

2 Principles about the Legitimacy of the Administrative Acts

Once the invalidity of certain laws, or entire legislation, is admitted for one of the above-mentioned constitutional reasons, the unquestionable consequence of the illegality of all the executive acts of the administration of such laws inevitably ensues.

So, when we see the Mishnah sages proclaim the invalidity of all tax laws,[763] we must infer they also consider the individual acts by which the state secures its tax collections and the possible confiscations of property of unlawful defaulters.

Conversely, considering the tax laws, valid in principle as any other, the Talmud scholars[764] deem illegal only the collections whose rate has not been previously set by the government, namely the collections unauthorized by a legislative provision (opinion by Shemuel Jarchinai himself as reported by R. Haninà Bar Kahanà); or, as R. Jannai's school views, the collection by a tax collector not in possession of a regular authorization to exercise

761 *Levush*, ch. 369. The passage is reported by Hermann Rosenthal, in the *Jewish Encyclopedia*, entry Jaffè, Mordechai, translated as follows: "The maxim *Dinà Demalchutà Dinà* is fully treated in § 369, and defined democratically by the statement that "only that government is legitimate in which the king's seal of authority is voluntarily acknowledged by his subjects: otherwise he is not their king, but a robber gathering imposts by force, whose edicts have no legal value." At the present time I do not have this text within reach, but given the identity of the whole paragraph, I am certain that the word translated here as "seal of authority" is, in fact, the "matbea'" used by Maimonides and by Caro. Now, though it derives from the verb "tava'" that means "to imprint," it is never found in the sense of a seal, but always in that of "coin." Thus, to translate more elegantly, Rosenthal moved away from the concept of the author who, in Maimonides' footsteps, intends the currency as an expression of sovereignty.

762 Mordechai Jaffè's (b. in Prague ca. 1530, d. in Posen in 1612) *Levush* is constructed on the model of the *Turim* and of the *Shulchan 'Aruch*, and the paragraphs of these works match up even though Jaffè gave different names of the various parts of his work. See H. Rosenthal's article, cit., in *Jewish Encyclopedia*, entry Jaffè Mordechai.

763 See the passages cited above, footnotes nos. 714–717.

764 Babylonian Talmud, Bavà Kammà, f. 113a = Nedarim, f. 28a, reported above, footnote no. 720.

his office; or finally, according to R. Ashè, the collections made by a gentile (nochrì) taxman.[765]

As an outline and concerning a particular activity, i.e., the collection of public tributes, we already see a reflection of the fundamental requirement of political life, that is to expect that the activity of the government and its officials is carried out within the law, both to the object and the subjects who exercise it.[766]

Therefore, the sages of Talmud outline the arbitrariness of government actions about taxes as emanating from incompetence and law violation. On the other hand, they consider legitimate all taxes imposed by the state within the limits of the law and collected by duly authorized (Jewish) officials.

They also consider the forced surrender of trees to construct bridges for everyday use as legitimate, although specifically imposed only on individuals.[767]

---

765 This last opinion appears to be strange. As Rabbinowicz notes about this issue, *Legislation civile du talmud traduite et annotée, Traité Babá Kammá*, Paris, 1877, p. 465, no. 2, "il est impossible d'admettre que R. Aschè désigne par cet mot tous les païens, car il veut mettre d'accord le passage avec l'opinion de Semuel qui dit ques les lois des autorités païennes sont obligatoires pour les Juifs: or les lois païennes obligent les Juifs de payer l'impôt aux péagers païens, par conséquent les israelites doivent les payer." Cf. nevertheless the passage of Maimonides cited below here, footnote no. 770.

766 It is interesting to compare what Ranelletti, *Istituzioni di diritto pubblico*, 5th ed., Padua, 1935, p. 135 writes, outlining the features of the modern "rule of law": "The financial administration organs cannot set the tax amount arbitrarily, nor shall the debt collector or other official demand the amount he wants; but they can only ask for what the law permits and in the forms established by it."

767 In fact, as an example of the application of Shemuel's principle: "the law of the State is the law," another scholar, Rabbà, reports the following. The government – he notes – uses to force individuals to give up a certain amount of palm trees with which bridges are built for public use. If we would consider the tax imposition as illegitimate, and we would therefore believe that, legally, the ownership of the individuals over the cut trees and turned into bridges has remained, then we should consider the trees themselves altogether as the epitome of theft and thus prohibit the use of the bridges as sinful. This is according to the general rule that prohibits drawing benefits from stolen items – the use of bridges. The fact that this prohibition does not exist is evidence that the action of the state was considered to be legitimate and such as to annul, *de jure*, the right of the individual owners. A colleague of Rabbà, Abajè, objects to this reflection, stating that even without considering it a legitimate state action, it might be thought to be a – tacit –relinquishment by the owners of their trees taken away from them. But Rabbà replies that it is unclear how such renunciation can happen: instead, the act of the government should be accepted as legitimate: indeed, its legitimacy should be recognized even in the case (which is precisely what interests us) that, against the orders of the king, the officials do not make the cutting down proportionately among all owners, getting instead the material from the property of a sole owner. And this, Rabba explains, because the affected owner has the right to make good of his losses at the expense of all the others

In a nutshell, the concept is already here of expropriation not based on law but legitimized by a cause of public utility.

The French tossafists do not depart at all from the Talmudic principles, and they, too, assert that only the lack of a preventive delimitation – that is to say legislative – of toll rates, turns the "law of the State" (*dinà demalchutà*) into "state violence" (*hamsanutà demalchutà*).[768] Maimonides adheres as well to the same principles. He is not satisfied to examine only the issue of taxes, but takes into consideration any act detrimental to the property of individuals, and starting from the reworking of the Talmudic passages mentioned above, steps forwards to set general principles through a more extensive exemplification.

Neither for Maimonides nor any of the Talmud sages was any collection carried out by an official

a) Who is Jewish and honest;[769]
b) Who acts based on a rate fixed by law;
c) Who is regularly appointed to his office[770]

to be considered a robbery, but rather a regular exercise of government power, aimed to fully legitimize the passing of ownership of the goods removed:

---

and it is his fault, not the state's if in the end he does not exercise it. Babylonian Talmud, Bavà Kammà, f. 113b: "Shemuel says: the law of the State is the law. Rabbà says: in fact, they cut trees down and out of them they make bridges on which we pass. Abajè replies: maybe the owners gave up their trees. Replies Rabbà: If we would not say: the law of the State is the law [i.e., in this case, the action of the state is legitimate], how can they renounce? [i.e.: if we would not base the annulment of the private owner's lordship over his asset on the legality of the expropriation, how could we consider such annulment to have occurred, since in fact no spontaneous waiver has ever taken place?]. Behold: [to support the illegality of the action of the state, it can still be objected] the officials do not act like the king wants, because the king says: go and take from everyone and they take from just one. [To which it is replied] the king's messenger is like the king and does not bother to take from all: it is they [the owners affected] who hurt themselves [by not claiming from others].

768 See the passage cited above, footnote no. 722.

769 Cf. above, footnote no. 765. It is unlikely that in practice this requirement was requested.

770 Maimonides, *Mishneh Torah*, Ilchot Ghezelà Veavedà (Norms on robbery and lost items), ch. 5: "The taxman it is considered a robber when he is a Gentile or unauthorized, or appointed by the king without the toll to exact having been determined, so that he can exact or leave what he wants. On the contrary, if a fee is decided by the king, who established ⅓ or ¼ or an established fee to be charged, and the fee is levied on behalf of the king by a Jewish collector known for his fairness and for not adding anything to what the king has established, he who collects is not presumed to be a robber because the law is the king's law; and also, refusing to pay this fee is a crime because it steals what belongs to the king, whether he is a Gentile or a Jew." The text corresponds entirely to the Talmudic one (Babylonian Talmud, Bavà Kammà, f. 113a = Id., Nedarim, f. 28a) cited above, footnote no. 720.

The fact that taxes are claimed from anyone who holds the land at harvest time, even if he is not the owner, does not detract from the legality of taxes.[771] The state's expropriations of properties for failure to pay royal property tax weighing on the properties themselves are likewise to be considered legal. On the other hand, the expropriation of property for non-payment of personal expenses, such as the poll tax [TN: head tax or capitation, i.e., taxation per head] is conversely to be considered illegal; except in the case that law expressly establishes the legality of such acts.[772]

Next to the collection of taxes and the expropriation related to them, other cases of ablation of private assets are considered legitimate and precisely:

1) The confiscation of assets following a conviction under a general law.[773]
2) In particular, the confiscation of assets of an official who has rebelled against the king's authority.[774]

In these cases, where the executive action relies on a legislative precept and takes place within the limits it poses, the legality of the action itself is out of the question, and the ownership of the seized object is legitimately removed from the original owner and transferred to the new one, who purchased from the government. "But on the other hand – continues Maimonides – if a king has taken a house or a field from a subject against the law, he is a robber, and the owner can reclaim the property from the person who had bought it."[775]

771 Maimonides, ibid., "So if a king has imposed a fee on the citizens – or a fixed fee on everyone year after year, or a certain quantity on every field – or if he has decreed that anyone ... who will be found in the field at the time of the threshing floor (= harvest) will have to pay the fee, whether he is the owner or not, or similar things, it is not robbery and the Jew who collects for the king is not a robber and he is an honest man, provided he does not add, change or take anything for himself."

772 Maimonides, ibid., "Therefore the tax collectors of the king and his officers who sell the fields for the tax set on the fields sell well. Conversely, the individual fee cannot be collected but from the individual himself who is affected by it, and if [the taxman] sold the field for the price of the poll tax, he did not sell well, unless such is the law of the king."

773 Maimonides, ibid., "If the king has decreed that anyone who transgresses an order exposes himself to the confiscation of assets, ... it is not robbery, etc."

774 Maimonides, ibid., "And so a king who was disgusted with one of his servants or ministers of the province and confiscated his field or home does not commit robbery and can enjoy the property he appropriated, and he who buys from the king, the property becomes his and the former owner cannot take it away from him because it is the right of every king to seize the patrimony of ministers who have irritated him, and the king removes the engagement [cancel the right of the private individual] on these assets that become like nobody's property, and he who buys them from the king has an untouchable right on them."

775 Maimonides, ibidem.

Apart from the hypotheses considered above of ablations based on law, based on the Talmud,[776] Maimonides finally considers the expropriation of particular assets, such as trees or houses, to be legitimate for the reason of public utility.[777]

Maimonides' doctrine is accepted in full by his commentator, R. Vidal of Toulouse, who clarifies that the confiscation of goods from people sentenced must be executed "according to the established law," in which case the validity of the action detrimental to the property is out of the question.[778] Furthermore, he adds that Maimonides' opinions on the recognition of acts by the government within the limits of the law and the disavowal of others have found full concurrence in the statute after him.[779]

Focusing on the exact text, another commentator, Meir ha-Cohen (12th century), applies the theory to the frequent hypothesis of real estate abandoned by Jews in case of a popular uprising against them and requisitioned by the state. In this case, not being based on a general law, the government's action is declared illegal, with the known consequence, in the privatism field, of allowing the original owner the opportunity to sue anyone who purchased the estate from the government, for the return of the estate (upon reimbursement of the price paid).[780]

Similarly, government confiscation of holy books is considered illegal by R. Eliezer Ben Joel ha-Levì of Bonn (died around 1238); the buyer must return them to their original owner.[781]

776 See above, no. 767.

777 Maimonides, ibidem, at the end: "If a king has ordered the trees cut down from owners to make a bridge, it is permitted to cross the bridge even if he has ordered his servants to cut a quantity from each and they have cut them all down from only one owner; and likewise, if he ordered to tear down houses to make roads or walls, it is permitted to use those roads and walls."

778 Vidal di Tolosa, *Maghid Mishnè*, on Maimonides' *Mishneh Torah*, commentary to Ilchot ghezelà veavedà, ch. 5: "A king who was disgusted with his servants, etc. Meaning: according to the established law, as he writes further on. This is clear because the assets of those sentenced to death belong to the king, as it is said in ch. nigmar haddin (Babylonian Talmud, Sanhedrin, ch. 6)." The text is reported by Josef Caro, *Bet Josef*, commentary to *Tur*, ch. 369.

779 Vidal di Tolosa, ibidem: "All those who had to decide have already approved this; and this is a true principle because the State law is the law but the State robbery is not; and in this case the stuff is stolen and the owner has the right to reclaim it; and this is explained in many places." The text is reported by Josef Caro, passage cited in the previous note.

780 Meir ha-Coen, *Haggaot Maimonijot*, Warsaw ed., 1882 (glosses to Maimonides' *Mishneh Torah*; authorship is not absolutely sure), commentary to the Ilchot ghezelà veavedà cit. text, ch. 5. Also reported by D. M. Shohet, *The Jewish court* cit., pp. 116–117.

781 Mordechai Ben Illel, *Sefer Mordechai*, on Bavà Kammà, f. 113a, §§ 190–194: "It seems to Raavià [R. Eliezer Ben Joel ha-Levi] that if one has left books in a city and fleed, if a Jew

The clear Maimonides-style organization of these constitutional principles associated with ownership encountered a great deal of good fortune: adopted in its fundamental lines by Asher Ben Jechiel[782] in his commentary on the Talmud,[783] we see it then reported in full in the two major successive codifications: R. Jacob Ben Asher's *Tur*[784] and R. Josef Caro's *Shulchan 'Aruch*. The former duly underscores the standard requirement for the legality of the state's action concerning taxation and confiscation: i.e., this action is supported by

bought them he must return them, [and will be compensated] up to the price paid. So also according to Rashì, who explains that the norm of compensation applies to books, etc."

782 Talmud scholar born in Western Germany in 1250, died in Toledo in 1328, a disciple of R. Meir Ben Baruch from Rothenburg, author of commentaries to the Mishnà and Talmud, of a volume of responses and of collection of rules (*Alachot*). Known under the names of Rabbenu Asher, Asherì and Rosh. See Gotthard Deutsch in *Jewish Encyclopedia* entry Asher Ben Jechiel.

783 R. Asher Ben Jechiel, *Commento al Talmud*, commentary to Nedarim, f. 28a: "Shemuel says: the State law is the law, and it is forbidden to defraud the Jew who has bought the king's taxes. And how have the sages allowed to defraud him allowing a tender? This is a tax that has no fixed rate and in this case, it is not said that: the State law is the law; because only in a matter that concerns all citizens the king acts lawfully, but not in a matter that is not equal for all, such as when [the taxman] takes a little from one and a lot from another, or when, having no fixed rate, he takes more than what the king wants. In this case, the whole action is unlawful." R. Asher argued, however, that even in the event of unlawful action, the dispossessed owner was not entitled to take action and the tacit waiver on his part was always to be admitted. R. Asher ben Jechiel, op. cit., commentary to Bavà Kammà, f. 113a, gloss to "en poretim" of the Mishnà (Bavà Kammà 10, 1, see above no. 769): "It is written in the tossafot that the Mishnah would be consistent with the opinion of the sages opposed to R. Shim'on, who say that for robbery resulting from an undetermined tax there is no renunciation by the owner. However, it seems to me that a waiver on the part of the owner should be presumed for everything that the taxman and the tax collector cash, even when there is no fixed rate. Nevertheless, it is despicable to take money from a place assigned to the robbery [the taxman's strongbox]."

784 R. Jacob ben Asher (called *Ba'al Ha-Turim* = author of the Turim), son of R. Asher Ben Jechiel just mentioned, was born in Germany and emigrated with his father to Toledo, where he died ca. 1340). He is well known in particular for a four-part codification called *Tur* (Order) or *Arbà turim* (Four orders), the most important after Maimonides' *Mishneh Torah*, before the appearance of Josef Caro's *Shulchan 'Aruch*. *Editio princeps* of the entire work: Piove di Sacco, 1475. First editions of the single parts: part 1 (Tur Orach hajim) Mantua 1476; part 2 (Tur Jorè de'à) Mantua 1476 for one third, completed in Ferrara 1477; part 3 (Tur Eben ha'ezer) Guadalajara s. a.; part 4 (Tur Hoshen mishpat) Piove di Sacco cit. ed. Two other complete editions and seven of separated sections between 1475–1495. See Max Seligsohn in *Jewish Encyclopedia* entry Jacob ben Asher, and Buchholz, op. cit. (above, footnote no. 721,), pp. 253–254.

general and preventive law;[785] the latter reports the chapter of *Mishneh Torah* word for word, with only some slight deviations in expounding the norms.[786]

Finally, not too distant from Maimonides' point of view is his contemporary R. Tam, who, in contrast to the authors mentioned so far, admits the validity of the fees not laid down at a precise rate, but subordinates that validity to the existence of a state of war or other serious public needs.[787]

Now let us pause for a moment: from all the texts considered, the essential requirement to which the Jewish doctrine subordinates the recognition of the government's acts, i.e., the dependence on law and the obligation not to overstep the boundaries thereof, appears to be very clear.

By setting that requirement, Jews affirm their awareness of the subjects' right to compliance with the judicial norms in force by the state bodies.

It is interesting to note how this right is affirmed in such a clear-cut manner, and with expressions remarkably similar to those of the Jewish sages, in all declarations of rights from the earliest ones of Carolingian age, to modern constitutions.

Remaining within the medieval era, to which the Jewish texts we have mentioned belong, the comparison is very useful of the texts themselves and of the drafting of those charts of freedom and exemption that, substantially born as pacts among subjects on the one hand and monarchs and feudal lords on the other,[788] constitute the most direct progenitors of the modern constitutional charts.

785 R. Jacob Ben Asher, *Tur*, Hoshen Mishpat, ch. 369, no. 14, Sabbioneta ed., 1553: "The king's law is the law in all that he has established for the whole kingdom; This is said for a general matter that he ruled on all citizens of the State, such as when he imposes a fixed fee for each year or for each individual; or such as the confiscation of property of one who transgresses a given order, or the confiscation of the home or the field of one who has incurred in the king's wrath. In these cases, the goods confiscated by the king are not stolen property and one can buy them because the confiscation of the rebel's assets is the same law for everyone. But a king who against the State's law takes possession of a house or a field of an individual is a thief like any other, and it is forbidden to purchase from him."

786 R. Josef Caro, *Shulchan 'Aruch*, part 4: Hoshen Mishpat, ch. 369, nos. 2–9.

787 Israel Isserlein's *Sefer Terumat haddeshen* [finished in 1519], Antwerp, 1523, Daniel Bambergo ed., § 341: "And in the notes to Asherì [R. Asher ben Jechiel], ch. 1 of Bavà Mezi'à' on behalf of Mariah (?), who writes on behalf of Rabbenu Tam, [it is said that] all taxes that the ruler collects, even those that are undetermined, such as those for the needs of the troops or for other great needs, all are named "dinà demalchutà" [i.e., they are all legitimate], etc."

788 Mochi Onory, op. cit. below, pp. 60 et seqq.

As we learn from more recent studies on these charts,[789] the guarantee to the subjects against the state's illegal coercions is at the heart of the fundamental rights of the individual set by those very charts.[790] In those documents that Mochi Onory quotes in great quantities and studies with outstanding sharpness for the 10th to the 12th century, we find uniformly sanctioned the obligation for state bodies to refrain from any action contrary to the laws. By this obligation, "a sphere of activity free from *extra legem vel sine lege* actions of civil servants under the guarantee of permanent control over the legality of a certain provision of theirs or a certain claim of theirs" is judicially ensured to the subjects.[791] The obligation and consequent guarantee are set for all areas where the state exerts its activity: "that is both concerning the administration of justice, and in tax matters, as well as for the rules safeguarding physical integrity of the people and personal freedom or enjoyment of property."[792] Officials cannot "aliquid exquirere quod injustum aut contra legem videtur,"[793] must judge "secundum quod lex jubet,"[794] cannot take into custody anyone "nisi per legem,"[795] cannot "sua bona per vim tollere ... nisi secundum quod lex praecipit":[796] in short, whatever their rank and in any expression of their authority, they must act within the insurmountable barriers posed by law.[797]

Also, in the doctrine of the Church, this duty of the *princeps* or his subordinates to act within the limits of the law is clearly affirmed. Just like Maimonides, we see St. Thomas deal with the criteria for legality of the government's acts, in the "quaestio" regarding robbery, and establishes, just like the Jewish scholar, there is no difference between the robbery carried out by a private individual and an illegal and violent collection by the government.[798]

789 Robert V. Keller, *Freiheitsgarantien für Person und Eigentum im Mittelalter*, in *Deutschrechtliche Beiträge* hrg. K. Bayerle, XIV, Heft 1, Heidelberg, 1933; Sergio Mochi Onory, *Studi sulle origini storiche dei diritti essenziali della persona*, Bologna, 1937.

790 V. Keller, op. cit., pp. 188 et seqq.: Mochi Onory, op. cit., pp. 167 et seqq.

791 Mochi Onory, op. cit., p. 168.

792 Idem, p. 169.

793 Idem, ibidem.

794 Idem, pp. 172 et seqq.

795 Idem, pp. 194, no. 4 et seqq. pages.

796 Idem, pp. 264 et seqq. The legal collection in tax matters is specifically guaranteed by the Mathildic papers. See the texts ibidem, p. 175, no. 21.

797 Idem, pp. 343, 349 and passim.

798 St. Thomas, *Summa theologica*, 2nd of part 2, q. 66, art. 8: "Utrum rapina possit fieri sine peccato ... Preterea terrarum principes multa a suis subditis violenter extorquent, quod videtur ad rationem rapinae pertinere. Grave autem videtur dicere quod in hoc peccent, quia sic fere omnes principes damnarentur. Ergo rapina in aliquo casu est licita. Respondeo: ... Principibus potestas publica committitur ad hoc quod sint justitiae custodes; et ideo non licet eis violentia et coactione uti, nisi secundum justitiae tenorem,

Instead, the intermediate Roman doctrine allegations do not appear precise because jurists have to cope with contradictory Roman laws enacted in different periods and influenced by conflicting political conceptions. These jurists do not always manage to harmonize them in a unitary system. In terms of operational state action of ownership transfers, the Roman law had provided at an earlier time that, in the event of forced sale of an estate or movable property for unpaid taxes, the buyer would be free from the risk of a claim by the expropriated owner only if the sale had been made in compliance with all the formalities required by law. Otherwise, the claim could remain valid for as long as thirty years.[799] It is the same principle by which the Jewish sources abide, apart from the difference of the thirty-year prescription that they do not mention.

Later on, the limitation period of possible action was reduced to five years. Finally, Emperor Zeno suppressed the very possibility of action, declaring "statim securi" those who had received anything from the public revenue, by whatever designation: only a four-year action against the public revenue itself was permitted.[800] This was tantamount to declaring a property transfer made by the government valid, regardless of the government's compliance with the rules of law, and to authorize the courts to accept the government's action, even when illegal, that made that transfer effective, as the ground for an exception to a reclaim action that might have been submitted. Justinian upheld the norm by extending its significance.[801]

---

et hoc vel contra hostes pugnando, vel contra cives, malefactores puniendo, et quod per talem violentiam aufertur non habet rationem rapinae, cum non sit contra justitiam. Si vero contra justitiam aliqui per publicam potestatem violenter abstulerint res aliorum, illicite agunt, et rapinam committunt, et ad restitutionem tenentur ... Si principes a subditis exigant quod eis secundum justitiam debetur propter bonum commune conservandum, etiamsi violentia adhibeatur, non est rapina; si vero aliquid principes indebite extorqueant per violentiam, rapina est, sicut et latrocinium ... Unde ad restitutionem tenentur, sicut et latrones, et tanto gravius peccant quam latrones, quanto periculosius et communius contra publicam justitiam agunt, cuius custodes sunt positi."

799 C. 7, 39, 1 of Diocletian and Maximian, undated. See C. 4, 46, 2 (of Diocletian and Maximian) and 3 (y. 337).

800 C. 7, 37, 2.

801 C. 7, 37, 3 (y. 531). See Ist. 2, 6, § 14: "Edicto divi Marci cavetur eum, qui a fisco rem alienam emit, si post venditionem quinquennium praeterierit, posse dominium rei per exceptionem repellere. Constitutio autem divae memoriae Zenonis bene prospexit iis, qui a fisco per venditionem aut donationem vel alium titulum aliquid accipiunt, ut ipsi quidem securi statim fiant et victores existant, sive experiantur sive conveniantur, adversus autem sacratissimum aerarium usque ad quadriennium liceat intendere iis qui pro dominio vel hypoteca earum rerum, quae alienatae sunt putaverant sibi competere actiones. Nostra autem divina constitutio, quam nuper promulgavinus, etiam de iis qui a nostra vel

On the other hand, at around the same time, the principle was reaffirmed that the rescripts contrary to the *jus generale* were deemed entirely invalid and rejected by court judges while only the general constitutions were scrupulously followed.[802]

Facing such antinomies of Roman laws,[803] intermediate jurists could not but draw contrasting inferences, appealing each to a different text to support their respective theses. Confronted with the Justinian law on the sale by the Public Revenue Office, Accursio, a rigid guardian of legality on the part of the government, considers the sale valid only if the Office believes in good faith that the Public Revenue is the owner of the item; otherwise, the property remains to the *dominus* who can always reclaim it.[804]

Similarly, referring to the same law, the *Summa Codicis* subordinates the validity of property transfer to the existence of a "justa causa" in the government's act of expropriation.[805] Of course, these requirements of *bona fides* and *justa causa*, although attributed to Roman sources, are, in fact, innovations introduced by Accursio and the author of the *Summa*. This in a process similar to that noted above, inducing the Talmud scholars to see those distinctions

---

venerabili augustae domo aliquid acceperunt haec statuit, quae in fiscalibus alienationibus praefata zenoniana constitutione continetur."

802 C. 1, 22, 6: "Omnes cuiuscumque maioris vel minoris administrationis universa nostrae reipublicae judices monemus, ut nullum rescriptum, nullam pragmaticam sanctionem, nullam sacram adnotationem, quae generali juri vel utilitati publicae adversa esse videatur, in disceptatione cuiuscumque litigii patiantur proferri sed generales sacras constitutiones modis omnibus non dubitent observandas. Imper. Anastasius." C. 1, 9, 7: "Rescripta contra jus elicita ab omnibus judicibus refutari debent nisi forte aliquid est quod non laedat alium et prosit petenti vel crimen supplicantibus indulgeat." (y. 406)

803 One might deny the existence of an antinomy by noting that the two aforementioned laws prohibit the recognition only of the rescripts contrary to the law; while expropriations and Tax Revenues' sales are not executed by rescripts. They still are, nevertheless, administrative acts *contra legem*, and in the practice of the registries and theories of medieval jurists, under the term of the rescript, any expression of the sovereign will for a single case was included, without distinguishing. On this point, see the exact observations by Nicolini, op. cit., pp. 181–182.

804 Accursio, in C. 10, 4, gloss "distrahatur": If the Tax Revenue Office has a share of property on a thing, it can validly sell it. "Sed quid si nullam partem habet fiscus et vendit? Respondeo: aut credit suam et statim emptor est securus (ut C. 7, 37, 3); aut scit alienam et non prejudicat domino [that is the sale is invalid]; nam ideo praejudicat quia partem habet ut hic, ergo ubi non habet non praejudicat." Nicolini, op. cit., p. 243.

805 *Summa codicis*, book VII, ch. 27. De prescriptione quadriennali: After four years, he who has received from the Tax Revenue Office is "securus"; "Sin autem aliquis sciens rem alienam esse et ex nulla justa causa a principe accipiat, nulla ratione tueri potest quominus rem restituat ... ne inde iniuriarum sumatur occasio a quo [the Prince] iura initium sumpserunt." Nicolini, op. cit., p. 246; Carlyle, op. cit., vol. II, p. 73.

as already existing in the Mishnah, when actually they are modifications set by them.

For the theory of the government acts, Bartolo does not consider the two laws cited by Zeno and Justinian (C. 7, 32, 2 and 3). Instead, concerning the aforementioned norm on the rescripts (C. 22, 6, 1), he sets clear general principles, establishing, in perfect harmony of logic construction and exemplifications with Maimonides, that the *princeps* can take away something from a private individual either by the general norm – that is by an executive action endorsed by law – like confiscating the property of a convicted person, or *exercendo jurisdictionem* – which falls within the general rule – or finally by an administrative act relating to a particular case not contemplated in the general law. However, in that case, the reasoning for public utility must be produced.[806]

Therefore, for Accursio, the author of the Summa, and Bartolo, just like for Maimonides, government action by which a property is taken away from an individual and transferred to another individual must either be endorsed by general law, or, in its absence, by a cause of public utility. Outside these two hypotheses, the act itself is arbitrary and the purchaser, sued by the original owner, "nulla ratione tueri potest quominus rem restituat."

Against this opinion, which found many followers,[807] the opposite emerges soon, always notably based on Zeno's abovementioned law. Thus in this law, Baldo finds an argument against those who argue that the emperor cannot take away the *dominium* of one thing from one and give it to another "sine causa"; and clarifies that such inference can concord with the principle of the nullity of the rescripts *contra legem*, restricting such nullity to rescripts without the "non obstante lege" derogating clause.[808] even more markedly Angelo

806 Bartolo, in C. 1, 22, 6: "Circa hoc an princeps possit mihi auferre dominium rei meae, dic: 1) aut vult mihi auferre diminium jus commune condendo, et potest ...; 2) aut vult mihi auferre jurisdictionem exercendo, et potest ...; 3) aut vult mihi auferre privilegium alteri concedendo, et tunc *a*) aut vertitur in hoc publica utilitas, et potest ..., *b*) aut non vertitur publica utilitas, sed sola voluntas: tunc regulariter non potest." Cf. Nicolini, op. cit., pp. 185 and 222.

807 On the requirement of the cause in the expropriation by rescript, see Nicolini, op. cit. pp. 284–309.

808 Baldo, in *l. Omnes C. de quadr. praescr.* (C. 7, 37, 2), no. 1: "Pretendens causam onerosam vel lucrativam a fisco modo quocumque qui excogitari possit perpetuo est tutus; sed domino contra fiscum datur regressus usque ad quadriennium ... Hic est casus contra illos qui dicunt quod non potest imperator rem meam per privilegium alteri concedere, et auferre mihi dominium; et subaudi: "sine causa," quia ubi causa subesset, nulla est dubitatio ... Nec obstat supra, *de precibus Imper. offer. l. rescripta* (C. 1, 19, 7) ubi rescripta et privilegia per quae absorbetur jus alterius, nihil vaient ... quia concedo hoc, nisi habeant clausulam derogatoriam "non obstante lege" tunc ergo non tenent." The opposite interpretation of

degli Ubaldi states that the emperor may "auferre bona privatorum etiam sine causa," even adding: "et qui contrarium dicunt mentiuntur."[809] He does that, relying not only on the Justinian's law, substantiating that of Zeno (C. 7, 37, 3), but also on the Pandects fragment *Item si verberatum* (D. 6.1, 15, §2) concerning the allocation of private funds by the emperor to *milites*,

This opinion, although less followed, does not remain wholly isolated.[810]

3 Principles about the Validity of the Judicial Proceedings

So far, we have dealt with the attitude of the Jewish judicial doctrine towards the state's legislative and administrative acts. Now, it is time to consider the orientation towards the third power of the state: the judiciary.

While being typically quite open-minded in recognizing the constitutionality of laws and the legitimacy of executive acts, the Jewish scholars were instead constantly averse to the recognizing the competence of state courts in cases between Jews. According to Jewish tradition, in a dispute between Jews, the parties must turn to the rabbinical court if this, recognized by the state, operates in the same state concurrently with the civil court. If, on the contrary, there is no absolute rabbinical jurisdiction, the two litigants must refer the cause to a rabbi or to a simple Jew who shall rule as arbitrator.[811]

This norm is reflects the constant aspiration by Jewish scholars to see the Jewish judicial and normative autonomy recognized by the state. Bringing civil cases before state courts means not only showing contempt for the judicial autonomy but also endangering the normative autonomy, given that the state may very well determine to pronounce its judgments not according to Jewish

this passage given by Nicolini, op. cit., p. 247, attributing the introduction of the requirement of *justa causa* in the expropriations to Baldo, is certainly due to an oversight. On the value of the derogatory clauses, see Nicolini, op. cit., pp. 197–209.

809 Angelo degli Ubaldi from Perugia, *Commentaria in Digestum*, Venice, 1580, in D. 6, 1, 15 § 2. Nicolini, op. cit., p. 302 and notes.

810 Nicolini, op. cit., p. 302, no. 3.

811 Cf. for all Leon da Modena, *Historia dei riti hebraici*, part II, ch. 6, re-ed. in *Rassegna mensile di Israel*, January 1933, p. 389: "Nascendo differente e litigi di qual si sia cosa, nella maggior parte del mondo sono giudici li Rabini principali, o vero che si compromettono di volontà, ai doi, o tre arbitri communi amici. Li giuditii seguono conforme ciò ch'anno dichiarato li Rabini in molti volumi, nella parte ultimamente detta *Cosen amispatt*, e quantità d'allegationi in casi occorsi, detti *Seelod Tesciuvod*, cavati per lo più dall'Esodo, cap. 21, comincia: "Haec sunt judicia quae propones eis"; e li seguenti cap. 22 e 23 e dal Deuter. 22. 23. 24. 25 e secondo poi la retta mente dei giudici, che giudica rispetto la persona, il caso e il tempo."

civil law, but according to its own civil law: which means completely removing the validity from the Jewish civil law. The scholars, therefore, forbid Jews to bring cases before state courts under threat of severe spiritual sanctions; and this also for the simple defense of the principle of judicial autonomy, even when the state judges according to Jewish law, respecting normative autonomy.

These principles are repeatedly stated in the Talmud and Midrashim in the homiletic exegesis of Exodus 21, 1[812] On the other hand, it is unclear whether the ban on Jews to turn to non-Jewish judicial authorities also harbors the declaration of nullity of all rulings that may have been issued by such authorities. In general, the texts establish the ban and only in the Mechiltà[813] is the question of whether the pronunciations made by the pagan courts, i.e., the state courts, should be taken for good. In response, the prohibition on this point is repeated in the form of an interpretation of the text of Exodus, and the text of the Mishnah, 9.8 Ghittin, is then cited, pointing it out as a reflection of the prohibition itself, which proclaims the invalidity of pagan sentences in divorce matters. On this same non-validity, other later Palestinian[814] and Babylonian scholars[815] are in agreement.

In the eyes of Jewish doctrine, the principle of nullity of pagan pronouncements in divorce matters is inevitable. Conversely, it cannot be affirmed with confidence that all the judicial activities of the state in civil matters, when exercised between Jews, appeared null and void to the Talmud scholars and that, therefore, the judgments of state courts were considered inconsequential by the rabbinical courts. The prohibition against appearing before state courts in preference to Jewish ones was there, under stern threats, but it seems that, once one had turned to them, apart from spiritual penalties, their sentences were recognized as valid, and the dispute already ruled was regarded as not re-proposable being it *res judicata*. The only exception regarded the cases of divorce considered a too delicate matter and too connected with the ritual to be evaluated by non-Jews.

812 Babylonian Talmud, Ghittin, f. 88b; Midrash Tanhumà, Mishpatim, f. 91a and 93a; Mechiltà, f. 81b (Nezikin, sect. 1). These texts are reported above, footnote no. 313.

813 f. 81b cit; above, footnote no. 313.

814 Jer. Talmud, Ghittin 9, 9, text reported above, footnote no. 324.

815 Relying on Graetz's *History of the Jews*, American ed., vol. III, p. 92, Greenstone, entry Conflicts of Law, writes in *Jewish Encyclopedia* that in the seventh century of the common era, seeking Jewish women to obtain letters of divorce from their husbands using Mohammedan courts, the Babylonian Gheonim Hunai and Mar Rabà introduced several reforms in the Jewish laws concerning divorce in order to prevent such action by the Jewish side, thus making these appeals to state courts superfluous.

Later, while the ban generally persisted with the same severity,[816] there are explicit declarations of validity of judgments by state courts. Thus, Izhak Ben Moshè from Vienna, called *Or Zarua'*, affirms that "the decision of a state court that was not in conflict with the Jewish law is valid if the two litigants, in agreement and without coercion by the state, have given their preference to the secular court to the decision of their dispute."[817] Jehudà Hassid Ben Shemuel goes as far as to affirm that where the Jews are scattered and in small numbers, the judgment of a state court is preferable to that of unqualified local Jewish judges.[818]

---

816 The prohibition is repeated by all the scholars. Cf., e.g., the takkanà (ordinance) of the 12th century French rabbis, among whom Jacob ben Meir (R. Tam) and his brother Shemuel ben Meir, quoted by Finkelstein, *Jewish selfgovernment in the Middle Ages*, New York, 1924, p. 156 and the July 1225 provisions of the rabbinical synod of Mainz, Graetz, *Geschichte der Juden*, vol. VI, p. 199; vol. VII, p. 24. Still, in 1800 the statutes of the confraternity *Hevrà Kadishà* of Szegedin forbid to their members to appear before state courts. Löw, *Dinà* etc. cit., p. 356.

817 Izhak da Vienna, called Or Zarua', Bavà Kammà, Arkaot section 3, 4, 6. The quotation is by Shohet, op. cit., p. 99, to whom I leave the responsibility of it, since checking on that is now impossible to me.

818 Jehudà Hassid Ben Shemuel [lived around 1200], *Sefer Hassidim*, Berlin 1891, 1301. Quotation as above by Shohet, op. cit., p. 101. Interesting is an opinion of the tossafot and of R. Izhak ben Perez, reported by R. Josef Colon, *Sheelot utshuvot* cit., no. 188, according to whom anyone who has contractually obligated himself by public deed drawn up by public officials of the state may no longer apply to the Jewish court for a dispute relating to the contract itself, but must inevitably turn to state courts: he has in fact voluntarily left the Jewish law, and therefore "he is not given heed anymore for this case because the state law is the law." R. Colon argues that this principle can possibly apply only to those private acts "for which one could have Jewish Chancellor and witnesses [that is, that he could, get them drawn up according to Jewish law], because in this case, one should really say: since he left the Jewish law and has linked himself to the other, he manifests the intention of wanting to be judged according to their law; but regarding anything related to the king himself [i.e., mandatory rules of public policy], as in this case where one has unavoidably to follow the rule of the king [i.e. one has to turn to the state notaries for the drawing up of the deed], it cannot be said: since he left, etc., because he could not do otherwise; and the same opinion it is also shared by R. Shimshon from Chinon. In addition, R. Asher [ben Jechiel] in a consulting expressly says that even if in a contract it is written that a party can sue the other in either court, if he brings the matter before the gentile court he is a desecrator and therefore must turn to the Jewish court only, and also in the Tur [by Jacob ben Asher] it is written that if the debtor tells the creditor: you can sue me in the gentile court, the creditor [if he does so] is excommunicated, because by having said that the debtor does not mean to annul the din torà [Jewish law; it is supposed in fact that the gentile court will not apply this law], but only to reinforce the assurance that he will pay up."

The two greatest codifiers, namely Maimonides and Josef Caro, while reaffirming, on the one hand, the generic prohibition against turning to state courts, even by mutual agreement, consider it legitimate to turn to them with the permission of the rabbinical court, permission to be requested by the plaintiff if the defendant refuses to appear in the rabbinical court.[819]

It is quite clear that in these cases when appearing before the state court is deemed lawful from a Jewish point of view, the judgments issued by such courts are considered valid. In cases brought before state jurisdiction against the Jewish provisions, on the other hand, in the absence of explicit statements by the sources, the question remains that the rabbinic doctrine may not recognize the validity of judgments with which such cases are decided.

But as a rule, Jewish sages upheld the approval of the state acts based on the principle of "dinà demalchutà dinà," where the word "dinà" (law), taken in the broader sense of "manifestation of the will," included all legislative, administrative and judiciary acts and they carefully listed all the exceptions to this general principle. Therefore, nothing having been said about the judgments of state courts and despite the ban mentioned earlier to bring cases before these courts, we can assume that once enacted, such judgments had to

819 Maimonides, *Mishneh Torah*, Ilchot, Sanhedrin (Norms on the tribunals), ch. 26, § 7 = Josef Caro, *Shulchan 'Aruch*, Hoshen Mishpat, ch. 26 § 1 and 2: § 1. It is forbidden to bring the causes before gentile judges and in their courts, even if it is a cause they decide according to Jewish norms. It is forbidden even if the two litigants agreed to be judged by them. He who appears to be judged by them is evil and it is like he would insult the Torà and raise his hand against it. § 2. If the Gentile [the State] has the power (?) and the defendant is powerful as well and [the plaintiff] cannot be saved with the Jewish court, he should first sue him to this latter court; if the defendant does not want to appear, then he should apply for an authorization from the rabbinical court and take the case to the gentile court." For other minor rules, see Caro, ibid., §§ 3 and 4. Compare this to the similar provision of the rules of the Jews of Castile of 1432 (Ordenamiento formado por los procuradores de las aliamas hebreas, Valladolid, y. 1432, published by Isidor Loeb in *Révue des Etudes juives*, vol. XIII, 1886, pp. 187 et seqq.), cap. III: "No Jew or a Jewess will bring a person before a court, whether ecclesiastical or secular, that is not of our faith, even if such court decides according to the law of Israel, except for matters relating to the payment of taxes or levies or cash or other rights of our Lord the King, or of our Lady the Queen or of money or a right of the Church or of a local lord or lady. He who will break this law will be excommunicated ... and will pay 1000 maravedis to the Jew who sued him or to whom the Rabbi of the Court will determine. But if a Jew refuses to appear in court after three summons, the Rabbi and the judges of the Jewish community may give permission to summon him before the non-Jewish court." The text is reported also by Finkelstein, *Jewish Self-government in the Middle Ages*, cit., pp. 361–362.

be considered valid, so as to make cases already decided by them before the rabbinical court inadmissible.

•••

Until the late Middle Ages, as a rule, the administrative duty to ensure that public faith was applied to acts between individuals, i.e., the same office that was later handed over to notaries, was the courts' responsibility. Since the most ancient times, Jewish doctrine recognized such activity of the State as legitimate and thus admitted the formal validity of the acts concluded before the courts, even if the form did not correspond to that required by Jewish law: only a few acts, given their specific nature, were excepted.[820]

We will deal with this principle in the following pages concerning the deferment question.

•••

Summing everything up, we can establish the following points:

1) In certain periods, there is a contrast between Jewish constitutional principles and those set by the legislation and doctrine of the Christian states.
2) Having these constitutional principles some reflections in the field of relations between individuals, the contrast between them in the decision of civil cases between Jews ends up falling into the broader sphere of conflict between Jewish law and state law. Any possible dispute arising between two Jews about the ownership of an asset taken away by the state from one of the two and then handed over by the same state to the other, or indirectly received by the latter, can have a different outcome. In assessing the (legislative or administrative) act with which the item at the center of the dispute had been expropriated, the outcome may depend on the court's application to which one had turned, of the Jewish constitutional criteria or non-Jewish ones.
3) In the absence of precise jurisprudential information on similar cases, since the constitutional criteria were a matter of public law, it seems safe to presume, as we have already said, that the state court adopted the policy set by Roman laws and by the doctrine of civil law; and that the application of Jewish principles took place only in the rabbinical courts.

820 Mishna, Ghittin, 1, 5. See this text further on, footnote no. 823.

If, as it is likely, this had happened, it was not, however, without offense to the judicial logic, since with two concurring jurisdictions either of which one could turn to, this would have imposed theoretically equal rulings, that is, practically based on the application of the same norms. Hence, to be effective, the unity of legislation should have had to cover private law and all the rules of public law somehow relating to relations of private nature.[821]

821 The conflict between personal norms and local norms regulating confiscations and expropriations is considered also by modern internationalists. Usually, the matter concerns exiles claiming from the location of their residence abroad the property of chattels, which for political reasons their state has confiscated transferring them to foreigners or citizens who later also expatriated with the goods in question. If the court empowered with the cognizance of the cause considers the provisions on the basis of which the confiscation has taken place as illegitimate because in contrast with the local constitutional principles and with those of public order, the goods at issue are assigned to their former owner. Otherwise, the latter's claim is rejected and the right of the new owner is confirmed. In the praxis, there are decisions in both ways. On this point, see Fedozzi, *Il diritto internazionale privato. Teorie generali e diritto civile* in *Trattato di diritto internazionale*, vol. IV, Padua, 1935, pp. 659–661.

CHAPTER 10

The Deferment Question

1 The Form of the Acts[822]

The earliest mention of Jewish sources of the relationship between Jewish law and state law in the private field is found in the Mishnah, in the divorce treaty (Ghittin, 1.5).

It states there that, although, by Jewish law, Gentiles cannot witness agreements drawn up between Jews, and therefore any deed undersigned by them is invalid, the acts issued by state courts are considered valid even if undersigned by Gentiles. However, deeds of divorce and liberation of slaves make the exception, as for them, the public form of the deed cannot compensate for the lack of undersigning formalities by Jewish witnesses. A part of the doctrine rejects the exception and considers that the public nature of the measure is such that always compensates for the lack of the requirement for witnesses to be Jewish, even in the event of divorce and liberation proceedings.[823]

However, it is insisted on the need to recognize as valid only the deeds drawn up in court, such as public offices par excellence and thus such as to provide every guarantee of perfect legality.[824]

822 Regarding the systematic processing of the material included in this chapter, I would like to warn that by the expression "form of the acts" I mean including only the peculiarities inherent in the scriptures. Following the best civil law doctrine, I do not consider as formal elements either the various means of conclusion of the contracts or even less so the more extensive category of the means of right acquisition. This paragraph will therefore be devoted to those peculiarities; the rest will be mentioned in the following paragraph.

823 Mishnah, Ghittin, 1, 5: "All acts that are drafted in the courts of the Gentiles shall be valid except for the letters of divorce and of slave liberation. R. Shim'on says: these are valid too; they were mentioned [as invalid] only if drawn up by private [Gentiles, instead of public officials]." Similarly, Babylonian Talmud, Ghittin f. 11a: "It has been taught: on behalf of R. Josè, R. El'azar said: so R. Shim'on said to the sages of Sidon: about the acts drawn up in the courts of the Gentiles, R. 'Akivà [first half of the second century] and the sages agree that, although the signatories are Gentiles, they are all valid, including the divorce and slave liberation acts. They disagree only in the case that [such documents] are drawn up by private individuals, etc."

824 Babylonian Talmud, Ghittin f. 11a: Rabina [d. approximately 422 C.E.; see *Jüdisches Lexikon* entry Rawina] intended to declare valid a document which had been prepared in an assembly of Aramaeans. Rafrem [about the same era] said to him: We have learned: the courts. [i.e., the acts undersigned by Gentiles are valid only if they are issued by the courts].

 DOI:10.1163/9789004627154_013

The reason for the distinction between these two acts (divorce and liberation of slaves) and all others regarding the possibility of acceptance of public form in the absence of Jewish witnesses undersigning, draws its origin from the nature of the two transactions. Being these unilateral, they are finalized with a written deed alone. Since it constitutes the very substance of the trade, such deed must be encircled by every formal guarantee, and therefore not even the seal of authenticity stamped by the court is sufficient: the undersigning of Jewish witnesses is a *conditio sine qua non* for the validity of the deed.

Concerning the validity of the public deed drawn up by Gentiles, the Babylonian Talmud, commenting on the passage in the Mishnah, is precisely in this order of ideas, noting the strangeness of the lack of distinction between a sale and a donation. That the general rule applies to a sale, a transaction perfected with monetary payment where the act is not but a mere proof – the sages note – it is understandable, but it is hard to understand a similar open-mindedness about donation. In this latter, in the absence of the price, the written deed constitutes the very essence of the transaction and would therefore need the same formal guarantees required for the letter of divorce and act of slave liberation. Logically, an act undersigned by Gentiles should be null and void also in the donation. It can, however, be considered valid according to the letter of the text of the Mishnah and applying Shemuel Jarchinai's principle to the case: the law of the State is the law. But its invalidity can also be sustained by expanding the significance of that text, and making it sound like: "except for deeds similar to the acts of divorce," rather than just: "except for the acts of divorce."[825]

It is interesting to note that on applying the formula "locus regit actum" even modern treatises of International Law distinguish between the forms of solemn acts and those of not solemn acts. By reasoning quite similar to the aforementioned by Talmud sages, in this respect, Laurent distinguishes

825 Babylonian Talmud, Ghittin f. 10b: "The Mishnah sets a comprehensive rule in which no distinction between sale and donation is made. But in the sale, the buyer acquires the object from the moment he payes in their [sc.: of the judges of the state court] presence, and the document is only a proof: because if he had not paid the money in their presence they would not hurt themselves [i.e., they would not have taken the responsibility of drafting a false claim]. Whereas in the donation, with what does he purchase? Indeed, isn't it with that document? But this document is a valueless crock [i.e., it is invalid]. Shemuel says: the State law is the law. [Thus the act, valid according to the state forms is also valid from the Jewish point of view]. Or you can answer, if you want: instead of reading, in the Mishnah: "except for the letters of divorce," read: "except like for the letters of divorce." [That is: from the rule of the validity of the public acts undersigned by Gentiles exclude not only the acts of divorce and of liberation, but all acts of the same nature; that is, consider the mention of two acts as explanatory rather than peremptory]."

between acts of sale and donation. "The writing – he notes[826] – formed to establish a sale, serves only as proof and is not necessary either for its validity or its existence; Whereas in donation, the form is the precondition for the contract to exist. Solemnity is therefore essential for the judicial act, as in the eyes of the law, the act has no existence whatsoever unless written in the forms that the law has established. However, in solemn contracts, form affects substance and consensus. The latter does not exist unless expressed in the forms required by the law; if these forms are not respected, there is no consensus, and therefore – no contract."

Setting the same distinction between acts where the writing serves as proof (such as a sale) and those where writing constitutes the very substance of the transaction (such as a donation), the Talmud believes that the formal requirements of the former could also be applied to local law (as long as the public form is heeded). Conversely, for the latter, where the form – to express the concept in Roman-style words – "dat esse rei," the Talmud considers it logical that the formal requirements themselves are governed by personal law, i.e., by the Jewish law. Accordingly, deeds should be considered void if they lack this underwriting obligation by Jewish witnesses as demanded by Jewish law. Furthermore, it is only after having elaborated this just concept that tribute is paid to the tendency of the jurist Shemuel, favorable, in principle, to the recognition of state law. While also recognizing the contrary theory as sustainable, the Talmud admits that even in donations, where the written act constitutes not a proof but actual substance of the transaction, the deed itself is to be considered valid even if a gentile public official compiles it, and thus lacks that requirement for the witnesses to be Jewish as prescribed by Jewish law.

However, in this Talmudic passage, it should be noted that the assumption is that in any sale, only the payment is the constituent element of the transaction and that the act is simple proof. In contrast, the act is always the only constitutive element in the donation.

In reality, the general principles of Jewish law about the perfection of contracts of sale and donation are quite different. The Mishnah (kiddushin 1,5) declares that "the real estate can be purchased with one of the three following means: the payment, the written act, the appropriation; the movables just by appropriation. Elsewhere (Bavà Batrà 9.7), it states that "in the verbal distribution of the goods, whether done by a healthy or ill person, the beneficiary cannot purchase real estate but by ordinary means, that is, the [symbolic]

826 Laurent, *Principles de droit civil*, vol. 1, no. 99. Cf. Di Stefano Napolitani, *La massima "locus regit actum."* Palermo, 1883, pp. 40–49, and Fedozzi, *Il diritto internazionale privato. Teorie generali e diritto civile*. Padua, 1935, pp. 252–253.

payment, the written act, the appropriation; and the movables only by appropriation." That means the verbal distribution alone is void and that the donation can only be accomplished by the means mentioned above. Likewise, marriage is understood as the purchase agreement of the wife and thus accomplished (kiddushin 1.1) "by one of the three following ways: money [given to the woman to marry her], the act of marriage, the appropriation [by coitus]. In the Gemara, another purchase means is mentioned, common to both movable and real estate, consisting in giving any object, mostly a handkerchief (*sudar*, from Latin *sudarium*) from the purchaser to the seller. As it comes into the seller's possession, that object determines *ipso jure* the purchaser's entry in possession of the purchased goods, even if the actual price has not been paid, nor has the deed of purchase been drafted, nor has the deed of purchase acts of possession been realized.[827] This "*Kinyan Sudar*" (purchase of the handkerchief), a symbolic substitute for payment of the actual price, or memento of a time when money did not yet exist, and bartering was the only possible

827 Babylonian Talmud, Bavà Mezi'à, f. 47b: "How is the *Kinyan* done? Rav says: with the objects of the person who buys, because the buyer wants the seller to permanently purchase the object. Levì says: with the objects of the seller because he shares the opinion of R. Jehudà who intends the passage of Ruth [4, 7; v. n. 8] like this: the avenger of the blood gave Booz the shoe; but the rule follows the Rav's opinion. The *Kinyan* is done with valuables worth even less than one perutà [a coin of the lowest value]. R. Nachman includes fruits and R. Sheshet includes them, etc." Mention of *Kinyan* also in Babylonian Talmud, Kiddushin f. 3a and f. 13a and Bavà Mezi'à f. 7a. Maimonides, *Ilchot mechirà* [norms on selling], ch. 5, § 5. "Lands, slaves, cattle and all other movables, each of them is bought by bartering (halifin); and this is what is called Kinyan; and the essence of this way is that the buyer gives the seller an object whatsoever and tells him: buy all this in exchange for the courtyard goods or the wine or the animal or the slave which you have sold to me for so much. As soon as the seller has raised the object and has bought it, the buyer acquired that land, or wine, or beast, or slave, even though he has not yet made the act of drawing to himself what he buys and has not given the price; and neither can later have regrets about it. § 6 … the *Kinyan* is not done with the objects of the seller but with those of the buyer." Josef Caro, *Shulchan 'Aruch*, Hoshen Mishpat, ch. 195, § 1: How is the *Kinyan* done? He who buys gives the person who sells an object whatsoever and says: buy this in exchange for the land or movable that you have sold or donated to me. When the seller draws this item toward himself, the buyer has purchased and so also does the beneficiary, wherever the sold or donated goods are located, even though there has been neither payment nor drafting of a deed, nor an appropriation and although there have not been any witnesses. 2. An object is needed there, even if it is not worth a perutà. Forbidden things, fruit, coins and things of the seller are excluded."

way of buying,[828] is a means of purchase known in ancient Jewish law[829] and then seems to disappear to reappear in the era of the Amorites,[830] becoming of everyday use only in the Middle Ages. Neither Maimonides nor the Gemara mentions it along with the other three means of concluding contracts[831] but

828 It is not easy to determine if this is a symbolic price, that chronologically followed the real price which would have been paid in ancient times, or rather a survival of the barter, the matrix of all contracts. In Germanic law, the launegild (*lohngeld*) is most likely a symbolization of the price, but with other peoples, similar payments seem original and non-derivative.

829 Ruth, 4, 7: "And this was an ancient practice in Israel relatively to redeeming or bartering or to finalize any contract: one would take his shoe off and gave it to his fellow, and this was the testimony in Israel." The Jewish scholars from the Talmud onward (Babylonian Talmud, Bavà Mezi'à, f. 47b cit.; Talmud Kiddushin, ger, 1, 5) all agree that this method of purchase and the *Kinyan Sudar* are basically the same things. And also from the scientific point of view, the thing seems to be certain. However, chronologically, a certain solution of continuity between the two institutions is indeed there.

830 On this issue, Asher Gulak, *Jesodè ha-mishpat ha-'ivrì* [The fundamentals of Jewish law], Berlin, 1923, (4 vols. in Hebrew) vol. I, p. 106, writes: "The purchase by means of the shoe has given rise to the purchase method by means of the delivery of a cloth (*sudar*), a system that developed at the time of the Amorites and that has been adopted in Jewish law to date. In the Talmudic era, the delivery of the *sudar* was seen as the replacement of the price of the purchased object, as some kind of fake trade-in. The buyer would give the seller a *sudar* or another object of his property and with the exchange of this object, the seller would transfer the property of the object purchased to the buyer. The system of purchasing by means of the *sudar* is based on the handing over of the shoe as described in the book of Ruth. However, in the Mishnah this purchase system is not clarified and also at the time of the early Amorites it is not sufficiently understood, so much so that Rav and Levì [Babylonian Talmud, Bavà Mezi'à, f. 47b; Jer. Talmud, Kiddushin 1, 5] discuss how it should be performed, whether with objects belonging to the buyer or to the seller. One can surmise that the acquisition by the shoe was forgotten and was then renewed at the time of the early Amorites. Support for this conjecture can be found in a passage of the Talmud of Jerusalem [Kiddushin 1, 5 = Midrash Ruth rabbà, 4, 7]: "At the beginning, one purchased by means of the shoe, as it is said in Ruth, 4, 7, etc. ... then one purchased by means of *kezizà* [another symbolic form of purchase in which the cracking (*kezizà*) of walnuts would represent the breaking of the possession; the text is repeated in Jer. Talmud, ketubot, 2, 10] ... afterward they purchased by money, or written deed or appropriation." At the time of Gemara the purchase by means of *sudar* became the most common one and wherever the expression "*kanù mijadò*" [they bought from his hand] or "*kinyan*" [buying] in general is found, it refers to the *Kinyan Sudar*. A few lines on the *Kinyan Sudar* are also written by M. W. Rapaport, *Der Talmud und sein Recht*, IV, *Formen der Obligation*, in the *Zeitschrift für vergleichende Rechtswissenschaft*, vol. XV, 1902, pp. 187–188, and by Josef Kohler, *Darstellung des talmudischen Rechtes* in the same *Zeitschrift*, vol. XX, 1907, p. 206, the latter jotted down hastily and not without inaccuracies.

831 Maimonides, *Ilchot Mechirà*, ch. 1 in princ. = Mishnah, Kiddushin 1, 5: "The real estate is purchased by money, or written deed, or by appropriation; the movable property only by appropriation."

separately,[832] and only in Jacob Ben Asher's Tur are four means of purchase cited: the three of the Mishnah and the *Kinyan Sudar*.[833] It is worth noting that the institution is essentially identical in nature and functions to the Germanic launegild,[834] the Roman *arrha*,[835] and similar givings which are at the basis of the conclusion of contracts, especially those free of charge among many primitive peoples.[836]

Finally, the Talmud itself admits that if there is a particular customary form to conclude purchase contracts, such as a mark placed on the object to buy, the

832 Maimonides, *Ilchot Mechirà*, ch. 5, § 5 above mentioned, no. 6.

833 Jacob Ben Asher, *Tur*, Hoshen Mishpat, ch. 190: "The real estate is purchased by means of one of these things: money, written deed, appropriation, *Kinyan Sudar*." = Caro, *Shulchan 'Aruch* hoshen mishpat, ch. 190. Cf. Leon da Modena, *Historia dei riti hebraici*, part 2, ch. 6, re-published in *Rassegna mensile di Israel*, January 1933, p. 389, which reflects the Italian praxis of the 16th century: "Every contract is finalized by each of the parties touching the edge of the cloth or of other witnesses' drape, almost in guise of a oath, called *chinian sudar*, which means the purchase of the drape." The original nature of the *Kinyan Sudar* here is no longer understood.

834 Which is also a price, that later became symbolic and represented by an object whatsoever, a coat, a pair of gloves, a shirt or similar. Once the launegild is given the negotiation is perfected and as the obligation arises on the parties to deliver the item on one hand, and deliver the real price on the other hand. The best pages on launegild are those by Schupfer, *Il diritto privato dei popoli germanici con speciale riguardo all'Italia*, vol. III, *Le obbligazioni*, Città di Castello-Rome-Turin-Florence 1909, pp. 173–181 and 230–233. Schupfer points out that the launegild is first used in sales and then, as it becomes a purely symbolic price, extends to other causes, especially to the donation and other negotiations with no charge involved, where it persists longer than in negotiations involving high costs, in which the real price replaces it. With that, Schupfer appears to assume that the object is symbolic of the price and chronologically posterior to it; and not that the price is a transformation of the item, used exclusively in ancient times. But the issue is not resolved. On the launegild see also Pertile, *Storia del diritto italiano*, 2nd ed., vol. XIV, pp. 579–583 and Siciliano-Villanueva in *Digesto Italiano*, sub voce. In Jewish law, the *Kinyan Sudar* remains, as a means to close a deal, in addition to the donation, also in onerous contracts, alongside the real price, the deed, or the appropriation.

835 As demonstrated by Tamassia, *Il launegildo in Grecia*, in *Archivio giuridico*, XLIV, 1890, pp. 371–373 and 379, by archaic *arrha* it is understood that in origin it is too the price and only later it became a simple guarantee and a penalty in case of recess. Also the *arrha sponsalicia*, which enters the late Roman law from the Jewish law through the nomocanons of the eastern Church, is nothing more than the original price of the bride (the biblical *mohar*). Volterra, *Studi sull'arrha sponsalicia*, part 3, Rome, 1930, pp. 1 and seqq. For some traces of similar payments in Greece, see Tamassia, op. cit., pp. 373–378.

836 Post, *Giurisprudenza etnologica*, It. transl., pp. 456 and 505 (Samoans, Tlingit, etc.); Wilutzky, *Vorgeschichte des Rechts*, vol. II, Berlin, 1903, pp. 74–75 (Polynesians, Bantu, Hottentots).

purchase made in this way should also be considered completed from a Jewish standpoint.[837]

Suppose the transfer of ownership is done indifferently in one of the ways listed. On the one hand, this means a written bill of sale can indeed sometimes be a mere proof testifying that the conclusion of a contract occurred through payment or appropriation by the buyer, or *Kinyan Sudar* or something else; or is in itself an element of completing the contract.[838] Reciprocally, on the other hand, it means that in the donation, the deed is not always the only way to set the deal in motion, but this can also be accomplished with the *Kinyan Sudar*, with the appropriation of the donated item, or by other customary means when the deed remains a simple proof.[839] When interpreting the *mens* [mind] of the

---

837 Babylonian Talmud, Bavà Mezi'à, f. 74a. And on the basis of this text, see Caro, *Shulchan 'Aruch*, Hoshen Mishpat, ch. 201, §§ 1 and 2.

838 That the written deed alone may be the perfecting element of the deal is controversial among the Talmud scholars, who conclude however affirmatively: Jer. Talmud, Kiddushin, 1, 5, following the passage reported by Gulak (no. 830 above): "[It can be purchased] "by written deed," it is said. R. Jirmijà had thought to have to say that the written deed is enough to purchase when no money is there to be paid (i.e., when it is a matter of donation); but when the contract involves a payment of money (i.e., when it is a sale), the purchasing will be made only by means of payment of money. R. Jona and R. Josè deny this both claiming that, even before the payment of money, the purchase has been perfected by means of the contract." Together these two scholars, and with them R. Johanan, against R. Abà's opinion in agreement with that of Shemuel, maintain that even the mere payment of money, without redaction of the deed, is sufficient to finalize the contract. (ibid.). Also the Babylonian Gemara (f. 26a) of the same text of Kiddushin 1, 5 contains the same discussion: "whence does it come that one purchases with money? Hizkija said: from the verse of Jeremiah [32, 16] that recites "fields are purchased with money." I shall say [it was objected to him] that they cannot be bought as long as there is no deed because the passage continues: "a leaflet be drafted and sealed"? [Hizkijà] replied: If the verb to buy would follow these two verbs, then it would be as you say. However, since "be bought" is written first, it is the money that makes the buying and the deed is a simple guarantee. Rav said: that the money alone is enough to make the buying it is said only where the deed is not drafted, but where it is drafted, the money alone does not make the purchase. But if it is explained and said: if I want to purchase with the money only, "then he is free [to do so]; and after handing over the money he cannot change his mind anymore [having the contract already being perfected]. Where is it established [that the purchase is done] with the deed? From Jeremiah's verse [32, 11]: "I took the purchase leaflet." Shemuel said: that it is the document that makes the buy has been said only for the deed of donation; but in the sale, the buying is done only when the money is handed over. Whence does it come [that the purchase is done] with the appropriation? Hizkijà said, from Jeremiah's verse [?]: Stay in your cities of which you have taken possession"(!). Mobile assets are purchased only with the appropriation. Whence is this coming? From the verse [Leviticus, 25, 14]: "When you make a sale or a purchase removing from the hand of the seller."

839 The opinion of the text of Ghittin f. 10b that considers the donation to be concluded only by means of the document and therefore excludes the validity of the deed signed

Talmudic jurist, rather than referring to the distinction concretely brought up between acts of purchase and sale and acts of donation, it is necessary to refer the rule in general about the validity of documents drawn up by public officials to the distinction between *ad probationem tantum* and *ad substantiam* acts. In the quoted text of Ghittin 10b, according to an opinion (the second one), only acts representing the simple evidence of a legal transaction, but not those in which the transaction actually takes place, are valid if they carry the signature of the gentile public officials. According to the opposite opinion (the first one) the distinction should not be made, and all acts should be declared as valid as a consequence of the principle of Shemuel; except for the two that are listed in the Mishnah.

Concerning the same question, the post-Talmudic Babylonian sages (the *Gheonim*) show absolute determination and deny validity to all the acts issued by the state authorities.[840]

Conversely, Maimonides[841] backs the opinion expressed in the mentioned Talmudic text, rejecting the application of the principle "dinà demalchutà

---

by Gentiles is the same one expressed by Shemuel in the aforementioned text. But that the donation, besides by means of the document, is concluded by the other ways of purchasing sees the medieval authors in agreement. So says also Maimonides, op. cit., Ilchot Zechijà Umattanà, [rules on purchase and donation], ch. 3, who equalizes sale and donation, saying: "If one makes a donation to another, the beneficiary does not acquire if not by one of the ways by which the buyer acquires the object bought; i.e. in case of a movable he does not buy until after having done the raising or the move to draw [the item] towards himself or another of the ways by which one buys movables. In the case of real estate or slaves, he does not buy until he operates the appropriation, as the buyer does, or the donation deed reaches his hand. The purely verbal donation is not valid." Jacob Ben Asher, *Tur*, Hoshen Mishpat, ch. 241 expresses himself in the very same way. It is interesting to note that while in the Talmud it is claimed that in the donation the written deed is sufficient to operate the conclusion of the deal and there are even those who believe that it is the only way, in medieval Germanic law the deed has a hard time acquiring such an autonomy. Liutprand also establishes (ch. 73) that the donation deeds that do not contain the mention of the launegild are not valid: which is to say that it is the launegild the means for perfecting the deal, whereas the deed does not have but a simple guarantee value.

840 *Teshuvot ha-Gheonim*, Harkavy editor, 1887, Berlin, 278, 424, 491; *Teshuvot Gheonè mizrach uma'arav*, J. Müller editor, Berlin, 1888, p. 199. I am drawing these two quotes, without the possibility of cross-checking them, from Shohet, op. cit., p. 96.

841 Maimonides, *Mishneh Torah*, Ilchot Malvè Velovè, [Rules on creditor and debtor], ch. 27: "A contract, in any language and character it may be written, if it is done according to the rules of the Jewish contracts so that they cannot be falsified nor have additions or subtractions, and if the witnesses are Jews who are able to read it, then is valid ... Conversely, every contract undersigned by Gentiles is not valid. The exceptions are the purchase contracts and those of obligation as long as [the buyer] gave the money before them [the

dinà" to the donation acts and other acts not constituting a simple proof. He establishes the following points:

1) As a rule, only an act drawn up following the Jewish law's formal and substantive requirements is valid. For example, the presence of two witnesses[842] and the quality of their being Jews are a formal imperative requirement. However, neither the Hebrew language nor the Hebrew characters are required.

2) The non-Jewish form – i.e., the possibility of subscribing by less than two witnesses and by non-Jewish witnesses – is permitted for purchase and sale acts and obligation acts (*hov*), as acts that constitute a simple proof. In such acts, mention must nevertheless be made of the delivery of the sale price or the obligation money, precisely to prove that the act was perfected with this delivery and not with the writing, which is only a declaration. To be valid, the document drawn up under non-Jewish form must be a public act emanating from the court or the public notary.[843] Maimonides rejects a more restrictive view of his teachers, who admitted the validity of non-Jewish form only for sale and not for the obligation.

3) The acts in which the script itself creates the negotiation, precisely the acts of "confession, renunciation, donation, transaction," are therefore considered invalid if prepared according to non-Jewish form, even if they are public acts (i.e., subscribed by non-Jewish witnesses).

---

judges or the notary] and they write in the contract: before us this fellow gave to that fellow this much as the sale price or the money of the bond and as long as these contracts are made in their [the Gentiles'] tribunals; but [the contracts made] in the place where they gather to the have legal discussions without validation of their judge have no value whatsoever. And also Jewish witnesses are necessary who testify that these Gentiles are the contract's witnesses and also that the judge has validated their testimony, and that they are not known as corruptible. But if any one of these things is missing in the contracts undersigned by the Gentiles, the contracts are completely worthless; and so are the contracts of confession (הודאות), donation (מתנות), transaction (פשרות) and waiver (מחילות) made with gentile witnesses, even when all the things above mentioned are there. My teachers decided that also the obligation contracts made by them [the Gentiles], even when the money was paid in their presence, are invalid, as valid are only contracts of sale if the money was paid in their presence: but I disagree on that."

842 See for all of them Leon da Modena, *Historia dei riti hebraici*, part 3, ch. 6, in *Rassegna mensile di Israel*, re-edition, January 1935, p. 389: "Non vien data tra loro [gli ebrei] niuna autorità a notari pubblici, se non il scrivano val per un testimonio e con doj testimonj si forma et è valido qual si voglia scrittura di negotio, di testamento, di matrimonio, di repudio e d'ogni altra cosa immaginabile. Per valersene poi in ogni tempo e luogo chi vuole vi fa far una legalità da tre altri, quali si chiamano giudici del caso."

843 Maimonides (ibid.) however also admits the validity of a contract of sale or an obligation drawn up in a non-Jewish and non-public form if the title is delivered by the seller to the buyer or by the debtor to the creditor before two non-Jewish witnesses who can read and read it upon delivery. But the content must be governed by Jewish law.

Maimonides thus follows the second of the two opinions expressed in the Talmud, denying that for acts of donation – and typically for others that constitute the substance of negotiation – drafting by a notary is valid; regardless of whether or not a general rule of the state imperatively requires a public act for the donation.

Others, too, espouse this view, considering that Shemuel's principle that "the law of the State is law" cannot be invoked but on "things that are advantageous to the king," i.e., concerning rules issued given an interest of the state. However, they cannot be invoked with those purely private interests, like donations. They note that in the Talmud itself, the principle is mentioned only about norms where the king's interest is at stake. To this end, they cite Bavà Batrà f. 54b passage – pointing to the royal law that prescribes the chirograph to validate the sale of real estate – noting the fiscal motive underlying this; and Bavà Kammà f. 113b passage – admitting the validity of state law on the confiscation of palm trees for the construction of bridges for public use – underlining the public nature of the provision. As a result, they conclude that even when general law prescribes a notarial act to conclude the donation, from a Jewish standpoint, this does not validate the notarial act itself, as the law deems no state interest: what good comes to the king by having the donation made with a form rather than otherwise?

Several scholars oppose this argument, mainly three Spaniards: R. Shelomò Ben Aderet,[844] R. Nissim Gherondi and R. Moshè Ben Nachman. They indicate that the Talmud adopts the principle of "the law of the State is the law," also concerning hypotheses where the king's advantage is absent entirely. For example, the case presented in Bavà Batrà f. 55a of the Persian law relating to a 40-year-long usucaption. From this, they infer the appropriateness of recognizing the form prescribed by state law as valid also in relations where no public interest is at stake: to make the recognition acceptable; it is sufficient that the law is binding. Therefore, also in donation, if the law requires recourse to the notary, the deed drawn up shall be valid *jure hebraico*. Unable to admit that a concept different from their own is expressed in the Talmud, the three scholars state that in the mentioned text of Ghittin f. 10b, there is no contrast but complementarity between the first opinion – admitting the deferment for donation in accordance with the principle of Shemuel – and the second opinion – that does not admit it, considering all acts where writing is the constitutive element of the negotiation as excluded from the deferment. In fact,

844 Born in Barcelona in 1235, died in 1310. Author of responses and glosses (hiddushin = novels) to various Talmudic treatises. See sub voce Moritz Kayserling in *Jewish Encyclopedia* and J. Epstein, *The responsa of Shelomoh Ben Aderet*, London, 1935.

the first refers to the case in which, for the donation, there is the king's order to use a public act, while the second refers to the case in which such order is missing.

Of course, it is nothing but one of the usual cases of forced interpretation of Talmudic text to project what is a new solution into it.[845]

---

845 R. Shelomò Ben Aderet, *Hiddushin*, Venice ed., D. Bomberg, 1523, on Ghittin f. 10b (footnote no. 825 above): "And if you want I will say that one must read in the Mishnah: "with the exception of the bills of divorce," that is to say: with the exception of any document in which all the substance of the negotiation depends on it, such as the cause of repudiation and the document of donation which resembles that of divorce which is invalid." Some say that the two opinions are at odds with each other because for Shemuel with the contract of donation made by the court of the Gentiles there is a purchase, whereas in the other opinion there is no purchase even where the order of the king is there. Conversely, some others explain that they are not at odds, but rather Shemuel's opinion refers to where the order of the king is there, and the second opinion refers to where the king's order is not there. And this seems to be well-founded because to the best of our knowledge in general, and with more reason here, "dinà demalchutà dinà." In opposition, some reject this point of view, because "dinà demalchutà dinà" is not said but in things that are advantageous to the king, such as the one said in ch. Hezkat ha-Battim at the end [Bavà Batrà f. 54b]: the king orders that land shall not be purchased but with a written deed, that is to say, that [the buyer] sign the deed and register it so that he [the king] could get [for the registration fee] what is established by him. In fact, we also say: you have proof [that it is said: dinà etc. only when there is an advantage for the king] from what it is said [Bavà Kammà f. 113b]: they cut palm trees down and make them into bridges on which we pass, etc. On the contrary, here the king does not benefit from this law. But this is wrong because in ch. Hezcat ha-Battim [Bavà Batrà f. 54b] it is also said: "Rabbà said: these three things were said to me by Ukbà bar Nehemià, etc."; which means that Rabbà considers the usucaption lasting 40 years according to the Persian law as state law, that is to say, that it is state law and that the king has ruled that the purchase prescription for the Gentile last 40 years: then what benefit and interest are there for the king?" We know that Nachmanides follows the same point of view from Izhak Ben Sheshet, *Sheelot utshuvot* (*Consultations*), Riva di Trento ed., Cristoforo Madruzzi, 1559, cons. 203, who also reports the different opinions: "And now I will let you know the difference of opinions of the commentators about the acts compiled by the gentile notaries. We read [Mishnah Ghittin 1, 5]: these are valid except for bills of repudiation, and the Gemara [bab., f 10b] notes that there is no difference between sale and donation, and questions: "it is fine for the sale, in which the essential is to give the money and the written deed is a simple proof, but for the donation, what does one buy with? With the deed? but this is worthless. Shemuel says: *dinà demalchutà dinà*; or read, if you like: with the exception of those contracts that are like bills of repudiation." Maimonides' opinion is that the second opinion is in contrast with that of Shemuel because the latter says that the contract of donation perfected not with money but with the sole document is valid upon the principle: *dinà* etc.; whereas for the second opinion it would not be valid and another contract would be needed, signed by Jewish witnesses. Maimonides decides following the second opinion – contrary to Shemuel – in ch. 27 about the rules of the lender and the seller (malvè velovè). And although we ascertained that [as a rule] the principle: *dinà* etc. applies, and also Maimonides agrees

From all this muddle of arguments, there seem to be four dominating views concerning the validity of documents prepared by courts (or notaries).

1st) All these acts are valid, except those of divorce and the release of slaves, exhaustively enumerated. (Mishnah and some Talmudic scholars).

2nd) On the contrary, all these acts are invalid. (Opinion of the Gheonim, which remained without follow-up).

3rd) Acts where the negotiation to which they refer is accomplished by other means are valid and are simply evidence. Conversely, those where the negotiation itself is properly motivated are invalid, even if resorting to the notary is established by the state with a mandatory norm. (Opinion of another current of Talmudic sages and Maimonides).

4th) The invalidity of the notarial form shall be declared for other acts, in addition to the two listed in the Mishnah (divorce and release), only when the state does not impose resorting to the same form with a mandatory norm. Contrarily, in the presence of such a norm, the invalidity must not be extended to acts other than the two mentioned above. (Opinion of the three medieval sages).

The scholars then adopt one view or another to resolve practical cases.

So does Izhak Ben Sheshet.[846] Called to decide about the validity of a notarial deed of donation, he considers it completely valid "because it states that the *Kinyan Sudar* was done." That is, the *Kinyan* itself concluded the negotiation, and the script is a simple proof of it. He reports all other viewpoints for sheer conscientious doctrinarian.[847] Likewise, in another consultation concerning a will made before a notary, having reported the various theories, Ben Sheshet

on that, this is said for cases where the king has an advantage, but it is not said for private cases; and this is the understanding of the second opinion. According to Nachimanides, Ben Aderet and those after them, the second opinion is not at odds with that of Shemuel that the donation done with contract signed by Gentiles is valid for the principle: *dinà* etc. because Shemuel intends the Mishnah like this: when the order by the king is there, then also the acts of donation are valid, while with the words: "read, if you like, etc.," the Mishnah is linked to the case in which the order by the king is not there. When, on the other hand, the order is there, then the donation too is valid. Conversely according to Maimonides, for the principle: *dinà* etc. [whether or not there is an order by the king, the beneficiary] has not bought anything and in order for him to buy, the *kinyan* is necessary." Similarly, R. Nissim Gherondi, *Commento* cited to Alfasì [R. Izhak Fez] (on ghittin see ch. 1) f. 557, expresses himself in a language even more twisted than that contained in these two texts, which do not stand out anyway for excessive clarity.

846 Born in Valencia in 1326, died in Algiers in 1408. Author of consultations, printed for the first time in Constantinople, 1546–47. On him, see J. Broydè in *Jewish Encyclopedia*, at this entry.

847 Izhak Ben Sheshet, *Consulti*, Riva di Trento, Cristoforo Madruzzi, 1559, cons. no. 203; see above, footnote no. 845.

concludes it is valid "because it is not the act that makes the purchase. ... but the word of the testator that makes the purchase ... and the written deed is a simple proof; the notary is thus believed when he says he has given these dispositions; and the deed is regarded as an act of sale."[848]

In consultation no. 478, the same author expressed the same opinion. In accord with the provision already mentioned in the Talmud, Bavà Mezià f. 74a,[849] it is admitted that the contract, concluded with the traditional local form of a handshake, must be deemed sealed, as if it had been concluded with the *Kinyan Sudar*. Therefore, the written deed has the nature of simple proof and is valid although drafted by gentile notaries.[850]

Subsequently, the same principle is reiterated by R. Asher Ben Jehiel in one of his consultations, on which his son, R. Jacob Ben Asher, bases a rule of Tur.[851]

Bearing in mind that, according to Jewish law, an ill individual can make a universal donation of his assets, fully or partially, provided that he declares to do so for 'cause of death,' without the beneficiary having to express acceptance by way of *Kinyan Sudar*; R. Asher concludes that the written deed testifying to the above is a simple proof and valid even if it is done according to non-Jewish laws. However, if an individual, even an ill one, donates part of his property

---

848 Idem, cons. no. 51. The act naturally needs "to be done in accordance with their laws, because it will not be valid for us if it is not valid for them."

849 Above, footnote no. 837.

850 Izhak Ben Sheshet, cons. no. 478. Benamozegh, *Delle fonti del diritto ebraico* etc., cit., p. 184. Of the local customary forms aimed at perfecting the contracts also from the Jewish viewpoint, the Talmud (Bavà Mezià, f. 74a) does not name but the distinctive tag. The handshake is mentioned only in later sources. Fehr, *Deutsches Recht und jüdisches Recht*, in *Zeitschrift der Savigny Stiftung*, Germ. Abth., vol. 39, 1918, pp. 316–318, observes that the first codification that mentions it is Jacob Ben Asher's Tur (published in 1340); and he argues that it is a reception of German law, explained by the fact that R. Asher Ben Jechiel's father and teacher of R. Jacob was born in Germany and lived there for a long time, migrating to Spain only in old age. Against this thesis S. Bialoblocki, in *Enc. Jud.*, entry Handschlag, notes that what R. Asher describes on the handshake in his comment to the aforementioned Talmudic passage (Bavà Mezià, f. 74a) is asserted not in the name of the German Talmudists, but in that of Chananel from Kairowan. It is noteworthy that one cannot speak in any case of reception of norms of local law into Jewish law, but only of recognition of the validity of those norms: a completely different thing.

851 R. Asher Ben Jechiel, in R. Jacob Ben Asher, *Tur*, Hoshen Mishpat, ch. 253, § 50: "A donation by an ill person of all his possessions or even part of them when he disposes of by cause of death, a donation that needs no *kinyan* [*sudar*] and is purchased with the word, is valid [even though written] according to non-Jewish laws; but the partial donation of an ill person who does not dispose of by cause of death, and there is no *kinyan* so that then everything would be bought with the delivery of the act, if this is done according to non-Jewish laws, it is not worth a hoot." Castelli, *Nullità*, etc. cit. p. 70. Benamozegh, *Controreplica* cit., pp. 152 and seqq.

without declaring it is done for 'cause of death,' the beneficiary must give the *sudar* to seal the deal. If not, the written deed becomes the element by which the negotiation itself is perfected, hence not valid unless drawn up under Jewish rules.[852]

Also, that of the *Shulchan 'Aruch* is modeled after the conclusion of the Tur. It stipulates that acts by which an ill person disposes of all his possessions, or only partially so, provided that he declares that the provision is decided *mortis causa*, are valid even if drafted by a notary, given that the provision would be valid even without the writing, which is just a simple proof. Furthermore, since testamentary provisions are always made for after death, Caro concludes that all testaments of ill persons made by gentile notaries are valid.[853]

In general, Caro follows Maimonides, i.e., he explicitly excludes the validity of deeds of donation, confession, transaction and renunciation, carefully declaring, however, that the exclusion is limited to those among the instruments that for their content appear to be not simple but essential elements of the contract.[854]

In his note to Caro, Moshè Isserles reiterates the concept based on several of the opinions we have already considered, but at the same time affirms the need to keep as valid without distinction all the instruments "where there is an order of the king to draw deeds before notaries."[855]

852 For the Jewish testamentary rules, see above, footnotes 662–671.

853 Caro, *Shulchan 'Aruch*, Hoshen Mishpat, ch. 253, §32: "The testaments that were made in the courts of the Gentiles are valid because – says the *Tur* – anything that even an ill person orders verbally, or even when he makes a partial donation but says that that happens for cause of death, is fully valid even without it being put in written."

854 Caro, *Shulchan 'Aruch*, Hoshen Mishpat, ch. 68, §§ 1 and 2 = Maimonides, *Mishneh Torah*, Hilchot Malvè Velovè, ch. 27 (footnote no. 841 above), except for the following modification: "But if in contracts signed by Gentiles any one thing of all these is missing, they are worth absolutely nothing: and so are the donation contracts, where the formula is e.g., "my field is given to you" so that the essence of the purchase is in the instrument, and the [gentile] witnesses have signed it; and so are the confession contracts drawn up e.g., just like this: one admits to another to be his debtor, and so are acts of transaction or waiver made with Gentiles as witnesses. Although all the aforementioned things are there, the contracts are worth absolutely nothing."

855 Isserles, note 2 to Caro, *Shulchan 'Aruch*, Hoshen Mishpat, ch. 68, 1: "Some say that [with regard to the validity in case they are compiled by gentile notaries] the acts of confession are like acts of loan [i.e., they are valid] (Bet Josef [comment of Caro to *Tur*; it is understood at the same ch. 68 of Hoshen Mishpat] on behalf of R. Shelomò Ben Aderet's and R. Nissim Ghirondi, Ghittin ch. 1 [footnote no. 845 above]). And so, acts of waiver shall be valid even if made by notaries (R. Izhak Ben Sheshet, cons. no. 142); and so, with regard to the donation in which the purchase is fulfilled with the *kinyan* [*sudar*] or by appropriation (*Bet Josef* [ibid]), as long as you admit in front of the notary that the act is not but a simple proof, anything that is done before them is valid (*R. Nissim Gherondi*, on Ghittin

Overall, in practical cases, those called to decide base their arguments primarily on the distinction between acts *ad substantiam* and acts *ad probationem tantum*, and on the distinction between acts for which the public form (notary) is specified by state law and acts for which this rule does not apply. Nevertheless, the tendency to recognize all the notarial deeds as valid with occasional admission of elements concerning not the form as much as the very substance of the deed becomes more and more consolidated.[856]

---

ch. 1). Therefore if an ill person made a will before gentile notaries, all that he ordered is valid (R. Izhak Ben Sheshet, cons. no. 51 [footnote no. 848 above]), as will be explained later on in the ch. 253, § 22 [footnote no. 853 above]. But wherever there is order of the king to write the acts before notaries, all contracts made before them are valid, even those of donation, pursuant to the principle: *dinà demalchutà dinà*. And the more so where the custom of rendering them valid is established (R. Izhak Ben Sheshet, cons. nos. 493 and 478; *Ben Josef* [ibid] on behalf of R. Shelomò Ben Aderet; *Maghid Mishnè* [comment by Vidal of Tolosa to Maimonides' *Mishneh Torah*] ch. 27 of the creditor's and debtor's rules; see also ch. 369 further on)."

856 So towards the end of the 18th century, R. Daniel Terni, Rabbi of Florence considers a testament made in Florence before a notary valid, especially since in the Grand Duchy of Tuscany the public act was prescribed for taxation reasons. Terni also believes – and it is with this that he shows to accept a local rule of law no longer relevant in the form but in the very substance of the law – that the testament cannot be undone but by another testament. "It seems to me – Terni writes in *Ikkarè ha-Dat*, Florence, 1803, pp. 70 and seqq. – that the heirs of the widow do not have reason to argue that the testament is invalid because done in the offices of the Gentiles, because Caro, at ch. 232, §32 [see footnote no. 853 above] decides that it is valid; and even if one can find some decider that considers it null and void, in our case he will admit that it is valid for the principle: *dinà demalchutà dinà*. In fact, although in 1693 the Grand Duke of Florence gave permission to judge the [civilian] causes among Jews according to Jewish law, yet, in 1746, on December 2, he issued an edict throughout his dominion stipulating that all contracts of donation, confession and obligation drawn up in favor of one in order to have effect from the time of the donor's death, although cited in the testament, have no validity and are null and void. In order for them to have validity, they must be drawn up by the public notary, who shall record them in his register, and send the transcript to the archive with the name of the donor and the beneficiary and the amount of the donation. Now, this provision was for the benefit of the Duke and his exchequer because he who was receiving the donation had to pay a fixed fee of 7¾%, having ordered that this provision be observed by all, without exclusion of the Jews. Also Maimonides, who considers the act done by gentile courts as valid only if it is a sale or a loan, but not a will, admits that in our case, it is valid in virtue of the principle: dinà demalchutà dinà. This is because the Duke issued a decree to his advantage, explicitly saying at the end of ch. 1 about the rules of rechijà umattanà that one must judge according to the law of the king because all causes of money where there is an order of the king must be dealt with according to their laws [see footnote no. 876]. The author of Bet Avraham says: for the decision it is obvious that for R. Asher Ben Jechiel, R. Moshè Ben Nachman, R. Shelomò Ben Aderet, R. Nissim Ghirondi, R. Jacob Ben Asher author of the *Tur* and for most decision-makers

It is finally noteworthy that the recognition of the local (public) form of the scripts is almost always done with an optional and not mandatory character: i.e., the parties may resort to public notaries for their scripts, but they have no obligation to do so and retain full faculty, if they so prefer, to follow the Jewish form. The choice of the one or the other of the two forms, recognized as equally valid, is referred to as the contracting parties will.

Only R. Moshè Isserles intends the referring, when it is admitted, as obligatory, i.e., as exclusive of the Jewish forms.[857] Based on the misinterpretation of consultation by Izhak Ben Sheshet,[858] his opinion remains completely isolated.[859]

---

of Romagna, Tuscany, Venice, Lombardy, France, Piedmont and London, the contracts made by the courts of the Gentiles, also those of donation, are valid for the principle: *dinà demalchutà dinà*, because [public officials] are incorruptible and have the order of the king. R. Menachem 'Azaria Fano [Rabbi of Mantua, 1548–1620] concludes by saying: "We are certain that the notaries say the truth because woe to them if they were suspects. The heirs are also wrong with regard to the second of the reasons given, that is, that having the testatrix lived after the disease the testament is invalid [which would be the principle according to the Jewish law]. On the contrary, it is valid because she set the condition that [her will] take effect after death, and the testaments made by means of the public notary are never null by law because the testatrix said and requested to be put in writing that this is the last will and another testament should be required to revoke it [this in accordance with the principles of Roman common law]."

857 Isserles, note 2 to Caro's, *Shulchan 'Aruch*, Hoshen Mishpat, ch. 68, § 1 (as a result of the passage just cited in footnote no. 855): "And every contract declared as valid by the principle: the law of the State is the law, if it is not written properly according to their laws, even if it is valid according to ours, it is not valid, because we do not declare valid with more breadth than them (R. Izhak Ben Sheshet, cons. 51); and the same is true the other way round, if it is invalid according to our laws and valid according to theirs (R. Joseph Colon, cons. no. 188); but there are those who think differently."

858 As we have seen (above, footnote no. 848), Ben Sheshet only meant to say that, once the validity of the notarial form of a given act was admitted, if the parties opted for it, it was necessary to verify that the form itself was carefully observed in the drawing up of the act. But this did not exclude the recourse to the Hebrew form if the contractors so preferred. The reciprocal rule, where if the local form is not admitted and the Hebrew form is not respected then the act is invalid, may be appropriate and intuitive but, as one can easily understand, is not reversible.

859 It will appears clear from this paragraph that all matters debated by the rabbinic teaching about the limits of recognition of the local law concerning the form of acts correspond in all respects to those that use to be discussed in Roman and modern doctrine of International Law, about the limits of the rule "locus regit actum." It is well known that it is argued for example whether the rule should be limited to acts drawn up before judicial authorities and registered, with the exclusion of private acts (for all, see Bar, *Teoria e pratica del diritto internazionale privato*, Buzzati transl., vol. 1, Turin, 1915, pp. 346–348, who reports all the intermediate doctrine) or to acts *ad probationem tantum*, with the exclusion of those *ad substantiam* (idem, op. cit., pp. 349–350). It is furthermore debated

2 The Substantive Law

It should be noted that the principles set by the sources investigated so far refer only to the conflict between Jewish law and state law concerning the form of acts. The principles of various conflicts in substantive law are dealt with elsewhere. Hence, the texts mentioned above have sometimes been invoked inappropriately to support the validity, *jure hebraico*, of deeds drawn up by notaries according to the state's substantive law and contradictory to Jewish law. Someone further argued that the formula "dinà demalchutà dinà" undoubtedly meant the total recognition of state law, including private law.

Benamozegh, for example, in his lengthy opinion regarding a case debated in Tuscany in the eighties of the last century between the heirs of a Tunisian Jew living in Jewish law, seeks, by all means, to show that the referral by the Jewish law to state law was at any time unlimited and never set a distinction either between form and substance of the acts or between public and private norms.[860] However, be it a lawyerly and not a doctrinal exercise, it is not convincing despite the lavish and most disorganized apparatus of quotations.

Benamozegh opponent in this cause was Castelli, who dismantled the arguments into pages just as lawyerly but somewhat more straightforward,[861] concluding by limiting the strength of the principle that "the law of the State is law" to the recognition of public law.

It is noteworthy, however, that even when observed in a strictly scientific manner, two different viewpoints had previously been already issued: Holdheim,[862] Krochmal,[863] and Jellinek[864] spoke in favor of interpretation in the sense of the total referring, whereas Frankel[865] and Löw[866] had insisted over the inconsequence of this idea, arguing that Jewish law could not voluntarily set its own condition of desuetude, and therefore the formula had to be understood as valid only within certain boundaries (public law, rights linked to government acts, feudal rights, acts of public offices).

---

on the optional or mandatory character of the rule (ibid., pp. 355–360). See the authors cited above, footnote no. 826.

860 Benamozegh, *Delle fonti* cit., pp. 84–203, in partic. pp. 135–136, 145 et seqq., 201. Some reservations on p. 116.

861 Castelli, *Nullità secondo il diritto ebraico* etc., cit. pp. 65–84, in partic. p. 76.

862 *Ueber die Autonomie der Rabbinen und das Prinzip der jüdischen Ehe*, Schwerin, 1843, p. 60.

863 See Jewish magazine (inaccessible to me) *He-chalutz*, I, 1852, pp. 80 et seqq.

864 See Jewish magazine *Neuzeit* (of Vienna), 1862, no. 1.

865 See *Zeitschrift für die religiösen Interessen des Judentums* (of Berlin), I, 1844, p. 275.

866 Löw, *Dinà demalchutà dinà* cit., in *Gesammelte Schriften*, vol. III, Szegedin, 1893, pp. 347–358.

Recently this divergence of views has manifested itself anew.

In his paper on the Jewish court in the Middle Ages, based on an extensive review of Talmudic and medieval texts, Shohet concluded in the sense of Benamozegh and of the others cited. It seems to him "that a careful study of the sources should settle the question beyond doubt that the principle of dinà demalchutà applies to all civil cases."[867]

Finkelscherer, on the other hand, having studied Talmudic passages concerning the relationship between Jewish law and local Persian law, was convinced that by setting the mentioned principle, Shemuel Jarchinai did not intend to perform a total referral to state law, nor did he act in earnest to transform the Jewish law upon the example of the Persian law, as some would claim.[868]

The last author who dealt with this question is Herzog, at the beginning of the first volume of his treatise on Jewish law.[869] He noted that, based on the sources it would seem that the recognition of state norms is to be intended as restricted, in the private area, to the "*dinè mamonot*," i.e., to property rights. Yet, it is challenging to delineate the boundary between the part of state law recognized and the part rejected.

Such disparity of opinions among modern scholars indeed corresponds to similar disagreements already expressed in the doctrine and practice of medieval decision-makers, among whom decreeing where the borders should be set in recognition of the local private law was always a doctrinal and debated issue.

Within the limits of our possibilities, it is appropriate that we seek here to examine the primary sources related to this matter dispassionately.

In the Talmud, the conflict between Jewish law and state law is certainly not resolved in the sense of a total referral. As we have seen, within certain limits and conditions, the sages recognize the validity of the state tax rules (Nedarim f. 28a and Bavà Kammà f. 113a.) and the public law in general.

Nevertheless, regarding the norms of private law, things proceed differently: for the form of acts, limits are set and, as we know, discussions are extensive (Ghittin f. 10b); as for the substance, the conflict is dealt with in respect to some particular points (which is enough to exclude the will for a total referral to local regulations), and with exclusive reference to asset law (property and obligations).

867 Shohet, *The Jewish Court in the Middle Ages*, cit., p. 112.

868 Finkelscherer, *Zur Frage* cit., pp. 381–383 in partic.

869 Herzog, *The Main Institutions of Jewish Law*, cit., pp. 24–32.

In the Mishnah, the prevalence of Jewish law over state law is established only for some secondary rules concerning hiring.[870] In the Jerusalem Gemara, the state law is not even mentioned. In the Babylonian Gemara, there are only

1) Recognition of the means allowed by the local customs for the conclusion of contracts, and those allowed by Jewish law.[871]
2) Precise referral to the Persian law for a small detail on the subject of riparian properties.[872]
3) Discussion on the referral to state norms regarding means for purchasing of real estate property.

This last point, which is the most important, is treated in Bavà Batrà f. 54b and 55a.[873]

---

870 Mishnah, Bavà Mezià, 7, 8: "The keepers of orchards may eat [of fruit] by State law, not by Jewish law." Ibid., 7, 1: "If one hires workers and tells them to start early and finish late in those places where it is not customary to begin [the work] early and finish it late, he is not entitled to force them: in places where it is customary to feed them he must feed them; where it is customary to provide them some other food to go with the bread, he must provide them; everything according to the customs of the country." See ibid., 9, 1: "if one takes a field [for rent or sharecropping] from a fellow, where it is customary to prune, he must prune; to weed out, he must weed out, to plow after harvesting, he must plow; everything according to the customs of the country."

871 Babylonian Talmud, Bavà Mezià, f. 74a. See above, footnote no. 837.

872 Babylonian Talmud, Bavà Mezià, f. 108a. (Shemuel Jarchinai's prescription): "He who takes possession of a piece of land on the bank of a river is impudent but it shall not be taken away from him. But now the Persians write: you have purchased it until the necks of the horses are emerged above the water, if another comes by and takes possession of it, it shall be taken away from him." It seems to me that this provision has to be interpreted as follows: according to Jewish law, the property of land not far from the bank of a river does not draw with it the property of the related coastal strip, which remains generally res nullius and can therefore become the property of the first occupant. However, given that according to the Persian law the property of such a land also involves property of not only the coastal strip but also of the river "until the necks of horses emerge above the water," the Jews shall adhere to this rule and refuse to recognize the occupation of the coastal strip, because it is a former private property, as an appendix to the main property.

873 Babylonian Talmud Bavà Batrà f. 54b: "On behalf of Shemuel, R. Jehudà said: the property of a pagan is in the same condition as a deserted land: whoever occupies it first becomes its owner. The reason is this: as soon as the pagan receives the money, he ceases to be the owner, whereas the Jew does not become owner as long as he does not get the deed of sale. Therefore, [in this time gap] the land is like it were deserted and the first occupant becomes its owner. Abajè said to R. Josef: But did Shemuel really say that? Has not he established: The State law is the law? Now the king has ordered that the land cannot be bought if not by means of a written deed. R. Josef replied: I know nothing about this. I only know about a dispute in Dura di-ra'avata [Dur on the Tigris, Obermayer, *Die Landschaft Babyloniens*, p. 142 in M. Simon, English translation of the Talmudic treatise Bavà Batrà, London, 1935, p. 222, no. 8], where a Jew bought a piece of land from a pagan and another Jew came along and worked a small piece of it, and when the dispute was

As laid down by Shemu'el Jarchinai, a scholar reports here the principle by which, in the case of a property sold from a Gentile to a Jew, the Gentile ceases to be the owner as soon as he receives the money; whereas the Jew does not buy the property until the time he has in his hands the chirograph [writ] of purchase. Hence, in the interim between payment to the Gentile and drawing up the deed to the Jew, the estate becomes a *res nullius*, and anyone may own it by occupation.[874]

Around this principle, a discussion heats up among the sages. Some declare themselves in favor of the recognition of the provision. In support, they cite several cases where it had a practical application, having recognized the occupant's right in preference of the buyer who has not yet got hold of the writ of purchase. Contrariwise, others declare themselves against such recognition by stating that concerning the means of purchasing real estate, it is the State's law that must prevail, and this requires that the purchase be accomplished by employing a legal transaction concluded with a written deed (without of course that in the transfer of the property those solutions of continuity be there that enable the purchase by occupation), or, as others note, by means of the forty years prescription of acquisition, or, in the case of lands derelict

---

brought before R. Jehudà, he allocated the land to the latter. Abajè replied: Are you talking about Dura di-ra'avata? Here the fields belong to people who go away and do not pay the levy to the king, and the king has ordered that anyone who pays the levy will have the usufruct of the field. [Usufruct is meant here in the sense of ownership as long as the original owner does not return and by reimbursing the levies paid, re-acquires possession of the land]. R. Hunà bought a field from a pagan and a Jew came along and worked a part of it. [After a dispute arose] this Jew went before R. Nachman, who confirmed his entitlement to the property ... f. 55a. R. Hunà ben Albin let them know that if a Jew buys a field from a pagan and another Jew comes along and occupies it [before the buyer has the purchase deed in his hands], we [the sages] do not take the property away from him, and R. Abin and R. Elai and all our teachers agreed on this point. Rabbà said: These three rules were referred to me by Ukbà Ben Nehemiah the Exilarch: the law of the State is the law. The Persians buy property through a 40-year usucaption; he who buys from those riches who received the land ownership from the treasury by paying taxes, buys legitimately, as long as they are lands transferred for land tax. Conversely, if it is a personal tax [the transfer by the treasure is not legitimate, and therefore] the purchase is not valid."

874 This provision, in contrast with the principles governing property transfers between Jews (see on this Mishnah, Kiddushin, 1, 5; pp. 224–225 above) is part of that set of norms which, by Jewish law, govern the relations of the Jews with the Gentiles, and of Gentiles among themselves and correspond exactly to the Romans' *jus gentium*. On these norms, see the old classic work of John Selden, *De jure naturali ac gentium juxta disciplinam hebreorum*, London, 1640, Argentières 1665, Leipzig and Frankfurt 1695, reprinted by Ugolini, *Thesaurus Antiquitatum sacrarum*, Venice 1744–1769, t. 27, pp. 471–1381. With the norm in question, Selden deals on p. 1216 of the Venice edition, drawing it from Caro's elaboration, *Shulchan 'Aruch*, Hoshen Mishpat, ch. 194.

for inability to pay taxes, with the occupation and the payment of taxes due. Suppose an estate has been allocated to the occupier. It is noted that it shall be under this final state provision related to the unpaid taxes and not under the principle put forward.[875]

In an attempt to give a systematic form to the Talmudic discussion, by turning it into an actual precept, Maimonides reconciles the two opposing opinions. He states that in the hypothesis considered, following the Jewish law is possible only when, for transferring estate ownership rights, the state does not impose certain forms. When such imposition exists, it is to the norms of the state that one must adhere exclusively "because in all financial matters it is judged according to the law of the king."[876]

Elsewhere, Maimonides explicitly admits the state law's validity concerning the purchase of lands derelict for the inability to satisfy tax charges.[877] Continuing on the same line of thought, he also establishes the rule that, albeit the more modern Jewish law, prohibits slavery, "If the king has decreed that

875 It is interesting to note that even in the Roman Empire, during the period corresponding to that of the Jewish scholars mentioned here, a law was issued attributing the ownership of estate derelict for excessive tributes to those who would occupy them and promise, for the future, to pay such tributes (C. 11, 59, 11, year 400). From the same era (years 388–392) there was also a law that granted the ownership of the deserted lands to whoever would occupy them and cultivate them within two years from the occupation. On the two Roman laws, see Rotondi, *Scritti*, vol. III. pp. 55 et seq. and Perozzi, *Istituzioni di diritto romano*, 1930, vol. I, pp. 694–695.

876 Maimonides, *Mishneh Torah*, Ilchot, Zechijà Umattanà [Rules on purchase and donation] ch. 1: "If a Gentile has sold mobile goods to a Jew, or has bought mobile goods from a Jew, he buys with the tradition or orders them bought with the tradition or with money; as for the real estate, however, he does not buy it from the Jew but with the document, nor does he order it bought but with the document, because one does not get backing but from the instrument. So if a Jew bought a field from a Gentile and handed over the money, and before he took possession of it another Jew takes possession just as it is done with the assets of a foreign resident, the latter Jew has made a legitimate purchase and only repays the money to the former, because at the moment that the Gentile has taken the money he has lost the property and the Jew has not purchased it as long as he has not received the contract, so that these assets are like assets of the deserted, and anyone who takes possession of them buys them lawfully. But this is said only where the king does not have a law known to all. On the contrary, if the law of the king and his rule prescribe that the rights to a property are acquired only by he who draws the contract or gives money or whatnot, he must follow the king's rule because in all money matters it is judged according to their law." The passage is reported without variants by R. Jacob Ben Asher, *Tur*, Hoshen Mishpat, ch. 194 and by Caro, *Shulchan 'Aruch*, Hoshen Mishpat, ch. 194.

877 Maimonides, op. cit., Ilchot Ghezelà Veavedà [Rules on stolen and lost things], ch. 5: "If the king made the law that when one pays the tax on a field this belongs to the person who pays the fee if the owner shirked and another pays the tax to the king and enjoys the fruits of the field, it is not a robbery but he is the owner until the landlord comes back because the king's law is the law." Caro, *Shulchan 'Aruch*, Hoshen Mishpat, ch. 369, § 10.

anyone who pays the fee for a man [who is not able to pay it] can become master of this individual for whom he paid if a Jew has paid the fee for a poor man, this poor man must serve him more than enough because the king's law is the law, but shall not work like a slave."[878]

The generalization that Maimonides makes based on the Talmudic text that defers to the law of the State "in all patrimonial issues," has no follow-up in later French and German doctrines, which are generally much more reluctant to admit the authority of local law in the field of private relations.[879]

The deferral, set by some scholars concerning some particular points, is dismissed entirely by others who restrict the recognition of state law only to fiscal and administrative norms.

R. Eliezer from Metz (d. 1198), taking to the letter the Talmudic text, declares as prevailing the provisions of the state law regarding the purchase of real estate utilizing the 40-year usucaption and to defaulted tax payments.[880] R. Eliezer Ben Joel ha-Levi (from Bonn),[881] and R. Izhak Or Zaruà (from Vienna)[882] declare themselves like-minded.

878 Maimonides, ibid. = Caro, ibid., § 11.

879 Besides, the weight to be attributed to Maimonides' expression "in all money matters," is not very clear. If taken literally, it would make the entire Jewish law concerning real rights and obligation rights worthless. The fact that Maimonides himself deals extensively with the patrimonial material and does not mention, not even in the rules of real estate transfer (Ilchot mechirà, ch. 1 and 2) the referral to the state norms, shows that the Spanish scholar did not intend to decree a complete referral. But it is very difficult to understand what limits he meant to set for such a referral. In favor of the interpretation in the sense of the complete referral are Benamozegh, *Delle fonti*, cit., pp. 136–141 and Shohet, op. cit., p. 112. Herzog, on the other hand, op. cit., pp. 28, 376, 390, remains unconvinced. It is certain, however, that Maimonides refers exclusively to the state norms of binding nature.

880 Eliezer of Metz, text quoted above, footnote no. 726: "We do not say that his law is valid but for the lands and in the norms inherent to them ... as it is said in Hezcat ha-Battim [Babylonian Talmud, Bavà Batrà, f. 55a] that the statute of limitations is up to 40 years, or if it said: whoever gives the tax be he the one who draws benefit from the land, etc."

881 Mordechai Ben Hillel, *Sefer Mordechai*, Bavà Kammà, § 190 (comment to Bavà Kammà f. 113b): "R. Eliezer Ben Joel ha-Levì writes: in any case only for the lands it is said: *dinà demalchutà dinà*; and [he adds that] there are those who say that also in other money matters it is said: *dinà* etc.; but no decision is taken." Moshè Isserles, *Notes to Caro, Shulchan 'Aruch*, hoshen mishpat, ch. 369, § 8, so reports the opinion of Rabbenu Asher Ben Jechiel (on Nedarim, ch. 3) and of Mordechai (Bavà Kammà, § 190 cit.), who reproduce the statements of R. Eliezer Ben Joel ha-Levì: "There are those who say that the principle: dinà demalchutà dinà does not apply but to taxes and levies relating to immovable property, that is, when the king orders that Jews do not live in his land if not in a given way; but in other matters, it does not apply."

882 R. Izhak Or Zaruà, III, Bavà Kammà 447; Shohet's uncontrollable quote, op. cit., p. 112, no. 4.

Following the local norm, R. Izhak Ben Perez settles a dispute over the extension of the period of mandatory detention of the pledge by the distrainee creditor, leaning, with apparent confusion between form and substance, on the text of the Talmud, Ghittin 10b, which admits the validity of local forms of the scriptures as long as they are drawn up by public officials.[883]

Against the pronouncement of this last scholar stands R. Jacob Israel, based on several valid arguments;[884] and R. Baruch of Worms establishes the general principle that "the law of the State is the law" does not involve the referral to the norms of private law governing the relationships between individuals.[885]

---

883 Mordechai Ben Hillel, *Sefer Mordechai*, Nezikin, § 196: " R. Izhak Ben Perez decided that if a Jew pawns an item with a fellow Jew, the creditor is not required to store the item more than a year, but after this period, he can sell it and collect his credit with the proceeds, according to State law (dinà demalchutà) concerning loans at interest that Jews make to the Gentiles. And he ruled in this sense in the case of an individual who had pawned books with a fellow. Having the creditor sold the books after the year, the debtor sued him; and R. Izhak Ben Perez determined that the debtor was not entitled to have anything on the basis of the state law, and brought the Ghittin, Mishnah "Kol ha-Shetarot" [1, 5, see above, footnote no. 823] as proof, where the Gemara decides that the State law is the law according to Shemuel's opinion." R. Izhak Ben Perez decision then becomes the rule. See e.g. R. Moshè Isserles, *Notes to Caro, Shulchan 'Aruch*, Hoshen Mishpat, ch. 73, § 14: "Where the practice is there that he who loans to the Gentile cannot sell the item pawned before a year, this same rule is applied also to the Jew who has loaned to another Jew who pawned an item, because in this the practice is followed." See the same principle in the note to the ch. 369, § 8.

884 R. Jacob Israel, consultation mentioned by Caro, *Bet Josef* on *Tur*, Hoshen Mishpat, ch. 369. R. Jacob objects to R. Izhak Ben Perez, that the support by the Ghittin text is not sufficient, since, on the other hand, from the texts of Bavà Kammà f. 113b [see above, footnote no. 767], Bavà Batrà f. 54b [see above, footnote no. 873] and from the interpretations of Mordechai, on Bavà Kammà f. 113b, §§ 190–194, of R. Asher on Nedarim f. 28a [i.e., from the interpretation of Eliezer of Metz, see above footnote no. 880] and others, it is deduced that the principle of Shemuel applies only to immovable property and for matters in which there is "king's advantage." Furthermore, that state provision on pawns should be disregarded also because unconstitutional: R. Jacob Israel says "it is not a lex fixed by the ancient generations and is not written in their statutes, but it is actually against their law. Moreover, it is not a general law not for the whole kingdom, but only for those who loan at interest, not for all other merchants. Finally, the government does not force to sell the pawned items but gives the lender the right to do so: now, what is not imposed is not state law, etc."

885 R. Baruch Ben Izhak of Worms, *Sefer hat-Terumà*, in R. Josef Colon, *Consulti*, no. 66: "I have by tradition from my teachers, received from the French, that one cannot say "dinà demalchutà dinà" except in matters of the king, such as his streets, taxes and levies; but in issues between private individuals, they have not said: *dinà* etc. A proof of this is that it is said [Babylonian Talmud, Bavà Kammà f. 113b; see above, footnote no. 767]: "Shemuel says: the State law is the law: in fact, Rabbà says, they cut palms and make bridges, etc." Therefore,

However, R. Izhak Ben Perez is not the only one who confuses the substance of the acts with the form. Many times, before notaries or other state officials draw up a contract with observance not only of the form but also of the substance of the local law (let us think, for example, about a notarial testament that calls a daughter to inherit concurrently with male siblings) contrary to Jewish law, Jewish scholars and judges tend to declare it valid and apply it precisely on the basis on the cited text of Ghittin 10b. R. Shimshon from Chinon, a French scholar (ca. 1290–1350), reacts wisely against this tendency, as he points out that contracts drawn up by non-Jewish notaries are declared valid only in the sense that they are reliable, that is, with regards to the form; but as for the substance, it must be decided according to Jewish law, and any possible clause, added to the contract, by which the parties bind themselves to be judged according to the law of the State, is null and void.[886]

The same considerations are made later by R. Joseph Colon, Rabbi of Mantua (d. 1480), who agrees with the opinions of R. Shimshon of Chinon, noting that from the words of the latter: "it is remarked that the contracts by gentile notaries were recognized as valid only in the sense that we see them as reliable but by no means such as to change the *Din Torà* (i.e., the Jewish

---

the principle: *dinà* etc. does not apply but to issues of roads, that is to matters of the king; but in a Jew's business with another, one should not decide with State's laws because its laws [of the State] were established only for its matters.

886 R. Shimshon from Chinon (Maharshak) in R. Josef Colon, *Consulti*, no. 188: "So I found written in the name of Chinon: About the contract valid in their courts, that has an expression according to which, by their law, it would be ruled in favor of Reuben whereas by our law it would be ruled in favor of Shim'on [fictitious names equivalent to so-and-so], it seems to me that one should not go according to their laws because if we say that we declare their contracts valid it is because they don't hurt themselves [i.e., they do not take upon themselves the responsibility of declaring false things, see the text of Ghittin 10b, above, footnote no. 825], etc. [sic, in Colon]. Anyway, it seems that one does not go [according to their law] because the expression "don't hurt themselves," for the contract is of no use except to say that we believe them, etc. [sic]; and if it is said *dinà demalchutà dinà* it is just like the example of the ch. *hagozet* [Bavà Kammà f. 113b, see above, footnote no. 767] that is, the principle applies to measures of public policy. In fact, it is said there: they cut palms and make bridges and we pass on them. Therefore, let's say that Shim'on wins the cause if this contract is done according to our laws, he must win even if it is done according to their laws, even though, according to their laws, on the basis of this contract he should be the loser. The objection that in the contract was written: "provided that he be judged according to their laws" is not valid because we say to him: you brought the damage upon yourself [knowing that the clause was invalid as contrary to Jewish principles]; because if we say that the contracts made in the courts of Gentiles are valid, it means that we have faith in them [as to form] but not that we follow them [as to substance]." Colon adds that this text by R. Shimshon from Chinon is not complete: he had to report it as he found it.

law)."[887] Colon also cites the opinion of R. Eliezer of Metz,[888] claiming that the principle "dinà demalchutà dinà" does not apply but to lands, and the text of Bavà Batrà f. 54b from which it is deduced that "even in money matters if it is said: dinà etc., that is only in matters of taxation and customs of the king's laws." Colon concludes: "that in the case of public taxes, it is said: dinà etc., but for a private issue, it is certainly not said: dinà etc., because otherwise you would – God forbid – abolish all Jewish laws."

The Spaniard R. Shelomò Ben Aderet also moves within the framework of the same principles. He talks about an opinion he issued relating to a dispute that arose between a father-in-law and his son-in-law following the death of their respective daughter and wife. Through the state court, the father-in-law had asked the son-in-law to return the dowry given to the late daughter on the ground that although, according to the Jewish law, the wife's heir is her husband, nevertheless, since it was well known that the court of that town also judged Jews according to gentile laws, in taking wife there, the Jew was in a way tightening a tacit pact with her to follow these laws in the relations with each other. Ben Aderet replies that although it is a patrimonial matter and thus a private pact would be admissible, according to the principle: "every deal in money matters is valid," nevertheless, the idea of the unspoken pact of referral to the state norms cannot be admissible; and likewise it is not permissible to appear before the state court to see these rules applied, being that contrary to the general prohibition to appear before non-Jewish courts, prohibition set precisely in order to avoid seeing applied the gentile law instead of the Jewish one.[889]

---

887 R. Joseph Colon, *Consulti*, Venice ed., 1519, no. 188, p. 223v: " As for the purchase of land, it is correct, says Colon, to claim that the land is properly purchased with a contract of theirs [= drafted by their notaries] given that of the land purchased it must be said: *dinà* etc., because the king says: be his land properly purchased with a contract made in his courts. But as to whether someone who is the owner of the contract is or not the loser in the cause [i.e., a matter affecting the substance of the relation], it not the case to say: dinà etc."

888 See above, footnote no. 880.

889 R. Shelomò Ben Aderet in Caro, *Bet Josef*, Hoshen Mishpat, ch. 26, in the end: "So writes R. Shelomò Ben Aderet who was summoned to rule on the case of a father whose daughter had died and who had requested the return the dowry from his son-in-law by means of the court of the Gentiles, with the argument that, though according to Jewish law the husband is his wife's heir, since everyone knows that [state judges] rule according to the Gentiles' laws, whoever marries a woman there is as if he had forfeited this pact. R. Shelomò Ben Aderet replied that in any relation concerning money, the private pact [notwithstanding the Jewish law] is valid and in truth [the sages] said that such a pact is

In another consultation on the same issue, Ben Aderet poses the principle that the referral should be restricted to "the law of the kingdom," i.e., to public norms and private norms "where there is an order by the king" (meaning: the mandatory, compulsory rules of public policy). As for private matters regulated by "the law of the rules," i.e., by the private law, there should not be referral

made in this matter; but using it in practice like that because it is a state norm in truth seems to be forbidden, and that is what the Torah warns against saying [e.g., 21, 1; cf. the texts cited above, footnote no. 313]: "These are laws that you shall put before them," not before the Gentiles, even though both sides agree and the matter concerns money. This is because the Torah did not allow the people [the faculty] to hold in great value the statutes of the Gentiles and their laws, nor to appear before them to be judged in things where their norm is like the Jewish norm. ... And God forbid from saying that we, the Holy People, can act according to the ways of the Gentiles and their norms! [that is, following the laws of the Gentiles in everything, even in non-mandatory private law]. ... And I say that anyone who claims that this is permitted because it is *dinà demalchutà* (the State's law) is wrong and he is a robber and the verse [Ezekiel 33, 15] applies to him: the wicked restores what he has taken by robbery and he is one of those who uproot the laws of the perfect Torah. And [indeed if it were so] we wouldn't have need any longer for the holy books composed by Rabbì [Judah ha-nassi '] and after him by Rabina and Rav Ashè [i.e., Mishnah and Talmud, that is the entire corpus of Jewish law] and they would teach their children the gentile law and would make colorful altars [Ezekiel 16, 16] in their temples, God forbid! Be nothing like that occurring in Israel, that the Torah don a bag [i.e., be deprived of its force] for them!" The opinion of Ben Aderet becomes the norm in Moshe Isserles' note to Caro, *Shulchan 'Aruch*, Hoshen Mishpat, ch. 369, §11 in the end: "If one takes a wife in a place where it is judged according to the laws of the Gentiles and the wife dies, neither can her father nor her other heirs say: anyone who takes a wife takes her in accordance with the [local] customs and the cause is judged with the laws of the Gentiles [decreeing] that with the woman's death, the husband is not the heir or something like that. And "the law of the State is the law" does not apply here, because this is not said if not in a matter in which the king has an interest, or when it is an injunction upon the citizens; but not in the sense that the ruling be done according to the laws of the Gentiles, because if it were so, every Jewish law would be null and void." In conclusion, Ben Aderet admits the referral of public law and binding private law to the state norms, but he does not admit it for non-binding private norms. And although in patrimonial matters, and thus also in the institution of dowry, Jewish law allows the deferral to its rules by private individuals, nevertheless, Ben Aderet says, it is forbidden to let such possible referral assume the character of referral to the law of the State, not being this reference allowed except for the mandatory provisions. The Roman norms applied also in the intermediate period regarding the restitution of the dowry can be found in D. 24, 3; C, 5, 18; C. 5, 13. See for example l. 4 C. 5, 18 (y. 223): "Dos a parte profecta, si in matrimonio decesserit mulier ad padrem redire debet."

"because if you do not say so," he concludes – "you repeal – God forbid! – all Jewish laws."[890]

As for Izhak Ben Sheshet, whose views concerning the form of the acts we already know, he touches on the question of the conflict between the substantive Jewish rules and local rules in another of his consultation.[891] In the case of a guardian appointed by a state court, rather than a Jewish court, he decides that the guardian's duties and obligations be regulated not according to Jewish law but according to what the court has established when granting the guardianship. These obligations translated into the duty, not imposed by Jewish law, to report an account of his management annually.[892] Ben Sheshet also recognizes the validity of contracts concluded under local custom forms.[893]

We have already had the opportunity to learn Caro's decisions about different points of interest for us: on the subject of a referral to the rules of the state, only some minor paragraphs should be quoted, relating to customs in matters

890 R. Shelomò Ben Aderet, in Caro, *Bet Josef*, Hoshen Mishpat, ch. 26 in the end: "Says R. Shelomò Ben Aderet in his response as to dinà etc.: Be aware that they did not say it but in that for which there is an order of the king, and in things which are subjected to the laws of the kingdom (*dinè ha-malchut*): because like we have the laws of the kingdom (*mishpetè meluchà*), as Samuel [the Prophet] said to Israel, so in other nations, the kings have known laws (*denim jedu'im*) and with reference to these [our sages] said that their laws are valid laws. Conversely, the laws by which they judge in the courts are not part of the laws of the kingdom (*mishpetè meluchà*), but the courts judge otherwise, according to what they find in the codices (books of judges = sifrè dajanim); because if you don't say so, you would, God forbid, abolish all the laws of Israel." This scholar, who lives under the Spanish monarchy, clearly wants to distinguish between laws issued by the king, pertaining to public law or to mandatory private law, and the Common Roman-Canon Law, based on the *Corpus Juris Civilis* and *Corpus Juris Canonici* (the books of the judges), including especially the permissive rules, that can be waived by the will of the parties.

891 No. 324, ed. cit. Riva di Trento, 1559.

892 I do not think that the consulting no. 52 directly touches our theme, as it concerns an inheritance between Conversos living in Majorca under the presumption of Catholics. The Jewish rules of succession, says Ben Sheshet, would be implemented "if the will had been done between Jews where the Jewish law is applied; but this testator dwelt in Majorca in the presumption of Catholic and therefore the woman who has to inherit is considered Catholic and all purported heirs are Catholics and even if they were Jews they should act according to the laws of the Gentiles, because the community of Majorca so has disposed." It should be noted that the repeal of the Jewish civil law by a community, albeit limited to the area of its jurisdiction, appears as a fact absolutely without precedent and should probably be explained as a consequence of the forced mass conversion of the community itself, which remained then secretly alive.

893 Cons. no. 478 based on the Talmud, Bavà Mezi'à f. 74a cit. See above, no. 277, no. 16.

of work,[894] the return of certain items found[895] and the law enforcement on the debtor's assets authorized by decree of the competent authority.[896]

•••

With an examination of the largest possible number of texts, we have just concluded the presentation of the rules on referral found in the doctrine and legislation of medieval Judaism. At this point, someone may ask: by establishing that Jews live according to their law, does the state refer exclusively to their substantive law or does it also accept their norms on the conflicts between personal law and local law? In other words, does it or does it not accept the referral when Jewish law requires it? This problem is well known to the modern experts in international private law for the case of foreigners.

Unfortunately, adequate documentation of practical cases is unavailable, and we cannot give an answer based on facts. We are, however, inclined to answer the question in the affirmative.

We can report that in a lawsuit discussed between a father and his sons for the inheritance of their mother before the Tribunal of Venice in 1697 (a dossier which survived in its entirety),[897] after gathering elements about the *status*

894 *Shulchan 'Aruch*, Hoshen Mishpat, ch. 331, § 1: "If one relocates from a place where it is customary for workers not to work from dawn to dusk, to another place where this practice exists or vice versa, and hires workers, he must act according to the custom of the location where the workers were hired."

895 Ibid., ch. 259, § 7: "Whoever saves objects from the lion or the bear, and the sea that withdraws 10 or 15 parasangs and floods every day (sic), all objects he finds, as well as those from the river overflow, are his [of the finder], even if the owner is there and claims those things for himself." Isserles' note: "but it is appropriate to return, although by law he is not required to return these lost things. If the king or the tribunal has decreed [the obligation to return] he must return under the principle: the State law is the law."

896 Ibid., ch. 104 § 2. With respect to the creditor who has not claimed his credit on time, it is provided: "If the public announcement said this: anyone who believes he is entitled to these goods presents his titles, and anyone who does not present them lose his rights if it was used like that, it is the state law and his rights have lapsed"; Isserles, note ibid, "and likewise if one had collected ... and the other would claim that he had collected unlawfully and that he was not his debtor, since he collected in accordance with the laws of the state, what he has collected is his."

897 Venice State Archive, Inquisitorate for the Jews, no. 39, in the dossier relating to causes among Jews entitled: "Cases in favor of children who are heirs of their mothers' dowry and not the husbands and fathers, respectively." In the same envelope there are two other dossiers regarding: a) "dowry cases in favor of husbands"; b) "cases about husbands taking illegal possession of their wife's dowry." In the same place, no. 38, is a dossier: "Rights and cases in favor of husbands for the inheritance of the dowry excluding children under the Jewish rights." On the conflict between the two norms, see above pp. 167–168.

civitatis of Jews to establish which law to apply,[898] and after becoming knowledgeable on the Jewish substantive rules relating to the controversy,[899] the judges ask and obtain two opinions from the friars, former Jews who are competent in Rabbinic Law. Interpreting the principle "dinà demalchutà dinà" in a broader sense than usual, these experts affirm that even in succession rules, although Jewish law overrides the *jus commune*, it is overruled by local royal or statutory norms.[900]

---

898 Laerzio Cherubini's *Bollario* Tome I, p. 721, § XIII (disposition of Paul IV) and the passages already known to us by Marquardo Susani, *Tractatus de judies*, part 2, ch. 2 and ch. 4 (see p. 171 above) are cited.

899 The Biblical norm on the succession "Numeri, hebraica Vaiedabber 27, 7" is mentioned: then a handwritten sheet follows with the succession rule "taken from the book called in Hebrew Massecht (sic = Talmudic treatise) Bavà Batrà in ch. 8 quoted ...: Both the son and the daughter are equal in their mother's assets."

900 The texts of two declarations are as follows: I) It is very true what other time we, the undersigned on August 21, 1693, in the cause between St. Domenico's Fathers and Maroni Jewish brothers, i.e., in faith attest that among the Jews the right and observance exist that the father excludes the children from their mother's dowry. This general rule, however, is not valid when in the instrument or dowry an arrangement to the contrary is provided, or when the statutes of the city provide otherwise in the matter of any succession: in this case, the Jewish law will always give way to the special statute of the city, also according to their laws, for which the decree of the country and the statutes of the kingdom and state should be observed, thus excluding the Jewish law with the following sentence in the Hebrew idiom: *dinà demalkutà dinà*; and we do certify this in pure truth, ready to confirm it with our oath. Faithfully: Paulus Loria, Carlo Amadio Gentili P. P. The notary's authentication follows. – II) I, the undersigned attest it to be the truth that in places and cities where the Jews have the privilege of using their rights, this is intended in that they can observe their aforementioned rights and customs in concurrence with the jus commune, because when there is a special statute of the city and places aforesaid and Decrees of Princes, their rabbis command: *dinà demalcodà dinà*: that means that these Jews too are obliged to observe the arrangement of the statutes and the decrees of the Princes of cities and places above mentioned and that their rights cease, and this truth I am ready to confirm in any most valid way, etc. I, Francesco Franchi, attest all the above for the full knowledge that I have of the aforementioned law. The authentication of the notary Joseph de Rachelis, of Mantua, follows, June 15, 1697, confirming the Declaration of "Franciscus de Franchis Renatus, alias Leo quondam Alexandrii de Fintiis." Quite different from that contained in these statements is the opinion expressed by Rabbi I. M. Hazan (op. cit. above, footnote no. 702) in the memorandum submitted in 1851 to the civil court of Ancona, concerning a dispute between Jews in a matter of succession. Hazan argues that the cause must be treated according to Jewish law and denies that, in inheritance matters, for the Jewish law the principle of referral to local law is valid, being this a field that has no connection with the public interest (pp. 65–74). In the same way, he reports (p. 83), so have decided previously: the rabbinate of Venice for a cause of succession disputed in Ragusa (opinion of David Pardo [1719–1792], *Michtam Ledavid* [*Consulti*, Thessaloniki, 1769], p. 232, no. 3) and the Rabbi of Leghorn David Azulai [1724–1806]

Whether the judges applied the principle of the referral (and therefore, the local statutory norms) or the substantive norms of Jewish law, is unknown.[901]

(*Josef Omez* [*Consulti*, Leghorn, 1798], no. 7) for a cause on the same matter disputed in Ancona.

901 Also concerning the conflict about the substance of the juridical institutes, the identity of the problem discussed by the rabbinical doctrine and of those treated by medieval and modern International Law specialists is clear. It is difficult to research the concept of public policy in the former as well as in the latter, so as to determine which of the Jewish laws (and, respectively, of the foreign laws) regarding private relations must in any case yield to territorial norms. The rabbis speak of norms "in which there is command of the king" or "an interest of the king," and similarly the other ones resort to the concepts of public policy, public interest and the like, distinguishing lastly between internal public policy norms (mandatory only for citizens) and international public policy norms (mandatory also for foreigners). But if it is clear that the rabbinic doctrine remains quite vague and often in the dark, it cannot be said either that modern writers have so far come to outline clear-cut and precise categories in the problem in question.

PART 3

The Jurisdictional Autonomy

CHAPTER 11

General Principles

The swings of the judicial doctrine around the point of the application of Jewish law appear to be possible and comprehensible only wherever the civil courts are the only ones competent to decide the disputes between Jews. Logically, however, they cannot take place where the state recognizes the jurisdiction of the rabbinical court as concurrent with its own for resolving such disputes.

I have already mentioned this matter several times: obeying a particular precept,[902] Jews often prefer to entrust the decision of their civil lawsuits, rather than to the state's courts, to arbitrators – mostly rabbis – chosen among themselves by mutual agreement. Of course, these arbitrators decree according to Jewish law.[903] Their judgments are given regular execution by the state bodies, of course, as the parties' consent is expressed in the forms generally required for the arbitration. Up to this point, the submission to the Jewish norms is purely consensual and, as always in the arbitrations like in any other private convention, such rules on which the decision is based cannot conflict with the state norms of public order. For example, divorces cannot be pronounced, nor can marriages contracted in prohibited degrees of kinship be considered valid, or the like: i.e., nothing can be decided that is contrary to mandatory laws of the state. The same disputes brought before the state court may be decided by it under local law, without this meaning any offense to the judicial logic, given that the state may ignore the Jewish personal statute and consider the norms based on which arbitration pronunciations are issued as simple contractual clauses created by the litigants' concordant will. It should be noted that even today while the state does not recognize the Talmudic-Rabbinic Law, nothing prevents two Jews from agreeing to submit themselves to the arbitration by a third Jew, authorizing him to issue his ruling, within the insuperable limits of the imperative state laws, under Jewish law. It shall not be said that the state recognizes this right by executing the arbitration ruling.

---

902 See above footnotes nos. 522–529.

903 Even though in the compromise the arbitrators are simply charged to rule "de jure," the doctrine is still concordant in considering that by this it is meant Jewish law. Similarly in the compromise between Christians the mere indication of ruling "de jure" is interpreted as referring to the statutory law and not to the common law. So says Carlo Ruini, *Responsorum sive consiliorum tomus secundus*, Venice 1571, cons. 4, pp. 7–8; M. A. Sabelli, *Summa diversorum tractatuum*, Venice 1707, entry judeus, p. 730, no. 6.

 | DOI:10.1163/9789004627154_014

However, things would be different if the state had recognized a coercive nature of the arbitration, i.e., if, with the state's consent, a party could force the other to appear before arbitrators ruling by Jewish law. In this case, the arbitration would become an absolute jurisdiction, and Jewish law would turn into a necessary personal statute, which would be imposed on the defendant even against his will, only on the initiative of the plaintiff. It happened many times in the period and locations that fall within the limits of our study.

Realizing the constant aspiration of the Jewish authorities, the governments have often recognized the coercive character of Jewish arbitration, which grew to change its character turning it into jurisdiction.[904] Gradually then, the three arbitrators chosen every time, one by the plaintiff, the other by the defendant forced by the plaintiff's request, the third one by the other two,[905] were usually replaced by actual courts with a fixed seat, large staff, specific days for the hearing, etc.

The government sometimes decided on the exclusive competence of these Jewish courts for all civil disputes between Jews, also establishing the unappealability of the judgments pronounced by them. In these cases, it is clear that the personal Talmudic-rabbinical statute became exclusive for the Jews.

More often, however, the Jewish jurisdiction was intended as concurrent with that of the state, i.e., the plaintiff was allowed to choose freely between the two courts, and the appeal to civil courts was also admitted for the rabbinical court rulings.

In these cases of concurrence of the two jurisdictions and competition with each other, in different degrees, for the same sentence, could the state court still rule according to a law different from that used by the rabbinical court? It is clear that it could not, since in so doing, in establishing the litigation's

904 The Italian doctrine, however, is opposed to this concession of coercive arbitration, since it constitutes precisely a jurisdiction. For Susani, in *Tractatus de judeis*, ch. VI, nos. 21, 23, 24, 25, pp. 47–48, the Jews can be arbitrators but not judges. Neither then "arbitri necessarii ex forma statutorum disponentium quod causae inter affines vel consanguineos debeant compromitti ... cum huiusmodi arbitri habeant jurisdictionem." Similarly, Sessa, *De judeis*, cit. p. 144, basing himself both on the Roman law of 398 (C. 1, 9, 8) and on those of Piedmont, where, as we will see, the coercion of Jewish, arbitration, granted for a few decades, was later revoked in 1667. On the other hand, in *Tractatus de juribus judeorum* cit., pp. 427–428, basing himself on the Germanic praxis, Beck recognizes that "auch die jüdische Barnosen [Parnassim = heads] einiger massen eine Jurisdiction über die Juden, mit hoher Approbation und Genehmhaltung der Landes-Obrigkeit, die Juden in Schutz nimmt, in gewissen Fallen, exerciren"; which is limited to internal disputes.

905 In compliance with the provisions of the Mishnah, Sanhedrin, 3, 1, which prescribes a team of three for civil trials and stipulates that the election take place precisely in this way.

relation, the plaintiff would have always been allowed to choose, between the two jurisdictions, the one that applied the law most favorable to him in the case into question.

Therefore it is safe to posit as logical, at least in a normal situation, the following point: whenever we find a rabbinical court recognized by the state – whether as mandatory arbitration or fixed jurisdiction – concurrent with that of the state or even competent in the first instance but liable, in its verdicts, to be appealed to the state court, whenever, that is, the civil court is empowered with the faculty to judge disputes between Jews that could have been or already had been examined by a Jewish court in the first instance (as chosen by the plaintiff), we can safely infer that verdicts of this tribunal take place exclusively according to Jewish law.[906] More briefly said: the recognition of the rabbinical arbitration as compulsory is necessarily connected with the exclusive ruling of the state courts, under the Jewish personal statute concerning all the relations that fall within the jurisdiction of such obligatory arbitration.

Based on this reasoning, I have strongly contested Juster's assertion that the Roman courts in Palestine and other provinces that I have tried to determine with accuracy, concurrent with the Jewish courts that remained active until 398, after 212 ruled according to the Roman Law. It is unreasonable that verdicts given by courts before which one could appear by choice could be issued according to different laws without severely offending logic and justice. So, either it should be admitted that Jewish courts ruled according to Roman law, which is absurd since such courts were recognized so that they could apply the special private law statute, or it should be admitted that Roman courts ruled according to Jewish norms, a notion supported by numerous documents.

The same reasoning applies as well to any other epoch: once the periods and reasons when a real rabbinical jurisdiction was recognized are made clear, we can deduce the chronological and topographical limits of the exclusive application of Jewish law by the state courts concurrent with rabbinical courts or ruling on their verdicts in instances of appeal.

This reasoning cannot be reversed, that is, it cannot be deduced from the lack of Jewish jurisdiction that state courts did not use Jewish law. As a matter of fact, the sole application of this right on the part of the civil courts is

---

906 Compare Fischer's and Dohm's the texts mentioned above, footnote no. 315 and ch. VIII of Leopold's II dispatch to the Jews of Mantua of January 2, 1791, that admits the rabbinical obligatory arbitration and appeal to civil courts, adding "however that the court shall take into account, as it is understood, the Jewish laws that served as basis to the first instance." (Printed copy, personal property.)

a widespread phenomenon, without any recognition of parallel rabbinical jurisdictions.

Instead, it is noteworthy that sometimes the suppression of previously functioning Jewish jurisdiction was also patently meant to suppress Jewish law. That was the case with the Roman law of 398, which turned the Jewish courts into simple arbitrations, affirming the obligation for Eastern Jews to appear before state courts as "romano communi jure viventes." The same happened with the Persian disposition, who, in 474, suppressed the rabbinical courts to eradicate the law and the Jewish religion itself. So, likewise, the abolition of Jewish courts was accomplished by the enlightenment-authoritarian or democratic governments at the end of the 18th and early 19th centuries. That abolition symbolized the general intention of making autonomous bodies of any kind, and their related personal legislations, disappear, as they were incompatible with the state's new individualistic concept.

In all three cases, the abolition of the jurisdiction also applied to the law. The consequence was the complete cessation of any doctrinal activity around such law for lack of the natural impulse stemming from its practice. As we have seen, Roman law determines the closing of the Palestinian Talmudic canon. Persian law draws with it the closure of the Babylonian Talmudic canon and, consequently, of the entire Jewish judicial and ritual tradition centered in Babylon after the closure of the Jerusalem canon. This tradition will only be revived later, again in Babylon, under the rule of the Arabs. And the abrogative laws of a century and a half ago lead to the demise of both the Jewish practice and judicial doctrine from across Western Europe, in brief marking, precisely according to the desire of legislators, also the decline of the Hebrew language itself, which from the judicial life had drawn its main nourishment.

Here is now the information that I was able to collect about the rabbinical jurisdiction in Italy in various periods, starting from the Roman era until the 19th century.[907]

907 Some scarce and confused information on this point can be found in Pertile, *Storia del diritto italiano*, vol. III, 2nd ed., Turin 1894, p. 215, no. 94; Scherer, *Die Rechtsverhältnisse* cit., pp. 280–285 and Salvioli, *Storia della procedura civile e criminale*, Milan 1927, p. 116. For the rabbinical jurisdiction in Germany, especially with regard to its persistence in the 19th century, see Stobbe, *Handbuch des deutschen Privatrechts*, vol. I, 3rd ed., Berlin, 1893, pp. 386–389.

CHAPTER 12

From the Roman Period to the 13th Century

1 The Roman and Byzantine Period

As I have endeavored to show above,[908] the Jews were not allowed to have either normative or judicial autonomy except in the eastern regions of the empire, most likely Syria, Palestine, and Egypt. The abrogative law of 398 (C. 1, 9, 8) concerns only these regions.[909] Romans and Byzantines alike do not seem to have granted the Italian Jews the right to use Jewish law or, much less so, the faculty of judging by it. The reference of the Talmud to a *bet din* (tribunal) in Rome, chaired by R. Mattatià Ben Heresh, a 2nd-century scholar, is too vague to establish accurate deductions upon it and should be seen as a symbolic act of arbitration rather than actual jurisdiction.[910]

2 The Ostrogothic Period

According to the most logical interpretation, in my opinion, Ch. 143 of the edict of Theodoric[911] stipulates the recognition of both autonomies in question. Therefore, it seems legitimate to say that since 512, when the edict itself was promulgated, the Jews of Italy were able not only to organize the internal relations of civil nature according to their laws but also, in the event of a controversy, to apply this law in their own courts. Unfortunately, however, all details on this subject are missing.

3 The Longobard Period

As I have already pointed out,[912] we do not have any precise documentary element for this period concerning the problem we are interested in. Therefore, the grain of truth that is fair to assume in the fanciful news of Achimaaz from

908 See above, pp. 79–107.
909 See above, pp. 86–87.
910 See above, footnote no. 321.
911 See above, pp. 108–110.
912 See above, pp. 111–116.

 | DOI:10.1163/9789004627154_015

Oria makes only probable but does not authorize with certainty any deduction of the existence of a normative and jurisdictional autonomy enjoyed by the Jews living in Longobard territories.

4 The Carolingian Period

The state's recognition of Jewish civil law in this period is absolutely out of the question.[913] The existence of judicial autonomy is also clearly evidenced by the provision of the *Lex romana utinensis* (II, 18) and *Epitome Monaci* in l. 10 C. Th. 2, 1. By decreeing the requirement for Jews to turn to state courts to decide cases that may arise with Christians, the faculty, if not the obligation, for internal causes to resort to arbitration of its own can be deduced.[914]

Much later, such jurisdiction is also documented in German territories.[915] However, in Italy, there is no textual evidence. In fact, while attesting to the recognition of the Jewish law, Sicilian documents from the 12th and 13th centuries show it was not applied by Jewish courts but by state jurisdictions.[916]

913 See above, pp. 117–125.

914 See above, pp. 118–119.

915 See above, pp. 118–122.

916 See above, pp. 124–126.

CHAPTER 13

From the 14th to the 19th Century

1 The Kingdom of Sicily

The earliest recognition of a particular Jewish statute in this period takes place in Sicily under the Aragonese Government.

As we have already seen, in the earlier period characterized by the coexistence of several peoples on the island, the principle of legal personality was valid for all citizens, and the Jews fully benefited from it. Even after the disappearance of the Arabs and the merger that occurred between Latins and Greeks, Jews continued living according to their own laws. However, the area of application of Jewish law seems to have shrunk considerably compared to the previous period, as demonstrated by the limited competence by subject given the special Jewish jurisdiction, which can be found in documents starting from 1392.

On June 22, 1392, in the chapters granted to the Judaic quarter of Syracuse, King Martino stated that in matters of dowry, a Jewish scholar should judge according to Jewish law.[917] Similarly, in the following year, upon request of the Judaic quarter of Palermo, the king reiterates the custom that "si aliqua questio seu lis ducitur inter judeos aliquos dicti regni ad invicem, ratione matrimonii seu alia quavis causa" be decided "secundum legem eorum et ipsorum judeorum ritus" and if the parties felt burdened by the ruling of the (Jewish?) judge of the first instance, each of them could "appellare coram quatuor sapientibus et duodecim secretariis dictae aliamae Panormi." Furthermore, upon one of the parties' taking legal action these judges "possint aliam partem compellere ad faciendum judicium coram eis prout fuit hactenus observatum";[918] which confirms the perfectly judicial nature of these decrees.

In 1395, albeit within limited competence, the Jewish jurisdiction was extended to the whole of Sicily upon the appointment of a single general Jewish judge (*dajan kelali*). King Martino, at the request of many communities and

917 G. and B. Lagumina, *Codice diplomatico dei Giudei di Sicilia*, Palermo, 1885–1909, doc. 76, June 22, 1392, request by the Jews of Syracuse: "Item per evitari omni inconvenienti et errori, petimu ki di loru dotarii per auctoritate regia si dija judicari in omni casu secundu li tenuri e comandamentu di la legi mosayca, lu qualu judiciu haja a fari lu mastru ki sirrà di la loru ligi cum li soy statuti, non obstanti omni altra constitutioni in la judeca facta in li tempi passati li quali siano derogati ipso facto."

918 Idem, doc. 95, May 12, 1393.

 | DOI:10.1163/9789004627154_016

individual Jews, "cum multociens inter judeos ad invicem et in judeos moveantur et vertantur ac eciam emergant questiones et causae tam civiles quam criminales sive mixte que de sui natura terminari et decidi debeant secundum eorundem judeorum legem, ceremonias et observantias et que proprie per judeos in premissis peritos debeant decidi et terminari," appoints M.ro Josef Abenafi as single judge for these causes throughout the island, as long as they are causes between Jews "et que de sui natura terminari corrigi puniri et decidi debeant secundum legem et observancias seu ceremonias Judeorum."[919] Of the other civil and criminal causes "Judeos predictos tangentes" the Christian "protector judeorum" Condissalvo Daycosa is appointed judge, with the authority to intervene also in the ruling of M.ro Josef.[920]

The office of general judge that the Jews ask to be entrusted exclusively to persona grata to the main Jewish quarters, in Palermo, Messina, and Syracuse,[921] then passes on to Rays from Ragusa,[922] then, in 1415, to doctor Isac of Mosè from Marseille.[923] In his absence, he is replaced, limited to the Jewish

919 Idem, doc. 123. To the jurisdictional functions, other ones, administrative and of control over all the giudeche of the Kingdom are added. All the many scholars who more or less extensively treated the history of the Jews in Sicily dealt with this judiciary. The first among them was Giovanni Di Giovanni, *L'ebraismo nella Sicilia*, Palermo, 1748, pp. 109 et seqq. Leopoldo Zunz then followed on his footsteps, *Zur Geschichte und Literatur der Juden*, 1845, pp. 510 et seqq. = *Storia degli Ebrei di Sicilia* (Perreau transl.), in *Arch. stor. siciliano*, vol. IV, 1879 and in a separate reprint, Palermo, 1879; La Lumia, *Gli ebrei siciliani*, in *Studi di storia siciliana*, II, Palermo, 1870, pp. 14–16; Güdemann, *Geschichte der Erziehungswesens und der Cultur der Juden in Italien während des Mittelalters*, Vienna 1884, pp. 275–276; Lionti, *Le magistrature presso gli ebrei di Sicilia*, in *Arch. stor. siciliano*, IX, 1884, pp. 195 et seqq.; Idem, *I ministri della religione presso gli ebrei di Sicilia*, ibidem, X, 1885, pp. 128 et seqq. The broad mass of new documents brought to light by [G and B.] Lagumina, op. cit., now makes the recourse to the older works unnecessary. On Lagumina's basis, Quinto Sinigaglia, *La condizione giuridica degli ebrei in Sicilia*, in *Rivista it. per le scienze giur.*, 41, 1906, p. 98. For some – second hand – news on the *dajan kelalì*, see also Scherer, op. cit., p. 283.

920 Idem, doc. 125, February 20, 1395.

921 Idem, doc. 151, March 5, 1398. Chapters asked of King Martino by Josef Abenafi on behalf of all the Kingdom's giudeche: "Item, signuri, ki conzosciacosakì lu officiu di lu judiciu ebraycu appellatu infra ipsi dayan sia statu per la vostra signoria conchessu a Mastru Josep phisicu vostru a supplicacioni de li dicti jammi [aliame = Jewish communities] ki in lu tempu erano obedienti; et conzosiacosaki si lu dictu officiu fussi conchessu ad alcunu non cum bona intentioni seguitaria grandi dampnu, supplicano ki di za inanti lu dictu officiu non sia datu ni optenutu per alcun exceptu per supplicacioni di tri principali zudechi di lu dictu regnu, videlicet di Palermo, Messina et Syracusa."

922 Ibidem mentioned, doc. 272, Nov. 24, 1416.

923 Idem, doc. 256, June 18, 1415. Queen Bianca prohibits every official from getting involved in the functions of the new "judice et assessore delle giudeche" and "super iis que per legem mosaycam inter judeos et judeos aguntur."

quarters of Mineo and Vizzini, by Sadone di Gaudio, a Jew from Mineo,[924] and then finally, in 1420 for the whole of Sicily by the doctor Moisè de' Medici Bonavoglia.[925]

This however partial avocation of civil cases between Jews to a single judge chosen among themselves, affected both the competence of city courts and that of the bishop's courts, resulting in numerous protests against the new judiciary.

The city of Messina was the first to mention that it was in contrast with the privileges prohibiting any citizen from suing another "alibi quam intus civitatem" before the stratigoto [criminal court judge], local judges or bishop; privileges that Jews also enjoyed. Furthermore, the aforementioned Jewish official tried to extend his jurisdiction with provisions reinforced by threats of spiritual sanctions, which constitute a severe abuse.[926] Consequently, the city of Messina was removed from the jurisdiction of the Jewish judge.[927] Meanwhile, similar protests arose by the citizens of Palermo[928] and the Jewish University,[929] jealous of their autonomy and quite displeased to see themselves placed under the control of a single supreme magistrate, especially sustaining its severe financial burden.[930] The king, facing this united front, decided to abolish the office of general judge altogether: which occurred on June 6, 1421.[931] Due to new pressures to the contrary, less than two years later, the king reinstated the office of *dajan kelalì*, appointing the very same M.ro Moisè de' Medici for life. The repealing, the king warns, had occurred

924 Idem, doc. 272 cit. On February 19, 1417 (ibidem, doc. 277) the officials are ordered to assist him in his judicial functions; and it is permitted to appeal to the queen against the sentences that he issued.

925 Idem, doc. 293, June 9, 1420. For the name, see doc. 301, June 6, 1421.

926 Idem, doc. 297, December 1420.

927 Idem, doc. 300, June 1421. Protest of the citizens Palermo: "Infra lu annu presenti uno Judeu medicu di Missina nomine mastru Moyse tacita veritate si havi impetratu unu privilegiu di li magnifici olim vicerè di essere judichi generali di tucti li Judei di li judechi di lu regnu di Sicilia et volendu exerciri lu dictu officiu a la judeca di Messina ki è sua secunda patria originali non li fu permissu et ora esti vinutu in la dicta chitati di Palermu et sua propria auctoritate et de facto voli exerciri lu dictu officiu dichendu ki è lu so officiu, havi jurisdictioni per tuctu lu regnu et ki non bisogna esseri chitatinu cussì comu lu officiu di lu mastru justiczeri, ecc."

928 Idem, ibidem.

929 Idem, doc. 301, June 6, 1421.

930 Idem, doc. 305: "... officium judicatus universalis judeorum Regni Sicilie supradicte quod ebrayce appellatur dyan helalì cum omnibus jurisdictionibus, lucris, provisionibus, emolumentis honoribus ad dictum officium spectantibus et pertinentibus et praecipue unciarum auri annuatim trigintasex exsolvendarum ..."

931 Idem, doc. 301 cit.

inadvertently, without consideration of the benefit for the Jews in having their disputes decided by a judge "de gremio ipsorum in lege potissimum et moribus comprobatum, pocius quam per judicem alterius legis et morum aliorum penitus diversorum."[932] The Jewish community, however, always hardly tolerating the violation of their autonomy by the *dajan kelalì*, tried again in 1433 to obtain the abolition of that office,[933] which they finally managed to obtain in an unspecified time.[934] But it was only for a short period: on October 22, 1438, the king reinstated the office putting in charge of it once again M.ro Moisè de' Medici Bonavoglia,[935] without then being persuaded by a new request of abolition submitted the following year by the city of Palermo.[936] After the death of Bonavoglia, on March 31, 1446, the Office of *dajan kelalì* was passed on to doctor M.ro Iosue Ben Nachrim;[937] and two of his lieutenants had jurisdiction over the islands of Malta and Gozo.[938] New protests, however, reached the court: and as a consequence of them, in 1447, first the jurisdiction of the above-mentioned judge over the Jewish community of Messina was removed,[939] and a few days later, upon payment of a large sum by all the Sicilian Giudeche (Jewish Quarters), the office was abolished entirely and, as it seems, for good.[940]

The jurisdictional attributions were transferred together with the administrative ones to the heads of the respective Giudeche;[941] and to these they remained until 1493, which marked the complete and definitive expulsion of the Jews from the Kingdom of Sicily.[942]

In the documents considered, it is said explicitly that the civil jurisdiction of the *dajan kelalì* is not complete, but practiced only in matters that

932 Idem, doc. 305, January 12, 1423 executive of royal order of November 18, 1422.

933 Idem, doc. 337, July 29, 1433: "comu sapeti tutti li Judehi di questu regnu per essersi liberati di la jurisdictioni di mastru Moyses foro taxati pagari certa suma, ecc."

934 In doc. 359, March 9, 1439, it is said: "officium ecc., restituimus et tornavimus sive de novo dictum officium formavimus et ereximus." Therefore, there was indeed an abolition.

935 Idem, doc. 359, March 9, 1439, executive of the royal provision October 22, 1438.

936 Idem, doc. 360, June 30, 1439.

937 Idem, doc. 371, April 30, 1446, executive of the provision March 31, 1446. For the name, see doc. 374.

938 Idem, doc. 372, May 12, 1446.

939 Provision January 16, 1447, made executive on May 23, 1447 (doc. 378).

940 Provision February 1, 1447, mentioned in doc. 374 of May 9, 1447. Sinigaglia, op. cit. p. 98 states that the office of general judge was suppressed for all the giudeche except for that of Palermo. But the sources agree in talking about a complete abolition. See doc. 374, 375, 379, 380. The sum paid was 600 ounces (doc. 379, June 5, 1447).

941 As it was requested in the petition May 9, 1447, doc. 374. Confirmation on November 15, 1491, doc. 846.

942 Provision March 31, 1492, for Spain, which became executive in Sicily on January 12, 1493. Sinigaglia, op. cit., p. 101.

"de sui natura terminari et decidi debeant secundum eorundem judeorum legem."[943] These certainly include matrimonial matters,[944] patrimonial relations between spouses,[945] and so much freedom is left to the Jews in this field that even polygamy, however subject to license, is admitted.[946] Jewish notaries recognized by the authorities draw up documents concerning the issues mentioned above according to formal and substantive Jewish norms.[947] Since the sources admit the latter's competence for drawing deeds of donations,[948] it is legitimate to deduce that the state recognized Jewish norms in institutions beyond the strictly matrimonial field.

2 The Kingdom of Naples

During the 14th and 15th centuries, in the Kingdom of Naples, the vitality of Jewish laws appeared to be restricted only to matrimonial relations. The drafting of the dotal instrument (*Ketubà*) had been usually entrusted to Jewish

943 Doc. 95, 123, 125, etc., cited.

944 Doc. 95 cit.

945 Doc. 76 cit. A confirmation of it is in a decision on a dispute risen in 1455 between Jews of Sciacca. Having Moisè Namahan (sic) died after making the donation inter vivos of all his possessions to his grandson David Namahan, his wife Esther disputed the validity of that donation alleging that the local Christian law stipulated the communion of assets between spouses, and therefore her aforementioned husband could not have freely disposed of the common patrimony without her consent. A verdict by the (Christian) judge of the Jews ruled in her favor. But at the death of Esther, having she left in inheritance her husband's assets allocated to her by the judgment to her grandchildren, David went back to claim those assets, this time getting a letter by the viceroy in which it was declared that the custom of the fusion of the patrimony of husband and wife had to be valid only for Christians, not for Jews. As a result of that, the ruling was overturned, the donation recognized and David was allowed to take possession of the assets in dispute. Ibid., doc. 169, June 26, 1455.

946 Doc. 264, June 3, 1416, see above, footnote no. 576.

947 Doc. 169 cit. See the diploma of the viceroy Ferdinando of October 12, 1485, published by Lionti, *I ministri della religione* cit., pp. 134–135, doc. 2.: "Pro Monachi Simey et Moysi lo Ricco Judeis de tera Castri Realis. Perchi havimu havuto noticia chi in la Judeca de quissa terra non è persona certa et stabilita chi hagia de notari et scriviri li repudii et convencioni di matrimoni chi sub vocabulo ebraico vocatur la yidubà (ketubà), chi in dies accadino infra questi Judei; de chi verisimilmente porria per alcun tempo esseri prejudicio per cui avessi bisogno di tali atti ... costituimo et ordinamo chi vui et nixuno altri digiati scriviri et notari li dicti atti chi de cetero accadiranno in la dicta Judeca." The diploma is confirmatory of another identical one granted on July 8 of the same year by Archbishop of Messina, published by Güdemann, *Geschichte* cit., p. 338.

948 Doc. 169 cit.

notaries,[949] albeit there were also examples of dowry contracts signed before Christian notaries.[950]

Disputes in matrimonial matters were the sole competence of Jewish judges who handed their rulings according to the Mosaic law. In that matter, recourse to these judges was not optional but mandatory: the party who intended to initiate the cause appealed to the government to obtain the appointment of Jewish judges, and the requested authority was promptly provided.[951]

It lasted until the Jews were expelled from the Kingdom in 1541.[952]

3 The Papal States (except Ferrara)

It seems certain that Jews were never granted the right to set up rabbinical courts in that territory. Regarding civil matters, both internal and vs. Christians, from 1524 uninterruptedly[953] until 1834 and beyond,[954] in Rome they appear to be subject to the competence of various state courts, particularly the court of the Vicariate.

4 The Grand Duchy of Tuscany

4.1 *Leghorn and Pisa*

Until the end of the 16th century, the duchies of Tuscany did not recognize any particular jurisdiction for Jews in their territory. The community of Florence

949 Ferorelli, *Gli ebrei nell'Italia meridionale dall'epoca romana al Sec. XVIII*, Turin, 1915, pp. 110–111. The Latin translation of a *ketubà* of year 199 = 1439 (not 1428, as it is said there) is reported.

950 Idem, pp. 112–113.

951 Idem, p. 114.

952 Idem, pp. 233–240.

953 See the text of the "Riforma dei tribunali di Roma," March 1, 1611, on which Vogelstein and Rieger, *Geschichte der Juden in Rom*, Berlin, 1898, vol. II, p. 196 [base themselves]. It is unclear to me how the latter can write: "Die Bestimmung enthielt eigentlich nicht Neues, sie war aber des endgültige Todesurteil des jüdischen Civilgerichtes," since there is no previous trace of rabbinical courts; and I cannot believe that a persistence can be considered of that 2nd century jurisdiction – which we excluded – that would have lasted for as long as 1400 years without leaving any trace.

954 *Regolamento legislativo e giudiziario per gli affari civili dello stato Pontificio*. Motuproprio November 10, 1834, § 368. The tribunal of the Vicariate has exclusive jurisdiction over non-commercial causes of the Jews.

was founded in 1437,[955] and throughout the 15th and 16th centuries, it was the only significant community with regard to civil disputes. Since the beginning of their settlement there, Jews appear to be subject to the exclusive local jurisdiction of the Otto di Guardia e Balia.[956] Apparently, the Jewish personal status is recognized in force only in matrimonial issues, whereas Roman and local law applied in all other legal relations amongst Jews.[957]

On June 10, 1593, Duke Ferdinando de' Medici opened the gates of Leghorn and Pisa to Greek, Turkish, and Jewish merchants and those of any other nation, allowing them to settle in those cities on very advantageous terms. Ch. 25 of the well-known privilege[958] empowers the Massari of the two communities of twofold jurisdiction, dealing with both civil and criminal matters:[959] completed the former for internal relations; restricted the latter to common minor offenses committed between Jews, and violations in religious matters.[960] Execution of the Massari's judgments was the bargello's [captain of justice] duty.[961] For disputes between Jews and members of other nations, Christians or others, and for more severe crimes, the ruling was the responsibility of the conservatore magistrate court.[962]

955 U. Cassuto, *Gli ebrei a Firenze nell'età del Rinascimento*, Florence, 1918, pp. 18 et seqq.

956 Idem, ibidem, p. 197. The provision dates 1478.

957 Idem, ibidem, p. 203.

958 Published in *Collezione degli ordini municipali di Livorno corredata dagli statuti della sicurtà e delle più importanti rubriche delli statuti di Mercanzia di Firenze*, Leghorn, Carlo Giorgi ed., 1798, pp. 237–255; and in Cantini, *Legislazione toscana raccolta ed illustrata*, Florence, 1800–1808, vol. XIV, pp. 10–19. Part VI of the *Collezione* cit. contains the "*Regolamenti ebraici*," an account of which is accomplished by Ermanno Loevinson, *Le basi giuridiche della comunità israelitica di Livorno*, in *Bollettino storico livornese*, year I, 1937, no. 2 (8 page reprint).

959 "Che i vostri massari ebrei nelle vostre sinagoghe habbino autorità di decidere, terminare e porre pene che parerà loro secondo il rito e modo vostro ebraico, tutte le differenze che nasceranno tra un ebreo e l'altro, e che possano mettere le vostre solite terminationi et altre censure a modo loro, volendo in ciò che la giurisdizione e l'autorità del detto nostro giudice sia deminuita, e quelli massari possano de fatto mandare in esilio tutti quelli ebrei che a loro paressero scandalosi."

960 This is better specified in the provision of August 5, 1650 (*Collez.* cit., p. 305): "Nelle criminali fra gli stessi ebrei la cognizione e terminazione di esse si aspetti ai loro massari, fuori che nei casi dove s'inferischino pene di morte, galera, mutilazione di membri o frusta et in qualsivoglia causa di omicidio, percosse o ferite dalle quali ne segua storpio di alcun membro o cicatrice apparente in faccia volendo che questi casi accettuatisi si aspettino al tribunale di V. S. (il Conservatore)."

961 Ch. 33 of priv. 1593 = ch. 14 of Cosimo's III motuproprio, December 20, 1715 (*Collez.*, p. 316).

962 Ch. 10 and 34 of privilege 1593; ordinance of 1650.

The Massari's exclusive civil jurisdiction was confirmed in 1645 with an interpretative "document" of that ch. 25[963] and continued uninterrupted throughout the 18th century.

Of interest is a conflict that arose in 1720 in Leghorn between this jurisdiction and the Court of the Wards (i.e., "miserabiles personae"), as a result of the exclusivity of competence of each of them, attributed to the former for Jews, by the aforementioned privileges, and to the latter for widows, orphans and the wretched by *l. unica C. quando imperator* (C. 3, 14). Relying on his quality of *miserabilis persona*, being blind and weak-minded, a man named Elia Pais de Leon sues another Jew, David de Medina, before the Court of the Wards. However, due to the defendant's opposition, on November 20, 1720, this court pronounces its incompetence, referring the case back to the court of the Massari, arguing that it was a dispute between Jews. De Leon stands his ground, and consequently, on October 9, 1721, de Medina appeals to the government, asking that the adverse ruling of the Court of the Wards be enforced. The petition was successful, and accordingly, the Grand Duke decrees "that in the causes of Jews against Jews of Leghorn, the Massari should be the privative judges of their Nation despite the provision of *l. unica C. quando imperator*.[964]

The voluntary recourse of the parties or the government delegation to Christian judges, however, remains free, in which case, as established in 1767, except for expressed derogation from Jewish privileges, "all acts until the judgment is issued shall be made by the Registrar of the court of the Jewish Massari."[965]

A precise procedure to be followed before the Leghorn court is finalized with the motu proprio of March 29, 1787, which establishes the following points:

1) For bringing a cause in the first instance before that Court, the authorization of an auditor of the civil tribunal of Leghorn is required.
2) Up to the sum of L. 200, the decisions will be final without counting the cost. For the causes of a more significant entity, appealing to the same Massari will be permitted after obtaining the auditor's authorization. Before re-discussing the case, the Massari shall decide by decree on the admissibility or inadmissibility of the appeal and its nature (suspensive or devolutive); except upon an appeal to the auditor against this decree.
3) Once the ruling on the appeal has been made, if the judgment of the second instance is in line with that of the first, any ordinary remedy shall

963 Mentioned in the ordinance of 1650.

964 *Collez.* pp. 321–323.

965 Leghorn governor's communication to the massari, Sept. 17, 1767, about the cause Jacob and Emanuel Ergas vs. Daniel Saccuto. *Collez.* pp. 329–330.

cease. If the first ruling is revoked, a new appeal to the Massari shall be the responsibility of the person who lost, prior authorization of the auditor or, depending on the importance of the cause, of the entire court.

4) The "Din Torah"(the pronouncement in accordance with Jewish law) must be requested by the plaintiff in the judgment of the first instance "within 15 days from the day he presented the first draft of contradiction or exception, and once these terms have expired, it will no longer be possible to request it."

If not requested in the first instance, it will no longer be possible to request the "Din Torah" in the the second or further instances. And when this was requested and granted in the first instance, a rehearing of the case to rule on the first or subsequent appeals, that is to say, the office of the judge-rapporteur, shall no longer be the responsibility of the auditor of Leghorn court or of the auditors of Florence's Rota. Rather, it "will be brought before the magistrate of the Massari according to the vote of other rabbis."[966] This, of course, so that these judges won't have to take the trouble to examine Jewish norms for a verdict that they themselves will not issue.

In these rules, the incongruity of the choice of law left to the plaintiff is particularly noteworthy, since he can thus enjoy an undue advantage, being able to prefer the law that is most favorable to him.

The trend toward the civil and political elevation of the Jews as individuals, that had begun at the end of 1700, in Leghorn does not correspond to the abolition of the ancient autonomies of the community. So much so, that as a case perhaps unique in the 18th century, certainly unique in Italy, in 1780 city Municipal Council membership is granted not to individual Jews, but to the Jewish nation as an entity, by means of its representative.[967] Care is taken at the same time to establish that the board's meetings shall not be held on Saturdays and Jewish holidays.[968]

The Jewish court remained active throughout the century and beyond, and was abolished only in 1808 by the French.[969] The Grand Duchy's government, restored in 1814, re-establishes all the ancient Jewish privileges but confirmed the abolition of jurisdictional autonomy, already incompatible with the new public law concepts.[970]

966 *Collez.* pp. 334–335. The obligation is added of drafting all judiciary acts in Italian.

967 Edict of March 20, 1780. Archive of the Jewish Community of Mantua, dossier 207, no. 117.

968 Ordinance of August 10, 1780. Ibidem, same dossier and number.

969 I. Rignano, *Della naturalizzazione acquistata in Toscana col mezzo della ballottazione*, cit., in *Archivio giuridico*, vol. 44, 1890, p. 395.

970 Sovrano motuproprio of Nov. 17, 1814: "S.A.R. and I. ... without prejudice with regard to the abolition of civil and criminal jurisdiction, for which the individuals of the Jewish nation,

4.2 *Florence*

In the 16th century, having grown both in number and importance, the Florentine Jewish community aspired to achieve the same judicial privileges enjoyed by the communities of Pisa and Leghorn. A request to that effect made in 1639 obtained a favorable outcome. On July 31 of that year, the government granted "to the supplicants Jewish Massari, the authority to decide, terminate and impose penalties that will seem best to them according to the Jewish ritual and custom in all disputes that may arise between Jews, in the same way, it is granted to the Massari of Pisa and Leghorn." Here too, there is a civil and criminal jurisdiction: but it is enjoined to the Massari that "before sending to exile any Jew who in their opinion is scandalous, they will have to wait for the approval of the competent bodies."

The jurisdiction so established is practiced uninterruptedly over the course of the century and the next one, as attested by a number of various provisions relating to it. Interesting among these is ch. 37 of the October 30, 1778 rescript that commands the Massari of the Jewish nation of Florence and the other Jewish nations of the Grand Duchy to fix the hearing days and public sessions for the causes to be heard before them, with the obligation to comply with the general legal provisions applied in the other state courts.

Also relating to the whole state is the Grand Duchy rescript issued on October 15, 1782 by a call which states that "in every court of the Massari of the Jewish nation in Tuscany, in disputes treated there in both first and second or further instance, the orders valid for all other courts of the Grand Duchy with regard to the causes' probative and decision-making terms must be heeded."

In Florence too, as elsewhere, next to the execution of the contentious jurisdiction, that of the voluntary jurisdiction is in parallel attributed to the Massari. Among other things, this is demonstrated by a rescript of February 10, 1785, in which the right to interpose the mundualdi [male guardians] to Jewish women in internal affairs between Jews is validated and confirmed for the future to the Massari of the Jewish nation of Florence.[971]

---

like all other subjects, shall be equally subject to the laws and orders of the Grand Duchy and shall have to resort to the ordinary courts, confirms for the remaining matters to the aforementioned Nation the privileges granted by his predecessors before the French government with several rescripts, motuproprii and regulations already issued respectively with regard to the Jews of Leghorn, Pisa and Florence as well as to those living in other parts of Tuscany." Rignano, ibid.; and already before I. E. Rignano, *Sulla attuale posizione giuridica degli israeliti in Toscana*, Florence, 1847, p. 16.

971 I draw this news from a "Memoria sui tribunali ebraici di Firenze" sent on January 19, 1786 by Cesare Lampronti, Chancellor of the University of the Jews of Florence, to the Jewish

The same provision is repeated for Pisa and Leghorn on March 31 of the same year.[972]

Here too the abolition of judicial autonomy is carried out by the French government in 1808.

5 The Duchy of Piedmont

At first, Piedmont Jews were subjected, in both civil and criminal matters, to the jurisdiction of their place of residence.[973] Any possible rabbinical ruling had been perceived as simple arbitration.

Later, in 1582[974] and 1603,[975] Jews obtained state support for sanctions against those opposing the internal ruling, indicating a step towards recognizing it as a proper jurisdiction. The final step was accomplished in 1616, when Duke Carlo Emanuele I, granting the Piedmont community's wishes, decreed the obligatoriness and established the exclusivity of the Jewish jurisdiction for all civil matters, giving the judgments of the rabbinical courts an absolute, irrevocable character.[976]

---

community of Mantua, and preserved in the archives of the latter community, *Dossier* 210 no. 27.

972 *Collezione* cit., p. 334.

973 Duboin, *Raccolta per ordine di materie delle leggi, provvidenze, editti, ecc. ... della Real Casa Savoia*, T. II, Turin, 1825, p. 697. Disposal of Amedeo VIII.

974 Duboin, op. cit., privilege of December 4, 1582, pp. 316–317: "Più gli abbiamo concesso ed accordato che occorrendo che nascesse qualche differenza o controversia fra essi Ebrei, che sia in facoltà tanto dell'attore che del reo ricorrer da loro Rabì tanto abitanti nei stati nostri che fuori per ottener opportuna provisione come è solito farsi tra loro Ebrei e conforme all'antica legge loro, e che detti Rabì possino liberamente usar dell'autorità loro in astringer chiunque fosse renitente all'osservanza dei loro ordini, anche per via di scomuniche sendo spediente, ed esse scomuniche pubblicare, mentre però che niuno sia levato nè tirato fuori della giurisdizione e stati nostri, ecc."

975 Borelli, *Editti antichi e nuovi di sovrani prencipi della Real Casa Savoia*. Turin, 1681, part III, Book XV (Degl'infedeli). Privilege of December 15, 1603, ch. 42, p. 1232: "Esse inibitioni non obstanti possano essa Università e Banchieri vecchi haver ricorso da' loro Rabbini, ai quali si dà ogni autorità necessaria per decidere tra loro, sì in questo, come in ogn'altre cause loro, conforme alle loro leggi, ecc."

976 Decree of October 7, 1616, Borelli, ibidem, pp. 1244–1245: "Carlo Emanuele I, per gratia di Dio Duca di Savoia, etc. Veduta nelle udienze nostre l'allegata supplica, e suo tenor ben considerato, ricordevoli dei privilegi concessi all'università delli Hebrei residenti nei nostri stati, specialmente nel capitolo 42 in quale concessimo che potessero detti hebrei in caso di differenza o lite fra di loro, per tal decisione elegger arbitri hebrei, overo andar dalli Rabini loro per ottenere giustitia conforme alle loro legi, e riti, obligando ognuno d'essi a tale osservanza; Onde avendoci detta università significato che vi sono alcuni

The system so posited, which was also confirmed in the privileges of 1626,[977] lasted for a few decades, but in 1667 it was abolished. The rabbinic jurisdiction was restricted to disputes in religious matters, with faculty to appeal to the Conservatore of the Jews. From that moment on, the responsibility for handling all civil cases between Jews, formerly the duty of rabbis, lay on him. The rabbis could thus only pronounce arbitration verdicts, which could also be challenged.[978]

---

delli sudetti hebrei che non solo hanno contravenuto e contravengono, ma di più dichiarato non voler obedir alli detti privilegi, capitolo e parte, o sia capitulatione seguita nella congrega fatta in Asti sotto li otto maggio 1614 con assistenza dei delegati nostri, la qual contiene altresì la materia del detto capitolo 42 e di più, che dopo la decisione delli arbitri o Rabini, non si possi più appellare, nè haver raccorso alcuno da qualsisia nostro magistrato, ministro od ufficiale; Hora intendendo noi che ogni cosa s'habbi da pontualmente osservare, et obedire; ci è parso ordinare, dichiarare e comandare, si come per le presenti, di nostra certa scienza, piena possanza, et autorità, partecipato il parer del nostro consiglio, ordiniamo, dichiariamo, anzi comandiamo a tutti gli hebrei abitanti nei nostri stati, che in conformità dei privilegi loro sudetti del detto capitolo 42 di congrega delli 8 maggio sudetto, ogn'uno in caso di liti, dispareri e differenze fra Hebrei debba eleggersi arbitri per la decisione d'esse et haver raccorso da loro Rabini per ottenerne il giudicato, conforme alli predetti riti e legi hebraici, prohibendo ad ogn'uno d'appellar innanti dei nostri magistrati, ministri et ufficiali, standosene ognuno fermo sopra quanto sarà da essi in tali differenze deciso e terminato sotto pena di scudi 200 d'oro al Fisco nostro applicandi per ognuno, et ogni volta che si contrafarà oltre che dichiariamo nullo, et invalido ogni atto che ne seguisse avanti cui si sia in contrario; evocando però sin'hora tutte le cause e liti mosse e da muoversi ovunque e da chi si sia, et avanti qualsivoglia magistrato, nanti detti arbitri, o Rabini eligendi, perchè così richiede il beneficio d'essa Università, e pur medesimamente delli hebrei litiganti; che tal è il voler nostro. Dat. in Torino li 7 ottobre 1616."

977 Decree of August 23, 1626, Duboin, ibidem, pp. 342–343: "Et primeramente permettiamo loro di poter continuare l'uso dei loro riti hebraici ... et anco di poter eleggere fra loro arbitri per terminare stragiudicialmente le differenze tra essi potessero nascer, e di congregarsi insieme, et proceder, ordinare et stabilire circa i negotii loro secondo gli occorrenti, astenendosi però di far fare esecutioni, conferir tutele, o far altro simile atto che possa inferir giurisditione, ma il tutto si farà dal loro Conservatore o Vicecons., secondo le richieste et nominationi loro, etiandio fondata ne' loro riti: potranno però impor pena di scomunica conforme alli detti riti per maggiore osservanza di loro privilegi e costitutioni come sopra fatti, come anche continuare secondo i medesimi riti la ricognitione delle scritture et istrumenti hebraici."

978 Interinazione [ratification] of the Senate of Nov. 23, 1667 which confirms and partially modifies the decree of 1603, Borelli, ibidem, p. 1258: "Al capo 42 dei privilegi predetti, confermati per rescritto delli 7 ottobre 1666 (sic; most likely 1616) et al capo primo del rescritto delli 23 agosto 1626: l'autorità dei Rabini si limita alla decisione delle differenze cerimoniali, dalle sentenze dei quali come dal laudo delli arbitri si farà l'appellatione al Conservatore in caso d'aggravio, al qual conservatore spetterà la cognitione di tutte le altre cause, e dalle sentenze del conservatore si dovrà appellar al Senato."

6 The Marquisate of Monferrato

The Gonzagas, Duchies of Mantua and Marquises of Monferrato, issued different laws in the two small states subjected to their domain, also with regard to the Jews. The coercibility of Jewish arbitration in civil matters is recognized in Monferrato several decennia before Mantua, that is – since 1539,[979] and the recognition persists for the entire period of the Gonzagas' sovereignty, repeated in all the decrees of tolerance. These specify that the will of one of the contenders is enough for the other to be forced to accept the arbitration: he is obliged to that by the same Conservatore of the Jews, who can punish him in case of persistent refusal. If the elected arbitrators do not accept the position, or if the parties do not reach an agreement on the arbitrators' choice, these are appointed by the rabbis, and in that case, are no longer permitted to refuse the ruling. This, obviously, occurs according to Jewish norms; and is unappealable. The enforcement of the verdicts is the responsibility of the authorities in the position of governor.

Finally, in all provisions it is reiterated that criminal matters are entirely competence of the ordinary jurisdiction.[980]

Interesting in this regard is a trial in Casale Monferrato, about which we learned from a consultation of the jurist Francesco Bursati.[981]

Abramo Sacerdoti, a Jew from Casale, accused by another Jew, Emanuele, of adultery and procured abortion, brings about the formation of two (?) rabbinical courts and elects three judges, in order to elicit a judgment in each of the courts on the allegations raised against him. But, accused by Emanuele himself to have usurped, with the establishment of these courts, the state jurisdictional authority, he is arrested for lèse-majesté in accordance with *l. 3 ff. ad legem Juliam majest.* (D. 48, 4, 4).

Bursati, his lawyer, tries to exonerate him by stating that the jurisdictional activity "vulgo beth din nuncupata" is within the Jewish rituals and is practiced

979 Salvatore Foà, *Gli ebrei nel Monferrato*, Alessandria, 1914, pp. 121 and 159. Decree of July 28, 1539 of Federico and Margherita Gonzaga, ch. 11: "Item che accadendo lite o controversia civile per qualunque causa si sia tra loro ebrei, che si allegano due dottori ebrei overo due arbitri ebrei quali habiano a veder sopra tale differentia et litte secondo la loro legge et ordini et quelli che contrafaranno il presente capitolo incorreranno in pena di 5 ducati ... Ma accadendo causa criminale vadano al nostro giudice deputato a questo."

980 Art. 10 tolleranza 1560 = art. 9 toll. 1570 = art. 6 toll. 1576, 1587, 1588, 1592, 1603, 1611, 1614, 1623, 1626, 1637, 1638, 1652 = cap. 2 ° toll. 1662 = cap. 9 ° toll. 1678, 1689, 1703, Foà, op. cit., ibidem.

981 Francesco Bursati from Mantua, *Consiliorum sive responsorum liber secundus*, Frankfurt a. M., 1579, cons. 152, pp. 119–124.

by the Jews "ubique per Italiam." It is then not comparable to that of an ordinary court, because "in hac hebreorum convocatione non fit erectio tribunalis, cum ibi nemo tanquam judex ordinarius sedeat pro processus compilatione justitiaeve administratione sed tantum conveniunt ad perficiendum illum actum super quo solummodo convocantur a partibus." In addition, the laws of Casale expressly allow Jews to set up courts and exercise the jurisdiction over contentious and voluntary matters.

However, this attempt to legitimize the *Beth-Din's* competence also for criminal matters, expressly restricted by law to civil matters, failed, and Abraham is condemned, as seen in other sources.[982]

7 The Duchy of Milan

The provision mentioned above, adopted in 1639 by the Gonzagas for Monferrato, reproduces verbatim chapter 6 of the privileges granted by Francesco II Sforza, Duke of Milan, to the Jews of his state on November 24, 1533. The chapter provides that in disputes between Jews, the contenders must choose two arbitrators, and they will decide the cause according to Jewish laws.[983]

With the Spaniards replacing the Sforzas in 1556, Cardinal Tridentino, governor of Milan, renewed the concession made to the Jews by the Sforza in 1533 for twelve years, reiterating the provision pertaining to coercive arbitration.[984]

982 In a court case between the University of the Jews of Mantua and the Treasury, discussed in 1578, the issue of the legality of setting up the *Beth Din* was also brought up. In the depositions of many witnesses, collected in Mantua and Cremona, it is unanimously declared to be customary for many years among the Jews of Padua, Mantua and Cremona to set up *Beth Din* in causes relating to tutorage, matrimonial matters, "scalzamenti" rites [acts of refusal of the levirate], divorces and oaths. This, however, "antequam Abraam fuerit condemnatus Casali." Jewish Archive of Mantua, *Dossier* 1, no. 58. Also the question of the community of Mantua, dated September 10, 1577, addressed to Duke, so that nothing of wrongdoing be seen in the constitution of *Beth Din* for the objects listed above, must be a reflection of the sentence itself. The consent is given "facta fide coram Senatu ita fuisse observatum antequam Abraam fuerit condemnatus." Jewish Archive of Mantua, ibidem.

983 "Che occorrendo lite o controversia per qualunque causa tra loro hebrei, che se ellegono duy doctori hebrei overo due arbitri hebrei, qualli habbiano ad vedere et giudicare tale differentia secondo la loro legge et ordini: et se alcuno hebreo contrafarà alli presenti capitoli, che cascha in pena de libre 20 etc." These chapters have remained unknown to C. Invernizzi, *Gli ebrei a Pavia*, in *Bollettino della società pavese di storia patria*. See pp. 191–240 and 281–319. A copy is stored in Mantua, Jewish Archive, *Dossier* 1, no. 4.

984 Invernizzi, op. cit., p. 293.

8 The Duchy of Ferrara

In Ferrara, the transformation of the Jewish judgment into necessary jurisdiction is accomplished twice and twice revoked, within a short time.[985] Two distinct periods of operative rabbinical courts exist, more than a century apart.

The first period begins in 1575.[986] On October 11 of that year, the deputies of the Italian and German communities of the Jews of Ferrara, gathered in the meeting in the main synagogue, deeming "che fosse opera ben fatta il provvedere che questa Università avesse continuamente una residenza di tre persone intelligenti che avessero cura di fare osservare gli termini necessari al vivere hebraico circa alli cibi liciti et inliciti et ordinationi di congiunger matrimonii e disgiungere, e far sì che non venghi tutto il giorno a far rumori nelle sinagoghe per interesse che habbia qualsivoglia hebreo l'uno con l'altro per conto di dare e havere, e astringerli ciascuno d'essi a chiamar arbitri insieme, hanno fatto elletione delli tre infrascritti, cioè messer Laudadio di Valmontone, messer Samuel del Vecchio e messer Cesare Finzi," assigning to them jurisdictional authority for 19 years, with the obligation to hold a hearing for half an hour every Monday and Thursday. This resolution is forwarded to the Court of the Elders with the request of approval and application of the mandatory rule, which is then granted on November 5. Although the privilege does not encounter the favor of all Jews, it remains in force for several years; and it is not until 1559 that someone begins to see in it an exorbitant concession "in diminutione della jurisditione dell'ill.mo Signor Duca." As a result, this privilege is abrogated and it is ordered to the Jews "che non ardischino proporre alcuna nomina nè fare alcun precetto, per la quale alcuno sia o possa essere sforzato andare dai giudici hebrei et levarsi dai tribunali cristiani." The prohibition is repeated again in 1564 by the bishop and by the judge of the elders.[987]

From this time, for over a century, no mention of Jewish courts is made, and the possible pronouncements return to have a character of pure arbitration.

We must wait until 1671 to hear again of civil causes between Jews, referred by the government to the rabbis of Ferrara for the ruling.[988] Then in 1676, the

---

985 Idem, op. cit., p. 319.

986 Later corrected by V. Colorni from erroneous "1525" (see Judaica Minora, Giuffrè 1983, p. 723).

987 For all that see Balletti, *Gli ebrei e gli Estensi*, Reggio Emilia, 1930, p. 95, no. 4.

988 Archive of the Jewish Community of Ferrara – Academy of the Rabbis, *Closet* 3, *Shelf* 2, no. 5, 1671, January 21: "Em.mo e R.mo Principe. Li Rabbini della Natione hebrea di Ferrara humil.mi Servi di V. E. si rendono incapaci all'esecutione dei di Lei riv.mi comandi per la disobbedienza che corre nella Natione nelle cause, civili, che nascono nella medesima e che vengono commesse dalla benignità di V. E. agli Oratori, dove che supplicano la

community presented a supplication to Cardinal Chigi, papal legate, asking for the rabbinical jurisdiction to be recognized for internal civil causes not exceeding five lire. The requested privilege was granted that same year and later confirmed with other rescripts of the subsequent papal legates who raised up to five scudi the court's authority so recognized; and lay down its organization and procedure, empowering the rabbis to punish those who had civil judgment preferred over the Jewish one. The jurisdictional function is entrusted to three rabbis who were obliged to hold a hearing for two hours a day – an hour in wintertime – after studying the Law. The summons, examined and accepted by the rabbis, were transcribed in the special register by the registrar and then summoned to the parties by the usher. The absentee was fined one scudo per day in favor of charitable organizations. Judgments were final and transcribed by the registrar, whose authority of certification was considered equal to that of a public notary. The latest confirmation of this privilege takes place in 1700 by Cardinal Astalli legate. In 1708, with the changing of the legation, the guild of notaries, perceiving in the Jewish jurisdiction a usurpation of public authorities harmful to its rights (and above all, quite obviously, to his honoraria) presents to the new legate a memorandum in which the guild states that "gli Ebrei, contro le Bolle Pontificie, leggi canoniche e civili hanno eretto una specie di tribunale con deputare giudici, destinare le hore giuridiche, per tutto l'anno et ellegere persone che sotto il nome di scrivano registrano atti e sentenze e faccino qualunque altra cosa concernente la professione di pubblico e legale notaro, giudicando essi giudici deputati fino alla somma di scudi cinque inclusive, omni appellatione remota, senza restringersi quanto alla facoltà di giudicare per altre somme maggiori" and calls for the abrogation of the privilege.

In another memorandum, the Jews raise objections to the notaries' reasons, arguing that the rabbinical jurisdiction is not a usurpation but relies on a specific state permit. They also insist on its benefits, saving the parties in question the high costs of civil suits.[989]

natural clemenza della E. V. habilitarli, che secondo nasce gli eventi possino more hebreorum censurarli con pubblica mortificatione, che riceveranno la gratia ecc." The license is granted on the aforementioned day and is renewed on February 23, 1672, upon instance of Massaro Emanuel Budrio.

989 I am drawing all this information about the second period of activity of the rabbinical court of Ferrara (1676–1708) from M. Roberti, *Privilegi forensi degli ebrei in Ferrara*, in *Atti e Memorie della R. Accademia di Scienze lettere ed arti di Padova*, vol. XXIII, 1907, pp. 160–162, who, in turn, drew from a manuscript by the notary Giuseppe Malucelli, *Breve racconto dell'abolizione dei tribunali degli ebrei introdotti*, stored in the Ferrara municipal library (Ms., *Cl. I*, no. 422).

The reasons put forward, however, do not have sufficient strength. Faced with the insistence of the notary guild, which produced a second memorandum supporting its viewpoint, Cardinal Casoni revoked all Jewish privilege that same year (1708), stating that no right "competisse, neque competere hebreis ipsis, exercendi jurisdictionem aliquam in cognoscendo vel decidendo causas cuiuscumque generis salva facultatem (sic) arbitrandi inter hebreos hinc inde consentientes, sine tamen facultate exequendi, sub pena nullitatis, carceris ac alii, arbitrio S. E."

Nor does it appear that this state of affairs has subsequently undergone further changes.[990]

9 The Duchy of Modena and Reggio

The establishment of a rabbinical court in the community of Reggio does not seem to go beyond 1657. Four years later, to better define its attributions and fix its procedure, the Jews of Reggio submitted to the Duke a text of provisions that, once approved, were used thereafter for a regular and well-defined explanation of judicial activity in civil matters.[991]

These rules empowered a college composed of two of the three pro tempore Massari to judge (elected by rotation among the members of the Restricted Convocation,[992] plus a rabbi) and established the appropriate rotations so that members of that college were re-assigned every three months. The judges were to sit twice a week and were assisted by a Chancellor (notary) and an usher (sacristan) (art. 1).

As for the jurisdiction, it had been established that the college should judge all cases not exceeding the sum of 50 lire. For higher sums, the parties had to entrust the decision to the judges or choose other arbitrators. The judges themselves had to appoint the arbitrators if the parties neglected to do so within the allotted time limit. In the compromise in arbitration, which would be registered with the Registrar, to avoid conflicts about the validity of acts, it was established "che tutte le scritture vulgari et in idioma Christiano habbino forza come permette il stilo della città e mercatura"; which, in relation to what we

990 And yet, in 1737 and 1743, supplications are again addressed to the papal legate, in order to obtain that the rabbis be entrusted once more with the cognizance of civil causes. Archive of Ferrara Jewish community, location cited, nos. 24 to 30.

991 See annex, document No. 9.

992 On these courts and their authorities, see Balletti, *Gli ebrei e gli estensi*, Reggio Emilia, 2nd ed., 1930. Cf. also my work: *Le magistrature maggiori della comunità ebraica di Mantova*, in *Riv. di Storia del diritto italiano*, vol. XI, 1938, pp. 93–101.

have said about the principle: the law of the State is law, is to be understood as limited to the form of the acts themselves (art. 2).

For the revision of the pronouncements of the three judges or arbitrators, an appeal was allowed to the other members of the Restricted Convocation, which would have been composed of six, if the three colleagues issued judgments, and of nine if external arbitrators passed judgments outside the Convocation (art. 3). After the rules for disqualification of judges – due to kinship or other reason – (art. 4) and for the deposition of the texts (art. 5), it was established as a fundamental point of the trial that, had the parties failed to appear within the period allocated, after two summons, the usher would have reported to the judges, and if no evidence of urgent impediments was presented, the verdict would have been pronounced in absentia (art. 7).

Before moving on to the executive branch, the ruling had to be countersigned by the state judge (art. 12).

The rules added a request for authorization to excommunicate those who may attempt to oppose the established jurisdictional rules by illegal means (art. 8) and authorized taking adequate measures against judges who were found guilty of misconduct (art. 9). Finally, in the book of the judges, it was added that all contracts concluded between Jews for house rentals or other things, were to be registered free of charge by the Registrar, so that they will obtain a validity equal to that "d'ogni sorte d'istrumento" (art. 11).

All this organic and precise complex of norms appears to regulate for several decennia the activity of the rabbinical court of Reggio. Only in 1738, in a series of new provisions proposed by the community, which the Duke agreed to and turned into law, do we find a somewhat different regulation, based in every detail on the system in force in the community of Mantua.[993]

As stated in chapter 9 of these regulations, Jewish arbitration was imposed on the litigants at the behest of one of the parties. Only when the other party rejected the choice, or when no agreement was reached on the election of the third party, or when the elected candidates were rejected, the Accademia Rabbinica Maggiore of the State had to take care of appointments, so that any dispute between Jews would always be decided according to Jewish law, even when the parties included orphans, widows or charities, in derogation from the judicial privileges granted to the *miserabiles personae* by the *jus commune*.

The verdicts of the arbitrators would be deemed final and binding, and the parties could not turn to any other court, thus preventing an indefinite continuation of quarrels. The execution of the sentences would have been the duty

---

993 See appendix, doc. 10.

of state bodies, subject to an authorization received "de' ministri e giudici di S. A." The chapter combines two provisions from Mantua: chapter 14 of the February 27, 1626 decree,[994] reported verbatim, and the commission of June 21, 1672.[995] It is most likely taken from chapter 11 of the October 4, 1700 decree of Ferdinando Carlo Gonzaga,[996] which in turn combines numerous former provisions related to the rabbinical court of Mantua.

Apart from the documents mentioned above, I could not find any other about Reggio, except for a ducal decree of 1779 requiring the Jews of Scandiano to depend exclusively on Reggio Rabbinic Academy in the decision of any cause of theirs.[997]

As for Modena, I was unable to track down anything, but the judicial autonomy granted to the community of Reggio makes it safe to presume that a similar recognition also to the Jewish community in the capital of the Duchy was highly likely. It was also proven by the reference in the aforementioned decree of 1738 to an Accademia Rabbinica Maggiore having jurisdiction over the whole state.

Actually, a further provision of 1851 (art. 9) "conferma nei ministri della religione israelitica in Modena e Reggio la facoltà ad essi attribuita da precedente sovrana risoluzione di decidere sull'articolo di rito e culto nelle cause degli ebrei per matrimonii, divorzii e loro dipendenze."[998]

Thus, reduced in its authority, the jurisdiction of the rabbinical court remained in Modena and Reggio until the state's annexation to the Kingdom of Italy.

10 The Venetian Republic

The Venetian government, just like the Papal one, appears at any time to be hostile to the repeated Jewish attempts to achieve an autonomous jurisdictional power.

Scanning the registry of the internal deliberations of the community of Padua in the 16th century, one can find repeated references to the

994 Jewish Archive of Mantua, *Libro M*, f. 54v. See further on, pp. 285–286.

995 Ibidem, *Libro M*, f. 88v. See further on, p. 289.

996 Ibidem, *Libro M*, f. 117v. See further on, pp. 290–291.

997 Ibidem, *Dossier* 181, no. 28.

998 Law of Francesco v, October 25, 1851, in *Codice civile per gli stati estensi*, 2nd ed., Modena, 1852, p. 374.

prohibition of turning to state courts for civil disputes, under penalty of excommunication,[999] and the obligation to choose arbitrators, and submit to the decision of the judges, specifically elected by the community and adjoin periodically to carry out their judicial function.[1000] However, it does not seem that the government had ever recognized the coercive character of the Jewish judiciary, forcing a reluctant party to obey the ruling. As collegial, predetermined and fixed, it remained a judiciary of arbitrators, which defendants unimpressed by excommunication threats could refuse, and its judgments could not have been given in absentia.[1001]

Briefly mentioning this function, Morpurgo[1002] does not question the problem of its precise nature. Ciscato, on the other hand, asserts that the

999 Jewish Archive of Padua, Basevi, *Compendio delle parti*, [deliberations] *dei registri della comunità*, manuscript ibidem, no. 54, ch. 13: revision of the part 25 tisrì 1578: One shall not bring any Jew before the tribunal of the State without the permission of the leaders of the community, under threat to the offender of being declared unworthy of any religious practice, of being unable to eat ritually pure meat and of being outcast by everyone as excommunicated, as long as he does not mend his bad actions in the way that will be prescribed to him by R. Shemuel Archivolti. The part is confirmed on 24 nissan 1589 (no. 334) and repeated in energetic terms on 3 adar 1595 (no. 522). However, in case of persistent refusal of the debtor to fulfill his commitment, the lender will be able to get permission to take his case before civil courts (No. 308, 4 av 1588; see above, footnote no. 819).

1000 Ibidem, no. 2, tisrì 1577: The leaders of the Jewish University shall judge every civil dispute up to 12 lire, and shall have the obligation to go to synagogue every Sunday after the afternoon prayer, for ruling on disputes that may be referred to them. No. 54, ch. 14, confirmation. No. 45, 26 Hesvan 1580: the election is decided of a Jewish court before which all matters between private individuals shall be referred. This court shall consist of three judges: R. Shemuel Archivolti, R. Abraham Heilprun and Shimshon Coen. Their deliberations will be respected as if enacted by the Grand Sanhedrin. However, should an individual believe that, by being directly or indirectly an interested party, one of those judges would not examine his reasons with the due impartiality, he will be able to get him replaced by one of the leaders of the University, and the same shall be done in the absence or impediment of one of the judges. They will have to meet at least once a week to receive complaints that may be submitted. No. 219, 6 adar 1586: election of three judges and one alternate. No. 257, 25 teved 1587: ban on appealing to the rabbinical court of Venice against the decisions of that of Padua. No. 284, 4 Shvat 1588: election of three judges. No. 308, 4 Av 1588: jurisdiction attributed to the heads of the community for controversy up to the sum of 2 ducats; obligation to choose arbitrators for greater sums. Etc.

1001 This is demonstrated by the permission to turn to the civil tribunal in case of the debtor's default; which would not make much sense if the Jews could pronounce judgments inter nolentes, endowed with executive force. Besides, in one of the mentioned resolutions (no. 54, ch. 11) it is explicitly said that "after the parties have laid out their reasons before the judges [showing in this way their mutual consent], the decision of the latter will have the force of a compromise made between the Jewish laws and those of the State.

1002 Edgardo Morpurgo, *L'Università degli Ebrei in Padova nel XVI secolo*. Reprint from *Bollettino del museo civico di Padova*, y. XII, dossiers 1, 2 and 3, Padua 1909, p. 14: Nel 1577 i Capi erano *giudici ed arbitri* in qualunque controversia, etc."

government *did* recognize the rabbinical judicial autonomy, limited to minor disputes. However, he does not provide any textual support to substantiate his claim,[1003] disproved by the prescribed submission of the causes between Jews to the jurisdiction of Christian judges.[1004]

This negative conclusion about Padua can be perfectly explained considering the strong opposition that the community of Venice met from the government whenever it tried to impose the rabbinical judicial on its members. In the pretension of the community to prohibit turning to civil court by the threat of ex-communications, and set up their courts, Venetian officials saw, in addition to an impairment of individual freedom, an affront to state authority and usurpation of public functions and objected to that repeatedly. Thus, in 1581, under the penalty of 200 ducats and 18 months in prison, the Cattaveri banned the proclamation of such excommunications and the setup of courts.[1005] This, however, achieved no great effect, as demonstrated by the new ban on judicial usurpations, established on April 26, 1606, threatening more severe sentences for judges and parties alike.[1006]

On February 13, 1622, the Jewish community managed to obtain recognition for a small portion of authority, consisting in the competence entrusted "ai capi di strazzaria d'Ebrei di giudicar le differenze che per causa di strazzaria [trade in cast-off clothes] vertiscono fra essi Ebrei con altri particolari." That concession lasted for just over a year and was revoked on June 13, 1623. Four years later, however, on September 10, 1627, the revocation was rescinded by decision confirmed on March 31, 1628. Before the end of thar very year the Cattaveri, considering "quanto sia grave il pregiudizio che risulta al pubblico decoro, all'autorità de magistrati, et all'esemplar forma dell'amministrazion d'una incorrotta giustizia," definitively annul such faculty of the "capi di strazzaria," "acciocchè non d'altronde che da ill.mi magistrati, et ex.mi Consegli di questa Serenissima Repubblica sia riconosciuta la potestà d'atti giudiziarii, siccome comporta l'autorità pubblica e riputazione di qualsivoglia magistrato."[1007] Following new Jewish attempts, this provision was repeated more than a century later, on April 12, 1745;[1008] while in 1706, the Portuguese Jewish community

1003 Ciscato, *Gli ebrei in Padova*, Padua, 1901, p. 178.

1004 The judge of L'Aquila up to 25 liras. From 25 liras up, the only judge for the Jews is the podestà. Ciscato, ibidem, p. 179.

1005 State Archive of Venice. Inquisitorate to the Jews, *Envelope* 39: printed booklet titled "*Scomuniche abbolite dal Magistrato Ecc.mo del Cattaver*," no. 2, p. 5. See appendix, doc. 4.

1006 Ibidem, no. 3, p. 8. See appendix, doc. 5.

1007 All this can be drawn from the last provision dated November 17, 1628. Ibidem, no. 5, pp. 12–13. On November 20, the "termination" is notified to Bondi dall'Osto, Elia Richetti, Elia Luzzatto and Donato Spiera, Jews and heads of the ghetto's "strazzaria."

1008 Ibidem, no. 7, pp. 15–16. See appendix, doc. 8.

of the city, having arrogated the right to conduct judicial activity, and after having actually carried it out, the Cattaveri intervened again, censuring the abuse and annulling the decision.[1009]

Repeatedly frustrated, as incompatible with the right of every citizen to judicially protect their own interests, were the bans placed by the community to appeal to civil courts against the taxes imposed on its members by the community itself.[1010]

It is worth reminding that the constant opposition to recognizing Jewish judicial autonomy does not imply any parallel opposition to the recognition of Jewish civil law. In fact, it was applied without any problem by civil courts.[1011]

11 The Duchy of Mantua

The Jewish community of Mantua, which came into being around the end of the 14th century,[1012] constantly grew, reaching approximately 2000 souls at the end of the 16th century,[1013] thus constituting one of the most important centers of Italian Jewry for three centuries.The Gonzaga Dukes, and later the Austrian government, granted the community all its desired autonomies. In the administrative and jurisdictional sphere, these reach such an extent comparable only to the situation of the Tuscan communities. The richness of the ancient archive documents of the Mantua community, their impeccable order and the help provided in researching the vast and valuable repertoire of all preserved materials[1014] allowed us to reconstruct here, with delicate precision, the history of jurisdictional autonomy from its first appearance to its final decline.

1009 Ibidem, no. 4, p. 10. The "part" of the Portuguese community is from March 1, 1706 and starts with the words: "De orden dos Signores do Maamad." The decision of the Cattaveri is from the following March 26. See appendix, doc. 6.

1010 Aforementioned provision of February 14, 1581; avogaresque meddling, ibidem, no. 6, p. 14, June 20, 1721. See appendix, doc. 7.

1011 See above, footnotes nos. 683–686.

1012 See my work *Prestito ebraico* etc., in *Rivista di Storia del Diritto italiano*, vol. VIII, 1935, file 3, pp. 444–458.

1013 See my work *Le magistrature maggiori della Comunità ebraica di Mantova*, in *Rivista di Storia del Diritto italiano*, vol. XI, 1938, file 1, p. 92. On the population of the community, see Repertorio of the Archive of the community (cf. following note), vol. VIII, pp. 75–80. Sporadic figures are available for the period 1591–1790.

1014 The archive includes documents from 1522 to 1810. The sheets are collected in chronological order in 274 numbered folders, the books are marked with alphabetical letters. This arrangement was made by Rabbi Bonajuto Isac Levi (1722–1808) from Mantua, to whom we owe the compilation of the repertoire, a most patient and admirable work, in ten large volumes which, exhibits, analytically in Italian, under different headings, the content of

From the start, in Mantua as elsewhere, the rabbis held several activities of voluntary jurisdiction in matrimonial and tutelage matters, establishing themselves in a three-person court (*Beth Din*) according to Jewish law.[1015] The State, however, totally ignored this activity which retained a merely private character. The court case brought against Abramo Sacerdoti in Casale, for abuse of jurisdiction in the criminal area, caused the authorities to focus their attention also on the functions of the *Beth Din* in the civil realm. Fearing that the legality of such functions could be called into question, the community prevented such investigations by asking for permission to exercise it. The Commissioner did not refuse but, unwilling to take any risk, granted the requested permission for one time only.[1016] Aspiring for unlimited and comprehensive recognition, the community was not satisfied and on September 10, 1577, insisted once more. "Occorrendo spesse volte all'improvviso – it writes – per interesse dei pupilli, o in casi di matrimonii, di divorzi, o scalzamenti, o giuramenti di vedeve sopra lor carte nuziali far certe subite dichiarazioni secondo il rito già celebrato per tutto l'hebraismo, et occorrendo parimente secondo il loro stile far riconoscere alcune loro scritture hebraiche e ricevere testimonianze per gli ebrei, così terreri come forestieri, le quali cose tutte convien fare alla presenza di tre o più eletti che in tali casi chiamano *ben din* che significa costituzione di giudizio," the community will be grateful to the Duke if he will want "far dichiarazione che liberissimamente possano secondo il rito ebraico costituire le persone che in così fatti casi hanno di bisogno." This time the permission is granted, "facta fide coram senatu ita fuisse observatum antequam Abraam fuerit condemnatus."[1017]

---

each documentindicating the place of it on the side. All the material written mostly in Hebrew remains thus easily accessible.

1015 In the aforementioned consultation no. 152 produced in defense of the Jew accused of abusing criminal jurisdiction, Bursati from Mantua paints a picture of the rabbinic activities in matters of voluntary jurisdiction which, albeit outlined with respect to the community of Casale, fits very well any other community of the time. The rabbis set up Beth Din: "1) in dando tutore pupillo mortuo hebreo patre; 2) dum prestatur sorori, seu uxori fratris mortui – consensus nubendi; 3) in recognitione scripturae manu alicuius propria firmatae; 4) pro repulsa infamiae illatae; 5) pro falsitate testis demonstranda; 6) dum repudium datur; 7) in protestando alicui; 8) quando dotes restituuntur; et multis aliis in causis, quae brevitatis causa omitto."

1016 April 15, 1577, Arch. Isr., *Folder* 1, no. 46. Permission to the rabbis, granted for this time only, enabling them to set up a court according to Jewish tradition, appoint guardians and curators, proceed to the division of property left behind by the dead for the contagion, examine deflowered unmarried women, and perform other acts according to Jewish rite.

1017 Arch. Isr. *Folder* 1, no. 50. The letter is published by L. Pegna in *Rassegna mensile di Israel*, vol. VII, no. 12, April 1933, p. 556 (from the original preserved in the Gonzaga Archive of Mantua).

In a court case of the following year, between the University of Jews and the tax authorities, the question of legitimacy of the *Beth Din* was brought up again for discussion and several dozen of Jewish and former Jewish individuals were summoned, in Mantua and Cremona, to testify on the point in question. They all agreed that ab immemorabili, at least until the sentencing of Abramo, in Mantua as well as in Cremona and Padua, "si è servato et si serva fra ebrei che si fanno tribunali ebraici come si dice *ben din* nelle cause nelle quali si tratti per interesse dei pupilli, matrimoni divorzii e scalzamenti e giuramenti de vidue sopra le lor carte nuptiali, per recognizione de alcune scritture ebraiche et examine de testimoni per hebrei così terrieri come forestieri, acciochè quelli che si voleno valler d'essi tribunali et ciò si contiene in quelli dove ha bisogno possi verificare et justificare che le cose se contengono in detti tribunali sono vere."[1018]

So far we are still in the field of voluntary jurisdiction.[1019] There was no government recognition in the field of litigation, meaning that the rabbinic pronouncements may have only been issued as arbitrations, subject to the agreement of the parties and stipulation of the compromise.

Things changed, however, even before the end of the 16th century. In fact, in the privileges granted by Duke Vincenzo Gonzaga to the University of the Jews of Mantua on October 25, 1590, at ch. 4, the arbitration in civil matters for the internal causes was made obligatory,[1020] which meant, as it has been noted many times, giving these arbitration pronouncements a character of real jurisdiction concurrent with that of the State.[1021] Such obligatoriness, as

1018 Isr. Arch., ibid.

1019 Another permission for one-time only is granted by the Commissioner to the rabbis on January 17, 1578. The license is given to form the Beth Din for the division, in accordance with Jewish law, of the inheritance of the widow of Vita Cases. Arch. Isr. *Folder* 1, no. 51.

1020 Arch. Isr., *Book M*, sheet 4: "In tutti i casi nei quali di ragione sono tenuti gli hebrei c'hanno differenze tra loro di elegger arbitri hebrei perchè esse differenze siano conosciute hebraicamente, dichiariamo et vogliamo che se una parte dimandarà arbitri, l'altra che ricuserà debba esser sforzata con precetti multe et altri rimedi di ragione del predetto Comessario a far l'eletione, sì che secondo il loro rito et nonostante cosa in contrario habbiano da star al giudicato d'essi arbitri, con questo però che per l'esecutione che occorrerà farsi et per ogn'altro atto in contraditorio debba tutto esser spedito con l'intervento e l'autorità del medesimo Comissario."

1021 In fact, if a party will request the arbitrators, the other one will not be able to refuse the choice. But if the same party will prefer to sue the opponent in the state court, their cause shall be discussed before the latter. The plaintiff has thus the choice between the two jurisdictions.

it was clarified shortly afterwards (1594), did not concern only causes between relatives,[1022] but any sort of controversy between Jews.[1023]

The crucial step for the transformation of arbitration into jurisdiction had already been accomplished: other steps would follow later, aimed at completing the metamorphosis and replacing the board of individuals elected on a case-by-case basis by the parties, with a stable judiciary, dependent on the community and directly remunerated by it.

On August 22, 1620, the community asked the Commissioner,[1024] (to which he consented on December 11),[1025] to allow the Vicinia Ristretta[1026] to prepare a list of names that the rabbis shall put into a ballot-box and then draw arbitrators for civil causes by lot, upon each request. The rabbis would be able to change those drawn up, if rejected because of kinship, or deemed unsuitable by them.

Even more explicit rules can be found in the Decree of February 27, 1626, ch. 14, where the aforementioned provisions of 1590 and 1594 were repeated, adding that "non concordando le parti nel far l'elettione degli arbitri, o d'un terzo facendo bisogno, overo non trovandosi chi vogli esser arbitro, habbino i Rabini della Accademia hebraica maggiore di Mantova a deputar essi gli arbitri, overo il terzo come sopra, come meglio a loro parerà, e quelli destineranno siano tenuti esser arbitri, et nonostante cosa alcuna in contrario siano esse differenze sempre conosciute hebraicamente, et habbino le parti da stare al giudicato di essi arbitri, con questo però che per l'esecutioni che occorreranno farsi debba essere con l'autorità et ufficio d'esso Signor Commissario."[1027]

The Faculty of the rabbis of the Academy (*Jeshivat ha-rabbanim*) appears to be restricted here exclusively to the appointment of arbitrators in some cases of need. However, from a document that followed the aforementioned decree

1022 For which in general the statutes prescribe coercive arbitration, see Susani, *Tractatus de judeis* cit., pp. 47a–48 (see above, footnote no. 904).

1023 Arch. Isr., *Book M*, folder 6. Privilege August 15, 1594. The aforementioned chapter of the privilege of 1590 "s'habbia da intendere indistintamente in ogni sorte di differenza, e tra ogni sorte di persona hebrea tanto congionta di sangue quanto non congionta, et conforme alla ragione hebraica."

1024 Arch. Isr., *Book S*, folder 66.

1025 Arch. Isr., *Book M*, folder 51v.

1026 The smallest of the three deliberative bodies of the community, see my study *Le magistrature*, etc. cit., pp. 464–473. The other ones are the Vicinia Maggiore and the Vicinia Generale.

1027 Arch. Isr., *Book M*, folder 54v. This chapter was published by A. Bertolotti, *Curiosità storiche mantovane*, no. 196, *La corte di cassazione ebraica*, in the magazine *Il mendico*, December 1st, 1890, The decree is confirmed on December 10, 1626 (Arch. Isr., *Book M*, folder 59v.) and on February 17. 1628 (ibidem, folder 62v).

by a few months, it is learned that while keeping the principle of inappeallability of the verdicts of arbitration, the right to resort to the rabbis had normally been accorded to the parties that were believed to have been weighted down by the arbitrations. Akin to the supreme court, the rabbis could review the cause according to the law and whenever recognized as ill-judged throw out the verdict, referring it to a new arbitral examination. In the event that the appeal was instead rejected when the cause itself was well-judged, no further revision was possible.[1028]

Once the cases had been brought before Jewish judges, the state court should thus always have had to declare itself incompetent: instead, it often happened that a party, dissatisfied with the Jewish verdict, having exhausted all the allowed attempts, ended up taking the case before the civil court, in the hope that this would re-examine the dispute and decide not according to Jewish law but according to Roman and local rules, more favorable to that party in the case in question.

To work around this bad habit that made disputes endless and wound up in blatant iniquities, the community asked, in 1659, that all Jewish causes, decided or to be decided, be referred solely to the jurisdiction of Jewish arbitrators.[1029] That did not only mean their wish to avoid appealing to state courts for causes already examined previously by the arbitrators themselves, but also to exclude the concurring of the two jurisdictions from the very beginning, totally taking away from the state court the faculty to judge in civil matters between Jews.

1028 See the document May 19, 1626 published by Bertolotti, op. cit., ibid., and reported above, footnote no. 522. The Academy's rabbis declare that since the appeal by Cuzzar was rejected, the arbitration ruling in the Cuzzar-Colorni lawsuit is res judicata and cannot, therefore, be subject to further revision.

1029 Arch. Isr., *Folder* 33, no. 62, October 15, 1659: "Vedendo l'Università delli hebrei umilissima serva di V. A. Ser.ma che molti hebrei, contro li rescritti e privileggi spetialmente concessi per titolo oneroso a essa Università da V. A. Ser.ma e da Ser.mi suoi antecessori, procurino con diversi mezi et anco con rescritti et comessioni della medesima Altezza di fare che le loro differenze non siano terminate da arbitri hebrei et a rito hebraico, ma da giudici christiani et a diverso rito, con infinità di spese et isterminio delle proprie cose, il che anche è occorso e tuttavia occorre nelle differenze vertenti tra Lustro e fratelli Norsa con Israel e fratello parimenti Norsa, che doppo diverse sentenze e lungo litiggio di molti e molti anni con rigiri et cavillij sono di nuovo sempre da capo. Per ciò per rimediare a cotanti disordini et vietare tali isterminii, supplica l'A. V. Ser.ma restar servita di commettere che tutte le cause vertenti e possano per l'avenire vertire tra hebrei ed hebrei et anco quella di detti Norsa siano da arbitri ebrei terminate, in conformità di detti decreti et privileggi et ciò non ostante qual si voglia sentenze de altri giudici date et rescritti e comessioni da qualsivoglia hebreo ottenute dalla medesima A. V. Ser.ma et cosa che li sia in contrario; che della gratia ecc. ecc."

Responding to such request with the formula "servemtur privilegia hebreis concessa exceptis causis in quibus judices christiani sunt delegati," it seems the government had actually intended to establish, aside from a few modest exceptions, the exclusive authority of Jewish jurisdiction.

Shortly thereafter, it would also lose the last remnants of its primitive character of arbitration, to take up those of a genuine court.

On May 18, 1661, it was disposed in the privileges that the Vicinia Ristretta, with the consent of the Commissioner, who could not refuse, would have the faculty for choosing judges for cases not exceeding 30 scudi.[1030] Accordingly, on the 1st of Iyar of that same year, 1661, implementing the concession, the aforementioned Vicinia appointed three judges plus two supplementary ones for a period of one year, conferring to them a jurisdiction of up to 30 scudi. For cases above that amount, parties would have had the right to choose arbitrators, whose judgments (both judges and arbitrators) would be deemed final and given without the function of counsel for the defense, except for causes of women and orphans, as per the rules of the State.[1031] Thus, the rabbinical court, whose members were periodically renewed, could be regarded as stably founded.[1032] However, it should not be forgotten that the judicial activity did

---

1030 Arch. Isr., *Book M*, folder 87v. Decree of Carlo II: "Vertendo qualche differenza fra gli Ebrei di essa Università così terrieri como forestieri fino alla somma di scudi 30, possi la Convocazione Vicinia Ristretta di quella ellegere persona o persone che habbiano autorità di terminarla e definirla in conformità de' ritti hebraichi, con che però ne venga partecipatto il commissario destinato da noi agli ebrei dal quale non dovrà denegarsi l'assenso."

1031 Arch. Isr., *Book Am*, folder 70, § 5.

1032 The list of members of the court, both active and supplementary, clerks and ushers with their salaries from 1661 to 1804 is available in the aforementioned *Repertorio Levi*, vol. IV. The appointment next to this first one occurs with the following Commissioner Decree of December 10, 1664 (Arch. Isr., *Book Am*, folder 35. no.13): "Carlo Conio Senator ducale et comissario generale delli hebrei di Mantova et suo dominio. Inherendo al decreto concesso da S. A. S. all'Università delli hebrei sotto li 18 maggio 1661 oltre il cap. 14 del Ducal decreto dell'anno 1626 intorno al stare ad arbitri et all'eletione di quelli nelle differenze vertenti tra essi Hebrei; A richiesta dei magnifici Salomon da Fano, Iseppe Josue Jona et Sansone Finzi, Massari della medesima università concediamo auttorità alli Rabini Vidal Norsa, Salomon Formigine, Leon Provenzali, hebrei elleti dalla Convocazione Ristretta della medesima Università, che tutti tre uniti possino giudicare et s'intendino deputati per arbitri nelle cause però solamente che non eccedino la somma di scudi trenta. Et in caso di impedimento o di recusatione legitima di alcuno et alcuni di essi s'havranno per elletti per subentrare Rabi Isaia Mirami et Rabi Simon Fano pur elletti a questo effetto dalla medesima Convocazione; con auttorità parimente alla medesima Convocatione, mediante però la nostra saputa, di subrogare et agregare presso loro altri ocorendo secondo li loro riti, come di permutare tutti o parte di quelli conforme farà bisogno, et nelle

not start at this time but has been practiced since arbitration became obligatory, i.e., since 1590. Not the stability of the collegium but the obligation to turn to it by the will of only one of the litigants is what gave it the nature of actual jurisdiction, with the right and duty to judge even in default of the defendant. Therefore, I believe that the decision of the Vicinia dated December 6, 1666, to grant the court the right to issue decisions in absentia was not the first of its kind:[1033] by its very nature, the court was entitled to hold such a faculty already since 1590 and there was no need for it to be recognized by a special provision.

The transformation of the mandatory arbitration into a special permanent court constituted for the community the culmination of lengthy efforts to strengthen its judicial autonomy. All that remained was to ardently defend this autonomy, trying to counter all the recurring attempts of individuals to frustrate it for personal gain. Indeed, individual losers in the lawsuit do not refrain from resorting to the civil courts in the hope of getting a new trial; and the community must quite frequently ask for confirmation of the principle of exclusivity and inappealability of Jewish pronouncements.[1034] This

---

cause che eccederanno la soma sodetta de scuti trenta dovrassi osservare la forma del supradetto capitolo 14 del decreto dell'anno 1626, al quale non intendiamo con la presente nostra di punto pregiudicare nè aportar pregiuditio alcuno ala nostra giurisditione, nè all'ufficio nostro; et vaglia durante la suddetta Convocatione. Di Mantova li x zenaro 1664."

1033 Arch. Isr., *Book Am*, folder 83, § 3. Provision of the Vicinia Ristretta (in Hebrew, as all the minutes of the meetings are): "Ancora decisero in quella adunanza, – poichè videro alcuni individui che non badavano a far ciò che veniva loro imposto, quando erano chiamati innanzi al tribunale, di venire cioè subito a sentire le parole dei giudici; che anzi gettavan quell'ordine dietro le spalle e voltavano il tergo sicchè era tirato indietro il giudizio non tenendo essi conto dell'ingiustizia che commettevano – di porvi riparo, affinchè la giustizia non ne ricevesse danno e convennero col consenso di tutti che se uno fosse citato dall'usciere a comparire davanti alle Eccellenze del tribunale per due volte (e non si presentasse), il tribunale avesse il potere di giudicarlo in contumacia e di fare la sentenza coi motivi del solo avversario a suo scapito. Ciò purchè non fosse stato impedito da un caso di forza maggiore plausibile e accetto al tribunale."

1034 May 25, 1668. Arch. Isr., folder 37, no. 11. Request for the following provision: "che oltre il dover gli hebrei far elettione d'arbitri hebrei et star al giuditio di quelli et che le loro differenze siano sempre conosciute conforme il rito hebraico come pur dispongono i decreti, che terminate le differenze tra di loro – niun eccettuato – da detti arbitri, et reviste in caso di bisogno dalla sodetta Accademia siano quelli voti o sentenze inappellabili con doversi la parte a quelle acquetare senza poter pretendere altre revisione, ma solo esseguire l'effettuazione col mezo del loro Sig.r Comissario, aliquo non obstante, al fine di troncare li cavillii et che non resta campo e forza a quelli riceverà la sentenza contraria tornar di nuovo ad inquiettar la parte per strusiarlo et destrugerlo et con spesa scausarli isterminio." And at the foot of the page: "Habeatur sermo et observentur decretal."

principle was then subject to two exceptions: the *miserabiles personae* (widows, orphans, charitable institutions, etc.) that in accordance with the l. *unica C. quando imperator* (C. 3, 14) enjoyed the right to appeal to a special court; and those who, with the ducal rescript, obtained the delegation of their cases to the Christian judges. The community perceived these breaches left open in the wall of its autonomy as dangerous and waged war against them, succeeding quite well on both fronts. Regarding the *miserabiles personae*, on June 27, 1668, the community asked that the norm decreeing exclusive judgment up to 30 scudi, except for the right to resort to the revision by the Academy (or, as we add here, by a reviewer chosen by the litigants), be posed to all causes between Jews, including those of minors, orphans and charitable institutions.[1035] The request was granted, and the provision, confirmed on June 21, 1672,[1036] was practically applied in 1676, when in a lawsuit involving a Jewish widow and other Jews, having the Senate declared "che la vedova possa appigliarsi a quel foro più li sia in grado sopra il fondamento che per il *jus comune* gode la vedova l'elettione del foro," the community requested and obtained that the exclusive obligatoriness of the Jewish court be intended as extended also to the widow.[1037]

About the referral of causes between Jews to the commissioner or other state judges, for "rescriptum principis," the community first imposed the ex-communication on those who dared beseeching rescripts of that kind;[1038] then it even claimed the abolition of the institution of referral, asking that "là dove si rescrive Dominus Commissarius provideat, o: justitiam faciat, s'intenda dover star fermo il rito e arbitramento ebraico."[1039] On June 21, 1671, Ferdinando Carlo granted the requested favor, decreeing the absolute exclusivity of Jewish verdict "nonostante fossero stati fatti atti in altro foro."[1040]

And whenever the private persevered in trying to obtain decrees of delegation, the community did not fail to intervene promptly to cancel the attempt and obtain confirmation of the principle of exclusivity of Jewish jurisdiction.

1035 Arch. Isr., folder 37, nos. 17–18.

1036 Arch. Isr., *Book M*, folder 88v. = Arch. Gonzaga, S. II, *Envelope* 3390, dossier years 1672–1696.

1037 Arch. Isr., *Book M*, folder 89, July 16, 1676. For a similar jurisdictional conflict in Leghorn, see above, pp. 267–268.

1038 Arch. Isr., *Folder* 38, no. 52, June 1672. The commissioner, however, decrees the nullity of such anathemas.

1039 Arch. Isr., *Folder* 38, nos. 53–54, June 18 and 20, 1672.

1040 Arch. Isr., *Book M*, f. 88v. cited.

This happened, for example, in 1687,[1041] and 1702,[1042] and in both cases the community came out victorious.

Apart from these provisions taken in relation to individual cases, the jurisdictional privilege was solemnly confirmed in the same terms as the decree of May 18, 1661, the decrees of June 6, 1682,[1043] and October 4, 1700, ch. 11.[1044]

Defended in this way from the competition from other jurisdictions, the Jewish court found itself burdened by a considerable amount of work. It was, in fact, responsible for civil cases of members of a community of about 2000 individuals who derived most of their living from commerce and who, living crammed in a small neighborhood, could not help but bump into each other and so often quarrel.

Therefore, the need to specify and complete the Talmudic-Rabbinical norms relating to both procedural and some points of substantive law, adapting them to the local needs, became soon clear.

The proposal to draft these procedural rules and rules of substance, intended to represent with respect to the general Jewish laws what the local laws represented with respect to the Roman-Canon Laws, originated from the authoritative Rabbi Moisè Zacuto in a meeting of the Vicinia Generale of February 3, 1676. The outline of the small dual code was then presented to

1041 Arch. Isr., *Book M*, f. 104, October 7, 1687. Having Lazzaro Padoa, involved in a cause with Simon Fano, got "con furberia" a decree that remitted the cause to the Commissioner, against the privileges, decree later annulled and attempting he now to bring again the cause before the Commissioner on the grounds that the testimony of Christians is necessary and that the Jews judge without the appropriate procedure, "il che tutto è insussistente perchè gli hebrei giudicano molto bene con quelle figure di giuditio che richiedono i propri riti e senza spesa veruna," the University of the Jews requests that the cause be ordered to be decided by Jewish arbitrators according to their rites, and that the Christian witnesses be heard by the Commissioner who shall then transmit the result of the testimony to the Jewish arbitrators. It furthermore requests that in general, in case of disputes between Jews when a rescript orders that the Commissioner do justice "s'intenda sempre la giustizia esser d'astringere gli hebrei al giudicato de li arbitri hebrei il che non possa il commissario ricusare di fare ad istanza di una delle parti."

1042 Arch. Isr., *Book M*, f. 115v., June 21, 1702 = Arch. Gonzaga, *S. II, Envelope* 3389, dossier 1702–1717. Following the community's action brought against those who attempt to evade mandatory arbitration, it is directed to take action in the sense required, that is "doversi qual si sia causa vertente tra hebrei niun eccettuato terminare hebraicamente dall'Accademia o arbitri hebrei ancorchè fossero seguiti atti in altri fori." June 28, 1702 (Arch. Isr., *Book M*, folder 116v.): Decree stating that the delegation granted to Raffael Fano refers only to the causes with Christians, having those with other Jews to be brought before the arbitrators or the Academy. In general, it is established, that such delegations are to be intended as referring only to the causes with Christians, not to those with Jews.

1043 Arch. Isr., *Book M*, folder 101.

1044 Arch. Isr., *Book M*, folder 117v.

the Duke Ferdinando Carlo who, with his May 29, 1676 decree, approved the decisions taken to establish rules on the points mentioned and precisely: "la prima di dare una norma delle clausole, condittioni, e cautioni che dovranno osservarsi in qualunque sorte di scritture hebraiche, secondo la loro qualità per la sussistenza di esse; la seconda di dichiarare specialmente gli authori che dovranno essere seguitati nelle decisioni delle controversie che possano accadere fra detti hebrei, et dei modi che dovranno tenersi dagli arbitri parimente hebrei nel concludere, e decidere ogni sorte di cause; la terza di porre alcune regole per l'ordine dell'elettione degli stessi arbitri, e de' procuratori, del formare il processo, dar copia delle scritture et altre cose concernenti l'ordine del giuditio, et i meriti delle liti; e la quarta di trovar rimedio per la pronta revisione delle sentenze che saranno date dagli arbitri, in quei casi nei quali ha luogo la revision."[1045]

The drafting of these rules, without any doubt by the rabbinate of Mantua, occupied the rest of 1676 and 1677. On January 19, 1678, permission to print was granted[1046] and the booklet was published shortly after with a foreword by Moshè Zacuto, under the title "שודה דדייני" (Shudà Dedajanè = judges' arbitrate), divided into two sections, the first concerning the judiciary system and the civil procedure (שפות השופטים ופרושת המשפטים), the second relating to the requirements of written acts as means of evidence (תקנות וגזרות לסדרי שטרות).[1047]

To these rules, still in procedural matters, some others were added in 1684, on the subject of *cautio judicatum solvi* [TN: payment of security for legal costs] and denunciation of a new work. Having the possibility been confirmed for the court to try in absentia,[1048] it was established that in case the defaulting party intends to make use of the option of the revision before the Academy or before the same arbitrators, it must first pay the amount of the conviction to the other party, which however must present a guarantee of availability for two months;

1045 Arch. Isr., *folder* 41, no. 18.

1046 Ibidem.

1047 A copy is preserved in Arch. Isr., ibidem. The booklet is listed by Eisenstadt, *Repertorium* cit., no. 2431, with the wrong date 1652. Here (no. 2427) is also mentioned a script about it (to which I was unable to access) by Abraham Kahanà, – להיסטוריה הישראלית באיטליה
בצדו קונטרס: שודה דדייני שפות השופטים ופרושת המשפטים תקנות וגזרות, לסדרי שטרות
In 175–190 מע (ב"סרת) 'ג זרוגה'
(*For the Jewish hisory in Italy. About the booklet "Arbitrio dei giudici etc.,"* see Jewish magazine *Ha-goren* [subtitle: *Abhandlungen über die Wissenschaft des Judentums*, herausgegeben von S. A. Horodetzki, vol. III, Berditscev, 5602 = 1902, pp. 175–190 [The magazine was published from 1898 to 1911]).

1048 Already repeated on November 7, 1677. Arch. Isr., *Book Am*, folder 113, § 3.

and that in case of a new work, a month be allocated to anyone who wanted to prevent it, so as to terminate the cause. If unsuccessful, perpetual silence would be imposed on it and the other party would be able to undertake and continue the work in question.[1049]

In the same year, an important innovation was made in the very substance of the jurisdictional system, as the rabbinical Academy was granted the faculty not only to simply review the decisions of judges or arbitrators, rejecting or confirming them from the pure legal standpoint but also, in case of refusal of the arbitrators or of their disability to judge the cause directly.[1050]

With this last provision, the structure of the Jewish judicial body remained permanently established and no further changes were made for almost a century.

In 1707, in Mantua, the emperors of Austria succeed to the Gonzaga house and they confirmed to the Jews the whole lot of privileges they had enjoyed under the previous rulers.[1051]

The special court is especially confirmed in art. 11 of the dispatches of Emperor Charles VI on April 16, 1715, January 15, 1725 and November 9, 1733.[1052]

In 1737, at the request of the new Governor of Mantua and the Duchy, the university of the Jews outlined its internal governance rules, drawing, with regard to the jurisdiction, a precise framework that is worthwhile to report in full. "Dalla predetta Convocazione Ristretta – it is written – vengono destinati o tre o cinque giudici legali periti del rito ebraico, alli quali spettar debba la giudicatura delle differenze nascenti tra un ebreo e l'altro con facoltà di promulgare i loro laudi diffinitivamente, denominandosi questo corpo sotto il nome di Accademia. Et in oltre dalla stessa Convocazione Ristretta viene creato un altro corpo di giudici di tre persone legali denominati Bed din in ebraico (che val a dire luogo destinato per la giustizia), ma a questi è ristretta la facoltà di non poter giudicare che per solo scudi 30, da L. 6 havendo la revisione i loro

1049 Arch. Isr., *Book Am*, folder 132, § 7, 1684, Rosh Hodesh Sivan.

1050 Request of the University of the Jews of January 3, 1684 (*Book Am*, f. 135v, § 3. Favorable opinion by Sen. Gobio, on May 20, 1684 (*Folder* 46, no. 9 = Arch. Gonzaga, *S. II*, *Envelope* 3389, dossier 1672–1696). Ducal commission May 25, 1684 (Arch. Isr., *Book M*, f. 103. In the July 7, 1667 decree (Arch. Isr., *Book M*, § 10) it is made clear that, as they all form "un sol corpo d'università," with regard to the interpretation of the rites and of the law the Jews of the State must depend on the rabbinic Academy of Mantua only and not on other foreign ones.

1051 Capitulation April 10, 1707, art. 40. Instructions by the General Commissioner to the Mantua Commissioner, ch. 10, August 30, 1707; provisions of the local authorities July 10, 1713 and March 29, 1715. These provisions are mentioned in a memorandum of the rabbinical Academy dated July 15, 1795 (Arch. Isr., *Folder* 242, no. 34).

1052 Cited memorandum.

laudi all'Accademia; distinguendosi che questa è concessa per comissioni ratificate negli onerosi decreti; et per il bet din si riportano annualmente le licenze del Signor Senatore Commissario agli ebrei, che si dirà in appresso il suo incombente per li medesimi. Resta poi in balia delle parti tra ebrei colitiganti di non valersi nè dell'Accademia nè del bet din, ma bensì di scegliersi un giudice per parte ebreo, e farsi da questo giudicare, che si chiamano arbitri, e che poscia, in caso discrepante, o pure non acquetandosi una delle parti al laudo, ha poi la revisione la Accademia sodetta. Per l'esecutioni poi delle sentenze sopradette sia dell'Accademia che del bed din e degli arbitri, resta riservata singolarmente ad un sogetto dell'Ecc.mo Senato, il quale viene creato annualmente in giro, col Signor Presidente inclusivo; e questo si denomina il Signor Senatore Commissario degli Ebrei, al quale, a più delle sodette esecutioni, è conferta la giurisditione di giudice, havendo le sue sentenze la revisione a lo eccelso senato suddetto, il qual Signor Senator Commissario però ha per tali sue incombenze una consueta onoranza da parte di questa Università di L. 720 annue, oltre gli onorari soliti delle sentenze."[1053]

In the form described here in detail, the judicial autonomy is confirmed by Maria Theresa in the privileges of March 10, 1742,[1054] and September 21, 1752,[1055] while on May 1st, 1764, the Governor-General, Count of Firmian reaffirmed the principle of the inappeallability of the arbitrators' and the Academy's rulings.[1056]

The reform movement that Maria Theresa and her son Joseph II started, inspired by the principles of enlightened absolutism, a movement aimed at the progressive crushing of the autonomous bodies standing between the individual and the state, leads to the abolition on December 1st, 1772, of as many as 12 of the 14 special jurisdictions of the Governorate of Mantua. Only the Mercantile Court and the "cosidetta Accademia Ebraica per le cause che insorgono fra di loro [ebrei] e che sogliono decidersi con le costituzioni particolari della loro nazione" survived.[1057]

Some windows of the closed castle of Jewish autonomy, however, must have yielded to the blow of the new winds that hit all public institutions: on April 30, 1779, in the text of the new privileges, the right for individual Jews to appeal to the Council of Justice against the judgments, decrees and acts of the Jewish arbitrators was granted by Maria Theresa "perchè, sentiti prima dal

1053 Arch. Isr., *folder* 99, no. 64.
1054 Cited memorandum.
1055 Arch. Isr., *Book Bb*, ch. XI.
1056 Cited memorandum.
1057 Arch. Isr., *folder* 185, no. 62.

medesimo gli arbitri, venga innanzi allo stesso consiglio ammessa la revisione o riduzione ad arbitrio." Also, in homage to l. *unica C. quando imperator*, the *miserabiles personae* were relieved of the absolute obligation to turn to Jewish jurisdiction.[1058]

Perceiving these new principles as a dangerous attack on prerogatives that had lasted two centuries, the community rushed to draft a lengthy memorandum, dated September 16, 1779, where it tried to oppose, with various arguments, the decreed innovations,[1059] to no avail. Nor did an appeal submitted for the same purpose five years later, directly to the Emperor, have better luck when presented by a delegation that had gone to Trieste for that specific purpose on a visit by the sovereign.[1060] In fact, the arguments contained in this appeal were expressly rebutted in a series of observations made by Marquis Zanetti, a senior official.[1061]

While fretting about this modest limitation brought upon its judicial autonomy, the community did not know that a more severe blow was being prepared for it: the complete abolition of their autonomy. In 1781, a decisive offensive against all Jewish national prerogatives was initiated by Joseph II: in homage to the new political principles, opposed to the old ones, the civil elevation of the Jews as individuals was promoted, but they were required to renounce all their national peculiarities. "Jews as individuals must be given everything, Jews as a nation, nothing," Clermont-Tonnerre will say at the National Assembly during

1058 Arch. Isr., *Book Cc*, ch. XI.

1059 Arch. Isr., *folder* 182, no. 52. The innovation "con infinito pregiudizio della Nazione sconvolge l'usato sistema." The main argument claimed here is the difference in procedure and the difficulty for state judges to get acquainted with Jewish norms according to which the sentence must be enacted: "Tutt'altro che sia nel civile egli è l'ordine dei giudizi nel foro ebraico, e in tanta diversità come ottenere che le cause, in questo ebraicamente conosciute, in quello poi similmente abbiansi a rivedere? Diverse pur sono e non di rado discordi le massime di giudicare, che gli ebrei traggono dall'antica legislazione di Mosè, dalla tradizione de' Padri loro, dalle interpretazioni de' Rabini, dall'esempio dei propri giudicati, dall'indole della Nazione, dagli oggetti d'industria e di commercio che tutta formano la loro occupazione, dalla stessa persino circoscrizion di luogo, entro cui astretti sono a doversi contenere; diverse, giova ripeterlo, e non di rado discordi son queste massime da quelle appresso i giudici e tribunali della Provincia comunemente stabilite e ammesse. Or una lite dagli arbitri o dai Rabini tra Ebrei giudicata con que' principii di giustizia che da tante partono e sì disparate fonti, se all'esame passi di giudici e Tribunali, che altri ne adottano, e di questi difficilmente aver ne possono la debita e sicura contezza, come fia che venga appresso gli uni e gli altri l'affare istesso conformemente conosciuto e deciso?"

1060 March 16, 1784. Arch. Isr., *folder* 195, no. 25. The document is no longer available there. It has become known from *Repertorio Levi*, vol. IV, Giudizio civile ebraico, sub anno.

1061 May 25, 1784. Observations against the appeal etc. Arch. Isr., *folder* 195, no. 26.

the French Revolution[1062] a few years later, and Joseph II did not think differently on the second point while proceeding with great caution in individual concessions.[1063]

During 1781 and 1782, it was imposed on Jews from many regions of the Empire to abandon the Hebrew language in all legal acts and, in general, business acts, replacing it with the language of the country, being excluded from the ban only the divine service. The Jewish schools were also radically transformed and assimilated into local ones, with regard to the system and the teaching material, always with the precise objective of denationalization.[1064]

These reforms, introduced in the Kingdom of Bohemia, aroused the enthusiasm of a publicist from Mantua, the count Giovan Battista Gherardo d'Arco, who drew inspiration from them to compile a booklet titled "*Dell'influenza del ghetto nello stato.*"[1065] In that script it is contended the harm that comes to the community from the isolation in which, compared to other nations that make up the state, the Jewish nation is maintained by restrictive laws and, above all, by the autonomies that were recognized to it. Applauding unconditionally to the provisions on the language and on the schools, D'Arco also attacked the jurisdictional autonomy, as one of the fundamental "principles of the division and detachment of the ghetto from the state in which it exists. "Oltre trovarsi ne' Rabbini – continues D'Arco – consolidata un'autorità politica e civile indipendente dall'autorità di chi regge lo stato, la quale derivando ne' medesimi dalla religione, acquista un grado di forza superiore ad ogn'altra; si presiede da essi ad un corpo d'intera nazionale magistratura, composto di tredici e talor quindici dei principali del Ghetto, che arbitri della lista (?) si chiamano. L'autorità di questo corpo, quantunque nascosta trovisi e velata

1062 Session of December 21, 1789. Simon Dubnov, *Histoire moderne du peuple juif*, vol. I, Paris, 1933, p. 100.

1063 On the policy of Joseph II towards the Jews, see Dubnov, op. cit., vol. I, pp. 30–37.

1064 Provision for Bohemia, November 2, 1781, available in Italian in *Gazzetta di Mantova*, 1781, nos. 47 and 48, November 23 and 30 = *Codice ossia collezione sistematica di tutte le leggi e ordinanze emanate sotto il regno di S. M. I. Giuseppe II, stampata in Vienna nel 1785, ed ora tradotta dal tedesco da* Bartolomeo Borroni, Milan, 1787, T. VIII, p. 45 = D'Arco, op. cit.further below, part I, pp. 140–144. The same provision for the Jews of Gorizia and Gradisca, November 24, 1781 (Arch. Isr. of Mantua, *folder* 88, no. 28). License for the Jews of Vienna and Upper Austria, January 2, 1782, ch. 15 (Arch. Isr., *folder* 189, no. 5). The provision is extended a little later to Mantua (Arch. Isr., *folder* 187, no. 31. The document, cited in the repertorio Levi, l. cit. is no longer available there. The date of May 13, 1781 given by Levi is for sure erroneous, having the provision been made foremost for Bohemia.

1065 G. B. Gherardo D'Arco, *Della influenza del ghetto nello stato*, Part I, Venice, G. Storti, 1782, 144 pp.; Part II, Venice, T. Bettinelli, 1785, 71 pp. The name of the author appears only in the preface of the publisher Storti.

sotto la denominazione modesta di arbitramento, e talor anche sotto l'equivoca denominazione di Accademia, all'autorità corrisponde però tuttavia di un positivo tribunale di privata giurisdizione giudiziaria. Inappellabili sono infatti i giudizii dell'arbitramento od accademia, di rado n'è concessa la revisione interna, giammai tollerata l'esterna appellazione al foro cristiano: il ricorso a questo proibito anzi trovasi onninamente dalla minaccia delle scomuniche, la forza atterritrice delle quali già è noto quanto estendasi fra gli ebrei. Vero è che privo sembra a primo aspetto siffatto tribunale giudiziario della forza coattiva, ma tuttavia sostanzialmente non è, giacchè a ministri ed esecutori de' propri decreti può vantarsi di avere gli uffizi pubblici dello stato: in seguito dell'informazione sua ottiene in fatti l'Accademia da questi per la maggior parte parzialissimi degli ebrei il braccio forte all'adempimento dei propri decreti."[1066] "L'abuso – the writer presses on – è propriamente l'unico fondamento di quell'interna giurisdizione, onde in molte province godono gli Ebrei; dal medesimo cangiata si è del tutto la natura degli arbitri, della cui esistenza presso gli ebrei trovasi veramente qualche indizio nel codice di Giustiniano [allusion to l. 8 C. I. 1,9] ma quegli arbitri non avevano autorità che qual loro la davano le parti contendenti; non era perpetua ma temporanea, non aveva coattività, nemmeno era inappellabile come ora, divenuto in certa guisa emulo del foro urbano, e quasi gareggiante con esso quel tribunale interno che arbitramento si dice, ed in qualche parte anche accademia a profanazione di tal nome."

D'Arco concludes by saying that the repeal of this harmful autonomy is imposed out a necessity, and comes as a logical corollary from the mentioned regulation for Bohemia "che tutto spira massime di fraternità e d'uguaglianza, che tutto tende ad avvicinar nazione a nazione, a rimuover dall'una e dall'altra quelle forze centripete, che le allontanano, e a rivolgerle come a un centro comune." And to be complete the provision invoked must decree not only the abrogation of the court but also of the very same Jewish civil law "e la riduzione del ghetto alla soggezione delle leggi stesse cui obbedisce la nazione, in mezzo alla quale esiste." "Nè solo alla nazione – it is said in conclusion – in mezzo alla quale trovasi un ghetto favorito e sostenuto da privilegi e prerogative, riuscir dee l'abrogazione propizia , ma all'ebrea eziandio nullameno. La parità ed uguaglianza di situazione che da ciò a derivar viene, dee necessariamente recare agli ebrei il massimo dei vantaggi, qual si è quello di ridurre insensibilmente gli abitatori dello stato a riguardarli con quell'occhio stesso,

1066 Op. cit., I, pp. 77–78.

con cui in grazia appunto della parità dei diritti e delle obbligazioni i medesimi si riguardano fra loro scambievolmente."[1067]

D'Arco's booklet, designed to meet the full favor of Joseph II, was probably read and meditate at Court; and certainly it was not incorrect to say that, with regard to jurisdiction, it coincided fully with the ideas of the Emperor and perhaps hastened its translation into practice: the fact is that in the same year, 1782, with announcement of July 11,[1068] the total repeal of both the Jewish law and jurisdiction was established in Austria. The measure was then extended on August 25, 1783 to Poland and Bohemia,[1069] and was finally made general by an interpretative decree of May 23, 1785.[1070] In Lombardy, however, in virtue of some circular letter that failed to reach us, this decree apparently did not have an immediate application and it was not until February 11, 1786 that the emperor ordered the repeal of all special jurisdictions in the duchies of Milan and Mantua, with the sole exception for the commercial tribunal.[1071] The Jewish community of Mantua was truly appalled by this new blow dealt to its autonomy, and hastened to draft a new memorandum in order to obtain, if not the repeal of this provision, at least some easing measure. "Gli ebrei – it is said in this memorandum[1072] – sono finora vissuti e vivono tuttavia, per quanto spetta all'interna loro polizia, conformemente a quel che prescrivono le Leggi date loro da Mosè, a quello che stabilirono le antiche tradizioni dei padri loro, a quello che interpretando e giudicando fu costantemente insegnato e deciso dai loro Rabbini. Di qui è che per matrimonii, per successioni, per contratti e per quasi tutto ciò che spetta agli atti ed impegni diversi della vita civile siansi finora regolati con principii e massime diverse ed in gran parte discordi

1067 Op. cit., I, pp. 135–137. An anonymous *Difesa contro gli attacchi fatti alla Nazione ebrea nel libro intitolato: Della influenza del Ghetto nello stato*, Pavia, 1784, 191 pp. is devoted to the refutation of D'Arco's work. Its author, quite obviously a Mantuan Jew, rebuts point by point the arguments adduced by D'Arco, and vigorously defends (pp. 84–88 and 175–178) the privilege of jurisdictional autonomy of the community, observing how, far from being unfair, it is based on precise sovereign concessions and is "tutto analogo all'essere speciale di questa nazione, che, distinta in altri capi principali, dee pure, per quanto riguarda alla giurisprudenza interna, regolarsi giusta la propria dell'ebreo codice, vantato e rispettato in tale materia dai legali tutti di buon senso e dal Selden in particolare (*De jure naturali et gentium*)."

1068 *Codice ossia collezione*, cit., VIII, p. 59. Similar inaccurate provisions are found in the already cited license of January 2, 1782, ch. 25 (Arch. Isr., *Folder* 189, no. 5).

1069 Mentioned in a letter from Trieste to the community of Mantua, dated July 6, 1785. Arch. Isr., *Folder* 198, no. 16.

1070 *Codice ossia collezione*, cit., X, p. 56 = Arch. Isr., *Folder* 198, no. 16.

1071 Edict of February 11, 1786 "per la pianta e organizzazione dei tribunali" §§ VI and VII. Cited in the aforementioned memorandum, in note 62.

1072 Arch. Isr. *Folder* 210.

da quelle della comune giurisprudenza: ed ecco perchè siasi resa e si renda necessaria una giudicatura nazionale. Di fatti o vuolsi in una controversia la qual insorga tra ebrei, prescindere da quel che o dispongon le proprie leggi o stabiliron le consuetudini, e l'amministrazion della giustizia involverebbe una manifesta ingiustizia, perchè si verrebbe con ciò a declinare dall'intendimento di quelli che disponendo o contraendo intesero di confermarsi alle massime che erano le sole regolatrici degli atti loro; o si vuole che il giudizio debba esser a queste coerente e conforme; e come ottenerlo da giudici e tribunali non istruiti di quella particolar giurisprudenza che ad essi dovrebbe servir di norma nel giudicare? Nè da ciò può dedursi che dunque convenisse assoggettare gli ebrei per gli atti civili alle leggi della Provincia. In primo luogo non cesserebbe l'inconveniente per tutto quello che seguito sia o siasi fatto nel tempo che le proprie consuetudini e le leggi erano in osservanza e vigore. Secondo, questo rovescio di massime e di principii metterebbe la massima parte di ebrei in una confusione e incertezza troppo contraria al buon ordine ed alla tranquillità di qualunque corpo sociale. Terzo, avendo molti atti civili un'intima relazione con quanto ha di dogma e di disciplina la loro religione, un sì fatto provvedimento verrebbe ad angustiarli in una parte in cui la ragione ed il sovrano stesso li vuol liberi e affatto tranquilli. Potrebbesi creder forse opportuna la compilazione di un codice, il qual contenendo ed esponendo le proprie leggi e consuetudini servisse ad istruzione dei giudici della Provincia. Ma questo corpo di legislazione perchè tutto comprendesse quanto sia necessario a conoscere o decidere ebraicamente le cause tutte degli ebrei un'opera sarebbe di lunga meditazione e di non facile esecuzione; ma questo non dispensa i giudici e i tribunali della Provincia da un nuovo studio per essi difficile certamente e fastidioso; ed essi non consumati in questo studio come il sono in quello della civile giurisprudenza rimarrebbero tuttavia esposti a poter errare o nell'intelligenza o nell'applicazione di queste nuove leggi." The memorandum went on, describing the economic benefits that the existence of the national judiciary always brought to the Jews, given that the judgment was absolute free, and added that if the commercial jurisdiction was preserved, a stronger reason was there for the Jewish one to be maintained, too, having uses intrinsically much more peculiar than the commercial ones, and that precisely for this reason was also maintained in the duchies of Modena and Tuscany.

The arguments of which the memorandum abounded, however valid and exposed with insight, were unhelpful to change a decision already made irrevocably. Mindful of this, the Jews of Mantua then tried to circumvent the obstacle going back to the offensive no longer frontally, but sideways; instead of the restoration of the actual jurisdiction they only asked for the faculty of the rabbinical Academy, to be consulted as advisors in all cases brought before the tribunal by contending Jews. In the mood for goodwill, the sovereign adhered to the request of the community with the provision of July 3, 1786.[1073]

In this way, the use of Jewish law in the decision of such causes was ensured, and also the jurisdiction "ejected from the door, comes back through the window," wrapped under the veil of just providing expertise: in fact, powerless in getting involved in the sea of troubles of the Talmudic-rabbinic sources used in the consultancy, the civil judges could not but comply in full with the rulings of the latter.

That went on for four years, until in 1790, the death of Joseph II and the ascent to the imperial throne of Leopold II Grand Duke of Tuscany, known for being very favorable to the Jewish autonomies, rekindled in the Mantuan community hopes for a full restoration of the jurisdictional privileges. In view of the issuing of a new decree of tolerance,[1074] a delegation sent to the Court of Vienna in order to present several requests of that community did not fail to insist on the matter of the tribunal. Finally, it had the satisfaction to see its wishes fulfilled around such an important point.

On January 2, 1791, in the new privilege issued by the emperor for the Jews of Mantua, with regard to the jurisdiction, the return to the situation that existed before the repealing decree of February 11, 1786 was expressly established. That meant restoring the rabbinical court to its full authority, with the sole exception, in homage to Maria Theresa's provision of April 30, 1770, of the faculty to review the judgments by the Council of Justice and relieve the *miserabiles personae* from the obligation to turn only to that court.[1075]

On September 8 of the same year, the community, with great satisfaction, went ahead with the election of the Academy Court, composed of three rabbis and two merchants, and of the lower Court (*Beth Din*) composed of two individuals and a rabbi of the Academy, to be renewed every year, plus an usher, 2 record keepers and 1 apprentice.[1076]

1073 "S. M. fa rimettere la compiegata supplica con promemoria degli individui della Nazione ebrea di Mantova a codesto R. Tribunale d'Appello, ordinando al medesimo nelle ricorrenze di mera perizia di permettere alla suddetta nazione di assumere il sentimento degli individui componenti la così detta Accademia a norma del supplicato. Comanda pure al mentovato tribunale di diramare la presente risoluzione alle prime istanze, e renderne intesi li detti supplicanti. Milano 3 luglio 1786." (Arch. Isr. *Folder* 210, no. 3). Controversial interpretation in the Viterbi cause, August 1786. Clarification of the Tribunale Superiore of Milan dated September 13, 1786 (ibid.).

1074 Arch. Isr. *Book Di*, f. 25, October 24, 1790.

1075 Ch. 8 of the privilege, released in print. (From a copy in my possession.)

1076 Arch. Isr. *Folder* 230, no. 42, f. 25.

The rhythm of the work interrupted for half a decade thus resumed and for another four years no new obstacle appeared on the horizon.

Only in 1795, some doubts arose in the Court of Appeal about the nature of the rabbinical court and the possibility in its decisions to comply with the Jewish substantive and procedural rules[1077] and the community was requested to make clarifications and explanations in that regard. On behalf of the community, the rabbinical Academy replied by means of a memorandum drafted by Rabbi Bonajuto Isac Levi,[1078] where the entire history of the court was redone since 1682, the current composition and operation was illustrated[1079] and the compliance with the procedural rules stipulated with a general character by the sovereign's regulations was guaranteed "compatibly with the observance of national rites, forms and customs."[1080] About this episode, it should be noted that neither the questions nor answers were very precise: it is quite unclear what the Court of Appeal intended to establish, nor does the memorandum seem to respond to the point: in each line, only the perception of danger is

1077 Arch. Isr. *Folder* 242, no. 34. The doubts are as follows: "1st) Se l'Accademia degli Ebrei possa erigersi, come ha fatto, in tribunale di prima istanza fra la sua nazione; 2nd) Se non sia già deciso dal Ces. R. dispaccio di loro tolleranza datato 2 gennaio 1791 che i giudici ebrei possono atenersi anche nel ordine giudiziario alle loro forme e riti; 3rd) Se non convenga sentire l'Accademia eccitandola a somministrare i fondamenti del rito, delle forme e leggi ebraiche che si osservano sia nelle decisioni, sia nel ordine."

1078 Arch. Isr., ibidem.

1079 "L'Accademia consta di tre rabbini il primo dei quali ne è l'anziano ossia il capo. A questi sono aggiunti due negozianti per i necessari lumi nelle cause mercantili, le quali in certi rapporti per disposizione del rito nazionale, decidonsi consentaneamente alle leggi, ed alla pratica del commercio. Sonvi altri due mercanti soprannumerari ossiano alcuni, i quali suppliscono a completare il numero dei giudici che per la definitiva non può essere minore di tre. Le cause che non eccedono le 180 lire Provinciali si giudicano, secondo l'inveterata pratica, da uno dei tre rabbini per turno annuale, unitamente ad altri due mercanti. Il personale subalterno consiste: 1° in un cancelliere e vice-cancelliere, che assistono al protocollo degli esibiti, alla spedizione degli atti, alla custodia dei medesimi in Archivio, alle sessioni e ad ogni altra relativa incombenza; 2° in un altro cancelliere addetto all'ufficio delle cause minori; 3° in uno scrittore aggiunto; 4° in due portieri che intimano gli atti alle due parti, e fanno fede dell'intimazione, e coll'incarico delle materiali occorrenze del luogo."

1080 "Per rapporto finalmente alle precedenze, ed alle circostanze con cui l'Accademia procede a giudicare le emergenti controversie, oggetto su cui cade l'ultima parte del superiore eccitamento, può l'Accademia rispettosamente assicurare il R. Tribunale di non iscostarsi dalle formalità e metodo che per la trafila degli atti prescrivono il sovrano regolamento, e le sopravenute modificazioni ed appuntamenti, compatibilmente però con l'osservanza dei riti e forme e consuetudini nazionali che per indispensabil dovere di religione e coerentemente al Clementissimo dispaccio servir devono inalterabilmente di base ai giudizi ebraici."

felt, and the desire to avoid, at a time so contrary to the maintenance of all autonomies, especially the jurisdictional ones, any question that could shake the recently strengthened foundations of the Jewish court, or anyway disturb its functioning.

As hoped by the community, the episode did not have any consequence, and with no further shocks, the year 1797 was thus reached, which temporarily marked the end of the Austrian rule over Mantua. From the French who took over, in favor, as we have said, of the individual emancipation of the Jews, but absolutely opposed to their national autonomies, in parallel to the emancipation itself proclaimed in Mantua on January 21, 1798,[1081] we would expect the repeal of the Jewish tribunal. Instead, in the turmoil of events, it escaped the attention of the new dominators and continued to operate as in the past, both in this period and later, following the brief period during which the Austrians had returned (1799–1801).

However, it was inevitable that one day or another some circumstance would arise such as to attract the attention of the French authorities on the Jewish jurisdiction: and that day would not mark but the end of an institution that according to the canons of democratic individualism was in general considered as a privilege contrary to the proclaimed principles of equality.

What the Jewish community always dreaded eventually manifested itself in 1804; and it was from a member of that very same community that the blow came about, which would bring down the secular jurisdictional autonomy.

The matter developed like this: in a lawsuit against the community, a woman, a certain Malcà Sonnino, widow Trabotti, in the interests of her minor children, turned to the Tribunal instead of turning to the Jewish Academy: but the Tribunal, agreeing to the exception opposed by the community, claimed lack of jurisdiction, maintaining that, being that a cause between Jews, the judgment in the first instance was the responsibility of the Academy, according to the provision of paragraph 8 of the January 2, 1791 diploma of Leopold II.

Defended by the attorney Petrali, the widow appealed against the court's declining, arguing in her grievance, among other things, that the Academy's ruling must already be considered as abolished, as the diploma on which it was founded is abolished. "Quel dispaccio – Petrali writes – è un diploma di tolleranza che privilegi accorda all'Università degli ebrei, ma la costituzione li ha parificati in tutto agli altri cittadini della repubblica e ha fatto cessare l'Università degli ebrei[1082] e in conseguenza abrogato del tutto il cessato diploma

1081 Luigi Carnevali, *Il ghetto di Mantova*, Mantua, 1884, pp. 42–43.

1082 In reality, it has only changed its name to "Azienda economica ebraica" (Jewish Economic Company).

suddetto, non potendosi supporre tolleranza o privileggi ove tutti son cittadini eguali e non esistono disparità di diritti."

The community immediately became aware of the seriousness of the attack, which transcended the single controversy by striking at the very basis of its autonomy, and trieed forcefully to respond to Petrali's arguments before the court, insisting on the point that the political equalizing of the citizens did not logically bring about the abolition of the autonomies of the groups in general and of the Jewish group in particular. "La costituzione – it writes – parificando in massima i cittadini ha confermata implicitamente per gli ebrei la parificazione di cui godevano in virtù del dispaccio di Leopoldo II, ma essa non è discesa a circumscrivere alcun particolare loro diritto, nella guisa stessa che lascia finora intatti alle provincie i loro statuti municipali; ed è tanto lontano che la parificazione politica degli ebrei renda incompatibile la sussistenza dell'interno loro giudizio nelle cause civili, che il celebre ministro e scrittore mons. Dohm di Berlino, mentre nel suo aureo trattato "Réforme politique des Juifs" propone il suo piano con cui mettere gli Ebrei perfettamente a livello degli altri cittadini non trova il menomo inconveniente ed anzi approva che si abbia a conservar loro il diritto di aver giudici ebrei di prima istanza, in riguardo a quello che, come ei lo dice, invincibile attaccamento di questa Nazione alle leggi ed ai costumi dei suoi padri."[1083]

Faced with a matter of such importance, the Court did not wish to pronouce directly and decided to submit the question to the Minister of justice "se possa o no continuare nell'attuale sua consistenza l'Accademia ebraica, massime dopo la legge 28 luglio 1802" (concerning the organization of the tribunals).[1084]

Alarmed by the turn of events, having a foreboding of a negative response to the question, in the meeting of 19 May 1804, the community decided to send a commission composed of 4 influential Jews to Milan, led by Rabbi Abram Vita Cologna and Lazzaro Berla, to see the Minister and save the Academy in extremis.[1085]

A week later, assisted by lawyer Maggi, the commission obtained a hearing, not by the Minister but by the secretary general Riva. The latter – as Cologna and Berla reported on the same evening in a letter to the Community[1086] – acted very courteously in the form, but in substance he turned out to be anything but favorable to the acceptance of the thesis proposed, on the reflection

1083 All this in Arch. Isr., *Folder* 271, no. 37.

1084 Arch. Isr., *Folder* 273, no. 33, packet no. 12.

1085 Ibidem. Cologna shall later be vice-president of Paris' Sanhedrin (1807). Dubnov, *Histoire moderne du peuple juif*, cit., I, p. 155.

1086 May 26, Arch. Isr., *Folder* 271, no. 37.

that the particular law and the particular judgment were contrary to human rights and equality enshrined in the Constitution. And to Cologna's observation that for Jews "è dogmatico anche quello che altri riguardano per oggetto di mero diritto civile" – as Cologna writes – while keeping smiling he replies "che una società i cui principii non possono amalgamarsi con le leggi dello stato, dovrebbe andarsene a casa sua."

The talk had decided the fate of the Jewish jurisdiction; and the official communication of the repeal followed within a few days, even before the commission's departure from Milan. Its members were left with the consolation of a thank-you letter from the community, aware that if the deal fell through it was not due to their fault but to the force of absolutely invincible circumstances.[1087]

And so, in a definitive manner, the judicial autonomy of the Jewish community of Mantua came to an end. With it, the Jews also lost the use of their law which state tribunals no longer applied. In Mantua, like anywhere else in the West, at the start of the 19th century, Jews paid for their individual rights of freedom and equality by renouncing their centuries-old autonomies. With the loss of these autonomies, their principal defensive barriers failed, and slowly but inevitably, they began the journey toward a complete breakdown.

1087 June 4. Ibidem: "Potete ben credere se ci ha al vivo commosso l'infausto esito nel noto affare dell'Accademia; ma non siamo meno grati al vostro maneggio e diligenza pel buon successo, e se è andato male non è da incolparne che la natura purtroppo infelice dell'affare stesso. Avete annesso il proclama del commissario oggi pubblicato, e sarà bene che prima della partenza v'informiate se per le cause incoate ma non decise, sia necessario di reintrodurre nuovamente gli atti nanti al foro competente, giacchè fin qui non si ha alcuna disposizione sul proposito."

Appendix of Documents

I

Conferral of Mantua citizenship to the Jew Saul of Spain
(Archive Gonzaga of Mantua, Books of the Decrees, III, page 337, year 1431, November 19).

Johannes Franciscus de Gonzaga Mantue etc. Imperialis Vicarius Generalis. – Condescendentes supplicationibus Sauli de Yspania ebrei habitantis in Civitate nostra Mantue continentibus in effectu ut dignemus ipsum ad civilitatis nostrae Mantuae beneficium admittere. Harum tenore, vigore nostri arbitrii et plenitudinis potestatis quibus publice fungimur in dicta nostra civitate Mantue eiusque districtu ac omni modo jure et forma quibus melius scimus et possumus ex certa scientia et animo deliberato, eundem Saulum eiusque filios et descendentes facimus et creamus cives civitatis nostrae Mantuae, ipsosque ad notri gratiam et civilitatis dictae nostrae beneficium admittimus civitatis recepimus et aggregamus. Ita et taliter quod amodo ipse filii et descendentes sui sicut cives et pro civibus civitatis nostrae predictae habeantur, teneantur, tractantur et reputentur. Et sic haberi, teneri, tractari et reputari volumus et mandamus. Et quod fruantur et gaudeant omnibus et singulis exemptionibus dignitatibus preeminentiis et prerogativis quibus alii antiqui et originarii cives civitatis nostrae predictae fruuntur et gaudent; auctoritatem quoque habeant plenam et lincenciam omnimodam de cetero acquirendi habendi et retinendi in dicta nostra civitate Mantue eiusque districtu bona quaecunque mobilia et immobilia atque jura sub quocunque titulo. Et de ipsis acquisitionibus et juribus notarius quilibet mantuanus licite et impune publica possit conficere instrumenta, unum et plura quotquot fuerint necessaria et opportuna; omnesque acquisitiones et contractus sub titulo facti et faciendi per ipsos in civitate nostra Mantuae eiusque districtu valeant et plenam roboris obtineant firmitatem perinde ac facti forent per originarios cives civitatis nostrae predicte describantur quoque in laribus civium civitatis nostrae predicte modo forma consuetudine nostrorum civium predictorum; non obstantibus ad predicta vel aliquod predictorum aliquibus legibus civilibus vel municipalibus; statutis, provisionibus, reformationibus, consuetudinibus, ordinibus, vel decretis nostris et Communis nostri Mantue factis vel etiam faciendis; et precipue non obstante statuto posito sub rubrica "De alienacionibus prohibitis" vel etiam statuto "De Cronicha Concilii Maioris" per totum aut alio statuto vel jure quod haberetur predictis obsistere quovismodo. Quibus omnibus et aliis quae obstare possent quantum in hac parte totaliter derogamus et esse volumus derogatum. In quorum testimonium presentes fieri iussimus nostrique sigilli impressione muniri.

 | DOI:10.1163/9789004627154_017

Datum Mantue XVIII Novembris 1431. Venturinus de Arivabenis, etc., visa signatura pro, fiat, scripsit.

II

Conferral of Mantua citizenship to the Jew Bonaventura son of the late Salomone (Archive Gonzaga, Books of the Decrees, VI, page 7, year 1432, April 19).

Johannes Franciscus dt Gonzaga etc. Annuentes supplicationibus nobis humiliter porrectarum per Bonaventuram hebreum quondam Salomonis incolam civitatis nostre Mantue. Harum tenore, vigore nostri arbitrii et de nostre plenitudine potestatis quibus publice fungimur in dicta nostra civitate eiusque districtu ac omni modo jure via et forma et causa quibus melius scimus et possimus ex certa scientia et animo deliberato, eundem Bonaventuram eiusque filios presentes et futuros et descendentes facimus admittimus, recipimus et creamus in cives et ad civilitatis beneficium et gratiam civitatis nostrae Mantuae, Ita et taliter quod ipse Bonaventura eiusque filii et descendentes presentes et futuri sint cives et in civis civitatis nostrae habeantur, teneantur, tractentur et reputentur. Et sic teneri haberi, tractari et reputari volumus atque mandamus. Quodque fruantur et gaudeantur omnibus et singulis exemptionibus privilegiis et prerogativis quibus fruuntur et gaudent cives civitatis nostrae Mantuae; auctoritatem quoque habeant plenam et licenciam omnimodam ac potestatem habendi de cetero acquirendi et perpetuo retinendi in dicta nostra civitate Mantue eiusque districtu bona quaecumque mobilia et immobilia atque jura sub quocunque titulo; omnesque contractus et acquisitiones per predictos fiende valeant teneant eiusque sint roboris et efficaciae ac si facta forent per originarios cives dicte nostre civitatis Mantue. Et de ipsis acquisitionibus atque juribus notarius quilibet Mantuanus publica possit unum et plura conficere instrumenta quot fuerint opportuna. Et describantur quoque in laribus civum nostrorum civitatis eiusdem; non obstantibus etc. Datum Mantue XVIII Aprilis 1432. Guido de Cambiatoribus, secretarius visa suplicatione. Signatum dicta die manu domini: pro; fiat.

III

Conferral of Mantua citizenship to the Jew Beniamino and his son Angelo (Archive Gonzaga, Books of the Decrees, VI, page 30, year 1434, February 23).

Johannes Franciscus marchio Mantue etc. pro illustrissimo ducali dominio Capitaneus Generalis etc. Condescendentes supplicacionibus nobis exibitis per

Begnaminum ebreum habitatorem Hostilie et Angelum eius filium qui nobis supplicarunt utdignemur eos creare cives civitatis nostre Mantue pro acquisitis et acquirendis; harum tenore, vigore nostri arbitrii et potestatis nostre plenitudinis, quibus publice fungimur in dicta nostra civitate Mantue eiusque marchionatu et districtu, ac omni modo, jure, via et forma, quibus melius scimus et possumus, ex certa scientia et animo deliberato, eosdem Beniaminum et Angelum et eorum filios et descendentes presentes et futuros admittimus, facimus et creamus cives civitatis nostrae predicte Mantue; ipsosque ad civilitatem dicte nostre civitatis et eius beneficium reducimus et aggregamus. Ita et taliter quod ammodo ipsi Begniaminus et Angellus, ac eius filii et descendentes sint cives et pro civibus civitatis nostre predicte habeantur, teneantur et reputentur, et sic haberi, teneri, tractari volumus et reputari; ac fruantur et gaudeant omnibus et singulis exemptionibus dignitatibus, preminenciis et prerogativis, quibus alii antiqui et originarii cives dicte nostre civitatis fruuntur et gaudent; ac auctoritatem habeant et plenam licenciam et bayliam omnimodam de cetero acquirendi, habendi et retinendi in dicta nostra civitate eiusque marchionatu et districtu bona quaecunque mobilia et immobilia, atque iura sub quocumque titulo, et de ipsis acquisicionibus et juribus notarius quilibet mantuanus possit et valeat libere et impune publica conficere instrumenta, unum et plura quotquot fuerint necessaria et opportuna, omnesque acquisiciones et contractus facti per ipsos et faciendi in futurum per eos et descendentes suos predictos in dicta nostra civitate eiusque marchionatu et districtu valeant et plenam roboris obtineant firmitatem perinde ac si facti forent per originarios cives nostros et dicte nostre civitatis; describantur quoque in laribus civium civitatis nostre predicte, modo forma ac consuetudine nostrorum civium predictorum; non obstantibus aliquibus legibus civilibus vel municipalibus, reformationibus consuetudinibus, ordinibus vel decretis nostris et Communis nostri Mantue factis aut faciendis; et precipue non obstante statuto posito sub rubrica "De alienacionibus prohibitis," statuto per totum sub rubrica "De cronicha concilii maioris" aut alio quocumque statuto vel jure quod haberetur predictis obstare quovismodo. Quibus et omnibus aliis quae obstarent vel obstare possent ex certa scientia et de nostre plenitudine potestatis derogamus et esse volumus derogatum et mandamus eciam si talia forent de quibus mentionem specificam fieri operteret. In quorum testimonium presentes fieri iussimus nostrique sigilli impressione muniri. Datum Mantue die XXIII februarii 1434, XII indicione.

Venturinus de Arivabenis prefati Illustrissimi Domini Marchionis secretarius subscripsit visa supplicacione signata manu prelibati domini Marchionis pro, fiat.

At the foot of the page: "In simili forma Amedeo de Cremona [non ebreo], XXII maii 1436.

Vigore supplicacionis signate fiat."

IV

(State Archive of Venice – *Inquisitorato agli Ebrei*, Envelope 39; printed booklet titled "Scomuniche abbolite dal magistrato Ecc.mo del Cattaver" no. 2, p. 5).
Terminazion del Capitolar Cattaveri
1581 _ 14 Febraro

Ancorchè sia per li Predecessori nostri altre volte è statopubblicato, sia a contemplazione d'altri magistrati che ricercorno, come anche per intiera consecuzione della giurisdizione nostra, et in una parola per riputazione di questa ben instituita Republica, che non fusse alcun Ebreo di qual condizione esser si volesse, che avesse ardir di pubblicar, o far pubblicar nel Ghetto scomuniche, che proibissero qual si voglia Ebreo di poter camparir d'avanti Magistrati Christiani per poter usare delle ragioni sue come era ed è giusto, e conveniente, et non erriger Tribunale nel suo Ghetto, et per forza di scommuniche, e maledizioni, violentar li poveri oppressi di star al detestando Juditio loro, quali ingiuriosi, e tirannichi modi, oltre che erano di diretto contrarii alla felice libertà di questo eccell.mo Dominio, erano anche di eterna oppressione a quelli Ebrei quali desideravano la giustizia di questo Stato. Pur non obstante questa Santissima provisione, adesso più che mai usano maggior tirannide della prima, credendo loro non esser compresi questi suoi abominevoli eccessi dal sopradetto Proclama, ancorchè la ragion di quello sia universalissima, e chiaramente proibisca, che alcun non sia tirannizado da qualsivoglia per via di scomuniche e maledizioni … Là onde mossi gli Clarissimi Sign.Timoteo Valier, Matteo Sanudo, e Lunardo Rimondo Onorandi Giudici di Cattaver a quali spetta la cosa degli Ebrei, di queste insolentissime audacie, nè essendo conveniente che tali possedono Imperio in questa Città secondo la legge della qual tutti li Cristiani come Ebrei son tenuti viver, non essendo appresso lei differenza di persone in fatto di Giustizia. Con la presente Terminazione hanno terminato, che non sia alcun Ebreo di qual condizione esser si voglia, il qual ardisca metter alcuna Parte a ballottarla, over publicarla per cavar denari, si per causa di strazzaria, come anco in qualsivoglia altra causa in detto Ghetto, nella quale si faccia menzione di pena de scomunica espressamente o tacitamente, giuramenti maledizioni contenute nel Libro dele Leggi, biasteme, o altre simili, acciochè cadauno che si tenirà aggravato possa liberamente senza alcun impedimento ristorarsi con la giustizia di questo stato, e questo in pena di ducati 200, la metà del qual sia dell'accusator, e l'altra metà *ad pias causas*, e di star mesi 18 in presone serado, alla qual sottozazerdebbano sì quelli che metteranno Parte contraria alla presente Terminazione, como ancho quelli che la ballotteranno, over publicheranno, registreranno, et esseguiranno, proibendo in tutto, e per tutto sotto l'istessa pena, l'essecutione della sopradetta Parte nel modo come in quella è stato espresso, et ogni ordine, e licenza che fosse data contro la presente terminazione non sia de alcun valor et a perpetua memoria hanno terminato sia registrata nel Capitular del presente Officio, et sia pubblicata nel Ghetto.

Die 14 februarii 1581 R. P. Praeco publicasse ut supra in Ghetto Hebreorum etc.

V

(Same site, same booklet, no. 3, p. 8)
Altra Terminazion Cattaveri contro Ebrei
Adì 26 Aprile 1606

Avendo pressentito da molte parti li Clar. Signori Piero Grimani, Stefano Belegno, Zorzi Pisani H. Giudici di Cattaver, che nel Ghetto delli Ebrei di questa Città vengono da loro Ebrei contro la mente del Principe, delle leggi et antiche terminazioni, Proclami et Ordini di quello Clar. Magistrato erreti Tribunali, Magistrati, Giudici, Notari, et altre cariche, et statuendo giorno delle udienze, giudicando indifferentemente tra loro si cause civili come criminali, assolvendo, condannando, concedendo suffragii, ponendo Parti, et inamissibilmente quelle eseguendo contro l'inobbedienti, in modo tale, che a guisa di tiranni astringendo con Scomuniche, Giuramenti, Maledizioni le Parti a dover da loro esser forzatamente giudicati, et vanno a poco a poco formando una nova, et piccola Republica.

Onde Sue Signorie Clariss. come Giudici eletti dal Maggior Consiglio, et per legge dell'Eccell. Senato, et dell'Eccelso Consiglio dei Dieci per la custodia, e governo delli Ebrei di essi Ghetti, vedendo in ciò esser bisogno di opportuna provision sì per la giurisdizion del loro magistrato come d'altri, et per decoro di questa buona instituita Republica, hanno con la presente terminato, che se da qui innanzi alcun Ebreo sii chi si voglia ardirà in qualsivoglia luoco di questa città o accidente (sic) giudicar tra loro Ebrei liti di stabili, et affitti di case di ghetto, et altre cause, e differenze civili, o criminali aspettanti al predetto Clarissimo Magistrato di Cattaver, et ad altri Magistrati, cadino in pena sì li giudici che giudicheranno, sì nodari, scrivani, o altri che notassero detti loro atti, o sentenze o accetteranno scritture dalle parti, sì nonzoli, cantarini, o altri che esse parti citassero, o facessero intervenire, come anche quelli che da loro si lasciano giudicar di ducati duecento, et d'anni tre di gallera per cadauno, et per cadauna volta che contrafaranno. E se alcun Ebreo, o Ebrea per qualsivoglia causa ardirà far publicar Scomuniche, Maledizioni, o Giuramenti contra alcun Ebreo, si ottenuta in questa città dalli loro Rabbini, come in qualsivoglia Loco, o Persona, cadino in pena sì li Rabbini che la concederanno, otteneranno, e faranno publicar, il Nonzolo, Cantarini, o altri che la pubblicheranno, come anche quelli ad istanza di chi fossero pubblicati, et contra di chi fossero pubblicati, non ne facendo di ciò consapevole la Giustizia il giorno seguente, di ducati duecento per cadauno, et per cadauna volta, et d'esser banditi per anni 25 di questa Città tra il Menzo et il Quarner, la qual pena pecuniaria sia divisa la metà del denonciante qual sia tenuto secretto, et l'altra metà *ad pias causas*. Et se alcun delli predetti Rabbini, Scrivani, Nonzoli, Cantarini, o parte interessati veranno a denunziare in questo Clar. Officio alcune delle predette contrafazioni, o contrafacenti, non solo li sarà immediatamente concessa la sua impunità, e sarà secretto, ma avrà il beneficio della condanna come si è detto, oltre che essendo una delle parti sarà in tutto e per tutto libero dalla sentenza, o condanna, che in tal caso contro di lui sarà stata fatta.

Però se alcun Ebreo, o Ebrea per strettezza di parentela o per qual altra si voglia causa vorrà far publicar scomunica nelli Ghetti contra alcuno, debbano comparir con quelli che desiderano in scrittura davanti S. S. Clariss., et officio loro, che quelle conforme all'antico instituto del predetto Magistrato le saranno concesse.

VI

(Same site, same booklet, no. 4, p. 10)
Parte presa nel capitolo degli ebrei ponentini e terminazioni Cattaveri che depena detta parte con riserva di proceder criminalmente.
Adì primo marzo 1706
De orden dos Segnores do Maamad, etc.
Omissis
Adì 26 marzo 1706

Gli Illustr., et Ecc.mi Sig. Cattaveri infrascritti, veduta e ben considerata la retroscritta Parte temerariamente proposta da Capi della Nazion Ponentina, e presa nel loro Capitolo con poco rispetto ai Tribunali erreti dal S.M.C. a quali era, ricorrendo, pronto il ricorso, anzi errigendo indecentemente nel loro Capitolo Tribunale, e posposti li riguardi, e le conseguenze in relevantissima materia, che costernerebbe il sostentamento dell'Università, hanno appassionatamente espresso condanne come in quella con scandalo, et mall'esempio, hanno perciò unanimi, e concordi terminato, che detta Parte illico sia penitus abbolita, sicchè non ne viva memoria, risservandosi di proceder criminalmente etc. Salvi sempre li ricorsi a detta Nazione, quando potessero giustificare la diffamata infedeltà al Tribunale di giustizia.

E d'ordine etc. la presente fu annotata sopra il Libro di dette Parti al margine della Parte depennata sottoscritta da Sue E.E.

Lorenzo Pasqualigo Cattaver
Marc'Antonio Falier Cattaver
Pietro Sagredo Cattaver
Gio. Maria Tomasini not.

Tratta dal Libro delle Parti della Nazion d'Ebrei Ponentini principia 1691, 22 settembre, e termina 6 settembre 1711 a c. 210t.

1721. Simile depennazione in altro Libro a c. 156 della suddetta Nazione etc.

VII

(Same site, same booklet, no. 6, p. 14)
Intromissione avogaresca
Die 20 Junii 1721

Capitulum 23 Partis captae in Universitate Nationis Theutonicae Judeorum, quo cum summa publicae pottestatis offensa impeditur omnis recursus ad magistratus competentes, tam super methodo exactionum, quam super executione et gravaminibus ejusdem methodi, violenti quadam et propre inaudita formalitate, tenoris ut in eo; tamquam Capitulum aperte iniuriosum Publicae Pottestati, contrarium Decretis Excell. Senatus 1699, 30 Januarii, et 1720 5 Octobris, nec non naturali et innegabili libertati, quae competit unicuique recurrendi ad suum Principem, praecipue super tam gravi et publica materia. Intromisit Illustr. D. Marcus Antonius Delphino Honorandus Advocator Communis, et hoc viso Capitulo supradicto, nec non Decretis Excell. Senatus dierum 1699, 30 Januarii, et 1720, 5 Octobris, et ex officio. Mandamus etc.

Ex Libro Intromissionum secretis Off. Advoc. Com.
Fides Jo. Baptistae Lenzi Ad. Com. Not.
Antonius Costantini Coad.

VIII

(Same site, same booklet, no. 7, p. 15)
Altra terminazion Cattaveri
Adì 12 Aprile 1745

Gli Illustrissimi et Excell. Signori Cattaveri infrascritti

Restando espressamente vietato con terminazione di questo Excell. Magistrato sin dal 1628, 17 Novembre alli Cappi della Strazzaria degli Ebrei di questa Città giudicar qual si sia differenza per occasione di strazzaria, e rilevandosi dal presente Eccel. Magistrato continuarne tuttora l'abuso con offesa dell'authorità de' Magistrati a quali soli spetta la potestà degli aiti giudiziarii, quindi è che Sue E.E. unanimi e concordi hanno terminato, e terminando comandato, che inherendo al sentimentodella sopraferita Terminazione 1628 sia risolutamente prohibito a cappi sudetti il dar sentenza nelle differenze, che mai vertir potessero tra essi Ebrei per occasione di detta strazzaria come da altro, dovendo chiunque usar in via giudiziaria le proprie ragioni in pena di D. 50 a trasgressori, oltre le nullità d'ogni atto contrario alla presente Terminazione, con proibizione, in oltre di pubblicar per questo o per qual sia altro motivo Parte di qual si sia sorte con menzione di scomuniche, o maledizione, annullando anzi qualunque scomunica, che fosse stata pubblicata, o si trovasse registrata, acciò chi si sentisse aggravato possa liberamente ricorrere a Tribunali di Giustizia in ordine alla sopra menzionata Terminazione 1628, et altra 1581, 14 febraro, et acciò non possa de cetero di chi si sia fingersi ignoranza sia la presente intimata ai cappi della strazzaria, e registrata nelle loro Mariegole, perchè sia in ogni tempo inviolabilmente esseguita, et sic etc.

Nicolò Pizzamano Cattaver
Gio. Battista Zazari Cattaver
Zorzi Manolesso Cattaver
Adì 30 Aprile 1745

Refferì Bonifaccio Fante haver intimato la controscritta Terminazione a Benedetto Malta per nome suo e Collegio in tutto e per tutto come in essa e ciò ex officio. Tratta da simile nel Libro delle Parti a c. 67t.

IX

"Ordini da servarsi dall'Università di Reggio nella terminazione delle loro cause civili a rito ebraico."
(State Archive of Reggio Emilia – Archive of the Jewish Community – Repertorio Bassani IV, p. 10).

Havendo la benignità dell'A. V. Serenissima concesso all'Università degl'Ebrei suoi devotissimi servi e fedelissimi sudditi il poter decidere e terminare le diferenze che vertano o possano vertire fra di loro a ritto Ebraico; ricorrono a' piedi di V. A. S. supplicandola a concedergli grazie d'ordinare a' suoi ministri che facciano osservare l'infrascritte regole concertate tra loro nella Città di Reggio, non solo dagli habitanti in detta Città, ma anche da tutti quelli, che concorrono con quelli di Reggio ne' pagamenti che si fanno all'A. V. S.

Regola, con la quale desiderano gli Ebrei che si terminano le differenze, liti e controversie che accaderanno tra un Ebreo e l'altro more Aebreorum; nel modo e forma già conceduta da S. A. Ser. all'Università degl'Ebrei, affine di troncare la strada a' discrepanti, e che non s'abbino da valere della forza, per levarsi dal filo della giustezza, contro la mente del Ser.mo Padrone, come da un'ordine dato sotto li 20 Decembre 1657 si vede.

Primo: Essendo la Congregatione ristretta in 9 Persone, che saranno Massari tre di loro ogni sei mesi, dovranno dua di Loro servire per Giudici in compagnia d'un Dottore lo spaccio di sei mesi continovi, e ne primi tre mesi servirano li duoi più vecchi, e per gl'altri tre che restano a compire il corso de sei mesi dovrà uscire il più giovane de detti due vecchi et entrar l'altro in compagnia del più vecchio, et in tal forma sempre si dovrà continuare di sei mesi in sei mesi; e questi dovranno col Dottore unitamente risiedere duoi giorni della settimana; da Pasqua sino alla frascata la Domenica e Giovedì, subito finito l'Officio grande e vi staranno un'hora per sentire se vi è alcuna differenza, e dalla frascata fino a Pasqua a hore di notte in detti giorni nel loco destinato; et in detto tempo ci dovrà stare il notaio e Sagrestano per chiamar chi farà bisogno.

Secondo: Le suddette compagnie, che di mano in mano le toccarà esercitare la loro funcione, per differenze che non eccederanno la somma di L. 50 possino e debino terminarle senza forma di processo, et in altre cause di maggior somma se le parte interessate concordamente consentiranno che li dettitre elletti giudichino e terminino le loro differenze in punto Iuris, et in forma d'accordo, dichiarando, che tutte le scritture vulgari et in idioma Christiano, habbino forza, come permette il Stilo della Città, e Mercatura, e si dovrà farne nota in un libro, che a tal effetto dovrà formarsi, che resterà in custodia delli Giudici, e Notaio, e la suddetta partita servirà per compromesso in forma, et in ogni caso che le parti interessate non concordassero, che li sudetti tre elletti terminino le loro differenze, sarà carico de medemi elletti d'astringerli a pigliare Arbitri, uno per parte, assignandole il tempo, che le parerà conveniente per far l'ellezione, spirato il quale, e qual si sia di Loro non havrà fatta l'ellezione o vero fosse spirato il compromesso, sia in libertà di detti Giudici l'assignarle un'altro termine, overo assignarle un'altro Giudice e stare alla Loro determinazione.

Terzo: In caso di doglianza doppo seguita la sentenza che sarà data o da una delle sudette tre compagnie o d'altri Arbitri, che ellegessero conforme li casi dovranno gl'altri sei tutti uniti sentire la causa e fondamenti delle doglianze, e giudicare se vi sia causa di revisione e determinare il modo che si dovrà tenere, et in caso di revisione dovrà esser giudicato dagl'altri sei, mentre però che la prima sentenza sia stata data dagl'altri 3, ma quando nella sentenza non vi fosse intervenuto alcuno delli 9, dovranno intervenirvi tutti 9, e lo stesso modo si dovrà, in caso cha da una delle parti fosse ricercato di voler copia del Processo, ancorchè a ritto Ebraico non vengha permesso se non in cause urgenti.

Quarto: In caso che venesse qualche diferenza avanti li sudetti 9 elletti e che per parentella o altre cause non le sia permesso dal ritto Ebraico d'intervenire nella giudicatura o che alcuno di loro fosse absente o impedito, debba subentrare in luogo di quello o di quelli, altri delli 9 nominati e le cause che fossero principiate da una di esse compagnie, ancorchè non fossero finite, dovranno essere da quelli medemi terminate, ancorchè siano spirati li sei mesi della sua carica.

Quinto: E per provedere nel miglior modo possibile che sia somministrata retta giustizia, si dichiara che li Giudici elletti non possino ascoltare le parti nelle cause che sono elletti per giudicare, se non nel luogo della residenza, et alla presenza degl'altri dua Compagni, o almeno d'un altro che così comporta il ritto Ebraico.

Sesto: E per le spese che potessero occorrere per riconoscimento delli Rabini, e notaio, acciò non s'habbino le parti a consumar in dette spese, s'havrà riguardo dalli detti 9 Deputati a ridurle alla minima quantità, che si potrà per benefitio publico.

Settimo: Et quando saranno comparsi avanti gl'elletti qual si sia che habia differenze con altri, e che se gli sia fatto intendere col mezzo del Sagrestano a dover comparire e che non venga, si dovrà far chiamare la seconda volta, e non venendo al tempo che le sarà assignato, dovrà il Sagrestano far la relatione alli Giudici, e quando non facci constare con prove evidenti, impendimenti urgenti, dovrà sententiarsi sopra le dimande dell'altra parte.

Ottavo: E perchè l'esperienza ha mostrato che vi sono state persone discole, che non ostante la prohibitione di non valersi della protezione di qual si sia Christiano nelle differenze che vertono tra un'Ebreo et l'altro, ad ogni modo si sono valsi della forza per avvantaggiare i suoi interessi contro il dovere, al che non si può rimediare per diversi rispetti; si farà pubblicare nelle Sinagoghe che chi preterirà, s'intende incorso in pena della scomunica Ebraica, nella forma che dispone la legge e rito Ebraico, e che dalla benignità del Serenissimo Padrone vien conceduto alla Nazione.

Nono: E se bene si deve proponere che nelli sudetti elletti e da ellegersi non sarà chi contravenga a gl'ordini già dati si dichiara che in ogni caso si scoprisse o si venesse in cognitione con verità, che qualcheduno havesse preterito e commesso mancamento contro il giusto, dovrà rappresentare il fatto avanti la convocatione ristretta la quale per la prima volta sarà in loro arbitrio di condonare e ammettere il mancamento con quel castigo che le parerà, e parendole rimmettere e confirmare nella carica quello che havrà trascurato, ma se commetterà novo mancamento dovrà essere publicato per le Sinagoghe il delinquente, ne mai più potrà haver carica nè Uffici nell'Università.

Decimo: E per assicursi ch'il tutto passa con buon ordine e che non sia perso il rispetto a quelli che devono giudicare, si dovrà deputare due persone che in caso de' trasgressori, habbino da ricorrere dal Serenissimo Padrone e da suoi ill/mi Ministeri per ottenere gl'ordini per il dovuto castigo e condanare conforme ai casi, come anche per l'esecutione delle sentenze.

Undecimo: Che tutte le fittarezze di case et ogni altro contratto et accordo facessero insieme duoi Ebrei e che verranno a farli notare sopra il Libro delli Giudici, sia valido al pari d'ogni sorte d'instromento, e questo per oviare ogni sorte di spesa che le sarà notato dal Notaio alla presenza de detti Giudici gratis.

Duodecimo: Quando detti elletti havranno fatto un gravame per far esequire quello havranno determinato overo per far osservare quello havranno determinato gli Arbitri, sia obligato l'Ill/mo sign. Giudice sottoscriverlo ancora lui subito, come si è usato fin'hora per darlo in mano agl'esecutori, e lo stesso si praticherà anche con quelli che habitano fuori di Reggio e concorrono con gl'habitanti in detta Città.

Concedit, approbat et observari mandat Dominus, ut petitur, ad placitum tamen S. C.
Ioannes Turrius, die XXII iulii 1661.

(further below): si concedono et si aprovano da S. A.

X

Decree of the Duke of Modena for the Jewish University of Reggio Emilia – April 23, 1738.
State Archive of Reggio Emilia – Archive of the Jewish University. Repertorio Bassani, XIII, p. 6).
omissis

Che per ogni e qualunque differenza che possa nascere fra un Ebreo e l'altro e qualsisia di loro tanto congionti di sangue come non congionti, se una parte addimanderà Arbitri e l'altra li ricusi, quella che ricuserà debba essere da Ministri e Giudici d S. A. Serenissima forzata con precetti penali e poi con molti ed altri rimedi di ragione più valevoli a far l'elezione, e conseguentemente a comparir nanti gli Arbitri, e non concordando le Parti nel fare detta elezione degli Arbitri e di un terzo, facendo di bisogno, ovvero non ritrovandosi chi voglia essere arbitro, abbiano li Rabini dell'Accademia Ebraica maggiore dello Stato a deputare essa gli Arbitri, ovvero il Terzo come sopra, e come meglio essi Rabbini parerà, e quelli che a ciò destineranno sieno tenuti essere Arbitri, nè possino ricusar di essere: sicchè secondo il rito degli Ebrei e non ostante cosa alcuna in contrario, le sudette differenze sieno sempre Ebraicamente conosciute, e debbano le Parti stare al giudicato d'essi Arbitri; con questo però che le esecuzioni che occorreranno farsi debbano essere coll'autorità ed uffizio de' Ministri e Giudici di S. A. Ser./ma; e questo capitolo abbi luogo indistintamente ancora nelle cause de' Pupilli, Opere Pie e Vedove, Ebrei, Ebree, non ostante qualunque disposizione in contrario del Jus commune; siccome pure alle sentenze date da detti Arbitri Ebrei, debbano le Parti talmente acquietarsi e stare al loro giudicato, di modo che la causa resti e s'abbiper onninamente terminata, nè alcuna delle Parti debba più essere ascoltata in qualsiasi Foro e Tribunale, e ciò affinchè la stessa Nazione possa quietamente attendere senza forma di Litiggio ai loro trafici, e non stancarsi e distraersi in liti, e consumarsi in dispendi.

Si concede.
omissis
(at the end): Matteo Maria Borghi April 23, 1738
Registrato ecc.
Gaetano Giudotti Cancelliere Ducale
Domenico Maria Giacobazzi 16 novembre 1740
Giuseppe Macchione cancelliere Ducale

Index of Authors Cited

www.ingramcontent.com/pod-product-compliance
Lightning Source LLC
Chambersburg PA
CBHW051401240926
51852CB00002B/77
9789004677616